THE
Illustrated
ENCYCLOPEDIA OF
CARTOON
ANIMALS

THE
Illustrated
ENCYCLOPEDIA OF
CARTOON
ANIMALS

JEFF ROVIN

PRENTICE
HALL
PRESS

NEW YORK LONDON TORONTO SYDNEY TOKYO SINGAPORE

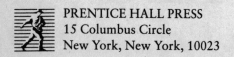 PRENTICE HALL PRESS
15 Columbus Circle
New York, New York, 10023

PRENTICE HALL PRESS and colophons are registered trademarks
of Simon & Schuster Inc.

Library of Congress Cataloging in Publication data
Rovin, Jeff.
    The illustrated encyclopedia of cartoon animals / by Jeff Rovin.
      p.   cm.
    Includes index.
    ISBN (invalid) 0–13–275561–0
    1. Cartoon characters—United States. I. Title.
  NC1766.U5R6 1991
  741.5'0973—dc20   91–31171
                                                             CIP

Designed by Robert Bull Design

Manufactured in the United States of America

10 9 8 7 6 5 4 3 2 1

First Edition

INTRODUCTION

It's fun to speculate what Aesop might be doing if he were living in the twentieth century instead of in Greece ca 620 to 560 B.C.

The teller of wonderful animal tales, such as the well-known *The Fox and the Grapes* and the lesser-known *The Bat and the Weasels*, among many others, Aesop would have been at home writing comic books. If he'd had any artistic talent, he might have gone into animation. Many of the stories spun by Walt Disney, Sheldon Mayer, Charles Schulz, and others have the charm, engaging characters, and moral content of the old fabulist's tales.

However, wonderful as his stories are, Aesop himself was just continuing an ancient tradition of humanizing animals. Just as many of the animal stories of the Brothers Grimm, Hans Christian Andersen, and the seventeenth-century French anthologist La Fontaine were inspired by Aesop, tales identical to those told by Aesop have been found on Egyptian papyruses dating back to 1500 B.C. Stories of anthropomorphic animals certainly date even further back: Gods with animal attributes are as old as civilization itself.

Why this ancient fascination?

Much of it was our ancestors' awe of the power, grace, and ferocity of animals. (And fear as well: The serpent, after all, helped to cost Adam and Eve Paradise.) The ritualistic slaughter of healthy bulls and rams in Egypt, and buzzards by the Acagchemen Indians of California, was an effort to protect them symbolically from the infirmity and dependence of old age. In so honoring these creatures it was hoped that the gods in their likeness would look favorably on the reverent and grant them strength and prosperity.

At the same time, people gave animals voices and bipedal gaits and used them in stories to underscore human strengths and failings. This represented a kind of shorthand for the storyteller: There was no need to go into much background if you had a wolf and a pig as your main characters. The wolf got the hisses and the pig got our sympathy. The use of animals also enabled storytellers, especially those who passed tales orally from generation to generation, to employ melodramatic gestures and expressions that would have been silly ascribed to people. (Try to picture the convict Magwitch instead of the wolf wearing the nightgown of Little Red Riding Hood's grandmother.) Animals also made it possible to hold an audience of all ages—children with the flamboyant characters and adults with the metaphors.

Throughout the centuries, humanized animals not only played a vital part in myths and legends but in literature as well, works of ethical loftiness like Jonathan Swift's *Gulliver's Travels* (the land of the Houyhnhnms was inhabited by intelligent, talking horses) and George Orwell's *Animal Farm,* mighty adventures such as Rudyard Kipling's *The Jungle Book* and Edgar Rice Burroughs's *Tarzan,* and delightful frivolity such as Beatrix Potter's tales of Peter Rabbit, Squirrel Nutkin, Benjamin Bunny, Jemima Puddle-Duck, Pigling Bland, and their kind.

Animals help to make tales timeless: Unlike the manners and fashions that date other great works, cats and rabbits are the same today as they were when Lewis Carroll gave them voices and human personalities in his adventures of Alice.

The late nineteenth century saw the birth of two new media, comic strips and motion pictures, and it wasn't long before each became infested by animals. But the move wasn't a simple transfer. An evolution took place.

The numbers of drawings needed to produce an animated cartoon, and the pressures of doing a daily comic strip or monthly comic book, dictated a "look" that was simpler than the illustrative technique used by Tenniel for *Alice's Adventures in Wonderland* or the realistic paintings of Beatrix Potter. Figures and expressions were caricatured and, freed from the more "realistic" treatment of animals in the past, writers came up with plots that were equally exaggerated. Moreover, because the comic and theatrical cartoon presentations were by necessity shorter, they tended to be gag driven rather than dependent on a great deal of plot. That made animal stories more comical than they'd been in the past, and in a world soon to be engulfed with world wars and a fiscal depression, funny animals became a beloved and much-needed respite. They didn't put an end to animals in literature: There was, and always will be, an audience for adult novels like Richard Adams's *Watership Down,* or for children's books such as E. B. White's *Charlotte's Web* and the timeless works of Dr. Seuss. But cartoons are now the accepted lingua franca of animals, the media of greatest impact and widest appeal. We understand how Donald Duck feels when he loses his temper or how Snoopy is warmed by the thought of long-lost family. It would be pretentious to call these vignettes psychodramas—nonetheless, it *is* cathartic to watch Wile E. Coyote's best efforts leave him with an anvil on top of his head. We all know the feeling, and it's good to be able to laugh at it.

This book is a compendium of the famous and not-so-famous animal characters who were created for the various cartoon media, animals both humorous and "serious" (e.g., the horse **Black Fury** and the amazing **Rex, The Wonder Dog**). Also included are a wide selection of animals who were spawned elsewhere but gained equal or greater fame on the screen or in the comics, such as Winnie the Pooh, Brer Rabbit, and Babar the Elephant. (Although cartoons have been made from Kenneth Grahame's *The Wind in the Willows,* Dr. Seuss's *The Cat in the Hat,* George Selden's *The Cricket in Times Square,* and other classic animal tales, their impact has been far, far less than the seminal works and they have not been given entries.)

Likewise, fanciful animals have been kept to a minimum. While it may seem niggling to include talking ducks, Dino the Dinosaur, the flying Dumbo, and hybrid creatures such as the Wuzzles, yet bar Howdy Doody's bizarre bird Flub-a-dub and Marshall Rogers's enchanting birdlike comic book character Foozle, a true cartoon animal is a singular creation: a creature whose entertainment value depends on our familiarity with its real-life counterpart and the absurdity of transposing human values and behavior to that known quantity. Without that point of reference, a creature is simply a cartoon character—not necessarily unfunny, but lacking that added depth. Besides, unicorns and dragons alone would practically double the size of this book.

Also excluded are the pretenders: Batman, Catman, Ant Man, Fly Man, the Rhino, Spider-Man, Web Woman, and others who have animal powers and even dress up like them . . . but are people. (*Strange* people, to be sure . . . but people nonetheless.)

We've also stretched the definition of *cartoon* just a tad to include the likes of Pokey (Gumby's horse) and Kermit the Frog and other Muppets. While these characters have appeared in cartoons, they're better known as clay figures and puppets, respectively. Yet, they beckoned. For their physical structure notwithstanding, they're as personable, expressive, and volatile as their cartoon counterparts.

A few of the more popular and unusual foreign animals have been included, underscoring the fact that the United States isn't the only country with a weakness for dogs, chickens, and stinkbugs. Speaking of which, there's no getting around it: Some very, very minor characters cried out for their own entries. While minor characters are usually discussed in the "Comment" section of similar major entries (frogs with frogs, and so on), a few, such as The Peckers and Ralph, the Righteous, Radical, Rasslin' Rhino, are so unusual that attention had to be called to them.

Finally, a word about the illustrations. We've illustrated only those characters who have not been overexposed in other media or if there was a new twist on an old favorite (like **Minnie Mouse**). Besides, it seemed redundant to publish another shopworn illustration of Garfield when Suicide Squirrel and Beppo the Super-Monkey were begging for recognition.

Each entry in this book is broken down as follows:

Pedigree. This section is a thumbnail description of who or what the animal is.

Biography. The biography includes the story of the animal's life and times, nemeses and friends, outstanding exploits and habits, a physical description, and, wherever possible, a family tree and known relatives.

Comment. Facts about the creation of the character, its historical significance, the media in which it appears, and other important information are included under this heading. Minor cartoon animals of the same ilk are also mentioned here. Cross-referencing can be found in the appendix, where all the animals have been grouped according to species.

An animal referred to in **boldface letters** anywhere in the text has its own entry elsewhere. If two or more *major* animals share the same name (i.e., Sandy), the earliest is designated (1), the next (2), and so on. Numerical designations have not been applied to minor animals: The Spikes alone would have brought us perilously close to the edge of a precipice we'd better not approach.

The Encyclopedia of Cartoon Animals was designed as a reference book, but it was also written to be browsed through and read for a laugh, for nostalgia, or as a guide through some of the more offbeat byways of popular culture.

It was also written as a tribute to the talents and inventiveness of people like Winsor McCay, Jim Henson, Mel Blanc, June Foray, Ub Iwerks, Dik Browne, and so many others who took what Aesop and others left us and pushed it in imaginative new directions. Not only have they given us a century of delight, they've enriched our culture in ways we're only just beginning to appreciate.

THE
Illustrated
ENCYCLOPEDIA OF
CARTOON
ANIMALS

THE AARDVARK

Pedigree. Long-suffering anteater of theatrical cartoons.

Biography. The seedy looking Aardvark has a problem: Like **Wile E. Coyote**, he's determined to eat prey who happen to be a lot smarter than he is. In this case, his would-be victim is the Ant, a little red bug with a Joey Bishop voice. The quadrupedal Aardvark tries everything he can think of to draw the little bipedal bugger up his nose, but usually ends up with a snootfull of TNT, nails, or other unpleasant objects.

Comment. The series was created by DePatie-Freleng. There were seventeen cartoons produced from 1966 to 1971; when they came to television, they aired on *The New Pink Panther Show* (see **The Pink Panther**). John Byner provided the voices for both characters.

ACE, THE BAT-HOUND

Pedigree. The crime-fighting aide to the comic book superhero Batman.

Biography. While driving through a wooded area on their nightly patrol, the superheroes Batman and Robin spot a German shepherd drowning in a river. Rescuing him, they find that he had been "knocked groggy." They take him home. The next day, in his civilian identity as Bruce Wayne, Batman places a "lost dog" ad in the paper. Meanwhile, when the Dynamic Duo receive an emergency call from police headquarters and set out in the Batmobile, the dog joins them. They don't have time to turn around and take him back, but Batman is afraid that "anyone seeing this dog will recognize him, from that forehead mark, as the dog Bruce Wayne advertised," which will "imperil our secret identities." Thus while the Caped Crusader checks in at police headquarters, Robin digs into the "black cloth tool bag" and makes both a black mask and collar bat-symbol for the dog, to disguise his true identity. Shortly thereafter, while the heroes are battling convict Bert Bowers, it's the dog who grabs the con's coatsleeve "in true police dog style" and enables them to arrest him. Later, Wayne receives a call from someone who says that the dog in the paper "looks like John Wilker's dog, Ace." Going to Wilker's home in the suburbs, they find the place ransacked and learn that Wilker, an employee of the Gotham Printing and Engraving Company, has been missing for two days. He's obviously been kidnapped, and it's just as clear that Ace was hurt trying to defend his master. With Ace's help, they track Wilker to the lair of counterfeiters, who were going to force him to work for them. Wilker is freed, and Batman borrows the skilled animal several times over the next few years. Eventually, Wilker takes a job that requires a great deal of travel, and he asks Wayne if he'd like to take the dog permanently. Wayne happily agrees, and improves the dog's effectiveness as a law enforcer by building a special stand so that Ace can slip his own mask on. He also places a small receiver inside the animal's collar; whenever Batman needs the dog, he simply activates a transmitter located inside the heel of his boot. The dog's most harrowing adventure occurs when his head is grazed by a criminal's bullet and he suffers selective amnesia. Because he was hurt by a man in a mask, he comes to hate anyone wearing a mask, Batman included. When Bat-Hound is finally apprehended, his memory is restored through surgery.

Comment. The canine crime fighter first appeared in DC Comics's *Batman* no. 92 in 1955. Most of his adventures took place over a nine-year period. See also **Rex, The Wonder Dog.**

ACTION ANT

Pedigree. Martial arts insect of the comics.

Biography. When the mysterious "blue mist" spread through the world, it killed off (apparently) all human life, and mutated insects and reptiles. Now intelligent and articulate, they have their own primitive civilization. On the one hand, there is the evil Master Skito and his ninja mosquitoes. On the other, there is Action Ant, defender of the Crystal Village and of the bug Queen Beatrice. Ant's aides are those other martial arts titans Mighty Mantis and Leapzard. All wear traditional Oriental garb.

Comment. The *Karate Kreatures* comic book was created by Michael DePasquale, Jr., and began publication from MA Comics in 1989. See also **Atom Ant.**

ADOLESCENT RADIOACTIVE BLACK BELT HAMSTERS

Pedigree. Comic book mutations.

Biography. When "radioactive cosmic jello [*sic*]" is discovered in our solar system, Dr. Cosby fears it will fall to earth and cause millions of deaths. Unfortunately, probes are unable to return with samples of the gel. Thus on April 1, 1977, Polish hamsters Bruce, Chuck, Jackie, and Clint are sent into space onboard a NASA rocket packed with explosives. Their mission is to pilot directly into the jello and self-destruct (pressing the "Kiss Your Ass Goodbye" button). The hamsters do so, but instead of dying, they're mutated and blasted back to earth. They land in Tibet and are found by a mystic, Master Lock. Because their arrival fulfills an unspecified prophecy, the holy man takes them to a monastery where, over the next eight years, the hamsters are trained to become masters of the martial arts and weapons. Their individual personalities emerge, and they are different indeed. Chuck is an intellectual "into Gandhi, no nukes, and Debussy," although if you "get him riled . . . he'll beat you into next month." Bruce is a "car enthusiast, an ace doctor and a mechanical whiz." Jackie "hasn't hit puberty yet. His favorite author is Dr. Seuss and his greatest desire is to visit 6 Flags Over New Delhi." However, he's "awesome in hand to hand combat." The excitable Clint is a "mover, a shaker [craving] non-stop action." When their tutoring is complete, the quartet returns to the United States "to cleanse the world of vermin" (although if their training fails, the hamsters are not above jumping onto an adversary's head and biting his ear). Even though the hamsters are human in nature and walk upright, they're still physically hamsters and eat only lettuce. Their most famous battles have been with the terrorists of the PLO (Pot-Luck Organization), and with the transvestite Wilhemina Fisk, the Queenpin of Crime (a parody of Marvel Comics Kingpin).

Comment. The characters' magazine was first published by Eclipse Comics in 1986; it lasted nine issues and a handful of one shots. A companion title, *Clint, the Hamster Triumphant,* ran for two issues. The characters were created by writer Don Chin and artist Parsonavich.

ALBERT THE ALLIGATOR

Pedigree. Friend of Pogo Possum, and star of comic books, comic strips, television, and a motion picture.

Biography. Initially, Okefenokee Swamp was the dominion of the somewhat hostile Albert the Alligator and a little black boy named Bumbazine—the only one who expresses any liking for the carnivore. Pogo and the rest of the cast were more or less in the background, supporting players to Albert's ongoing quest for food. Indeed, many of them nearly made it onto his menu; even other alligators weren't immune, as he threatened, once, to gobble down young Alexander Alligator. (He backed down when the spunky Alexander cried, "Drop away! I hope I is tough!") Unliked, the bipedal cigar-smoker soon decides to leave the swamp for the city *(Our Gang no. 6),* but as a "talkin' gator" he's a freak much in demand among humans, and he returns to Okefenokee. Albert is finally befriended and defended among the animals by Pogo Possum *(Animal Comics no. 11),* which occurs one issue after Albert uncharacteristically helps to chase a tiger from some defenseless little animals. Over the next few issues, he helps Pogo get rid of some unwelcome relatives, helps chase a nasty mosquito from the swamp, and does battle with a bear. In turn, Pogo and several other animals come to trust Albert enough so that when strange voices begin emanating from within his body, they don't hesitate to enter his mouth in search of the cause (as it happens, a bunch of mice had crawled inside and made a home of Albert, mistaking the sleeping alligator for a log). Although Albert never gives up his love of food, he becomes more and more a gourmand instead of a predator. By the time he moves from comic books to a comic strip, he's a fully socialized member of the swamp: In one of his first appearances, he actually allows a widowed bird to move into his mouth and, after a while, to build a nest, because she finds his maw so "cozy." Later that year, when he accidentally swallows a "frog-child," he allows Pogo to push a ladder down his throat, climb in (with a lighted candle on the possum's head), and go searching for the tadpole. This new, reformed Albert describes himself as "handsome, brilliant, an' modest to a faretheewell." Creator Walt Kelly's assistant, George Ward, describes him more succinctly as a "loveable big blowhard" and, indeed, his bombast has a way of creating problems where there was only peace before—such as the time he owed the local shopkeeper, the stork Mr. Miggle, "a few measly trillion" dollars, and rather than try to make a dent in the debt, bad-mouthed him to others. His bluster not-withstanding, Albert has revealed himself to be a creature of many bonafide talents. He plays the Sousaphone, flute, and banjo, although he's a failure as a composer (not in his view, of course); he can read, but not write (when Pogo comments that the book he's reading is upside-down, the words come from Albert's mouth . . . upside-down); and he's a pitcher to be reckoned with on the swamp baseball team—but his fielding leaves something to be desired, because he tends to catch balls with his mouth and swallow them.

Comment. See entry on Pogo for details about Albert's history in the media.

ALIEN DUCKLINGS
Pedigree. Comic book superducks from another world.

Biography. Fleeing from the evil Overloads [*sic*], a quartet of white, energylike beings known as Amps leave the Greenway Galaxy. Their ship is nearly destroyed by a pursuit craft from Lord Volteater—but the foursome manage to crash-land on earth. Because they can't survive long in our atmosphere, they look quickly for "the dominant species and clone" similar forms from tissue samples. Unfortunately, they've landed on a farm; Twobee, Beebee, and Eyebee choose ducks, and Beea selects a pig. They realize their mistake too late: They haven't enough energy to assume another form. Still, they can think and talk like before, and make the best of things. Beea sees an episode of *Kung Fu* and uses his energy to transform his pig-self into Master Po, the Philosopher Pig and martial arts master; Eyebee goes to the library, reads, and becomes Webster, the Avian encyclopedia; Beebee rents videocassettes and absorbs everything he's seen, from old Steve Martin routines to *Honeymooners* episodes, and can access any personality whenever he wishes; and Twobee goes to a comic book shop, emerging as costumed Aquaduck, who is "psychically linked to the metawaves of nearby fish," thus making him "the most powerful superduck the universe has ever seen."

Comment. There were four issues of *Alien Ducklings*. This ingenious, very funny comic was written by Cliff MacGillivray, drawn by Andy Ice, and published by Blackthorne in 1986. The ducks were parodied in the publisher's *Laffin Gas* no. 4 in 1986 as Alien Hamsterlings. Another flock of space ducks can be found in *Quad Star Comics Presents* no. 1: *The A.D.A.* from Quad Star Comics in 1989. Three human aliens, Jerry, Dave, and another Dave, are forced to flee their solar system when it's invaded "by a mad group of ducks." Rocketing to earth, the humans are pursued by ducks who, disguising their duck shapes, pose as doctors, lawers, teachers, and politicians: Only the three alien humans can tell real people from duck-people and form the Anti-Duck Association, devoted to exterminating the aliens.

THE AMERICAN RABBIT
Pedigree. Motion picture superhero.
Biography. When Robert Rabbit is born, a wizened old rabbit visits his parents and remarks, "He could have quite a future ahead of himself." As the parents exchanged confused glances, the elderly rabbit vanishes, then shows up again a few years later and watches the young, gray, bespectacled hare shine in a rugby match. Sometime later, he passes by the house when Robert is playing the piano. He only smiles, and savors the boy's achievements. While Robert is at a picnic with his parents, he's off kicking around a rugby ball when he sees a boulder fall off a cliff. Running to warn his folks, who are directly beneath it, he suddenly begins to trail a vaporous American flag . . . which suddenly enrobes him like a bizarre tattoo (his ears are blue and speckled with white stars, his body is covered with horizontal red and white stripes). Golden roller skates appear on his feet, and as Robert races ahead, he suddenly takes flight. He flies up under the boulder and pushes it away, saving his parents. When he alights, the old rabbit appears—dressed, now, in a wizard's robe. He explains that Robert has been selected for a sacred role: inheritor of "the Legacy. For as long as time itself, our quiet little village . . . has provided a special hero to make the outside world a better place." Leaving home (and his proud but teary-eyed parents), Robert heads to (all-animal) San Francisco, where he lands a job at the nightclub Panda Monium, run by Theodore "Teddy" Panda and his aide Bunny O'Hare. Unfortunately, all is not well in Frisco. The bike-riding Jackals demand "insurance" money from local establishments, trashing those that don't pay. Teddy refuses to bow to extortion, and the bikers destroy Panda Monium. Bunny organizes a unity march among all the local animals, and the parade riles the bikers' boss, Vultor, a fat man with glowing eyeglasses and a collar and tie pulled right up to the rim of these spectacles—pulled so

high that none of his face is visible. Vultor's constant companion, a buzzard, flaps off and, during the march, he pecks apart the cables supporting the Golden Gate Bridge. Fortunately, Robert is able to sneak off, become the American Rabbit, and knot the strands together before the span collapses. Later, Vultor torches a paddle-wheel steamer where unemployed Panda, Bunny, Robert, and Ping Pong the benevolent gorilla have gone to get work. American Rabbit saves them again, after which the group decides to move to New York. Vultor follows them and, in time, the American Rabbit tracks him to the Statue of Liberty—which the villain has rigged with TNT. The rabbit punches the man, who deflates, and Robert learns the horrible truth: The buzzard was doing a ventriloquism act. He's actually in control . . . and, worse, is sitting atop the plunger of the detonator. Reluctantly, American Rabbit backs down. And it turns out this isn't all Vultor has done: He's rigged a Doomsday Switch to New York and threatens to destroy the city if it doesn't surrender to him (quite a leap from simple extortion, and something never fully explained in the plot). The animal citizens become his slaves, the Jackals serve as savage police, and American Rabbit is plagued with guilt. Enter the old rabbit, who picks Robert up in a cab and tells him to find a way to stage a "power play" of his own. The taxi leaves Robert off at a travel agency, where he sees a poster of Niagara Falls. Bingo! He becomes the American Rabbit, flies to the dam whose waters power the city's electricity, and fires electricity from his fingers to cause the water to flow up—away from the turbines. The Doomsday Switch is rendered inoperative, and when Vultor comes to investigate, the hare flies after him. The buzzard speeds north, the American Rabbit close on his tail feathers. The chase ends when it begins to snow and ice forms on Vultor's wings. The self-described "supreme anarchy" crashes inert to the ground. When last seen, Robert and Bunny are arm-in-arm.

Comment. Stewart Moskowitz created the characters seen in *The Adventures of the American Rabbit*. The Clubhouse Pictures presentation was brought to the screen by Japan's Toei Animation and released in 1985.

AMOS MOUSE

Pedigree. Mouse star of Walt Disney theatrical featurette *Ben and Me*.

Biography. According to a mouse tour guide show-

ing off a statue of Amos in modern-day Philadelphia, the church mouse was "responsible for the great deeds attributed to Benjamin Franklin." Born and raised in Philadelphia in the old church on Second Street, Amos was the eldest of twenty-six children who lived behind the paneling in the vestry. The mice slept in shoes in the crowded hole, and life was hard . . . so, in the winter of 1745, Amos ran off to give the family one less mouse to feed. However, as he puts it, "Jobs were scarce, especially for a mouse, for we were a downtrodden race." Nearly frozen and starved, he stops in to see printer Benjamin Franklin. When Franklin shatters the lenses of his last pair of glasses, Amos uses his sharp teeth to fit in pieces of lenses from another pair, thus inventing bifocals. He gets a job with Franklin inking the presses (sleeping comfortably on a quill pen at night) and during the next few days not only invents the Franklin Stove and comes up with the idea to publish a newspaper, the *Pennsylvania Gazette,* but takes advantage of his diminutive size to spy around town and get news. When Franklin goes out, Amos rides inside his hat (there's a small door so Amos can step out onto the brim) and is thus able to "offer advice without being seen by others," such as helping the absentminded Franklin remember people's names. In their spare time, Amos answers Ben's mail while the publisher and inventer "putters around with his experiments." One of these catches Amos by surprise. Franklin attaches a box to a kite and sends Amos aloft— ostensibly to make him "the world's first flying reporter." Amos later said that he was "so enthralled with the spectacle spread out below, that I failed to notice a sharp pointed wire fixed to the kite just above my head." A storm cloud arrives and the kite gets zapped: Amos crashes to earth and, furious at having been used as Franklin's guinea pig, stalks off . . . electrical sparks shooting from his body whenever he steps in a puddle. Amos moves back with his family. Years pass; the mouse is in the forefront of the movement for independence, and during the summer of 1776 Ben comes calling for him, begging him to return, to help him make the "big decisions." Amos agrees, but only if Ben will sign a paper granting the mouse certain rights. While Amos is drafting it at Ben's shop, Thomas Jefferson enters, moaning about his inability to come up with an opening for the Declaration of Independence. Glancing at Amos's contract, Franklin reads, "When in the course of human events . . ." and—eureka!— Jefferson leaves with his opening line. Today, only the mice are shown the statue of Amos. But to them (and us), he stands tall in American history.

Comment. The charming 1953 film was written by Robert Lawson and Bill Peet, directed by Hamilton Luske, and narrated by Sterling Holloway. Dell published a comic book adaptation in 1954.

ANDY PANDA

Pedigree. Popular star of theatrical cartoons and comic books.

Biography. For the first nine cartoons of his career, Andy is a young, black-and-white furred, mischievous cub living in the forest with his big, lumbering father. There, plots revolve around everything from fishing to dealing with pygmies. With *Goodbye Mr. Moth* (1942), not only is Andy on his own but he's out of the woods and living in a roomy suburban home. In what's probably Andy's funniest cartoon, *Dog Tax Dodgers* (1948), **Wally Walrus** comes to Andy's door to collect the $3 due on all pet dogs. Because Andy doesn't want to part with the money, he tries every trick he can think of to keep Wally (and Wally's trained dog-finding flea Itchy) from learning about his pet Dizzy—a gangly mutt with a mop of red hair. In the end, not only does Wally find out about the dog, but Dizzy is honest enough to admit that she's just had a litter of eight puppies. Andy promptly faints. Other cartoons revolve around Andy trying to grow a victory garden, working as an air-raid warden, and creating music in the classic shorts *The Poet and Peasant* (1946) and *Musical Moments from Chopin* (1947), both Oscar nominated. The former is wildly entertaining, as Maestro Andy Panda conducts the Hollywood Washbowl Orchestra and everything that can go wrong does, including a frog getting under Andy's flowing red wig, a bird and then a cat alighting on the baton, a wolf chasing a duck around the podium, and Andy getting a pitchfork in the seat, which causes him to soar into the stratosphere—though he continues to conduct while parachuting down using his wig. Also nominated for an Academy Award was *Fish Fry* (1944), which chronicles Andy's efforts to get a gold fish home from the pet store, despite the efforts of a hungry cat to steal it. In comics, Andy is frequently teamed with the rambunctious Charlie Chicken. Andy's attire consists of red trousers, with yellow shoes and gloves. His voice has both the sound and cloying sincerity of Judy Garland in *The Wizard of Oz*, although his humble manner—down to averting his face and digging his toe into the floor when

embarrassed—is reminiscent of *Mickey Mouse*. Although Andy was a successful character, the highlight of his career was the cartoon *Knock Knock* (1940), which introduced audiences to **Woody Woodpecker.**

Comment. Searching for a character that had never been done in cartoons, producer Walter Lantz created Andy after reading about the arrival of a panda at the Chicago Zoo. (In fact, in the first Andy cartoon, *Life Begins for Andy Panda,* Andy's father warns him never to leave the forest, or "hunters will capture you and put you in the newsreel." Andy starred in twenty-eight cartoons from 1939 to 1949. The cartoons came to television in 1957 as part of *The Woody Woodpecker Show* on ABC. Over the years, Andy's voice was provided by Bernice Hansel, Sarah Berner, and Walter Tetley. In comics, Andy first appeared in Dell's *Crackajack Funnies* no. 39 in 1941. He began starring in Dell's *The Funnies* with no. 61 (1942) and remained with that title (along with other Lantz characters) when it became *New Funnies* (no. 65); it suspended publication in 1962 with no. 288. Andy also starred in fifty-six issues of his own Dell comic (1943 to 1962), and guest starred in other titles. Other cartoon pandas were seen on the 1982 CBS Saturday morning show *Pandamonium* [sic], about a trio of talking pandas who, with their human teen pals, thwart the schemes of the extraterrestrial fiend Mondragorr. See also **Peter Panda.**

APE

Pedigree. Ape companion of television's inept George of the Jungle.

Biography. The title song says it all: "When he gets in a scrape / he'll make his escape / with the help of his friend / an ape named Ape." The cultured, literate, naked brown gorilla is truly the brains of the duo, helping George as he battles various jungle nemeses, from evil witchdoctors to hunters to unscrupulous developers. Not that Ape is always more effective than George: He is apt to spend so much time calculating the exact spot to hit a prison wall to effect a jailbreak, that the prospects of getting away are dim. Ape's most valuable asset is his ability to beat his belly to send drumlike signals through the jungle. He calls it his "tum-tum tom-tom." Also living with the pair are George's mates Stella and Ursula.

Comment. Ape's voice and mannerisms were inspired by those of 1930s film star Ronald Colman.

Paul Frees provided the voice for this Jay Ward (**Rocky and Bullwinkle**) creation. Also seen on the series were two other animals: George's pet elephant Shep, so named because George is convinced he's just a "big, gray, peanut-loving doggie," and the all-important Tuki-Tuki bird, which carries word to George of happenings in remote parts of the jungle (although exactly how is a mystery, because its entire vocabulary consists of *ah-ah, ee-ee, tuki-tuki*). There were sixteen George of the Jungle cartoons in all; the series aired on ABC on Saturday mornings from 1967 to 1968. All of the characters appeared in the two issues of Gold Key's *George of the Jungle* comic book (1968 to 1969). Another segment on George's show was **Super Chicken**.

THE ARACUAN BIRD

Pedigree. Magical, slightly insane bird nemesis of Donald Duck.

Biography. With flamingolike legs, a long bill, a billowing T-shirt (the colors change from film to film) and a broomlike head of red "hair" shooting back from its head, the bird's appearance, manner, and even its voice are reminiscent of Walter Lantz's **Woody Woodpecker**, who had shot to prominence five years earlier. The bird made his screen debut in Walt Disney's feature-length cartoon *The Three Caballeros* (1945). During the segment "Aves Raras," Donald watches a movie showing the strange birds of South America. The Aracuan Bird is introduced as "one of the most eccentric birds you have ever seen"—an understatement, as the irrepressible bird walks off the screen and along the projector beam, then goes back and marches up and down trees in the jungle. Spotting a delicately built, newly completed nest of the hardworking Marrequito bird, it pauses to drop a "last straw" on top, causing the nest to fall apart. All the while, the mischievous bird sings a short, staccato melody over and over, its everpresent theme song. **José Carioca** arrives and the bird comes back and snatches his cigar; after pronouncing the redhead "a very stupid fellow," José takes Donald on a train trip to Brazil. As they ride the rails, the Aracuan Bird is spotted lounging on the tracks, forcing the train to send its cars onto different tracks to avoid it. The pest's next appearance was in a short subject, *Clown of the Jungle* (1947), in which Donald enters the woods to do some nature photography. The bird arrives singing, vanishing into the ground, popping up again like weed, then disappearing. Donald forgets about it until he tries to take a

picture of a hummingbird. Dressed like a Cossack, the bird dances in front of Donald's lens, ruining the picture, then leaves and returns with a seltzer bottle to blast Donald. When the furious duck gives chase, it speeds away on a nonexistent motorcycle. Later, it dangles a fake bird in front of Donald, luring the camera-wielding duck up a tree. When Donald reaches the top, the bird crowns him with a hammer. Back on the ground, it escapes by drawing a door in a boulder and running away. The door, of course, does not work for Donald. The bird's final big screen appearance was in *Blame It on the Samba,* a lively segment of the feature film *Melody Time* (1948). When the bird pours a drink for Donald and José, keyboardist Ethel Smith is visible in the large glass; the birds dive in and join her. The Aracuan Bird is soon up to his characteristic tricks. He pokes a match beneath her foot to make the music livelier; satisfied with the results, he repeats the procedure with a stick of dynamite. The organ explodes, although Ethel never stops playing as the pieces fly through space, finally tumbling down and reassembling.

Comment. In addition to its screen appearances, the bird also popped up in Donald Duck comic books. The character apparently inspired the red-haired Firebug, an arsonist bird who made life difficult for the Junior Woodchucks in **Huey, Dewey, and Louie** comic books.

THE ARISTOCATS

Pedigree. Quartet of cats from the Walt Disney film of the same name.

Biography. In turn-of-the-century Paris, mother cat Duchess and her kittens Berlioz, Marie, and Toulouse are the beloved pets of wealthy Madame Bonfamille. When the elderly woman summons her lawyer and instructs him to write a will that will leave all she owns to the cats—with her butler Edgar to inherit everything "at the end of *their* lives"—the eavesdropping Edgar is enraged. (He not only calculates how long each cat will live but adds in the fact that each has nine lives. That *really* depresses him.) Dropping sleeping pills into the cats' milk as he warms it that night, he waits until the cats are asleep, then shoves them into a basket, mounts his motorbike, and heads into the country. However, he stirs the dogs Napoleon and Lafayette, who detest intruders. In the madcap chase that ensues, Edgar loses the basket, but doesn't dare stop for it. He heads back to the city, confident the cats won't be return-

O'Malley (left), Duchess, and her kittens . . . a k a **The Aristocats.**

ing. All the jostling awakens the cats, but a thunderstorm sweeps through the marsh in which they've landed, and they stay put. Come morning, the cats begin the seemingly hopeless task of trekking home. Fortunately, they run into the wastrel ginger alley cat Jack O'Malley, who is smitten with Duchess and offers to lead her and her kittens back to Paris. Climbing a tree, O'Malley waits for a milk truck to pass by, then leaps on the windshield and terrorizes the driver, who jams on the brake, stalling the engine. The four cats climb aboard, but when the truck lurches and Marie falls out, O'Malley is forced to scoop her up, race after the truck, and jump on with her. Meanwhile, in Paris, the cats' close friend, the mouse Roquefort, has been searching for them. While the dejected rodent commiserates with Madame's horse Frou-Frou, Edgar walks in, happy as a songbird. He confesses the crime to the horse (who he doesn't think can understand him, naturally), and Roquefort overhears. Back on the milk truck the cats are forced to flee when the milk man spots them lapping up his wares. They follow a train track, and after a close encounter with a train deposits them in the river, they're helped ashore by a pair of geese, Amelia and Abigail. The birds lead them to the outskirts of Paris, and after a stay with some friends of O'Malley's—jazz musicians Scat Cat, Chinese Cat, English Cat, Italian Cat, and Russian Cat—Duchess and her kittens head for home. Upon their arrival, Edgar shoves them in the oven, and Roquefort—who's been watching Edgar—asks Duchess what to do. She sends him to get O'Malley, who, with the help of the jazz cats and Frou-Frou, close Edgar inside a trunk and ship him to Timbuktu. The reunion with Madame is a happy one, and not only does O'Malley move in with them, but the woman establishes a foundation for all the alley cats in Paris.

Comment. The charming film *The Aristocats* was released in 1970. It was originally written to serve as a two-part show on the TV series *Walt Disney's Wonderful World of Color,* but Disney wanted it made as a theatrical feature. It was the final animated film whose production he was to authorize before his death. Eva Gabor provided the voice for Duchess, Phil Harris was O'Malley, Dean Clark was Berlioz, Liz English was Marie, and Gary Dubin spoke for Toulouse. Among the other animals, Sterling Holloway was Roquefort, Nancy Kulp was Frou-Frou, and Scatman Crothers was Scat Cat. A comic book adaptation of the film was published by Gold Key in 1971, and the junior cats starred in Gold Key's *The Aristokittens,* nine issues of which were published from 1971 to 1975. Gold Key also published nine issues of *O'Malley and the Alley Cats* from 1971 to 1974.

ASTRO

Pedigree. Fun-loving dog of the future on television's *The Jetsons.*

Biography. Astro is the big, blue Great Dane owned by the Jetson family of the Sky Pad Apartments of the twenty-first century. Able to stand upright when need be, he can also speak a few words in his gruff voice (enough to make himself understood). What he says boils down to the fact that, like most dogs, Astro enjoys being treated like a human, leading George to comment that he has "a distorted view of a man and dog relationship." (George felt more charitable toward him, however, when the dog became wealthy in *Millionaire Astro.)* To date, Astro's only real crisis has been in *The Coming of Astro,* when, newly arrived in the household, he fails to stop a prowler (a cat burglar, of course). The Jetsons get an electronic guard dog, Lectronimo—although, in the end, Astro proved himself more valuable than the robot. Those who only know Astro as the Jetsons' pet are familiar with only half the story. On *Astro and the Space Mutts,* he works with the dogs Cosmo and Dipper and journeys through space with the human Space Ace, an intergalactic lawman. Although the dogs are clods, they manage—somehow—to help their long-suffering master.

Comment. Hanna-Barbera's *The Jetsons* premiered in prime time on ABC in September of 1962, each episode lasting a half hour. The show ran only a single season, but has been in syndication ever since. A new series aired from 1985 to 1988, also in syndication, making a total of seventy-five Jetsons episodes in all. A special, *The Jetsons Meet the Flintstones,* aired in 1987. Don Messick was the voice of Astro in all of these episodes. *Astro and the Space Mutts* aired in 1981, part of the *Space Stars* cartoon show on NBC. Messick again provided Astro's voice, Frank Welker was Cosmo, Lennie Weinrib was Dipper, and Mike Bell was Space Ace. The dog has also been seen in the feature-length Jetsons theatrical cartoon, released in 1990, in which George is given a promotion and transferred, with dog and family, to the Orbiting Ore Asteroid. The dog also appeared in the thirty-six issues of *The Jetsons* comic book, published by Gold Key from 1963 to 1970.

ATOM ANT

Pedigree. Superpowered insect of television fame.

Biography. The theme song doesn't exaggerate when it says, "He's rough, he's tough, and bad guys yell, 'Enough!' " Atom Ant is one tough cookie. Headquartered in a long, winding anthole located beside a mighty oak tree in Antsville, the mighty bug derives his powers from an Atom Smasher, which he keeps in his lab, although he also pumps up his muscles by lifting weights. Thanks to power boosts from computers and radios, Atom Ant can pick up distress calls on his antennae and is also attuned to every panic button in the nation. Whenever he becomes aware of a problem, he reads up on the villain in question in his *Crook Book,* dons his red jersey emblazoned with a purple *A,* purple tights, and a white crash helmet, and soars into the sky crying, "Up and at 'em, Atom Ant!" If the hero needs to travel vast distances in an instant, he simply steps into the atom smasher and is quickly teleported. The insect is strong enough to hold up a falling skyscraper, or press several tons; watching him lift a ten-ton steamroller once, a character was moved to exclaim, "That ant isn't human!" Among the insect superhero's many adversaries are Crankenshaft's Monster, Karate Ant, Ferocious Flea (whose motto is, "If ya can't beat 'em, bash 'em"), Godzilla Termite, Killer Diller Gorilla, and Anastasia Antnik. In his off-hours, Atom Ant enjoys reading comic books about himself, watching television, and reading *The News*.

Comment. Hanna-Barbera's *The Atom Ant Show* debuted on NBC in 1965 (after he and **Secret Squirrel** were introduced in a prime-time special). There were twenty-six episodes, which were later syndicated as part of *The Banana Splits and Friends*. Howard Morris was the voice of Atom Ant. Gold Key published one issue of an Atom Ant comic book (1966). See also **Action Ant**.

ATOMIC BUNNY (a k a ATOMIC RABBIT)

Pedigree. Superpowered comic book rabbit.

Biography. An inhabitant of Bunnyville, Atomic Bunny gulps down U^{235}-irradiated Carrot Cubes to acquire superpowers and protect the town from harm. Chief among his powers are the ability to fly, superstrength, and the ability to use his ears like an extra pair of hands. When he isn't fighting his archenemy Sly Fox, the rabbit can be found giving young rabbits rides through the air or helping the military solve various problems (like putting steering wheels on parachutes to help control drift). Whether powered or not, the black-furred hare is always in uniform, which consists of a white *AB* on his pink-furred chest (a tattoo?); an orange cape with a blue lining; and a belt, in whose buckle he keeps his Cubes. The tough-as-nails hero has a fluffy white tail and a pink face.

Comment. The Charlton Comic was published from 1955 to 1959; the Al Fago creation was called *Atomic Rabbit* for its first eleven issues, then *Atomic Bunny* through no. 19 (apparently an attempt to capitalize on the success of **Bugs Bunny**). See **Atomic Mouse** for a comment on the titles' back-up features.

ATOMIC MOUSE

Pedigree. Third supermouse to hit the comic books (following **Supermouse** and **Mighty Mouse**).

Biography. Atomic Mouse helps the 1,999,999 Precinct keep order in peaceful Mouseville. (The police are pictured as dogs and pigs, years before the latter became a slur.) By popping a single U^{235} pill, the mouse acquires superstrength, the ability to fly through air and space at the speed of lightning, and supersenses. What's more, the effects of the pills are cumulative: The more the mouse takes, the stronger he gets. The hero's archenemy is the evil cat Count Gatto, who's assisted by the feline Shadow. The two commit everything from mundane crimes like bank robbery to more exotic robberites like stealing the

pot of gold at the end of the rainbow, but always end up in jail. (Because they keep escaping from prison, Atomic Mouse begins devising new ways to keep them out of trouble, such as flying them to Faraway Forest on the other side of the world, locking their heads in boards so kids can throw balls at them, and trapping them inside a spray of water that, as cats, they hate.) The duo has also been known to call on Gatto's sister Gertie, the witch, for her help . . . although she's so dumb she always proves more of a hindrance than a help. Atomic Mouse is also the voice of reason in Mouseville. Once, when a spaceship landed in the town and a giant mouse emerged, Atomic Mouse refused to attack the creature. He told the panicky populace that giantism did not mean that visitor was evil. Sure enough, the extraterrestrial introduced himself as Myko from Saturn, and was indeed benevolent. The mouse's ally is a dog named Professor Invento; the mouse occasionally uses the scientist's time machine to right wrongs in different eras. Atomic Mouse's sometime sidekick is Li'l Mouse, who is nonsuperpowered (see "Comment"). Atomic Mouse wears a black costume (although in some comics, it looks as if this were his fur, not fabric), with a white *A* on his chest, white gloves and spats, and yellow trunks. He wears a red cape, which is sometimes fringed with blue. And mark those calendars: The first day of every month is Atomic Mouse Day.

Comment. The Charlton Comics character was created by Al Fago and appeared in *Atomic Mouse* nos. 1 to 54 (1953 to 1963) and again in its own title, which ran five issues (1984 to 1986). The mouse also appeared in all three issues of *Giant Comics* (1957) and in other Charlton titles. Famed artist Neal Adams was one of the ghost artists on the strip. Executive editor/artist Fago was responsible for many animal features that appeared in *Atomic Mouse, Zoo Funnies* (twenty-eight issues, from 1945 to 1955), and also in the comic featuring **Atomic Bunny**. These include Goofy Rabbit, a tall, pink hare whose abilities fall far short of his assessment of them; Li'l Mouse, a practical joker when he's away from Atomic Mouse; Simon Skunk, who can turn a simple outing like fishing into a disaster; Punchy the Crow of Zooville, a kindly bodybuilder who gets into adventures with his friends, the slick, con artist Blackie Crow, the ambitious Shorty Squirrel, the gentle Bruno Bear, and others; Tubby Hippo, who is also of Zooville and has adventures with the sly Gate Gator; Leon the Lyin' Lion, a prevaricator whose tall tales have a way of backfiring (out camping with friends, he lies about a giant mosquito he fought once, his self-aggrandizing fib causing every mosquito within earshot to grow irate and attack); and the denizens of Farmer Gray's Red Barn, who include Augie the Dog (unrelated to **Augie Doggie**), Prudence Platypus, Martha Mole, Dorie Duck, and Mr. Owl.

AUGIE DOGGIE

Pedigree. TV father and son dogs.

Biography. Augie Doggie wears a green sweater (no pants) and lives with Doggie Daddie, who wears a blue collar (nothing else) in a small suburban home. Augie, who is half the size of his father, is a clever science whiz; Daddie, whose voice sounds like that of Jimmy Durante, is a former vaudevillian and bird dog. In short, the two are nothing alike, yet their affection for one another is unshakable. This is evidenced not only by their actions but by their ornate, poetic way of addressing one another. Doggie Daddie is the lesser offender: While he concludes many lines with declarations like, "My son, my son" and "favorite son," he also murders the language, using words and phrases such as "al-you-min-i-mum" (aluminum), "Do my eyes perceive me?" "As a matter of factual," "Foinishins" (furnishings), "toe-may-tee-o" (tomato), and comparatively minor offenses like "foist" and "ting." (Doggie Daddie's best line was inspired when he was trying to catch up on the news and Augie butted in. Daddie called him, "My newspaper-readin'-interruptin' son"). However, it's Augie who regularly comes up with the florid turns of phrase. He constantly refers to his father as "Dear old dad," often embellishing or amending it as, "Old tuckered-out dad," "Dear old under-pressure parent," "Mon papa," "Father who knows all," "Poverty-stricken dad," "Grown-up dad of mine," and the like. In their cartoons, one is always coming to the rescue of the other. Occasionally, the problems are self-imposed. In *Ro-Butler*, Augie builds his father a robot servant for Father's Day. When Daddie breaks the controls, the automaton goes dangerously haywire. In *Party Pooper Pop*, Augie would rather sit in his room, studying science, surrounded by his banners from Yale, MIT, and Harvard, than go to a party; Doggie Daddie draws on his own experience on the stage and as a self-professed lady killer to teach his antisocial son how to comport himself at a party. In one of their best efforts, *Growing, Growing, Gone,* Daddie

thoughtlessly chuckles while reading Augie's fanciful autobiography and, declaring "I abhor ridicule," the little dog runs away. Doggie Daddie poses as a ghost, an outlaw, and Robin Hood to try and scare the boy into returning; nothing works, however, until the pooch runs into Peggy Poodle. Her advances terrify him, and he's home in a flash. More often than not, however, the dogs' problems come from outside. In *Peck O'Trouble,* Daddie is having a terrible time doing his taxes, and Augie is having an even worse time trying to keep things quiet, as a fly, Augie's sneezes, and finally a pesky woodpecker annoy "dear old dad." In *Hum Sweet Hum,* Augie is slated to conduct the singing Humboldt Hummingbird in a TV concert; however, Chops the Cat has other ideas, posing as Santa, a voice coach, and so on, in an effort to eat the bird. *Dough Nutty* pits them against crook Lefty Louie, whose counterfeiting machine Augie has found. *Swats the Matter* finds the dogs besieged by a trio of mosquitoes; the enemies do battle with a flyswatter, hot coals, pans, Flit, a toilet plunger, and, finally, swords—prompting Daddie to groan, "Why couldn't we have mosquitoes that play chess?" *Fuss N' Feathers* has Augie go out to the hen house where Cleo Elizabeth (a tip of the hat to Liz Taylor fans) is sitting on a giant egg that, unknown to Augie, has fallen from a zoo truck. Out pops an ostrich, who wreaks havoc in the household. *Good Mousekeeping* pits the two against a determined mouse (the weapons, this time, are a shotgun, bowling ball, room filled with mousetraps, fishing rod, and mallet). *Skunk You Very Much* has a polecat follow them home from the woods. *It's a Mice Day* costars Philbert Mouse, who is living at the house with the dogs' blessings. When the mouse takes ill, Augie concocts a formula to shrink himself to the mouse's size so he can nurse him. Daddie also takes a swig, at which point Bad Cat arrives to eat them all. Luckily, Augie is able to make a growing formula, after which he shrinks the cat and makes him move in with the mouse.

Comment. Hanna-Barbera produced forty-five Augie Doggie cartoons. They aired on *Quick Draw McGraw* (see entry), which was aired in syndication, beginning in 1959. Daws Butler provided Augie's voice, and Doug Young was Doggie Daddie. According to the characters' creator, Mike Maltese, "I called the little guy Augie Doggie because Augie rhymed with Doggie and it sounded good."

AVENGER

Pedigree. Eagle aide to the TV superhero Birdman.

Biography. Based in Central City, the superhero Birdman derives his powers from the Egyptian sun god Ra. Whenever he's in need of assistance (i.e., cut off from the power-giving rays of the sun), he uses a communicator on his neck to summon Avenger. The bird is powerful enough to carry Birdman if need be, and is especially useful when it comes to swooping down and disarming villains who are attacking Birdman. Avenger wears an Egyptian neck piece, and although it can understand Birdman's instructions, it can only answer, *skree! skrawww! grawk!* and the like. Birdman, Avenger, and the young Birdboy are headquartered inside a volcano.

Comment. The characters appeared on Hanna-Barbera's *Birdman and the Galaxy Trio,* which began airing on NBC in 1967. There were thirty-eight episodes in all; the characters also appeared in several issues (starting with no. 1) of Gold Key's comic *Hanna-Barbera Super TV Heroes,* which ran seven issues in 1968 to 1969. The Galaxy Trio were superheroes in a separate cartoon. Another "law-eagle" was Legal Eagle, a comical figure with a tin star and a porkpie hat. He appeared on Filmation's *The New Adventures of Fat Albert* (1987).

AZRAEL

Pedigree. Cat owned by the sorcerer Gargamel, nemesis of the diminutive Smurfs.

Biography. The little brown cat—who behaves like a real cat, unable to speak or walk upright—lives in a castle with its master (and, later, with his apprentice Scruple) and goes wherever Gargamel goes, helping him try to capture and/or destroy Smurfs. More than once, Azrael has spoiled a perfect trap (such as a concealed pit filled with spikes, or one of Gargamel's disguises) by meowing excitedly and giving its presence away.

Comment. The cat and the Smurfs were created by Belgian cartoonist Pierre "Peyo" Culliford in 1957 and made their debut in the weekly comic magazine *Spirou,* which was distributed throughout Europe. The name of his little blue elves had an unusual genesis: Peyo was at a restaurant and couldn't think of the word *salt,* so he asked his companion to pass the *schtroumpf,* which is Flemish for "whatchamacallit." He remembered the word because it had made him and his friend laugh; when he came up with his comic strip characters, he thought, "Maybe it will make other people laugh too." He was right. The characters came to NBC television as the Smurfs. The Hanna-Barbera show aired on Saturday mornings beginning in September 1981 and was an immediate hit. Scruple debuted on the show in 1986. A feature-length animated film, *The Smurfs and the Magic Flute,* a French-Belgian coproduction made in 1975, was released in the United States in 1983. Hanna-Barbera also has produced a half-dozen prime-time Smurfs specials, the best of which was the first one, *The Smurfs Springtime Special.* In it, Gargamel learns that he can create gold by boiling six Smurfs in molten lead. Don Messick provides the voice of the cat. Marvel published three issues of a Smurfs comic book from 1982 to 1983. Azriel is the name of several figures in the Old Testament; Azazel is one of the names of the Devil.

BABAR THE ELEPHANT

Pedigree. Literary light who has become a TV and
motion picture star.

Biography. Born in the Great Forest, Babar lives
there until his mother is slain by a hunter. Fleeing to
the city, he is adopted by a wealthy, elderly woman
who dresses him in wonderful clothing and sets him
up in a lovely home. He is soon joined by his cousin
Celeste and her younger brother Arthur—but the
Great Forest beckons and, eventually, the pachyderms return. There, Babar and Celeste are wed and
become the king and queen of the elephants.

Comment. The character was created by author/
artist Jean de Brunhoff (1899 to 1937), whose first
book was *L'Histoire de Babar, le petit elephant*, published in 1931. (It was published in English as *The
Story of Babar*.) The rich color in the oversize book
enhanced the wonderful tale, and was followed by
Le Roi Babar (1933, *Babar the King*), *ABC de Babar*
(1934, *Babar's ABC*), *Les Vacances de Zéphir*
(1936, *Babar's Friend Zephir*), and the posthu-
mously published *Babar en famille* (1938, *Babar at
Home*), *Le Voyage de Babar* (1939, *Babar's Travels*), and *Babar et le Père Noël* (1941, *Babar and Father Christmas*). The author's son, Laurent, has
continued the series, writing nearly thirty volumes,
the first of which was *Babar et ce coquin d'Arthur*
(1946, *Babar and that Rascal Arthur*). Although his
fame derived from the books, Babar has gained new
fans thanks to the Home Box Office (HBO, cable
television) cartoon series, which premiered in 1989
and consists (thus far) of fifty-two half-hour episodes (produced by Nelvana Productions and by the
Clifford Ross Company.) *Babar: The Movie* was released by New Line Cinema in 1989. The film re-
counts a chilling event that Babar faced on his first
day as king: the threat of the villainous Rataxes and
his army of blue rhinoceroses. Aided by Celeste, Arthur, and the monkey Zéphir, Babar builds a Trojan
mammoth to scare off the fiends. The cartoons are
drawn in a style identical to that in the books. Commenting on the enduring success of the property,
Laurent de Brunhoff says, "Children like elephants
and the warm family life. There's a lot of love between the characters, and that's very appealing to
kids."

BABBIT AND CATSTELLO

Pedigree. Cartoon parodies of comedians Abbott
and Costello.

Biography. In their cartoon debut, *A Tale of Two
Kitties* (1942), Babbit is a tall, lean cat with white
feet and hands; Catstello is a dumpy, black cat with a
white belly. Catstello is kindly: When Babbit tells
him to climb a tree and catch **Tweety**, the cat replies,
"I like boids. I'll go hungry first." But the con cat
Babbit convinces his dull-witted friend to make the
effort, and the rest of the cartoon is devoted to
Catstello's failed attempts by ladder, springs, wings,
and TNT to bring the bird down. In the next cartoon, *A Tale of Two Mice* (1945), the characters are
no longer cats but mice, trying to carry a hunk of
cheese past a vigilant cat. In their third and final cartoon, *The Mouse Merized Cat* (1946), the duo are
still mice trying to get cheese past a cat. This time,
Babbit uses hypnosis to persuade his partner that
he's a tough dog.

Comment. These exquisitely animated Warner
Brothers short subjects were lost in the shadow of
the studio's more popular **Bugs Bunny** and **Porky
Pig**. Mel Blanc provided a remarkable facsimile of
Costello's voice; Tedd Pierce did a properly low-
keyed copy of Abbott.

BABY HUEY

Pedigree. Diapered, superstrong duck featured in
comic books and animated cartoons.

Biography. The intellectually dense and headstrong
Baby Huey lives in suburban Duckville with his surprisingly tiny mother and small, timid, derby-
wearing dad. One *big* duck, Huey hatched from his
egg (already wearing a blue bonnet, blue bow tie,
blue shirt, and diaper) able to talk—albeit rather im-
maturely. Over the years, the duck has never graduated from phrasing such as "That I will dood,
mama." His favorite expression is "Duh." However,
there are compensations. Huey is incredibly strong:
He can fling an airplane into the skies and can, with
ease, straighten an iron bar bent with effort by the
mighty "Crowbar" McQuack, the "World's Strong-
est Duck." Although Huey will eat anything, he is
partial to apple pie and carries around a ten-gallon
baby bottle. Everything in Huey's world is duck ori-

ented, from the explorer Christopher Columduck to the automobile Quackillac.

Comment. Huey's first comic book appearance was in Harvey Comics's *Casper, the Friendly Ghost* no. 1 in 1949. The hefty duck's own magazine began in 1956 and lasted ninety-nine issues. He also starred in thirty-three issues of *Baby Huey and Papa* (1962 to 1968) and fifteen issues of *Baby Huey Duckland* (1962 to 1966). He appeared in eleven Famous Studios/Paramount theatrically released cartoons from 1951 to 1959.

BABY SNOOTS
Pedigree. Tiny elephant of comic book fame.
Biography. Baby Snoots's parents are circus elephants. They want their offspring to be a musician in the symphony (he studies trumpet with Professor Fortissimo), but Baby wants to be in the circus. Overhearing them argue, intinerant Uptite Mouse frightens Baby Snoots just before a show: The elephant bolts from his parents, runs to center ring, races up to the trapeze, swings across, and falls into a bucket of water, all to great applause. Unfortunately, the ringmaster fires the three elephants and they leave with Uptite in tow . . . against Papa Elephant's wishes. They return to their small house in the woods (Uptite settles into a tin can outside), the only walking, talking animals in an otherwise human world. The family never returns to the circus, and the baby elephant gets into all kinds of trouble—largely because, unlike most elephants, Snoots has a terrible memory. For example, sent to town to buy pizza and butter, Snoots puts the pizza rather than the butter in ice to keep it fresh. He's also naive and trusting: A pair of crooks convinces him to help rob a mansion in exchange for a booking at Carnegie Hall. Fortunately, the streetwise Uptite is always on hand to help Snoots from a jam. The little blue pachyderm dresses in a diaper and bonnet; Uptite wears only a small baseball cap. (The mouse refers to Snoots as an 'elefink," and to himself as a "meece" . . . the latter "borrowed" from **Mr. Jinks.**) Papa Elephant does little more than read the newspaper, while Mama Elephant is always cooking (blueberry pancakes and apple pie are her specialties).

Comment. The name was inspired by the radio character Baby Snooks; the elephant/mouse relationship is similar to that in **Dumbo.** The character starred in twenty-two issues of its own Gold Key

comic book (1970 to 1975), as well as in eleven issues of the company's *March of Comics* (1971 to 1982).

BAGGY PANTS
Pedigree. Little-known TV cartoon cat.
Biography. Dressed like Charlie Chaplin's Tramp, complete with a cane and moustache, the silent cat enjoys tame adventures as he tries to make friends or lend a hand on a movie set, at the circus, in a haunted house, on the beach and in other mundane settings. Despite being rebuffed by one and all, the cat retains a sunny disposition.

Comment. De Patie-Freleng produced thirteen episodes of the cartoon, which aired on *Baggy Pants and Nitwits* on NBC in 1977. The sight gags (there was only music and sound effects) are reminiscent of **The Pink Panther,** although not as inspired. The Nitwits were based on the popular park bench characters created by Ruth Buzzi and Arte Johnson for TV's *Laugh-In.*

BALOO
Pedigree. Literary character turned adventure cartoon star.
Biography. The big, benevolent bear befriends the human boy Mowgli, who is raised by a wolf family in the jungles of India. Baloo is particularly helpful protecting Mowgli against the boy-eating panther Shere Khan. The bear later turns up in a rather different environment: as pilot of the Sea Duck, a seaplane licensed by Higher for Hire, based in Cape Suzette. At his side are the plucky young bear navigator Kit Cloudkicker and the lion mechanic and stevedore Wildcat, while the bear Rebecca Cunningham and her daughter Molly handle things back at the office. Their nemesis is the air pirate Don Karnage, a fox, and his crew, which includes the dogs Dumptruck and Mad Dog. The strings of evil are pulled, behind the scenes, by evil Cape Suzette multimillionaire businesscat (who else?) Shere Khan.

Comment. The characters were introduced in Rudyard Kipling's *The Jungle Books* (1894 to 1895), a collection of animal tales for children. They were brought to the screen in Walt Disney's 1967 animated feature *The Jungle Book*. Twenty-three years later, Disney introduced the adventures of the airborne Baloo and his friends in the syndicated TV series and comic book *Tale Spin*.

BAMBI

Pedigree. Deer star of a novel and a Walt Disney film.

Biography. As the film begins, the rabbit Thumper scurries around the forest, informing one and all that a new Prince has been born: Bambi, son of the great Prince who leads all deer. After a few days, Bambi is up and out, learning to walk and meeting the denizens of the wood, most notably Thumper—who drums a hollow log with his rear legs and says proudly, "I'm thumpin'. That's why they call me Thumper." With Thumper's help, he also learns a few words, like bird, butterfly, and flower. While sniffing the flowers, Bambi comes nose-to-nose with a young skunk whom he innocently calls Flower; although Thumper gets hysterical, the skunk says, "He can call me Flower if he wants to," and the name sticks. On Bambi's next outing, he's less awkward and stilt legged than before—although you wouldn't know it when his deer Aunt Ena arrives with her daughter Faline. Bambi hides behind his mother's legs, and has to be coaxed to come out and play with the young doe. He finally does so and they romp together until the Great Prince passes. It's the first time Bambi has seen his father, and he's struck speechless by the imposing figure. Come winter, Bambi is shown the wonders of the season by Thumper—although he never quite gets the hang of skating, and ends up splayed and spinning on the ice. He does learn to eat the bark from trees and doesn't like it. Thus he's overjoyed when his mother takes him out one day and, pawing through the snow, finds new grass. They eat—until Bambi's mother smells the presence of Man. Telling her son, "Run, Bambi! Don't look back—keep running no matter what, to the thicket!" she sets off. Bambi heads home, thinking she's behind him, and when he arrives, he says breathlessly, "We made it! We made it, mother! We—Mother?" She isn't there. Instead, the Great Prince steps up and informs him, "Your mother can't be with you any more. Now you must be brave and learn to walk alone." The two walk off together, in silence. When spring arrives, Bambi's sporting a small rack of antlers, and his friends Thumper and Flower also look more mature. Indeed, they *are* more mature, as first Flower, then Thumper, fall in love. (Or as Friend Owl puts it, they "become twitterpated.") After fighting off rival buck Ronno, Bambi asks Faline to "stay" with him; she gladly agrees. All is well until fall, when a group of hunters arrives. The animals head to the hills, but a pack of hunting dogs corners Faline. Bambi rushes back and saves her, holding the dogs at bay while she runs. He isn't able to stop the hunters, however, and from somewhere in the distance a shot rings out. Bambi goes down, hit in the leg, yet no hunter comes: A campfire has run wild and set the forest ablaze. The Great Prince rushes over and yells at Bambi to get up; dazed, the deer obeys and follows his father through the inferno to the stream, where he's reunited with Faline. Come spring, when foliage returns to the charred woods, the Great Prince tells

The title credit for Bambi Meets Godzilla. *Courtesy* MARV NEWLAND.

Bambi he loves him and sets out alone to look for "a resting place." Standing alone, Bambi takes his place as the proud, Great Prince of the forest.

Comment. Bambi's voice changed as he grew; the voices were provided by Bobby Stewart, Donnie Dunagan, Hardy Albright, and John Sutherland. Peter Behn was Thumper, Bill Wright was Friend Owl, Paula Winslow was Bambi's mother, and Fred Shields was the Great Prince. In addition to a film adaptation, Dell's *4-Color* comic published the one-shot *Bambi's Children* (no. 30). Thumper also had his own title, in the rather curious teaming *Thumper Meets the 7 Dwarfs* (no. 19). The original novel *Bambi* was written by Felix Salten (pen name of Siegmund Salzmann) and first appeared in Germany in 1923. It was published in the United States in 1928, subtitled *A Life in the Woods*. The plots and characters are similar, and the animals speak in the novel much as they do on the screen (although the novel also features talking leaves, something Disney wisely avoided). Salten published a sequel *Bambi's Kinder* (*Bambi's Children*) in 1939.

Bambi made an unauthorized return to the screen in Marv Newland's masterful 1969 short subject *Bambi Meets Godzilla,* in which the titles crawl over a pastoral scene of the deer grazing. When they end, the monstrous foot of Godzilla crushes Bambi into the earth. The end titles crawl. In a non-Newland sequel, *Bambi's Revenge* (1970), a little hoof pokes from under Godzilla's toes, gives him a hotfoot, and the reptile leaps off.

THE BANANA SPLITS
Pedigree. Costumed animal stars of live-action television and comic book adventures.
Biography. The Banana Splits are rock musicians Fleegle (a dog), Snorky (a small elephant), Bingo (a gorilla), and Drooper (a lion). All wear what look like batting helmets with a banana stuck in the top: Fleegle wears a big bow tie, Drooper has spats, and both Snorky and Bingo are garbed in vests. All but Fleegle wear shades. The group lives in an apartment, where their rehearsals are constantly annoying their neighbors. The band travels around in their Banana Buggy, and their gigs are usually the starting point for their many adventures. In the *Dear Drooper* segment of the show, the lion is able to indulge his penchant for jokes. Posing questions like "Who invented spaghetti?" he'll answer, "A guy who used his noodle." The theme song is typical of the general mindlessness of the show, as the Splits sing:

One banana, two banana, three banana, four.
Four bananas make a bunch and so do many
more.
Four bananas, three bananas, two bananas, one.
All bananas playing in the bright warm sun.

Comment. *The Banana Splits Adventure Hour* was Hanna-Barbera's first try at a live-action series. As creator Joe Barbera explains it, "The show simply evolved when we decided to make some of the characters we were drawing larger and thereby give them more charm." Whether he succeeded is questionable; the costumes were less versatile than Muppets, and looked flabby and amateurish. The show ran on NBC, Saturday mornings, from 1968 to 1970 (following a prime-time preview). Paul Winchell was the voice of Fleegle, Don Messick was Snorky, Daws Butler was Bingo, and Allan Melvin played Drooper (the identities of the actors in the costumes is not known). Gold Key published nine issues of a Banana Splits comic book (1969 to 1971). An earlier bunch of animal rockers were the cartoon dogs The Beagles, long-eared rockers Stringer and Tubby, whose gigs invariably got them into trouble. Produced by Total TV Productions and Lancelot Productions, *The Beagles* debuted on CBS in 1966. There were twenty-six cartoons in all.

BANDIT
Pedigree. Faithful dog of TV and comic book star Jonny Quest.
Biography. Adventurer/scientist Dr. Benton Quest and his eleven-year-old son Jonny travel around the world with fellow researchers looking for scientific and archaeological artifacts. Jonny and the pint-size Bandit are inseparable, and the dog's *Grrrs* and *Yips* usually tell the youngster that danger is near. When Jonny is in trouble, Bandit will stop at nothing to rescue him. The white dog has black circles around both eyes, making it appear as though he's wearing a mask . . . like a bandit.

Comment. Hanna-Barbera's *The Adventures of Jonny Quest* first aired on ABC in 1964. There were twenty-six half-hour adventures; these were played straight rather than comical. Artist Doug Wildey created the characters; Don Messick provided the dog's bark. Another thirteen adventures were filmed in 1987, and twenty-six more are being considered for the future. Gold Key published one Johnny Quest comic book in 1964; a series from Comico, begun in 1986, prominently features Bandit in most adventures and has lasted more than thirty issues.

BANSHEE
Pedigree. Horse ridden by Marvel Comics western hero, Ghost Rider.

Biography. Schoolteacher Carter Slade is the scourge of villains in the old west. Coating a costume with "glowing dust" from a meteor, he rides forth as the irridescent Ghost Rider (later, Night Rider). Carter also sprinkles his horse Banshee with the powder, causing the animal to glow.

Comment. One of the least successful Marvel Comics western heroes, Ghost Rider first appeared in *A-1 Comics* no. 27 in 1950. He got his own magazine in 1967, which ran for seven issues. He has appeared sporadically in the Marvel lineup. Another Marvel avenger was the Black Rider, who rode the horse Satan through the pages of his own magazine from 1950 to 1955. See other Marvel Comics cowboy horses **Cyclone, Nightwind,** and **Steel.** See also **Black Fury** and **Sandy** (2).

BARFY
Pedigree. Pet dog in the "Family Circus" comic strip.

Biography. A grayish mutt, Barfy lives with Billy, Dolly, Jeffy, PJ, and their parents. Most of the time, Barfy just sits around, watching the highjinks of the family, scratching his back on the grass, or enjoying being petted. Sam, a small brown and white stray, ar-

Barfy with Sam (top) and Kitty. © KING FEATURES SYNDICATE.

"That was the pencil sharpener for heaven's sake, not the can opener."

rived next: The kids were nervous wrecks as their mother had the dog's description broadcast over the radio. When no one claimed him, he stayed . . . drawing initial jealousy from Barfy. However, the two dogs are nothing alike. Sam is more adventuresome, and enjoys taking baths with the kids or hanging around the dinner table for scraps. Brown and white Kittycat boldly wandered in the front door one day and also stayed, making the dogs envious because, as Dolly put it, "Cats are allowed up on things but dogs aren't." The last animal to join the strip was the pet rabbit Snowball. None of the animals speaks, nor do readers know what they're thinking . . . except for the occasional "?" when, for example, Dolly chides the cat, "Lost your mittens? You naughty kitten! Then you shall have no pie." (When dad announces he's off to "the rat race," Dolly also pipes up, "Kittycat wants to go too!")

Comment. Barfy has been a part of Bill Keane's one-panel daily strip since its inception in 1960. Sam joined the family on January 26, 1970, Kittycat became a permanent member on April 22 of the following year, and Snowball arrived on April 17, 1976. All were based on pets in the Keane household.

THE BARKLEYS
Pedigree. All-dog version of TV's *All in the Family.*

Biography. Dog Arnie Barkley is a bus driver who isn't afraid to voice his rather traditional view of things, from women's lib (he'll play sports with his sons, but not his daughter) to keeping up with the Joneses (or in this case, the Beagleses), to crime—much to the displeasure of his liberal daughter, two sons, and long-suffering wife, Agnes.

Comment. There were thirteen half-hour episodes of this De Patie-Freleng series, which aired on NBC from 1972 to 1973. The messages—largely of tolerance and charity—were straightforward enough for children to grasp. Henry Corden was the voice of Arnie, Joan Gerber was Agnes, Steve Lewis handled Chester, Julie McWhirter was daughter, Terri, and Gene Andrusco was young son, Roger. *All in the Family* was also the basis for the cartoon series *Wait Till Your Father Gets Home* (syndicated, 1972), about the human Boyle family. The only animal featured here was the pet dog, Julius.

BARNEY BEAR (1)
Pedigree. Moderately successful animated cartoon character of the 1940s.

Biography. The pear-shaped, lumbering, slow-talking bear lives in the woods and hasn't a malicious bone in his body, although he's constantly getting into trouble due to circumstance (trying to hibernate and being bothered by normal woodland activity), lack of forethought (taking timber that belongs to the local beavers, and having them come and gnaw down his abode to get it back), miscalculation (underestimating the resourcefulness of a fish he's trying to eat), or simple ineptitude (trying to grow a victory garden). Barney walks upright and wears trousers.

Comment. There were eighteen Barney cartoons from 1939 to 1952, produced by MGM. The original, pastoral look of the cartoons was replaced by a sharper design and more gags as the series wore on. Over the years, Billy Bletcher and Paul Frees were the principal voice of Barney, although animator Rudolf Ising contributed his voice as well. The bear also appeared in comic books featuring **Tom and Jerry.**

BARNEY BEAR (2)
Pedigree. Young comic book bear whose adventures teach him Christian lessons.
Biography. Barney lives in a house in the woods with his parents, and invariably becomes involved with woodland creatures who are confused or unhappy because they don't *"pray* and *trust* God!" In one adventure, the bear is washed down a stream to a land where all of the animals are like something out of Alice's Wonderland, moving backward or in circles. Barney learns that there are no families here, and declares, "No wonder things are so *mixed up!* Everybody needs *parents* to help them grow up!" Barney wears blue coveralls; all of the animals talk and wear clothing.

Comment. There were six Spire comics about Barney published from 1977 to 1981. Although Barney's father is almost identical to the cartoon **Barney Bear (1),** this Al Hartley creation is unrelated. There's a curious inconsistency in this series that preaches against hunting, but has the bears fish to put food on the table.

BARNEY THE INVISIBLE TURTLE
Pedigree. Comic book sleuth.
Biography. Standing approximately six feet tall, the bipedal Barney wears athletic shoes and a scarf, smokes a cigar, and assists his human partner, detective Ted Gavin, of Detroit. Barney deems his invisibility vital to their success, because, as he tells Ted, "You've got absolutely *nothing* going for you." True enough: Barney is constantly at dumb Ted's elbow,

telling him everything he should be doing. For example, cornered by thugs, Ted is distracted when he reaches into his pocket and finds "A fish. It must've got in there when I was in the lake." Barney replies, *"Quick*—throw it at them—it'll take 'em by *surprise!"* Barney rarely plunges into a dangerous situation himself, preferring to coach from the sidelines. Their cases range from finding missing persons to stopping rampaging robots.

Comment. The character appeared in one issue of his own magazine, published by Amazing Comics in 1987. Creator Rick Rodolfo says, "The inspiration for this, of course, was the old Jimmy Stewart movie *Harvey."*

BASIL OF BAKER STREET
Pedigree. The great mouse detective of a novel and a Disney film.
Biography. In the year 1897, England was getting set to honor the mouse-monarch Queen Moustoria, who was about to celebrate her fiftieth year on the throne. Dr. David Q. Dawson (a mouse) arrives just in time to celebrate the Diamond Jubilee, and is looking for a place to stay. Meanwhile, little Olivia Flaversham (also a mouse) is celebrating her birthday, for which her toy maker father, Hiram, has built her a near life-size mechanical mouse. Suddenly, an evil bat flaps in and, while Olivia hides in the closet at her father's urging, the intruder makes off with the elder Flaversham. Sobbing, the little girl leaves in search of the legendary mouse detective Basil, who she hopes can help her. But she's unable to find his home, located in the cellar at 221B Baker Street, and as she sits sobbing in the rain, Dawson finds her. He knows where Baker Street is and gladly takes her there; the housekeeper (mousekeeper?) Mrs. Judson admits them. (*Note:* Sherlock Holmes's housekeeper is named Mrs. Hudson.) After the newcomers wait for a while, a beggar arrives. But it's actually Basil, who had been in disguise for an investigation. Doffing the garb, he listens as Olivia explains what happened. Basil is convinced that the bat was Fidget, the peg-legged employee of "my archenemy Ratigan," who believes that he should be king. Basil vows to find his hideout and rescue Hiram. Elsewhere, at that very moment, the rat Ratigan is busy explaining to his flunkies that he will soon be the new ruler of England: He plans to abduct the queen and replace her with a Hiram-built robot who will name him king. (In case anyone doubts that Ratigan has the necessary ruthlessness to carry out his plan, he summons his immense cat Felicia and has her eat the

drunk little mouse Bartholomew.) That mean streak proves valuable, because Hiram refuses to build a mechanical queen. To help persuade him, Ratigan sends Fidget out to kidnap Olivia. However, not only does the bat fail (Olivia sees him first) but Basil, Dawson, and the girl find Fidget's cap in the snow. Basil brings it to the bloodhound Toby, who sniffs the cap then gives them a ride as he follows the scent. He tracks Fidget to a toyshop, where the bat is busy collecting items Hiram will need to build the robot. Unfortunately, the bat is able to grab Olivia and get away . . . but at least he leaves his list behind. Basil does a chemical analysis and learns that it came from *The Rat Trap,* a pub on the Thames. Disguised as a sea captain and his mate, Basil and Dawson head over. Alas, Ratigan's guards recognize them and subdue the pair, leaving them in a trap unique in all the world. The mice are bound and left in a mousetrap. As a record plays, the arm draws a string tighter. When the cord knocks over a glass, a marble will fall out and knock over an ax that not only will slice off their heads, but will activate a gun and crossbow. Concurrently, Hiram has built the robot mouse. Ratigan takes it to the palace, makes the substitution, and plans to feed the queen to Felicia—while, back at the pub, Basil manages to maneuver the mousetrap so that the ax cuts them free. They dodge the other weapons and, freeing Olivia from her bottle-prison, hitch a ride to the palace on board Toby. Basil saves the queen as Fidget is about to hurl her into the cat's mouth. The Dog chases Felicia away and Basil runs onto the celebration platform, just as the bogus queen names Ratigan king—and the rat begins reciting changes in the way the country is to be run (beginning with higher taxes and the restoration of slavery). Basil kicks the robot queen to pieces and the rat grabs Olivia and makes off in his dirigible. Basil, Dawson, and Hiram pursue on a platform carried aloft by party balloons bundled inside a flag. Although Ratigan pushes Fidget into the Thames to lighten the airship, the hasty flight causes him to crash into the Big Ben clock tower. After a wild chase through the gears (a superbly animated sequence), Ratigan falls into the river—presumably to his death. Returning home and seeing Olivia and her father safely off, Basil names Dawson his official assistant . . . as a mysterious figure arrives and asks for the detective's help in solving a crime. All of the characters in the film wear garb appropriate to humans of late nineteenth-century England.

Comment. Barrie Ingham was the voice of Basil, Val Bettin was Dr. Dawson, Candy Candido was

Fidget, and the incomparable Vincent Price was Ratigan. Susanne Pollatschek provided the voice for Olivia, and the delightful Alan Young was her father. The 1986 film was based on Eve Titus's 1974 novel *Basil of Baker Street.* That was, in fact, the name of the film until several months prior to its release; the failure of the live-action feature *Young Sherlock Holmes* suggested to the Disney people that Holmesian-based films might be off-putting at the box office.

BATFINK
Pedigree. TV bat superhero.
Biography. Deciding to become a crime fighter, a not terribly imposing bat dons huge metal wings (which double as shields) and, with the assistance of Super Sonic Sonar and his Japanese aid Karate, goes out on board the Batillac (a Volkswagen with stylish but nonfunctional wings in back) whenever the police chief calls on the hot line. During his career, Batfink has battled the likes of the Robber Hood, Rainmaker, Brother Goose, Cinderobber, Daniel Boom, the Thief from Baghdad, Jerkules, Napoleon Blown Apart, Roz the Schnozz, the Mean Green Midget, the Sonic Boomer, and Whip Van Winkle. However, his archenemy is Hugo a Go Go, a wacky scientist.

Comment. Inspired by the success of TV's *Batman,* this Hal Seeger (**Fearless Fly**) production flew into syndication in 1966 with ninety-six episodes. Bob McFadden was the voice for both characters. The name was derived from the expression *rat fink,* which was popular at the time.

THE BEAGLE BOYS
Pedigree. Criminal dogs in the Disney comic books.
Biography. The four ex-cons (who walk upright and are more human than canine) are identified only by the numbers on their orange sweaters: 176-167, 176-617, 176-671, and 176-761. They also wear black masks and blue trousers and caps. Although the four, unshaven dogs look the same, there *are* differences; for example, 671 is the brightest of the dumb bunch, 167 likes poetry (his favorite anthology is *Crime Rhymes*) and 761 has curious culinary tastes, i.e., catsup on ice cream and peanut butter pizza with gravy. For years, they tried every way they could think of to steal the Money Bin of **Scrooge McDuck.** Indeed, it got so bad that Scrooge installed a special Beagle Alarm System, just "to keep tabs on the terrible Beagle Boys." (They got around it by hiring decoys—"rejects" who hadn't made it into their esteemed ranks.) The Beagles have a book of by-

laws, which also contains their crime tips (the first of which is "Make sure all guns are loaded"). Concurrently, they were also the chief adversaries of **Super Goof**. Among their crimes were stealing animals from zoos so they can make a fortune by opening their own zoo in a country that "doesn't have a single zoo" (not only did Super Goof foil them, but they'd have gone broke anyway: They had chosen an African nation). Today, led by their brawny, tough-as-nails mother "Ma" Beagle, the villains are regulars on the TV series and in the comic book *DuckTales* and are once again devoted to stealing Scrooge's Money Bin. (Now, however, there are seven dogs, of all different shapes and sizes—presumably, some of the rejects made the grade.)

Comment. The characters first appeared in *Walt Disney's Comics and Stories* no. 134 in 1951, starred in forty-seven issues of their own magazine from 1964 to 1979, and appeared in various one-shot titles as well as *Super Goof*. They were created by legendary **Donald Duck** artist/writer Carl Barks.

BEAKY BUZZARD

Pedigree. Minor star of Warner Brothers theatrical shorts.

Biography. The gawky, toucan-beaked Beaky made his debut in 1945 in *The Bashful Buzzard,* in which the mother buzzard sends her children out to fetch dinner . . . instructing the fumbling Beaky to get, at the very least, "a butterfly or a little worm." Trailing his siblings to a farm, he gets stuck on the weather vane and has to be rescued by mom. (Meanwhile, the other birds have brought home a cow—with the milking farmer still attached—a dog *and* hydrant, and more.) Beaky goes after a bumblebee and gets stung in the process. While soothing his wound in a pond, he gets into an argument with what he thinks is a diminutive creature . . . but which is, in fact, a huge winged dragon. The monster chases Beaky into the skies; somehow, the bird manages to subdue it and presents it to his startled mother. In 1950, a somewhat more aggressive (although no luckier) Beaky returned in *The Lion's Busy* (a title that hasn't a thing to do with the cartoon, but is terrific nonetheless). In it, Beaky follows Leo the Lion around, trying to kill and eat him. After several close calls, the panic-stricken Leo goes into a cave and doesn't come out for years, by which time Beaky "can't eat nothing anymore but marshmallows." Later that year, in *Strife with Father,* continuity is forgotten as Monte and Evelyn Sparrow find and adopt an aban-

doned egg, which hatches into Beaky and causes problems in the treehouse.

Comment. The unrelated buzzards Pappy and Elvis appeared in the Warner cartoon *Backwoods Bunny* (1959), determined to make a meal of **Bugs Bunny**. Another buzzard, Walt Disney's Ben Buzzard, was the costar of the 1943 Donald Duck short *Flying Jalopy,* as an unutterably seedy used-plane salesbird.

BEANS

Pedigree. Theatrical cartoon cat; original teammate of **Porky Pig**.

Biography. The chubby, often impish, bipedal black cat in overalls first appeared in *I Haven't Got a Hat,* tossing a cat and dog on a piano to disturb the schoolhouse recital of snooty Oliver Owl. Oliver gets revenge by unloading a fountain pen full of ink on Beans, who falls on a bench, which flings him and a can of paint into the school. Coated with ink and paint, the two make up. But that's the only lull in Beans's action-packed career. In his second appearance, *A Cartoonist's Nightmare,* an animator falls asleep and ends up in his drawing, where he and Beans face the likes of Battling Barney, a kangaroo, and Spike the Spider. He faces Oliver again in his next cartoon, *Hollywood Capers.* Posing as Oliver Hardy, Beans gets into a movie studio and creates havoc on the set of a film the owl is trying to direct. In his fourth adventure, Beans wins the hand of Porky's Pig's daughter (see **Porky Pig** for details). Beans was also teamed with **Ham** and **Ex** in a pair of cartoons: The twin dogs are said to be the cat's nephews!

Comment. The cat's debut cartoon in 1935 also marked the first appearance of Porky Pig. The two were intended to be a team (Porky and Beans), but the pig far outshined his partner, even when Beans was the featured player. The cat starred in seven Warner Brothers cartoons before being retired in 1944.

BELFRY

Pedigree. Comic book nemesis of Spooky, the Tuff Little Ghost.

Biography. A humanoid bat with huge bat ears who wears formal attire, a ratty top hat, and a purple cape. Belfry lives in a cave and is devoted to annoying the ghost Spooky, for example, by pouring honey on him and letting ants crawl all over him. Belfry's goal is to run the ghost out of town so he can take over Spooky's Spookville home. Invariably, however, the bat's plans backfire.

Comment. The bat appeared primarily in one- and two-page gags in Harvey Comics *Spooky*, which began publication in 1955, and in other Spooky and Casper the Friendly Ghost titles. Another bat named Belfry was seen in the Filmation TV cartoon series and First Comics comic book *Ghostbusters*, which is unrelated to the film of the same name (Filmation's live-action *Ghost Busters*, sans Belfry, aired on Saturday mornings in 1975 to 1976 and predated the hit movie of the same name). The pudgy-cheeked, soft-spoken bat hung out with the heroes at their headquarters in the 1986 incarnation. Also seen in the Filmation live-action series, cartoon, and comic book was the strong, obedient gorilla Tracy.

BELVEDERE

Pedigree. Comic strip dog.

Biography. A brown mutt with black spots, Belvedere (a male) is owned by the Dibbles of suburban Floogle County. A food fanatic, Belvedere has petitioned the government to start a bone-stamp program, has perfected boomerang tossing to steal meat from the barbeque, is very fond of wine, and even bakes (his rum cakes spout geysers when sliced). His doghouse undergoes regular renovations, whether it's to accommodate an L-shaped sofa, to turn it into a penthouse and install an elevator, to add rockers so

© Field Enterprises, Inc., 1979

" HE SAYS HE WON'T FETCH THE PAPER. HE'S OVERQUALIFIED. "

he can be rocked to sleep, or to change it to look like a fire hydrant. A sporting dog, Belvedere frequently goes hunting with owner Orville, and enjoys croquet, pool, golf, Monopoly, and other games. However, he regularly cheats at cards, usually with the help of the other household pets, Jezebel, the cat (who bends her tail in the shape of cards held by other players) and Chi Chi the parrot, who looks more like a toucan (she reveals the numbers using puffs of cigar smoke). Belvedere's veterinarian is Dr. Barkum, who has had to deal with such bizarre maladies as removing a swallowed hand grenade. One of Belvedere's most annoying habits is barking at cars using a megaphone; his most outrageous stunt has been to steal a construction derrick and use it to fish. Belvedere refuses to fetch newspapers, insisting (through the parrot, who can talk) that he's overqualified. For a musical instrument, he plays the gong, much to the dismay of his family. Whenever and wherever the Dibbleses go traveling with the dog, whomever they're visiting always pretends to be out.

Comment. George Crenshaw's witty one-panel daily strip was inaugurated in 1974.

BENJAMIN BEAR

Pedigree. TV cartoon bear.

Biography. The conceit of the story is that all of the teddy bears in the world are alive, and only pretend to be limp and lifeless. Otherwise, Benjamin Bear says, "No one would tell us their problems, or cry on us when they feel bad." However, according to the narrator, "One day, each year, when all the stars in the nighttime sky are just right . . . something magical happens." The bears leave their sleeping owners and, by hook or crook, go to a remote wood (apparently in France) where they hold a picnic. Benjamin Bear—well spoken, alert, and dressed in a tight, red vest—is an old hand at this, and his job is to lead Sally's teddy bear Wally to his first picnic. Mailing themselves to a nearby post office, they walk the rest of the way, stopping only when they find a human, Amanda, crying in the woods. Now, teddy bears have three all-important rules: to be a good listener, never to let people see them move, and never to tell anyone about the picnic. But naive Wally feels bad for the girl and talks to her. She explains that her

George Crenshaw's self-impressed pooch **Belvedere.** © FIELD ENTERPRISES.

teddy bear Doc is missing and she's heartbroken. Having broken rule number two, Wally blows rule number three by telling her that Doc's at the picnic and offers to take her there. Benjamin is furious with his ward, but they make Amanda up to look like a bear and lead her to the picnic. There, in a moment of exuberance, the girl leaps up and her makeup falls away; at once, all of the bears "go teddy," dropping where they are. Amanda begins to cry about what she's done, and Wally shouts at his dozens of comrades, "Teddy bears aren't supposed to make children cry!" That does the trick, and while the bears slowly awaken, Doc comes to Amanda. The feasting and frolicking resumes, and a good time is had by all. Benjamin and Wally make it home before dawn and resume their roles as teddy bears.

Comment. The featurette was inspired by the 1913 song "The Teddy Bear's Picnic" by John W. Bratton and James B. Kennedy. The movie was directed by Bill Speers from a script by Derek Dorio and Dan Lalande, based on a story by Gerald Tripp and Darson Hall. Jonathan Crombie was the voice of Ben, Marsha Moreau was Amanda, and Stuart Stone was Wally. The Lacewood Productions film was syndicated in 1989. Another bear who was seen one time only in an animated featurette was Oliver Bear, star of the 1983, forty-five-minute-long Dutch film *The Dragon That Wasn't . . . Or Was He?* Set in modern-day times, it features the conceited, rich, portly, and unimaginative Oliver Bear, who doesn't believe that his servant has really seen a dragon on the castle grounds. However, Oliver become a believer when he finds what he thinks is a beach ball and takes it inside: The ball is really a giant egg and it hatches, relasing a baby dragon, which causes considerable turmoil at Oliver's big party.

BEPPO THE SUPER-MONKEY

Pedigree. Comic book lab animal from Krypton, home world of Superman.

Biography. When scientist Jor-El learned that the planet Krypton was soon to explode, he set about designing a rocket that would carry his family to safety. Beppo the monkey was "the experimental monkey [Jor-El] used to determine whether his son could survive space conditions," subjecting him to a cosmic ray chamber and other experiments. When Krypton was on the verge of destruction, Jor-El sent his son to earth, where he became Superman; Beppo, no fool, stowed away onboard the rocket. Upon reaching earth, he, too, acquired superpowers, a virtue conveyed by earth's yellow sun (as opposed to the red sun of Krypton). Possessing powers such as superstrength and the ability to fly, Beppo wears a red cape and trunks and an ill-fitting blue shirt with a red *S* on a yellow field. Along with **Comet the Super-Horse, Krypto,** and **Streaky the Super-Cat,** Beppo is a member of the crime-fighting Legion of Super-Pets.

Comment. Beppo first appeared in DC Comics's *Superboy* no. 76 in 1959. Some accounts refer to Beppo as having been a passenger on an early test rocket, instead of a stowaway.

BERNICE, THE WHIFFLE HEN

Pedigree. Bird who predates Popeye in his own comic strip.

Biography. The flying, yellow-feathered Bernice is a "lucky hen." Thus when friends Castor Oyl (Olive's brother) and Ham Gravy (Olive's boyfriend) find her, they decide to take Bernice to the casino located on Dice Island. They know there's no way they can lose. The two men buy a boat, then search the waterfront for someone to pilot it: They hire a squinting sailor named Popeye, who made his debut in the strip . . . and in American folklore. Olive joins them on the voyage, and not only don't Castor and Ham become wealthy, but Popeye and Olive quickly take over the strip from them!

Comment. Bernice first appeared in the *Thimble Theatre* comic strip in 1929. She was created by E. C. Segar. Another animal that has appeared in the strip is Bernard, one of 328 vultures who live with Popeye's foe the Sea Hag on Vulture Island. See also **Junior.**

BERT RACCOON

Pedigree. Star of TV cartoon series.

Biography. Bert lives in Evergreen Forest, which is "quiet, peaceful, serene . . . that is, until Bert Raccoon wakes up." Bert is a reporter for the local newspaper the *Standard,* and his sense of adventure and inquisitiveness usually get him into trouble with other denizens of the forest. His close, long-suffering friends are the raccoons Ralph (his publisher) and Melissa (his girlfriend). Other pals include the little sheepdog Broo, the big dogs Schaeffer and Sophia, and the bespectacled, bow-tied Cedric the Aardvark. When any or all of them need to get away from the pressures of the village, they retire to the clubhouse, a shack deep in the woods. The only dark spot in the daily life of Evergreen is the presence of Cyril Sneer, a pink, cigar-chomping aardvark, and Cedric's father. Cyril lives in a castle and loves nothing more than money. (To the tune of "I Dream of Jeannie," he sings, "I dream of money that I'll never share . . ."). The only time he ever softened was when he encountered the young runaway raccoon Bentley, whose plight reminded him of his own troubled youth (and whom he talked into going home). Cyril's aides are three nameless little pigs. Other animals who inhabit the forest are Mr. Knox, a crocodile; the wealthy chicken Lady Baden-Baden; and Mr. Mammoth, a very successful business-rhinoceros. Bert wears a red sweatshirt with a big yellow *B* on the front, has a voice reminiscent of Popeye's, and loves peanut butter.

Comment. The characters first appeared in the 1983 featurette *The Raccoons and the Lost Star,* in which Cyril (tough to take seriously in his Napoleon-style hat) goes to a distant world and plots to imprison all the animals on earth, after which he plans to conquer the planet, assisted by his pigs as officers and bears as soldiers. The plan is thwarted by the raccoons and by the three dogs. A half-hour series was introduced in 1987, produced by Hinton Animation and the Canadian Broadcasting Corporation. Len Carlson provides the voice of Bert. Kevin Gillis created the characters.

BERTRAM
Pedigree. Horse star of cartoons and a popular videogame.
Biography. Bertram is the brave all-white horse of the medieval knight Sir Dirk the Daring, who is in the service of King Ethelred (and in love with the potentate's daughter, Daphne). An excellent "bloodhound," Bertram can track anything virtually anywhere, and refuses to desert his master even in the most unpleasant situations—as when the evil Phantom Knight turns the warrior into a dog (Bertram simply nudges Dirk all the way to the hut of a wizard who can help him) or when the sorceress Sevilla uses her magic to "control anything on two legs" (Dirk blindfolds himself, unsheathes his sword, and has Bertram lead him right to the vile lady). Extremely clever and resourceful—he once rolled a huge boulder in front of a cave to trap enemies within and, another time, helped Daphne use a shovel to erect a catapult—his whinnying sounds almost like English words, which Dirk and Daphne understand.

Comment. The characters first appeared in the

Cinematronics arcade videogame *Dragon's Lair* in 1983. That game featured short animated sequences each of which ended in a crisis: The player selected one option from several. If it was the correct choice, the game went on until (after passing through forty-two different rooms) Dirk rescued Daphne from the dragon. If not, the game ended abruptly (usually with Dirk's death by horrible means). The superb animation was handled by Don Bluth Productions. The format was translated to a TV series of the same name in 1984 by Ruby-Spears Enterprises. Because television isn't interactive (yet), the wrong choices in each half-hour adventure were shown to the viewer first, along with their dire results, after which Dirk, naturally, made the correct decision.

BERT THE TURTLE
Pedigree. Civil defense mascot.
Biography. Wearing a bow tie and a civil defense helmet, the loping, bipedal turtle hosted cartoons about what to do in the event of enemy attack. Bert spoke like an old man, and his motto was "Duck and cover." The enemy was never represented as humans but as other animals, i.e., a monkey dropping a load of TNT near Bert.

Comment. The character appeared in government-made films from the middle to the late 1950s.

BIANCA
Pedigree. Pet goldfish of **Mickey Mouse**.
Biography. The black and orange goldfish appeared in just two shorts. In *Mickey's Parrot* (1938), the talking bird manages to become trapped in the cabinet under the goldfish bowl. Elsewhere, **Pluto the Pup** hears the bird's tirade and rather witlessly assumes that it's Bianca who's giving him a tongue-lashing. Pluto comes over to teach her a lesson, but backs off when Bianca leaps from the bowl and bites his nose. In *Lend a Paw* (1941), Mickey's love for a stray kitten makes Pluto jealous. To get the cat in trouble, Pluto places it beside Bianca's bowl, hoping the feline will upset it. The cat does just that, and causes the bowl (with Bianca and water still inside) to land on the floor, Mickey comes running, but instead of automatically blaming the cat, he asks Bianca what happened. The fish points with a fin and burbles the dog's name, causing the plan to backfire.

Comment. Another Disney goldfish was Cleo, who was featured in *Pinocchio* (1940) (see **Figaro** for details).

THE BIG BAD WOLF

Pedigree. Huffer-and-puffer of several Walt Disney shorts.

Biography. Walking upright, with his matted coat of black fur and tattered blue pants held up by suspenders, the Big Bad Wolf came to the screen in the Oscar-winning Silly Symphonies cartoon *The Three Little Pigs* (1933). His would-be victims: the flute-playing Fifer Pig, who would rather play than work and quickly builds a house of straw; the violin-playing Fiddler Pig, who's also not from the workers and constructs his house of sticks (and who wears a French sailor's suit very similar to the one later worn by **Donald Duck**); and the piano-playing Practical Pig, who builds his house of brick (the pigs' names did not evolve until the animals made their fourth short subject). After he blows down the homes of the first two pigs, he's thwarted by the bricks of the third; shimmying down the chimney, he's welcomed by a cauldron of boiling oil on the other end, and runs off shrieking. However, the cartoon was so popular that Disney brought back the quartet in the next year in *The Big Bad Wolf*. This retelling of the Little Red Riding Hood story has the wolf (who now wears a ratty top hat) dressing up as Granny and secreting himself in the old woman's cottage. But before he can eat Riding Hood, Practical Pig uses freshly (and fiercely!) popping popcorn to drive him away. Although twice-burned, the wolf returns—with help—in *Three Little Wolves* (1936). This time, the Big Bad one and his three wolf children—each of whom dresses like their slavering dad—disguise themselves as Little Bo-Peep and her sheep and make off with the two wimpy pigs. Luckily, Practical Pig has designed a Wolf Pacifier for just such an emergency, and once again beats back the carnivore. Still unwilling to give up, the Wolf and his offspring are at it again in *The Practical Pig* (1939)—although in truth, the wolf has by this time become more of a hapless comedian than a true menace. Disguised as a mermaid, he nabs Fiddler and Fifer while they're swimming. Depositing them with his children, the Wolf tells them not to eat the pigs until he's nabbed Practical Pig. The little wolves can't resist *preparing* dinner though, and stuff the Pigs inside a pie crust crammed with potatoes. When they pepper the pie, the pigs sneeze and flee in the hail of potatoes. Meanwhile, Practical Pig has managed to snare the Wolf in a lie detector he's built. Learning the location of his brethren, Practical helps them make good their flight. The Wolf and Pigs made a brief appearance in *Thrifty Pig* (1941), and the pigs alone had guest spots in *All Together* and *Food Will Win the War*, both in 1942.

Comment. The story of the Three Little Pigs is a folktale of which the origin is unknown. It was first written down by nursery rhyme collector J. O. Halliwell in 1853, but remained unpublished until Joseph Jacobs issued his *English Fairy Tales* in 1890. The pigs' famous reply to the wolf's request to open the door—"not by the hair of my chinny-chin-chin"—appears in this version, along with the wolf's legendary reply, "Then I'll huff, and I'll puff, and I'll blow the house in." The wolf is cooked in the original tale as in the Disney tale, but there is one significant difference between the two: In the original story, the ravenous wolf eats the first two pigs. Billy Bletcher provided the voice of the Wolf, and Frank Churchill wrote the theme song of the first short, *Who's Afraid of the Big Bad Wolf*, which became an optimistic anthem of the depression era. The Wolf and the Pigs had a brief posttheatrical life in comic books. The Three Little Pigs had their own issue of Dell's *4-Color* (no. 218) in 1949, in which the Wolf sprays Practical Pig with a potion brewed by Snow White's witch, "a concoction that'll make a smart pig dumb"; the Pig manages to break the enchantment, after which he finds a magic lamp whose genie flings the Wolf through the air. The pigs join the Mounties in the second tale and battle marauding bees in the third. The Wolf also appears in one-page gags throughout. The Wolf and one of his offspring also appeared in the *Li'l Bad Wolf* strip, which was a popular back-up feature in *Walt Disney's Comics and Stories* beginning in 1945, lasting from no. 52 to no. 203. *The Further Adventures of the Three Little Pigs* ran as part of the "Silly Symphonies" Sunday strip from January to August 1936; it launched the short-lived *Practical Pig* strip, which debuted in May 1938. ("Silly Symphonies" was responsible for featuring many characters Disney had featured in cartoon shorts or was considering for the screen. Among these were **Dumbo** and **Ferdinand the Bull**, "Max Hare and Toby Tortoise" (1934), "Peculiar Penguins" (1934), "The Life and Adventures of Elmer Elephant" (1935, which inspired the later, unsuccessful "Timid Elephant" strip), "Ambrose, the Robber Kitten" (1935), and "Bucky Bug"—the title character inaugurated the strip on January 10, 1932. Bucky is a ladybug who ended his twenty-six month stay in the strip by marrying the June bug.

BIG BIRD

Pedigree. Towering feathered costar of TV's *Sesame Street.*

Biography. Standing eight feet, two inches and perpetually six years old, the "canary" has three fingers on each hand, three toes on each foot, yellow feathers, a yellow beak, Ping-Pong ball eyes, three feathers jutting from the top of its head, and orange legs with five reddish, fleshy rings around each. Big Bird lives "all alone" (if you discount the teddy bear Radar) in a fenced-in nest in an alley on Sesame Street (see **Kermit the Frog** for details on the show and other animal denizens). Preferring to be with friends rather than hunt for worms, his closest animal pals are the elephantine Snuffelupagus and the dog Barkley; his human friends include Gordon, Susan, Maria, Linda, Luis, Olivia, Bob, and Tanya. Big Bird is a gentle creature who enjoys roller skating and has a strange habit of bending down and looking backward through its legs. Despite reading *Newsbeak,* the bird is very naive, for example, when Big Bird goes to give something to Mr. Hooper of Hooper's Store and is informed that he died, the bird casually remarks, "I'll give it to him when he comes back." The human members of the street have to explain, very precisely, what death is. Likewise, Big Bird has to be told what pregnancy and adoption are (naturally, to the benefit of the children watching the show). Only once, however, has Big Bird ever faced a truly grave crisis. That occurred in the theatrical film *Sesame Street Presents Follow That Bird* (1985). Contacted by Miss Finch of the organization Feathered Friends, Big Bird is told that the Dodo family of Oceanview, Illinois, wants to adopt him. Wanting a home more than anything, Big Bird bids a sad farewell to Sesame Street—and finds that Donnie, Marie, Dad, and Mama Dodo are not just dumber than he is, they're quite possibly the dumbest creatures on earth. (Dad Dodo is constantly spouting questionable wisdom, e.g., "You have to come home before you can leave.") Profoundly disappointed, and missing his friends, Big Bird runs away from the comfortable Dodo birdhouse on Canary Road (take *that,* John Steinbeck!) and heads back east. However, he is not only stalked by the angry Miss Finch, but by circus owners Sid and Sam Sleaze. The Sleazes manage to cage the bird, paint its feathers blue, and put the poor captive on display as the Blue Bird of Happiness. Luckily, one of the kids in the audience recognizes Big Bird, calls Sesame Street, and the bird's pals come to collect their friend (after a frantic car chase—hence the title of the film.) Although Miss Finch comes up with another family for Big Bird, the youngster refuses to leave . . . ever.

Comment. Over the years, on television and in the movies, Carroll Spinney has played Big Bird. In addition to the starring motion picture, Big Bird was in a TV special, *Big Bird in China,* which was filmed on location, and had a cameo in *The Muppet Movie* (1979). In *Sesame Street Presents Follow That Bird* (1985), Sally Kellerman was Miss Finch and Laraine Newman was Mommy Dodo. Brilliant *Second City Television* (*SCTV*) alumni Dave Thomas and Joe Flaherty were the Sleazes. Incidentally, Big Bird and his *Sesame Street* colleagues aren't present in the foreign versions of the program. Produced in their respective countries, these shows feature their own Muppet stars: Samson Bear appears on Germany's *Sesamstrasse,* the seven-foot-tall parrot Montoya (essentially Big Bird with dark green feathers and an orange top) is seen on Mexico's *Plaza Sesamo,* a blue-feathered version named Pino, with a sidekick mouse and dog, are featured on Holland's *Sesam Straat,* a pink porcupine is the star of Spain's *Barrio Sesamo,* Beav Beaver appears in Canada, and so on.

BIGGY RAT

Pedigree. Bitter enemy of TV's **King Leonardo.**

Biography. Headquartered in a shack perched precariously atop a mountain, Biggy Rat and his assistant Itchy Brother constantly plot the overthrow of Itchy's brother, King Leonardo of Bongo Congo. Dressed in a trench coat and floppy hat, Biggy Rat talks like Edward G. Robinson, packs a pistol, and is always chomping on a cigar. Tall, skinny Itchy has a voice like Ed Wynn, a mangy mane, and fleas all over his body, which cause him to scratch constantly. Both animals walk upright.

Comment. The characters first appeared on Leonardo Productions's *King Leonardo and His Short Subjects,* which aired on ABC from 1960 to 1963. Biggy and Itchy appeared in most of the 103 episodes. Jackson Beck was the voice of the rat, and Allen Swift was Itchy.

BILL THE CAT

Pedigree. Cat-star of the comic strip "Bloom County."

Biography. The flea-bitten orange cat was introduced in the strip by young Milo Bloom, who remarked "Never ones to pass up a hot trend . . . we're introducing a new character. Meet Bill the Cat! He's all we could find but I'm sure you'll learn to love him." Raised in "the green, gentle hills of Dubuque, Iowa," Bill left his home and his girl Sally for New York to become a cartoon star. After being rejected by several prestigious strips, he went to "Bloom County," and quickly earned fame and big bucks. Drink, drugs, and "free-basing 'Little Friskies' " followed, after which his friends dug in their heels and "pulled him back from the brink." For a time, it was presumed that Bill died in a car crash on Route 66, where he was said to have been going 140 in his Ferrari. But an investigative book by Bob Woodward *(Frazzled)* suggests otherwise, and it's discovered that Milo had gone to the wreck, retrieved Bill's tongue, and gave it to his young friend Oliver Wendell Jones, who found that "there were still living genetic thingumajigs and DNA doohickeys" in the tongue. After creating several Bill-like monsters, the little scientific genius recreated the cat. He ran for president (see below), lost, then ran off to be a Rajaneeshee cultist in Oregon (as Bhagwan Bill). Saved by Milo and **Opus the Penguin,** he becomes a Republican and begins dating Jeane Kirkpatrick, which upsets his friends more than anything else. Bill has starred in the films *Orangestoke: The Legend of Bill, Lord of the Monkeys; Terms of Bill's Endearment;* and an untitled slasher film. The cat has run for president twice on the National Radical Meadow party ticket, losing in 1988 only because he "barfed a hairball on Connie Chung." Bill's dialogue in the strip consists primarily of *Ack ack ack* as he consistently chokes on said hairballs.

Comment. See **Opus the Penguin** entry for details on the comic strip.

BILLY THE KID
Pedigree. Comic book goat-cowboy.
Biography. A law-goat of the old west, Billy lives in a small, neat shack outside of Drygulch, rides the valiant horse Paint, and is always coming to the aid of the town's inept Oscar the Sheriff, an ostrich. Not only is he a superb shot, but he can lasso a runaway stagecoach and drag himself onboard. Among Billy's most desperate foes have been the dog Eagle Eye Buzzard, a gambler who tried to sabotage the local sled races; the "wicked eastern crook" Snakeye Snazzy; and that trio of robber-gobblers Jed, Buck, and Hack, a k a the Terrible Turk Brothers. In one adventure, the turkeys lashed Billy to a tree and set it on fire; luckily, he was able to reach a flaming branch and burn the rope off his wrists. Billy wore a yellow shirt, black vest, red neckerchief, woolly white trousers, brown gloves and boots, and a blue ten-gallon hat over his curled horns. There was usually a cigarette hanging from his thin goat lips.

Comment. Billy was a costar in Fawcett's *Funny Animals* comics, which lasted ninety-one issues, from 1942 to 1956. His own title lasted three issues (1945 to 1946). Other characters that appeared in the magazine included another goat Kid Gloves, the world's "slickest confidence man"; the Battling Bantam, a k a "the fighting fool," a cocky rooster who fancied himself a tough guy but always got his comb handed to him; and Benny Beaver. Young Benny is one of the most industrious little fellows in all of Funny Animal Land. He lives at home with his parents, is a struggling actor who makes the rounds with pal Fuzzy Bear, holds down a job as builder with his uncle Bill Beaver, and enjoys reading in his spare time. He dresses in blue coveralls and a red cap. See also **Hoppy, the Captain Marvel Bunny; Sherlock Monk;** and **Willie the Worm.**

BIMBO
Pedigree. Early cartoon star, and sidekick to Betty Boop.
Biography. Bimbo is a bipedal pup with a round muzzle, huge eyes, a coffee bean nose, and small ears that look like they came off Adam West's Batman cowl. He first appeared on his own in the Song Kar-Tunes series, which were begun with *Oh, Mabel* in 1924 and introduced the soon-to-be-famous gimmick of a bouncing ball appearing over the words of a song (the theater organist would play along with the silent film). Between the choruses were various bits of animated action, such as Bimbo playing a trombone in *My Old Kentucky Home* (1926). The dog was promoted to a starring role in the Song Kar-Tune *La Paloma* (1930), in which his appearance is dramatically different: He has white fur instead of black, his nose is the size of a doorknob, and his ears are long and lying flat along the side of his head. He's also become rather libidinous by now, heading south of the border to woo a lady dog. That reputation was strengthened by his first nonsinging role, as the star of *Hot Dog* (1930), in which he's tooling along in his car when he spots a buxom roller-skating lass. He stops to pick her up and she comes along, only to leave when he attempts to kiss her. Undaunted, Bimbo drives after her, gets arrested for speeding, and charms the court by testifying in song, while strumming his banjo. In his next cartoon, *Dizzy*

Dishes (1930), he doesn't have much time to cavort with his female costar, a singer: He's a waiter at a busy all-animal restaurant, and there's no time for anything but the patrons. As it happens, that costar was soon to become a major star: she's Betty Boop . . . although not yet the Betty we all adore. She's a humanoid *dog* with jowls and long, floppy ears (these evolved into her famous earrings). Bimbo is back on the love boat with his and Betty's next appearance, in *Barnacle Bill* (1930). As a sailor came ashore, he visits Betty in her apartment and they sit on the sofa, with the shade drawn. Outside, lady-cats are aghast—until the shade opens and the two are seen playing checkers. Betty went from dog to person in the 1932 cartoon *Any Rags*. Although Bimbo had gone back to being a little black pup (with a too-small shirt that rode up above his navel) and starred in a few other shorts, such as *Herring Murder Case* (1931)—as a detective who arrests brawny Gus Gorilla for killing a fish—and *Bimbo's Initiation* (1931)—he falls through a manhole and becomes embroiled in the rites of a secret cult—he became more and more a supporting player to the increasingly popular Boop-Oop-a-Doop girl. By the time they made the musical *Minnie the Moocher* together in 1932, it was Betty who was really the star. As for Bimbo, he was essentially neutered, becoming her goggle-eyed pet and helper rather than her lover.

Comment. Some historians consider Bimbo and Fitz to be one and the same character, to the extent that they mistakenly refer to Fitz as Bimbo. (He's *a* bimbo, but that's hardly the same thing.) The two dogs couldn't look less alike, and while Fitz obviously inspired Bimbo, and the animators gave them many of the same mannerisms, they're different characters. As for Betty, artist Grim Natwick, who first drew her in her dog days, says he used "a French poodle for the basic idea of the character." In addition to starring in 102 cartoons, Betty and Bimbo appeared in a short-lived comic strip that ran from 1934 to 1935 (daily), and from 1934 to 1937 (Sundays). Their comic book career consists of collections of her comic strips, as well as a 3-D comic book published by Blackthorne in 1986.

BISKITTS
Pedigree. Tiny TV dogs with a mission.
Biography. The series is set in an unspecified century in the past, although everyone—including the talking, bipedal, foot-tall Biskitts—wears medieval clothing. As the narrator puts it, "Hidden deep in a swamp lies tiny Biskitt Castle, home of the smallest dogs in the world. For years, kings have entrusted their royal treasure to these pups." The monarchs don't know where the dogs keep the treasure, although they can access it when needed. Unfortunately, the present ruler is the "wasteful" King Max, and the Biskitts won't let him near his wealth. Thus with the help of his royal jester Sheckey, and his bloodhounds Fang and Snarl, Max is always trying to find out exactly where the castle is located. He comes closest to pinpointing their island in the marsh when he gives them the Trojan Biskitt, a wooden dog that contains flares attached to a timer. Fortunately, the rockets fire all at once, and the figurine takes off—right for Max—making it impossible for him to follow. Complicating matters for both the Biskitts and Max is the green-eyed wildcat Scratch, who lives in a cave and is constantly trying to catch and eat the little dogs. Max and his dogs are constantly on the lookout for the cat, because without the Biskitts he'll never find his treasure. Also on the prowl are huge swamp bears, which eat cats, people, and Biskitts alike. When they're not occupied with the shenanigans of King Max or Scratch, the dogs spend time collecting tar to patch the castle roof, gathering ingredients for their special flea powder, or joy-riding on the backs of frogs, storks, or snakes. Individually, the Biskitts include Lady, Blabber, Scat, Bump, Bones, Shiner, Flip, Downer, Mooch, the Valley-Girlish Wiggle, and the leader Waggs. (Waggs has a sense of humor: Asked if he's injured after a battle, he replies, "It only hurts when I bark.") The best episode featured a third-party crook, a greedy dragon that stole the hidden treasure chest and took it back to Dragon Mount. Hobbit-like, the Biskitts had to venture to the monster's lair and reclaim it, after first arming themselves with that legendary weapon, the Bone in the Stone.

Comment. Hanna-Barbera's *The Biskitts* premiered on CBS in 1983, for a short Saturday morning run. Each adventure lasted a half hour. Darryl Hickman was the voice of Waggs, B. J. Ward was Lady, Jerry Houser was Shiner, Peter Cullen was Fang and Scratch, Kenneth Mars was Snarl, Henry Gibson was Downer, and Dick Beals was Scat. Another bunch of unbearably cute medieval Hanna-Barbera dogs were the Paw Paws, who showed up on the syndicated *The Funtastic World of Hanna-Barbera* in 1985. These were Princess Paw Paw (voice by Susan Blu), Mighty Paw (Bob Ridgley), Brave Paw (Thom Pinto), Laughing Paw (Stanley

Stoddart), Wise Paw (John Ingle), Trembly Paw (Howard Morris), and the bad dogs Dark Paw (Stanley Ralph Ross, a former writer on the *Batman* TV series!), Bumble Paw (Frank Welker), and Slipper Paw (Leo DeLyon).

BITSY
Pedigree. Dog owned by the comic strip baby Marvin.
Biography. Marvin is the son of Jeff and Jenny Miller, and Bitsy is their dog. Bitsy was put out in the backyard when Marvin was born, and, according to Jenny, "still feels he's in competition with Marvin for our affections." For Marvin's part, although Jeff tries to convince his two-year-old son that "a boy and a dog just naturally go together," Marvin muses to himself, "I think you've got me confused with a flea." Truth is, it's mostly Bitsy's fault that they don't get along and, these days, the dog would prefer to be left outside on a cold night than be brought inside with Marvin. Bitsy has also been known to sit around, sucking on a baby bottle, trying to convince the Millers that, like Marvin, he has needs.

Comment. Tom Armstrong's strip premiered in August 1982. Other pets in the present-day comic strip pages are the well-behaved poodle Ribbons and the slovenly mutt Haywire in Carpenter and Wallterstein's "Ribbons" (for the pampered poodle, a nightmare is dreaming that "someone put *dog food* in my dog dish!"); Dogbert, the quiet, tiny white dog owned by the equally timid Dilbert in the Scott Adams strip "Dilbert"; Chubb and Chauncey, the *Odd Couple*-like dogs owned by Abby in Vance Rodewalt's "Chubb & Chauncey"; Virgil the rabbit-chasing hound in Rechin and Wilder's "Out of Bounds"; and the bespectacled white thrill-seeking dog Custer in Rich Torrey's "Hartland" ("Ya big dummy!" his master says. "That's a balloon! It's meant to be held, not *eaten!!*" Custer considers this, then thinks, "It's a good thing, too! They taste terrible!"). Other animals are Jake, the snide pet rabbit of young Ophelia in Heidi Stetson's "Ophelia and Jake" ("What happened to my crocuses?" the woman cries. Still chewing on one, the hefty gray rabbit thinks, "They croaked."); Bumper, the big, dumb, playful bulldog owned by the stars of Ralph Dunagin's and Dana Summers's "The Middletons"; Howard Huge, the massive, food-craving St. Bernard in the late Bill Hoest's single-panel cartoon of the same name ("Howard," reads the sign inside the refrigerator, "these are the kids' school

lunches—*do not eat!*"); Mostly, the mostly Siamese cat, and Smilie, the big dog owned by George and Dorothy Baxter in Ted Key's "Hazel," which began running in *The Saturday Evening Post* in 1943. There are also Rivets, a playful white-and-black terrier whose eponymous strip debuted in 1952, created by George Sixta (and followed by three comic books); Fred Basset, the pensive, white-and-brown hero of Alex Graham's "Fred Basset," which premiered in 1965 ("I do like to see them enjoying a gay time over the festive season," he reflects sarcastically as his owners painfully recover from a series of Christmas parties); and Lucky, who stars in Ray Helle's "Life with Lucky" strip, which runs in the *National Enquirer*. The black dog has a white belly and face, and a knack for getting into trouble: Only boxing gloves tied to his paws can keep him from raiding food cabinets, and nothing the Dogwood Obedience School teaches him ever seems to work.

BLACK FURY
Pedigree. Horse star of his own action comic book.
Biography. The magnificent Black Fury, "king of wild horses," is the leader of a herd that dwells in Montana in the last century. His adventures range from fighting a sadistic rancher who wants to tame him, to battling an albino wolf that wants to eat him, to warding off the effects of drinking at a poison pond, to helping an "old bum" by letting the man ride him and thus earn the respect of the townsfolk. Whatever he's doing, Black Fury is always suspicious when he detects "man smell," and nothing sends him into a rage faster than the "the hated scent" of gunpowder. Black Fury is the strong, silent type: There are no thought balloons to reveal what's on the horse's mind.

Comment. Incredibly, Charlton Comics's writers came up with enough stories for *Black Fury* to last fifty-seven issues (1955 to 1966). Another horse star, albeit far less popular, was Thunderhoof, who starred in various William H. Wise titles such as the one-shot *America's Biggest Comics Book* (1944). As for horses that didn't originate in the comics, Dell had a virtual monopoly on the herd, publishing thirty-six issues of *The Lone Ranger's Famous Horse Silver* from 1952 to 1960, inspired by *The Lone Ranger* TV show; twelve issues of a *Fury* comic book (1957 to 1962), based on the adventures of the TV horse; seventeen issues of *Roy Rogers' Trigger* (1951 to 1955), inspired by the cowboy's TV series; ten issues of *Mister Ed, The Talking Horse* (1962 to

1964), based on the TV series; and ten issues of *Francis The Famous Talking Mule*, based on the movie character, from 1951 to 1960.

BLACKIE BEAR

Pedigree. Decadent comic book animal.

Biography. "The lazy and yawning" bear is constantly in need of money and always looking for an honest, but easy, way to get it. Once, when he was duped into assisting a pair of thieves, the victim—hippo "Billion Bucks" Van Smythe—comments, "The poor fellow . . . may be a *fool,* but he is no *felon.*" Blackie is all-black, save for his white belly and face, and pink muzzle. He is never without his black derby and black bow tie.

Comment. The character appeared in DC Comics's *Funny Stuff* beginning in 1944.

BLIP

Pedigree. Monkey sidekick to the TV hero Space Ghost.

Biography. Named after the only word he can say, Blip partakes in adventures with teens Jan and Jayce and the white-garbed interstellar police officer Space Ghost, who travel the universe onboard the *Phantom Cruiser,* battling villainy. Blip can fly thanks to a jet pack on his back. Although he's bright, his mind isn't well developed enough to receive telepathic signals. The foot-long monkey has a tail longer than his entire body, and wears a yellow costume with a blue front, blue boots, a red belt, and a black domino mask.

Comment. The character appeared on Hanna-Barbera's *Space Ghost,* which began airing on CBS in 1966. There were forty-two episodes in all. Blip also costarred in nos. 3 to 7 of Gold Key's comic *Hanna-Barbera Super TV Heroes,* which ran seven issues from 1968 to 1969.

BOBO, THE DETECTIVE CHIMP

Pedigree. Gumshoe comic book monkey.

Biography. An extremely bright chimpanzee, Bobo was owned by animal trainer Fred Thorpe of Florida. When Thorpe was murdered, sheriff Edward Chase investigated . . . and ended up keeping the intelligent monkey as a pet. However, Bobo proves to be more than just a pet, his uncanny crime-solving abilities earning him a place as Chase's "little deputy." Bobo's reputation spreads quickly: As one thug puts it, "That's him—*Detective Chimp*—the only one in town that could ruin our racket!" Bobo can't speak, although he thinks in English so readers know what's on his mind. And there's a great deal on his mind, everything from, "Big muscles . . . exercise . . . *bah!* My *brains* are good enough!" and—while examining his bank book—"Flat broke! I've been squandering too much money on banana splits!" In his later years, Bobo met **Rex, The Wonder Dog** and the two found and drank from the Fountain of Youth. There's no telling what the future holds for the newly young chimp.

Comment. The DC Comics character first appeared in *The Adventures of Rex, The Wonder Dog* no. 4 in 1952. Although the stories are realistic and the plots serious, Bobo and his dialogue are handled tongue in cheek.

BOGEY

Pedigree. The parrot-companion of the comic strip character Ug.

Biography. No one knows what the big, brown, hairy biped Ug is, other than the fact that he's an "often confused, temperamental and emotionally immature creature" who thinks that the three basic food groups are chocolate, vanilla, and strawberry. As for Bogey, he's a smart green parrot who rides on top of Ug's head or shoulder and looks after him as they roam the city and country. He's the kind of guardian who refuses to let Ug go to the movies and expose himself "to all that tasteless and unhealthy trash" (the concession stand), although when they do go to see *The Birds,* Bogey can't resist growling quietly at the woman sitting next to them, scaring her out of her mind. At the beach, Bogey will keep an eye on Ug, yell out, "Wave!" and watch with frustration as the hirsute brute shakes a hand at him—and gets clobbered by a wave. Bogey is also a philosopher, commenting seriously about everything from the future ("People just hope the future isn't any worse than the present") to guilt ("It ruins your self-confidence, increases your insecurity and generally makes you even more depressed") to human nature ("Sometimes people can be cruel! Sometimes they'll just zero in on one thing about you and use it for nothing more than cheap sport!"). Ug will usually respond to these observations with complete misunderstanding or with a joke. A regular costar in the strip is Bogey's friend Merv the Snake, a hard-luck character (walks through poison ivy, can't turn the pages of an interesting book, and so on).

Comment. The comic strip by Tom Wilson, Jr., debuted in 1985. Wilson is the son of Tom Wilson (**Fuzz**).

BONER'S ARK

Pedigree. Anthropomorphic animal-filled ark of comic strip fame.

Biography. Captain Boner and his wife Bubbles are in charge of this modern-day ark, which the inept captain can't seem to steer back to shore. Like a comic strip *Ship of Fools*, human foibles are examined through the antics of Dum-Dum (gorilla), Lookout (giraffe), Cubcake (koala), Priscilla (pig), Spot (dog), Duke (penguin), Aarnie (aardvark), Officer Otter, Mr. Fix-it (pelican), Ho-Ho (crow), Mom (goose), Rex (dinosaur), Sandy (stork, the ship's cook), Hippo (the restaurant waiter), Hyena (the marriage counselor, whom Boner and Bubbles visit regularly), Snooky (boa), Mr. Bug, Homing Pigeon the navigator (his sense of direction is worse than Boner's), the Orangutan, the Polar Bear, the Skunk, the Lion, the Kangaroo, the Donkey, the Rooster, the Mouse, and the Sheep. Incidentally, when you go to the ark restaurant and order a chocolate moose . . . that's exactly what you get.

Comment. "Boner's Ark" was created by Mort Walker in 1968. Walker originally wrote and drew the strip as "Addison"; Frank Johnson is now at the helm. Another animal-compendium strip of this era is Robert Bollen's "Animal Crackers," which is set on a wildlife preserve in Africa and centers on the adventures of the inept lion named Lyle.

BONGO

Pedigree. Walt Disney cartoon bear.

Biography. Dressed in a fezlike cap, red jacket, and blue bow tie, Bongo the Wonder Bear is a unicycle-riding circus bear that loves to perform—but he loathes his human owners, who keep him locked in a tiny cage and treat him badly. Having had enough, Bongo shakes his cage until the lock breaks, and he unicycles away. Finding himself in the woods, he mingles with the other animals and tries to imitate their habits, failing and drawing their laughter. A thunderstorm, a near-fall off a high cliff (precipitated by a sneeze while he's unicycling), and a clumsy effort to snare a fish leave the bear dejected. He's about to return to the circus when he meets the lady bear Lulubelle and they fall in love. But their nuzzling is interrupted by the arrival of the brawny, Quasimodo-like bear Lumpjaw, who covets Lulubelle. The big bear is about to pound Bongo like a drum when Lulubelle intercedes. She goes to slap Bongo—which, in bear lingo is a sign of love—but

strikes Lumpjaw instead; the big bear takes it to mean that the lady is infatuated with him, and Bongo leaves, dejected. However, the look on Lulubelle's face tells him who she's really in love with. Cycling back, Bongo starts a fight with Lumpjaw and beats him using all kinds of circus tricks. The big bear ends up in the river after a logrolling confrontation, and the film fades out with the little bears sitting on adjoining trees, which bend to form a heart.

Comment. The character was created by novelist Sinclair Lewis expressly for Walt Disney's feature film *Fun and Fancy Free* (1947). The section was introduced by **Jiminy Cricket**; Dinah Shore narrated. Due to the pedestrian plot, blandness of the bear himself, and straightforward animation, the Bongo section pales beside the wonderful *Mickey and the Beanstalk* segment.

BOO

Pedigree. Ghostly cat belonging to TV's Funky Phantom.

Biography. Back in the Revolutionary days, Jonathan Muddlemore and his cat were fleeing the British and hid inside a grandfather clock in their mansion in East Muddlemore in New England. Locked inside the clock, the two perish there. Cut to the present: A trio of teenagers—Skip, April, and Augie—enter the old mansion to escape a storm; when midnight tolls, the clock releases the captives, henceforth known as the benevolent Funky Phantom and Boo. Together, the quintet roam the land righting wrongs and battling evil ghosts and apparitions such as the Headless Horseman. Accompanying the group is Skip's crabby bulldog Elmo.

Comment. Hanna-Barbera's *The Funky Phantom* debuted on ABC in 1971; there were seventeen episodes.

BOO BOO BEAR

Pedigree. Cartoon companion of **Yogi Bear**.

Biography. Small, light brown, eternally cheerful Boo Boo lives in his own, small cave in Jellystone Park. Unlike Yogi, Boo Boo wakes up from hibernation each spring gleeful, happy to welcome the new season. Also unlike Yogi, Boo Boo is a caution: He constantly warns his friend not to break the law and try to steal food, although Yogi never listens. Boo Boo's only attire is a small, blue bow tie.

Comment. See entry on **Yogi Bear** for rundown of Boo Boo's TV and comic book appearances.

BOOTLE BEETLE

Pedigree. Disney cartoon bugs.

Biography. Bootle Beetles have an antlike body, little green wings that lie flat on their back, a pair of antennae, and tan shoes. When first seen in *Bootle Beetle* (1947), an elderly, bespectacled Bootle Beetle is puffing on his pipe and reminiscing to young Ezra Bootle Beetle about the time he ran away and faced such woodland dangers as falling pine cones, weariness (2,000 Bootle-miles equals sixteen inches) . . . and **Donald Duck.** The drake is out looking for bugs to add to his collection, and the bug gets trapped in a jar; fortunately, he's able to escape by bracing himself inside the lid and fleeing when Donald opens the seemingly empty container. The bug and Donald are more mutually supportive when stranded on an island in *Sea Salts* (1949), but it's business as usual in *The Greener Yard* (1949), when the insect (reminiscing to Ezra yet again) talks about the time he ventured into Donald's yard for food and the duck nearly killed him. A third Bootle Beetle, Herman, is the assistant to **Ludwig Von Drake** (who says he likes insects better than people). Herman not only travels around the world with the duck but is charged with the important task of operating the movie projector at Von Drake's many lectures.

Comment. The name Bootle Beetle was inspired by a racehorse named Beetle Bootle. Dink Trout provided the voice for the bug.

BORIS THE BEAR

Pedigree. Realistic comic book talking bear.

Biography. Boris lives in a treehouse and is the pet of a young boy named David. A comic book fanatic, Boris becomes sick and tired of all the knockoffs of **Teenage Mutant Ninja Turtles** (i.e., Puerile Phosphorescent Pugilistic Prairie Dogs, Beardless Breeder-Reactor Boxing Bobcats, and Immature Isotopic Internecine Inchworms). Arming himself with a knife and an Uzi, he goes out to find and "slaughter" these animals. His early victims include Sloberus (**Cerebrus**), the Tampa Mice (**Miami Mice**), the Juvenile Deviant Hard-Shelled Assassins (the Turtles), and so forth. Subsequent issues pit the bear against characters from other comic book genres (robots, Marvel Comics superheroes, and so on), and also had Boris living bear versions of some of the most famous stories from comics: His battle with the Bear-Slayer, a robot, parodied Spider-Man's fight with a similar foe; at other times, Boris himself became superhero parodies such as the Punishbear (the Punisher) and the Rocketbear (the Rocketeer). His most famous adventure was the multipart Ninja Wars.

Comment. The character appeared in his own Dark Horse Comics magazine beginning in 1986; Nicotat Comics took over beginning with no. 13. The series ended with no. 21. Boris was created by James Dean Smith, and the stories are juvenile fun for those who don't know the tales and conventions being parodied, amusing satire for those who do. Back-up strips occasionally featured animal stars, such as Wiggy Worm and Doubtful Donkey. It isn't known whether this is canonical, but in the first issue of **Wacky Squirrel**'s magazine, it was revealed that a Dr. Frankenstein-type scientist and his hunchbacked aide (patterned after actors Colin Clive and Dwight Frye) created the bear in a laboratory. After they taught him about science and other "difficult concepts," he discovered comic books on his own. In this particular tale, the squirrel goes out to slay the bear before he eliminates every other character in comicdom. On the subject of comic book bear heroes, a short-lived character was Corban the Barbearian, a comic book spoof of Conan the Barbarian. Corban roams an unknown, primitive world and is on a perennial search for the magical Frost Stone. On the way, he partakes in daring adventures such as a battle with a giant spider and a run-in with an evil siren. The bear is bipedal, can talk, and dresses in a black leotard with a fur cloak. Phil Green's creation appeared in just two issues of *Corban the Barbearian,* published by M. E. Comix in 1987. It's a very amateurish comic book.

BOWZER

Pedigree. Comic strip pooch.

Biography. The brown, lean, red-nosed retriever belongs to the lazy, perennially unemployed Moose Miller. Because Moose rarely has any money, the dog regularly steals food: Stumbling on picnickers, he'll take a bit of food, pretend to die, and wait until the "poison" food is discarded to eat it; fetching a stick, he'll return with a chicken from someone's campfire. Bowzer enjoys swimming in neighbor Chester Crabtree's swimming pool, but is otherwise as slothful as its master, even to the point of refusing to fetch his slippers (Bowzer simply barks at the cat, who corrals the mice and orders *them* to do it). Another of Moose's pets is the "Chicken-Stealing Parrot"

Boris the Bear—*duly alarmed and ready to deal death.* © JAMES DEAN SMITH.

Polly, which regularly dive-bombs Chester's grill and returns to Moose with the goodies—despite the presence of Chester's bulldog Buster, whom the bird regularly outwits (when Chester plots to trap the bird beneath the grill cover, Polly times its attack so that the lid slams on the dog). As the strip developed, the Miller household became a menagerie, much to the dismay of Moose's long-suffering wife, Molly. Son, Blip, and daughter, Cindy, keep a big, yellow goat, ducks, a horse, a cat, a frog, a goldfish, a pig, a raccoon, a porcupine ("Where are you going with that cake?" Moose asks, to which Blip replies, "It's for my porcupine . . . to show him how much I love him . . . because I can't hug him"), and a stork, which roosts on the roof.

Comment. Bob Weber's charming "Moose" saw the light of day in 1965. A quarter century later Moose continues to do nothing, although (happily) Weber still entertains! Weber's son, Bob, Jr., is responsible for **The Pigglys.**

BOY
Pedigree. Homeless dog in an early comic strip.
Biography. The little, yellow terrier walks on all fours and is the constant companion to the hobo Pete. The pair have only two goals in life: food and shelter. Selfish people, cruel circumstance, and the police officer O'Leary usually get in their way, although the harshness of the strip is softened by the comedic means through which the destitute duo try to obtain their ends. For example, a cook (recurring character Linda) agrees to give them food, if Pete will take her to a football game. He agrees and is fed. The next day, Linda is all dressed up and Pete takes her to the stadium . . . bypassing the gate and leading her to a hole in the fence. He's rewarded with more food: a knuckle sandwich. The dog got his name rather informally, coming when the hobo said, "Here, boy!"

Comment. The characters were created by C. D. Russell and first appeared in the Sunday comic strip "Pete the Tramp" on January 10, 1932. It was discontinued in 1963. Boy had his own short-lived strip, "Pete's Pup."

BOZO
Pedigree. Pet dog of early Warner Brothers cartoon star Buddy.
Biography. Curiously, this dog is never the same from cartoon to cartoon. In the first Buddy cartoon *(Buddy's Day Out)*, he's called Happy, and is badgered by Elmer, the baby belonging to Buddy and Cookie. The next time the dog appears *(Buddy and Towser)*, he's a white dog named Towser, whose job is to guard a chicken coop. The dog becomes Bozo in his third cartoon *(Buddy the Dentist)*, in which he has a toothache that his master tries to cure; he remains Bozo for his final screen appearance *(Buddy's Lost World)*, in which they are shipwrecked on an island inhabited by dinosaurs and cannibals, and are rescued from the human-eaters' pot by a friendly apatosaur. In his latter two incarnations Bozo was white with a black left ear and a black spot on his back.

Comment. The dog's cartoons were released from 1933 to 1935.

BRAIN
Pedigree. Dog-assistant to the gimmick-laden cartoon sleuth Inspector Gadget.
Biography. The mutt is an indispensable aide to the intrepid, trench-coated detective, who is based in a pleasant suburban house that he shares with his niece Penny. Able to walk on two legs, or run fast enough to keep up with a car, the dog is a master of disguise, having impersonated everything from a rock star (right down to the shades and earrings) to a nurse (complete with a wig and breasts . . . although Brain *does* keep his collar on). The intelligent Brain can't talk, although the tone of each *rawr* speaks volumes. His coat is orange; he has white ear tips and a red nose.

Comment. The half-hour-long *Inspector Gadget* cartoons went into syndication in 1983 and continue to be a popular attraction. The show may have the longest production credit of any in history: It's a DIC production in coproduction with FR3 and Nelvana, in association with Field Communications, LBS, TMS, and Cuckoo's Nest. The character was created by Jean Chalopin, Bruno Bianchi, and Andy Heyward. Don Adams, of *Get Smart* fame, is the voice of the inspector.

BRAVEHEART
Pedigree. Sidekick to a truly bizarre TV cartoon detective.
Biography. The Inch-High Private Eye works for the Finkerton Organization, which provides security and does investigations. Although the trench-coated Inch-High is himself hapless (much like Maxwell Smart of TV's *Get Smart*), he is well served by his niece Lori and his Gomer Pyle-like aide Gator. However, most useful of all is his "capable, cunning canine companion in crime fighting," the St. Bernard

Braveheart. The dog is actually rather dumb; however, he's smarter than the rest of the bunch and is usually the first to catch onto a criminal's scheme. When he does so, he barks and uses sign language to explain what he's figured out. The only word Braveheart can say is *Uh-huh*. Inch-High frequently rides about on the dog's head or hidden in his fur. Braveheart has a keg strapped to his neck, in which the sleuth keeps his many disguises and crime-fighting gadgets. He boasts three hairs standing up on his head, and his tongue is always hanging stupidly from the side of his mouth. He can stand on his hind legs when he has to.

Comment. The Hanna-Barbera series of half-hour adventures aired on NBC in 1973. There were thirteen cartoons in all. The series featured voices provided by such luminaries as Jamie Farr and Ted Knight. John Stephenson provided Braveheart's voice.

BREEZLY AND SNEEZLY

Pedigree. Animal inhabitants of the North Pole.
Biography. Breezly Bruin is a confident, optimistic polar bear. Sneezly is a pessimistic seal with a perennial cold, and they have just one ambition: To get out of the frigid wastes and into the warmth (and food stores) of the U.S. military installation, Camp Frostbite. Despite various deceptions, the chilly duo is invariably foiled by the colonel and his men. As Sneezly is regularly heard to say each time Breezly explains one of his schemes, "The colonel's not going to like it." Breezly is dressed in a scarf and winter hat with ear flaps.

Comment. The Hanna-Barbera characters first appeared on *The Peter Potamus Show* in 1964; twenty-three episodes were produced. Howard Morris and Mel Blanc were Breezly and Sneezly, respectively. These characters were an attempt to capitalize on the studio's popular **Yogi Bear.**

BRER RABBIT

Pedigree. Hero of literature and of a Walt Disney motion picture and comic books.
Biography. When young Johnny comes to stay on his grandmother's plantation, he is upset and disoriented; his mother is staying with him, but his father—a man to whom his newspaper career means everything—is not. When Johnny runs away to try to reach his father, he's joined by the elderly black worker Uncle Remus. A wise man, Remus always tells Johnny about how the headstrong young Brer

Rabbit tried to run away from the Briar Patch (Remus segues into the animated segment by singing the Oscar-winning song "Zip-a-Dee-Doo-Dah"). Caught in a trap laid by Brer Fox, he hangs upside down while the fox runs off to sharpen his ax. But along comes dumb Brer Bear, who enquires what the rabbit is doing. Brer Rabbit says he's "makin' a dollar a minute" scaring the crows from the cornfield. Wanting to earn some of that booty, the bear releases Brer Rabbit and takes his place. When Brer Fox returns, he's livid; he grabs the rabbit, the bear leaps into the fray, and in the ensuing confusion Brer Rabbit is able to creep away and return home. The moral, Remus tells Johnny—just as he says he told Brer Rabbit— is that "you can't run away from trouble." Johnny returns home and, in time, gets into an argument with some local ruffians over ownership of a puppy. (The boys are doing this simply to make Johnny's life miserable.) Remus takes him aside and tells him about the time Brer Fox constructed a Tar Baby to trap Brer Rabbit. When the hare strolls by and the tar figure fails to return his "Howdy," he goes to bust the mute Tar Baby "wide open." Naturally, he becomes trapped in the muck, and is carted off by Brer Fox. While preparing the rabbit for dinner, Brer Fox and Brer Bear get into an argument: The latter wants to use his massive club to smack the rabbit's head "clean off" for all the trouble he's caused. The fox wants his head in place so he'll know exactly what's happening to him when they skin him alive. Seeing an opportunity to outwit his foes, Brer Rabbit encourages Brer Bear to knock his head off, or Brer Fox to skin him, but adds, "Whatever you do, please, please Brer Fox, please don't fling me in dat Briar Patch." The fox is intrigued: If the hare is so frightened of that, that's exactly what they'll do with him. Naturally, as soon as he's freed and tossed into the wiry patch, he gets away. Johnny picks up on the moral of this tale, and when the ruffians threaten to go to Johnny's mother in the matter of the dog, he tells them to go right ahead, but to please not tell their own mother. Naturally, this is what they do, and their mother smacks them good for their mischief. When the boys come looking for Johnny to pay him back for having tricked them, Remus lifts the spirits of the battered boy and his compassionate girlfriend, Ginny, by telling him another tale. This one finds Brer Rabbit bound up in Brer Fox's den. When the fox places the hare over the crackling fire, the rabbit begins to laugh; mystified, the fox asks why. Brer Rabbit tells them that he recently visited his Laughing Place, and that just thinking about it makes him chuckle. He adds that everyone has a Laughing Place and, against Brer Fox's wishes, Brer Bear unties the rabbit and tells him to take him to their Laughing Place. Brer Fox leads them to a bee hive, in which Brer Bear gets tangled up and stung; the fox begins to laugh and, furious, the bear begins pounding him. The hysterical Brer Rabbit confesses that this is *his* Laughing Place, and he goes free as the angry bees chase Brer Fox and Brer Bear away. Johnny and Ginny are happy, now—but not for long. Johnny has a close encounter with an angry bull, which leaves him near death. But he recovers and, in the fade-out, he, Ginny, Remus, and Brer Rabbit himself walk singing into the sunset. Other characters who make brief appearances in the cartoon segments are Brer Fish, Brer Frog, and Brer Possum. Brer Rabbit is dressed in a shirt and trousers; Brer Fox wears an undershirt, vest, trousers, and farmer's hat; Brer Bear is dressed in a shirt and floppy hat.

Comment. Brer Rabbit was featured in animated segments of the film *Song of the South* (1946). Johnny Lee was the voice of Brer Rabbit, James Baskett was Brer Fox, and Nicodemus Stewart was Brer Bear. Baskett also starred as Uncle Remus. Brer Rabbit was also the star of several comic book stories which appeared in three issues of Dell's *4-Color,* as well as various other one shots. The first of these (*4-Color* No. 129, 1946) was an adaptation of the film. Later tales were originals, featuring the hare versus the fox and introducing supporting characters such as Sis Goose, Brer Turkey Buzzard, Brer 'Gator, Brer Crow, and the hare's mother, Mammy Rabbit. The screen and comic book character was very much like the Brer Rabbit created by Joel Chandler Harris for his book *Uncle Remus, His Songs and His Sayings; the Folk-lore of the Old Plantation,* published in 1880 (although the title page says 1881). The section of the book titled "Legends of the Old Plantation" chronicles how Brer Fox is constantly chasing Brer Rabbit, but as narrator Uncle Remus says, "Brer Fox ain't never kotch 'im yet, 'en w'at's mo', honey, he ain't gwineter." In addition to the famous Tar Baby story, Chandler tells of how Brer Tarrypin manages to knock out Brer Fox, how Brer Rabbit boils Brer Wolf to death, how Brer Tarrypin beats Brer Rabbit in a race, and how Brer Rabbit finally manages to kill Brer Fox. Harris wrote a sequel, *Nights with Uncle Remus* (1883), as well as the children's books *Uncle Remus and His*

Friends (1892) and *The Tar Baby and Other Rhymes of Uncle Remus* (1904).

BRONTO
Pedigree. TV dinosaur.
Biography. When young teen pilot Tod has airplane trouble, he bails out and lands in a jungle where prehistoric life still thrives. Astride the four-foot-tall baby brontosaurus Bronto, Tod—a k a Dino Boy—teams with the caveman Ugh and fights a variety of foes, including the Treeman, the Worm People, the Rock Pygmies, and the Mighty Snow Creature. The letter *B* is on a patch on the side of the Bronto's reins.

Comment. There were only eighteen episodes of Hanna-Barbera's *Dino Boy,* which aired on *Space Ghost* on CBS beginning in 1966. Another friendly dinosaur was seen in the Hanna-Barbera series *Valley of the Dinosaurs* (CBS, 1974), in which the archaeologist Butler family (including their dog Digger) are swept down the Amazon River and dumped into a prehistoric world. There, they befriend the cute stegosaurus, Glomb.

BRUTUS
Pedigree. Lion pet on TV cartoon show *Roman Holidays.*
Biography. Brutus lives with the Holiday family, which consists of Forum Construction Company employee Gus, his wife, Laurie, and their kids, Happius and Precocia in A.D. 63 Rome. They reside at the Venus DiMillo Arms, 4960 Terrace Drive, Pastafasullo, Rome. The lion has a huge mane and enjoys playing and bathing in the Holidays' tub. Their landlord, Mr. Evictus, is not happy to have the lion on the premesis.

Comment. The series was Hanna-Barbera's unsuccessful attempt to recreate the success of *The Flintstones.* Each episode ran a half hour; there were thirteen in all. The series aired on NBC for one season (1972 to 1973). Daws Butler (**Huckleberry Hound**) provided Brutus's voice. Gold Key published four *Roman Holidays* comics in 1973.

BUBBLES
Pedigree. A comic book dog.
Biography. Bubbles belongs to Betty Cooper, costar of the Archie comic books. She is a white mutt with a black spot on her back; her left ear is also black. The dog is seen primarily in sight gags, e.g., scratching fleas off herself and onto Archie. The dog wears a heart-shaped name tag.

Comment. The dog appears primarily in the Archie Comics publication *Betty and Me,* which began publication in 1965.

BUCKY O'HARE

Pedigree. Spacefaring comic book rabbit.

Biography. Bucky is a green-furred, spacefaring rabbit who lives in a dimension parallel to ours and captains the intergalactic frigate *Righteous Indignation,* aided by his crew Dead-Eye Duck (a scowling duck), Jenny (an Aldebaran "witchcat"), and the non-animal, ambulatory alien eyeball Blinky. He's also joined by earth boy Willy DuWitt, who is able to get to the animal dimension thanks to a photon accelerator in his bedroom. Among the space scum the heroes have battled are the bipedal Toads, the Betelgeusian Berserker Baboons, and the Metaphysical Mice, who possess extraordinary powers of teleportation.

Comment. Bucky and company began appearing in *Echo of Futurepast* No. 1 (1984), published by Pacific Comics and, later, by Continuity Publishing. The characters were created by Larry Hama in 1978, with an assist by artist Michael Golden. Other science fiction animals arose (and died) in the early 1980s. These included the denizens of the comic book *Tales from the Aniverse,* which Arrow Comics began publishing in 1986. It featured outer space stories starring the likes of Retro Ram and his Rocket Rangers (Mustella Mink, Drakestar, Armeil O'Dill, later joined by Platimaticus Letrapuss and Thalla Marit); the feline Ms. (Arda) Chevious and her partner, the muscular lady space-goose Ganda; the foxy Varcel, leader of Varcel's Vixens, consisting of the bird Talon, the lizard Squamata, the horselike L'Ming, and the catlike Lola; and tales of the *S. S. Heep,* a space station occupied by the likes of the security-skunk Keystone, horselike administrator Miss Tails, her secretary Charolette (a goose), bartender-dog Barky, and that old goat Admiral Kilda. Renegade Press offered a four-issue run of *Strata* in 1986, which starred Clarence the Squirrel, the armored Arthur the Beaver, and other woodland mammals interacting with humans on adventures in outer space. There was also one issue of *Entropy Tales* from Entropy Enterprises in 1985, featuring the (aborted) series *Star Fox* starring the space foxes Jennifer Dawn Logan and Kes Jurorko.

BUFORD

Pedigree. TV dog-detective.

Biography. According to the theme song, "Here comes help! Here comes action! Here comes Buford!" Unfortunately, these are all mutually exclusive. It takes a lot for his teen pals Cindy Mae and Woody to get the pink bloodhound moving, although when they do, he has a unique trait: His nose flashes red whenever he's onto a clue. The dog is southern-born and speaks in a guttural monotone. His flesh hangs in deep folds on his bony frame; when he stops short, it has a way of collecting around his head. Buford wears a rebel cap and his beat is rural, swampy Pendike County, where he has solved such mysteries as *The Vanishing Stallion, The Man with the Orange Hair, The Case of the Missing Gator,* and *The Missing Bank.* More often than not, it isn't the baddies who are the stumbling blocks, but the thick-skulled sheriff and his aide Goober.

Comment. Unlike **The Hunter** and others, Buford wasn't bipedal and more human than dog. Hanna-Barbera's *Buford Files* was part of the show *Yogi's Space Race,* which premiered on NBC in 1978. The same segments were repeated on the show *Buford and the Galloping Ghost,* which aired on NBC in 1979; there were only thirteen episodes of the show. Frank Welker was the Gomer Pyle-like voice of Buford. The Galloping Ghost was about a cowboy battling the supernatural out west. See also **Yogi Bear.**

BUGS BUNNY

Pedigree. Arguably the greatest of all cartoon animals: a confident, brainy, lovable con artist with class.

Biography. Technically, Bugs Bunny arrived in the Warner Brothers short *A Wild Hare* (1940). However, he was an evolution of the wacky, buck-toothed rabbits that had appeared in three previous cartoons: *Porky's Hare Hunt* (1938), in which the hyperactive, unsophisticated white rabbit looks more like a rat with long ears; *Hare-um Scare-um* (1939), another hunt film in which the still overly frenetic gray rabbit called Bugs drives the hunter and his dog crazy, assaulting them with everything from disguises to a joy buzzer; and *Elmer's Candid Camera* (1940), recounting Elmer Fudd's attempts to photograph nature while being badgered by a more temperate gray rabbit. However, it wasn't until *A Wild Hare* that the personality, general appearance, mannerisms, and ever-present (although never fully eaten) carrot all came together as the modern Bugs. Although more pear-shaped and with a rounder head than today's rabbit, this unflappable Bugs subjects Elmer to the kind of well thought out, mildly sadistic tricks that were to become his trademark. In addition, the Oscar-nominated cartoon featured the first of many big, wet kisses Bugs would plant on others over the years, grabbing Elmer by the cheeks and holding his face in place, not to mention Bugs greeting him with what may now be the world's most famous rhetorical question, "What's up, Doc?" Bugs crossed swords with Fudd again in his second cartoon, *Elmer's Pet Rabbit* (1941), in which Fudd buys the hare at a pet shop and brings him home. The rabbit is unhappy with the fenced-in accomodations out back and, inviting himself into the house, makes himself at home—regardless of how many times his owner tosses him out. Later that year, Bugs's third cartoon, *Tortoise Beats Hare*, handed him one of his rare humiliations: **Cecil Turtle** beats him in a race, leaving Bugs confused and frustrated. It was one of the few times Bugs was anything other than completely in control of a situation. Elmer remained Bugs's chief adversary over the years, in cartoons such as *Wabbit Twouble* (1941), in which Fudd tries to enjoy an outing in Jellostone National Park; *The Wabbit Who Came to Supper* (1942), about another hunting trip; *The Wacky Wabbit* (1942), with Fudd as a gold prospector; *Fresh Hare* (1942), starring Elmer as a Mountie in pursuit of the infamous rabbit; and *The Hare-Brained Hypnotist* (1942), with Fudd using hypnotism for hunting (note how the number of Bugs cartoons increased in 1942, a result of the rabbit's extraordinary popularity). Other cartoons are *The Old Grey Hare* (1944), which looks at the rivalry as it will be in A.D. 2000 ("What's up, Prune Face?" asks Bugs), and then has the two winded old-timers reminisce about their first meeting, as babies; *The Unruly Hare* (1945), starring Elmer as a surveyor who's disturbing the rabbit; *Hare Tonic* (1945), in which Elmer buys the rabbit to make stew (Bugs muses, "I gotta stay and heckle that character!"); *Hare Remover* (1946), with Fudd as a chemist who turns his dog Rover into a wild animal, then tries to do the same to Bugs; and *Easter Yeggs* (1947), with Bugs delivering "Technicolor hen fruit" for the weary Easter Bunny while trying to avoid becoming Elmer's "Easter wabbit stew." In *Slick Hare* (1947), Humphrey Bogart sits down at Elmer's restaurant and orders rabbit, pronto (after a mad chase, Bugs

finally puts *himself* on the platter when sexy Lauren Bacall joins Bogey). *Hare Do* (1949) featured Fudd armed with an army surplus "wabbit detector"; and there were many others. Arguably the greatest of all these—perhaps the finest Bugs Bunny cartoon of them all—is *What's Opera, Doc?* in which Elmer hunts Bugs onstage in a wonderful cartoon riposting Wagner's *Ring* operas. (Imagine Elmer singing "I'm killing a wabbit" to the opening bars of "Ride of the Valkyries," and you'll get the flavor.) Elmer isn't Bugs's only foe, nor is our own era his only bailiwick. The rabbit makes hash of an intrepid little Indian in *Hiawatha's Rabbit Hunt* (1941, an Oscar nominee) and fights off a lion in *Hold the Lion, Please* (1942; Bugs has a wife in this cartoon). Other nemeses include **Beaky Buzzard** in *Bugs Bunny Gets the Boid* (1942, great title) and Nazi leader Herman Goering in *Herr Meets Hare* (1945). Bugs meets mustachioed gunslinger Yosemite Sam several times, beginning with *Hare Trigger* (1945) and continuing with *Buccaneer Bunny* (1948), *Bugs Bunny Rides Again* (1948), *Mutiny on the Bunny* (1950), and many others. Bugs has run-ins with the Gas House Gorillas, a baseball team against whom Bugs plays all positions in *Baseball Bugs* (1946, and boasting a classic scene showing Bugs's indomitability: When a Gorilla whacks a ball with a tree trunk—the ball Bugs needs to make the last out—the intrepid rabbit hops a bus to a skyscraper, goes to the roof, scales a flagpole, flings his mitt up, and snares the ball); with Rocky and Hugo, the gangsters (Edward G. Robinson and Peter Lorre, respectively) in *Racketeer Rabbit* (1946); a bruiser of a boxer in *Rabbit Punch* (1948), in which the rather unorthodox fight lasts 110 rounds (the exasperated champ finally ties the unstoppable Bugs to a train track) before Bugs breaks the film and ends it; with McCrory the Scotsman ("What's up, McDoc?") in *My Bunny Lies over the Sea* (1948); Sir Pantsalot, a medieval knight, in *Knights Must Fall* (1949); with witchdoctor I. C. Spots, who requires a rabbit for one of his concoctions in *Which is Witch* (1949); with the child-eating Witch Hazel in *Betwitched Bunny* (1954); and with Paul Bunyan and his huge dog Smidgen, whose garden Bugs invades in *Lumberjack Rabbit* (1954). Bugs usually gets the upper hand through guile. However, in *Hare-um Scare-um*, Bugs is dressed as a female dog, to woo a hunting dog. This begins a minitrend of cross-dressing—an outgrowth of his innate hamminess, his desire to be shocking, and to charm male adversaries and put them at a disadvantage. Among the cartoons where Bugs was seen in drag were *What's Cookin', Doc* (1941), impersonating entertainer Carmen Miranda; *Hare Ribbin'* (1944), as a mermaid; *Bugs Bunny Nips the Nips* (1944), as a geisha; *Long-Haired Hare* (1949), as a teenage girl; *Hare-Trimmed* (1953), as a bride; and *Now Hare This* (1958), as Red Riding Hood. Apart from women, Bugs has also appeared as a number of other characters, including the heroic *Super Rabbit* (1943) who, thanks to a "super-vitaminized" carrot developed by Professor Canafrazz, becomes a powerful, costumed, airborne rabbit who tackles the rabbit-loathing Cottontail Smith; *Jack Wabbit and the Beanstalk* (1943; see **Daffy Duck** for Bugs's other trip up the vine); the Masked Marauder, a carrot-stealing wild west pest in *Buckaroo Bugs* (1944); a concert pianist in *Rhapsody Rabbit* (1946), a mouse foiling his performance of a *Hungarian Rhapsody* by Liszt (see **Tom and Jerry** for a quite similar cartoon); an astronaut in *Hardevil Hare* (1948), in which he meets Marvin Martian (see **Daffy Duck** for more on Marvin); a Revolutionary War soldier battling Hessian Sam von Schamm (Yosemite Sam) at the Battle of Bagel Heights in *Bunker Hill Bunny* (1950); the "mascot" of Columbus in *Hare We Go* (1951); a circus performer who gets on the wrong side of Bruno the bear in *Big Top Bunny* (1951); and a draftee in *Forward March Hare* (1953). Much of what we know about Bugs's youth comes from two cartoons. In his interview with Lola Beverly in *A Hare Grows in Manhattan* (1947), he talks about his childhood on New York's Lower East Side and how his survival instincts were honed by constant hounding from dogs. In the more revealing *What's Up, Doc?* (1950), he tells the Disassociated Press that he studied piano and music as a youngster, had bit parts in several Broadway shows, teamed with vaudeville star Elmer Fudd, and was ultimately discovered by Warner Brothers. *Hare Splitter* (1948) reveals that he has had a girlfriend named Daisy Lou, ignoring the fact that he is married (or perhaps divorced?). At present, disregarding all previous relationships, his girlfriend is the sweet Honey Bunny. Bugs's only other known relatives are his young nephew Clyde (*His Hare Raising Tale*, 1951, and *Yankee Doodle Bugs*, 1954, among others), and his cousin Herman in San Francisco.

Comment. Bugs was named after his original director, Ben Hardaway, whose nickname was Bugs, while the expression "What's up, Doc," came from the childhood memories of Tex Avery, who directed

A Wild Hare. The late Mel Blanc provided the character's voice, which he said came from combining "the toughest voices I know," Brooklyn and the Bronx. Bugs has starred in 173 Warner Brothers cartoons, made guest appearances in 11 others, and was also seen in the 1988 theatrical film *Who Framed Roger Rabbit* (see **Roger Rabbit**). There have been four feature-length Bugs Bunny films, compilations of his greatest shorts: *Bugs Bunny Superstar* (1975), *The Bugs Bunny/Road Runner Movie* (1979; Bugs gives a tour of his home and reminisces in new footage), *Friz Freleng's Looney Looney Looney Bugs Bunny Movie* (1981), and *Bugs Bunny's 3rd Movie: 1001 Rabbit Tales* (1982). The framing story of the latter features Bugs and **Daffy Duck** as rival book sellers for Rambling House Publishers—a good vehicle for Bugs to read stories to prospective client Sultan Sam (a k a Yosemite Sam), and to roll those old cartoons. On television, Bugs first appeared in *Bugs Bunny Theater* and *Bugs Bunny Cartoon Show,* which debuted in New York and Los Angeles, respectively, in 1956, showing theatrical cartoons starring Bugs and the other Warner Brother characters. The prime-time series *The Bugs Bunny Show* featured new adventures and aired on ABC from 1960 to 1962; it went into reruns on Saturday mornings and ran until 1975. Over at CBS, *The Bugs Bunny/Road Runner Hour* debuted in 1968, showing theatrical cartoons until 1977; *The Bugs Bunny/Road Runner Show* premiered in prime time on CBS in 1976, and replaced the hour-long show on Saturday mornings the following year. It ended its run in 1981. Presently, the rabbit is represented on Saturday mornings with the enormously popular *Bugs Bunny and Tweety Show* (see **Tweety**). The hare has also appeared in twenty prime-time specials since 1976, consisting of old and new material. Among these have been *Bugs Bunny's Easter Special* (1977), *Bugs Bunny in Space* (1978), *How Bugs Bunny Won the West* (1978), *Bugs Bunny's Valentine* (1979), *The Bugs Bunny Mother's Day Special* (1979), and *Bugs Bunny's Wild World of Sports* (1989). In comic books, Bugs appeared in the first and most subsequent issues of *Looney Tunes and Merrie Melodies Comics,* 246 issues of which were published by Dell from 1941 to 1962, and then starred in 245 issues of his own magazine, published from 1942 to 1983 by Dell and then Gold Key (with no. 86). The fifth issue of the Looney Tune comic book featured Bugs as the Super Rabbit, an adaptation of his motion picture guise. The Steven Spielberg TV cartoon series *Tiny*

Tunes features the adventures of Bugs, Daffy, Porky and so on as six year olds. It premiered in September 1990.

BULLDOG DRUMHEAD

Pedigree. Ineffectual comic book canine detective, parodying author H. C. McNeile's gentleman-adventurer Bulldog Drummond.

Biography. The portly, distinguished, whining Bulldog is an inept sleuth and a hypochondriac (in just one panel he complains, "I'm just wracked with pain . . . I can't straighten up. And—and now I'm having trouble breathing" followed in the next panel by, "Oww! My corn!"). Bulldog fights criminals so expert that "even their teeth are well drilled," yet he always manages to triumph . . . by accident. In one notable escapade, the hero inadvertently ties his suspenders to his shoelace. As he's being dragged outside a criminal's speeding car, his suspenders pop off and slingshot his shoe smack onto the felon's head. Bulldog is occasionally assisted by the scrappy cat Oliver Wendell McDuffy, whose father Drumhead sent up the river.

Comment. The character appeared in DC Comics's *Funny Stuff* beginning in 1944.

BULLET

Pedigree. Comic strip Mutt belonging to Snuffy Smith.

Biography. When wealthy Barney Google ran into the wilds of Kentucky, he met the hillbilly characters that would eventually replace him in his own strip: Snuffy and his wife Loweezy (joined, later, by nephew Jughaid). Bullet is a light brown mutt with dark brown spots on his back and ears, and he's described by Snuffy as "th' goodest friend I ever had in all my borned days." Despite the testimonial, if Bullet sees a lady dog, he'll desert Snuffy in a flash. Other animals who appear in the strip include Jughaid's pet frog Lucifer, the pesky razorback hog Ol' Snort, and the mule Aunt Sukey.

Comment. Snuffy and company first appeared in the "Barney Google" strip in 1934 (see **Spark Plug**). When creator Billy De Beck died in 1942, his assistant Fred Lasswell inherited the strip. Today, the strip is known as "Barney Google and Snuffy Smith." The characters were also seen in fifty TV cartoons, syndicated in 1963.

BULLET CROW

Pedigree. Comical comic book superhero.

Biography. Dressed in blue, with a red cape, red gloves, and a blue-and-yellow bullet-shaped helmet, Bullet Crow is headquartered in a "highly sophisticated laboratory and playroom . . . at the very tip of Mount Crowlympus," a headquarters "cleverly disguised as a big toaster" so that no one will assume it to be the lair of a superhero. Assisted by the tiny Coronary Canary and the costumed heroine Bonnie Bunny, the "Fowl of Fortune" spends much of his time battling and trying to rehabilitate the evil Edmond Eagle. When he's not fighting criminals, Bullet Crow stays in shape by facing the weapons in his Danger Room.

Comment. The frenetic character first appeared in one-page strips in the fan magazine *The Comic Reader*, beginning with no. 166 in 1979. It stayed with *The Comic Reader* until the magazine's demise

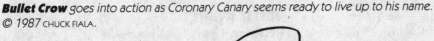

Bullet Crow goes into action as Coronary Canary seems ready to live up to his name. © 1987 CHUCK FIALA.

five years later. Bullet Crow graduated to his own two-issue Eclipse magazine in 1987, which reprinted many of the adventures. Bullet Crow was created by Chuck Fiala.

BULLSEYE AND TRICKY JOHN

Pedigree. TV dogs parodying Hawkeye and Trapper John from the series *M*A*S*H*.

Biography. Bullseye and Tricky John are dog Mounties, members of the Mangy Unwanted Shabby Heroes squad, which is stationed *waaay* up north and is responsible for keeping other animals in line. Among the loonies they deal with are the French, female-chasing wolf lumberjack; a polar bear who recklessly snowmobiles around; the huge clumsy Bruce Moose; and a coyote who wants to be a police dog. Assisting Bullseye and Tricky John are the voluptuous poodle Coldlips; the nerdy radio operator Sonar, a dachshund; Major Sideburns, Coldlips's lover; Lupey, a hot little chihuahua; Colonel Flake, the Harry Morgan type airedale; Hilda, a Great Dane who takes guff from no one; and General Upheaval, a by-the-book Peke.

Comment. The characters appeared on Filmation's *M*U*S*H,* one of the segments on *Uncle Croc's Block* (see **Fraidy Cat,** for details). Robert Ridgely provided the voices for Bullseye, Tricky John, Sonar, and Hilda. Ken Mars was everyone else.

BUNNY AND CLAUDE

Pedigree. Minor Warner Brothers theatrical stars.

Biography. As the theme song puts it, "Bonnie and Claude, this rabbit and his broad," race around the nation in their roadster, stealing carrots. Dressed just like their motion picture counterparts—Claude in a stylish suit, tie, and hat (with his rabbit ears poking up through the brim), Bunny with a beret, cigar, blond hair, and brightly painted lips—the outlaw rabbits are the stars of *Bunny and Claude* (1968) and *The Great Carrot Train Robbery* (1969). In the first, the bunnies sally forth from their hideout in Pop's Flophouse to rob carrots from shops. They're chased by a big-bellied, nameless, Southern sheriff with a handlebar moustache (and a voice extremely reminiscent of that of Yosemite Sam's)—who, at one point, disguises himself as a giant carrot in a failed effort to trap the pair. The second cartoon really belongs to the sheriff, who tries various, unsuccessful ways to board the carrot train the thieves have commandeered. Flatly animated, the cartoons depend more on puns than on typical Warner Brothers

(Wile E. Coyote) sight gags: When the sheriff corners the duo at Pop's, he yells, "Come out, you rat!" A rodent emerges with its hands raised. Another time, Claude surveys vegetable booty they've stolen and says appreciatively, "Twenty four carrots. Not a bad haul."

Comment. The first short was a send-up of the studio's hit film *Bonnie and Clyde* (1967). Mel Blanc was the voice of Claude and Pat Wodell was Bunny.

BUNSON BUNNY

Pedigree. Comic book rabbit created by Walt Kelly of **Pogo** fame.

Biography. While walking through the forest of Wood Land, Bunson and his father find a book called *Christmas Stories.* Because neither of them can read, they take the book to Mr. Owl—who's "very good at reading the pictures," but not the words. Mr. Weevil, Mr. Frog, and the other animals are also unable to help, but when all the animals are together they decide to have a Christmas party at "the ol' tumble-down shack" and invite Santa. Bunson writes to him on a leaf, which they mail to the North Pole. Santa can't help but notice the leaf as it spills from a bag loaded with Christmas letters, and he elects to go. Needless to say, his cheery nature and gifts make for a memorable Christmas. Bunson is wide-eyed and innocent, wanting nothing more than to have a happy Christmas.

Comment. The characters appeared just once, in "Christmas Comes to the Wood Land" in *Four-Color* no. 91: *Santa Claus Funnies* in 1945, published by Dell. The animals are much less stylized than in the "Pogo" strip, but the characterizations and dialogue are superb, making the children's story a sheer delight. See also Kelly's **Elfalump.**

BUSTER BUNNY

Pedigree. Comic book bunny.

Biography. Buster is a spunky young hare who thrives on fun. He enjoys camping (right next to the house, though, so he can go inside and eat), and going to the movies (as long as someone else is paying, because he never has any money). The white (later, gray) bunny always wears a red sweatshirt and black trousers.

Comment. Buster appeared in sixteen issues of his own magazine from Standard Comics (1949 to 1953), and also appeared as back-up feature in comics starring **Supermouse.** See **Hamton** for another Buster Bunny.

BUTCH

Pedigree. Romantic rival and general nemesis of Pluto the Pup.

Biography. The big, blue-gray bulldog has a studded collar, massive black eyebrows, a big mouth filled with wicked-looking teeth, and a mean disposition . . . although it must be said that his anger toward Pluto is not entirely unfounded. In their first outing together, *Bone Trouble* (1940), Butch spies Pluto trying to make off with one of his bones. The bulldog chases Pluto to a fair, where, in the hall of mirrors, Pluto is able to create monstrous images that send Butch running—and (unjustly) leave Pluto with the bone. The bulldog loses another bone to Pluto in their second cartoon together, *T-Bone for Two* (1942), and, worse, loses him the affection of the dachshund Dinah in their next three cartoons. He rebounds from a series of bit parts with *The Purloined Pup* (1946) as a dognapper (some comeback!) who has made off with a puppy and is tracked down and hauled off to prison by Pluto. He has a meatier part in the O'Henry-ish *Pluto's Purchase* (1948), in which the bulldog does everything he can to try to steal a salami **Mickey Mouse** has sent Pluto to buy. The upshot: Pluto manages to deliver it to Mickey, who turns around and gives it to Butch for his birthday. Butch's other screen appearances have been largely insignificant.

Comment. Butch costarred in eleven short subjects.

BUTTONS BEAR

Pedigree. Star of the featurette *A Chucklewood Easter.*

Biography. Buttons is the son of Bridget and Abner Bear. Upon waking from hibernation in the cave the Bears share with the Fox family, Buttons sets out with his friend Rusty Fox to reacquaint himself with their homeland, Chucklewood Park. There, they find Ranger Jones putting up signs announcing the coming of Easter. The animals ask what Easter is, and Jones tells them all about the Easter Bunny and Easter eggs. Excited by the concept and wanting to be involved, the animals run off and steal eggs from the nests of Edwina Duck, Gertrude Turtle, Winnie Woodpecker, and others—unaware how frantic their actions leave the mothers. Back in the cave, the boys stash the eggs, then sneak out and clandestinely follow Skipper and Bluebelle Rabbit as they make their yearly pilgrimage to the hidden cave of the Easter Bunny. Meanwhile, the mother animals have

contacted Ranger Jones about the stolen eggs, and he alerts the park population to watch for them. Rusty's father George finds the eggs in the cave, and he and Abner return them. At the same time, Buttons and Rusty are discovered in the rabbit cave and put on trial for trespassing. Luckily, the Easter Bunny chooses to be lenient, sending the boys back to the park so they can see the suffering they've caused among the egg-laying mothers. Buttons and Rusty are truly repentant, having learned, as the Easter Bunny puts it, "to keep your noses out of other critters' nests!"

Comment. Written by John Bates, the half-hour cartoon was produced and directed by Bill Hutten and Tony Love. It went into syndication in 1986.

BUZZ-BUZZ BEE

Pedigree. Resolute little foe of **Donald Duck**.

Biography. With a stinger longer than his little legs, and a head considerably larger than his little bean-shaped torso, Buzz-Buzz may not look much like a bee . . . but he's the pride of the breed. In *Inferior Decorator* (1948), Buzz-Buzz sees flowers on Donald's wall, unaware that the duck is simply hanging wallpaper. After several run-ins with Donald, the bee becomes stuck in the paste and must summon his hive mates to give him a hand (and Donald a stinger). Buzz-Buzz makes sure **Pluto the Pup** gets the point in *Bubble Bee* (1949), when the dog destroys his hive to get at the gumballs Buzz-Buzz has been stealing from a machine and stashing. (The script is woefully unenlightening as to why a bee is hoarding bubble gum. Presumably, he likes to chew it.) The bee once again has to deal with Donald when the duck attempts to steal his honey in *Honey Harvester* (1949); the two cross stinger and beak once more in *Slide, Donald, Slide* (1949), when Donald wants to listen to baseball on the radio, and the bug wants to hear music (he has a long-haired "maestro" coiffure for the occasion) and in *Bee at the Beach* (1950), fighting over a place in the sun (the bug triumphs). *Bee on Guard* (1951) finds Donald once again trying to take the bee's hard-earned honey, while *Let's Stick Together* (1952) features world-weary Donald and the bee reflecting on their old (stock footage) battles.

Comment. The name Buzz-Buzz has been retroactively assigned to the insect by the studio. Forerunners of Buzz-Buzz include the bee which flies into Donald's flute and buzzes **Mickey Mouse** in *The Band Concert* (1935) (when the mouse-conductor tries to shoo the bee with his baton, the orchestra goes mad trying to keep up); and the bee in *Moose Hunters* (1947), which gets into the (truly wretched) female moose costume Donald and **Goofy** have donned to try to lure a male moose. Another cartoon bee, this one in TV advertising, is the mascot of Honey Nut Cheerios breakfast cereal. Introduced in 1986, he has an orange head and black-striped orange body. Like all bees, this one has tiny wings and big white shoes.

BUZZY THE CROW
Pedigree. A wily bird of animated cartoons and comic books.
Biography. A bird who can think on his talons, Buzzy—who wears a straw hat, has a gold tooth, and talks like Eddie "Rochester" Anderson—is always looking for a way to destroy the cat who's trying to eat him (and who talks like Jack Benny). He's done things such as buttering him up and shoving him into a bottle, leading the screaming cat into a library where the librarian bops him, and lighting three cigars and using them like rocket boosters to launch the cat skyward. Buzzy lives in a birdhouse on the property where the cat lives with its unseen master.

Comment. The characters made their debut in the Paramount Noveltoon *Stupidstitious Cat* in 1947, in which Buzzy uses everything at his disposal do fill the cat with fear, i.e., smashing a mirror, spilling salt, and even painting the cat black to send him running away in fear. A handful of cartoons followed, such as *Sock-a-Bye Kitty, As the Crow Lies, Cat-Choo, Better Bait Than Never,* and *No Ifs, Ands, or Butts.* The characters made their comic book debut in *Paramount Animated Comics* no. 1 in 1953; they appeared mostly in two-page chases in this and other Harvey Comics titles, although they did star in one issue of *Harvey Hits* (no. 18, 1959). Although Buzzy wasn't as successful as other Paramount cartoon characters, such as **Herman the Mouse, Baby Huey,** and Casper the Friendly Ghost, he enjoyed a longer career than some of the more obscure characters created by the studio in the late 1940s. The concept behind the Noveltoons was that characters the public enjoyed would be developed by the studio. Unfortunately, Blackie the Lamb, Inchy Inchworm, Herbert the Dog, Finny the Goldfish, Louie the Lion, Kitty Cuddles, Snapper (a photojournalist dog . . . or a "news hound," as he described himself), Tommy Tortoise and Moe Hare never made it beyond one or two cartoon shorts.

CALVIN AND THE COLONEL

Pedigree. A team of TV cartoon animals.

Biography. The Southern duo consists of the dull-minded, cigar-smoking bear Calvin Burnside, and his wily companion, Colonel Montgomery J. Klaxon, a fox. Together, they get into fairly pedestrian adventures involving thieves, money, jobs (the colonel usually gets Calvin to help him without pay), and even one of the colonel's former beaus. Other characters include the colonel's wife, Maggie Bell, and her sister, Sue.

Comment. Although changing values would never have allowed *Amos 'n' Andy* to appear in an animated cartoon, that's more or less who these characters were: The voices were provided by Freeman Gosden and Charles Correll, who had created the original radio characters. Kayro produced twenty-five episodes for syndication in 1961; Dell published two issues of the comic book in 1962.

CAP'N CATNIP

Pedigree. Comic book crime fighter, aided by his sidekick Womble, the Wonder Gerbil.

Biography. A millionaire in Petropolis, Cheshire A. Catt is disgusted by "the ever increasing rise in big crime." Thus he dons a yellow costume with a red cape and cowl and becomes the ferocious Cap'n Catnip. His "faithful junior accountant" Freddie becomes the orange-garbed Womble, and is constantly pointing out to people, "I am not a mouse! I'm a gerbil!" In their first (and only) adventure, the heroes battle Ratman and the thieving Jet-Pack Cats, who steal the plans for "a nuclear-powered mouse trap." Chief among the weapons Catnip brings to bear against them are catnap gas ("All the good guys hold your breath!" he shouts) and their supersleek Kitty Kar. The heroes are aided briefly by the black-and-blue costumed Ms. Kitty and her striped sidekick Tiger. Inspector Drummond (a bulldog, of course) lends a hand on behalf of the police.

Comment. The characters appeared just once in Charlton Comics *Charlton Bullseye* no. 2, in 1981. Also appearing in that issue were **Neil the Horse** and Jack Bunny. The latter is a trusting young hare who falls in with Wernher von Bluebird, a rocket scientist working on a rocket sled in the middle of the woods.

Jack helps the scientist guard the site against Russian spies.

CAPTAIN JACK

Pedigree. Suave cat hero of adult comic books.

Biography. The unflappable gray-furred space adventurer of the year 2200 is the commander of an intrepid crew, which consists of the hound Herman Feldman and his tiny, red, devil-tailed dog sidekick Beezlebub [sic] and an android, the terrier-faced "man" Adam Fink (a parody of writer Otto Binder's classic robot Adam Link). Among their adventures have been the rescue of an astronaut, Stanley Tomcat, who was launched into space and never returned (he's found living on an idyllic alien world that he doesn't want to leave); Herman's near-death experience, in which he visits heaven (God really *is* the Almighty Dollar); and a stay with raccoons Fred and his contentious daughter, Janet, the only denizens of a farming planet, to help with the harvesting (a comic book version of *The Rainmaker*). A gambler and bon vivant, the captain is rarely without a cigarette holder and natty uniform.

Comment. The characters were created by Mike Kazaleh and first appeared in Fantagraphics Books comic book *The Adventures of Captain Jack,* which began publication in 1986. The comic also features the adventures of Boris and Morris, the Dingbats: vampire bat rock singers. Another science fiction cat comic book was the one-shot *Watchcats,* a parody of DC's successful series *Watchmen.* In this 1987 comic book from Harrier Publishing, a team of superheroic cats is both stalking and being stalked by a killer. The cats are Gus, Hatrack, Professor New York, and Carrie. Assisting them is the flying robo-dog Rover.

CAPTAIN TEDDY

Pedigree. Costumed comic book superhero.

Biography. Originally, Captain Teddy was Captain Titan, a mighty hero. Unfortunately, the evil Purple Brain imprisoned Titan's mind inside an inert, toy teddy bear; only by merging with its owner, suburbanite Arthur Quinn, can he become a hero once more. The union is achieved when Quinn utters the word, "Contract." In this form, the hybrid Captain

*The mighty **Captain Teddy** shares his wisdom.*
© CHARLES RUTLEDGE.

Teddy has a human torso with a teddy bear head; he wears a red-and-blue costume and cape. Known as "the toy wonder" and "the plaything without fear," he can fly, has super strength, and can't be harmed by gunfire. His only foes have been the Buddy Bears, **Care Bears** parodies who go berserk and become machine-gun–toting soldiers of fortune.

Comment. The character appeared just once, in the only issue of Paragraphics *Boffo Laffs* in 1986. The comic book is historic for having been the first to boast a hologram on the cover. The delightful character was created by Charles Rutledge. See also Superted.

CARE BEARS

Pedigree. Toys turned media superstars.

Biography. The Care Bears are fuzzy, little animals who live in the clouds, in the magical realm known as Care-A-Lot. They take turns using a telescope, and whenever they spot a sad child somewhere, one or more of the bears head to earth (floating or driv-

ing a cloud car). If their ebullient presence and gentle prodding fails to improve the child's mood, they can always resort to the Care Bear Stare—a quasi-hypnotic technique that never fails to bring joy! The bears are Tenderheart, Birthday Bear, Cheer Bear, Funshine Bear, Wish Bear, Friend Bear, Bedtime Bear, and Good Luck Bear. Each of the bears is a different pastel color and has a happy design on its chest appropriate to its name (a rainbow, a cupcake and birthday candle, a heart, a four leaf clover, and so forth). Naturally, each bear specializes in the activity after which it is named. There's also a resident grouch: blue Grumpy Bear, who has a raincloud on its chest and always carries an umbrella, convinced it's going to rain. When the bears need to communicate with one another, they use—what else?—their C.B. radio.

Comment. Created in 1981 by Those Characters from Cleveland as a line of greeting cards, the characters became enormously popular stuffed toys and were propelled into an extraordinary career in various media (for which many of the details about the bears' powers and Care-A-Lot were devised). In motion pictures, they've been seen in *The Care Bears Movie* (1985), in which not just the Care Bears but the Care Bear Cousins (Noble Heart Horse and Gentle Heart Lamb, among others) battle the Evil Spirit of Magic; *Care Bears Movie II: A New Generation* (1986), which introduced the Care Bear Cubs (Baby Tugs, Baby Hugs, and so on) and the Care Cousin Cubs and typical doings in the Kingdom of Caring; and *The Care Bears Adventure in Wonderland* (1987), in which they follow Alice through the looking glass. They had their own Saturday morning ABC series in 1986, *The Care Bears Family,* as well as a half-hour seasonal special first aired in 1988, *The Care Bears' Nutcracker Suite,* a tale of how the wicked three-headed King of Mice not only conquers Toyland, but turns the Care Bears into wood (one must assume there's no market for Care Boards). Since 1985, the Marvel Comics line of juvenile Star Comics has had considerable success with the *Care Bears* comic book. A year before the Care Bears came to television, another bear family debuted on CBS: *The Berenstain Bears,* the stars of Stanley and Janice Berenstain's long running line of children's books. Their earthbound creatures live in treehomes in Bear Country, whose economy is based on honey instead of money. The focus of the cartoons (and books) are the young Sister and Brother Bear, Papa Bear, and Mama Bear. Also in the cast are Handybear Gus, Miss Honeybear (the teacher), and others. However, the focus is on the family, and the interplay between these characters is real and often touching—as opposed to the unadulterated schmaltz of the Care Bears. Another character that evolved from a line of greeting cards was Hallmark's little girl Rainbow Brite, who lives in Rainbow Land and owns a magnificent white horse named Starlite. The horse has a rainbow mane and tail, and a yellow star on its forehead; it can fly, and carries Rainbow to earth where she spreads sunshine around—she also uses her magic powers to help kids in trouble (there's a whole lot of originality going on here!). Stormy is also an inhabitant of Rainbow Land, and she rides her purple steed Sky Dancer to spread rain. Outside of cards and toys, the characters appeared in a 1985 animated motion picture *Rainbow Brite and the Star Stealer,* and in a DC Comic book adaptation of same. Far less successful was American Greetings Get Along Gang, six young bipedal animals: Montgomery (a moose, and the leader), Dotty (a dog), Zipper (a cat), Bingo (a beaver), Woolma (a lamb), and Portia (a porcupine). The team enjoyed brief notoriety in six issues of a Marvel Star comic book in 1985. In 1988, Cine Group produced a similar syndicated cartoon series, *The Little Flying Bears.* The winged bears protected the environment and other animals in twenty-six half-hour episodes.

CASUAL T. CAT

Pedigree. Cat seen in the safety commercial, *The Shocking Adventure of Casual T. Cat.*

Biography. A baby is on the floor, playing with an electrical cord, eyeing an outlet. Along comes the bipedal, brown cat Casual. Baby grabs the cats tail, plugs it in, and Casual is fried. Lesson: "Childproof your home."

Comment. The public service spots began airing in 1989, produced by the American Academy of Pediatrics. The figures were created by Will Vinton Productions, using Claymation. Love that name: Casual T. Cat.

CATTANOOGA CATS

Pedigree. Live action Saturday morning cats.

Biography. Rock-and-roll felines, Cheesie, Kitty Jo, Scootz, Groovey, and Country introduce cartoon segments featuring other characters, and also partake in short live-action skits of their own.

Comment. The Hanna-Barbera series premiered on ABC in 1969. The identities of the actors in the costumes is not known; the voices were provided by Julie Bennett (Cheesie and Kitty Jo), Jim Begg (Scootz), Casey Kasem (Groovey), and Bill Galloway (Country). Also seen on the show were the cartoon escapades of Auto Cat and *It's the Wolf,* about the misadventures of **Mildew Wolf.** Other shows involving costumed animals included *The Bugaloos* (from Sid and Marty Krofft in 1970), four insect musicians—Joy, Courage, I.Q., and Harmony—living in Tranquility Forest; and the syndicated *The New Zoo Revue* (from Barbara Atlas and Douglas Momary in 1972), about the human-size Freddie the Frog, Henrietta the Hippo, and Charlie the Owl.

CAVE BIRD

Pedigree. Prehistoric bird of TV's Captain Caveman cartoons.

Biography. Little is known about this roughly foot-tall orange bird. It lives inside the hollow club of the prehistoric superhero Captain Caveman, who was frozen during the Ice Age and thawed in modern times. When the hero needs something the bird has stashed away—items as diverse as a flint and a jackhammer—the top of the club pops open, an extender arm emerges, and the bird gives the caveman a hand. The dodolike bird usually isn't happy to be disturbed, however, and invariably makes some snide comment about "Cavey's" ineptness.

Comment. The characters first appeared on *Scooby's All-Star Laff-A-Lympics* in 1977 (see **Scooby-Doo**). They got their own show, *Captain Caveman and the Teen Angels,* on ABC in 1980 (twenty-four adventures) and also costarred that year on *The Flintstones Comedy Show.*

THE C.B. BEARS

Pedigree. TV cartoon version of *Charlie's Angels*—with bearness instead of bareness.

Biography. The titular Bears are the clever leader Hustle, the dumb Bump, and the diminutive but exuberant Boogie, and they're based in a garbage truck. Whenever there's a crime or mystery, a woman named Charlie calls them over their C.B. radio and they go to work. Among the cases and situations they've handled are *The Valley of No Return, Drackenstein's Revenge, The Invasion of the Blobs,* and *The Missing Mansion Mystery.*

Comment. The Hanna-Barbera characters appeared on their own show, which debuted on NBC in 1977; there were thirteen episodes. Daws Butler was Hustle's Phil Silvers-like voice, Henry Corden was Bump, and Chuck McCann played Boogie. Susan Davis was the voice of Charlie. Other segments seen on the hour-long *C.B. Bears* show were *Heyyy, It's* *the King* (see **The King**); *Undercover Elephant* (see **Undercover Elephant**), and *Blast Off Buzzard,* a series of silent sight gags in which the buzzard tries to catch and eat a snake named Crazy Legs as it winds through the desert and environs (your basic **Road Runner** clone).

CECIL TURTLE

Pedigree. Star of a trio of Warner Brothers theatrical cartoons.

Biography. When **Bugs Bunny** reads the title of his 1941 cartoon *Tortoise Beats Hare,* he's furious: "Why these screwy guys don't know what they're talkin' about!" he rages, then challenges the tortoise, Cecil, to a race. Unbeknownst to the arrogant Bugs, however, Cecil arranges for his cousin Chester to have a bunch of their friends to help him win the race. Thus regardless of what impasse the rabbit throws up along the way, the turtle remains in the lead. And, of course, he's there at the finish line ahead of Bugs. When Bugs wonders if he's been tricked, ten turtles admit, "It's a poss-i-*bil*-ity!" Indignant, Bugs stews for a while then demands a rematch in *Tortoise Wins By a Hare* (1943). Donning a disguise, Bugs chats with the turtle, asking how he manages to move so fast (ignoring the fact that Cecil cheated to win the first race). The tortoise reveals that it has to do with his "air-flow chassis" and, encouraged, Bugs goes home and builds himself a metal shell. He dares Cecil to race again, and the tortoise accepts. Meanwhile, gangsters bet "everything we got" that the rabbit is going to win. To ensure that he does, they intend to waylay the turtle. Naturally, Cecil dresses as a hare, and when Bugs runs by the thugs whack him. Manfully continuing, he is violently impeded many times. When Cecil wins, Bugs pulls off his shell and yells, "What are you doing? *I'm* the rabbit!" Flabbergasted, the bad guys shoot themselves. The duo's next and last meeting is in *Rabbit Transit* (1947). This time, Cecil has equipped his shell with rockets, and he jets past the startled Bugs. Through subterfuge, the lead changes hands several times, until Bugs *finally* wins. However, because Bugs was doing over the speed limit, Cecil summons the police, who cart the champ away.

Comment. Cecil is the only cartoon character who has ever repeatedly bested the wily rabbit!

CEREBUS THE AARDVARK

Pedigree. "A mean and lethal aardvark" of comic books.

Biography. A three-foot-tall, hard-drinking, greedy, gray-furred, sword-swinging, talking earth-pig, Cerebus battles wizards, monsters, and various villains while searching for treasure in a "preindustrial" human world of Lower Felda, which consists of sprawling countryside and seedy cities like Boreala and Beduin. Unquestionably, the strangest character he has met in his travels is the insane costumed vigilante, the Cockroach (a caricature of the superhero Batman). After first spotting him, Cerebus muses, "There's only *one* thing more idiotic than running around in a mask after dark in a *snowstorm . . .* and that's *following* someone in a mask after dark" (no. 11). Another bizarre character is a spoof of Marvel's monster the Man-Thing, as Cerebus battles the mucky giant Woman-Thing (no. 25).

Comment. The character was originally going to be called Cerberus, after the vicious, three-headed dog of Greek mythology. But the publisher got the name wrong while taking notes, and the misspelling stuck. Originally a parody of Conan, Cerebus's magazine first appeared in 1977, published by Aardvark-Vanaheim Press; more than 150 issues later, it remains a popular title. The character was created by Dave Sim, whose innovative art shifts skillfully between the moody and the spectacular.

CHARLIE THE TUNA

Pedigree. Advertising mascot for Star Kist tuna.

Biography. Wearing a beret and shades, the hip tuna is determined to be chopped up and crammed into a can of Star Kist. To prove that he has class, he learns music, studies art, plays sports, reads poetry—and is always rewarded with a fish hook that lowers down the printed message, "Sorry Charlie." As the announcer explains, "Star Kist doesn't want tuna with good taste. Star Kist wants tuna that tastes good." The blue-skinned Charlie swims, although he also stands on his tail, which looks like legs. He also has arms.

Comment. The character was introduced in 1961, the creation of the Leo Burnett agency. He has been seen in nearly 100 different advertisements. Actor Herschel Bernardi provides his voice.

CHAUNCEY CHIRP

Pedigree. Comic book bird who tries to survive the hazards of life in the woods.

Biography. "Chirpy" lives in a nest with his folks, but spends most of his time bumming around with the bluejay Johnny Jay. (As one bird puts it, "I always knew that Mrs. Chirp's son would be a disgrace.") Their foe is Humphrey "Blowhard" Bohawk, a juvenile delinquent bird who wants to lead them into trouble. The yellow Chauncey has a black head of "hair" and wears a collar and string tie.

Comment. Chauncey appeared occasionally in Eastern Color Printing's *Jingle Jangle Comics* throughout the 1940s. Other characters in the forty-two issue run of *Jingle Jangle Comics* included Benny Bear; the kangaroo Susie Spring, her son Junior, and their noisy foe Willie Woodpecker; and the Very Royal Lion, who thinks only of food (he once improvised an aria titled "The Big Hunk of Cheese").

CHESTER CHEETAH
Pedigree. Advertising mascot for Chee-tos snacks.
Biography. Insisting that other cheese snacks "ain't nothin' but fluff," the star of TV and print advertising is constantly doing what he can to get ahold of a bag of Chee-tos. He invariably fails (e.g., he'll set off after a Chee-tos truck on a motorcycle, invariably failing to notice the open manhole between them). The hip cheetah wears black sunglasses, red trunks, and white sneakers with an orange spot on the side.

Comment. The character began appearing in advertising in January 1989. His single-mindedness is reminiscent of the **Trix Rabbit.**

CHILLY WILLY
Pedigree. Penguin star of theatrical cartoons and comic books.
Biography. Rarely uttering more than a word or two, and always wearing the same red-and-white beanie, the foot-tall Chilly Willy lives in an igloo in Coldernell, Alaska. His needs are simple: Money, warmth, and food. Most of the cartoons revolve around getting these, despite impasses presented by other animals. These rivals range from the otherwise good-natured, drawling Smedley the polar bear, to the nameless dog that guards the fur pelts in a local warehouse. Widely considered to be the best of the Chilly Willy cartoons are *The Legend of Rockabye Point* (1955) and *Half-Baked Alaska* (1965). In the former, Chilly and Smedley vie against one another to steal the catch off a local fishing boat, all the while trying not to wake the ship's dog; in the latter, Chilly abandons the shoeshine stand he runs in the middle of the tundra to try his hand at more lucrative trades, such as playing the piano in a local bar, working as a blacksmith, and cutting hair.

Comment. Chilly was created by director Alex Lovy, but was redesigned and successfully launched by animator/director Tex Avery. Avery later said, "You couldn't do anything with a little fuzzy, wuzzy penguin." Therefore, Avery says, he tried to get humor from the supporting characters, "the dumb dog, or the dumb sea gull, or the dumb polar bear." Walter Lantz produced forty-eight Chilly Willy cartoons between 1953 and 1972. Daws Butler provided the penguin's high, little voice. These cartoons came to television in 1957, when ABC premiered *The Woody Woodpecker Show.* Chilly also appeared as a back-up feature in many of the comic books that starred **Woody Woodpecker,** such as *New Funnies,* which also featured such minor Lantz characters as Billy and Bonnie Bee. Chilly also starred in nine issues of his own, published by Dell under its *4-Color* banner (1956 to 1962). Another comic book penguin of far less note, Willie the Penguin, starred in six issues published by Standard Publishing from 1951 to 1952.

THE CHIPMUNKS
Pedigree. Trio of singing rodents on records, television, and film.
Biography. David Seville (see "Comment") is a handsome young songwriter and manager of the Chipmunks, who live with him in a large home. The three singing stars are Alvin, the self-styled leader of the group, who wears a baseball cap and a voluminous red sweatshirt with a big, yellow *A* on the front and is self-impressed, canny, stubborn, and mischievous; chubby Theodore, who stops eating and laughing only long enough to sing; and brainy Simon, who wears horn-rims and should know better than to follow Alvin into trouble—but does so anyway. When something does go wrong or things are too quiet in the house, one can always count on hearing David's cry, *"Alllll-vinnn!"* The group's adventures often involve revenge (against their martinet of a baby-sitter or grouch of a neighbor), but also take them far and wide as the artists travel nationally and internationally.

Comment. The characters were first heard on *The Chipmunk Song,* a k a *Christmas Don't Be Late,* in 1958; it was written by Ross Bagdasarian, who wrote under the "professional" name David Seville. Bagdasarian was originally going to call his characters the Butterflies, but children who heard tests of the voices (Bagdasarian's own, speeded up) thought they sounded more like chipmunks—undoubtedly due to their similarity to Walt Disney's popular **Chip**

'n' Dale. The characters were named after Liberty Records executives Al Bennet and Si Waronker, and recording technician Ted Keep. More records and merchandise followed the 4 million–copy hit, as did an animated TV series, *The Alvin Show,* which premiered on CBS in 1961. It remained on the network until 1965, after which it was syndicated as *Alvin and the Chipmunks.* NBC used the same name and cartoons when it brought the series back in 1979; the name was the same but the cartoons were new when the series returned to the network in 1983. In 1986, a feature-length animated film, *The Chipmunk Adventure,* updated Jules Verne's *Around the World in Eighty Days:* While David is in Europe, Alvin convinces the others to elude their housekeeper, Miss Miller, and enter a hot air balloon race. While competing against a trio of female chipmunks, the Chipettes, the boys also become involved with ruthless diamond smugglers. In comics, Dell published twenty-eight issues of *Alvin* from 1962 to 1973, along with various one shots, including *Alvin for President* in 1964, placing him in the ranks of **Bill the Cat, Huckleberry Hound, Pogo Possum,** and other as animals that have run for the nation's highest office.

CHIP 'N' DALE
Pedigree. Walt Disney's cartoon chipmunks.
Biography. First of all, how to tell them apart? Simple. Chip's the more sensible one with the black nose, Dale's the more impulsive and frivolous one with the red nose. The pair of chipmunks—brown-furred, with a black-and-white stripe down their back—first appeared in *Private Pluto* (1943). Voicing high, squealing, inarticulate sounds, they find, to their dismay, that the military has assigned **Mickey Mouse's** dog **Pluto the Pup** the job of protecting a pillbox in which they've been living and stashing nuts. The bulk of the cartoon consists of the chipmunks finding new ways to use Pluto to crack nuts (putting them inside his helmet and smashing down, firing him into the air and having him land on them, and so forth). In their second outing, *Squatter's Rights* (1946), they find themselves competing with Mickey and Pluto for the mouse's weekend cabin. After numerous confrontations, the chipmunks accidentally knock Pluto out and, while he's unconscious, they splatter him with catsup. Thinking his dog's been wounded, Mickey heads for the vet . . . leaving Chip 'n' Dale triumphant. The chipmunks didn't get their names or the ability to speak (albeit, as speeded up as their previous chatter) until the

third cartoon, *Chip an' Dale* [sic], in which they tackled their recurring foe, **Donald Duck,** for the first time, a rivalry that began when Donald went out to chop wood for the fireplace, unaware (not that he would have cared if he *did* know) that one hollow log was the chipmunks' home. The conflict continued through such cartoons as *Three for Breakfast* (1948) with pancakes as the prize (the buttering of the *roof* so Donald will fall is a classic), *Trailer Horn* (1950), with Donald camping nearing the chipmunks' home, and *Working for Peanuts* (1953), set in a zoo (see **Dolores**). The shapely chipmunk torch singer Clarice was introduced in *Two Chips and a Miss* in 1952, providing love interest (and someone to fight over). One of their most enjoyable adventures was *Pluto's Christmas Tree* (1952), which gave the Disney artists a chance to do some lovely scenic and lighting designs with the tree. Not that the cartoon is short on gags. The two best scenes were the chipmunks twisting the bulbs on and off to befuddle Pluto (when the dog pokes his nose up to sniff them out, Dale mistakes it for a bulb and turns it as well), and Dale, hiding from Pluto, disguising himself as a Santa Claus candle. Needless to say, Mickey comes along just then to light the figurines, and when Dale blows out the match, Mickey simply picks him up and lights his head using a flaming wick. Fortunately, Chip rushes along to put out his blazing partner. Chip 'n' Dale also serve with **The Rescue Rangers:** Unlike the naked chipmunks of the theatrical cartoons, Chip wears a leather jacket and fedora to go into action, while Dale dresses in a much less appropriate (although flashier) Hawaiian shirt.

   Comment. The characters' names were created by assistant director Bea Selck, who took it from eighteenth-century furniture maker Thomas Chippendale. They starred in twenty-three theatrical cartoons, and were seen in the 1983 featurette *Mickey's Christmas Carol.* Their voices were originally provided by Jim Macdonald and Dessie Flynn. In comics, the chipmunks have guest starred in numerous Disney magazines, as well as in their own title, thirty issues of which were published by Dell from 1953 to 1962, and eighty-three by Gold Key from 1967 to 1982.

CHIPS
Pedigree. A big, voracious comic book dog.
Biography. On his way home from school, wimpy third grader Randy Walters gets beaten up by a bully . . . yet again. However, he's also befriended by a

Chips, *a dog with a unique way of dealing with troublemakers.* © DOUGLAS POTTER.

nearly five-foot-long dog, whom he dubs Chips (because his spots look like chocolate chips). Chips is scarred and has a huge jaw full of angry-looking teeth; the first thing he does on reaching the Walterses' home is eat the pet cat, Fluffy. Reluctantly, Randy's parents allow Chips to stay. Randy goes to school the next day with a fresh sense of confidence, and while the dog holds everyone at bay, his master tears into the bully who beat him up the day before. Unfortunately, Chips has a nasty habit of eating children. Unable to control the boy or his pet, Mr. and Mrs. Walters move while their son's at school, leaving the boy and his dog to fend for themselves.

Comment. Douglas Potter's outré characters appeared in just one issue of *Chips and Vanilla,* published by Kitchen Sink Comix in 1988.

CINDY BEAR
Pedigree. Cartoon bear, girlfriend of **Yogi Bear.**
Biography. Jellystone Park's Cindy is a truly smitten bear: Although a well-bred southern belle, she continually tries to romance the charming but self-possessed Yogi Bear. When he's around, she implores him to whisper sweet nothings in her ear ("Nothin' . . . nothin' . . . nothin'," he teases, but Cindy laps it up just the same.) When they're apart, she can usually be found sighing and saying, "He loves me, he

loves me not," pulling petals off of flowers, always ending up on the former. Each time she awakens from hibernation, Cindy swears she's not going to listen to any more " 'We're just pals' or 'You're a good kid' stuff." She vows she's going to catch Yogi "in a tender bear trap" and get him to marry her. She constantly fails, but that doesn't stop the pretty bear from trying. Cindy is always dressed in a blue tutu, yellow scarf, and a flower in her hair, and carries a blue parasol. Her preferred brand of lipstick is strawberries. Much as Yogi is known for his signature phrase, "Smarter than the average bear," Cindy is prone to state, "I *do* declare!"

Comment. See entry on Yogi Bear for the rundown of Cindy's TV and comic book appearances.

CLARA CLUCK
Pedigree. Walt Disney chicken diva.
Biography. With a full bosom and equally expansive manner, Clara is one of the ear-ringingest opera stars of all time. Decked-out in a sunbonnet with an ostrich feather poking from the upturned brim, and covered with dark brown feathers on all but her breast, tail, and wings—which are white, white, and tan, respectively—Clara overwhelms an audience of youngsters in her first cartoon *Orphan's Benefit* (1934) and again in the 1941 color remake (her re-

fusal to stick strictly to the score makes life difficult for accompanist Mickey). In between, her performances in *Mickey's Grand Opera* (1936) and *Mickey's Amateurs* (1937) are also legendary. The only problem with the former is that the scene from *Rigoletto* is played with **Donald Duck.** When her partner is sent flying by **Pluto the Pup,** who's chasing a frog, the duck's rapier stabs Clara and for a glorious moment she sings at least an octave higher than Verdi had intended. When she comes down from the high notes, she—along with Donald, Pluto, and the scenery—come crashing down. Like true professionals, however, they crawl from the detritus to squawk out the last measure of music. In *Symphony Hour* (1942), Clara reveals another talent: She also plays the cello—badly.

Comment. Florence Gill provided the voice for the character; Clara was last seen in a cameo in the featurette *Mickey's Christmas Carol* (1983). It isn't known whether Clara is related to Lady Kluck, the huge, nonsinging chicken seen in Disney's 1973 feature *Robin Hood.*

CLARABELLE COW

Pedigree. Early Walt Disney character who never quite achieved stardom.

Biography. A skinny, bipedal cow with tiny horns, two large teeth, a big cowbell, Clarabelle is usually seen in puffy, frilly clothing. (Skirts were introduced to hide her voluminous udders, which caused censors some degree of concern.) In her first screen appearance (*Plane Crazy,* 1928), she has the ignominious distinction of trying to escape an airplane whose propeller threatens to de-udder her. The fact is, in most of her films, Clarabelle demonstrates the finesse of a landslide, whether she's dancing in *Orphan's Benefit* (1934) or bathing in *Mickey's Fire Brigade* (1935), blissfully unaware that her house is burning down. Her musical skills are legendary: In *The Barnyard Broadcast* (1931) she plays the piano, while her instrument is the violin in *Symphony Hour* (1942).

Comment. The prototype for Clarabelle first appeared in the short *Alice on the Farm* (1926), an early Disney series in which a live girl interacted with cartoon animals. Clarabelle starred in sixteen cartoons and had a cameo in the featurette *Mickey's Christmas Carol* (1983). She also costarred as the girlfriend of **Super Goof** in his eponymous comic book, although she didn't know that her neighbor and the superhero were one-and-the-same. It was

usually gossipy Clarabelle who read or heard of some crime and came over to inform Goof, who was invariably napping.

CLAUDE CAT

Pedigree. Minor star in the Warner Brothers theatrical firmament.

Biography. The gray-brown cat with a mass of hair poking from the sides of his face, and a tuft jutting over his forehead, made his debut with the mice **Hubie and Bertie** in the Oscar-nominated short *Mouse-Wreckers* in 1949. In the cartoon, the ace mouser is taunted by so many pranks—e.g., Bertie descending inside the chimney while Hubie holds a fishing rod, then smacking the cat and disappearing in a flash—that he comes to doubt his sanity and the mice take over the house. He fights the mice again in his second outing, *The Hypo-condri-cat* (1950), in which he proves himself to be deathly afraid of becoming sick, and is constantly taking medicine and wrapping himself in a blanket. Unable to pass up such an Achilles' heel, the mice not only convince Claude that he's ill and in need of an operation, but perform the surgery (using kitchen utensils and gardening implements), convince him he's died, and send him to heaven at the end of a balloon. He may not have much upstairs, but Claude is content at cartoon's end. In his next outing, *Two's a Crowd* (1950), the cat's life is upended when his master brings home a new pet: the floppy-eared Frisky Puppy, whose bark continually startles Claude. Filled with venom, the cat tries to torment the dog by using biscuits to lure it to the washing machine (the cat ends up inside) and attempting to blow the dog up with TNT disguised as sausage links (he only succeeds in blowing up the oil burner, which takes half the house with it). Thrown out by his understandably peeved owner, Claude gets satisfaction by sneaking back in, barking at the dog, and causing *it* to jump. Claude is more or less a supporting player in *Mouse Warming* (1952), as he gets in the way of romance between a boy mouse and the girl-next-door mouse, while it's another battle with Frisky Puppy in *Terrier Stricken* (1952). In his last screen appearance, *Feline Frame-Up* (1954), he tries to take advantage of his new cat-housemate, **Pussyfoot,** who's protected by the bulldog Marc Antony.

Comment. Living in the shadow of Warner's great cat **Sylvester the Cat,** Claude was unable to carve a niche for himself. Another unsuccessful Warner's would-be cat star was Conrad Cat, who starred in two cartoons in 1942: *The Bird Came C.O.D.* and *Porky's Cafe.* In the first, he's a delivery boy for the Arctic Palm Co. Bringing a plant to a theater, he pauses to play with a magician's hat, with *Sorcerer's Apprentice*-like results, as various animals emerge to torment him. In the second cartoon, he's a cook, Porky's a waiter, and an ant who gets stuck in a batch of pancake batter is the trigger for the destruction of many appetites and platters.

COLD BLOODED CHAMELEON COMMANDOS

Pedigree. A comic book featuring "genetic mutation at its finest."

Biography. At a "high-tech government lab," the chameleons are subjected to a formula developed by Dr. Poindexter: "a serum extracted from chameleon plasma . . . coupled with various forms of radiation." Soon after the treatments begin, the animals become more humanlike in appearance and intelligence ("Pardon me," says one to a scientist, "but do you have some Gray Poupon?"). They are trained "in self-defense and weapons use," becoming topflight warriors. Rivit possesses "increased strength and super-powerful legs," Nerves has "increased sense of danger, lightning reflexes . . . and a bit of hair to boot," Sarge has a "highly tactical military mind," and Radion can "change skin color [and] body shape." When Poindexter is abducted by the terrorist group Night Brigade, the chameleons travel to a "remote jungle fortress" to rescue him.

Comment. Like most of the **Teenage Mutant Ninja Turtles** send-ups, this Blackthorne Publishing title did not last long, four issues coming and going in 1986 to 1987.

COLT: THE ARMADILLO THAT WON THE WEST

Pedigree. Sharpshooting comic book animal.

Biography. As a baby, the armadillo was caught in an avalanche and emerged unhurt: It was then he realized that his "shell was stronger than a normal armadillo's." Wandering into a ghost town, he's found by an old prospector who names him Colt, raises him, and teaches him to walk on his hind legs, ride, use a lasso, talk, read, write, play cards, and shoot. The old man also gives Colt a donkey to ride. When his benefactor is shot by the crazed Joe Skinhead, Colt goes after the man, guns him down, and turns him in for the reward. Satisfied by the experience, Colt decides "to become a bounty hunter." Although Colt is an expert gunslinger, he is frequently saved by his bulletproof shell. Colt is approximately

five feet tall, and strong enough to lift a man over his head. Being an armadillo, he's also excellent at digging tunnels.

Comment. The eponymous comic book lasted just three issues, published by K-Z Comics in 1985. Tom Zjaba created the character.

COMET THE SUPER-HORSE

Pedigree. Pet horse of the comic book superhero Supergirl.

Biography. Comet was born a centaur, a creature with a man's head, arms and torso, and a horse's body: He was Biron the Bowman of the island of Aeaea in Ancient Greece. After Biron prevented the sorcerer Malador from murdering the sorceress Circe—Malador was attempting to contaminate Circe's spring when the centaur fired an arrow and shattered the vial—the sorceress sets about rewarding Biron by turning him into a man. But Malador tampers with the potion she prepares, and Biron becomes 100 percent horse with a cometlike mark on its back. Because Circe cannot counteract Malador's spell, she grants the white stallion superpowers, including immortality, and enables him to communicate with people via telepathy. However, Malador's wrath is not yet played out: He exiles Biron on a planet in the constellation Sagittarius (where else?), where the horse remains imprisoned by a "magical aura" until a spaceship bearing the teenager Kara passes by. (When the planet Krypton exploded, Kara and her family survived on a domed chunk of the world. When that was destroyed, Kara was rocketed to earth, where she joined her cousin Superman as the crime-fighting Supergirl.) "Repeller rays" from Kara's ship liberate Biron, who eventually tracks Kara to earth. In a strange development, the superhero dreams she's attacked by aliens and temporarily loses her flying powers. Comet comes racing along just in time to keep her from falling to her death, then "super kicks" the alien spaceships away from earth. Shortly thereafter, Supergirl dreams that he dives to the ocean bottom to pull a stricken submarine to safety, and also flies through the time barrier to World War II to save a U.S. ship from a kamikaze pilot. Deciding to go to the Supergirl Dude Ranch and do some riding to "get this obsession about that imaginary stallion out of my system," Supergirl—in her identity as Linda Lee Danvers—is shocked when she finds the horse there. After Comet gives her a ride through the skies, and tells her he knows who she really is (he shows her a picture of

Supergirl), the noble steed becomes Supergirl's pet and staunch ally. He continues to live on the Supergirl Dude Ranch. Years later, the sorcerer Endor of the planet Zerox gives Comet the power to become fully human "whenever a comet is visible in the sky." When this occurs, Comet assumes the identity of cowboy Bronco Bill. (Supergirl doesn't realize they're one-and-the-same, and is "sweet" on Bill.) In his superhorse identity, Comet originally took the cape from a large statue of Supergirl whenever he went into action. Now, he always wears the long, red cape attached to a blue harness (recently, it's been fastened in front with a red *S* in a yellow shield). Supergirl summons him when needed using superventriloquism. Perhaps his most valuable power is superintuition: If he senses there's someone around who doesn't like Supergirl, he lets her know. Along with **Beppo the Supermonkey, Krypto,** and **Streaky the Supercat,** Comet is a member of the Legion of Super-Pets. Not surprisingly, his favorite expression is, "Great Pegasus!"

Comment. The steed of steel first appeared in DC Comics's *Adventure Comics* no. 293 in 1962.

CONGORILLA
Pedigree. Comic book gorilla that swaps brains with a great white hunter.
Biography. A noted trapper-turned-ecologist, Congo Bill struggles in vain to save the life of Chief Kawolo, a witch doctor, who has fallen off a cliff. With his last breath the native rewards Bill by giving him a ring bearing the likeness of a gorilla, explaining that whenever Bill rubs it, he will be able to transfer his mind, for one hour, into the body of the tribe's chief deity, a golden gorilla. Bill has his doubts, but when a rockslide traps him in a cave, the

desperate adventurer rubs the ring—and finds himself elsewhere, in the ape's body. Hurrying to the cave, Bill frees his body. Rubbing a ring that the gorilla wears, Bill can return to his own body before the hour is up. There are only two drawbacks to becoming Congorilla: In this form Bill cannot speak and, worse, the ape's inferior brain is switched into Bill's human form. Thus he usually makes sure his body is locked up or tranquilized before he makes the transfer.

Comment. Congorilla swung onto the comics scene in DC Comics's *Action Comics* no. 248 in 1959 (although Bill had met the gorilla previously, in no. 224 in 1957, when the ape saved his life). Congo Bill himself had debuted in 1941, in *Action Comics* no. 37). He starred in seven issues of his own title from 1954 to 1955.

CONRAD
Pedigree. Comic strip frog.
Biography. While Conrad is hiding inside a log to escape his bookie, a portly blockhead of a princess sits down nearby. To get out of the marsh, Conrad tells her he's an enchanted prince. Dubious at first, the princess is convinced when she asks him to say something romantic, and he replies, "You don't sweat much for a fat girl." She carries him off to the palace, where the king promptly demands, "How do you plan to support my daughter?" Conrad replies, "A hydraulic jack," but the king lets him stay anyway . . . and secretly plots to get rid of him. Meanwhile, the courtship leaves Conrad uncomfortable ("Oooh . . . I have butterflies in my stomach," the princess coos. "So do I," Conrad answers. "I ate a caterpillar.") Not only does he find her unattractive ("I've dated worse-looking females . . . of course, they were frogs"), but he's especially ill at ease when

*Bill Schorr's **Conrad.***
© TRIBUNE MEDIA SERVICES:
Reprinted by permission.

she introduces her pet Fido—an alligator who has her believing he's a dog and who has culinary designs on Conrad. Apart from these people and pets, Conrad's pet peeves include frog jokes (he calls them "ethnic humor"), dragonflies (they really *are* dragons and tough to eat), and the moronic witch Aggie (instead of turning him into "a gallant prince," she transforms Conrad into "a gallon of prunes"). Conrad has a brother at Harvard—he's a lab experiment.

Comment. Bill Schorr's sarcastic, very funny frog debuted in 1985 and is one of the unsung gems of the comics page.

COOL CAT

Pedigree. Late entry into the Warner Brothers theatrical cartoon stable.

Biography. A bipedal tiger who wears a collar and necktie, the unflappable Cool first appeared in *Cool Cat*, hunted by the ineffectual Colonel Rimfire, who rides through the jungle on a four-wheel drive, robot elephant named Ella. Thwarted, the Colonel tries again in *Big Game Haunt*, pursuing the tiger into a haunted house where both are terrified by Spooky the ghost. The two have other tilts, at the Grand Prix, circus, and elsewhere, with Rimfire always coming out a loser. Cool also had adventures at college (*Bugged by a Bee*), where he impresses the girls with his athletic prowess (actually, he keeps getting stung by a bee), and with desert-dwelling Indians (*Injun Trouble*).

Comment. The cat appeared in six cartoons (1968 to 1969). The animation, gags, and characterization were not up to the standards of Warner Brothers (**Bugs Bunny, Road Runner**).

COSMO CAT

Pedigree. Superheroic comic book cat.

Biography. Deriving his powers from "cosmic catnip capsules," Cosmo is based in "a secret lab" on the moon, where he uses his telescopelike "telefinder" to "locate any poor soul in need of help." Finding one, he travels to earth via rocket (one that possesses a powerful blaster beam); once here, he can fly, has superstrength (he can throw a bull with ease) and possesses impenetrable skin (buzzsaws only tickle him). His adventures include defeating the evil human Professor Ratzoff, who is out to steal a shipment of artificial meat balls; using a jet-belt to help poor Dunky Duck learn how to swim; and riding a racehorse for a "female feline in distress" after

the jockey is kidnapped. His arch-nemesis is Horroface, an incredibly ugly human who wants to rule the universe. Cosmo wears a red sweatshirt with a yellow C on the front, blue tights, red boots, yellow gloves, and a green cape.

Comment. Cosmo first appeared in Fox Publication's *All-Top* no. 1 (1945), then starred in ten issues of his own comic book (1946 to 1947), three specials from 1957 to 1959, and ten issues of *Wotalife Comics* (1946 to 1947). The character was created and chronicled by Pat Adams. Companion strips included the adventures of the fleet Flash Rabbit and tales of Roscoe Bear, who has sundry misadventures in Redstone National Park (e.g., warming his seat over an open hole in the ground . . . only to learn, painfully, that it's Ol' Hotshot Geyser). A character similar to Cosmo is Super Cat, who wears a Supermanlike costume and battles wolves, bears, and so on in Norlen's *Animal Crackers* nos. 1 to 31 (1946 to 1950) and, later, in *Frisky Animals* nos. 44 to 58 (1951 to 1954).

COUNT DUCKULA

Pedigree. Vampire duck of TV cartoons and comic books.

Biography. Castle Duckula in Transylvania has always been regarded by the locals as a "foul fortress of fear and affliction," watched over by the grumpy John Gielgud-like butler-buzzard Igor and the giant, dumb canary Nanny, "a primeval, monstrous, irresistible force of energy." Once every century, when the moon is in the House of Asparagus, one of the counts of Duckula can be resurrected—and the duo prepare to do so now. However, in providing Igor with the ingredients for the rite, Nanny inadvertently brings catsup instead of blood. Thus when the green-skinned Count Duckula materializes, he shuns going to the village to "find a lovely maiden to bite on the neck" and opts, instead, for "a nice tossed salad." Yes: Igor has created "a vegetarian vampire." His voice is reminiscent of Jerry Lewis (no Transylvanian accent for this count); his hair is combed to the side in the shape of batwings, and he is wearing a cloak, vest, and bow-tie. The vampire sleeps in his coffin during the day (otherwise, he'd "crumble into a pile of dust") and rises at night (always disdaining Igor's invitation to sample a cup of Rh negative). He proves to be lovably inept at everything he does, whether it's trying to become a movie star (another Bird Reynolds), or attempting to fend off bankruptcy (a regular chore) by becoming an auto racer . . . and spending the entire episode trying to get a car to work. (The most inventive plan involves rubber bands attached to the automobile and the castle. The scheme misfires and launches only the duck, temporarily earning him the nickname "Boomerang.") Using the same "Mystic Coffin" in which he was brought back to life, Duckula can also teleport the castle from Mt. Cragmore to any place in the world, which also leads to many misadventures, most notably a run-in with Attila the Hen in Outer Mongolia. At home, Duckula's greatest foe is the vampire-hunting bird Dr. Von Goosewing. However, the vampire is in love with Goosewing's bird niece, Vanna Von Goosewing. Among the hired help, Nanny provides her share of comic relief by constantly falling through the floor ("much faster than taking the stairs"), walking through walls (doors "always get in the way when you're in a hurry"), and

otherwise doing things tail feathers-backward. (That tossed salad she made Duckula? She didn't bother taking the vegetables from the refrigerator first, but threw the icebox around.) Duckula plays the banjo to relax; Igor reads. In fact, the only time the usually unflappable Igor ever became agitated was when his favorite author, Edgar Allen Crow, dropped by the castle.

Comment. Cosgrove-Hall Productions's *Count Duckula* premiered in syndication in 1988. Due to their dry humor and ingenious characterization, the half-hour stories have taken their place in the distinguished company of **Road Runner** and **Rocky and Bullwinkle** as cartoons that appeal as much to adults as to children. David Jason is the voice of the count, while Barry Clayton provides always illuminating narration. Marvel's popular *Count Duckula* comic book began publication in 1988. Other vampire

Original model sheet for **Count Duckula.** *This is used by animators as a guide for drawing the character.*
© THAMES TELEVISION, *courtesy Neil J. Rosini, Esq.*

ducks include **Spider-Ham**'s foe Count Quakula, and the Filmation TV cartoon character Quacula. The latter appeared from 1979 to 1980 on CBS's Saturday morning *The Mighty Mouse Show*. More sinister than Count Duckula, Quacula wears a blue vest, a black cape with a red lining, sleeps in a coffin shaped like an egg, and lives in a castle owned by his lumbering bear sidekick. See also the vampire duck **Duckula**. Other animal vampires include Bunnicula, the vampire rabbit who is a popular children's book character and appeared in a half-hour syndicated cartoon; and Catula, who starred in one episode of *Hello Kitty's Fairy Tale Theater,* which aired Saturday mornings on CBS in 1987. *Hello Kitty* also introduced other stories, including characters such as the Wizard of Paws and Cinderkitty.

COURAGEOUS CAT

Pedigree. TV cartoon hero created by Bob Kane (*Batman*).

Biography. The anthropomorphic animals of Empire City can rest easy knowing that the heroes Courageous Cat and his sidekick Minute Mouse are on the job—heroes who have no superpowers per se, but triumph through superior deductive skill some of the time, and dumb luck most of the time. (Bound and imprisoned, the Cat clicks out the "Boy Scout code" with his teeth. Fortunately, a group of passing Boy Scouts hears him and set him free.) Nothing is known of the characters' pasts. They live in the Cat Cave high in the hills overlooking the city: When the police flash the "Cat Signal" on TV, the heroes jump into the sleek, red Catmobile and race into the night. At the touch of a button, this remarkable car can turn into either the Catplane or the Submobile; it contains skindiving equipment, spyglasses, a loudspeaker, and a carphone, among other gadgets. As for Cat, he packs an arsenal unlike any on earth. Among his seemingly endless supply of guns are a balloon gun (holding onto it, the hero can fly), refrigerated-air gun, flashlight gun, rope gun, magnet gun (it's not magnetic but *shoots* a stream of magnets!), cannonball-interrupter (as the name implies, it stops oncoming cannonballs), shark-repellent gun, sword gun, can-opener gun, umbrella gun, rivet gun, and bum's-rush gun (a pair of hands emerge on extenders and give villains the heave-ho). If all else fails, Courageous Cat keeps a feather in his belt to tickle villains. Minute Mouse is armed only with a water pistol. The feline hero dresses in a red bodysuit with a five-pointed star on the chest, black

trunks, a yellow belt and cape, and white gloves. Minute Mouse wears a green cape, a yellow bodyshirt, no pants, and white gloves. Among the heroes' skills: great swimming ability. Among their flaws: a serious fear of ghosts. Their foes include Frog (a gangster with an Edward G. Robinson voice), Professor Shaggy Dog, Rodney Rodent, Black Cat, and Professor von Noodle Strudel, a well-meaning scientist whose inventions usually fall into the wrong hands, such as the briefcase that has a nose and can literally smell the combination to any safe.

Comment. The Trans-Artist series was syndicated in 1961; there were eighty-five episodes. Bob McFadden provided the voices of both characters. The animation is stiff and the drawing unexciting, but the nutty gadgets and villains are entertaining enough.

CREEPY CAT

Pedigree. A bungling comic book cat from Marvel Comics's golden age.

Biography. Creepy has just one job at the home in which he lives: to catch the "smart aleck" mouse who lives there. But he's so incredibly dumb, the task is beyond him. For example, he allows the mouse to look over his shoulder while reading the book *How to Catch Mice.* On another occasion, after the mouse has put a lobster in Creepy's bath, the cat runs around, trying to get out of the house. The mouse tells him to jump out the window, and Creepy obliges . . . although the mouse neglects to point out that the window is shut. The glass does more damage than the lobster. The big, naked, orange cat is rare among comic book cats in that it has very sharp, visible fangs.

Comment. The strip appeared in the two issues of *Film Funnies* (1949 to 1950). Its fun, cruel violence reflected the success of the formula pioneered in the **Tom and Jerry** and **Bugs Bunny** cartoons.

CROW OF THE BEAR CLAN

Pedigree. Barbarian bear (barbearian?).

Biography. When his primitive village of anthropomorphic bears is attacked and destroyed by the reptilian Saurans, Crow is taken alive. With hundreds of other bears, they are taken to Castle Sauraz, where they will all eventually be eaten. Fortunately, Crow meets fellow prisoner, the fox Lamont Red, and is able to escape. Although he's devoted to slaying Saurans, the spunky bear has many adven-

tures, many of them with the bold lady-skunk Cinder, the mighty boar Tusk, the raccoon Shep, and the fox Whitey. Other breeds of animals include the Rhinos, who are brutish mercenaries.

Comment. Blackthorne's *Crow of the Bear Clan* began publication in 1986. It was created by Edward Luena and Ken Hooper, who also write and draw the magazine.

CRUSADER RABBIT

Pedigree. Star of the first cartoon series produced expressly for television.

Biography. A native of "the animal community" Galahad Glen, the diminutive but long-eared Crusader was assisted by his squire, Ragland T. Tiger—a k a Rags. Together, they fought such foes as Wetstone Whiplash, Dudley Nightshade, the two-headed dragon Arson and Sterno, Babyface Barracuda, and Belfry Q. Bat. Not only was "the brave little bunny" the brains of the outfit, but he had the remarkable ability to turn everyday objects into weapons, e.g., beer bottles found in a trash can into binoculars. As for Rags, he had brute strength and limited magical powers, which also served them well in their adventures.

Comment. Ragland was named after the 1917 song "Tiger Rag," though the series' theme song was "Ten Little Indians." The show was the first animated program created for television and featured four-minute segments that ended in a cliff-hanger; five episodes completed one story, enabling stations to show them in a half-hour slot or to run them throughout the week. The characters were created by Jay Ward and Alexander Anderson. They appeared in syndication in 1949 and, although they were still popular in 1951, a lawsuit over ownership of the cartoons caused production to come to a halt. When everything was squared away the series returned, with first-run episodes airing from 1957 to 1958, after which the cartoon went into syndication for just over a decade. Lucille Bliss provided Crusader's voice in the first series, Gigi Pearson in the second; Vern Louden was Rags in both. In comic books, the rabbit appeared in two issues of Dell's *4-Color*, nos. 735 and 805.

CUTEY BUNNY

Pedigree. Comic book rabbit superheroine.

Biography. Corporal Kelly O'Hare is a buxom, wise-cracking military recruiter who lives with her young sister, Taffy, in a modest apartment in Peoria. Visited by the Egyptian god Ra, Kelly is "anointed . . . Akeshti Unnuit [and] presented . . . with the mystic amulet of Ra." She becomes an enemy of evil, using the power of the amulet to transform herself into four distinct figures: Roller Bunny, who "can do about 200 miles per" on her "motorized skates"; Rocket Bunny, who can fly and is protected by a force field; a samurai; and the energy-generating Aunt Samantha. However, by issue no. 4, Ra has come to disapprove of these non-Egyptian guises, and adorns her with a more Middle Eastern, all-purpose Cutey Bunny costume. In this guise, the amulet grants "the bunny bombshell" the power to fly, super strength, and other powers. Her favorite expression is "Gosharooty." Foes and allies of "the crimebusting cottontail" have included the sinister Vicky, a fox who's "a double agent for the KGB . . . a triple agent for MI6, British Intelligence [and] a fourple agent for the CIA"; the X-Critters Zephyr, Cycat, Vermin, Clummox, and Nite Toddler (parodying Marvel Comics's X-Men); and the Nice Guy League of America (a send-up of DC Comics's Justice League of America) featuring Captain Huey (i.e. **Baby Huey**), Wunner Bunny, Plastic Spam (a stretchable pig), Sub-Moron (a shark), the Bitchin' Torch, and Bat Bat.

Comment. Kelly first appeared in J. Q. Enterprises' *Army Surplus Komikz* no. 1 in 1984. There have been seven issues to date. The risque but wildly inventive comic was created, written, and drawn by Joshua Quagmire. The comic's back-up feature was "Space Gophers, Inc.," a saga set in the third galactic age, when "a small group of furry bucktoothed reprobates" travel through space as intergalactic truckers.

CYBORG GERBILS

Pedigree. Comic book animals from the future.

Biography. In the year 2154, four cyborg gerbils are sent back to the present day to commit a murder. Their victim: Paul Hayman, Jr., a retarded man who will one day become a genius and cause the end of the world. They are also assigned to kill Professor Mandamus, the scientist who will make Paul a genius . . . and who also has his pet Vocal, "The world's *first* and *only* cyborg cat." The four gerbils—who, as one character puts it, "Look like little Rambos"—are the laser-toting Lester and Jezz, portly Ralph, and the hook-handed Edam.

Small but tough: The **Cyborg Gerbils** *in action.* © TRIGON COMICS.

Comment. Obviously inspired by the motion picture *The Terminator,* the comic book was published by Trigon Comics in England. Only two issues appeared, in 1986. Dave Greene and John Jackson were the cocreators.

CYCLONE
Pedigree. Stallion owned by Marvel Comics's western hero Two-Gun Kid.
Biography. After destroying the gang that had preyed on his late father and the Circle-H ranch, Seth Harder roams the land, righting wrongs as the Two-Gun Kid. His gray horse Cyclone is an important part of the team.

Comment. Midway through his 136-issue run, the Kid could be found riding the white horse Thunder. The Marvel Comics publication ran from 1948 to 1977. See other Marvel Comics cowboy horses **Banshee, Nightwind,** and **Steel.**

DAFFY DUCK

Pedigree. Insane, possibly psychotic, but beloved duck of cartoons and comic books.

Biography. Short, lisping, black-feathered, and slightly cross-eyed, with arms instead of wings, an extremely round bottom, and a white stripe around his throat, the nameless duck was launched to superstardom following a bit part in *Porky's Duck Hunt* (1937). In that black-and-white cartoon, **Porky Pig** and his beagle go hunting in a marsh. Porky shoots a duck, but when the dog brings it back, the duck comes to life, hooting and laughing his soon-to-be-famous *Woo-HOO! Woo-HOO!* Flipping the dog to the ground the duck taunts Porky with, "Don't let it worry you, skipper! I'm just a crazy darn-fool duck!" Then he pirouettes madly away, returning again briefly during the hunt when he generously shows Porky how to fix his jammed gun before going off like a top once more. Audiences loved the duck; as animator Bob Clampett puts it, "People would leave the theaters talking about this daffy duck." Daffy got his name in the follow-up film, the full-color *Daffy Duck and Egghead* (1938), in which an early prototype of the Elmer Fudd character stalks the duck with no more luck than Porky. Over the next few cartoons, Daffy became the slobbering figure we know today—taller, leaner with a trio of feathers sprouted from his head—although no less hyperkinetic or unpredictable. The only change was that, unlike the duck's occasional triumphant run-ins with hunters, Daffy more and more only *imagined* himself to be a slick, able operator. Warner Brothers's *truly* poised cartoon star was **Bugs Bunny**; more and more, Daffy became the oppressed rather than the oppressor, although he was too proud to acknowledge the fact that he constantly had (duck) egg on his face. His oft-uttered retort to those who had bested him was a terse, bitter, "You're de*thp*icable!" (Never was the contrast between Bugs and Daffy clearer than in their three face-offs: *Rabbit Fire* in 1951, *Rabbit Seasoning* the following year, and *Duck! Rabbit! Duck!* in 1953, as each tried various schemes to persuade hunter Elmer Fudd to gun down the other. Bugs was rarely outsmarted.) The turning point in Daffy's career came in 1942, with *Daffy's Southern Exposure,* when he opted not to migrate so he could see what "this win-

ter business" was all about. Facing the freezing cold and a hungry wolf and weasel, his mortality became clear to audiences. (When he *does* head south for the winter in *Thumb Fun* [1952], he refuses to exert himself by flying, but hitchhikes.) Later that year, *My Favorite Duck* actually ends with camper Porky dragging the vanquished Daffy behind him. In addition to his excitable, basically lazy nature, these things are known about the duck: He wears a bulletproof vest under his feathers (*To Duck or Not to Duck,* 1943); has a consuming passion for yams *(Tom Turk and Daffy,* 1944); enjoys taking bubble baths (*Ain't That Ducky,* 1945); was briefly the pet of a young girl named Agnes, whose father tried everything he could think of to get rid of the freeloader (*Nasty Quacks,* 1945); possesses an often uncontrollable urge to draw moustaches on faces on billboards and posters (*Daffy Doodles,* 1946); worked briefly selling cookbooks (*Along Came Daffy,* 1947), appliances (*The Stupor Salesman,* 1948 and *Design for Leaving,* 1954), and insurance for Hot Foot Casualty Underwriters (*Fool Coverage,* 1953); and was a baby-sitter for the Acme Baby-Sitter Service (*The Up-Standing Sitter,* 1947). Daffy is married, although his wife is seldom seen. In *Wise Quacks* (1939), he and Mrs. Duck have ducklings, one of which Daffy and Porky must rescue from a buzzard (the cartoon also reveals that Porky and Daffy have known each other since childhood). In *The Henpecked Duck* (1941), Mrs. Duck (in a flowered hat and skirt) goes to court to get a divorce after Daffy, practicing magic, causes the egg containing their next child to vanish . . . and replaces it with a doorknob, hoping to fool his wife. Fortunately, in court before judge Porky, the desperate Daffy is able to make the egg return, and all is forgiven. In *Stork Naked* (1955) Mrs. Duck has a name, Daphne, but the couple is childless . . . and Daffy is determined to keep it that way, setting up all kinds of weapons and impediments in an effort to keep the stork away.

In addition to his own adventures, Daffy has starred as a number of other characters. He was a prehistoric duck on the run from Caspar Caveman and his dinosaur Fido in *Daffy Duck and the Dinosaur* (1939). Knocked unconscious in *The Great Piggy Bank Robbery* (1949), Daffy imagines himself to be master detective Duck Twacy. Later, in *The*

Super Snooper (1952), he was Duck Drake, private eye, ear, nose, and throat. In *The Scarlet Pumpernickel* (1950), Daffy persuades a studio executive to let him play a leading man for once instead of a slapstick comedian. Thus Daffy gets to don a red mask and a Zorro-type costume and play the "masked stinker" who not only robs from the rich, but rescues Milady Melissa from the unwanted attentions of the Grand Duke (**Sylvester the Cat**). There's no prologue in *Drip-Along Daffy* (1951): He's a cowboy who rides into Snake Bite Center (astride his steed Tin Foil, a clever play on the Lone Ranger's horse Silver), intending to "clean up" the town. However, as chief heavy Nasty Canasta is about to cut him down, Drip-Along's sidekick Porky saves the day and is appointed sheriff . . . while Drip-Along becomes a street cleaner, literally responsible for cleaning up the town. Dazed after being butted by a goat, he imagines he's fighting the German navy as the costumed, caped Super American *(Scrap Happy Daffy*, 1943), although in *Stupor Duck* (1956), he is far more inept. Garbed in a red-and-blue costume and flashy cape, Daffy is a being from another world who's endowed with superstrength, invulnerability, and the ability to fly. Unfortunately, Stupor isn't very bright: Overhearing a TV soap opera about a fictional villain named Aardvark Ratnick, he assumes the character is real and flies off to squash his reign of terror. Naturally, this causes sundry problems: He tries to stop a building from being blown up, not knowing it's being razed to make way for a new city hall, then prevents a train trestle from being destroyed, unaware that it's a movie set. Perhaps Daffy's most famous role is that of Duck Dodgers, which he played twice: in *Duck Dodgers in the 24½th Century* (1953), and *Duck Dodgers and the Return of the 24½th Century* (1980; seen on TV only as part of *Daffy Duck's Thanks-for-Giving Specials)*. In the former, Duck is informed that the world is nearly out of "aludium fozdex, the shaving cream atom," and he must journey to Planet X to get more. He is joined, in this dangerous quest, by Porky and, together, they face Marvin Martian, who has come to Planet X to claim it for Mars. In the end, although Daffy wins, Planet X has been hacked and bombed to the size of a basketball. In the sequel, Duck is entrusted with the Rack and Pinion molecule, which is used to polish yo-yos. As if that weren't challenge enough, he must also deal with Marvin, who's bent on destroying the earth. Daffy was also cast as Jack in *Beanstack*

Bunny (1955), climbing the beanstalk with Bugs and facing a giant Elmer Fudd.

Comment. There have been 131 cartoons in which Daffy starred, one in which he costarred, and two with cameo appearances; he also performed a piano duet with **Donald Duck** in the 1988 theatrical film *Who Framed Roger Rabbit* (see **Roger Rabbit**). The late Mel Blanc provided the voice for the duck. Two feature-length Daffy compilations with new framing stories have been released: *Daffy Duck's Movie: Fantastic Island* (1983), a *Fantasy Island* spoof, and *Daffy Duck's Quackbusters* (1988), in which the duck inherits a fortune and opens a ghostbusting service. Daffy had his own short-lived TV series, *The Daffy Duck Show,* which presented the theatrical cartoons and aired on NBC on Saturday mornings from 1978 to 1981; and *The Daffy/Speedy Show* (with **Speedy Gonzales**), which NBC aired the following year. His TV specials have been the aforementioned Thanksgiving show in 1981, and *Daffy Duck's Easter Special* (1980), which featured three new cartoons. The duck was also seen on Bugs Bunny's many series. (See **Bugs Bunny** for further details). In comic books, Daffy appeared in the first and many subsequent issues of *Looney Tunes and Merrie Melodies Comics,* 246 issues of which were published by Dell from 1941 to 1962, and then starred in 145 issues of his own magazine, published from 1953 to 1983 by Dell and then Gold Key (with no. 31). Beginning in the second issue of *Looney Tunes* magazine, in 1990, Daffy began starring in the four-page comic strip *Bat-Duck*. By day, he's playboy Bruce Mallard; by night, he enters his Duck Cave, dons a costume similar to that of Batman, teams up with aide the Pork Wonder (**Porky Pig**), and fights crime. **Bugs Bunny** is Bruce's manservant Belfry, and **Foghorn Leghorn** is Police Commisioner Boredom. Also worth mentioning is a strange one-shot comic book called *Daffy Qaddafi,* published in 1986 by Comics U.S.A. In it, Moammar Qaddafi leaps from the window of his barracks during an attack, and ends up in Wonderland. There, with a familiar black duck as his guide (behaving more like Dickens's Ghost of Christmas Present), he is shown the real world—not the fantasy world of his own propaganda—and ends up in a state of mental collapse.

DAGMAR
Pedigree. Comic strip canary belonging to young Nancy.

Biography. Nothing is known about this bird, except that it sits in a cage and listens (or at least, seems to) whenever her young (about eight-year-old) owner speaks. Nancy also owns a turtle named Otto, a dog called Poochie, a cat named Kitty, Alvin the goldfish, and a budgie (not the same as the canary).

Comment. Nancy first appeared in the 1920s in Ernie Bushmiller's comic strip *Fritzi Ritz,* Fritzi being her aunt. Nancy was spun off on her own in 1938, and also appeared in comic books from 1949 to 1963, and in a series of Terrytoons cartoons in 1942 and 1943. The pets began appearing in the late 1940s. Other dogs that appeared in the strip were Connie, a dachshund so named because her long, narrow torso started in the middle of the strip and was "continued" in the last panel; Skinny's dog Happy (Skinny was fat, and Happy never smiled); and Fritzi's dalmation, who has no name.

DAISY
Pedigree. Household dog of the Bumstead family.
Biography. The lilac-colored, floppy-eared Daisy is usually found sitting under the kitchen table, behind an easy chair, beside the bathtub, or tagging along with a member of the Bumstead family (occasionally, playfully imitating the way they're standing) —an ever-present domestic touch to the household of Dagwood and Blondie, son, Alexander, and daughter, Cookie. When Daisy's involved with a storyline it's usually peripheral. For instance, Dagwood is sneaking in late one night after a card game, and she bites him on the nose ("I'll bet you're happy to know what a great watchdog we have," Cookie says as her dad's proboscis is bandaged). Daisy has had at least one litter of five pups, although they no longer live with the family.

Comment. The *Blondie* comic strip was created by Murat "Chic" Young and first appeared on September 15, 1930. For the first three years, adventures involved the courtship of Dagwood and scatter-brained Blondie Boopadoop; when they married, Dagwood was disinherited by his railroad tycoon father and they settled down, slowly building a family in a middle-class setting. In the late 1930s, Daisy was usually seen palling around with Alexander, then known as Baby Dumpling. Young died in 1973, and the strip has been continued by his son, Dean, and Jim Raymond. The dog also starred in seven issues of her own Harvey Publications comic book, *Daisy and Her Pups,* from 1951 to 1955.

DAISY DUCK
Pedigree. Girlfriend of **Donald Duck.**
Biography. In her screen debut in *Don Donald* (1937), Daisy barely resembles the lovely duck who has won Donald's heart, she of the long lashes and beguilingly lidded eyes, the ever-present big, floppy bow in her hair, the overly wide high-heeled shoes, and blouses with puffed shoulders (never a skirt or pants, though). In her first appearance, she's a Mexican woman named Donna, with a mantilla, a voice and appearance like Donald's . . . and a temper. During the course of the cartoon with the love-stricken Donald, she slaps him, hits him with a guitar, knocks him into a swimming pool, and dances on his photograph. She *would* have hit him with a vase as well had she not noticed his flashy red sportscar parked outside. When she finally agrees to go out with him and the car breaks down, the mortified Donna opens her handbag, withdraws a unicycle (!), and rides away. Donna resurfaced as Daisy in *Mr. Duck Steps Out* (1940), still with her Donald-like voice (barely

Dagwood Bumstead and **Daisy** *about to indulge in their favorite pursuit: napping.* © KING FEATUES SYNDICATE.

higher than his) but rather more flirtatious (although she turns from his advances when they're sitting on the sofa, her tail feathers crook and urge him over). Unfortunately, this first date is spoiled by Donald's nephews **Huey, Dewey, and Louie,** who sneak from the closet where Donald's locked them, go to Daisy's house, and jitterbug with the vivacious duck—at one point pulling Daisy from Donald's arms and substituting an ice cream cone. (Donald's eyes are shut and he doesn't know the difference! When he realizes Daisy's gone, he angrily flings the cone to the floor and, naturally, gets splattered with strawberry ice cream). By the time of her sixth cartoon, *Cured Duck* (1945), Daisy's quacking sounds are gone, replaced by a voice as smooth as a bell. (Good thing, too. The raspy voice is okay coming from raucus Donald, but it was never right for the very feminine Daisy.) In this cartoon, Donald throws an awe-inspiring (and quite hilarious) tantrum when he's unable to open a window in Daisy's house. Gently but sternly, she informs him that unless he learns to control his temper, she won't see him again. Ironically, though a mail-order course from the Institute of Temperism cures him, he makes the mistake of laughing at one of Daisy's typically outrageous hats . . . and learns that she has a temper worse than his! Her more selfish side is on display in her next cartoon, *Donald's Double Trouble* (1946), when she refuses to see Donald because she doesn't like his voice! Disconsolate, Donald spots a duck who's a dead ringer for himself . . . and has a sonorous voice to boot. He pays the man to take his place; unfortunately, the two fall for each other, and Donald finally attacks his double while the couple is in a tunnel of love. Furious at the deception, Daisy chases off *both* drakes. Donald's luck continues on its downward spiral as he tries to destroy **Chip 'n' Dale** for interfering with his romance in *Crazy Over Daisy* (1950), only to learn that she's an animal lover and, while throwing *him* out, gives the chipmunks a home. Daisy's most distinctive trait is her fondness for the most flowery and outlandish hats imaginable.

Comment. For a duck of such renown, it's surprising that Daisy has only costarred in twelve short subjects, along with a brief appearance as young Scrooge's lover in *Mickey's Christmas Carol* (1983). She's had more visibility, although still a decidedly secondary role, in comic strips and comic books. In the strips, the couple first met when Daisy moved into town (see **Donald Duck,** for the Disney Babies revisionism). They dated, and instead of riding Don-

ald to improve himself, Daisy took a more secondary role, exhibiting many of our cultural stereotypes of women: poor driving, cleaning house, inability to participate in sports, cooking dinner while Donald sits around, and so on. In comic books, although Gold Key's *Daisy Duck's Diary* was a failure (there were nine issues from 1954 to 1962, mostly published under the *4-Color* Comics banner), and her two one-shots with **Scrooge McDuck** are unmemorable, she was a solid supporting player in Donald's own titles. (The one time Daisy came to Donald for help with the cleaning, Donald was so afraid to tell her no that "he pried up the floor boards and crawled out under the house." She is indeed a force to be reckoned with!) The comics also introduced Daisy's three nieces, April, May, and June—little ducks with bows in their hair, Daisy-like shoes, and tiny black blouses. The finest Daisy stories were collected by Gladstone Publishing in the book *Donald and Daisy* in 1988.

DALGODA
Pedigree. Comic book dog from outer space.
Biography. Back in 2042, Project Cyclops—a program of searching for alien life forms—contacted beings from the planet Canida, thirty-two light-years distant. Twenty years later, spaceships left each world with an exchange occupant for the other. Now, a century after that, visits between the two worlds by diplomats are relatively routine. However, the arrival of Dalgoda on earth signifies a new era: The evil Nimp, from another world, intend to conquer Canida, and Dalgoda comes to earth to enlist military aide. The comic book saga followed Dalgoda's adventures in space and on earth (against ruthless politicians, terrorist robots, and the like). Dalgoda possesses a human body (albeit, covered with brown fur), a small tail, and dog's head (except for a goatee and handlebar moustache), and wears clothing. He can run on all-fours if necessary and can smell fear or truth on a person.

Comment. Written by Jan Strnad and drawn by Dennis Fujitake, the literate, beautifully illustrated *Dalgoda* was published by Fantagraphics Books and lasted for eight issues (1984 to 1986). Not so coincidentally, the letters of Dalgoda's name, rearranged, spell the title of one of the most famous of all dog stories, *Lad, A Dog.*

DANGER MOUSE
Pedigree. Heroic mouse of television, comic strips, and comic books.

Biography. Dressed in a white bodysuit with a yellow *DM* in a red circle over his heart and a black patch over his left eye, the white-furred mouse is "the world's greatest secret agent." Thrill seeking-crime busting was a career for which he seemed fated. At the age of one day, he climbed Mt. Everest and planted a flag on top. Educated at Cambridge, Oxford, Harvard, the Sorbonne, and Wurtemberg, he not only earned a double black belt in judo but became the world's greatest tennis player. The mouse drives about in a flying car, the Mark III, and is assisted by proper, bespectacled hamster, Penfold—a k a Agent Jigsaw, because he "always goes to pieces in a crisis." The two met while shopping for vegetables. Whenever there's trouble, Colonel K (a humanoid figure with a doglike face) of the Department of Intelligence contacts the mouse by videophone and briefs him; the rest is up to the hero. His greatest foe is the "evil amphibian," Baron Silas Greenback, a megalomaniacal frog with a crow aide named Stiletto.

Comment. The Thames Television character was introduced in 1981, and spawned a comic strip in *Look In* magazine the following year. A *Danger Mouse* story was also featured in each issue of Marvel's *Count Duckula* comic book beginning with no. 2 (cameo) and no. 3 (his own feature) in 1989.

DARKWING DUCK
Pedigree. Disney's superheroid star of TV cartoons.
Biography. When ordinary Drake Mallard dons a mask, slouch hat, and cloak, ("Look good while doing good" is his motto) he becomes Darkwing Duck. Assisted by the jut-jawed, accident-prone pilot Launchpad McQuack, and riding either the duck-faced jet Thunderquack or the powerful motorcycle Ratcatcher, Darkwing fights crime in the city of St. Canard. He often works for the secret organization SHUSH, whose rival group FOWL—the Fiendish Organization of World Larceny—includes such criminals as the evil toy maker Quackerjack and the half-duck, half-plant Bushroot. Other characters in the series include Darkwing's nine-year-old orphaned nieced Gosalyn, who lives with him, and his suburban duck-neighbors the Muddlefoots—Herb, Binkie, their bullying son Tank, and their brainy son Honker.

Comment. The characters made their debut in September 1991 on the syndicated *Darkwing Duck* series. Jim Cummings provides Darkwing's voices.

DARO
Pedigree. Comic book black panther, pet of Wild Boy.

Biography. In the middle of Africa, young David is to be killed by his Uncle Clyde so the elder man can collect his inheritance. But David gets away, and grows to be the jungle hero Wild Boy. Coming on a python and a black panther locked in battle, the loin-clothed youth stabs Bimba the snake to death, names the wounded panther Daro, and nurses him back to health. Thereafter, the two travel together, Daro ripping apart anyone who tries to harm his golden-haired master. He's also good at using his teeth to free Wild Boy whenever the youth gets tied up, and Daro's ability to track spoors also comes in handy. Other animals who regularly cross their path are Kimba the chimp (with whom Wild Boy can converse) and the powerful Ghoonga the elephant.

Comment. Daro's origin was revealed in the first of the fifteen issues of Ziff-Davis's *Wild Boy* (1951 to 1955).

THE DEFIANTS
Pedigree. Mutated comic book animals.
Biography. Years in the future, earth has colonized two worlds: Venus and Regis. To do manual labor on these worlds, scientist Arim Zola has produced a virtual slave breed known as manimals and hybrids—creatures with humanoid bodies and animal heads (and intellects). However, Level 2 Hybrids turn out to be smarter than expected and four males lead guerrilla-style warfare against the "power mad business conglomerates" based on Regis, specifically Telexx. The Defiants are Komodo (their leader), Felis (a cat), Lepus (a gun-happy rabbit), and Canis (a dog). The quartet hides out in the abandoned Barbadoes Gym, where they spend their spare time practicing martial arts.

Comment. The characters appeared in the Victory Comics magazine *Komodo and the Defiants*, which published two issues in 1987. Chris Etheredge was the creator of this amateurish title.

DEPUTY DAWG
Pedigree. Lethargic, inept law officer of TV cartoons.
Biography. Deputy Dawg is the latest in a long line of Mississippi sheriffs—however, none was quite so fumbling as he. Although things always work out for the best at the end of each cartoon, it's usually by accident. His most notable escapades involve foes such as Ty Coon (a raccoon in a bow tie), the Peach Pluckin' Kangaroo, th' Catfish Poachin' Pelican, the nearsighted Vincent Van Gopher, and semiregulars, the corn-stealing Pig Newton and Muskie Muskrat.

The portly, white bulldog wears short, tight blue trousers, a flat, black, wide-brimmed hat, and a black vest with a badge pinned low on the right side. Also seen in the cartoon is Deputy Dawg's young nephew, Deputy Elmer; the only human in the series is the Sheriff, to whom Deputy reports.

Comment. The characters were created by Larz Bourne. Terrytoons produced the first of Deputy Dawg's 105 cartoon adventures in 1960; most of these were produced for *The Deputy Dawg Show,* which was syndicated and, later, shown on NBC (1971 to 1972). There were also four theatrical cartoons produced (beginning in 1962) after the TV show proved so popular in the south and southwest that theater operators wanted episodes to screen. In all the cartoons, the character's syrupy drawl was provided by Dayton Allen. Dell published two issues of a Deputy Dawg comic book in 1961 and 1962 (part of its *4-Color* title); Gold Key offered a single issue in 1965. The character also costarred in the comic book *New Terrytoons,* published by Dell, then Gold Key. There were fifty-four issues between 1960 and 1979.

DESDEMONA
Pedigree. Cat from the "Mutt & Jeff" comic strip.
Biography. Desdemona belongs to Cicero, the son of Mutt. White with fine black stripes all over her body, Cicero can read but can't speak to humans—only to other animals—and enjoys sleep more than anything. For example, reading about military strategy in the newspaper, she realizes that the same principles can be applied to capturing mice. Carefully setting out cheese and lying in wait, she falls asleep while staking out the mouse hole. Desdemona believes in the rights of animals (she helps chickens brainstorm to find a way from being sent to slaughter), loves milk, and hangs out in Kat Alley—the one place she knows she won't be attacked by dogs. When she goes out, she usually dresses in a hat and coat. She's also incurably drawn to play, which is often destructive—whether it's swatting at the ornaments on a Christmas tree (causing every last one to fall), batting the cord attached to a shade (and getting wrapped around the bar when the shade snaps up), or knocking over a bottle of ink (and having to hang onto the top of the cartoon panel to keep from sinking in it). Unlike Shakespeare's ill-fated Desdemona, if this cat were accused of a crime, she'd be guilty. Possibly the most ingenious cartoon involved one-word descriptions of the action in each panel. The cat sets out *Cheese,* uses a fan to send the smell

into a mouse hole *(Breeze),* lets one mouse come out and sniff it *(Tease),* gives chase as the mouse runs *(Flees),* peers into the mouse hole *(Sees),* falls asleep there *(Z's),* continues to sleep as her tail is pulled through the hole and knotted on the other side *(Seize),* and then, with a *Wheeze,* begs with the mice to release her *(Please!).*

Comment. The character made its debut on December 3, 1933, in "Cicero's Cat," a strip tacked onto the Sunday comic strip "Mutt & Jeff." (Cicero had appeared with *a* cat on November 18, 1907, but it wasn't this cat.) The strip varied in length from one row of panels to a half-page for the first year, then settled into a two-row format for the next twelve years. It is presently just one row. She was the creation of Al Smith, who had just taken over as ghost artist/writer on Bud Fisher's popular strip. The cat also starred in one-page adventures in the *Mutt & Jeff* comic book, which had a variety of publishers from 1939 to 1965. The cat also has been referred to as Esmeralda—apparently a slip of the pen.

DICK DUCK
Pedigree. The duck dick of comics.
Biography. Based in a seedy office in a world of anthropomorphic animals, Dick wears a trenchcoat and slouch hat (even when he's indoors), and waits for business. Temperamental and volatile, he has been known to throw prospective clients out the window when they get his name wrong. One of his greatest foes was Moxie Mouse (a **Mickey Mouse** parody).

Comment. The character was created by Jim Engel, and the humor was—well, not always sophisticated (a bear walks in and announces, "I need a dick"). The duck appeared irregularly in one-page adventures in the fan magazine *The Comic Reader* throughout the late 1970s and early 1980s.

DINK
Pedigree. Huggable little TV dinosaur.
Biography. Although the brain cases of certain dinosaurs were beginning to grow larger in the late Cretaceous period, the stars of this series (which is apparently set in that period, due to the presence of a tyrannosaurus) are as articulate, clever, and frolicsome as contemporary human children. And, incongruously, as agile as well: Dink has been known to bat pitched coconuts with its tail, and grab a vine with its mouth and swing through the air—something neither its teeth nor the vine would have survived. So much for using Saturday morning fare

to educate kids. Dink is a small, green, blue-eyed apatosaurus (a k a brontosaurus) who pals around with other young dinosaurs: Scat, an alligatorlike thief; Flapper, a pteranodon who has trouble making soft landings ("Left most of the trees standing," an observer notes. "That's some improvement!"); Amber, a baby duckbill dinosaur; and Shyler, a bashful and softspoken little dimetrodon. They become involved in all kinds of adventures together, which usually involve getting lost, making new friends, or facing the threat of the towering adult carnivore Tyrannor, who dwells in Hunter's Grove. When the group is perplexed or distraught, they often turn for advice to the elderly sage, a white-haired prehistoric turtle named Crusty.

Comment. The Ruby-Spears series *Dink, The Little Dinosaur,* debuted on CBS in 1989. He followed in the fossilized footsteps of the lesser-known Denver, whose series *Denver, the Last Dinosaur,* was syndicated in 1988. The green biped, alive in the modern world and groovin' with contemporary kids, starred in half-hour adventures *(Chips N' Robbers, School Daze,* and *Dino-Star* among them) from Fries Entertainment.

DINKY DOG
Pedigree. The world's largest cartoon puppy.
Biography. Uncle Dudley despises dogs. So naturally, young Sandy and Monica don't just get a dog for a pet, they get a huge one. Although Dinky means well, he can't help stumbling over everything in sight, invariably infuriating Dudley. The exploits of the kids and their dog have taken them to the circus, to a haunted house, to Camp Kookiehaha, and to the baseball diamond. Dinky has also tried his paw at reporting, art, and acting.

Comment. The Hanna-Barbera character appeared on his own segment of *The All-New Popeye Hour,* and aired on CBS beginning in 1978. There were sixteen episodes in all; Frank Welker provided the dog's voice.

DINKY DUCK
Pedigree. Shy little duck of theatrical cartoons and comic books.
Biography. An orphan, the tiny, black Dinky spends his time roaming around, trying to find a home or employment, or just helping other animals. In the comics, he lives on a farm with the slave-driving Rudy Rooster, who makes Dinky do all the hard work.

Comment. Terrytoons produced fifteen Dinky cartoons from 1939 to 1957. They came to television as part of the syndicated *Heckle and Jeckle Show* in 1955; the characters were also back-up features in various **Mighty Mouse** comic books and in the fifty-four–issue run of Dell, then Gold Key's, *New Terrytoons* (1960 to 1979).

DINNY THE DINOSAUR
Pedigree. Cartoon pet and mount of the caveman Alley Oop.
Biography. Alley Oop is the gruff, strong, but likable defender of the Kingdom of Moo, which is ruled by the doltish King Guzzle. In his first meeting with the big (about twenty feet tall), purplish Dinny, the dinosaur grabbed Oop and tossed him in the air; the caveman landed on Dinny's back, right behind his head, and has been perched there ever since. Swinging a mean club, Oop battles enemies both within and without Moo; more often than not, it's Dinny's strength and ability to serve as a living battering ram

Dinny the Dinosaur
and Alley Oop prove
that dinosaurs were,
in fact, fleet creatures!
© NEWSPAPER ENTERPRISE
ASSOCIATION.

that saves the day. However, Dinny does draw the line at battling more powerful carnivores, preferring to run than fight. When Dinny disobeys his master and is rewarded with a conk on the head, the big dinosaur whimpers like a puppy. After six years of prehistoric doings, Oop, his love Oola, and Dinny are snatched by a time machine belonging to Professor Wonmug, and have adventures in many different eras.

Comment. Dinny was the first character created by Vincent T. Hamlin for his comic strip. A reporter in Texas, Hamlin kept hearing about fossilized dinosaur skeletons and decided to use prehistoric life as a basis for a new strip. According to Hamlin, Dinny was created by mixing "the body of a diplodocus with the spine plates of a stegosaurus and the head of a duck. For purposes of acceptable animation, I gave him the running gear of a mammal rather than a reptile." The dinosaur's master was created next, known only, then, as Oop the Mighty. Hamlin added the French "allez," dropped "the Mighty," and created Alley Oop. Their relationship was inspired by the tale of *Androcles and the Lion,* a story that dates back to the first century A.D. The strip first appeared on August 7, 1933; the characters have also starred in Alley Oop comic books published by Standard (eight issues, 1947 to 1949), Argo (three issues, 1955 to 1956), and Dell (two issues, 1963) and have been guest features in other titles. Dallas Frazier's "Alley-Oop" was a hit song twice in 1960. The characters came to television as a segment of the animated Filmation series *The Fabulous Funnies,* which aired on NBC from 1978 to 1979.

DINO THE DINOSAUR
Pedigree. Pet "runtasaurus" owned by the Flintstones.

Biography. Dino is a pinkish dinosaur with black spots on its back, a long neck, and a head with a big, round snout and three sprigs of black hair on top. He stands approximately five feet tall, can walk on four legs or two, and lives with cave family Fred and Wilma Flintstone of Bedrock, in Cobblestone County. Dino has a high-pitched yip and also has a nasty habit of running Fred down and licking him whenever his master comes home from work. Although loving, he manages to cause Fred considerable pain: He usually drops the (stone) newspaper on Fred's foot and, when he goes for a walk, becomes so excited that he drags Fred behind him . . . and often up and over the fence. Dino is a creature of diverse interests. Originally, he was keen to become a

motion picture actor like his hero, the TV star Sassy. However, after leaving home and trying to break into films, Dino returns disenchanted: Sassy, it seems, is a super-snob. (While Dino was gone, Fred was inconsolable, standing by a picture of Dino and weeping.) These days, Dino is content to stay at home and chase the pesky Cave Mouse; now and then, he goes out with the teenaged Pebbles (Fred and Wilma's daughter) and Bamm-Bamm (son of their neighbors, the Rubbles), using his sensitive nose to help solve mysteries of an eerie nature. Other pets seen in the TV series are the Rubbles' Baby Puss, a saber-tooth tiger; Hoppy the Hopperoo, a green, bat-eared kangaroolike creature who carries the children around in its pouch; and Snoots, a "snorkasaurus." A more fanciful regular introduced late in the series was the yard-wide Schneider the Spider. Lastly . . . did you know (or care) that Wilma's maiden name is Slaghoople?

Comment. *The Flintstones* was the first cartoon show created expressly for prime-time television. The Hanna-Barbera series, which was inspired by *The Honeymooners,* debuted on ABC in 1960, and had an astonishing run of six years (166 episodes). The characters have been recycled several times on different series, although rarely with distinction (such as *The New Fred and Barney Show* in 1979, and *The Flintstones Comedy Show* in 1980, which featured *Dino and Cave Mouse*—segments which were primarily chases—as well as the Hardy Boy-like adventures of *Pebbles, Dino, and Bamm-Bamm*). There was also a feature-length cartoon in 1966, *The Man Called Flintstone.* Chips Spam originally provided the voice for Dino. Russi Taylor is Cave Mouse. In comic books, Charlton published twenty issues of *Dino* from 1973 to 1977. As the *The Flintstones,* Dell, then Gold Key, produced sixty issues plus various special editions (1961 to 1970); Charlton published fifty issues (1970 to 1977); and Marvel Comics published nine issues (1977 to 1979). Marvel also began publishing *The Flintstone Kids* in 1987, in which little Dino was featured. It was based on the TV show, which ran from 1986 to 1988.

DIRTY DUCK
Pedigree. Underground comics duck.
Biography. This is a duck who likes human women, and will do just about anything to get them. In his first appearance, he poses as a violin teacher to lure the ladies to his lair; his first student knocks him out and dates his roommate, Weevil, instead. Things go

downhill from there. Weevil always gets the women, while the cigar-chomping duck is left with egg on his face. Even when Dirty tries to spoil things for the diminutive Lothario, his efforts backfire. In a restaurant, when a waiter brings a message to Weevil from an admirer, Dirty has him "tell her to drop dead." Wowed by this reaction, the lady strips and has herself served to Weevil on a silver platter.

Comment. The duck was created by Bobby London, whose character design and layout was patterned after the classic **Krazy Kat** (in particular, Mock Duck and Mrs. Kwakk-Wak). It made its debut in Hell Comics's *Air Pirates Funnies* no. 1 in 1971. The magazine lasted two issues, put out of business by a copyright infringement suit brought by Walt Disney Productions (for using Disney character look-alikes in sex-and-drug orgies). The duck then began a long and successful run as a one-page feature in *The National Lampoon*. His most unusual appearance was in the magazine's *Very Large Book of Comical Funnies* (1975). In "flip book" style drawings published on the edge of every page, Dirty tries unsuccessfully to pick up a stripper. (That irreverent magazine also published stories featuring Pigboy and Little Sneakers, a parody of Big Boy and **Nugget**; and a tale of the Nazi Gorilla, a giant ape which was killed and eaten by Martians.)

DIZZY DOG
Pedigree. Comic book dog from the 1950s.
Biography. Dizzy is a tubby little white dog with tiny black speckles on his back and sides, and a pair of large, triangular black ears that look almost like bat ears. His wardrobe consists of white gloves and a red bow tie, although he dons a derby when he goes out. Dizzy isn't a troublemaker. He enjoys lying on his hammock or going to the park and reading a newspaper . . . but, as with all good comic book animals, trouble always has a way of finding him. He'll buy a bottle of ketchup, take it home, and out will pop a genie. He'll let neighbor **McSnurtle the Turtle** pose him a riddle, then go nuts trying to figure it out. Dizzy's frequent rival is Amster the Hamster: The little rodent in the big top hat and frock coat is jealous of Dizzy's nice home and well-stocked refrigerator and has gone so far as to sneak up when the dog is sleeping and paint himself like Dizzy, and Dizzy like him, to steal the refrigerator from him. A hose was his downfall. In another tale, Amster actually jeopardized the dog's life by tricking Dizzy into insulting Ferrence the Fencing Ferret (great name!). The dog was forced to duel him, but was resourceful enough

to trick Ferrence into sticking his snout in the gun, thus ending the battle.

Comment. The character was created by the prolific and talented Sheldon Mayer, who contributed greatly to DC's roster of humorous and animal characters. Among the other Mayer animals that appeared in *Funny Stuff* and other DC animal titles were Bo Bunny, an innocent hare who gets into trouble when he does what his pal the fox tells him to (debuted in no. 75); the pesky Chip Chipmunk, who's always looking for an easy way to get food or cash; and the Brat Finks, a pair of miscreant mice who first appeared in *Fox and the Crow* no. 95 in 1965. The latter were fairly revolutionary by animal standards: Teen mouse Rudy dressed and behaved like a juvenile delinquent, while his little sister dressed sweetly and sprayed ink on the wall when their parents' backs were turned. See also Mayer's **Doodles Duck**.

DJUBA THE RED GORILLA
Pedigree. Ape-assistant to the comic book hero B'wana Beast.
Biography. Michael Payson Maxwell and Rupert Zambesi are college buddies who take a private plane to Africa to visit Rupert's people, the Zambesi. En route, the aircraft is struck by lightning and crash-lands on Mt. Kilimanjaro. There, they are spotted by Djuba. The ape trails the wounded men into a "burnt-out lava crater," where Rupert gives the more seriously wounded Michael rainwater to drink. Moments later, the gorilla shows himself, mumbles a few words ("Hummdari! Jabal Golokai!") and attacks; but Michael is miraculously healed as well as bigger and stronger than before, and is able to beat the ape into submission. Docile now, the ape presents Michael with a helmet ("Some ancient civilization with . . . science beyond ours made it," Michael speculates), which allows him to become "attuned" to the gorilla's mind and control the ape as well as all animals. Michael remains in the jungle as the superhero B'wana Beast; Djuba stays on as a keeper of the strange "serum" that Michael must drink to remain big and strong. If B'wana Beast is trapped for any reason, he can summon Djuba from miles away.

Comment. Djuba costarred with B'wana Beast in his two appearances in DC Comics's *Showcase,* nos. 66 and 67 in 1967.

DOCTOR WHOOT

Pedigree. Spacefaring comic book owl.

Biography. The time: the future. The place: USS *Space Ark,* a ship crewed entirely by anthropomorphic animals, and devoted to keeping the peace throughout outer space. Nothing is known about Doctor Whoot's past—although it's said that the wise owl "won a trip around the galaxy on a TV game show and got on the wrong ship by mistake." The smug, black-feathered bird is said to have stuck around only because the crew of the *Ark* is so dumb that he was able to "feel superior to everybody." Whoot is rarely without a copy of *The Reader's Digest Condensed History of Everything* under his wing. Other animals onboard include Captain Stone, an egomaniac fox and graduate of the Fur-Bearing Alliance (a k a Furball) Academy; Kitty, the cat first officer who graduated from Furball with honors ("so no one really knows why she got stuck on the *Space Ark*"); and Brooklyn (a weasel) and Slinx (a turtle), the ship's engineers.

Comment. The character appeared in all five issues of Apple Press's *Space Ark* comic book. Kenny Mitchroney's art is some of the most animated and expressive funny animal art since the golden age.

DOG (1)

Pedigree. A flea-bitten comic book dog in an Archie-style comic book.

Biography. Harvey Hooper is a teenager newly arrived in Midville and depressed about having no friends. While the movers move his family in, teens sitting in Cheerful Charlie's Cola Castle see a mangy,

Harvey, and the arrival of **Dog (1).**

brown dog wandering across the street. They run out to stop traffic so he won't be hurt; the animal wanders into the moving van, then slips out and enters Harvey's house while the kids give chase. Harvey spots the dog and it's love at first sight. Not only does Harvey acquire a pet, but he gets to meet other kids . . . and Midville suddenly seems far less desolate.

Comment. Dog was introduced in Marvel Comics's *Harvey* no. 1 in 1970 and stuck around for all six issues.

DOG (2)

Pedigree. Star of enormously popular "Footrot Flats" comic strip in New Zealand.

Biography. Dog is a sheepdog who watches over the spread of his master and friend, big, slovenly rancher Wal Footrot. When not doing his duty or trying to snare food, the dog spends time with Jess, his girlfriend, or with Wal. (He doesn't like Wal's inamorata, hairdresser Cheeky Hobson, though, and does everything possible to interfere with that relationship.) Other characters in the strip include the tough pig dog Major, with whom Dog also doesn't get along; Wal's brawny cat Horse, who's tougher than Major and Dog put together; Irish Murphy, a neighbor and a thief; Rangi, one of his sons, who wants to kill Dog for his hide; and Prince Charles, the pampered Corgi owned by Wal's Aunt Dolly. Dog has a black coat with a white belly, face, and extremities.

Comment. The comic strip was created by Murray Ball, and made its debut in New Zealand's *Evening Post* in 1976. It's unlikely to find a U.S. home, however, due to its graphic treatment (albeit, truthful and nonsensational) of butchering, animal birth, and the like as well as its forthrightness toward language and sex (both human and animal). A feature-length film, *Footrot Flats, The Dog's Tale,* was released in 1986 and became the top-grossing film in New Zealand's history. In it, not only must the dog deal with Irish Murphy, Cheeky, and Wal's preoccupation with wanting to play on a professional rugby team, but there's a swarm of vile rats that attacks the farm and Jess. The film was written and directed by Ball.

DOGAROO

Pedigree. The comic book "Dog of Wonder, the Dog from Down Under."

Biography. Raised by kangaroos in the Australian outback, the sheepdog ends up in an American kennel, where he's adopted by Stephanie and Sidney, the children of the local sheriff. Able to talk, hop, and toss a mean boomerang, the dog helps the kids help their father by catching local crooks. No one but the children know of the dog's amazing skills.

Comment. Created by Cliff and Robin Mac-Gilliray, the character appeared in one issue of Blackthorne's *Dogaroo* (1988).

DOG BOY
Pedigree. Underground comic book dog.
Biography. Dog Boy has a human body with the head of a dog; his live-in lover, Dog Girl, is entirely human, save for her floppy little ears and a black nose. Both are liberal nonconformists, although Dog Boy is far more blue-collar than his companion. An illustrator, Dog Boy eventually launches the newspaper *Graffiti*, a "radical newspaper." But while that's what he does for a living, the comic book focuses on more surreal adventures, such as his battle with witches hiding under his basement staircase, an encounter with a dog that bites his shoulder and won't let go for over a week, and a meditation in which he gets "in touch with my guts," angrily chasing away the "glebes" that are pulling his insides tight. Dog Boy's preferred beverage is "an ice cold beer . . . no glass," and his best friend is the human Knoot, an advertising executive.

Comment. Steve Lafler's Dog Boy originally appeared in Cat-Head Comics's *Guts* no. 3. He was given his own magazine in 1986, published by Fantagraphics Books.

DOGMATIX
Pedigree. Pet of the comic book and film hero Asterix.
Biography. In 50 B.C., the Romans have conquered virtually all of Gaul . . . save for Armorica. The tiny

Dogmatix becomes a message-bearer for Asterix. However, he's too young to grasp what he's supposed to do . . . so Asterix picks him up and carries him!
© DARGAUD S.A.

Dogaroo struts his stuff. © CLIFF AND ROBIN MACGILLIVRAY.

village is protected by Asterix, who acquires super-powers by consuming a magic potion brewed by the druid Getafix. Asterix's terrier puppy Dogmatix is small enough to fit in the palm of his hand and is as playful as he is dumb. When Asterix tosses away a massive building block, Dogmatix faithfully goes and chases it. In Egypt, when the hero accidentally breaks off the nose of the sphinx, he buries it so the Egyptians won't find out; Dogmatix "helpfully" begins digging it up again. In one adventure, the dog drinks some of the druid's potion and becomes powerful enough to defeat a wolf. Dogmatix is white with brown eartips and a stubby brown tail.

Comment. Created by writer Rene Goscinny and artist Albert Uderzo, the characters first appeared in the French magazine *Pilote* on October 29, 1959. There have been several feature-length Asterix cartoons, most notably *Asterix the Gaul* (1967), *Asterix and Cleopatra* (1968), and *Asterix and the Big Fight* (1989).

DOLLAR

Pedigree. The pet dog of comic book and TV star Richie Rich.

Biography. The white beagle with black ears belongs to the world's richest boy. Not surprisingly, black markings in Dollar's coat form small dollar signs. The dog can make only rudimentary sounds, like *Yum* and *Yich!* In his most famous escapade, Dollar stows away on a plane bound for the North Pole. When the ship crash-lands, he is adopted by an Eskimo family and becomes a very successful sled dog (wearing a heavy coat he found in the wreckage of the plane). While running from a polar bear, Dollar discovers an untapped oil field—which, when he's found by Richie, increases the boy's phenomenal wealth.

Comment. The Harvey Comics character first appeared in *Richie Rich* no. 65 in 1965. Dollar was also featured on *The Richie Rich/Scooby-Doo Show*, which premiered on ABC in 1980. Frank Welker provided the dog's bark.

DOLORES

Pedigree. Gentle pachyderm seen in a trio of Walt Disney shorts.

Biography. In her screen debut, *Tiger Trouble* (1945), the shambling, doe-eyed elephant is **Goofy's** mount and sole companion on a tiger hunt. By the time the sly tiger is through toying with the dull-witted hunter, Goofy is seen heading out of the jun-

gle with Dolores on *his* back. Somehow having become a circus animal in *The Big Wash* (1948), Dolores is due for a bath—and Goofy is the attendant whose job it is to give her one. She does everything she can think of to get out of it (including dressing as a clown, a disguise that could mislead only Goofy) but ends up in the tub just the same. Not that Goofy has triumphed: Dolores gets the "last word" when she sneezes, blasting Goofy into a pool of muck and leaving *him* filthy. In her final screen appearance, *Working for Peanuts* (1953), Dolores is now in the zoo where **Donald Duck** is in charge of her comfort. Meanwhile, **Chip 'n' Dale** are determined to make off with Dolores's peanuts. Although she and Donald try everything they can think of to drive the chipmunks off—which includes spitting peanuts from her trunk as though it were a machine gun—the pests come up with the winning idea of painting themselves white and having themselves taken into the zoo as rare albinos.

Comment. Apart from being sweet and fairly bright (for a Disney cartoon character, anyway), the elephant didn't have much of a personality. See also the Walt Disney elephant **Dumbo.**

DOMINO CHANCE

Pedigree. Comic book cockroach.

Biography. The approximately five-foot-tall, twin-antennaed, pink "Roach Extraordinaire" is an interstellar shipper who works primarily for Geoffrey Ogden Davies, "the richest man in known space." Dressed in a white parka and blue knee boots, Domino flies through the cosmos onboard the spaceship *Scarab* with his roach sidekick, Arnie. Together, they have more-or-less standard science fiction adventures, like battling a deadly life form on an asteroid, a not so relaxing stopover on an alien world, and enslavement on the planet Doin. A costar in the strip is Domino's friend, the human-roach hybrid "Troubles" Galore, a special agent whose criminal investigations regularly intercept the roach's path.

Comment. Kevin Lenagh's character was originally published in his own title by Chance Enterprises; nine issues appeared in 1984 and 1985. Amazing Comics took over the title in 1987.

DONALD DUCK

Pedigree. Quick-tempered legend of cartoons and comics.

Biography. Son of Quackmore Duck, Donald Fauntleroy Duck was born on Friday the thirteenth, on

Roach **Domino Chance** in his standard spacefaring garb. © KEVIN LENAGH.

a stormy March night. He lives in Duckburg at 13 Quack Street and first appeared in the 1934 short *The Wise Little Hen,* wearing his soon-to-be-familiar sailor's jacket (usually blue, but occasionally black in comic strips) and white or blue French sailor's hat, although he had a more gooselike body: long neck, long and narrow bill, wings with the hint of fingers rather than hands. In the cartoon, a mother hen goes from fat, lazy Peter Pig to Donald, asking them to help plant corn. Peter bluntly spurns her; Donald, dancing on the deck of a ship, at least comes up an excuse, uttering, "Who me? Oh, no! I got a bellyache." In the duck's second cartoon, *The Orphan's Benefit,* he has more of a part, trying to recite *Mary Had a Little Lamb* and *Little Boy Blue* in front of a roomful of young, inattentive mice. (Compare this to the similar cartoon debut of **Porky Pig.**) Donald loses his temper when one of the kids blows his nose . . . and, because audiences loved and identi-

fied with the duck, Donald hasn't regained it since. His appearance was barely modified for this film, although he got his big, arched eyebrows and modern, flared bill by his fourth screen appearance, in the classic *The Band Concert* (1935). (As Donald's temper and abrasiveness increased with successive cartoons, the animators rounded his body more and more, so that he would still cut a cuddly, likeable figure.) In *The Band Concert* (his first cartoon in Technicolor), Donald is an obnoxious vendor at conductor Mickey Mouse's outdoor performance of "The William Tell Overture." The two stars go to war, although the band continues to play. After costarring in twenty-one shorts, Donald got his own cartoon in 1937, titled *Donald's Ostrich,* in which he's a railroad stationmaster who must deal with an ostrich. Donald had many occupations over the years: a plumber *(Donald and Pluto,* 1936), an exorcist *(Lonesome Ghosts,* 1937), a messenger boy delivering a ticking bomb *(Donald's Lucky Day,* 1939), a construction worker *(The Riveter,* 1940), a tugboat crewman *(Tugboat Mickey,* 1940), window cleaner on a skyscraper *(Window Cleaners,* 1940), a firefighter *(Fire Chief,* 1940), a farmer *(Old MacDonald Duck,* 1941), a blacksmith *(The Village Smithy,* 1941), a soldier *(Donald Gets Drafted* and *Sky Trooper,* 1942; *Fall Out—Fall In,* 1943; and many others), a toy shop gift wrapper *(The Clock Watcher,* 1945), a forest ranger *(Old Sequoia,* 1945), a super-sales-duck after taking Ajax Voice Pills *(Donald's Dream Voice,* 1948), a logger *(Up a Tree,* 1955), and more. He's also been a singer (for which his duck voice was mercifully abandoned by the filmmakers), performing everything from opera *(Rigoletto* in *Mickey's Grand Opera,* 1936) to pop ballads *(Donald's Dilemma,* 1947, in which a mild concussion makes him a great crooner). Obviously, the explosive duck had trouble holding down a job. Just as clearly, there isn't a situation that the hot-tempered drake can't turn from worse to much worse. However, as the series evolved, Donald became more and more the typical suburbanite (living in Hollywood, California), whose comfort was constantly being threatened by his precocious nephews **Huey, Dewey, and Louie** (beginning with *Donald's Nephews,* 1938), missteps with his girlfriend **Daisy Duck** *(Mr. Duck Steps Out,* 1940, among many others), a lemon of a car *(Donald's Tire Trouble,* 1943), an escaped gorilla *(Donald Duck and the Gorilla,* 1944), a troublesome bird *(Wet Paint,* 1946), the pesky chipmunks **Chip 'n' Dale** *(Chip 'n' Dale,*

1947), a kangaroo (*Daddy Duck,* 1948), **Buzz-Buzz Bee** who is drawn by the floral wallpaper Donald is hanging *(Inferior Decorator,* 1948), a witch *(Trick or Treat,* 1952), and many more. Disaster dogs Donald even when he tries to grab a scrap of happiness, such as a day at the beach *(Beach Picnic,* 1939), a few rounds of his favorite sport, golf *(Donald's Day Off,* 1944), trying to add to his extensive bug collection [*Bootle Beetle,* 1947 (see **Bootle Beetle**)], camping *(Trailer Horn,* 1950), or flying model planes *(Test Pilot Donald,* 1951, and others). Among Donald's family members, several have appeared in cartoons, comic strips, and comic books—also usually to his detriment. These are his Aunt Fanny and cousin **Gus Goose;** cousin **Gladstone Gander;** sister Dumbella (Della in the comic strips), mother of Huey and his brothers; and uncle **Ludwig Von Drake.** His grandfather costarred just once, in *No Hunting* (1955): A buffalo hunter of the old west, the frontiers-duck steps from a painting and convinces Donald to get out of his chair and come hunting, with fruitless results. Appearing only in the comic strip and comic books is proper **Grandma Duck. Scrooge McDuck** is Donald's uncle. Donald occasionally works as Sky Warden in Duckburg, putting out fires in the Black Forest.

Comment. Although Donald was created as much to give the calm, rational Mickey Mouse a foil, there's a reason he endured: If Mickey represents our optimistic, cheerful side, Donald is the pessimist in us all—albeit carried to the extreme, as his dire outlook usually becomes a self-fulfilling prophecy. Donald came to the screen as a result of something Walt Disney heard on the radio show *The Merry Makers* in 1932: entertainer (and part-time milkman) Clarence Nash (1904 to 1985) was playing a tongue-tied duck reading *Mary Had a Little Lamb.* For more than a year, Disney had been wanting to give **Mickey Mouse** a friend named Donald Duck (a name derived when Disney was going through an alliterative phase, e.g., **Clarabelle Cow, Horace Horsecollar, Clara Cluck, Peter Penguin** and so on). It was Nash's recitation that caused it all to gel. After hiring Clarence and working with him to make the voice more expressive, Disney put the duck on the screen. It was animator Dick Lundy who came up with Donald's characteristic "tantrum" pose: head craned forward, one fisted arm held straight out, the other swinging at his side, one leg angled forward, the other straight beneath him as he bounced around madly. During his career, Donald starred in 164 short subjects, of which one—*Der Fuehrer's Face*

(1943)—won an Oscar (seven other Donald cartoons were nominated over the years). That short has Donald dreaming of what life would be like in Hitler's Germany, from overwork on the assembly line (where he screws the tops on bombs, artillery shells, and bullets—pausing to salute pictures of Hitler that roll by incessantly) to stale bread to vacations taken in front of a painted backdrop of the Alps. When Donald wakes in his own bed, at home, the effect is still stirring. Donald also guest starred in the feature-length films *The Reluctant Dragon* (1941; his recently released short *Old MacDonald Duck* was pared and included in the omnibus film), *Saludos Amigos* (1943; the segment *Lake Titicaca* has Donald touring the region, highlighted by a llama-back ride over a rope bridge that comes apart in midtransit, while in another segment, **José Carioca** takes him on a tour of South America), *The Three Caballeros* (1945; see below), *Fun and Fancy Free* (1947; the featurette *Mickey and the Beanstalk), Melody Time* [1948; the sequence *Blame it on the Samba* (again, see **José Carioca**)], and *Who Framed Roger Rabbit* (1988; Donald and **Daffy Duck** play piano in a nightclub, each trying to outdo the other). A strong case can be made for dubbing *The Three Caballeros* as Disney's finest feature-length film; certainly it's the most imaginative, *Fantasia* notwithstanding, and, at times, the most beautiful. The framing story has Donald receiving a huge parcel for his birthday. There are several gifts inside and he opens the first. It's a movie projector and film and, setting it up, Donald watches an animated documentary about the *Aves Raras* (strange birds) of the southern hemisphere. A lengthy segment tells how one of these, Pablo the Penguin, so loathes the cold that he leaves Antarctica and, "with a tenacity of purpose seldom found in a penguin," seeks happiness "on some tropical shore." Another segment introduces **The Aracuan Bird** after which the strangest bird of all appears. While out climbing in the Andes, hunting for condors, young Gauchito finds the nest of a "flying donkeybird" who measures five meters from wingtip to wingtip. Gauchito manages to get on "the Burrito's" back and, using a kite string, trains it to do all kinds of tricks. For its part, the animal is happy to stay, because it likes human food "much better than hay." Hoping to make a fortune with the donkey, Gauchito enters it in a race, the Gran Carrera; the animal blazes past the competition so fast that it's wings aren't seen. However, when the boy goes to collect the prize money, the donkey's wings pop from beneath the saddle and he's disqualified. The boy and his donkeybird fly off and, according to Gauchito, who's narrating, "neither him nor me was ever seen again as long as we lived." The next segment introduces José Carioca, who takes Donald on a tour of Brazil—where the duck falls passionately in love with (live-action) dancer Aurora Miranda—after which the birds are joined by **Panchito.** Together, onboard a flying "magic serape," the trio heads to Mexico for a visit. There—again combining the cartoon animals with live-action footage—Donald is wowed by the lovely ladies they constantly encounter, most of whom he addresses with his familiar "Toots." Donald cuts a mean rug in a Mexico City nightspot, but it's the visit to Acapulco Beach that undoes him. Leaping off the flying serape, Donald chases the bathing beauties across the sand, forcing his feathered companions to give chase. Donald's frantic single-mindedness leads from one terrific slapstick gag to another before his friends can haul him off. Later, Donald is smitten with a cactus that becomes a dancing woman; the other cacti come to life and dance with them, at one point Donald being trampled by little cacti in his own likeness. Back at home in the final segment, Donald is so wound up he dons a bull costume and battles bullfighter Panchito. Donald also played Scrooge McDuck's nephew Fred in *Mickey's Christmas Carol,* a featurette released in 1983. On television, Donald was always featured during the opening theme of *The Mickey Mouse Club* (1955 to 1959): ready to bang a gong at the end of the opening—and something always went wrong when he did. To wit, two of his nephews popping up from behind and firing squirt guns; a nephew running up and striking the gong with his own mallet before Donald can do so, stealing his thunder; the gong splattering when struck, as though it were packed with pie filling; the mallet vibrating when hit, causing Donald to reverberate; the gong falling to pieces at the feet of the stunned duck; the gong spinning like a top when struck, slapping his feathered derriere over and over; the gong making no sound when hit until Donald puts his ear to it, at which point it rings out; and Donald winding up as though to hit the gong, then banging a triangle instead. Donald was also seen in hour-long specials on the weekly Disney programs *Disneyland, Walt Disney Presents,* and *Walt Disney's Wonderful World of Color,* in shows such as *The Donald Duck Story, Donald's Silver Anniversary, A Day in the Life of Donald Duck, At Home with Donald Duck,* and others. These were all compilations of old cartoons strung together with

pieces of new footage. As famous as Donald became on the big and little screen, he was also a hit in comic strips and comic books. Donald first appeared in the "Silly Symphony" comic strip on September 16, 1934, beginning a serialized adaptation of his debut cartoon. On August 30, 1936, the subheading "Featuring Donald Duck" appeared on the Sunday strip; shortly thereafter, the strip became simply "Donald Duck." A daily Donald Duck strip was inaugurated on February 7, 1938, with Donald working as a zookeeper and being chased by hungry seals on day one, climbing a mountain and fighting an angry mountain goat on day two, trying in vain to hang a picture at home on day three, and so on. Bob Karp wrote the strip from the start through 1974; Al Taliaferro drew it until his death in 1969. In comic books, Donald appeared on the cover and inside of the first Walt Disney magazine, *Walt Disney's Comics and Stories* and regularly thereafter; Dell published the title from 1940 to 1962 when Gold Key took over (no. 264); Gladstone inherited the title with no. 511 in 1986, Dell inaugurated Donald's own magazine in 1940. Gold Key took over with no. 85 and Gladstone got it beginning with no. 246. Disney began publishing the title on its own in 1990. There have also been dozens of Donald one-shot comic books. Without a doubt, the most renowned artist to work on the comic books was Carl Barks. The comic book containing his first Donald art assignment *(4-Color* no. 9, 1942) is valued at close to $3,000 for a mint-condition copy, and Barks's many oil paintings of Donald and company are worth considerably more. The appeal of Barks's work is complex, but derives largely from the fact that there is real drama in the stories, whether Donald was searching for pirate gold, exploring an old castle, lost in the Andes, or working as a sheriff. Moreover, Barks gave Donald and the supporting characters nuances lacking in the action-oriented cartoons and punch-line directed comic strips. He also created a fully realized world of ducks—in particular, Duckburg (which internal evidence places either off the coast of California or on an island in the Atlantic Ocean, near Washington, D.C.). The geography and character of the quaint place (and neighboring Goosetown, Turkeyneck-on-the-Mohawk, and so on) is consistent and detailed: Like any small American town, there's a newspaper, the *Duckburg Bugle,* a thriving downtown, fairgrounds, a bowling team, the Duckburg Ducks (of which Donald's the captain), a TV station, groups like the drama club and the Rock Hunters' Association; and (naturally) a smelt delivery truck. While there are a lot of fowl—such as the big goose Mrs. Gobblechin—there are also other animals such as the boar P. J. McBrine, the crone-dog J. Crowsfoot Dryskin, and people who are just like humans except for the fact that they have small, round, black noses. (There are also *pet* dogs in Duckburg and a zoo with nonanthropomorphic animals.) In 1988, books and products featuring Disney Babies were introduced, suggesting that Donald and other members of the Disney menagerie all played together as toddlers. Donald—who is dressed the same, except for a bigger and brighter red bow tie—not only knew Daisy but took baths with her and shared her crib. These stories are cute and certainly profitable, but they cannot be considered canonical. See other characters in the Donald chronicles **Gyro Gearloose** and **Moby Duck**.

DOODLES DUCK

Pedigree. An ordinary, hearth- and home-loving comic book duck.

Biography. Doodles is a duck of simple pleasures: All he wants to do is sit at home and read in a bath or an easy chair. Unfortunately, his precocious nephew Lemuel is forever making noise with his "foghorn voice" or getting into trouble, thus depriving Doodles of quiet and solitude. (One time, Doodles launched a preemptive strike by shouting in Lemuel's ear, thus convincing the duckling that noise was bad news. Thus when the kitchen sink began to leak, Lemuel said nothing, and the resultant flood carried the house "clear across the country.") Doodles wears a black bow tie; Lemuel is always dressed in a red sailor's cap and bow tie. Other animals in Doodles's realm are the distinguished Gus the Goose, who walks with a cane and smokes a cigar; Amster the Hamster, who wears a top hat fully as large as his body; and the gullible Buttons, a rabbit.

Comment. Sheldon Mayer's creation first appeared as a back-up feature in no. 80 of *The Dodo and the Frog,* 1954.

DORIS THE PARAKEET

Pedigree. Bird-star of the comic strip "Kudzu."

Biography. Owned by the young man Kudzu, Doris has two passions in life: chocolate and wanting to escape Kudzu's mother, who's constantly hassling her to learn to talk (and to stop picking the chocolate chips from her homebaked cookies). Of the two passions, chocolate is the stronger . . . which is why she sticks around. As the little green bird puts it, she needs chocolate to "feel better. Then I gain weight,

my face breaks out . . .and I feel guilty." Depressed, she eats more chocolate to make her feel better again. Over the years, chocolate has given her a "hangover" (her belly, that is), made her explode ("It was worth it"), given her recurring fits of the d.t.'s, and caused her beak to fall off. She's eaten kisses without removing the foil, believes in buying American but eating Belgian, prefers dark chocolate with red meat and milk chocolate with fish, and once tried to freebase fudge. Doris's conscience appears regularly as a small asterisk at her side; she has no trouble ignoring it. Her one visit to Chocoholics Anonymous ended in disaster: She couldn't talk with her mouth full.

Comment. Doug Marlette writes and draws the strip, which began in 1985. For the botanical record, kudzu is a weedy vine that tends to grow wild and rampant.

DOZER

Pedigree. Cartoon dog belonging to Mr. T.

Biography. The big, gray bulldog works with Mr. T and his seven teenage friends as they solve mysteries around the world. Apart from the fact that the dog wears a rather ridiculous mohawk haircut, he's quite bright and has saved the group from mazes, cave-ins, and various other traps. It isn't clear whether the name derives from the fact that the dog likes to sleep, or is as strong as a bull(dog)dozer.

Comment. The *Mister T* [*sic*] cartoon series was a short-lived effort from Ruby-Spears. It aired on NBC in 1983 and Mr. T provided his own voice for the series. On the subject of marginally significant dogs, one mustn't forget Chu Chum, the canine aide to detective Charlie Chan on his series *The Amazing Chan and the Chan Clan,* a Hanna-Barbera series that was briefly seen on CBS in 1972. As for other animals that were added to cartoon versions of live-action series/characters, there have been plenty. Dribbles is the dog mascot of the Harlem Globetrotters from their first series (CBS, 1970), the dog Mop Top appears on *The Brady Kids* (ABC, 1972), Flash the dog lends a paw to the paramedics of *Emergency + 4* (NBC, 1973), helped along by the myna bird Charlemagne and the monkey Bananas. Chump is the pet chimp of Brad Brennan on *My Favorite Martians,* about a pair of extraterrestrials (CBS, 1973); Snubby the monkey belongs to Gilligan on *The New Adventures of Gilligan* (ABC, 1974); Brandon (a k a Brandy) is the setter owned by Punky Brewster (NBC, 1986, a cartoon adapted from the prime-time hit); Fugi is the dog belonging to *The Osmonds* (ABC, 1972); and their singing colleagues the Partridge Family have a robot dog named Orbit in *Partridge Family: 2200 A.D.* (CBS, 1974). Speaking of singers, Elvis was the name of the dog on the western series *Butch Cassidy and the Sun Dance Kids* (NBC, 1973). Finally, there's the duck, Gertrude, who keeps Cindy Lindenbrook company during her *Journey to the Center of the Earth* (ABC, 1967), a character inspired by the duck of the same name in the 1959 live-action film.

DROOPY

Pedigree. Star of vastly underrated theatrical cartoons.

Biography. Like many cartoon characters, such as the later **Huckleberry Hound,** Droopy lives in different time periods and holds different jobs, as the plot dictates. In all, however, he's a low-keyed, bipedal, white pup with black ears, a brown tail, a head of messy red hair, and jowls that hang nearly to his shoulders. His voice is soft and prissy, and, with rare exceptions, he shows extreme excitement by gently waving a tiny banner that he pulls from behind him, or by voicing a quiet cry of delight (the exceptions are noted below). Droopy is also magical: With no explanation (other than the fact that this is a cartoon) he can move from one spot to another, clear across the planet, in the blink of an eye. Indeed, physics regularly fail in the cartoons, as when the bulldog Spike writes on a blackboard and continues writing on the air, or loses his head out of sheer excitement. In Droopy's wonderful screen debut, *Dumb-Hounded* (1943), a killer wolf escapes from Swing Swing Prison. Droopy breaks from the pack of barking, hustling bloodhounds to pursue the nameless killer his own way. (In a marvelous throwaway scene early in the cartoon, Droopy nonchalantly passes behind a fire hydrant; when he emerges after the briefest pause, he smiles sheepishly at the camera and blushes.) The dog is waiting for the wolf at his apartment hideaway, and the wise con gets the seemingly dull-witted Droopy to "promise me you won't move." The wolf runs from the building, takes a car, train, boat, horse, and plane deep into the woods, to a cabin . . . where Droopy is waiting. "Ya moved, didn't you?" the dumbstruck wolf exclaims. When he demands to know how Droopy did it, the dog is no pushover: "Now, let's not get nosy, bub," he replies. After several chase scenes, Droopy finally gets the wolf by pushing a monstrously huge boulder off the top of a skyscraper right on top of the wolf ("Yes, you're right," Droopy says to the camera. "It

is gruesome.") Droopy gets his reward, and is ecstatic, breaking character by whooping and hollering and bouncing all over the place. The dog and wolf crossed swords again in *The Shooting of Dan McGoo* (1945), a send-up of Robert W. Service's *The Shooting of Dan McGrew,* in which they meet at the Malamute Saloon in Coldernell, Alaska, during the Gold Rush days and vie for the affections of human singer Lou. After a lengthy, very funny shootout, Droopy wins a kiss from the woman—and, again breaking character, shoots around the saloon like a rocket. He and the wolf have other notable confrontations, especially in the hilarious *Drag-a-Long Droopy* (1954), in which Droopy is a sheep herder and the wolf is a cattle rancher, both of them vying for the same grazing fields. The wolf's recurring inability to mount his horse is inspired. However, the high point of the short is a macho demonstration of marksmanship, in which the two adversaries choose increasingly more difficult targets to hit. Droopy backs down after the wolf blasts a fly off a mesa on the horizon; a small, high-pitched *ahhhh* can be heard as the insect dies. The dog's other major adversary is Spike, who costarred in what is arguably the best cartoon in the series, *Wags to Riches* (1949). Droopy and the bulldog both belong to a millionaire who, on his death, leaves his fortune to the dog who has been "loyal, upright, on-the-level, good-natured, smart, talented, clean-minded, has an eye for beauty, sober, a good scout, and brave as the knights of old." Spike thinks that means him; naturally, Droopy gets the money. However, the will stipulates that if Droopy dies, the estate passes on to Spike. Spike becomes Droopy's butler, and tries repeatedly to kill him—using gas, playing pin the tail on the donkey by an open window, placing an artillery shell inside a camera, chopping down a tree on the pup, painting a tennis court to look like a pool and erecting a diving board, rigging a rifle to the bathroom doorknob. Naturally, each trap backfires. Finally, when Droopy is sleeping, Spike lathers him up as a mad dog and calls the dog catcher to come and get him. But a fan blows the foam onto Spike, and guess who's carted off—truly mad, now. Other superb team ups with Spike were *Chump Champ* (1950) in which Spike, as Gorgeous Gorillawitz, competes against that "atomic flash" Droopy (from Kookamonga, it's revealed) to find out who's the "King of Sports." Again, all of Spike's treacherous schemes backfire, such as placing sharks in the pool, an anvil in the punching bag, a bomb in a sack for the sack race, and painting a white line into traffic during the track meet (cars follow the white line and mow Spike down). In *Droopy's Good Deed* (1951), the two scouts compete for a trip to Washington and an audience with the president. Spike tries to undermine all of Droopy's good deeds (for instance, by trying to lure him off the top of a skyscraper, running him over with a trolley, drowning him, burning him, and blowing him up with TNT). Droopy has a son, Dribble.

Comment. Creator Tex Avery says he designed Droopy as "a baby bloodhound. I didn't want too many wrinkles on his forehead [and] I wanted him on his hind legs. His name came from a droopy look on a bloodhound." Bill Thompson provided the character's voice, which was inspired by Mr. Whipple from the *Fibber McGee and Molly* radio show. MGM made twenty-four Droopy cartoons between 1943 and 1958; one of these, *One Droopy Knight* (1957), was nominated for an Academy Award. However, the series was at its peak—and an entertaining, brilliantly animated peak it was!—only through 1954. Beginning with *Deputy Droopy* in 1955, the animation was "flattened," the molded, full-bodied look sacrificed due to rising budgets. Droopy made a minor but memorable cameo in the 1988 film *Who Framed Roger Rabbit,* working as an elevator operator in Toon Town (see **Roger Rabbit**). It should be noted that many of the over-reactions of Roger—such as his eyeballs popping way out of his head, to the tune of cow bell sound effects—were based on the actions of the wolf in cartoons such as *The Shooting of Dan McGoo.* Droopy also costarred in comic books featuring **Tom and Jerry,** usually in one-page gags.

DUCKANEER
Pedigree. Pirate duck of the comic book high seas.
Biography. Dexter is a comic book artist who lives in an apartment in Quackersville. Working late one night on his comic book Duckaneer, he falls asleep and finds himself in the adventure, as the swashbuckling hero himself. In the beginning, Dexter is the abused cabin boy of a human pirate captain. Befriended and coaxed along by Katrina "Kitty" Hawkins, the captain's unhappy (human) mate, the duck reluctantly stabs the captain to death and takes over the ship. Unfortunately, the crew has no intention of "taking orders from a duck" and makes him and Kitty walk the plank. ("I guess we blew it, ducky," she apologizes just before they take the plunge.) Dexter awakes, then, and vows to get out of the comic book business.

Comment. The character appeared just once, in Star*Reach Productions's *Quack* no. 1 in 1976. Duckaneer was created by Frank Brunner.

DUCK "BILL" PLATYPUS
Pedigree. Star of satirical comic book series.
Biography. The platypus wears a stovepipe hat, smokes a cigar, and lives with a slew of misanthropic animals at the Labraya Mud Pots [*sic*] in Tasmania. He loves nothing more than lounging on his back in the hot mud. The more or less reasonable, if gruff, Duck "Bill" is the sanest animal in the area; most of the others are fanatics and loons of one kind or another. "Coffee" Coughlin is a mustachioed dog who's addicted to java; McQueen Butterfly is hooked on doughnuts ("Aw, cruel cruller, why do I love thee so?"); Konko is a brutish cop-gorilla from Borneo; radical preacher Brother Froghorn is out to break the local frankfurter cult, which worships the evil god Hott Doggoth and wears wienie beanies ("They're slaves to a string of satanic sausages!"); fox Krystal Kringle, a New Age advocate, dresses like Santa; Kuddly Koala does "cuteness exercises," because cuteness is "where the mean moolah is." There are also Tub the hippo, who owns the local beanery; condor Cal Condom; the human cultist Guru Guggenheim; and human scientist Dr. B. F. Muleskinner.

Comment. Duck "Bill" Platypus was created by Kyle Rothweiler and first appeared in Fantagraphics Books's *Critters* nos. 34 to 37 in 1989; Duck Bill had his own one shot in the forty-first issue. The characters and strip are reminiscent of **Pogo Possum,** an ensemble that deals with political subjects—although the Duck "Bill" cast is more off the wall (in a thoroughly entertaining way) than Pogo's team. Another platypus was the star of Cine Group's *Ovide and the Gant,* which was set in the South Seas and included Cy the Snake and Bobo the Dodo. There were thirty-two half-hour episodes produced for TV syndication in 1988.

DUCKBOTS
Pedigree. Comic book robot-ducks.
Biography. Bad news for Dr. Francis Drake of Drake industries: He's spent years working on S.D.I. for the U.S. military, under the mistaken assumption that it stood for Strategic Duck Initiative. As a result, when he unveils a trio of towering duck-robots to the military, they laugh in his face. To teach the government a lesson for mocking him, Drake programs the robots, Brant, Widgeon, and Merganser, "to perform

wanton acts of evil destruction." Their first act is to mash Drake to a pulp, after which the three robots go on a rampage, crushing cars and buildings, firing destructive "nullifier" rays, and flying about. Even the superhero Mr. Wonderful is unable to stop them.

Comment. The characters appeared in just two issues of their own Blackthorne title, published in 1987. That's unfortunate, because the comic was quite amusing. Cliff MacGillivray says he created the characters because he wanted to do a comic "with a group of evil, fowl characters."

DUCKULA
Pedigree. The first comic book vampire duck in continuing adventures.
Biography. The vampire duck wears formal attire and a long black cape; he has green eyes and speaks with a Transylvanian accent. In the first of his two adventures, Duckula uses "coldly logical science" in his lab to create life . . . along with copies of other magazines. In his second appearance, he destroys publications that don't feature ducks. His "hairy henchman" is the lumbering Bearzanboltz, a brown Frankenstein Monster-like bear who was "spawned by a freak explosion in a toy factory."

Comment. Scott Shaw's creation appeared in the first two issues of Star★Reach Productions's *Quack* comic book (1976 to 1977). **Daffy Duck** had faced a Duckula, previously, in an issue of his Gold Key comic book and was scheduled to play a different Duckula in an unrealized feature film. In addition, see the most popular of the vampire ducks, **Count Duckula.**

DUCKY DUCKBILL
Pedigree. A comic book dinosaur duck.
Biography. Ducky is an orange, bipedal dinosaur that has a duck's head and webbed feet. He also has humanlike arms and webbed fingers, and is able to speak. In his one adventure, the plucky dinosaur falls in love with the married Alice Saurus . . . unaware that the carnivore is trying to lure him to her dinner table. When she and her husband are about to eat him (raw, with green onions), Ducky persuades them to let him cook himself "with orange sauce." When he leaves to get the oranges ("only recently evolved," he notes,) Ducky doesn't bother to come back. Ducky's good friend is Bronty the Brontosaurus.

Comment. This clever gem of a strip was created by Larry Gonick and appeared in the only issue of Pacific Comics's *Wild Animals,* published in 1982.

Other animals that appeared in the magazine were Dumphy Duck, the No-Luck Duck, a would-be comic book star whose magazines keep failing; Lackluster Lizard, a puritanical reptile who refuses to appear in underground comics; Harry the Canary, who reflects on captivity; Bungalow Bill Bunny, who is always trying to be something he isn't (a tough-talking CB'er, or the masked Rabbit Marauder); and Crawford Crow, who philosophizes about life while his friend Fremont Frog enjoys riding his tricycle.

DUKE "DESTROYER" DUCK
Pedigree. Aggressive comic book mallard from another dimension.
Biography. A construction worker on a world of anthropomorphic animals, Duke is in Ginger's Joynt when another duck (implicitly **Howard the Duck**) vanishes, drawn away by "extraneous combustin'." Sobered by the shortness and unpredictability of life, Duke gives it all up to find "somethin' more appealin'." He enlists in the special forces, then goes to college and graduates magna cum laude with degrees in criminology, physical education, and abnormal psychology. Becoming a detective, he's shocked one night when the vanished duck staggers into his apartment. Near death, he explains that he'd been sucked "into another space-time continuum . . . wh-where ducks can't t-talk . . . and *pink primates* c-call all . . . the shots!" Before expiring, he says that the most vile entity there was Godcorp, a multinational company that used him to make money, then sent him to a lab to find out "what made me t-tick." Duke promises to avenge the duck's death and, climbing into a special ship and crossing "nega-space," travels to our world. After killing Godcorp chief Ned Packer, Duke remains behind to right other wrongs on our sick planet. Another of Duke's powerful foes was the paraplegic Dr. Paraquat and his pet parakeet, the megalomaniacal leader of a colony of slaves infected with a new strain of venereal disease, "black syph." Apart from a duck's head and feet, and a covering of white down, Destroyer Duck has the physique of a human bodybuilder. The duck wears trousers and a T-shirt and is never without his green wool cap.

Comment. The character was created by writer Steve Gerber and legendary artist Jack Kirby, and seven issues were published by Eclipse Comics from 1982 to 1984. The character was conceived to raise money for a lawsuit between Gerber and Marvel Comics (the prototype for Godcorp, one assumes) regarding ownership of **Howard the Duck.** The title and lawsuit were discontinued when "a mutually agreeable settlement" was reached. Another very aggressive comic book duck was the Midnite Mallard, who starred in nos. 6 and 7 of Target Comics *Midnite Skulker* (1987). The waterfowl was costumed like Batman: a gray bodysuit with blue boots, gloves, trunks, cape, and cowl. In this parody of DC's multidimensional housecleaning series *Crisis on Infinite Earths,* the bird uses the power of the mystical Brooch of Darkness to defeat the human superheroes Captain Airehead, the Orange Crusher, Wanda Woman, and others, his goal being to "mix all the infinite dimensions together . . . to create a world so complex and convoluted that only *I* could understand it." Fortunately, he's defeated by Captain Continuity. Other animals seen in the magazine include Millard Mallard (second cousin to Hewey, Dewey, and Lewey [*sic*] and kin to Man-Drake the Musician) and Gopher Gus, a humanoid gopher.

DUMBO

Pedigree. Flying pachyderm of a novel and Disney feature.

Biography. A squadron of storks braves a nighttime storm to bring bundles of joy to Florida, where the circus has its winter headquarters. As neatly tied bags float to earth around her, the elephant Mrs. Jumbo waits expectantly for hers; alas, it never comes. The next morning, while the animals are loaded onto the train for the trip north, Mrs. Jumbo is still watching the skies. Elsewhere, a hapless stork stops on a cloud, breaks out a map, and tries to find the circus. Fortunately, he sees the train passing below, and flies down. He delivers a bundle to Mrs. Jumbo in the elephant car, and while the four gossipy lady elephants Matriarch, Prissy, Giggles, and Catty look on, she unwraps the parcel. There's a baby elephant, and Mrs. Jumbo names him Jumbo, Jr. The other pachyderms think he's cute as can be—until he sneezes and his huge ears unfurl. They taunt him and call him "Dumbo," but his mother ignores them. She swaddles the babe in its ears, and cuddles up with it. The train reaches its destination in a raging storm, but men and elephants both work to raise the big top (a sequence of breathtaking fury and beauty). When the skies clear there's a parade, and Dumbo's in it; unfortunately, he trips over his ears, lands in a mud puddle, and the onlookers laugh. But that's not the worst of it. When the circus opens, kids come over and tease him, one blowing hard into his ears to see them billow. Mrs. Jumbo spanks the heartless boy with her trunk, and circus attendants rush over. She's

whipped and goes wild, hurling circus workers everywhere; roped and shackled, she's deemed a "mad elephant" and is locked in a cage. Dumbo is alone now, and can't help but overhear the other elephant ladies declare that he has "ears only a mother could love," and other cruel things. Observing the scene is a small mouse dressed in a ringmaster's costume and foraging for peanuts. Offended by their actions, he mutters to himself, "What's the matter with those ears? I don't see nothin' wrong with them. I think they're cute!" The mouse watches as the forlorn Dumbo walks over to the women-elephants, and they turn away; shocked, the mouse says, "So, you like to pick on little guys?" and runs after them, scaring the elephants good. Dumbo has crawled into a haystack to mope, and, coaxing him out, the rodent introduces himself as Timothy Mouse. He tells Dumbo that what the elephant needs is a good act to build some self-confidence. Overhearing the circus manager talking about an act involving an elephant pyramid, Timothy waits until the man is asleep, then whispers in his ear that Dumbo should be at the top of the pyramid. When the man awakes, eureka! He decides to put Dumbo on top of the pyramid. But the act is a disaster. Dumbo makes his entrance, slips, and collides with the bottom elephant. In a scene of unparalleled cartoon destruction, the pile of elephants collapses, destroying everything in the tent and finally pulling down the big top itself. For this, Dumbo is made to act with the clowns, leaping from the top of a burning building into a tub of goop. Dumbo is mortified after the first performance, and Timothy gives him a bath while trying to boost his spirits. They try not to listen to the clowns drinking and laughing at him in a nearby tent. Still, Dumbo begins to cry, and Timothy decides to take him to see his mother. In a scene second only to the death of **Bambi's** mother as a guaranteed tear-jerker, Mrs. Jumbo extends her trunk through the bars of her cage and rocks her teary-eyed son. Dumbo is happy, and he and Timothy return to their part of the circus where they drink from a trough . . . unaware that one of the clowns has inadvertently tossed a bottle of booze into it. The next thing Dumbo and Timothy know, they're seeing pink elephants with trumpets for trunks. And that's just for starters. The elephants break into smaller and smaller elephants, then become camels, snakes, belly dancers, canoes, fountains, skaters, and even dancing partners to electric arcs. Then it begins raining elephants in slow motion, pachyderms that slowly transform into clouds . . . and dawn. Timothy and Dumbo are awakened by the leader of the group of four other crows, who asks them what they're doing up in a tree. Timothy doesn't believe the bird, but when he and Dumbo look down—sure enough, he realizes they're way up in a tree. They panic and fall to the ground, and while they walk away, Timothy tries to figure out how they got up there. The crows suggest that maybe they flew. The mouse realizes, yes, that has to be it: Dumbo *flew* them up there. Realizing that a flying elephant would be "the ninth wonder of the universe" and an unqualified smash in the circus, he's determined to find out if that is, in fact, what happened. He and the crows lead Dumbo to the edge of a high cliff. One of the birds gives Dumbo a "magic feather," which he tells the elephant will help him to fly. The mouse and birds shove the elephant off the edge of the cliff, Timothy scurries into the small clown hat Dumbo is still wearing, and the pachyderm soars. Back at the circus, Dumbo once again takes his place atop the burning building— Timothy in his cap, the "magic feather" clutched tightly in his trunk. He leaps, and loses the feather; he also loses his confidence, and as they plummet earthward, Timothy gives him a fast, frantic pep talk. At the last possible second, Dumbo pulls out of the fall and flies over the tub of goop. As circus goers gawk, Dumbo dive-bombs the mean clowns, then makes a pass over a peanut vendor, sucks up a mass of peanuts in his trunk, flies toward the nasty lady elephants, and machine-guns them with peanuts. A succession of newspaper headlines announce that Dumbo sets an altitude record, that Dumbombers are being built by the air force (planes with Dumbo heads and wings), and, finally, that the elephant and his manager, Timothy, have just signed a fat Hollywood contract. But Dumbo stays with the circus— ensconced in his own sleek, private rail car where his freed mother lounges in comfort.

Comment. At sixty-three minutes, *Dumbo* is one of Walt Disney's shortest feature cartoons. Ed Brophy provided the voice for Timothy Mouse; Dumbo did not speak. The 1941 film was based on the novel by Helen Aberson and Harold Pearl, published in 1940 (Disney read the book in galley form). It's an excellent film, although unusually sloppy by Disney standards, e.g., noses, tail feathers, and other parts of characters disappear where animators forgot to draw them for several frames. However, that doesn't detract from the irresistible appeal of the feature. In comic books, Dumbo starred in sixteen issues of a gas-station giveaway in 1942, and in three issues of Dell's *4-Color*, among other one-shot titles.

See also the Disney elephant **Dolores.** In comic strips, the elephant had himself a new job in "The Substitute Stork," which ran for several months in the Sunday strip "Walt Disney's Treasury of Classic Tales." On television, the Disney Channel cable service has been airing *Dumbo's Circus* since 1986; the show is set in the circus and stars actors in animal costumes.

DYNOMUTT
Pedigree. Superhero dog of TV cartoons.
Biography. Bumbling sidekick to the costumed superhero Blue Falcon (whom he refers to familiarly as "BF"), Dynomutt is described by the theme song as being, "Stronger than a train with a so-so brain, he's fearless, scareless, a little too careless." The robotic Dog Wonder helps to fight crime in Big City, using supergadgets whose numbers are apparently endless. (Although they don't prevent Dynomutt from getting tired, and he has been heard to mutter, "I'm demanding I get a lube job every six months or one thousand bad guys—whichever comes first.") Among his powers are superstrength, derived from a "strength power pack" in his belt; the ability to stretch his torso to virtually any length at any angle; the ability to extend his head like a battering ram, suddenly and with great speed (also useful when he's relaxing, because he can fetch a stick without moving); legs that contain "dyno springs" to cushion him when he falls (which is sometimes from thousands of feet); a tail that also becomes a coil, allowing him to hop around like a pogo stick; a "dyno-automatic defrost cycle," which can protect him from frigid temperatures (useful when they fight the ice-generating Mr. Cool); a jet engine stored in his back for quick pursuit (he also has a propeller for hovering); a hacksaw, scissors, and even an electric shaver hidden in his hand; suction cup feet, which allow him to scale sheer walls; "dyno gift wrap" ability, which means his arms can extend to great lengths and wrap around a foe; a spotlight nose; sonar; a parachute (no doubt a backup in case his spring-legs fail); and many gadgets stored inside his chest, accessed by pressing its *D* emblem. These include a tool chest, a communicator, a television, a "mirrormatic" shield for reflecting enemy ray blasts, a "dyno dynamic automatic ice maker," and even the yellow pages. Dynomutt's controls are located in a panel in his back; if anyone tries to mess with them, a "dyno-antitheft circuit" is activated, and a pincer comes out and grabs the tinkerer. The canine hero is also a master of disguise, able to transform himself

into everything from a fishing rod to a chair to a vacuum cleaner to suck up evidence. Blue Falcon always carries additional power packs that, when plugged into the dog's head, can increase the animal's size and/or strength. The gray dog has a voice like Art Carney's Ed Norton; stands approximately four feet tall on his hind legs; and wears a blue-green costume referred to as the dog's "wonder wear," consisting of a cowl, short cape, boots, gloves, and a blue harness with a yellow *D* on the front. He usually walks on all fours, but can also stand upright. Dynomutt lives with the Falcon (a k a Radley Crown) in a penthouse apartment known as the Falcon Lair, which is where the mysterious figure Focus One calls whenever there's a case that requires the heroes' talents. The two get about town in the flying Falcon Car, which is hidden beneath a pool in the penthouse. Dynomutt is responsible for getting it out while the Falcon suits up; more often than not, the dim dog forgets to drain the pool, and the heroes hop into bucket seats filled with water. Among the heroes' greatest foes have been the Harbor Robber, Tin Kong, the Injustice League of America, the Red Vulture, the Wizard of Ooze, and the Queen Hornet.

Comment. Although Dynomutt's relentless stupidity has a way of grating, the constant flow of dopey gadgets is good for a laugh. The dog was created to capitalize on the popularity of a hound he very much resembles, **Scooby-Doo.** Hanna-Barbera produced sixteen half-hour adventures, which aired on ABC's *Scooby Doo/Dynomutt Hour* beginning in 1976. The character later guest starred on other series. Frank Welker provided the dog's voice; Gary Owens was Blue Falcon. Marvel Comics published six issues of *Dynomutt* from 1977 to 1978. The character also appeared in Marvel's *Scooby Doo* starting with no. 1 (all nine issues, 1977 to 1979) and *Laff-a-lympics* (all thirteen issues, 1978 to 1979).

EB'NN THE RAVEN

Pedigree. Comic book hit-bird.

Biography. Eb'nn—nicknamed the Slayer—has a muscular, human body (except for the layer of blue feathers), and a raven's head. Traveling about with his friend Jack Rabbit, Eb'nn says he hires himself out "for one thing, profit." However, he always manages to take assignments in which his victim deserves to be destroyed—such as the evil evangelist-bird Dr. Feelwell and his brainwashed minions. Dressed in a purple cape and tight gray costume, Eb'nn carries a sword and smokes a cigar.

Comment. *Eb'nn* no. 1 was published by Crowquill Comics in 1985; the comic switched to Now Comics with no. 3. The popular character was created by writer Mike Dimpsey and artist Chris Ecker.

Eb'nn the Raven in a characteristic snit. © CROWQUILL COMICS.

EEK AND MEEK

Pedigree. Comic strip mice.

Biography. Eek wears a bowler, is perpetually drunk and, when he isn't flat on his back asleep, he's playing the bugle. He has an opinion about everything. Meek wears nothing, is rather timid, plays the cello, and is perpetually mystified by the world. Together,

Howie Schneider's underrated **Eek** *(right) and* **Meek.**
© NEWSPAPER ENTERPRISES ASSOCIATION.

they make an ideal pair. Typical of their exchanges are these:

> MEEK: The Bill of Rights guarantees everyone the right of free speech!
> EEK: Oh, shut up!

And:

> MEEK: In my search for the girl best suited for me . . . I shall leave no stone unturned!
> EEK: Good . . . because that's probably where you'll find her.

Meek's girlfriend is the curly-haired Monique, whom he tries unsuccessfully to get to marry him; alas, she's sweet on Eek. The mice had one of their funniest exchanges on the subject:

> MEEK: Monique says she can't stand the sight of me.
> EEK: Fight back! Show her you got guts!
> MEEK: I did! Now she says she hates my guts!

Other mice in the strip are the hipster Cyrano, slumlord J. Paul Ghetto, the feuding Seymour and Bernice, the student Luvable (who was especially confused, in the 1960s, by campus unrest), and the sleazy insurance sales-mouse Fieldstone. The mice live in holes in the ground in a rather barren field.

Comment. Howie Schneider's wonderful "Eek & Meek" made its newspaper debut in 1965. "Eek & Meek" has always focused on the issues of the day, including censorship, the environment, equal rights, and welfare. After twelve years, though, Eek and Meek weren't reaching as wide an audience as they should have, and Schneider made the dramatic change of metamorphosing them into a pair of gawky young men!

EGBERT
Pedigree. Comic book chicken.
Biography. Egbert is a timid, clumsy chicken and is constantly being undermined by "his sly pal" the Count, a fox who dresses in a top hat, jacket and vest, bow tie, and spats. At first, the fox wanted to eat Egbert who, through dumb luck rather than guile, always managed to escape. Later, they became involved in various failed business enterprises. ("I asked for *ice*, Count. What's the idea of bringing me *water?*" The fox's reply: "I got this for *half-price!*") Skinny, with big eyes and a long neck, Egbert has a bulb-shaped body, yellow feathers, and a trio of black-tipped tail feathers. He usually dresses in a blue blazer.

Comment. The character starred in twenty issues of his own Quality Comics title, which lasted from 1946 to 1950.

ELECTRA
Pedigree. Pet owned by Cathy of the comic strips.
Biography. Cathy says she's lived alone long enough. She tells her mother that all her friends "hurry home from work to be with their husbands" and adds that she's finally ready to make a real commitment." Cathy's mother is thrilled until Cathy says, "I'm going to get a dog." She heads to the humane society, where a small, "brown, scraggly mutt"

Electra *trying to act cool . . . and failing.* © UNIVERSAL PRESS SYNDICATE.

sits in a cage, admonishing itself not to look too interested, or too blasé. Cathy picks it, then selects the name, which means "dazzling, brilliant beauty." Not surprisingly, Cathy's mother immediately assumes the role of "grandmother," spoiling Electra with toys and giving her daughter advice on how to raise it. Cathy's boyfriend, Irving, also undermines the training process, letting the dog up on the furniture, feeding her when she begs, and allowing her to chew on his sweater. For Electra's part, she's learned that Cathy is most generous with snacks and toys when the bathroom scale's been altered (clandestinely, of course, by using the nose to adjust the dial), and that the best way to train Cathy is to bug her in the middle of the night, "sleep deprivation [being] the foundation of all great obedience programs." Electra has also found joy in taking Cathy literally: Chastised for chewing on her master's shoes, the dog is told "never, never, never" to eat shoes again. So she goes right for the boots. Electra can be a pain in other ways: She is a terrible watchdog, loves to eat magazines, took a long time to housebreak (she thought the papers were out so she could read about **Snoopy**), and still refuses to heel. Nonetheless, Cathy treats her so well that Irving's decided he wants "to be reincarnated as a dog." People cookies are the dog's favorite food.

Comment. The dog was introduced in the strip in 1988, inspired by creator Cathy Guisewite's own dog, Trolley.

ELFALUMP
Pedigree. A comic book goblin-elephant from **Pogo** creator Walt Kelly.

Biography. Arriving in "a little hidden glen" by wagon, a group of goblins decide to make it their home. In addition to four shape-changing creatures there's Elfalump, a pink elephant wearing a military cap. While Elfalump is cooking dinner, a fairy crawls from under a cabbage leaf and tells the goblins that the fairy queen is a prisoner of the gnomes—the "sworn enemies" of goblins. Elfalump and the goblins wage war on the gnomes and rescue the queen, escorting her home in a wagon drawn by mice. The hot-tempered Elfalump is the most interesting of the five goblins.

Comment. The character appeared in the "Goblin Glen" tale in *Four-Color* no. 114, *Fairy Tale Parade*, published by Dell in 1946. The goblins have a decidedly Pogoesque look in this delightful story. See also Kelly's **Bunson Bunny.**

ELSIE THE COW
Pedigree. Mascot for Borden Company's milk products.

Biography. The brown Jersey cow, her big-eyed and smiling face staring out at consumers from a large daisy, is the wife of Elmer the Bull. The couple has twins, Beulah and Beauregard, born when Borden celebrated its centennial in 1957.

Comment. Elsie was created in 1938. When the logo appeared at the Borden exhibit in the New York World's Fair of 1939, fairgoers demanded to see Elsie in the flesh; a cow named "You'll Do Lobelia" was pressed into service. She remained a popular attraction at the fair and, afterward, on tour nationwide. The cartoon likeness appeared in magazine advertisements throughout the 1940s, and with the growth of television in the early 1950s, Elsie became an animated star of Borden commercials. Her mate Elmer was introduced in 1940. He finally galloped out from the shadow of being "Mr. Elsie" when he was named the mascot for the company's new glue product Elmer's Glue in 1951. Elsie starred in three issues of her own D. S. comic book from 1949 to 1950. After fifteen years in retirement, Elsie returned to TV in June of 1990 with an all-new animated ad.

EPIC
Pedigree. Hopeless mount of the bird-brained comic strip cowboy Tumbleweeds.

Biography. The word *swayback* could have been coined to describe this brown horse with the Moe Howard haircut and matted tail, which drags behind him for several yards. Utterly lethargic, the horse chews tobacco, and about the only time he moves is when he spits—usually after Tumbleweeds has played a tune on the guitar. Once, in order to get work from a local rancher, Tumbleweeds goes to Sagebrush Sam's Used Horses lot to try and trade Epic for a good horse. As soon as Tumbleweeds rides in, Sam says, "You're gonna offer to trade that four legged plug-ugly for one o' my horses! . . . I'm gonna laugh in your face!" Another time, Tumbleweeds leaves a "for sale" sign on the horse, gets no takers, and switches it to "finders keepers." He finally realizes, however, that he could never part with this "cavalry reject that lives on fermented oats an' brings snickers an' guffaws as we ride by!" Based in the appropriately named town of Grimy Gulch, Tumbleweeds is occasionally able to stir Epic to help him flee the local tribe of Indians and the unwanted advances of the homely spinster Hildegard

Hamhocker. Epic has a dry sense of humor, however, and enjoys stopping short, so Tumbleweeds goes flying over his head. Another animal seen in the strip is Beaumont the vulture, the mascot of Claude Clay, the town undertaker. A relatively recent addition to the strip has been Pajamas, a ragged-looking mutt described by Tumbleweeds as "the world's laziest dog," a dog who wants to howl at the moon but won't, because it's "too much effort."

Comment. Tom K. Ryan's "Tumbleweeds" is a wonderful send-up of western clichés. It first appeared in 1965. Another unfit comic strip horse is Loco. The timorous steed is owned by the Indian Redeye, and his cowardice frequently undercuts the brave's dreams of conquest and glory. Both appear in the Gordon Bess "Redeye" strip, which began in September 1967.

ERMA FELNA

Pedigree. Comic book space-cat and soldier.

Biography. Flight Commander Erma Felna is a humanoid cat and the leader of a unit in the space-spanning Extraplanetary Defense Force, the military arm of the planet-colonizing government ConFed. When the world of Derzon is invaded, the commander leads her troops into battle—rejecting the suggestion of her lover Tavas Ikalik to transfer off the active duty roster. Wounded during the successful battle, Erma is sent to Ekosiak to recover. There

happen to be hints of a local rebellion, and shortly after she's back on duty, Erma and her superior, the fox Colonel Hitzok, lead a team that defuses a terrorist's nuclear bomb in the heart of Hicho. Shortly thereafter, they suppress an uprising of animals who resent the military presence on the world. Hitzok is wounded during the assault, and Erma is placed in command of the Home Guard Troops as revolution seethes. While that's bad for ConFed, it's good for Erma, whose star rises and she begins her rise to an interplanetary command. Other soldier animals seen in the strip include Dael Valderzha, an otter; Colonel Jones, a duck; and Captain Itzak Arrat, a horse and a friend of the Felna family. Arrat is in charge of an EDF space destroyer, and his adventures among ore-pilferers in the Chishata Asteroid Belt comprise a major subplot of the saga.

Comment. The character made her debut in *Albedo* no. 0 [*sic,*] published in 1985 by Thoughts and Images. The saga lasted for all fifteen issues of the title, and was reprinted in the subsequent, short-lived *Command Review* (1987). Creator Steven A. Gallacci wrote a very literate, complex, politically intriguing tale that deserves more attention than it received. Gallacci was also responsible for the *Birthright* series that ran in *Critters* (see **Lionheart**). A slightly different animal soldier is Boomer Blue, the kangaroo fighter of the future in Innovation's *Newstralia* comic book (1989).

FARLEY

Pedigree. Contemporary comic strip dog.

Biography. The massive black-and-white sheepdog owned by the Patterson family is a typical gentle comic strip lug: He likes to sleep and eat (and not just the cake, but the birthday candles as well) and would rather drink from the toilet than from his dish. When sent outside to chase the cat away, he ends up singing with it, but when sleeping outside, he will chase cats from the garden when his owner is looking. He curls up on the sofa and refuses to be shooed away and snubs Barfo Bits for human food (although he can be fooled into eating the Bits if they're placed in a plate and scraped onto his dish). However, easygoing Farley can be vengeful: Left outside one snowy day, the dog howls and howls and no one lets him in. When young Elizabeth finally comes in from playing, the snow-covered dog walks over to her lazy brother Michael and shakes off on him. Of course, it's no wonder the dog is spoiled: El, the woman of the house, is constantly saying things like, "Does a wittle woofie want his ears scratched?" and "Does he want his tummy rubbed? Yes, he does!!"

Comment. The dog appears in Lynn Johnston's terrific daily and Sunday strip "For Better or For Worse," which debuted on September 9, 1979. The pet was based on Johnston's own sheepdog Farley; Johnston had previously drawn cartoon books beginning with *David, We're Pregnant!* in 1974, in which the pooch Ashley was seen occasionally.

FAT FREDDY'S CAT

Pedigree. Towering figure among underground comic cats.

Biography. The scrawny orange cat with the black-striped tail belongs to Freddy of the Fabulous Furry Freak Brothers (the other siblings being Franklin and Phineas). The cat—who has no name—loves prowling the city streets, making it with chicks and getting into fights (razor blade in hand, he sings, "I'm an *ornery* cuss / and I'm *so* full of *piss* / if I don't like your looks / I'll hit you with *this!*") When he stays at home, the cat loves to torture the local cockroach population (although he's been known to tell them where food is hidden, so Freddy will throw it out, enabling the cat to eat it). However, he loves to taunt Freddy most of all, not only with little misdeeds—sleeping on his face or urinating on his typewriter—but by clever tricks, such as doing all kinds of acrobat maneuvers, then sitting deadstill when his master's gotten the camera. Because the cat enjoys drinking from the toilet, he'll pee in the drink of anyone who forgets to flush. He's also been known to unplug the refrigerator when he doesn't like what's in his cat dish—again, forcing Freddy to ditch the spoiled food, thus allowing the cat and his friends to have a party in the alley. His pet peeves are dry cat food, a dirty litter box (in protest, he'll defecate on Freddy's pillow, in his boots, in flowerpots, or in the stereo headphones), and being called kitty. His most remarkable talent is the ability to detect the sound of Freddy's can opener opening cat food from blocks away. The cat talks to the reader, and occasionally to other human characters—although much to the cat's frustration, they don't understand him.

Comment. The clever and funny cat was created by Gilbert Shelton (**Wonder Wart-Hog**), and first appeared in "The Fabulous Furry Freak Brothers." That comic strip began appearing in the *L.A. Free-Press* in 1967, with the separate cat strip tagged on. The Freak Brothers moved to comic books in 1971, where their collected adventures lasted six very successful issues from Rip Off Press. Rip Off also published five issues of *The Adventures of Fat Freddy's Cat* (1977 to 1980), then resurrected the title in 1988.

FATKAT

Pedigree. Hedonistic, chubby comic strip cat owned by Trudy.

Biography. A black cat with long, crinkled whiskers, Fatkat is a feline who enjoys his leisure. His daily routine is: 1:00 P.M.—lunch, nap, look out window, nap, dinner, nap; 2:00 A.M.—meet the boys. Whenever he breaks his routine, it's invariably for mischief. He likes sneaking onto the scale, unseen, to jack-up Trudy's weight; staring intently out the window when Trudy's husband Ted is in the easy chair, waiting for Ted to come and see what's going on, then dashing into the chair; and reading **Mickey Mouse** comics to taunt his nemesis, the mouse Gaylord. Fatkat also enjoys the ladies, and has been a father at least once—but nothing pleases him as

Jerry Marcus's **Fatkat** *and his friend Gaylord.* © KING F
TURES SYNDICATE.

much as a bowl of cream. He does typical cat things like playing with string, albeit reluctantly. ("They throw you a ball of string and expect you to go into ecstasies!" he laments, then dives in. "On the other hand, it's hard to break a habit of centuries!") As for Gaylord, he's a cultured mouse in a cloak and top hat, who's always one-upping Fatkat, whether it's building a better snowman, or wearing a classier T-shirt (Fatkat is proud of his cat-shirt until Gaylord strolls by with one featuring the Battle of Waterloo). Another pet in the household is the big sheepdog Rodney, who belongs to Trudy and Ted's son, Crawford.

Comment. Jerry Marcus's characters debuted in the "Trudy" strip in 1963, although Fatkat didn't come along until 1974. The strip is still going strong.

FAUNTLEROY FOX
Pedigree. A middle-class, highly explosive animated cartoon and comic book fox.
Biography. Fauntleroy lives in a pleasant suburban house and drives a blue convertible. He is outwardly calm and rational, but is easily driven into wild rages by Crawford C. Crow, who lives in a tree on his property, drives a red convertible, and is always after food, money, or anything belonging to Fauntleroy. (The Fox once wailed, "According to this list I made, that crow has more of my belongings than I have!"). Crawford originally spoke with a strong Brooklyn accent, but that was later discarded. Perhaps the most ingenious of Crawford's schemes to get inside Fauntleroy's house was to print his own obituary in the newspaper, along with an ad announcing that his remains were available from the Stuffit Taxidermy Parlor. Fauntleroy read the notice and purchased the crow for his mantle—after which Crawford pretended to be his own ghost and had the run of the place. The only other problem in the Fox's life are fox hounds, which chase him now and then. (Once, coming to warn him of their approach, the Crow snidely remarked, "Be seein' youse aroun' sometime! Around some girlie's neck, dat is!") The brown-furred Fauntleroy always wears blue trousers, white gloves, and a red bow tie. The Crow wears a purple top hat and, in the early cartoons and comic book stories, smoked a cigar.

Comment. These characters were created by writer/director Frank Tashlin and made their debut in Columbia Pictures's theatrical short *The Fox and the Grapes* in 1941. In it, the Fox suffered various indignities while trying in vain to get grapes the crow dangles before him. There were sixteen cartoons in all (the last was released in 1949), and their madcap pace and semisadistic nature clearly inspired the tone of the later Warner Brothers cartoons (for example, **Road Runner, Daffy Duck,** and **Bugs Bunny**). In comic books, they first appeared in DC Comics's *Real Screen Funnies* no. 1 in 1945 and remained in that magazine until they got their own title in 1951. *Fox and the Crow* had a remarkable run of 108 issues, after which it was turned over to *Stanley and His Monster.* The characters also appeared in *Comic Cavalcade* beginning with no. 30 in 1948. A back-up feature in early issues of *Fox and the Crow* was *The Hound and the Hare,* which consisted of a dumb pup named Shep constantly chasing a canny orange rabbit. (A whistling tea kettle inside a hollow log is enough to convince the dog that the 5:15 is coming at him from inside the log.) Most foxes in comic books and cartoons have tended to be nameless, one-dimensional villains. However, in addition to Fauntleroy (and resembling him more than a little!), other foxes who had continuing strips of some note were Foxy Fagan, who starred in seven issues of his own Dearfield title (1946 to 1948), and Sharpy Fox, who starred in Marvel's *Comics for Kids,* which lasted two issues in 1945, as well is in various other titles.

FEARLESS FLY
Pedigree. Superheroic TV insect.
Biography. Hiram Fly is a timid little fellow who lives in "an unassuming matchbox" behind someone's picket fence. However, when trouble looms, he dons his big, square "supersonic glasses" and becomes Fearless Fly. Able to fly (what fly can't?), the hero is "speedier than a ray of light," has super-strength, and boasts X-ray vision, which penetrates everything but lead. His one weakness is spiders. Fearless Fly's foes include the 972-year-old Asian megalomaniac, the human Dr. Goo Fee; the seductress Lady Deflylah; Ferocious Fly; and Napoleon Bonefly. As Fearless Fly, the insect wears red trunks, a red shirt with a white *F* on the chest, and a brown helmet with antennae that form an atomic symbol that can spin and cut like a buzzsaw. The hero's girlfriend is Florrie; his best friend is Horsie the Horsefly.

Fauntleroy Fox and his nemesis, Crawford C. Crow, in a typical situation. © DC COMICS.

Comment. Hal Seeger Productions made twenty-six episodes of *Fearless Fly*, which were syndicated in 1965 on the *Milton the Monster Show*. Bob McFadden provided the voice. Other segments of Milton's show featured Penny Penguin, a well-meaning but clumsy young bird, and cowboy-sleuth Flukey Luke, who rode the horse Pronto. Gold Key published one issue of a *Milton the Monster and Fearless Fly* comic book (1966).

FEIVEL MOUSEKOWITZ

Pedigree. Motion picture star.
Biography. In Shostka, Russia, 1885, the Mouse-kowitz mouse family lives in a mousehole in the home of the Moskowitz human family. Young Feivel Mousekowitz and his sister, Tanya, delight in Papa's violin playing, as well as his tales of that mythical giant, the Great Mouse of Minsk, which chased all the cats away. They also revel in his tales of America, where "there are mouseholes in every wall." When a pogrom results in the burning of the village—with mustachioed Cossack cats attacking the mice while their human counterparts burn and loot—the Mousekowitzes head to Hamburg, Germany, and board a ship bound for America. During the passage, a storm strikes and Feivel loses the hat his father had given him, a cap that had been in the family for generations. He chases it, braving the waters sweeping the deck; losing his footing, he grabs a handy herring and is carried overboard. The Mouse-kowitzes continue the journey with heavy hearts, signing in at the mouse corner of Ellis Island and trying to begin their new life. Meanwhile, Feivel has managed to crawl inside a bottle and reaches shore. After the top-hatted seabird Henri gives him a bath and encouragement, Feivel sets out to try to find his family. Instead, he meets Warren T. Rat, who's assisted by the cockroach Digit. They sell the boy to the owner of a sweatshop, where the lad is put to work. But Feivel isn't beaten: That night, with the aide of fellow mouse Tony Toponi, he strings rags together, and they climb from the window to freedom. They pass an anticat rally the next day, where Tony falls for the organizer, Bridget. The sweet lady mouse suggests that Feivel see Honest John, a politician who "knows everybody" in town. Alas, he doesn't know the Mousekowitzes, so Feivel stays with Bridget (and Tony) at her loft in a water tower. The following day, at an even larger rally organized by Gussie Mausheimer, Feivel timidly suggests that a solution to the cat problem might be to build a Great

Mouse of Minsk. The mice agree, and work begins in an abandoned building at the waterfront (although Feivel's family is at the rally, they fail to see him because a big lady is standing in front of them . . . and they don't hear him because he whispers). En route to the waterfront, Feivel hears violin music from a sewer and, thinking it's his father, goes to investigate. Instead, he finds a bunch of cats with Warren T. Rat playing the music—only Rat's not a rat, he's a cat in disguise. Feivel is startled, yells, and Rat's poker-playing cats drop their hands and give chase. Caught and put in a bird cage, Feivel is freed by the big, puffy cat Tiger, who feels sorry for the kid. Not so the other cats: The mouse heads for the waterfront, Rat's feline felons in pursuit. Luckily, the Great Mouse is finished, and the rodents unleash the towering, wheeled, wooden figure. It crashes through the wall, spitting Roman candles and swinging its great tail, and the cats are backed up to the water. Warren T. Rat is carried off the pier when the mouse goes over, and the other cats flee. The fireworks start a blaze, and when firefighters arrive their hoses wash Feivel away from the triumphant mice. Tony calls for him, Papa Mousekowitz hears Tony, and, with Bridget, Mama Mousekowitz, and Tanya, they climb onto Tiger's back and go searching—Papa playing his violin. Feivel hears him, the family is reunited, Henri and his birds give the group an aerial tour of their new home—and the newly completed Statue of Liberty winks at the immigrant mice as they fly by.

Comment. Phillip Glasser was the voice of Feivel, Pat Musick was Tony, Cathianne Blore played Bridget, John Finnegan was Warren T. Rat, Dom DeLuise was Tiger, Madeline Kahn played Gussie, Nehemiah Persoff was Papa, Erica Yohn played Mama, Christopher Plummer was Henri, and Amy Green was Tanya. The characters starred in the 1986 Universal feature film *An American Tail*, which was superbly animated by Don Bluth and his staff, based on a story by Judy Freudberg, Tony Geiss, and David Kirschner. Steven Spielberg produced the film, which not only provided the mouse with his name (after the filmmaker's grandfather) but gave the film its lead feet and smarmy sentimentality. Disney characters tend to grow, change, and interact; Spielberg characters are either sages or wiseacres from day one, who move viewers by being subjected to contrived traumas. Feivel returned in a sequel, *An American Tail 2* in 1991, in which the heroic little mouse went west. See also Spielberg's **Littlefoot**. Bluth (see

1

2

1. *Not only are the* **ALIEN DUCKLINGS** *fun but, with tongue in cheek, the editorial (the "Intro-duck-shun") compared them favorably with Proust's* Swann's Way *and Ibsen's* The Wild Duck. © CLIFF MacGILLIVRAY AND ANDY ICE.
2. *From the left:* **ANDY PANDA**, **WOODY WOODPECKER**, *and* **CHILLY WILLY.** © 1957 WALTER LANTZ PRODUCTIONS, INC. *All rights reserved. *A registered trademark of and licensed by* WALTER LANTZ PRODUCTIONS, INC.
3. **ATOMIC MOUSE** *about to end the luck of Shadow (left) and* **COUNT GATTO**.
4. **BABY SNOOTS** *anchored by the grouchy Uptite Mouse.* © WESTERN PUBLISHING CO.

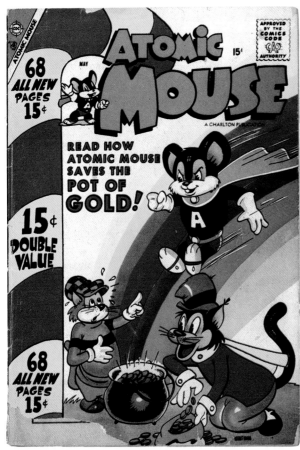

3

4

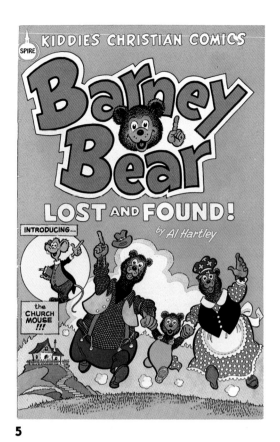

5

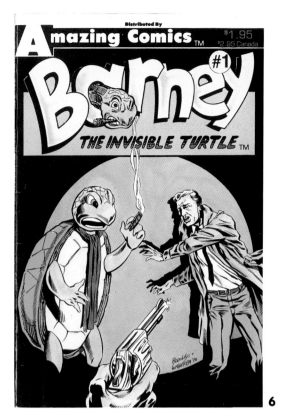

6

7

5. **BARNEY BEAR (2)** *and family.*
© Fleming H. Revell Company.

6. *That's Ted Gavin on the right, and*
BARNEY THE INVISIBLE TURTLE *on*
the left. © Rick Rodolfo.

7. **BELFRY** *gives Hot Stuff a hard time.*
© Harvey Publications.

8. *The burden of leadership—***BLACK**
FURY *frets over his herd in a time*
of drought. © Charlton Comics.

8

9

10

11

12

9. *The oh-so-mature* **CAPTAIN JACK**. © Fantagraphics Books.
10. **CHAUNCEY CHIRP** *(right) and his pal Johnny Jay.*
11. *The rip-snortin'* **COLT, ARMADILLO THAT WON THE WEST**. © K-Z Comics Group.
12. **COMET THE SUPER-HORSE, KRYPTO, BEPPO THE SUPER-MONKEY,** *and* **STREAKY THE SUPER-CAT** *tackle Superboy and members of the Legion of Super-Heroes.* © DC Comics.
13. **COSMO CAT**, *heroic. . .and verbose.*

13

14

15

16

17

14. *The dull-witted* **CREEPY CAT**.
15. **CROW OF THE BEAR CLAN** *struggles to make lizard shish kebab.* © EDWARD LUENA AND KEN HOOPER.
16. *A canine not to be trifled with:* **DALGODA**. © JAN STRNAD AND DENNIS FUJITAKE.
17. **DARO** *subdues a stranger.*

18. **DEPUTY DAWG** *puts Elmer to sleep (understandably) with a reading from Hist'ry of th' Dawg Clan.* © SPOTLIGHT COMICS. *Courtesy of Jim Main.*
19. **DESDEMONA** *calls for help in a panel from 1947.*
20. **DINKY DUCK**. *His terror comes from being told how often he'll have to be dunked in a fish tank in his temporary job as an advertising mascot.*
21. *Even stranded on an ice floe,* **DOLLAR**'s *sensitive sniffer detects food.* © HARVEY PUBLICATIONS. *Art by* ERNIE COLON.
22. *Sheldon Mayer's* **DOODLES DUCK** *and Lemuel.* © DC COMICS.

23

24

25

26

23. *Doug Marlette's*
    DORIS THE PARAKEET.
    © Tribune Media Services.
    Reprinted by permission.
24. *He's armed to the bill
    and he means business:*
    DUKE "DESTROYER" DUCK.
    Art © 1984 by Frank Miller.
25. *Fetch?* **DYNOMUTT**
    *simply stretches his neck to
    reach the stick.*
    © Hanna-Barbera Productions.
26. **EPIC** *may be a swayback,
    but he's in better shape than
    many of the people in
    Tom K. Ryan's strip.* ©
    Register and Tribune Syndicate.
27. *The philosophical*
    FEARLESS FLY.
    © Hal Seeger Productions.

27

28.

28. **FUMBLES** (note the foorwear!) gives Beverly
a hard time. © Hanna-Barbera Productions.
29. **GRANDMA DUCK**: not one for sloppiness.
© The Walt Disney Company.
All rights reserved.
30. The toothless **GUMMY** and his master.
© 1991 Marvel Entertainment Group.
All rights reserved.
31. The prognathous Katnip chases the feisty
HERMAN THE MOUSE. Note the knife and fork.
© Harvey Publications.

29

30

31

32. HOPPY, THE CAPTAIN MARVEL BUNNY, *with Benny Beaver visible through the left porthole, and Hoppy's nonsuper alter ego visible through the right.*

33. IRWIN, THE DISCO DUCK, *dances with Ringy of the Wibble Wabble Singers.* © Peter Pan Industries. *Courtesy Marty Kasen.*

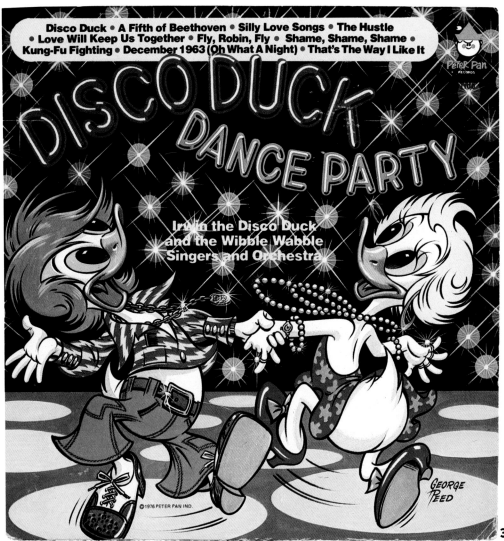

Bertram) is almost certainly blameless, as the former Disney artist's first feature cartoon, *The Secret of NIMH* (1982) was quite an achievement. Based on Robert C. O'Brien's Newberry Medal–winning children's novel *Mrs. Frisby and the Rats of NIMH* (1971), this surprisingly overlooked film tells the tale of supersmart mice (progeny of a victim of experiments at the National Institute of Mental Health) who've established a civilization in the field of Farmer Fitzgibbon. The film focuses on three tales: NIMH's efforts to get the mice back, a power struggle between the rat leaders, and the efforts of the widow Mrs. Brisby (Frisby would have been laughed off the screen) to move her family to safe ground, away from the farmer's plow. The three tales are skillfully interwoven, and there's real splendor in the characters of the Great Owl and the sorcerer rat Nicodemus. The climax, in which a magic charm is used to raise Mrs. Brisby's stone home (with her children inside) from the muck into which they've fallen is breathtaking.

FELIX THE CAT

Pedigree. The first true animated film star, also a hero of television, a comic strip, and comic books.

Biography. In his first cartoon, the three-minute-long *Feline Follies* (1919), Felix did little more than grow agitated as a clever little mouse outsmarted him (obviously inspired by the comic strip exploits of **Krazy Kat**). But artist Otto Messmer (see "Comment") did more with Felix than any animator had done with a cartoon character up to that time. As Messmer put it, using "a wink or a twist of the tail" or some other gesture, he was able to give Felix personality. Felix evolved quickly into an alternately fun-loving or brooding, pointy-eared loner of a black cat who, when faced with a problem, walked with his paws locked behind his back, head bent forward in thought. Felix's domestic arrangements are unclear: Sometimes he's living with a human family *(The Oily Bird,* 1928), many times he's living alone, in *Why and Other Whys* (1927) and *Felix Woos Whoopee* (1928) he's married to a white "Mrs. Cat," while in *Flim Flam Films* (1927) he even has children, whom he takes to the movies (his own, of course). Wherever he is, however, he has troubles and responsibilities aplenty. Many of these revolve around trying to get a good meal. Among them are *Felix Gets the Can* (1924), *Felix Dines and Pines* (1927), and the magnificent *Felix Revolts* (1924), in

which he leads all the cats in town on a strike, refusing to catch mice until the felines are allowed into kitchens and trash cans. Others have him working as a baseball batboy *(Felix Saves the Day,* 1922), struggling to get to southern California *(Felix in Hollywood,* 1922—a feat he achieves by using chewing gum to ruin peoples' shoes, thus getting a kickback from the shoemaker), saving Miss Muffet from a spider and helping the Old Lady in a Shoe find a new home in *Felix in Fairyland* (1923), dealing with barnyard animals *(Felix the Cat on the Farm,* 1925), and even facing ghosts *(Sure-Locked Homes,* 1927—the "ghosts" turning out to be shadows cast by a baby with a light). He also has some truly bizarre adventures, such as the time he tries to reclaim his pelt from the man to whom a tailor sold it *(Felix Trifles with Time,* 1925) or getting shoe polish and blackening himself in when the animator forgets to do it *(Comicalities,* 1928). In this cartoon, Felix also uses his newfound cartoonist's "powers" to draw himself a lovely female cat companion. When she rejects him, the intemperate cat rips her up. Felix also has the ability to use his (detachable) ears as scissors, or his tail as anything from a telescope to a clarinet to an umbrella to a baseball bat. In an inspired scene from *Oceanantics* (1928), he's staring pensively at a closed grocery store, wondering how to get in. He sees a door in a house across the street (the door is small, in perspective), stretches his tail to it, uses the appendage to remove the door, and places it in the wall of the shop, which he then enters. He's also fond of grabbing the *?* or *!* that regularly appear over his head and using them as a hook or sword to get out of a jam. In one cartoon he pulls an *8* off a sign and uses it as glasses, while in another he blows musical notes that are used to fuel a furnace. This stoic hero in unpredictable adventures changed greatly after his thirty-two year layaway from the screen: When he starred in an all-new series of cartoons made for television, his world had changed dramatically. He's rarely moody now—nor is there cause. Felix carries a carpetbag-style magic Bag of Tricks, from which he can pull just about anything he ever needs, including an airplane! Although he repeatedly must deal with the evil Professor and his bulldog assistant Rock Bottom, who are trying to steal the bag, they rarely pose a serious threat. Other foes Felix has faced on television include the Abominable Snowman, Martin the Martian, General Clang, the Leprechaun (several times, in fact), Redbeard the Pirate, the Sea Monster, and others. Felix's regular costar is Poindexter, the Professor's benign egghead nephew. These cartoons were fun, but with his Bag of Tricks, Felix rarely had to resort to the clever and/or desperate tactics that had made his silent adventures so appealing.

Comment. Felix was created by animator Otto Messmer, although it was Pat Sullivan, at whose animation studio Messmer worked, who claimed credit for the character. In any case, both men agreed that the character was inspired by Rudyard Kipling's "The Cat That Walked by Himself," one of the *Just So Stories* (1902). Felix's first cartoon was released in 1919, as part of the weekly, one-reel *Paramount Screen Magazine* package. Previously, animator John R. Bray had provided the animated segment; when he went to the rival Goldwyn studio, *Magazine* producer John King asked Sullivan to come up with a replacement. Sullivan passed the task on to Messmer, who, remarkably, turned out the cartoon at home, in his spare time. The cat had no name until 1921 and the release of *Felix the Cat.* Felix was coined by King, taken from the words *feline* and *felicity,* for good luck. In 1922, Sullivan took Felix from Paramount and signed with distributor Margaret Winkler who, later, was instrumental in the discovery of Walt Disney. Felix starred in 150 silent theatrical cartoons from 1921 to 1928. Sullivan failed to make the transition to sound, and the character was overwhelmed by the popularity of characters such as **Mickey Mouse.** He made a short-lived comeback in three sound, color cartoons released by the Van Beuren Studios in 1936, but his real return had to wait until he was rediscovered on television. Felix made a triumphant return in 260 new, four-minute-long cartoons produced by Joe Oriolo for a syndicated show that began airing in 1960. (The song guaranteed, "You'll laugh so much your sides will ache, your heart'll go pitter-pat—watching Felix, the wonderful cat!") Jack Mercer did all the voices for the TV incarnation. Felix also gained fame on television in another way: His was the first (still)

image broadcast on television when NBC inaugurated their experimental transmitter in New York in 1930. Although Felix was a bona fide cartoon star, he's also had a lasting impact on comic strips. His own Sunday strip debuted on August 14, 1923, followed by a daily strip on May 9, 1927. Messmer and (uncredited) assistants handled the strip until Joe Oriolo took over in 1954.

In comic books, Felix starred in a series of comic strip reprints published from 1927 to 1931 by McLoughlin Brothers, appeared in a variety of one shots, then got his own Dell magazine in 1943. Toby Press, then Harvey Comics, then Dell again had the book over the years; 118 issues were published through 1965. In 1989, Eternity Comics issued a Felix one shot in 3-D. Harvey published 7 issues of *Felix's Nephews Inky & Dinky* from 1957 to 1958. An all-new feature-length cartoon based on Felix's adventures was filmed in 1989.

FELIX THE PIG

Pedigree. A low-life among comic book pigs.
Biography. With a face very reminiscent of **Felix the Cat** (except for the pig's snout), the swine is the mascot of the fictitious rock band Womanizer. Offstage, little is known about the porker, save that he lives in a rundown apartment and has a girlfriend named Beaverlee, the former main squeeze of Felix's friend, the hip duck Platterpuss.

Comment. The character appears in the comic magazine *Paper Cuts,* two issues of which were published by Brainstorm Studios in 1988.

FERDINAND THE BULL

Pedigree. Bull of literature and Walt Disney's short *Ferdinand the Bull.*
Biography. When a group of men come to the farm in Spain to find animals for the bullring, all of the young bulls show off—except for Ferdinand, who wanders away and plants himself beneath his beloved tree, sniffing the flowers and smiling at the

Having stolen Platterpuss's girl, **Felix the Pig** *beats a hasty retreat.* © COREY HARRIS. Courtesy NEAL WARNER.

butterflies. Alas, this day he has the misfortune to sit on a bee, which causes him to run and charge about; the "talent scouts" are impressed, and take the bull to Madrid. On the day of the big match, the bullfighter waits in the center of the arena while Ferdinand enters timorously. Spotting flowers that have been thrown from the grandstand, the bull goes over to them, plunks himself down, and begins smelling them. The bullfighter implores him to get up and fight, but Ferdinand refuses. He's pulled from the ring, shipped back to the farm, and allowed to return to his tree and the flowers he loves so dearly.

Comment. Don Wilson narrated this Oscar-winning 1938 short. It was based on author Munro Leaf's *The Story of Ferdinand*, which was published in 1936. Disney's artists stuck closely to the book illustrations of Robert Lawson. There was a one-shot comic book based on the short (1938), and a comic strip sequel, "Ferdinand the Bull and the Robbers," which was published in *Walt Disney's Treasury of Classic Tales*.

FERDY AND MORTY
Pedigree. Nephews of **Mickey Mouse**.
Biography. In their only short, *Mickey's Steamroller* (1934), the two lads are dressed in nightshirts and are out for a walk with **Minnie Mouse**. Mickey leaves his steamroller to flirt with Minnie; while the adults are involved with each other, the boys climb from their carriage, commandeer the steamroller, and cause havoc up and down the street. The steamroller eventually plows into a hotel, where Mickey's nephews improvise a see-saw using their uncle's head and a board.

Comment. Although the characters had a short theatrical career, older if only slightly better behaved, they were regulars in the Mickey Mouse comic strip and comic books. Typical of the gags in the former is this: One of the boys wants to watch television, but Mickey wants him to practice the piano. The nephew's solution is to steal the rearview mirror from Mickey's roadster and clip it to the piano so that he can do both.

FIDO (1)
Pedigree. Very early dog of animated cartoons.
Biography. Fido is a cute but street-smart, conniving pup. Typical of his "ingenious" ideas is convincing Bobby to sell his balding father hair restorer by showing him how it works on a dog. Little does Mr. Bumps know that Fido secretly replaced a short-haired dog with a long-haired one for the demonstration (in *Bobby Bumps: Before and After*). In *Bobby Bumps Puts a Beanery on the Bum*, Fido literally makes a hostile cat eat its words by grabbing the word balloon above its head (see "Comment") and shoving it down the feline's throat. Other adventures in which Fido was prominently involved were *Bobby Bumps: Fido's Birthday, Bobby Bumps and His Pointer Pup,* and *Bobby Bumps Loses his Pup.*

Comment. Rather than cutting away to title cards as in silent films, the Bobby Bumps series, like many silent cartoons, simply adopted the word balloon conventions of the comic strips. The characters appeared in fifty short cartoons from 1915 to 1918, with one in 1925. They were produced by the Bray Studios, one of the first and most successful animation houses. Other Bray productions were the *Police Dog* cartoons (four in all, released in 1915), about a crime-busting pooch who "adopts" a patrol officer; *Goodrich Dirt,* the tales of a good-natured hobo and his happy-go-lucky dog (twenty episodes from 1917 to 1918); the five-cartoon series *Judge Rummy* (1921), about a dog judge (the character was created by Tad Dorgen, who also coined the term "hot dog"); and *Pete the Pup,* the adventures of a cartoon dog, combining live action and animation. Pete was created by Walter Lantz (**Woody Woodpecker**) and starred in ten *Hot Dog* cartoons (1926 to 1927).

FIDO (2)
Pedigree. Big dog owned by the comic strip king in "The Wizard of Id."
Biography. The fictitious, medieval kingdom of Id is governed by a rather rotten, short king—a king so small in stature that he must ride a dog instead of a horse. The king rides the brown dog with a saddle, and no one in the realm is permitted to refer to him as other than a horse. (Once, when the dog got loose and was captured, the king was informed he was being kept in the "horse pound.") Fido is a good dog except on fox hunts, when it joins the other dogs, dragging the king behind him. The king also has a pet python and another dog, which is trained to protect him from danger. Unfortunately, this dog is a chicken, and protecting the king means locking his teeth to some part of him and running away. Another animal in the strip is Cuddles, the small dog who belongs to Blanch, the wife of the king's wizard.

Comment. The strip, written by Johnny Hart (see **Jake**) and drawn by Brant Parker debuted November 9, 1964; the dog first appeared on March 24, 1969.

Fifi (right)—the slimmest dog on earth.

FIFI

Pedigree. Pet dog of the comic strip character Maggie.

Biography. When mason Jiggs and his washer-woman wife, Maggie, win the Irish sweepstakes, they become rich. Maggie becomes affected, Jiggs yearns for his old friends, and the two are in constant conflict. More often than not, Jiggs gets stuck dog-sitting for his wife's incredibly thin poodle, who looks more like a mosquito than like a dog. The spindly dog doesn't speak, or even move much. As a little girl, Maggie had a pooch named Rover; as a boy, Jiggs "had a mutt named Flea Flea." Another animal in the strip is Betsy the horse, who pulled a trolley on the Cass Avenue Line.

Comment. George McManus's "Bringing Up Father" first appeared in 1913. During McManus's tenure, it was one of the most popular comic strips in the nation; on his death in 1954, the strip limped along, its stature sorely diminished.

FIGARO

Pedigree. Cat seen in several Disney cartoons.

Biography. First seen in the feature-length *Pinocchio* (1940) as the pet cat of the woodcarver Geppetto, Figaro is a small, friendly black cat with a white streak down its breast. When Pinocchio fails to return home from school and Geppetto goes looking for him, Figaro comes along (as does the goldfish Cleo); all are swallowed by a whale, and are subsequently saved by Pinocchio. After a cameo appearance in the war propaganda film *All Together* (1942), Figaro returns—considerably different than he is in *Pinocchio*. In that film, he's so happy to see Pinocchio that he leaps into the goldfish bowl and kisses Cleo. Not now. In their first short together, *Figaro and Cleo* (1943), slinky, mean-eyed Figaro is a more traditional movie cat, out to bury Cleo rather than embrace her. **Pluto the Pup** and Figaro are teamed in the cat's next short, *First Aiders* (1944), in which **Minnie Mouse** (with whom Figaro is living now) practices her nursing skills solely as a plot device to leave Pluto trussed from head to toe so that Figaro can torment him. When Minnie goes out to buy more supplies, her home is all but wrecked as Pluto tries to get at the cat. In *Bath Day* (1946), a *very* reluctant Figaro is bathed and perfumed, then goes out and gets into a scrap with some alley cats. Result? When he comes home, he gets another bath. Figaro and the dog **Butch** fight to a draw in an effort to get at Minnie's bird Frankie in *Figaro and Frankie* (1947), while in *Cat Nap Pluto* (1948), the feline does everything he can to keep the exhausted party-dog from getting some sleep. Finally, in *Pluto's Sweater* (1949), the dog takes guff from Figaro, Butch, and other dogs about an ugly sweater Minnie has knitted and forced him to wear. After the dog falls in a pond, the sweater shrinks . . . and Pluto, gesturing, manages to convince the furious Minnie that far from being ruined, the shrunken sweater would be ideal for Figaro. Exit the cat, from the cartoon . . . and from further screen adventures.

Comment. The cat's purrs and snarls were the work of Clarence Nash (the voice of **Donald Duck**) and, later, Kate-Ellen Murtaugh. See also Pluto's cat foe **Milton**.

FISSION CHICKEN
Pedigree. Comic book superhero.
Biography. Dressed in a blue vest and trunks and silver bracelets, the cynical, superstrong, flying chicken fires destructive bolts from his fingers and chases evildoers from New Jersey and environs (where somehow, only walking, talking animals live). His pet peeves are having to tail villains ("Big pain in the ass to fly this slow"), "gettin' monster guts all over my costume," and running out of toilet paper in his apartment (in these cases, he's been known to rip down the wall of a neighboring lavatory). His recurring foes are the Vortoxians, "The Marketing Experts from Outer Space." Other foes have included Nuke Chicken, a creature every bit as powerful as himself; the gas-spewing Ether Bunny; and the giant spider Boogog. Among other characters who have appeared in the strip are the Fuzzy Cutekins (a **Care Bears** parody), Skippy Squirrelheart, Merry Moonmouse, Joyous Jackrabbit of Happyland, and the Middle-Age Generic Mutant Tortoises. The opening verse to the hero's theme song—sung to the tune of "Yankee Doodle"—is, "Fission Chicken is the champ / of all the action aces / he'll seize the villains like a clamp / and smash them in their faces."

Fission Chicken takes matters in wing.
© FANTAGRAPHICS BOOKS.

Comment. The character J. P. Morgan was introduced in *Critters* no. 15 in 1987. There was no origin; Morgan just leapt into the fowl's adventures. Fission Chicken continued in *Critters*: No. 39 was devoted entirely to the fowl's adventures. He got his own title in 1989. See the even more astounding *Super Chicken*.

FITZ
Pedigree. One of the first animated cartoon characters, dog-companion to Koko (a k a Ko-Ko) the Clown.
Biography. Fitz (who has also been referred to as Fido) is a little white dog with floppy ears and a big, black spot on its back. Fitz and its master literally come out of the animator's inkwell at the beginning of their cartoons, to partake in a wide variety of adventures. The dog is very much a secondary character in Koko's adventures, which include a trip to a haunted house, a run-in with Aladdin's lamp, and a visit to the circus. Among the more imaginative and surreal tales were *Koko's Earth Control* (1928), in which Fitz fiddles with a potentially destructive lever (a sign above it reads, "If this handle is pulled the world will come to an end"), and many stories in which Koko interacts with his animator in the real world.
Comment. The dog was created by artist Dick Huemer and was originally devised to come onto the

screen and conduct the theater's musical accompanist. Fitz is often referred to as **Bimbo,** a later character from the same animators. However, there's nothing to suggest that it's same dog; indeed, they look completely different. There were 125 cartoons in the original *Out of the Inkwell* series, which lasted from 1916 to 1929 (although neither character was given a name until 1923). The classic series was created by pioneering animators Dave and Max Fleischer, whose works include the magnificent, vintage Popeye, Betty Boop, and Superman series. Koko was revived for an awful series of TV cartoons syndicated in 1961, with the lady-clown Kokette joining the irrepressible duo.

FLIP

Pedigree. Dog belonging to comic strip teen Rusty Riley.

Biography. When his parents are killed in an accident, teenager Rusty is sent to an orphanage—from which he promptly flees with his terrier Flip. Reaching the home of millionaire Mr. Miles, Rusty is put to work as a stable boy, eventually being promoted to jockey and riding the racehorse Bright Blaze to numerous victories. Along the way, he and Flip keep criminals away from the mansion and the racetrack. Flip's most fur-raising adventure involved him being framed for the slaughter of Woolly Smith's sheep, and Riley's desperate efforts to prove him innocent.

Comment. Frank Godwin's *Rusty Riley* debuted on January 26, 1948 and was discontinued in 1959.

FLIP THE BIRD

Pedigree. Underground comic book bird.

Biography. The cigar-smoking bird in a tiny derby and sweater slinks around human neighborhoods stealing food. In his one adventure, he overhears Henry's wife telling her husband that she has to go to her bridge club meeting, and that when the interior decorator arrives he should stay out of the way. To "have some *fun* with this guy . . . and get a *free meal,*" Flip poses as the decorator, pigging out while sawing the sofa in half, planting a tree in the living room, bringing in a neon "Eat at Joe's" sign, tearing down a wall, and so on. When the real decorator arrives (a Salvador Dali lookalike), he kills the bird, stuffs him, and mounts him over the mantel.

Comment. John Pound's character appeared in Marvel's *Comix Book* no. 1 in 1974—the company's attempt to produce a newsstand underground comic. Although the effort was admirable, the results were so diluted as to be virtually toothless.

Other animals that appeared in the comic's five-issue run include **Myron Moose,** Marion McKay's All-Animal Orchestra—featuring Ollie Elephant on trumpet and Harry Horse on piano—and Dr. Pierre Rovere, a psychiatrist who happens to be a dog and helps other dogs.

FLIP THE FROG

Pedigree. Early animated cartoon frog.

Biography. Flip is a bashful, black-skinned character who is human, save for his frog's head. He is dressed in a cap, bow tie, trunks, shoes, and gloves and has buttons down his chest (!). Flip moves from locale to locale (often in a car with a face), and from odd job to odd job, as an excuse to become involved in various sight gags. The unassuming frog is especially fond of the ladies and won't hesitate to tackle a bully three times his size to protect or impress a woman. Flip—who doesn't speak—is the only animal in these otherwise human-populated adventures. Among his more impressive turns are as a prize-fighter in *The Bully,* as a bullfighter in *Bulloney,* dealing with a runaway robot in *Techno-Cracked,* pursuing a shapely secretary in *Office Boy,* and picking his way through a haunted house in *The Cuckoo Murder Case.*

Comment. In his first two cartoons, *Fiddlesticks* and *Puddle Pranks,* Flip was much more froglike, with webbed hands and feet. More grotesque than endearing, he was quickly changed into a more likable figure. There were thirty-seven Flip cartoons in all, released by MGM from 1930 to 1933. There was very little dialogue, the cartoons consisting primarily of music and sound effects. The character was created by Ub Iwerks, Walt Disney's first animator and the man who designed **Mickey Mouse.** Sadly, the Flip series flopped due to cost overruns and stories that were beautifully animated but lethargic in their pacing and far less inventive than the Mouse tales. After this defection, Iwerks went back to work for Disney, who never forgave him for having left. Iwerks died in 1971.

FLOOKY

Pedigree. Troll-dog of TV cartoons.

Biography. Flooky belongs to Blitz Plumkin, a troll of Trolltown (population 347). The dog is blue with orange spots, has a purple nose, yellow hair on its head, and long, erect ears bent at the tips. Constantly scratching its fleas, the dog can't talk and has a passion for "dog candy" and dog cookies. Among its most notable escapades was chasing a troll-cat around the new troll train, bumping into the controls, and causing the train to become a runaway (when Blitz and his girlfriend, Pixlee Trollsom, yell at Flooky to use the brake lever, he misunderstands and breaks the lever). In another adventure, Blitz accidentally uses magic to turn a troll-cat into a giant. Instead of chasing troll-mice, the cat chases Flooky and the trolls. It finally occurs to Blitz to turn the dog into a giant and thus end the threat. More dangerous by far was the encounter with the Trollness monster. Blitz, Pixlee, and Flooky go camping near Trollness Lake, where the dog indulges in his passion: fetching sticks. When the monster arrives and *also* enjoys fetching sticks, Flooky wisely steps aside.

Comment. The rather unimaginative *Trollkins* aired on CBS in 1981; it lasted just a single season. Each cartoon was fifteen minutes long. Frank Welker provided the barks and grumblings of the dog, Steve Spears was Blitz, and Jennifer Darling was Pixlee.

FLOP

Pedigree. A comic book cat with only one desire in life: canary lunch meat.

Biography. Flop is a chubby, black-and-white cat who wears a red bow tie and has just one goal in life: to eat Flippity, a little canary who lives in a cage at the house. Flop is forever devising new ways to get at the bird, such as building a ladder, cutting a hole in the attic floor and climbing down on a rope, and trying to stack boxes on top of chairs. Fortunately for Flippity, the hound Sam also lives in the house and he always arrives in time to save the bird.

Comment. Both visually and plotwise, these characters bear a striking resemblance to **Sylvester the Cat** and **Tweety.** Flop and company first appeared in DC Comics's *Real Screen Funnies* no. 1 in 1945. In addition to **Fauntleroy Fox,** the comic featured the adventures of Tito and his Burrito, the comedic adventures of a Mexican boy and his burro.

FOGHORN LEGHORN

Pedigree. Loud, blustery motion picture rooster.

Biography. The superintendent of the chicken coop on a farm, Foghorn has changed little since his motion picture debut in the Academy Award–nominated short, *Walky Talky Hawky.* In it, chicken hawk **Henery Hawk** leaves home to hunt chickens for the first time. He arrives at the Foghorn's barnyard: telling the dumb little bird that he, himself, is a horse, Foghorn directs his attention to his nemesis Charlie Dog, and tells him that's a chicken. ("Oy,"

Henery says with a Yiddish accent, "that's the biggest chicken I ever did see!"). After a series of slapstick misadventures, Henery ends up leaving with the dog, a horse, and Foghorn. The first two animals are calm and confident as the chickenhawk drags them away, but Foghorn is wailing and clawing at the ground. Somehow Foghorn survives, and in his second cartoon, *Crowing Pains,* he tries to convince Henery that **Sylvester the Cat** is actually a chicken. Henery remains unconvinced and elects to stick around until daybreak to see which one crows. Sylvester does, thanks to a book of ventriloquism Foghorn's been studying. Henery, Foghorn, and Charlie costarred in several other cartoons, after which Foghorn spent most of his time playing tricks on the dog. In one classic, *The High and the Flighty,* novelty salesperson **Daffy Duck** arrives at the barn and sells the rivals gags to use against one another. When he sells the same joke to both of them ("Pipe Full o' Fun Kit no. 7"), the two team up to destroy Daffy. A nameless weasel is another of the rooster's ongoing nemeses. Foghorn is big and white, with a brown head and tail feathers. In addition to his booming, southern voice, his trademark is repeating statements after injecting an *"Ah say,"* to wit: "What in—*Ah say,* what in the name of Jesse James is that?" and "Ah always—*Ah say,* Ah always wanted a son!" His favorite song is Stephen Foster's *De Camptown Races.* Charlie Dog is white with brown ears and a brown stripe down its back, and is described by the hardly unbiased Foghorn as "simpleminded." The rooster's favorite pastime is taking a plank, lifting the dog's tail, and whacking him repeatedly in the backside. The dog invariably chases and nearly chokes when he reaches the end of the leash. While he lies gasping for air, Foghorn usually adds insult to injury, for example, by returning with a croquet mallet and wicket and whacking the hound's head. Foghorn's occasional love interest is **Miss Prissy.**

Comment. Although not as well known or beloved as the other Warner Brothers characters (**Bugs Bunny, Road Runner,** and others), Foghorn has had an impressive career, starring in thirty cartoons between 1946 and 1980. Created by animator/director Robert McKimson, Foghorn was clearly inspired by the character Senator Claghorn from Bighorn of radio's *The Fred Allen Show.* Mel Blanc, who provided Foghorn's voice, insisted that the voice was also derived from "a hard-of-hearing sheriff" he'd seen in a vaudeville show. Charlie appeared in several cartoons on his own, usually playing an itinerant as in *A*

Hound for Trouble, in which he found himself in Italy looking for a master.

FOOFUR

Pedigree. Dog star of television and Marvel Comics.

Biography. Foofur is a homeless, gangly blue bloodhound who finds a deserted old home and moves in. There, he is joined by other homeless animals, as well as pets who sneak away from their masters for a visit. Although the group likes nothing better than to hang out, adventure is always just around the corner in the person of Mrs. Escrow, the real estate salesperson who's trying to sell the house. The animals always come up with some way to foil her, confrontations which are always preceded by a "bow-wow pow-wow" to determine strategy. (The woman doesn't know that Foofur lives there; her little dog Pepe does, but obviously can't tell her.) Occasionally, the animals must deal with other threats, such a crooks using the house for a hideout or the pesky Rat Brothers—Chucky, Baby, and Sam—who maintain that the house is their turf. The animals who come to visit Foofur include the European dog Fritz-Carlos, who enjoys regaling the others with tales of his ancestors, such as Uncle Fernando who served in the canine corps; the spindly, hip cat Fencer; the monstrously big and strong dog Louis (who belonged to a mean Dog-Pack—a street gang—until Foofur talked him out of it); the lady dogs Dolly (she's owned by one of the local super-rich), Hazel (who is compulsively neat), and Annabel (who's always running into things because she won't cut her bangs); and Foofur's young nephew, Rocki. Annabel's twin sister, Lulubel, also joined the group, once. The animals usually walk on all fours, and can only talk among one another.

Comment. The Phil Mendez character joined NBC TV's Saturday morning lineup in 1986. Frank Welker was Foofur's voice, Jonathan Schmock was Fritz-Carlos, Susan Tolsky was Annabel, Pat Carroll was Hazel, and Susan Blu was Dolly. Marvel published six issues of a *Foofur* comic book in 1987 and 1988.

FOXY

Pedigree. Early cartoon character from Warner Brothers.

Biography. A bipedal fox who looks like **Mickey Mouse**, except for his spats, fluffy tail, and ears—which are shaped like spades on playing cards. Foxy is an impatient, sometimes violent critter. At a saloon in his screen debut (*Lady Play Your Mandolin*)

he punches out his horse when the animal wants to dance. In his second cartoon (*Smile, Darn Ya, Smile*) he whips out a pin and punctures a heavyset woman who can't squeeze into a trolley. Foxy has an unnamed fox girlfriend who looks just like him.

Comment. There were only three Foxy cartoons, all of them released in 1931.

FRAIDY CAT

Pedigree. Haunted TV feline.

Biography. An alleycat, the skinny Fraidy has reason to shake in his paws: He's haunted by eight ghosts, his previous lives, who appear when he accidentally utters their name or number. When they arrive, they nag him to become one of them and are constantly doing things to hasten Fraidy's demise. For example, because only he can see them, they'll steal a bone from a big dog, who'll think Fraidy did it. Each of the dead cats has its own personality. Number one is the prehistoric Elafunt, two is the magician Kitty Wizard, three is the pirate Captain Kitt, four is the dashing Sir Walter Cat, five is the gunslinging Billy the Kitt, six is the undertaker Jasper Catdaver, seven is the ace pilot Captain Eddie Kittenbacker, and eight is the cool Hep Cat.

Comment. The filmation cartoon series was one of the segments on *Uncle Croc's Block,* in which Charles Nelson Reilly dressed in a crocodile suit and played the host of a children's program who doesn't like his job, but shows the cartoons anyway. His sidekick is Mr. Rabbit Ears, a bunny, played by perennial Burt Reynolds costar Alfie Wise. Alan Oppenheimer provided the voice for Fraidy Cat; the show aired on ABC from September 1975, until February 1976, and was a smashing failure. Also featured on *Uncle Croc's Block* were the segments *M*U*S*H* (see **Bullseye**) and *Wacky and Packy,* the saga of a caveman and his wooly mammoth on the loose in modern day New York.

FRED

Pedigree. Mascot of the title characters in the comic book version of the hit film *Ghostbusters*.

Biography. Fred is actually Ferdinand, a little black terrier who lives with Mrs. Van Huego at the Hotel Sedgewick. When he goes out, he occasionally hangs around with the ghost-fighting heroes and with the kids known as the Junior Ghostbusters. However, his best friend is the benign, little green specter Slimer, who comes and goes with impunity—and with whom Fred gets into numerous adventures in the quest of food. Whenever their forays bring them face-to-ghastly-face with a truly malevolent ghost,

Fred is able to operate the vacuumlike ghost traps by himself. Another animal that has been seen in the series is Manx, a cat who dines in the trash cans outside the Ghostbusters' firehouse headquarters.

Comment. The character first appeared in *The Real Ghostbusters,* which Now Comics began publishing in 1988, based on the 1986 film. Fred presently costars in the comic book *Slimer,* a spin-off title that began in 1989.

FREDDIE
Pedigree. Frog motion picture star.
Biography. A human-size frog with human limbs, hands, and feet, debonair Freddie is a French secret agent whose first mission is to find out why British landmarks are being stolen. Freddie's "assistant" is his computerized car, the Frogmobile . . . a k a Nicole.

Comment. The character is the star of the feature-length animated film *F.R.0.7.,* produced by Hollywood Road Film Productions for release in 1991. Freddie was created by Darko Markovic, his voice provided by Ben Kingsley.

FRITZ THE CAT
Pedigree. Legendary cat of underground comics and motion picture celebrity.
Biography. A slick, sex-maniac, drug-loving, crude cat in a world of cats, pigs, and other animals, the tabby walks, talks, and frequently gets to remove his clothing (usually a jacket, shirt, trousers, and necktie). He is often full of hollow compliments (to an aspiring singer after hearing her sing: "I'm paralyzed . . . with sheer ecstasy! I'll just lay here an' die quietly from too much love and joy!"), although he is painfully truthful with anyone who isn't the object of his affection (to the mother of his first girlfriend, Gabrielle, whom he genuinely loved until he got to deflower her: "You're not nearly as pretty as your daughter, but you have my undying gratitude for producing the dear girl!"). He doesn't take rejection kindly (when spurned by the lovely Della Pussywillow, he mutters, "Damn cold-hearted, egotistical, snooty-nosed, artificial phony dame!"), and the deepest reading he ever undertakes is *21 Different Ways to Cook and Serve the Housefly.* Not much is known about Fritz's past, except that his parents and sister live in a little shack from which he ran away after he was thrown out of school (although he later got a diploma in "the arts of magic.") Fritz is known to have committed incest with his sister on at least one occasion. Fritz later becomes a movie star (paralleling what happened to him in real life) and dies

(*The People's Comics,* 1972) when, in a jealous rage, the ostrich Andrea buries an ice pick in his head.

Comment. Created by Robert Crumb, the phony but endearing cat made his debut in an amateur comic the sixteen-year-old Crumb produced in 1959. The cat's first professional appearance was in 1964, in a comic strip in *Help!* magazine, although no name was given to the feline. In it, he's a rock star who eats a "teenage girl pigeon." Crumb drew the bulk of his Fritz material between 1960 and 1965, despite the fact that most of it was published much later in books like *Head Comix* (1968) and *R. Crumb's Comics and Stories* (1969). The public knows Fritz best due to Ralph Bakshi's X-rated animated cartoon feature *Fritz the Cat* (1972). An antiestablishment tract with sex thrown in, it bears only a superficial resemblance to the comic stories, and Crumb disowned it. In the film, a bathtub orgy brings the cops to Fritz's East Village pad. He escapes and they pursue; hiding in a synagogue, he's saved when the police get caught up by Jews dancing the Hora. Heading to Harlem, Fritz hides out with (and makes love to) Big Bertha, leaves town with his old flame Winston, falls in with Hells Angels, is caught in an explosion when the bikers attack a power plant, lands in the hospital, and seduces the ladies who come to visit. Fade out. The film was a financial success, although a sequel, *The Nine Lives of Fritz the Cat* (1974), was not. This time, Fritz is unhappily married. Smoking grass, he slips into reverie in which he makes love to his sister, works as Hitler's valet, rockets to Mars with the sex-crazed Thelma, and becomes involved in a war between President Kissinger and black-run New Jersey. The film was irreverent and shocking, but nothing more. Skip Hinant provided the voice of Fritz. Although Fritz is the most famous underground comic book animal, he isn't the only one. In addition to those with their own entries (**Dirty Duck, Fat Freddy's Cat, Pat th' Cat,** and **Toad**), there were also Dildo Duck and Frankie Rat, who had their own strips in the one-shot *Bicentennial Gross-Outs* (1976); Waldo the Cat, who appeared in the third issue of *Comix Book* (see **Flip the Bird**); the debonaire, monocled adventurer/thief Stan Croc, who was created by François Thomas and appears in *Heavy Metal;* Stewart the Rat, a foul-looking rodent who starred in his own "graphic novel" from Marvel's adult Epic line; topping him in sleaziness, Mickey Rat, a k a "the potentate of puke," a **Mickey Mouse** spoof whose title appeared twice in 1972 and once in 1980; and Larva 69, an ant who headlined the only issue of *The St.*

Louis Bug (1969). Another underground title—the most significant of all—was *Air Pirates,* which lasted for two issues in 1971. The comics portrayed various Walt Disney characters having sex and doing drugs; a copyright infringement suit brought by Disney resulted in a judgment against the publishers and the demise of the title. The defendants' claim, that the characters were "public figures" and thus suitable fodder for parody, was rejected by the court—an historic limitation of the protection afforded publishers under the banner of satire.

FRUIT STRIPE ZEBRAS

Pedigree. Advertising mascots for Fruit Stripe bubble gum.

Biography. Denizens of Fruit Stripe Land, the five zebras are white with fat stripes, the bands around each animal colored to represent one flavor of gum (lemon, orange, cherry, lime, and grape). The zebras talk, walk upright, and, needless to say, enjoy chewing gum.

Comment. The animals appeared in print and TV advertising throughout the late 1970s and into 1980.

FUMBLES

Pedigree. Dog-costar of TV's *Where's Huddles.*

Biography. A big sheepdog-type, Fumbles belongs to Ed Huddles, quarterback for the Rhinos. Fumbles wears a football helmet and always wants to get into the act, especially when the players have a scrim-

Fuzz: as big a loser as his master.
© UNIVERSAL PRESS SYNDICATE.

mage at home. Next door neighbor Claude Pertwee has a pet cat, Beverly, whom Fumbles enjoys chasing. Fumbles's sensitive nose is good for sniffing out lost footballs.

Comment. The Hanna-Barbera series aired prime time on CBS in the summer of 1970. There were ten half-hour episodes in all. Gold Key published three issues of a *Where's Huddles* comic book in 1971, and the characters also appeared in the company's *Hanna-Barbera Fun-in* no. 9.

FUZZ

Pedigree. Pet dog of the comic strip character Ziggy.

Biography. Short, bald Ziggy is a perennial loser; his small, white dog with a big black nose isn't much luckier. "His bite is worse than his bark," Ziggy says, and the sign outside Ziggy's home reads, "Don't Worry About the Dog." The animal came home from the first night of obedience school wearing a dunce cap. About the only initiative he's ever shown is to try to get Ziggy to celebrate his birthday seven times a year, since one year equals seven dog years. Ziggy's parakeet, Josh—which he bought for $5, marked down from $98—is somewhat more successful at the game of life. He has a social life (dating the clock cuckoo), he's sarcastic (when the phone goes *ding-a-ling,* he tells Ziggy, "That must be for you") and he's aggressive: He refuses to eat bird seed unless it's "got enough fiber in it," and during a run for the presidency decided to call Dan Rather "a weenie during a live interview" to get some attention. He also enjoys causing Fuzz to come running by doing his impression of an electric can opener, and making Ziggy jump by pretending to be a test of the emergency broadcast system. Ziggy also owns a precocious goldfish, who slops water all over when it does laps around the bowl and has been known to put Mr. Bubble in its water. As for Ziggy's pet cat, it's so frail it can't watch **Tweety Bird** cartoons without trembling, looks up to **Garfield** as a role model, and, not surprisingly, is a terrible mouser (the mouse came over to Ziggy one day and said they "were out of Cheez-whiz"). Of all the pets, only the bird and mouse speak. Only the bird and mouse have anything worth saying.

Comment. Greeting card artist Tom Wilson created the one-panel *Ziggy* strip in 1966, and tried unsuccessfully to sell it for two years. The cartoons were collected in a book, *When You're Not Around,* which came to the attention of Universal Press Syndicate. The strip was inaugurated in 1970.

GABBY

Pedigree. Comic book owl tree surgeon.

Biography. The green-feathered Gabby and the big bear Flabby are the owner and sole employees of We Do Anything, Inc.—tree surgeons who are starving because they haven't had a job in five years. When they finally get a call, they rush out to the city park to take care of a sick tree. When the pair try to inject the tree with a hypodermic that is filled with chlorophyll, they accidentally stab a squirrel who's living inside. Warfare erupts, the hostilities accelerating when Flabby vows to "make squirrel pie with [the] bushy-tailed creep." After the surgeons use tar, a cannon, and other means to try to destroy the rodent, a police officer arrests them for attempted massacre. Although the tree surgeons are sent to jail for thirty days, Gabby looks on the bright side: At least they'll be eating regularly. Both animals walk upright, wear clothes, and talk.

   Comment. The owl appeared in the only issue of Wham-O Manufacturing's oversize *Wham-O Giant Comics* in 1967.

GABBY GOAT

Pedigree. Obnoxious, early costar of **Porky Pig**.

Biography. Loud, ranting, and short, Gabby looks (and acts) more like a devil than a goat, with his thick, short, back-turned horns and perenially arched brow. Everything outrages the goat: He and Porky go camping in *Porky and Gabby,* and he screams at everything from the truck they're behind to a pesky bee to an outboard motor that runs wild. In *Porky's Badtime Story,* while the two try to get some sleep, everything from a rainstorm to another bee to a noisy cat work against them, while in *Get Rich Quick Porky,* drilling for oil makes the pair crazy.

   Comment. The Warner Brothers character appeared in just those three cartoons, in 1937.

GABBY GOOSE

Pedigree. Tiny bird of early theatrical cartoons.

Biography. Gabby is a nonstop talker, a tiny goose with a round head, huge eyes, tiny bill, and chickenlike torso. In his first cartoon (*I Wanna Be a Sailor*), Petey Parrot announces to his mother that he wants to be a sailor, and she's horrified. Petey's father was a sailor, and the lady parrot deems him a "high-seas homewrecker," a "sea-going slob," and a "rumsoaked old seagull." But Petey is undeterred, and builds a boat from a barrel. Gabby accompanies him, saving the day when a storm sinks the vessel. Gabby (here called Dippy) and **Porky Pig** go fishing in *It's an Ill Wind,* but are forced to seek shelter in an old yacht club when a storm whips up. Thanks to a stray dog and a turtle, the two are convinced the place is haunted. Finally, in *Porky's Hotel,* Porky and Gabby (now adorned with a sailor's cap and jacket) run a hotel to which the ailing old Gouty Goat comes for a rest. Naturally, the yakking goose eventually turns Gouty homicidal.

   Comment. Gabby appeared in just these three Warner Brothers cartoons (1937 to 1939). Although the goose is small—he's barely as tall as Porky's head—his endless babble makes him impossible for characters (or the audience) to ignore.

GANDY GOOSE

Pedigree. Gentle numbskull star of theatrical cartoons and comic books.

Biography. Gandy is a perennially sunny goose who means well, although he doesn't have what it takes to think things through. For example, he reasons that if a clothes washer can wash clothes, why not dishes? ("You must admit," he later says "you never saw such clean broken dishes!") After several cartoons in which he appeared solo (as a Chicken Little clone in *Doomsday,* as an inept Sherlock Holmes in *G-Man Jitters,* and so forth) he was joined by his antithesis, the perpetually cross and whining cat, Sourpuss. In their first outing (*The Magic Pencil*), Gandy finds a pencil that causes anything he draws to come to life. The goose is innocently amused and amazed, but Sourpuss sees the pencil as a means to live like a king; ultimately, his avarice causes it to be destroyed. The two serve together in the military during World War II (disastrously, as chronicled in *Night Life in the Army* and *Camouflage,* among others) after which they live together in a simple cottage in the woods. The adventures there range from fanciful (*Mother Goose Nightmare, Comic Book Land*) to the relatively ordinary (*Barnyard Actor*). As for Sourpuss, even when Gandy's not around to mess things up, the cat's temper invariably gets him into trouble. For example, when a dog comes to the door

Gandy Goose and his beloved Agnes.

selling sunglasses, the cat shoves him away. A fight ensues, Sourpuss gets two black eyes, and he's forced to buy the sunglasses to hide them. Gandy usually wears a vest, trousers, a bow tie, and a sailor's cap. The black cat's clothing varies. Both talk and walk upright. Gandy's girlfriend is the goose Agnes.

Comment. Terrytoons's Gandy was originally going to be called Willie, and was inspired by comedian Ed Wynn. Arthur Kay did an exceptional impersonation for Gandy's voice. Sourpuss's voice was inspired by Jimmy Durante; the cat's design was taken directly from a cat that had appeared in the studio's *The Owl and the Pussy Cat* in 1939. Gandy appeared in forty-one cartoons from 1938 to 1955; Sourpuss didn't join him until 1940. The cartoons were syndicated on television in 1971 as part of *The Deputy Dawg Show.* Gandy and Sourpuss appeared as a backup feature in the various **Mighty Mouse** comic books, as well as in Marvel's *All-Surprise,* twelve issues of which were published from 1943 to 1947.

GARFIELD

Pedigree. Selfish, hedonistic cat of comic strip and TV cartoon fame.

Biography. Garfield lives with the human cartoonist Jon Arbuckle, and loves food more than anything—lasagna above all, although he also likes coffee that is strong enough "to sit up and bark" and doesn't hesitate to nibble on Jon's fern when he wants a snack. He does, however, dislike cat food ("The bouquet leaves something to be desired"). Although chubby (he was five pounds, six ounces at birth, and weighs fifteen pounds now), Garfield doesn't con-

sider himself fat, just "under-tall." Next to eating, the cat enjoys sleeping, and frequently suffers what he describes as "nap attacks." Garfield detests Mondays, but more than that he hates dogs, a species he considers to be brainless; he also hates their "bone breath." (Not surprisingly, the cat's favorite movie is *Old Yeller.*) Naturally, early in the strip's run, Jon's friend Lyman comes to live with them for a while, bringing along his dog Odie—who ends up living with them when Lyman leaves. Odie's only crime is playfully barking at Garfield, usually rousing him from sleep . . . although Garfield hates the way the dog always turns around three times before lying down. Garfield is always playing cruel tricks on Odie, such as dribbling and then punting him, shoving him off the edge of the table, startling him so he'll run into something hard, riding him like a horse, blowing a dog whistle in his ear, bombarding him with light bulbs or flowerpots, stuffing the dog's own snout down his throat, and dropping a cake on his head (*that* was a sacrifice). Somehow, the slobbering, trusting dog always manages to survive and come back for more. Not so other household denizens. The chicken Nadine ended up in noodle soup, and one of Jon's belongings, the puppet Hondo, exited this world after insulting the cat. Jon's pet frog Herbie was eaten by Garfield, and his pet rabbit Slippers managed (with help) to get caught in a mousetrap. Garfield himself had a pet ant, Lyle, who was destroyed when he was caught ogling the cat's lasagna. (While ants are okay in Garfield's book, he's terrified of spiders.) One much-hated animal is the gray midget cat Nermal, "the world's cutest kitten." His cuteness annoys Garfield to no end, but he belongs to Jon's parents, so Garfield can't touch him. However, he *has* tried—and failed—to get the cat together with some tough street cats, so they'll rip him to pieces. Conversely, Garfield goes out of his way to protect Squeak the Mouse and his family from Jon—not out of affection, but because Garfield is afraid he'll be "out of a job" if the mice die. (Squeak is unrelated to **Squeak the Mouse**). Garfield's girlfriend is Arlene, around whom he tries to be very cool. However, hidden behind the hip palaver ("Yo, Arlene. Hey, ba-beee") is a scaredy-cat who would just as soon avoid her, because she enjoys conversation, which he hates. He also "cherishes" his bachelorhood. Garfield has a Gucci scratching post (although that does not stop him from shredding chairs and drapes), a teddy bear named Pooky, and a rubber chicken named Stretch. His one hobby is sitting on the fence and singing, which always results in a storm of debris being tossed his way. (Alas, Odie often comes along as the drum-playing Mr. Skins, which spoils things for the cat.) His only physical activities are chasing the mailman ("Why should dogs have all the fun?"), swimming in the bird bath (and scuba-diving in the punch at parties), and chasing ice cream trucks. Garfield has several secret identities: Amoeba Man (Garfield under a white sheet), who simply absorbs food; the Caped Avenger, who "searches out evil wherever it may lurk" (i.e., Odie or the mailman) and also steals food from Jon's plate; Orange Beard the Pirate (a favorite Halloween guise); and he was briefly a Wonder Cat Cadet, inspired by the TV show *Wonder Cat*. When he's outside, Garfield enjoys swinging on vines and pretending to be Tarzan. Garfield's only known relatives are his mother, his Aunt Evelyn, his Aunt Reba (who ended up as part of a tennis racquet), and his Uncle Barney. Barney went to the vet one day and came home as Aunt Bernice, which explains Garfield's hatred of vets (even though his vet, Liz, is among Jon's girlfriends). Garfield has two cat friends, Guido and Fluffy, whom he met while briefly incarcerated at the pound. Garfield never bathes or speaks; his thoughts—including his favorite expression, "Big, fat hairy deal"—are known to readers and other cats only. Finally, while it's clear that Garfield has six whiskers, what's not so obvious is that he has fourteen toes.

Comment. Jim Davis's enormously popular cat first appeared on June 18, 1978, and currently appears in an astonishing 2,000-plus newspapers nationwide and is translated into twelve languages.

He was named after Davis's grandfather, whose name was James A. Garfield Davis. Prior to creating Garfield, Davis tried to come up with a comic strip about a gnat. That didn't work out, and he shifted to a cat because he "noticed there were a lot of comic strip dogs who were commanding their share of the comic pages but precious few cats." Davis draws the strips eight to ten weeks in advance of publication. On television Garfield has spawned a Saturday morning cartoon show, *Garfield and Friends* (1988), as well as numerous prime-time animated specials. These half-hour adventures—many of which have won Emmy Awards—include the first, *Here Comes Garfield* (1982), *Garfield in the Rough* (going camping with Jon and Odie and meeting Billy Rabbit, Dicky Beaver, and a panther, among others), *Garfield in Paradise* (Jon and Garfield go to tropical Paradise World, where they have a very unhappy run-in with a volcano and with Chief Rama Lama of the Ding Dongs—although Garfield does enjoy meeting the lovely lady cat Mai Tai, who belongs to Queen Owooda), *The Garfield Halloween Adventure* (Garfield meets ghosts and experiences a rare moment of charity: He returns Odie's candy to him when the dog saves his life), *Babes and Bullets* (featuring Garfield as the private eye Sam Spayed), *A Garfield Thanksgiving* (the cat must diet at the worst possible time of year), *Garfield on the Town* (and in the pound), and *Garfield: His Nine Lives* (the feline plays a variety of different characters, including Cave Cat and Space Cat). Lorenzo Music provides the cat's voice (i.e., his thoughts). Garfield is also the star of more than a dozen best-selling books, which reprint the comic strips as well as a handful of originals; he made his first appearance as a balloon in the Macy's Thanksgiving Day Parade in 1984. Davis is also the creator of **Orson the Piglet**. Ironically, Davis owns no cats (his wife is allergic to them).

GAYLORD

Pedigree. The pet buzzard of the comic strip's Broom Hilda.

Biography. The witch Broom Hilda, her friend Irwin the troll, and Gaylord live in the Haunted Forest in the modern day, although exactly where has never been revealed. (A city of some kind lies just across the Troll Bridge, because Broom Hilda goes there now and then.) His wings hunched high, long pink neck bent low, glasses perched on his beak, and spats on his feet, Gaylord is an erudite bird who plays the tuba, reads everything from poetry to Freud to geology, and serves as straight man for the witch. When she announces that she's going back in time to see Attila, Gaylord says, "You find the savage splendor of his ruthless conquests fascinating, eh?" To which she replies, "The bum was my first husband and he owes me 1500 years back alimony." The witch also uses the buzzard's beak as a can opener when there isn't one handy. Gaylord is a vegetarian (his preferred food is cabbage, although he also enjoys a good cucumber sandwich) who lives in a gnarled, old tree. He is fond of bodybuilding, playing basket-

Gaylord, *Broom Hilda, and creator Russell Myers's perennial query: Who's brighter, human or beast?* © CHICAGO TRIBUNE/NEW YORK NEWS SYNDICATE.

ball, and yoga. Because he's especially well versed in "plant hybrids and the latest technology in chemical fertilizers," he has achieved scientific wonders, such as developing an apple tree that grows to maturity in one minute (unfortunately, its one huge apple falls from the tree and flattens him). Recently, Gaylord has become uncharacteristically status conscious (encroaching middle age?), buying a fake car phone for his car and explaining to Broom Hilda, "It's not *who* you call that matters, it's who people *think* you call." Gaylord's only known relative is his cousin Montrose, a juvenile delinquent ("He had a very traumatic egghood," says the vulture).

Comment. Russell Myers's brilliant and popular strip "Broom Hilda" debuted in 1970. Gaylord, the witch, and company were seen in their own segment of Filmation's animated series *The Fabulous Funnies,* which aired on NBC from 1978 to 1979.

GERIATRIC GANGRENE JUJITSU GERBILS
Pedigree. Mutated lab animals turned comic book crime fighters.
Biography. Gerbils Zeke, Duffer, Geezer, and Codger were raised in the Nuclear Nibbles Research Center and genetically bred by the government to serve "as a crime fighting force." Dressed in pink domino masks and matching harness, the martial-arts heroes fought crime in the 1950s, then retired. Now, thirty years later, government liaison Dr. Christina Proper pulls them out of the Grubby Acres Rest Home to continue their mission. Although they aren't as sharp as they used to be (Zeke is constantly falling asleep), they give each assignment their all.

Comment. The Gerbils were the stars of their own short-lived eponymous magazine, published in 1986 by Planet-X Productions. They were the first of many characters to parody the phenomenally successful **Teenage Mutant Ninja Turtles.** As writer/artist Tony Basilicato put it, "Instead of a young, energetic group of turtles, I'd create a race of farty old gerbils who were a little better than useless."

G.E.R.M.IN. SHEPHERD
Pedigree. Comic book dog.
Biography. Bought as a pup by Dr. Wallace Hill of the Boston Research Institute, the female German shepherd Juno was earmarked for experiments as part of the Genetic Engineering Research, Military Intelligence program. Hill's task was to create an incredibly intelligent breed of dog that could be used to spy in foreign countries, relieving human agents of dangerous missions. When Juno is impregnated,

*Jack Sparling's model sheet for Cerberus, the **G.E.R.M.IN. Shepherd.***

Hill uses chemicals and benevolent viruses to tamper with the embryonic puppies. Unfortunately, enemy agents destroy Hill and his lab . . . although Juno escapes. She has her litter, but only two puppies survive. They are found by police officer Martin Beckman, who takes them home with him. He names the male Cerberus, and has him trained as a police dog; the female, an albino, is called Winter, and lives at home with Beckman's wife, Patricia, and their daughter, Mindy. Needless to say, Cerberus becomes a crack crime fighter with almost supernatural strength, intelligence, senses, and agility.

Comment. The comic book character appeared in Seaboard Periodicals's *Thrilling Adventure Stories* no. 3 in 1975, created by writer E. C. Meade and artist Jack Sparling. Future episodes—plotted, but never drawn—featured Winter being snatched and trained to serve a crime kingpin, and Cerberus forced to hunt her down.

GERTIE THE DINOSAUR
Pedigree. One of the first animated cartoon animals.
Biography. There were actually two versions of Gertie. The first involved the participation of an actor (in this case, animator Winsor McCay himself). At the behest of the human "ringmaster," who stands to the right of the screen, Gertie the dinosaur (apparently an apatosaur) rises from behind a hill and lumbers into the foreground, pausing to swallow a boulder. After eating an entire tree, the dinosaur is bidden to make a "pretty bow," and bows to the left, center, and right. The ringmaster asks her to raise her right foot, and she obliges; when he asks her to raise her left, she petulantly refuses. He calls her a bad girl and she weeps copiously; softening, the ringmaster throws her a pumpkin, which she catches and eats in a single gulp (a real pumpkin was thrown behind the screen by the ringmaster, a cartoon pumpkin continuing toward the dinosaur's mouth). Now Gertie willingly raises her right foot, after which she digs her muzzle into the ground and eats the stump and roots of the tree. Gertie proceeds to dance on her hind legs and frolick with an elephant before finally allowing the ringmaster to climb onto her back, walking off with him as he cracks his whip. (Again, an animated proxy took the place of McCay, who stepped behind the screen). The second, more familiar version has a live-action prologue in which a group of men (McCay among them) visit the American Museum of Natural History in New York. Over dinner, McCay bets that he can bring a dinosaur to life using animation. Sketching a dinosaur on an easel, he does just that. Gertie

performs as before, although titles interrupt the action to explain why she's doing what she's doing.

Comment. The masterful *Gertie the Dinosaur* was created by newspaper cartoonist Winsor McCay using 10,000 separate drawings; it was first screened in 1914. McCay had intended the ten-minute-long cartoon to be part of a vaudeville act, but his possessive employer, newspaper magnate William Randolph Hearst, forbade it. Thus, his stage career aborted, McCay filmed the prologue and titles so the cartoon could stand on its own, then sold it to theaters. A sequel, *Gertie on Tour,* was never completed. Forerunners to Gertie had appeared in McCay's brilliant newspaper comic "Dream of the Rarebit Fiend": In 1905, a jockey mounted an apatosaur skeleton and entered a horserace ("If this thing don't win this race, I'm badly mistaken," says the rider from atop his intimidating mount); and in 1913, a Gertie lookalike ate a tree and boulders, then spit the latter at a yakky onlooker. Interestingly, McCay didn't animate just Gertie in the cartoon: Unlike modern animators, who lay figures down on an unchanging background, McCay painstakingly redrew the scenery in each frame! Thus when Gertie walks toward the lake to get a drink, the artist is able to make the ground sink a bit beneath her weight.

G.I. JACKRABBITS

Pedigree. A comic book menagerie of military special-forces animals.

Biography. The animal world is menaced by the Cowbras, powerful, subversive cows based in a castle atop Mount Cowbra in Tibet. Assigned to battle them are the gun-toting G.I. Jackrabbits, consisting of the crow Skywalker, who can fly and is "fluent in crow, chicken, swallow, and rabbit dialects"; Barbequed, a chicken who, although only three years old, is an "expert in wing to hoof combat"; Sergeant Tusk, a walrus, who fights only with a bazooka and is "trained extensively in gorilla warfare"; Rock n' Rabbit, an electronics and weapons expert who "is one of the pioneers of the carrot grenade"; Splash, a fish, who totes a hypercharged laser pistol and is "the first aquatic member" of the team; expert marks-rabbit Scarlett O'Hare, the first female member of the team; Quickfoot, a rabbit proficient in martial arts; and General Thumper, a rabbit who speaks every animal language and is the commander of the team.

Comment. The comic book characters were a send-up of the popular G.I. Joe characters—right down to the epithet, "A Real American Hare" in lieu of "A Real American Hero." Created by Adam Post,

Gertie the Dinosaur *sobs after being called a bad girl.*

the Excalibur Publications magazine published just one issue, in 1986. Other animals seen in the strip were the moose scientist Dr. Bullwinker and the government representative, a dog named Inspector Barker.

GLADSTONE GANDER

Pedigree. Comic book duck cousin and rival of Donald Duck.

Biography. In appearance, Gladstone is slightly different from his nemesis: a bit taller, with feathery black hair on his head and a slightly longer, less up-turned beak, he dresses in a blue jacket, fedora, and spats, and wears a black bow tie. In personality, the stuffy gander is every bit the hot-air-bag Donald is, constantly boasting or rashly promising this or that. In luck, however, Gladstone is far different from his hapless cousin. Whereas Donald always ends up a loser, Gladstone somehow manages to get on top. When the two first meet they're instantly competitive, which proves frustrating for Donald over the years: The itinerant Gladstone has attained financial security through luck (finding a diamond in the street; stumbling across a meteor laden with opals, sapphires, and emeralds; and so on). This gives Gladstone the freedom, if not the reason, to toot his own horn. When Gladstone boasts, "My doorknobs are solid *rubies*," it's a lie, but not as outrageous a prevarication as when Donald retorts, "Mine are solid *diamonds!* So big it takes two men to turn 'em!" The stories pit the two ducks against one another: trying to raise money for **Daisy Duck**'s club; entering a fishing competition, wooing Daisy, competing for parts in a play, and so forth.

Comment. The character was created by Carl Barks and first appeared in *Walt Disney's Comics and Stories* no. 88 in 1947. He evolved from the need, according to Barks, for "somebody that Donald was trying to outdo." A collection of stories, *Donald and Gladstone,* was published by Gladstone Publishing in 1989. Gladstone was never featured in any Donald Duck cartoons until the series *DuckTales* debuted in syndication in 1988. He also appears in the comic book *DuckTales*. Another cousin of Donald's, wealthy abstract artist Fred, was introduced in *Walt Disney's Comics and Stories*.

GNATRAT

Pedigree. Comic book parody of the superheroes Batman and Daredevil.

Biography. When Boo Swain was a boy, he was waiting for a bus with his mother and father (Tom, a comic book artist). The rats were mugged by a cat, who wanted the art; the parents fainted, and Boo swore to devote his "life to squashing punks and making the world safe for good comic books. And I won't *faint* like my sissy parents." Studying comics and toning his muscles to "unbelievable perfection," he becomes wealthy when his father dies. Deciding to become a costumed vigilante, he opts for a gnat costume when the insects fly through an open window. He is later joined in his crusade by Tadpole, a k a young Prick Jason, a frog who dresses up in a tadpole costume. When Boo isn't out fighting crooks—most notably the lizard Jerko (i.e., the Joker)—he lives in Stately Swain Manor in the Forest with his faithful dog servant Alpo. His love interest is Robin, a nearly human bird. Losing his eyesight in his third adventure, he became Darerat, a red-costumed superhero, to bring in the giant frog known as the Burger Kingpin, a fiend who ordered 72,000 pizzas and had them sent to Swain Manor, bankrupting him.

Comment. This exquisite parody ran through Dimension Graphics's *The Dark Gnat, Gnatrat,* and *Darerat/Tadpole* (1986 to 1987). The stories were written and drawn by Mark Martin. *The Ultimate Gnatrat,* published in 1990, featured the tacky lady hippo Lasagna Loves.

GO GO GOPHERS

Pedigree. TV western about animal genocide.

Biography. The setting is the west, shortly after the Civil War, and the bane of the life of Colonel Kit Coyote, commander of a U.S. fort in Gopher Gulch, are the small, buck-toothed gopher-Indians Ruffled Feathers and Running Board, his interpreter. Coyote and his sergeant, Hokey Loma (as in Oklahoma), want to exterminate the gopher population, and the two aggrieved animals stop at nothing to sabotage the fort and its operation, from monkeying (gophering?) with the telegraph and railroads to masterminding the Trojan Totem.

Comment. The Total Television/Leonardo Productions *Go Go Gophers* aired on the *Underdog* show, which premiered on NBC in 1964. There were forty-eight episodes in all. New York TV personality Sandy Becker provided the voice of Ruffled Feathers, George S. Irving was Running Board, and Kenny Delmar was Colonel Coyote.

GOLIATH (1)

Pedigree. Pet of the young TV star Davey.

Biography. Goliath is a gangly brown dog with a large, ungainly head, huge eyes and a big, flat nose. He lives with young Davey Hanson, Davey's younger sister Sally, and their parents Elaine and John. Goliath talks in a goofy voice to Davey; to everyone else, he just barks. (Although he says wistfully, "If they let me go to school, maybe everybody'd understand me!") The dog is there to serve as the young boy's conscience. He hangs around with Davey constantly, in town or in their treehouse, and if the boy is about to do something harebrained (such as leaving the house when he's supposed to wait for the plumber), the dog trots out his oft-spoken warning, "I don't know, Davey . . ." Otherwise, the dog's favorite expression is "Shucks!" Goliath is glad to help Davey with his chores (such as delivering newspapers), although his most important job around the house is guarding the garage when Davey's club is in session, keeping out girls. Mostly he likes to play and sleep (which he does with his big, floppy ears folded over his eyes). Even in the midst of an emergency, as when he and Davey are chasing a runaway truck, he'll say some something typically doglike: "I'm sick of all this running." Goliath is very good at following scents; he's also a proud pup and pretends to be able to read, even though he can't. (Being able to talk isn't good enough?) His favorite food is a good bone, but he also loves ice cream.

Comment. *Davey and Goliath*—which always ended with a clear moral lesson and/or an expression of someone's love for God—was produced by the United Lutheran Church in American and Clokey Productions (**Pokey**). The fifteen-minute-long episodes featured voices by Richard Beals and Hal Smith. The characters were created through stop-motion photography, the filming of articulated figurines one frame of film at a time.

GOLIATH (2)
Pedigree. TV dog who becomes a superpowered lion.
Biography. Living alone and tooling about on a motorbike, young Samson and his dog Goliath have miraculous abilities. Whenever he claps his enchanted bracelets together, the youth becomes the superpowered Samson. When he brings them together a second time, waves of magic wash over the dog and he is transformed into a huge lion, some seven feet long, whose roar literally causes the earth to tremble. In addition to great strength and the ability to take mighty leaps that border on flying, the lion fires power beams from his eyes, which cause objects to explode or can melt metal. Even more incredible is the change that comes over his right foreleg, which becomes an "electropaw," with razor-sharp claws

that can cut through metal. In his normal, wimp form, Goliath is white with black ears and a black spot on his back. He can bark, but not speak.

Comment. Hanna-Barbera's *Samson and Goliath* aired on NBC in 1967; the title was changed to *Young Samson* the following year, to avoid confusion with *Davey and Goliath* [see **Goliath** (1)]. There were twenty episodes in all. The characters were also featured in no. 3 of Gold Key's *Hanna-Barbera Super TV Heroes* comic.

GOOBER
Pedigree. A ghost-hunting dog of TV cartoons.
Biography. Goober is as sickly looking a dog as one is apt to find on television: Extremely thin, he has blue fur with a green tail and ears. Apparently an Afghan, he wears a stocking cap and has the remarkable ability to become invisible whenever he's frightened. This happens often, because the unwilling "specter detector" is teamed with the youngsters—Ted, Tina, and Gillie—who investigate reports of ghosts for *Ghost Chasers* magazine. Goober only barks to the characters on-screen, although he occasionally makes asides to the viewer; profound comments, such as, "This is ridic-a-lick-a-licalus." In his most noteworthy adventure, he acquired the cultured tones of Boris Karloff when a mad scientist switched his brain with that of the Frankenstein Monster. The team has also investigated the ghost of Captain Ahab seen hanging around a New England estate, and a spirit haunting the dude ranch of basketball superstar Wilt Chamberlain.

Comment. Hanna-Barbera's *Goober and the Ghost Chasers* premiered on ABC in 1973. There were just fifteen half-hour episodes. Goober was created to capitalize on the popularity of **Scooby-Doo**. The great Paul Winchell provided his voice.

GOOFY
Pedigree. Oafish but endearing Walt Disney character also known as "the Goof."
Biography. The bipedal, black-furred, droopy-eared dog with the huge pair of buck teeth and distinctive *uh-hyuck* laugh is one of the few cartoon characters whose ancestry is extremely well documented. Beginning with Caveman Goofy (a k a Neanderthal Goofy), the Goofy family tree continues through Horatio Goofy (508 B.C., "the noblest Goof of them all"), Demosthenes Goofy (who took a wrong turn with the Olympic torch and carried it around the world; he was an inept athlete as well), Nero Goofy (A.D. 636), Galus Goofy (commander-in-chief of the

royal barge in Egypt), Sir Cedric Goofy (1142; he was a squire whose boss, Sir Loinsteak, was accidentally knocked out before a joust against Sir Cumference, so Goofy took his place), Erik the Viking who explored the Arctic Ocean ("Starlight, star bright, gosh I wish I knew where I was tonight"), Leonardo da Goofy who knew the world was square and sent his son, Leo, Jr., to prove it (1491; the boy reached America but left because he didn't like cigars), Leonardo Goofy (1551, an inventor), Cortez Goofy (an explorer and adventurer), Pilgrim Goofy (1642), his grandson Percival Goofy [he went west as a scout and guide, took the name Buffalo Bill Goofy, and once had a showdown with the vicious Pistol Pete (see **Pete**)], naval hero John Paul Goofy, pirate Old Black Goofy, explorer Lewis Goofy (1807), sea captain and whaler Captain Ebenezer Goofy (who was such a fumbler that when he struck a match across his seat, he set his pants on fire, then tried to douse it—accidentally jumping into the gunpowder barrel beside the water barrel), lawman Wyatt Goofy (1880), Livingstone "Wrong Way" Goofy (who discovered the South Pole then later mapped the Sahara, where he became lost, used a magnifying glass to study his map, set it on fire, and squandered the last of his water in a doomed effort to extinguish the blaze), Amos Goofy (1869, Goofy's grandfather, and a railroad worker), aviation pioneer Wilbur Goofy (1901, he attached wings to a fuselage, cut a hole in the top and bottom, used suspenders to hold "the Goofy Glider" around him, then tried to get airborne using everything from a bicycle to a catapult to a kite to roller skates to TNT—the latter put him into orbit), Livingstone's grandson Hector (ringmaster for a circus, and best friend of **Dolores** the elephant), Edsel Goofy (1940s, an inventor of failed vehicles like the seesaw bike and a big booster of the pogo stick as a means of transportation), and, finally, Goofy's Aunt Matilda and his Uncle Joe Goofy, the latter a world traveler. Goofy also has a son, Goofy, Jr., and a wife, Mrs. Goofy, both of whom first appeared in *Fathers Are People* (1951), and a pet grasshopper named Wilbur who was introduced in *Goofy and Wilbur* (1939, Goofy's first solo cartoon). As for Goofy himself, he's had a long and eclectic career. In his initial screen appearance (*Mickey's Revue*, 1932), he was seen only as a laughing, peanut-eating member of the audience with a short and unkempt beard and wearing pincenez glasses, vest, and tattered hat; he looked

*An ancestor of **Goofy**: Demosthenes Goofy, who ran the Olympic torch in the wrong direction.* © 1983 THE WALT DISNEY COMPANY. *All rights reserved.*

far more scraggly than the Goofy of today. He was known, then, as Dippy Dawg, and although he was involved in other early cartoons (amiably helping **Mickey Mouse** prepare for *The Whoopee Party* in 1932, for example) and got a name change in *Orphan's Benefit* (1934), he didn't really come to the fore as what animator Art Babbitt calls "an everlasting optimist . . . a half-wit, and a . . . good-natured hick" until *Mickey's Service Station* (1935). In that film he helps destroy a car, not to mention himself: He mistakes his own long, snaking hand struck deep inside the engine as something unknown that needs to be whacked. Thereafter, according to a 1937 model sheet (i.e., a guide to the animators showing the character in various poses), Goofy was to be drawn "a little awkward and screwy—no matter what he is doing. When eyelids show—make one higher than the other to give a 'goofy' look." During his varied career, Goofy has been a firefighter (*Mickey's Fire Brigade,* 1935), an iceman who helps move an evicted Mickey (*Moving Day,* 1936), a clock-tower clock cleaner (*Clock Cleaners,* 1937), a boat-builder (*Boat Builders,* 1938), and much more. However, he is most famous for his many "instructional" films, in which the narrator uses Goofy's misexamples to demonstrate what *not* to do. Among these are a series of sports shorts, including *The Art of Skiing* (1941), *The Art of Self-Defense* (1941), *How to Play Baseball* (1942), *How to Swim* (1942), *How to Play Golf* (1944), *How to Play Football* (1944), *Tennis Racquet* (1949), *Goofy Gymnastics* (1949), and others; a miscellaneous selection, such as *How to Be a Detective* (1953), *How to Dance* (1953), and *How to Sleep* (1953); and his most famous series, a how-not-to-drive trilogy consisting of *Motor Mania* (1950), *Freewayphobia No. 1* (1965), and *Goofy's Freeway Trouble* (1965) (see also **Super Goof**).

Comment. Goofy has appeared in eighty-four cartoons, as well as in the feature-length omnibus films *The Reluctant Dragon* (1941; the segment *How to Ride a Horse*), *Saludos Amigos* (1943; the segment *El Gaucho Goofy*), and *Fun and Fancy Free* (1947; the segment *Mickey and the Beanstalk*). Goofy also took the part of Jacob Marley's ghost in the 1983 theatrical featurette *Mickey's Christmas Carol.* The dog's name came from Walt Disney's habit of describing his cartoon characters' predicaments as "goofy." The dog's distinctive voice was provided, first, by the late Pinto Colvig, then by Stuart Buchanan, Bob Jackman, and Hal Smith. A long-time regular in the Mickey Mouse comic strip,

Goofy has had a stagnant career in comic books. Except for *Super Goof* and costarring roles in a variety of Disney comic books, Goofy headlined only thirteen editions of Dell's *4-Color* comic book from 1953 to 1962. Goofy's kind of slapstick simply doesn't translate well to the print medium.

GOOFY GOOSE
Pedigree. A vacuous gander, even by comic book standards.
Biography. Lazy and hopelessly dim-witted, Goofy supports himself by doing odd jobs—although more often than not, he has to be coaxed to work by his industrious insect friend Julius. The bespectacled Goofy is always dressed in a black vest and red necktie. Other animals that inhabit Goofy's world are the obnoxious Calvin Cow, the dog Mrs. O'Grady, and Julius's cousin Andy.
   Comment. The DC Comics character appeared as the main backup feature to **Peter Porkchops**. A secondary strip featured Biggety Bear, who also was inept and perennially broke.

GORGON
Pedigree. Pet dog of the comic strip boy Barnaby.
Biography. Barnaby is a preschooler who has to deal with a pompous, cigar-smoking, often fumbling Fairy Godfather named O'Malley, parents John and Ellen who don't believe that the winged, middle-aged man exists—and a most unusual dog. The stray first appears in the woods, after which, "imbued with too much Christmas spirit, someone broke into the ASPCA shelter . . . and freed all of its 216 canine inmates." When Barnaby first finds the dog, it has treed the frightened Mr. O'Malley—who inadvertently gives it it's name when he calls it a "shaggy gorgon." Barnaby's parents let him keep the animal, who begins to talk soon thereafter ("didn't know I could do it," the affable dog confesses. "Never tried it before, I guess."). Unfortunately, as soon as he realizes he can speak, all Gorgon does is tell puns and shaggy dog stories. In his most amusing adventure, Gorgon, Barnaby, and O'Malley search for the dog's father, Rover, who used to live "with some people named Baskerville." They find him working as a local firehouse dog, and offer to let him live at Barnaby's "for his declining years." He stays until he learns that he'll be expected to take a bath.
   Comment. Crockett Johnson's strip "Barnaby" premiered in the New York tabloid *PM* on April 20, 1942, and was discontinued a decade later when

Johnson grew tired of the pressures of coming up with a daily strip. Gorgon first appeared on December 26, 1942. Seldom has a humorous comic strip had better characterization, or more entertaining dialogue. A gorgon is a snake-haired monster of Greek mythology—something this delightful dog definitely is not.

GORILLA GRODD
Pedigree. Sinister, superintelligent ape, foe of the comic book hero the Flash.
Biography. In 1862, a spaceship crashes in Africa, near the equator. The wreckage is found by a tribe of gorillas: Inside are a small, hairless, humanoid alien, and a multifaceted crystal orb. Rays from the orb, an "evolution/identity-caster," strike the gorillas, boosting their intelligence; two beams are especially powerful. One, "straight/pure," hits Solovar; the other beam, "warped/dangerous," strikes Grodd. Solovar becomes the Gorilla King and, under his guidance, the tribe builds the golden and glorious Gorilla City. Grodd, a scientific genius, secretly plots his overthrow. When a pair of explorers locates the city in 1873—while it's still under construction—the alien telepathically learns English, transfers this knowledge to Solovar's aide Kios, and Kios teaches Solovar. Alas, jealous Grodd compels one of the men to draw his gun and shoot the alien. The gorillas pounce on the explorer, killing him; the other makes it back to civilization, although no one believes his story about an ape city, and he's institutionalized. Meanwhile, the completed Gorilla City is "invisibly shrouded" to prevent humans from ever rediscovering it. But there's danger from within, as Grodd never gives up his dream to rule the city . . . and the world. Finally rebelling against Solovar in modern times, Grodd is defeated by the superfast human hero the Flash. Taking a second stab at conquest, Grodd first uses an evolution machine to push himself along the evolutionary track and become human (as though gorillas were an intermediary stage in human evolution, and not an offshoot of the same root!) Calling himself Drew Drowden, he leaves the city to destroy the Flash . . . but is once again defeated. Imprisoned in Gorilla City, the resourceful Grodd can't get out . . . so he commits suicide and transfers his soul into human William Dawson, whose body he subsequently transforms into an exact likeness of his old self. Grodd continued to fight the Flash until the superhero's death in 1985. (Incidentally, the apes eventually give up their isolationist policy and open a "gorilla embassy" in New York,

with apes representing them at the United Nations.)
Comment. The simian czar was introduced in DC Comics *The Flash* no. 106 in 1959. *Note:* In each issue all "phrases are loosely translated from the alien."

GRANDMA DUCK
Pedigree. Grandmother of **Donald Duck**.
Biography. Grandma Duck lives on a farm and occasionally comes to visit Donald, bringing her own form of martial law to the household, forcing her grandson and his nephews **Huey, Dewey, and Louie** to clean up. Back on her farm, she's one tough waterfowl, unafraid to stand up to Brer Fox and Brer Weasel, who regularly raid the chicken coop (see **Brer Rabbit**). She's especially hard on **Gus Goose**, the laziest hired hand this side of Duckburg (Grandma had **Gyro Gearloose** make her a "telepathic-fetcher" to summon the snoozing Gus so she doesn't have to yell for him). Huey and his brothers often come to help her, and she once had **Jiminy Cricket** come by to help get rid of the Corn Bugs, which were eating her crop. The elderly duck is awful when it comes to finances and overspends on the comfort of her animals, especially her horse, Dobbin. Ms. Duck's neighbor is the dog Farmer Bumpkin. Grandma wears reading glasses, blue high-buttoned shoes, a jacket with puffy shoulders and frilly sleeves, and keeps her white hair in a bun. Grandma is apparently Donald's maternal relative, because the paternal side of the family hails from Europe.
Comment. The strict lady duck first appeared in the Donald daily newspaper strip on September 27, 1943. After making his nephews scrub the backs of their necks, Donald and the boys go to pick her up at the train . . . where she scowls at Donald, brings him to a water fountain, and scrubs the back of his neck. She made regular appearances in Donald's strip and comic book—she was in most issues from no. 121 to 168—and also starred in seven issues of Dell's *4-Color* comic book *Grandma Duck's Farm Friends*. Grandma never appeared in theatrical or TV cartoons.

GRAPE APE
Pedigree. Giant gorilla of TV cartoons.
Biography. According to the theme song, the gorilla is "over forty feet high . . . just a little bit shy . . . but a superstrong guy." The giant, 2,000-pound purple gorilla travels around the country with his normal-size, soft-spoken dog friend Beegle Beagle—a former

carnival huckster who thinks he can make a fortune on the monkey. Grape sits on top of the car while Beegle drives, and the two get into all manner of adventures, whether it's agreeing to race the Triple X Double Whammy 8 sports car against a pair of cheaters, or Ape falling in love with a giant, blue gorilla parade balloon or having to deal with a Beegle lookalike who tries to take control of the ape for evil purposes. In all of their adventures, Beegle's more-or-less keen mind and Ape's inarguably great strength always prevail. Grape wears a baseball cap, tiny jacket, and a black bow tie. He speaks in a superdeep voice, is fundamentally monosyllabic, and usually ends each sentence by muttering his own name, for who-knows-what reason. But who'd ever tell him not to: He's so strong that he can push a mountain down one place and have it pop up in another.

Comment. The character appeared on Hanna-Barbera's *The Tom and Jerry/Grape Ape Show* in 1975; there were thirty-three adventures in all. Grape was seen in 1976 on *The Tom and Jerry/Grape Ape/Mumbly Show,* and in 1977 (for just September) on *The Great Grape Ape.* See **Scooby Doo** for guestshots. Bob Holt was the voice of the ape, and Marty Ingels played Beegle. Charlton published two issues of a Grape Ape comic book in 1976, and Grape starred in Marvel's *TV Stars* no. 1 (1978).

GRIMM
Pedigree. Comic strip dog.
Biography. Thirty years old in dog-years, and a truly modern dude (he puts Perrier on his Gravy Train), the little yellow hound lives with the goose Mother Goose and lives to chase anything: cars (he'll settle for a school bus, although he hates the stop-and-go nature of the beast), birds (on the beach, he sings, "I wish they all could be California gulls," and he's had the gall to play dead to lure over vultures), and, of course, cats. His second-favorite pursuit is tormenting the mail carrier, whether deflating the truck tires, tripping him, or sneaking behind him and barking suddenly. (When the mail truck and dog catcher's van collide, Grimm just sits there, smiling, and says, "Is this a great country or what?") He also enjoys chasing his tail (when he finally caught it, he stood there thinking, "Now what?") and playing poker (especially strip poker . . . that is, with Dagwood Bumstead, Hagar the Horrible, and Dennis the Menace), although he always loses: His wagging tail gives him away when he's got a good hand. High on the list of Grimm's dislikes are trips to

the vet (he's been known to sabotage the phone when Mother Goose calls for an appointment), wearing a collar (Mother Goose implores him to put the collar on . . . and, grinning, he says to it, "Hey, collar . . . you just won a million bucks!"), and Benji movies (he requires insulin before watching them). He honestly doesn't mind having fleas live on him (he jokingly refers to himself as "Fleas 'R' Us"), and especially enjoys when they throw him surprise parties (tiny streamers and balloons fly from the dog's fur). He's even been known to wait for them while they go shopping in flea markets. Attila, the pure-bred Persian cat, and Ham, a lazy pig, also live with Mother Goose, and Grimm himself has a pet: a goldfish named Lassie. His acquaintances include Carl, "A good Dane, but not a great Dane," and a trio of lady pointers (yes . . . the Pointer Sisters). His favorite TV show is *Carl the Wonder Poodle.* The best cartoon: the beer-commercial send-up with Grimm drinking from a toilet and remarking, "It doesn't get any better than this." Runner-up: Grimm staring at a fire hydrant with a "Wet Paint" sign, and declaring, "I think I will."

Comment. Mike Peters's "Mother Goose and Grimm" began in 1985.

GROVER GROUNDHOG
Pedigree. Costar of *Rudolph the Red-Nosed Reindeer* comic books.
Biography. Grover is a well-meaning little mammal who has a penchant for building bizarre contraptions, and also has a habit of screwing up whatever he touches. For example, he once turned a snow buggy into a rocket (complete with a drill for burrowing into mountains) to reach the distant Tailor Gnome and get Santa's toy bag repaired. In a different tale, he built a jet-propelled toboggan, which rocketed him into the lair of Wilbur the Wizard. Using Wilbur's magic wand, Grover inadvertently causes all the tools in Santa's workshop to turn into wild animals. On another occasion, he bumps into the neatly hanging harness of his friend Rudolph, reassembles it up all wrong, and causes it to snap during a run. The reindeer falls through a "sky hole," ends up in Topsy-Turvy land with its greedy Santa, and has to be rescued by Grover, who comes after him with a hot-air balloon. Once in a while, though, Grover's a victim instead of a perpetrator, as the time he bought a magician's Lucky Dragon Egg—which was really a Bad Luck Dragon the mage was trying to get rid of. Grover was also featured in one-page "How-to" features, which taught readers how to

draw, how to make paper airplanes, and so on. The buck-toothed, brown groundhog was always dressed in a snowcap, scarf, and mittens, although never in boots. Other animals who popped up in the stories include Pigeon Pete and his cousin Homer Pigeon, Ethel and Egbert Eagle, and, of course, Rudolph's fellow reindeers.

Comment. DC published fifteen issues of *Rudolph the Red-Nosed Reindeer* between 1950 and 1962. The series was inspired by the Robert L. May story, which was written in 1939 for a Montgomery Ward & Co. booklet, and by the 1949 Johnny Marks song based on May's tale. Most of the stories were written and drawn by Sheldon Mayer, who added some interesting wrinkles to the Rudolph saga, such as that "no reindeer can fly unless he is hitched to Santa's magic sleigh." While on the subject of Santa, more "revisionism" came from the W. T. Grant Co., which published a one-shot comic book in 1942: *The Adventures of Stubby, Santa's Smallest Reindeer.*

GUERRILLA GROUNDHOG

Pedigree. Mutated comic book animal.
Biography. Guerrilla Groundhog and his sidekick Maximilian Mole—who possesses superhearing—operate in our own human world. Based in a complex deep beneath the plains of the American Midwest, and aided by the human Gwen, they fight bizarre threats to the nation, such as the earth-invading Red Spot Commies, "Jovian sandworms with a profound sense of Marxist/Leninist ideology." The heroes move about underground by digging tunnels at superspeed, or cover greater distances using the Silver Gopher, a "magnetic railway [that] can manage ten thousand miles an hour." When they have to work in the seas, the heroes frequently call Cal Calamari, a giant squid.

Comment. The character had a short run in his own Eclipse Comics title, published in 1987.

GUMMI BEARS

Pedigree. Candy product turned into TV characters by the Walt Disney Studios.
Biography. Standing between two and three feet tall and dressed in medieval garb, the "dashing, daring, courageous, faithful, and friendly" bears drink Gummiberry juice, which gives them the ability to bounce "here and there and everywhere" to defend themselves or their friends. Years ago, the bears intermingled with humans. However, human greed—specifically, their attempts to learn the secret of the

juice—caused the bears to shut themselves off in underground tunnels. Now, in medieval times, the Gummi Clan lives in Gummi Glen in the kingdom of Dunwyn. (There are also Gummis who, when these European bears went subterranean, sailed "across the sea" and established New Gumbria.) The bears do all they can to help Gregor, the king of Dunwyn, in his ongoing battle against the evil Duke Igthorn of Drekmore, who wants to rule the world. Their only human friends are Cavin, a page at the king's castle, and the king's daughter, Princess Calla. The ranks of the little bears include the happy Sunni, big and responsible Tummi, crabby Gruffi, grandpa Zummi (keeper of the Great Book of Gummi, a tome of Gummi science and lore), Grammi Gummi (brewer of the Gummiberry juice) and youngest-of-all Cubbi—who, in one adventure, became so fed up with crime in the kingdom that he donned a cloak and mask and became the sword-swinging Crimson Avenger.

Comment. *Disney's Adventures of the Gummi Bears* hopped from the Heide candy lineup to the NBC Saturday morning lineup in 1985. The show was expanded to *The Gummi Bears and Winnie the Pooh Hour* in 1989. In addition to above-average animation, the show has a lush orchestral score. A comic strip, "Disney's Gummi Bears," went into syndication the same time the series premiered and is still in circulation.

GUMMY

Pedigree. The comic book alligator pet of monarch Royal Roy.
Biography. Most kids have pet dogs and cats; the incredibly wealthy Roy, prince of the tiny nation Cashelot, has a pet alligator who thinks he's a dog and occasionally lets out a *Bow wow! Woof woof!* Even though he's some seven feet long, Gummy isn't mean spirited; in any case, as his name implies, he's toothless. What's more, the animal has a nose more sensitive than that of a bloodhound. Gummy lives in a *very* long "doghouse" behind the castle and is not permitted to beg for scraps at the table. The animal is fond of knocking the crown from King Regal's head with a snap of his powerful tail.

Comment. Gummy waddled onto the comics stage in the first issue of Marvel Comics's *Royal Roy* in 1985. The magazine lasted just six issues.

GUS GOOSE

Pedigree. Cousin of **Donald Duck.**
Biography. The arrival of Donald's cousin Gus was

preceded by a letter from Gus's mother, Donald's Aunt Fanny. Fanny wrote that she was sending him for a visit, but tacked on an ominous P.S.: "He don't eat much." In fact, Gus never *stops* eating. The obese, dumb duck consumes everything in sight— even the Barking Hot-Dogs bought by the desperate Donald, which are guaranteed "to get rid of hungry relatives." The grinning gander departs only when every scrap of food is gone. Gus wears a red hat, bow tie, red waistcoat, Eton collar, with a blue shirt, and possesses the questionable talents of knitting spaghetti into a stocking before ingesting it and shuffling bread and meat like cards into a hefty sandwich.

Comment. Gus appeared in just the two theatrical cartoons, *Donald's Cousin Gus* (1939) and *Mickey's Christmas Carol* (1983), and made a few visits to the Donald Duck newspaper comic strip. Gus also had a costarring role in the Mighty Knight comic stories, which appeared in the comic book starring **Super Goof**. Here, he's portly but doesn't always eat, and proves to be quite resourceful when it comes to helping the adventuresome hero (when the evil Robber-Knight has Mighty Knight at bay, Gus sneaks ragweed to the fiend's horse, causing it to sneeze and unseat the villain). Another venue for the goose was the **Grandma Duck** comic book. He lived on her farm and was always asleep when he was supposed to be working.

GYRO GEARLOOSE

Pedigree. Scientist chicken in Walt Disney comic books.
Biography. Standing four feet tall with a carpet of red hair, Gyro wears spectacles, a yellow hat tied under his chin, a green vest, a white shirt buttoned to the neck, and brown trousers. The somewhat absentminded fowl is first seen hopping around on a pogo stick, a quart of milk strapped to his back, trying to invent "a new way to churn butter." Truth be told, Gyro has a knack for inventing impressive, but often useless, objects such as a worm-training device (leaving him a very unpopular citizen in Duckburg, because when he went fishing, there was little left for anyone else to catch), a firefly tracker, an old-leaf miniaturizer, a mind-reading robot, and a "sculptinker"—a moving work of art that self-destructs and "symbolizes that modern-type sculptoring is a big bust . . . no-talent stuff!" His proudest achievements are the think boxes, which make crea-

tures smarter and can also be used in reverse, to make creatures "unsmart." Later, Gyro becomes an inventor-for-hire. Customers (like **Grandma Duck**) send in orders for inventions and he comes up with them. Whenever Gearloose has a mental block, he clears it by hitting himself on the head with a hammer. About the only time he was daunted was when he tried to create an invention to guarantee an ant-free picnic: He ended up with walls and a roof on a platform . . . then realized, to his chagrin, that he'd built a house, which is "what people most want to get away from when they go open-air picnicking!" In the comics, his long-time professional rival was the crook Emil Eagle, who was always spying on Gyro and/or trying to steal his inventions. Gyro is presently in the employ of **Scrooge McDuck** on the TV series and in the comic book *DuckTales*. For Scrooge, he's come up with more useful inventions such as a time-altering device, a Reducto-Ray, automated factory equipment, and his most impressive effort of all: the Gizmo Duck supersuit, which enables the wearer to become a security guard *extraordinaire*. The silvery suit—which can only be activated by uttering the word *Blatherskite*—is bulletproof, fireproof, and knuckleproof; rides on a unicycle-like wheel; and contains such devices as missiles, a helmet copter, an umbrella, a vacuum cleaner, a telephone, a mop-o-matic, a toast timer that sings country western music, and a digital zucchini slicer (see **Scrooge McDuck** for further details). In both his old and new adventures, Gyro is assisted by the diminutive robot Little Bulb, who is literally a light bulb with wire arms and legs. Gyro lives in the south side of Duckburg (he was born on the north side, around 1920). His only known relative is his grandfather, Ratchet Gearloose, who worked as an engineer on Scrooge McDuck's paddlewheel boat *Dilly Dollar*.

Comment. The character first appeared in *Walt Disney's Comics and Stories* no. 140 in 1951, and appeared in five issues of his own Dell comic book from 1959 to 1962. Little Bulb debuted in 1956. Both were created by legendary Donald artist/writer Carl Barks. The most entertaining aspect of the strip was not just Gyro but the bits of incidental background business in which Little Bulb was involved, such as folding paper into an airplane and soaring off, rolling a doughnut with a stick, making faces at a mouse, packing batteries when setting out on the aforementioned picnic, and so on.

THE HAIR BEAR BUNCH

Pedigree. Trio of TV bears led by the irrepressible Hair Bear.

Biography. Wonderland Zoo is a nice place to visit, but a less-than-wonderful place for its denizens. The Hair Bear Bunch live in Cave Block no. 9, and have managed to turn their cave into a place of comfort: Hidden inside rocks and behind revolving walls are televisions, a refrigerator, easy chairs, and the like. But a cage is still a cage, and the bears constantly look for ways to get out of the zoo—such as dressing as a woman and her children or using a compressed air tank as a rocket. Naturally, their escapes make life difficult for Mr. Peevely, the curator, and his assistant Botch, who always ends up having to get the bears back (although their job is made easier by their unique Bear Radar device). At the zoo, the bears' best pals are Bananas the Gorilla and Fur Face the Lion. Hair Bear, the leader, wears a vest and an ascot, has a frizzy head of hair, and talks like Phil Silvers; Square Bear wears a shirt and is big and dumb; and Bubi Bear is small and exuberant.

Comment. The Hanna-Barbera cartoon was clearly inspired by the studio's earlier **Wally Gator** cartoons. *Help! It's the Hair Bear Bunch* premiered on CBS in 1971. There were sixteen cartoons in all. Daws Butler was the voice of Hair Bear, Paul Winchell was Bubi Bear, and Bill Calloway was Square Bear. When the series went into syndication in 1974, it was retitled *The Yo Yo Bears*. Gold Key published nine Hair Bear Bunch comic books from 1972 to 1974.

HAM AND EX

Pedigree. Likable twin pups of theatrical cartoons.

Biography. The duo first appeared in *I Haven't Got a Hat* (the debut cartoon of **Porky Pig**), singing the title song. Their second cartoon, *The Phantom Ship*, is considerably more exciting, as they explore a ghostship with their uncle **Beans**. In *The Fire Alarm*, their third and final cartoon, they're mischievous rather than cute, pulling pranks in the firehouse where Beans is employed. In the end, they steal a firetruck and cause massive destruction before being apprehended—and spanked! The dogs are white and bipedal, with a black spot on the left side of their torso and right side of their face.

Comment. The twosome starred in just these three Warner Brothers cartoons (1935 to 1936).

THE HAMM'S BEAR

Pedigree. Advertising mascot for Hamm's Beer.

Biography. The tall, smiling, chunky, bipedal bear and his friends—most notably, Big Moose—live in the woods of Minnesota, "the land of sky-blue waters" and home of Hamm's Bear. The early commercials featured the clumsy bear in short, slapstick routines, such as having a fishline tug-of-war with his own reflection in a pond (and losing), or conducting the Woodland Symphony Orchestra and getting pelted by acorns from the unappreciative Raccoon Twins. In the mid-1960s, he was appearing in live-action ads, and allowed to say one line: "It bears repeating."

Comment. Introduced in 1955, the bear's 100-plus commercials were originally seen just in the Midwest, which was where the beer was sold. He was shelved in 1968, then reemerged a decade later and went national.

HAMSTER VICE

Pedigree. Comic book crime fighters.

Biography. Because crime in the metropolis of Swamp Indigo is "so dense that it takes the place of nitrogen in the atmosphere," Hammy, Ben, and Wolph team to form Hamster Vice. Hammy is the commander; Ben is an explosives expert (he is most proud of his exploding rubber bands), and Wolph is a swordsmaster, whose flashing blade regularly sends the comic's "PG-13 rating down the toilet." The "furry fuzz" are based in an apartment building, which also houses their warrior girlfriends—respectively, Flash, Charity, and Rocks-Anne. Another crime-fighting team in the all-animal city is the Rooster Squad. Chief among their foes are racketeer Addam Antt, and the drug-running Young Adult Hybrid Underwater Subnuclear Shaolin Snakefist Kung Fu Leather Spiders, led by Mandok Spydor—who is "famous for doing business with a client . . . then *eating* him."

Comment. Dwayne J. Ferguson's characters debuted in their own Blackthorne Publishing comic book in 1986. It ran for eight issues.

HAMTON

Pedigree. Peewee version of **Porky Pig.**

Biography. Hamton is an indecisive young pig who is sure of only one thing: He likes to eat, and can usually be found chowing down at Acme Pizza and Hot Dogs. The porcine youth is shy and low on self-esteem, qualities he hopes to overcome at Acme Looniversity, where he's learning how to be funny . . . just like his distant relative Porky. Hamton's class-mates include Buster Bunny, a blue-furred hare who's related to **Bugs Bunny** and is nearly as smart and pre-cocious; pink-furred Babs Bunny, who has bows on her eartips and enjoys doing impressions of lady rock stars and celebrities; Plucky Duck, a green-feathered duck who, like **Daffy Duck,** has a huge ego and quick temper; Sweetie, a pink, diminutive version of **Tweety Bird;** Furrball, a pesky feline like **Sylvester the Cat;** Fifi, a petite skunk; Calamity Coyote, a miniature **Wile E. Coyote;** Little Beeper, a small Road Runner; and Dizzy Devil, a destructive Tasmanian devil who loves party and food . . . especially pizza rolls.

Comment. These characters first appeared in the *Tiny Toons* cartoon series which debuted in the fall of 1989. They have since become the stars of their own DC comic book, as well as numerous novels and an activity magazine.

HANGDOG

Pedigree. Pet dog in the comic strip "The Great John L."

Biography. John L. is a preadolescent who has one of the laziest dogs on earth. How lazy? He dreams about sleeping. Fleas have declared the top of his head a national forest, it's so stationary. Even with his head out the car window, Hangdog sleeps (al-though he hates spitting out the bugs afterward). And he doesn't go for a walk, he goes for a drag. Hangdog refuses to fetch sticks ("If he wants the darn thing so bad, why does he keep throwing it away?"), and although a girl says that he's probably "very wise," John L. insists that the animal can't stay awake long enough to complete a thought (listening to them, Hangdog thinks, "E = mczzzzzzz"). Fortu-nately, he's a great watchdog: His snoring drives prowlers away. Only meat can stir him from his leth-argy. John's baby brother often pretends to be the superhero Babyman. In these fantasies, he leaps on Hangdog's back and fancies the stationary dog as Lightning, the Wonder Horse. Hangdog can't talk to other characters in the strip, only to the reader.

Comment. Don Addis's charming "The Great John L." debuted in newspapers in 1983.

HASHIMOTO

Pedigree. Martial arts mouse of theatrical cartoon fame.

Biography. Living in a Japanese home, the scrupu-lously polite, soft-spoken, judo-practicing mouse wears traditional Japanese clothing as he tells folk-tales as well as his own adventures to reporter G.I. Joe from an American newspaper—tales such as *So Sorry, Pussycat, Spooky-Yaki,* and *Night Life in Tokyo.* Also seen in the cartoons were Hashimoto's family: his wife (known only as Mrs. Hashimoto) and young daughter, Yuriko, and son, Saburo.

Comment. Terrytoons produced fourteen car-toons featuring the mouse, from 1959 to 1963. John Myhers provided the voices for all the characters. Apart from interesting visuals occasionally reminis-cent of Japanese watercolors, and expansively pre-sented in CinemaScope, the cartoons were not extraordinary. There was one issue of Gold Key's *Deputy Dawg Presents Dinky Duck and Hashimoto-san* (1965); the character also costarred in Dell, then Gold Key's, *New Terrytoons* comic book, fifty-four issues of which were published from 1960 to 1979.

HEATHCLIFF

Pedigree. Comic strip, comic book, and TV cat.

Biography. Tough, violent, and misanthropic like his *Wuthering Heights* namesake, Heathcliff is a mischief maker with class: He practices his favorite pastime, spilling trash cans, while doing ballet steps; he carpools to the local fish market to beg or steal (seafood is his favorite food, and he once consumed an entire porpoise in a single sitting); he fills the birdbath with glue so he won't have to chase his pray; he is registered to vote; he frequently and reck-lessly hides in lion cages to steal their meat; he's been known to run onto football fields and snatch the ball just as a placekicker is about to boot it; and he once retained a lawyer to sue a restauranteur who refused to honor a fish-dinner contest Heathcliff had won. The cat's "favorite TV show" is sitting by the oven and watching turkey cook. Owned by the Nutmeg family (young Iggy and sister Marcy, and Grandpa and Grandma), Heathcliff hates mice above all, but he'll slash at "everything that moves," including falling leaves. His nemesis is the bulldog Spike, al-though there are few dogs (Spike included) who can stand up to the violent kitty. His girlfriend is Sonja, an attractive Persian cat whom he once wooed by setting out sardines shaped like a Valentine. The mice in the house (Harry is one of the few named) are fearful of going out for cheese, although their efforts at making peace with the cat have been in vain. Heathcliff's only fear is visiting the vet.

Comment. George Gately's feline premiered on September 3, 1973, and the single-panel daily strip and half-page Sunday strip remain a popular attraction in more than 1,000 newspapers. There have been nearly forty paperback collections of the cartoons. ABC's *Heathcliff and Dingbat* aired in 1980, followed by *Heathcliff and Marmaduke* in 1981. Mel Blanc provided the cat's voice, which was extremely reminiscent of **Bugs Bunny**—forgivable, given the cocksure nature of both. (Dingbat was a vampire dog with an Hungarian accent who appeared in the cartoon component *Dingbat and the Creeps,* which costarred Nobody—a pumpkin head with a baseball cap and sneakers—and the skeleton Sparerib. The trio worked—ineffectually—for Odd Jobs, Inc.) *Heathcliff the Movie* was released in 1985. In it, Heathcliff told stories to his three (unnamed) nephews and a mouse . . . all of whom were a captive audience (Heathcliff locked them in a cage). The stories involved Heathcliff using a timid lookalike named Henry to help him win an important footrace; the taming of a pair of martial-arts cats known as the Siamese Twins; a stay in an obedience school run by tough cat Corporal Bruiser; a battle with the Catfather, who moves into town and tries to become a local bully; a bout with the wrestler Boom Boom Pussini, who has eyes for Sonja; and the story of Heathcliff's father being released from jail and trying to go straight. For the first time, we learn that Heathcliff's hostility arises from having been raised in a bad neighborhood . . . to which he returns to help keep his dad out of police hands. Marvel Comics's enduring *Heathcliff* comic book began publication in 1985.

HECKLE AND JECKLE
Pedigree. Obnoxious talking magpies of theatrical cartoons, comics, and television.
Biography. Cocky, smirking, gag-playing twin birds, Jeckle speaks in a singsongy British accent, Heckle with a rough, New York voice. In every other way the magpies are identical, from their appearance—black feathers, occasionally with white bellies—to their quasi-sadistic natures to the fact that they call everyone "chum" or "old bean." Their frequent victim (it would be inaccurate to call the inept fellow an adversary) is a bulldog named Dimwit, who prefaces virtually everything he utters with a long, dumb, *Duuuuuh.* The stories usually have the duo taking advantage of Dimwit or another character, which results in a chase that lasts the bulk of the cartoon (and rarely draws sweat or even a look of distress from the cool birds). For example, they'll sell the dog a book guaranteed to make him smart. When the dog opens it and finds nothing but blank pages, the birds will claim he *is* smarter: He knows never to buy anything from them again. Thus begins the pursuit, which invariably causes Dimwit or another foe more harm. When they aren't bashing other animals, the magpies engage each other in glib if predictable repartee:

> HECKLE: I hate to say it, but we have only one choice.
> JECKLE: Oh no! Surely you don't mean . . .
> HECKLE: Oh yes I do . . . and don't call me Shirley.

Sure it's predictable, but that's part of the birds' charm. They're cool enough to wink at the audience, to tell old jokes with confidence. In fact, they're so cool they can acknowledge the fact that they're animated characters. For example, in *The Lion Hunt,* when they need to take a quick trip and a boat suddenly appears, one of them remarks, "My! Things happen quickly in a cartoon, don't they?" In *The Power of Thought,* one of them decides to "take advantage" of the fact that he's a cartoon character by transforming himself into any animal he thinks about. Likewise, with no explanation, one of them goes through *Sno Fun* doing a Humphrey Bogart impersonation.

Comment. The idea of doing animation's first twin characters was Paul Terry's, founder of Terrytoons, although it was his staff that came up with the idea of using birds. The names were a spinoff of an earlier Terrytoon cartoon, *Ickle and Pickle;* it isn't clear whether Heckle's name inspired his personality, or vice versa. Terrytoons produced fifty-two Heckle and Jeckle cartoons produced for theatrical release from 1946 to 1966; Dayton Allen, then Ned Sparks, provided the voice for both birds. These cartoons began showing up on television in 1955 on the syndicated *Heckle and Jeckle Show.* Adventures of **Dinky Duck** and **Little Roquefort** were also seen on the show. Filmation produced thirty-one new cartoons for *The New Adventures of Mighty Mouse and Heckle and Jeckle,* which aired on CBS in 1979. Frank Welker was the voice of the birds. In comic books, the magpies starred in their own title from St. John Publishing, which lasted thirty-four issues (1955 to 1959), and in four comics from Gold Key (1962 to 1963), three from Dell (1966 to 1967), and one from Spotlight (1987). The characters also appeared in many of the comics that featured **Mighty Mouse.** Dimwit had his own one-page features in many of these comics, which usually had him searching in vain for a bone, getting bullied by other dogs, and so on.

HENERY HAWK

Pedigree. Small but tough theatrical nemesis of Foghorn Leghorn, cartoon rooster.

Biography. Henery's screen debut *(The Squawkin' Hawk)* set the tone for the series. The young son of George K. Chickenhawk, Henery refuses to eat a worm his mother has brought for him. Sent to bed without dinner, he sneaks out of their treetop home to get food from a coop, ends up being chased by a rooster and has to be rescued by his mother. Back at the nest, the worm is writing his will . . . but Henery still won't eat him. He wants chicken. In his second cartoon *(Walky Talky Hawky),* he leaps from his folks' treetop home ("Someday, I guess I better learn to fly," he says, hitting the ground hard), and has his first run-in with the rooster **Foghorn Leghorn,** who convinces him that a dog is a chicken and that he, himself, is a horse. During the course of this cartoon, Henery demonstrates his inordinate strength and determination: He carries off a doghouse with the dog still in it, and, in the end, confused and angry, he ropes the rooster, dog, and a horse together and drags them home to find out which is which (reasoning, "One of dese tings has *got* to be a chicken!") And so it goes, in every cartoon, the chickenhawk going forth to get himself a chicken; unfortunately, he isn't always experienced enough to know what one looks like. On several occasions, Foghorn attempts to pawn off a dog and a cat on the tough but naive bird, and in *You Were Never Duckier,* Henery accidentally makes off with **Daffy Duck.** In his later years, Henery gets his act together and usually picks on just Foghorn. In his last appearance *(Strangled Eggs),* he's "abandoned" in a basket on the stoop of **Miss Prissy.** Prissy wants to raise Henery as a chicken but her boyfriend Foghorn wants the chickenhawk dead, and he tries any number of ways to dispose of Henery while seeming to train him to be a chicken. (For example, Foghorn disguises a hand grenade as an egg and persuades the chickenhawk to sit on it. Unfortunately, when Foghorn pulls the string attached to the pin, the grenade flies toward him. Later, after planting mines in the field and teaching Henery how to pick and scratch

for food, it isn't the chickenhawk who blows up.) Henery's head is slightly larger than the rest of his body, and he has a well-developed chest and arms. He's covered with brown feathers, and has a short but erect spray of tail feathers. He talks with a high-pitched but tough New York accent.

Comment. The Warner Brothers character was seen from 1942 to 1961. One of the studio's lesser lights, he appeared in just eleven cartoons.

HENRY LIMPET

Pedigree. Human-turned-fish in a live-action/animated feature.

Biography. In a prologue, naval Lieutenant George Stickle and a superior officer open a top secret file on Henry Limpet, to check on his last-known whereabouts. As they look up the information, the story shifts to World War II. Frail Brooklyn bookkeeper Henry Limpet is declared 4F because of his terrible eyesight. He's embarrassed not to be taking part in the war—especially when brash navy friend George Stickle stops by. It doesn't help matters that Henry's wife, Bessie, is taken with the sailor. The only bright spot in Henry's life is his fascination with fish. He hangs around the pet shop, maintains a large aquarium in his apartment, and reads "hundreds of books" about sea creatures. He even sings plaintively, at one point, "I wish, I wish I were a fish." Visiting Coney Island with Bessie and George, Henry is reading a book titled *Theory of Reverse Evolution,* which states that while fish evolved into humans, it may also be possible to go back again. Distressed with his life and curious about the theory, Henry—who can't swim—leaps off the pier. As soon as he's underwater, he's struck by a blue light and metamorphoses into a blue limpet (still wearing Henry's glasses). George dives in after him, but doesn't realize the fish is his friend; Henry is presumed to have drowned. Delighted with his new surroundings, Henry revels in them—until he's attacked by a shark. Screaming in panic, he unleashes a sound that chases the animal away—a cry that he subsequently dubs his "whale-busting sound." Nearby, the mustachioed hermit crab Crusty is darned impressed, especially when Limpet uses the blast to save him from an octopus. The crab accompanies Henry on his journey to find more limpets. They spot one who's been hooked by a fisherman, and Henry rescues it. The limpet, Ladyfish, is so grateful she wraps her body around his and wants to run right to the spawning grounds. But Henry thinks of Bessie and declines, stating, "It wouldn't be proper!" Shortly thereafter, Henry spots a Nazi U-boat, and, without showing himself, calls out to a U.S. destroyer, which he leads right to the enemy vessel. He offers to help the navy find other Axis subs—but wants George Stickle to serve as liaison. Stickle is seconded to the destroyer, set out in a raft, and Henry surfaces to have a chat with him (disappearing now and then to "go down for air.") Stickle is shocked by his friend's condition but, as Henry notes, becoming a fish has really made a man out of him. Thereafter, George communicates with Henry by dropping a hydrophone into the sea, and the toll among the German navy is high. (Needless to say, Bessie doesn't believe George when he tells her what has happened and gets to state the inevitable "There's something very fishy about this.") Meanwhile, the frustrated Germans develop torpedoes that can home in on "das Limpet," and they inaugurate the weapons as Henry is leading an important convoy to Europe. To make matters worse, a collision with a manta knocks Henry's glasses to the bottom of the sea, leaving him practically blind. Enter Crusty, who agrees to ride Henry's back and serve as his eyes. Of course, the two don't know about the torpedoes. When the U-boats arrive and the heroes realize that the projectiles can follow them, there's a moment of panic—until Henry realizes that he can cause the torpedoes to double back toward the subs and destroy them. When the U-boats have been reduced to scrap iron, and the convoy has completed its journey, Henry, George, and Bessie meet at the Coney Island pier. There, Mrs. Limpet gives her husband a new pair of glasses and they say good-bye, Henry assuring her that "Maybe all along I was meant to be a fish. Maybe nature just corrected her error." Cut back to the present: Stickle and his companion learn that Henry was last seen off the coast of Florida, and contact him to promote him to commodore, USN reserve . . . and to ask him to help in a program to train dolphins for the military. (Curiously, the film ends before Henry puts in an appearance. Either he's had enough of humans, doesn't find much merit to the Cold War, ran off with Ladyfish, retired in Florida, or all of the above. Or maybe Henry felt they were just pulling his fin, because commodore is not a rank used in peacetime.)

Comment. The 1964 film starred Don Knotts as Henry, Jack Weston as George, and Carole as Bessie. It was based on the little-known novel *Be Careful How You Wish* by Theodore Pratt. Dell published a comic book adaptation.

HENRY'S CAT

Pedigree. Cat of British TV cartoons.

Biography. Henry is never seen in the stories, which feature the bare, orange, cockney cat fantasizing about escapades in exotic locales, with himself as the hero and the recurring "evil sheep" Rambaba as his enemy. Typical is *The Lost World,* in which, while watching a Tarzan movie on television, the cat daydreams about being Tarzan. Swinging from vines and riding about on elephant-back, he prevents Rambaba from capturing the ninety-foot-tall ape King Konga, whom he wants to display in his Dinosaur Diner back home. Occasionally, the feline's real-life friends will partake in his imaginary adventures. In *The Great Adventure,* it's a thousand years in the future, and our hero is Captain Goodcat, commander of a spaceship known as the *Fabulous Flying Carrot.* At his side are Dr. Chris Rabbit, as well as an unnamed dog, pig, worm, parrot, snail, frog, mouse, and duck. Commander Sheepdog sends them on a mission to discover why stars are vanishing in deep space. Arriving on a distant world, Goodcat discovers that Rambaba has stolen them and plans to use them to erect a giant space sign advertising his new product: food made from recycled rubbish. Goodcat and his crew are imprisoned, but they persuade Rambaba's martian slaves to rebel and foil the lamb once more. Even in more reality-based episodes, such as *The Weather Man,* there's a strong fantasy element, as when he decides to become a weatherman to put an end to unpleasant days (a good way to get rid of a cold spell would be with a volcano, he concludes). He never does achieve his goal, although it's fun watching him and pal Chris rehearse by having Henry's cat walk around with a TV-shaped cardboard box on his head, or going into his routine when he notices a surveillance camera in the grocery store.

Comment. The fifteen-minute-long adventures began airing in 1984, produced by Bob Godfrey Films Ltd. and created by Stan Hayward. The stories feature very limited animation and are told solely through narration, but there is wit and charm here. The cartoons have been shown in the United States on cable television.

HERMAN THE MOUSE

Pedigree. Wisecracking mouse of theatrical cartoons and comic books.

Biography. It's a sad day in the mouse hole: Mouse after mouse on the Cheese Patrol is being slaughtered by a big, black cat as they boldly try to get food. The names of the dead mice are inscribed on the wall of the hole; the survivors are gaunt, weak, and disspirited. Suddenly, the silhouette of a fierce cat appears on the wall behind them. The mice panic—then breathe easier when they realize that it's only cousin Herman, newly arrived from the city and doing a hand shadow to get everyone's attention. Dressed in blue trousers, a straw hat, and bow tie, and carrying a cane, the jaunty, big-eared mouse talks like a Dead End Kid and refuses to accept the prospect of defeat. Striding over to the sleeping cat, he blows a trumpet in its ear, lets the feline follow him into a sack, then slips out a small opening in the other end and seals the bag. Herman drags the cat toward a well, but his victim extends a sharp claw and cuts his way from the bag: Thus begins a chase that ends in the cat's death by drowning—although at the fadeout, nine ghosts (one for each of the cat's lives) are seen chasing Herman. The mouse survives and faces other cats in subsequent cartoons, defeating each before the arrival of his permanent foe, Katnip. Brown-furred and sleepy-eyed, with a slow voice and a mind to match, Katnip is allowed to live. As one of the mice puts it, "If Katnip is kicked out, the folks will get another cat." Herman replies, "That's *dangerous!* You just *can't* get another cat as dumb as Katnip," to which the terminally dumb Katnip adds, "Exactly!" Now and then, Katnip hopefully chases Herman with a knife and fork, a pitiful spectacle indeed. Likewise, Herman still enjoys tormenting the cat: He's been known to slip into the kitty's mouth and pull out his tongue, so that when he bites down he'll perforate it.

Comment. Paramount's Herman appeared in thirty-three cartoons from 1947 to 1959. Katnip didn't arrive until the seventh cartoon, *Micecapades,* in 1952; Finny the Goldfish, not Herman, was seen in Katnip's second cartoon, *Feast and Furious.* Apart from these, it was Herman versus Katnip all the way. The cartoons came to television on *Funday Funnies,* along with **Baby Huey,** the sluggish Tommy Tortoise, Casper the Friendly Ghost and others; the show was syndicated in 1959. Arnold Stang provided the voice for Herman, and Sid Raymond was the voice of Katnip. In comics, Herman and Katnip first appeared in *Paramount Animated Comics* no. 1 in 1953. They also starred in four issues of *Harvey Hits* beginning in 1958 (nos. 14, 25, 31, and 41), and in short adventures that were published in other Harvey titles, such as *TV Casper and Company.*

HERO

Pedigree. Horse owned by the comic strip superhero the Phantom.

Biography. For 400 years, the mantle of the Phantom has been passed from father to son in the mythical Afro-Asian land of Bangalla. The purple-costumed hero lives in Skull Cave in the Deep Woods, and protects the natives and wildlife alike. He gets about by riding the magnificent white stallion Hero (his father's horse was Thunder), and is always accompanied by his gray mountain wolf, Devil.

Comment. The Phantom and his brood were created by Lee Falk and first appeared in newspaper comic strips on February 17, 1936. They went on to star in comic books published by David McKay, Harvey, Gold Key, King Features, Charlton, and, presently, by DC), and also starred in a live-action motion picture serial in 1943. Other horses (and canines) who accompany superheroes on their rounds include the black steed Hurricane and the black hound Thunderclap who ride with DC Comics's the Wild Huntsman; the genetically altered flying horse Aragorn who bears Marvel's the Black Knight about (he was replaced by the magical flying horse Valinor when Aragorn went to the superheroine Valkyrie); Captain Cleo, the dog who uses a small area rug for a cape and, pretending to possess superpowers, runs around with Captain Kentucky in a comic strip in the trade publication *The Comic Reader;* Lucifer, black horse of the western-style vigilante El Diablo; White Wind, horse of Fawcett's 1940s modern-day archer-hero Golden Arrow; Lockjaw, the genetically altered, five-foot-tall, half-ton bulldog who has worked with Marvel's Fantastic Four; Winged Victory, the flying horse of DC's modern-day "Lancelot" the Shining Knight; and Diablo, stallion ridden by the 1940s hero the Whip. There are also a falcon, Redwing, who accompanies Marvel's Falcon on his rounds and helps track fleeing thugs; and Bingo, the trained, superintelligent kangaroo who helps his human master fight crime as Kangaroo Man in three issues of their own comic book.

HILLBILLY BEARS

Pedigree. A simple (and simple-minded) TV cartoon family.

Biography. The Rugg family is a quartet of bears who live in a shack in the woods. The world-weary Maw Rugg is the one intelligent member of the family, and the only one who can understand big, lean, barely articulate Paw Rugg. Rounding out the family are tiny, energetic Shagg Rugg, their son, and teen daughter, Floral Rugg. The four bears dress in tattered clothing; the parent Ruggs smoke pipes, while the men wear big, pointed hillbilly hats. Among their adventures are run-ins with pesky animals as in *Rickety-Rockety-Raccoon, Woodpecked, Rabbit Rumble*, and *Going, Going Gone Gopher*, and a brush with (surprise!) Goldilocks.

Comment. The Hanna-Barbera characters appeared in their own segment of *The Atom Ant Show*, which debuted on NBC in 1965. There were twenty-six cartoons. Henry Corden was Paw, Jean Vander Pyl did the voices for Maw and Floral, and Don Messick was Shag. Another set of Hanna-Barbera bumpkins are Punkin Puss and Mushmouse, a cat and mouse who fight each other as well as common foes from ghosts to Bat Monsterson. These characters appeared in twenty-three cartoons, which were syndicated as part of *The Magilla Gorilla* show in 1964, and in one issue of a Gold Key comic book. Allan Melvin was Punkin's voice, and Howard Morris handled Mushmouse.

HIPPETY HOPPER
Pedigree. Popular Warner Brothers theatrical cartoon kangaroo.
Biography. Escaping from the zoo in *Hop Look and Listen* (1948), the baby kangaroo ends up in the cellar of the house where **Sylvester the Cat** is hunting for mice. When Sylvester tries to draws Hippety through a mouse hole, he's convinced it's a monster mouse and goes running from the house. Outside, a bulldog chides him for being a coward, and Sylvester reluctantly goes back. This time he actually gets on top of Hippety—and gets tossed outside. After Sylvester is bounced out several more times, the dog goes inside—where he meets Hippety's mother, Gracie, who's come for her child. The dog and cat are last seen headed from town. In his next screen appearance, *Hippety Hopper* (1949), the kangaroo is at the dock, waiting to be shipped to the zoo, when he prevents a mouse from committing suicide. The mouse explains that Sylvester has made his life so miserable death is the only way out. Hippety agrees to help him, and goes home with the rodent. Once again, Sylvester is trashed and the dog boasts that he'll take ballet lessons if a mouse can whip him. At the fadeout, both Sylvester and the hound are doing just that. Hippety escapes from the circus and slams the cat once again in their third team-up, *Pop 'em Pop* (1950), while their fourth cartoon together, *Who's Kitten Who* (1952), is fundamentally a rehashing of the first short. The rest of the series adheres to the same Sylvester-can't-lick-the-giant-mouse theme.

Comment. There were eleven Hippety cartoons in all.

HOBBES
Pedigree. Comic strip tiger.
Biography. Hobbes is a stuffed tiger and the "best friend" of six-year-old Calvin, who describes him as "on the quiet side . . . somewhat peculiar . . . a good companion, in a weird sort of way." (When he's in a bad mood, Calvin is apt to call him "fuzz for brains.") Whether the tiger is alive isn't known and doesn't matter (see "Comment"); he's alive to Calvin, and thus to the reader. Whether it was he or Calvin himself who cut off all the boy's hair in one strip, or tied him to a chair in another, is moot. Whether the carnivore really did eat Tommy Chesnutt for making fun of Calvin when he took the stuffed tiger to school is something we'll never know. (Although in this, we also have Hobbes's word: "Ugh!" the animal groans. "He needed a bath.") While Calvin is utterly unpredictable, Hobbes has a certain stability about him. He always cautions his chum against doing something harebrained, and recognizes these ill-advised schemes viscerally: Whenever Calvin announces a typically nutty scheme, Hobbes's tail "gets all bushy" from nerves. (Ladies also get a reaction from him, albeit far more favorable—especially if they're redheads with green eyes and long whiskers. Hobbes is on record as believing that when we die, "we play saxophone for an all-girl cabaret in New Orleans.") He also has a greater sense of responsibility, and regularly admonishes Calvin to "Read a book! Or write a letter! Or take a walk" instead of watching "tripe" on television. (Hobbes's resolve is not as great as his oratory, because he invariably ends up getting caught up in whatever Calvin is watching.) Withal, Hobbes also has his feral side. Although he's anxious when he and Calvin take frequent wagon or sled rides down the hill, he has trouble resisting a good snowball or water balloon, and sets his beeper watch to go off so he can hide and jump out at Calvin when he returns from school, bowling him over (reminiscent of Tigger; see **Winnie the Pooh**). Calvin's mother has said she's tired of sewing the tiger up after these violent encounters, but that hasn't put a stop to the roughhousing. Other facts about Hobbes: He doesn't believe in astrology, loves nothing more than "a big sunny field to be in," believes in running from danger ("It doesn't impress the girls

... but there's no sense impressing them and then getting killed"), is especially afraid of ghosts, is "always a little loopy when he comes out of the dryer," is a dynamo at Scrabble (with words like zygomorphic and nucleoplasm), yet is as bad at math as Calvin is ("I couldn't figure out this subtraction problem," he says while doing Calvin's homework, "so I put 'Atlanta, Georgia.' "). Hobbes is naked, save for the wintertime, when he wears a scarf to go out. Calvin also dresses him up on those rare occasions when the family goes out to eat. Calvin's young classmate Susie Derkins (a k a "booger brain") has a stuffed rabbit called Mr. Bun; it's not known whether the doll lives for her in quite the same way as Hobbes does for Calvin. However, she does find Hobbes "just *adorable!*" and enjoys hugging him—something the tiger enjoys even more.

Comment. "Calvin and Hobbes" was created by Bill Watterson and premiered in November 1985. Asked whether or not Hobbes is real, Watterson replies he's "more real than I suspect any kid would dream up," but adds that "the fantasy/reality question is a literary device, so the ultimate reality of it doesn't really matter." Tellingly, the tiger appears only as a stuffed toy whenever any other character is with him and/or Calvin in a panel; when Calvin takes photographs of Hobbes, he sees the living tiger but others see only the stuffed animal. It's probably coincidental, but the French theologian and leader of the Reformation, John Calvin, was a contemporary of the English philosopher Thomas Hobbes. The characters were humorously riposted in an issue of the comic book *Patrick the Rabbit,* in which Marco and his pet rabbit Patrick took the parts of the live rabbit Patrick and his stuffed boy Hives. The Fragments West title began publishing in 1989.

HOKEY WOLF
Pedigree. Fast-talking TV wolf.
Biography. Hokey is a dead-ringer for Phil Silvers's Sergeant Bilko, not only in voice and manner, but in the way he's constantly trying to con a nameless farmer and his watchdog Douglas. Hokey's devoted associate is the tiny fox Ding-a-Ling.

Comment. The Hanna-Barbera character appeared on his own segment of *The Huckleberry Hound Show* (1958), although it wasn't added to the series until 1960, replacing **Yogi Bear.** There were twenty-four episodes in all. Daws Butler provided Hokey's voice.

HOMELESS HECTOR
Pedigree. Dog featured in a very early British comic book.
Biography. The frisky little pooch hung out with humans Weary Willie and Tired Tim, mostly observing as the improverished pair living in modern-day Cockle Bay constantly searched for a way to make a pound.

Comment. The characters starred in the weekly comic book *Illustrated Chips,* which was first published in 1896. They remained a popular feature until 1953. Other British animals of comic books and comic strips include Tiger Tim, who made his first comic strip appearance in 1904, and got his own pictures-and-text magazine, *Tiger Tim's Tales,* in 1919; Pip, Squeak, and Wilfred—a dog, penguin, and rabbit—who starred in their own eponymous strip that began in 1919 and got them involved in adventures that ranged from publishing a newspaper to dealing with the communist Wtzkoffski and his dog Popski; the animals of Mrs. Bruin's Boarding School that, in addition to Tiger Tim, included Joey the Parrot, Willie Ostrich, Jumbo the Elephant, Georgie Giraffe, Fido the Dog, Jacko the Monkey, and others, all starring in the comic-style magazine *The Rainbow,* beginning in 1914; Dicky Duck, Rupert the Chick, and Robert Rabbit, all of whom starred in the weekly comics magazine *Chicks' Own,* first published in 1920; the talking, bipedal Korky the Cat, who starred in the weekly *The Dandy* from the very first issue (1937), and was constantly trying to nab fish without getting caught by cooks, the game warden, and others; Chimpo's Circus, which appeared in the weekly *Happy Days* from the first issue (1938) and, in addition to the monkey, costarred Crackle the Pig, Jum the Elephant, and Leo the Lion (the ringmaster); and Dogman, the ineffectual bipedal canine superhero who appeared in the black-and-white *Ally Sloper* comic magazine, four issues of which were published in 1976. Alfie the Space Tramp and the helmeted Wagger the Dog-Star Terrier also made a one-panel appearance in the first issue.

HOMER PIGEON
Pedigree. Bird of cartoon and comic books.
Biography. Dressed in a straw hat, bow tie, vest, and trousers, the Midwestern Homer is a gallant, simple-minded bird who lives in Birdville and is devoted to his shy girlfriend, Carrie Pigeon. Not a particularly interesting character, Homer is usually upstaged by his costars, as in *Swing Your Partner,* when he wakes

his horse to take him and Carrie to a barn dance. The unhappy horse climbs from bed muttering, "All day long I work like a horse. Now I have to drive this dope to a dance." After Homer inadvertently parks him in a pool of mud by the barn, the horse spends the rest of the cartoon fantasizing about how he's going to destroy the bird, from stomping viciously on his back to detonating a barrel of TNT under his nose. He finally settles for riding the cart beside Carrie, whipping Homer and having him pull them home.

Comment. Created by Walter Lantz (**Woody Woodpecker**), the bird appeared in just three cartoons, *Pigeon Patrol* (1942), *Swing Your Partner* (1943), and *Pigeon Holed* (1956). Dal McKennon provided the voice. Homer is reminiscent of Red Skelton's goofy radio character Clem Kaddlehopper. The bird also starred in a backup feature in Dell's popular comic book *Walter Lantz New Funnies,* beginning with no. 82 in 1944. A Lantz character that appeared exclusively in that comic book was Charlie Chicken, who looked somewhat like Woody, with a big red comb, short beak, and large eyes. Charlie lives in the barn of Farmer Homer Brown, where he likes nothing better than to "snooze under a tree." However, other animals or Brown himself invariably interfere with Charlie's plans. Unfortunately, whether Charlie is supposed to watch the cow Esmeralda, or deliver a note, he invariably screws up, inspiring Brown to say delightful things like, "Charlie, I'm going to hammer you through the floor."

THE HONEY-MOUSERS
Pedigree. Theatrical cartoon series spoofing television's *The Honeymooners.*
Biography. The stars of this short-lived series are the blustery Ralph Crumden, his long-suffering wife, Alice, and dimwitted friend Ned Morton and his wife, Trixie (Trixie is seen only in the last cartoon). In their debut short, *The Honey-mousers* (1956), the trio is suffering hard times because the house is unoccupied. Then Ned brings the good news: There are people moving in. The bad news: They've got a cat. The threesome build a Trojan Dog and head for the refrigerator; when the cat finally does attack, the feisty (and hungry) Alice simply raps it one. End of menace. In their second adventure, *Cheese It, the Cat* (1957), the cat's still around, and Ralph and Ned try everything they can think of (a toy tank, invisible ink, a flying champagne cork) to get over or around it. When they finally get the cake they're af-

ter and bring it back to the mousehole, dopey Ned inadvertently lights dynamite sticks instead of candles. They're able to get the cake from the hole—and blast the poor cat. Their last escapade, *Mice Follies* (1960), involves Ralph and Ned's efforts to get home from a late lodge meeting without waking their wives. Naturally, there's a pesky cat to make things difficult.

Comment. Warner Brothers also did a one-time, all-mouse parody of *The Jack Benny Story* titled *The Mouse That Jack Built* (1959).

HONG KONG PHOOEY
Pedigree. Kung fu cartoon dog.
Biography. Penrod Pooch is a bipedal, talking dog janitor who works for the police station in an all-human city. Whenever he hears Sergeant Flint or dispatcher Rosemary talking about a crime, he sneaks into his private room, which is hidden behind a vending machine, climbs into a filing cabinet, and dons an orange robe and black domino mask—the costume of Hong Kong Phooey. Grabbing his aide Spot—a yellow cat with purple stripes, who doesn't talk and is usually busy trying to catch mice—he leaps out the window and into a dumpster, where his car the Phooeymobile is hidden (the auto looks like a Model T with a pagoda top). Although he calls himself "the muscular master of martial arts," regularly consults *The Hong Kong Book of Kung Fu* tucked in his sleeve, and threatens to "deal out terrible justice," Hong Kong is a clod who learned his craft by correspondence course. Whenever he attacks a villain, he usually ends up doing a jump-kick from a window or into a wall. Even when he hits his target, he's ineffectual: When he and Spot are trapped inside a giant bubble, his kung fu blows fail to free them, and it remains for Spot to produce a pin to pop their prison. Things don't go much better when the dog summons his "kung fu powers of concentration": By uttering mystic phrases, he's supposed to be able to tap hidden knowledge. For example, while pursuing the candy-stealing Gumdrop Kid, he intones, "Chee-chee, chi-chi, chou-chou chum, now where's the kid whose name begins with Gum?" Instead of finding the felon, Phooey ends up having a wanted poster blow in his face. Fortunately, Spot figures out where the criminal is hidden. The truth is, if it weren't for Spot, Hong Kong would fail at everything he does. About the only thing Phooey does right is bang a small, magical gong, which transforms his car into a helicopter, reaper, and other vehicles. Among Phooey's foes are the magician Professor Presto (and his

pet crocodile Big Tooth), the Giggler, Mr. Tornado, Dr. Disguiso, and the Incredible Mr. Shrink.

Comment. Hanna-Barbera's dog starred in thirty-two cartoons, which aired on ABC from 1974 to 1976. He returned in *The Hong Kong Phooey Hour* on NBC in 1980. The adventures are standard fare, but the voices are unique: Scatman Crothers was Hong Kong and Joe E. Ross was Flint. Charlton Comics published nine issues of *Hong Kong Phooey* from 1975 to 1976.

HOPPITY

Pedigree. Star of historic feature-length film.

Biography. Hoppity is a grasshopper who wears a fedora and green jacket (his wings form the coat-tails), a striped shirt, shoes, and green trousers, and who alternately walks in a loping gait or hops. Hoppity—along with the likes of Mrs. Ladybug, Mrs. Stinkbug, Mr. Creeper, Mr. Bumble, and Bumble's daughter, Honey (Hoppity's bee-loved)—are members of a bug settlement located in "the lowlands," just a few feet from Broadway, in the yard of Dick and Mary Dickens, an aspiring songwriter and his wife. The Dickenses are quite poor, and in danger of losing their home; moreover, the iron fence is broken, and people (whom the bugs call "human ones") are constantly walking through the little village of matchboxes and cans, tramping the bugs' homes underfoot or burning them down with carelessly tossed matches. For protection during such incursions, the bugs rush underneath screwtop lids, slip into fountain pen caps, hide in purses, and so on. Still, as Mr. Bumble puts it, it'll only be a matter of time before the humans "trample us off the face of the ground." Enter Hoppity, who has been away for a while (where is never made clear; at school, presumably, given his rather collegiate look). When he returns, he declares that he's discovered "there's no place like home," and it becomes his top priority to make the bugs' homes more secure. Eavesdropping on the Dickenses, he learns that they're hoping a music publisher will buy his new song . . . a sale that will make it possible for them to keep the house and grounds. Returning to the town, Hoppity convinces the bugs to stay and see if the check arrives. Meanwhile, the corrupt, wealthy C. Bagley Beetle offers to let Mr. Bumble and his bee-utiful daughter move to his isolated "uplands" side of the property (where he lives magnificently inside the base of a fountain, sleeping in a bed made from a compact). His terms: Honey must marry him. She refuses, and Bagley and his henchbugs Swat the Fly and Smack the Mosquito

make life miserable for the insects, for instance, by clandestinely causing a lighted "smoke stick"—a cigar—to roll up against Mr. Bumble's Honey Shop, and stealing the check from the Dickenses' mailbox when it arrives, hiding it in a crack in the stoop. When a kids' hockey game nearly destroys the settlement, Hoppity and Mr. Bumble realize it's time to move. They find a mansion with a garden and, like an antennaed Moses and Aaron, lead the bugs to it. Unfortunately, paradise quickly becomes hell when the sprinkler turns on and washes the bugs and their possessions away. They return to the Dickens property, on which a condemned sign has now been posted. Hoppity is shunned and, while brooding alone, he overhears Bagley plotting to let all the bugs move onto his property, which has also been condemned, if Honey will marry him. Hoppity attacks, and although he's a strong young bug (delivering especially potent kicks), he is overpowered and stuffed inside the envelope with the check. Bagley makes his offer to Honey who, for the good of the community, agrees to marry him. However, during the ceremony, a plumb line destroys the church and the human ones arrive to begin building a skyscraper on the former Dickens lot. The stoop is torn down, Hoppity and the envelope are liberated, and the grasshopper valiantly drags the check to the mailbox, where it is picked up. While the $5000 check makes its way through the mails (no one seems to know where Dick has moved), the skyscraper rises. In the end, Dick's song is published and is a huge hit, he and Mary buy a penthouse atop the skyscraper and set up a garden, and the bugs move in. (As for Bagley, his thugs have to chop him out of mortar where he was trapped while the building rose.)

Comment. *Mr. Bug Goes to Town* was directed by Dave Fleischer from a script hammered out by no less than nine writers: Fleischer, Dan Gordon, Ted Pierce, and Isidore Sparber came up with the story, while Gordon, Pierce, Sparber, William Turner, Carl Meyer, Graham Place, Bob Wickersham, and Cal Howard wrote the screenplay. Stan Freed provided the voice for Hoppity, Ted Pierce spoke for C. Bagley Beetle, and Pauline Loth was Honey. The film was released by Paramount in 1941. Even though it was the fourth feature-length cartoon (after Disney's *Snow White and the Seven Dwarfs* and *Pinocchio,* and Fleischer's own *Gulliver's Travels),* it was the first animated feature ever to be based on an original story (which is probably why it took an army of writers to hammer out the plot and screenplay). The film failed due to a lack of support from Paramount, and the fact that bugs *can* be off-putting; it was reissued as *Hoppity Goes to Town*, which remains the film's title on television and videocassette. Despite sumptuous color and art direction, atmospheric lighting, and frequently breathtaking animation (the lengthy sequence in which the "human ones" use shovels and derricks to break ground for the skyscraper is seen from the bugs' point of view, and is simply stunning), the film suffers from bland characterization and forgettable songs—two areas in which the Disney features never fell down. Paramount pulled the plug on further features from Dave and his producer-brother Max (who had already made the studio a small fortune with their Popeye and Betty Boop shorts). Had the Fleischers been independent filmmakers, like Disney, they may have learned from their mistakes and contributed far, far more to the field of animation. The film was adapted for comics in *The Cinema Comics Herald* no. 1 (1941).

HOPPITY HOOPER
Pedigree. TV cartoon frog.
Biography. Hoppity is a sweet but trusting bipedal frog who, with his clever friend Waldo the Fox and lumbering Fillmore the Bear, will trying anything to make a buck. Roaming the countryside onboard a medicine show wagon, they've tried everything from prospecting to racing to peddling quack elixirs to entering (natch!) a frog-jumping contest. More often than not, they end up leaving town in a hurry.

    Comment. A creation of Jay Ward Productions (**Rocky and Bullwinkle**), the frog appeared in twenty-six cartoons, which began airing on ABC in 1964. The title was changed from *The Hoppity Hooper Show* to *Uncle Waldo* in 1965. Chris Allen was Hoppity's voice, Hans Conried was Waldo, and Bill Scott handled Fillmore.

HOPPY, THE CAPTAIN MARVEL BUNNY
Pedigree. The animal superhero counterpart to the human comic book superhero Captain Marvel.
Biography. The scrawny, pink-furred Hoppy; his girlfriend, Millie; and a good friend Zeke Squirrel dwell in Funny Animal Land (a k a Funny Animalville), a world situated not far beyond Planet Carrot. It's a place where timid animals such as rabbits, pigs, squirrels, and monkeys live in peace and contentment . . . as long as the carnivores leave them alone. While reading a *Captain Marvel* comic book, Hoppy wonders whether *Shazam*, the same magic word which turns diminutive Billy Batson into that mighty

hero, will transform him into a superrabbit. He utters the word and, to his surprise and delight, it works. Saying it again turns him back into Hoppy. Thus when predators rear their heads, Hoppy becomes the "mighty, flying cottontail," brawny Captain Marvel Bunny, endowed with superstrength, the power to fly, the ability to remain underwater indefinitely, "rocketlike speed," and a fondness for the exclamation, "Crunching Carrots!" Although many of Hoppy's adventures are relatively innocuous—like dealing with an imposter who is pretending to be Captain Marvel Bunny to woo a princess—a few are downright scary, as when Hoppy and Millie are captured by the slavering, sword-wielding Leopard Men, and another in which the evil Black Bill the Bear and his loggers try to drown them in a waterfall. The tales can also be political, such as the time the Four Flusher Ferry Service sabotaged a bridge built by Bill Beaver so that the ferry route won't be endangered. Hoppy's costume consists of a red bodysuit, a white cape with a yellow fringe, yellow gloves, belt, boots, and a yellow lightning bolt on his chest.

    Comment. Created and wonderfully drawn by Chad Grothkopf, Hoppy first appeared in Fawcett's *Funny Animals* no. 1 in 1942; Captain Marvel appeared on the cover to introduce the rabbit. Hoppy starred in most issues through no. 68, and also came to our world in no. 28 of *Marvel Family* in 1948, helping Mary Marvel stop a war between the Dog People and the Cat People of the planet Vesta. When several of the Hoppy stories were reprinted in the **Atomic Mouse** comic in the 1950s, copyright problems compelled the publisher to change Hoppy to Speedy, the Magic Bunny, and Shazam to Alizam. The lightning bolt was stricken from his costume. See also **Billy the Kid, Sherlock Monk,** and **Willie the Worm,** other *Funny Animals* characters. In addition to the superheroic **American Rabbit, Atomic Bunny, Cutey Bunny,** and **Thunderbunny,** there was the tall, lean Marvel Comics hero Super Rabbit, who wore a cape and a skintight costume with his full name rather awkwardly emblazoned across his chest, and saved endangered kittens and bunnies from carnivores. He first appeared in *Comedy Comics* no. 14 in 1942, appearing there and in other titles sporadically through 1948.

HORACE HORSECOLLAR
Pedigree. Early Walt Disney character.
Biography. The black, bipedal horse with hands and feet instead of hooves, ever-present horsecollar and

derby, and neighing laugh, is one of the most underused characters in the Disney menagerie. The cigar-smoking steed first appeared in the **Mickey Mouse** cartoon *The Plow Boy* (1929), and frolicked in the surf with **Clarabelle Cow** in his second outing, *The Beach Party* (1931). In *Barnyard Broadcast* (1931), he showed his musical talents for the first time: Decked out with a bow tie on his collar (this is, after all, a formal event), he plays both the violin . . . and a saw, by banging it with a hammer. His most memorable performance is in his fourth cartoon, *Mickey's Mellerdrammer* (1933), in which the Disney troupe stages *Uncle Tom's Cabin*. Decked out in a moustache and cruel sneer, he plays Simon Legree. As he's about to whip Mickey (playing Uncle Tom), the audience erupts with anger and the performance comes to a premature end. After that cartoon, Horace was once again relegated to relatively minor roles, as a rather unconvincing muscle-horse in *Orphan's Benefit* (1934), a drummer in *The Band Concert* (1935), blowing the French horn during *The Light Cavalry Overture* in *Symphony Hour* (1942), a Christmas caroler in *Pluto's Christmas Tree* (1952), and other similar cameos.

Comment. Horace appeared in sixteen shorts, and had a cameo in the featurette *Mickey's Christmas Carol* (1983). Why Disney never developed this or other early characters (such as Clarabelle) is not known. Apparently, his attention was monopolized by the ones that clicked with the public. As for the rest, they were "kept on the payroll" solely because they were recognizable if unspectacular supporting players. Other minor horses in the Disney stable include Thunderbolt, the drunken racehorse in the Mickey Mouse cartoon *The Steeple-Chase* (1933); the dazzling, vain racehorse Snapshot III and the nag of a steed Old Moe in the **Goofy** cartoon *They're Off* (1948; guess who wins?); and Rover Boy no. 6, who gives **Donald Duck** a hard time in *Dude Duck* (1951). In feature films, Disney horses have been Percy, Goofy's uncooperative steed in the *How to Ride a Horse* section of *The Reluctant Dragon* (1941); Widowmaker, the merry horse ridden by Pecos Bill in *Melody Time* (1948); Gunpowder, Ichabod Crane's timorous horse in the magnificent *Legend of Sleepy Hollow* segment of *The Adventures of Ichabod and Mr. Toad* (1949), and lazy, straw-hatted Cyril Proudbottom, Mr. Toad's horse in the *Mr. Toad* half of the film; Major, a horse who becomes a human coachman in *Cinderella* (1950); Samson, the brave, cheerful stallion ridden by Prince Phillip in *Sleeping Beauty* (1959); and the Captain,

the bucktoothed horse whose powerful kicks help save the kidnapped puppies in *101 Dalmations* (1961).

HOT DOG

Pedigree. The dog belonging to comic book character Jughead Jones of Archie comics fame.

Biography. The white mutt lives with its master in Riverdale, and, according to Jughead, is "sensitive. He cries if he's left alone." Like its food-crazy owner, the dog will bite just about anything—preferably, behinds—although he's terrified of cats. Above all, Hot Dog is confused by humans. He tells the reader in one story that the Joneses complain about bills, yet, "When I try to do my bit by discouraging (the mailman), everyone comes down on me like I was some sort of a barbarian!" He complains that when he sees a welcome mat, he takes the invitation literally . . . and is invariably chased away. He also doesn't understand why people bring food home from a restaurant, but "we doggies never get to see those doggie bags!" Hot Dog is in love with Zina, the poodle that belongs to local teen Veronica Lodge, and he regularly serenades her with heartfelt howls. (Being wealthy, the Lodges gave Zina a small "luxury canine condominium" to live in, and make sure she's bathed and shampooed three times a week. Hot Dog gets no more than two baths a year.)

Comment. Jughead has been a costar of the Archie comic books since 1941. Hot Dog got his own magazine, *Hot Dog,* in 1989. In it, Jughead's scientist-friend Dilton builds him a high-tech doghouse that not only dispenses food and water automatically, but has a telescope, radar dish, and other gadgets. It's the radar that gets Hot Dog involved in his first solo adventure: He picks up a distress signal from the extraterrestrial Astro-Mutts—Captain Bark Rogers, Luke Tailwagger, and Lieutenant Saluki—who are out seeking to destroy the evil Galacti-Cats and their leader Drak Batfang, who have been preying on the "peace-loving Moustians." Hot Dog has also been seen occasionally on the nine different Archie cartoon shows, beginning with *The Archie Show* on CBS in 1968 (he has been known to conduct the band when the singing Archies perform). Ol' Blue is another local dog, owned by Cap'n Petty. Also, see Archie's dog **Spotty**. Other animals that appeared in Archie's comic (beginning with no. 1 in 1942) were Cubby the Bear, Judge Owl, Squoimy the Woim, and Bumble, the Bee-tective. Comic book dogs that didn't gain the fame of Hot Dog include Butch the Pup, who appeared in DC's

1939 one-shot *New York World's Fair Comics;* Sniffy the Pup, who starred in fourteen issues of his own Standard title from 1949 to 1953; Spotty the Pup, who lasted only two issues from Avon in 1953, then managed only two more issues when he became Superpup the following year; and the riotous Black Terrier, who appeared in just one issue of Nedor's *Real Funnies* in 1943, spoofing the superhero the Black Terror.

THE HOUNDCATS

Pedigree. TV animals spoofing *Mission: Impossible.*

Biography. The bipedal Houndcats consist of the following secret government agents: Musselmutt, a big sheepdog-type with awesome strength; Dingdog, a southern-born daredevil in a Confederate uniform; Stutz, the leader, a cat who dressed like an automobile driver from the turn of the century; Puttypuss, a pudgy cat-master of disguises; and Rhubarb, an engineer/scientist/inventor dog who wears an oversize coat and a big, floppy hat. Driving a Stutz Bearcat known as Sparkplug, the Houndcats become embroiled in such exploits as *The Double Dealing Diamond Mission, The Ruckus on the Rails Mission,* and *The Great Gold Train Mission.* Despite the fact that each adventure is meticulously well planned, things always go way wrong. Fortunately, the Houndcats always emerge triumphant.

   Comment. The characters were seen on their own NBC show from 1972 to 1973. There were thirteen episodes of this DePatie-Freleng production. The voices were provided by Aldo Ray (Musclemutt), Stu Gilliam (Dingdog), Daws Butler (Stutz), Three Stooges member Joe Besser (Puttypuss), and Arte Johnson (Rhubarb).

HOWARD THE DUCK

Pedigree. Comic book star who became a motion picture disaster.

Biography. Howard is a denizen of Duckworld, located in another dimension. There, the evolution of ducks patterned the evolution of humans on our world—so much so that Howard speaks English. Howard's earliest aptitude tests suggest that he is "best suited to be a mortician," although it's soon discovered that he's a "potentially brilliant scholar." Sadly, he hates "the structured environment of school" and completes his education "in the streets, taking whatever work is available." He works, for a time, as a minstrel, as a boxer, and as a construction worker . . . although for the most part, due to "his

truculent tongue, his abrasive wit, and his low tolerance for occupational abasement," he's out of work. When the villain Thog causes a shift in the Cosmic Axis, which keeps the dimensions in balance, Howard is whisked from his world and brought to ours, plunked down in the Florida Everglades—which happens to be the crossroads of many dimensions. Howard becomes involved with the barbarian Korrek, a wizard, a sorceress, and the superheroic monster Man-Thing in the struggle against Thog. By the end of the battle, Howard has managed to get back into the interdimensional flow. Unfortunately, it doesn't take him to Duckworld, but dumps him in Cleveland, Ohio, on our world. There, he meets model Beverly Switzler and helps her escape the clutches of Pro-Rata, an evil accountant. The duck moves in with Beverly and, while trying to fit into our world, has a nasty habit of attracting all kinds of bad guys, from the giant Gingerbread Man ("Its candy eyes flame with . . . malice") to the insidious Dr. Bong (his head is shaped like a bell, his arm is a clapper, and he's half mad from constantly bringing the two together) to the sinister Morton Erg who, after taking a bubble bath in radioactive water, became the monstrous Gopher. Fortunately, the wily duck is skilled in the art of Quack-Fu, and invariably escape his foes (although to battle Dr. Bong, he donned a special suit of armor and briefly became the superhero Iron Duck). Disgusted with the sorry state of American society, and with human bias (especially against ducks), Howard made a failed run for president of the United States in 1976, on the All-Night party ticket (no. 7). The otherworldly waterfowl stands two feet, seven inches and weighs forty pounds. He has arms instead of wings, is rarely without a cigar, but is otherwise quite ducklike. For the first few years, his wardrobe consisted of a blue blazer, undersize fedora, and red tie with black polka dots. Later, he acquired trousers. His oft-heard cry of pain and despair is *Waaugh!*

   Comment. Howard was created by writer Steve Gerber and made his debut in Marvel Comics's *Fear* no. 19 in 1972. His own comic book lasted from 1976 to 1979 (thirty-one issues), became a large-size black-and-white comic book that ran until 1981 (nine issues), then became a full-color comic book again in 1986 and lasted just two issues. In 1986, Universal Pictures released a live-action film *Howard the Duck,* which cost $40 million, flopped, and replaced *Heaven's Gate* as the most embarrassing miscalculation in Hollywood history. George Lucas was the executive producer, and Willard Huyck directed. Nine different actors and two separate "stunt ducks" wore the awful, stiff-looking Howard costume at various points in the film. His voice is uncredited, but belongs to actor Richard Dreyfuss. Marvel published a three-issue adaptation of the film.

HUBIE AND BERTIE
Pedigree. Minor Warner Brothers theatrical stars.
Biography. A pair of goofy-looking mice with buckteeth and huge ears, the pair gnawed their way into cinemas in *The Aristo Cat* (1943). Pussy is a spoiled cat who's so mean to its private butler Meadows that the man up and leaves. Forced to look after itself, Pussy reads a book about cats and learns that they're supposed to capture mice. Encountering Hubie and Bertie, Pussy is told that a bulldog sitting in the yard is a mouse, and the cat goes out to eat it (armed with bread, no less). Pussy is sent flying. Returning to the book, the cat finds a picture of a mouse and chases the right animals. However, the cat collides with the dog and gets beaten up once again. Pussy awakes in its bed, thinking it was all just a dream . . . until the dog and mice emerge from the covers. The two rather bland mice stayed away from the screen until 1948, when, in *House-Hunting Mice,* they explore a Home of Tomorrow and are hounded by the automated devices therein. Their next offering, *Mouse Wreckers* (1949), was Oscar-nominated, and has them trying to convince **Claude Cat** he's insane so he'll ignore them. After blowing him up like a balloon and letting him whiz through the house; rebuilding a room while he's sleeping so that everything is upside down and he thinks he's on the ceiling; subjecting him to a bulldog and dynamite, among other indignities, they reduce the cat to a trembling wreck and are able to move in. They battle Claude again in *The Hypo-condri-cat* (1950), in which they convince him he's dead, and they have their final, bizarre showdown in *Cheese Chasers* (1951): Having overdosed on cheese at a cheese factory, the mice swear off the stuff, realize there's no reason to live, try to get Claude to eat them . . . and can't convince him it's on the level. He, in turn, realizes that *he'll* never be able to trust or eat another mouse again, and offers himself unto the local bulldog . . . who is similarly traumatized and goes out looking for the dogcatcher, the other animals chasing in turn.

Comment. While the cartoons are entertaining, these two characters don't have the qualities that made other famous "twin" teams endure, such as the sly charm of **Heckle and Jeckle**, the devotion of **Chip 'n' Dale**, or even the out-and-out cuteness of Pixie and Dixie (see **Mr. Jinks**).

HUCKLEBERRY HOUND
Pedigree. Emmy Award–winning TV dog.
Biography. The Southern-bred dog is something of a Walter Mitty, starring in a series of adventures that are widely separated in time and space. In one cartoon, he'll be a Northwest mountie tracking the nasty Powerful Pierre; in the next, he'll be fighting a dragon; after that, he may turn up fighting a bull, surfing in Hawaii, or putting out a fire. The only constants are his propensity for understatement (after a villain has literally pounded Huck's head into his body, the hound says, "Well . . . boxing ain't his weakness, that's fer sure"), unflappable nature (when the pirate Jolly Roger warns, "I'll break every bone in your puny body," Huck replies, "It's no use, Rog. You can't sweet talk your way outta this one"), droll observations ("Well, I declare . . . a hummingbird. Don't particularly care for that tune he's hummin', though"), modesty (in old England, when he's introduced with fanfare as that "courageous naval hero, Admiral Horatio Huckleberry," he ambles out and says, "Howdy, folks"), and the ability to recover immediately from any injuries, even if he's slammed face-first into the side of a cliff. There's one other constant: He's forever singing Percy Montrose's "Clementine" . . . off-key. The blue-skinned hound has black ears, a black nose, and black on the tip of his tail. When not in costume for an adventure, he is seldom without his straw hat and necktie.

Comment. This Hanna-Barbera legend was created after the producers heard voice man Daws Butler do his impression of a man from Tennessee who never got shaken up, regardless of what catastrophe befell him. However, there were other inspirations as well. The hound was to some degree based on a wolf character that had appeared in the 1953 MGM cartoon *Three Little Pups,* an animal whose drawling voice was also provided by Butler. His laid-back manner also owes something to popular TV star Andy Griffith. The dog was named after the berry which, thanks to Mark Twain, has come to signify bumpkinness. The character debuted in syndication in 1958. In its original run, there were fifty-five episodes of *The Huckleberry Hound Show.* Huckleberry has occasionally made cameo appearances in the cartoons of other Hanna-Barbera animals (for example, on *Yogi's Gang* from 1973 to 1975). In comics, Huckleberry appeared in forty-three issues of his own title from Dell, then Gold Key (1959 to 1970), eight from Charlton Comics (1970 to 1972), and various one shots, including the 1960 classic *Huckleberry Hound for President* in which, popular as he was on the stump, he backed out on election day eve because he didn't "know beans about *fishin'* . . . and I don't care a hoot 'n' a howl about *golf.*"

HUEY, DEWEY, AND LOUIE

Pedigree. Donald Duck's precocious nephews.
Biography. It began in *Donald's Nephews* (1938), with a postcard from Donald's sister Dumbella: "I am sending your angel nephews to visit you." (In the earlier "Donald Duck" comic strip of October 17, 1937, the sister was Della and it was a more detailed letter she sent: She was giving the boys to Donald until their father got out of the hospital. Seems "a giant

firecracker exploded under his chair.") In the cartoon, they arrived driving their tricycles through the front door (standing behind it, Donald was slammed into the wall); in the comic strip, they arrived quietly and rigged the doorknob to the front light, electrifying it; when Donald ran out screaming, they snuck in and put a bucket of water over the door, which spilled on their "Unca Donald" when he reentered. In any case, the three imps in their beanies and tight little sweatshirts had arrived. The rest of the short contains nothing but agony for the elder duck. The boys use their bikes and mallets to play polo in the house; blow a trombone to launch a tomato at a baby grand piano, causing it to close on Donald; and put Volcano Brand hot mustard in his pie, then douse his blazing bill with a fire extinguisher (Dewey trikes by and hits the dazed duck with a blast from his squirt gun for good measure). Donald

Huckleberry Hound holds court with (from the left) Dixie, Pixie, **Mr. Jinks**, Blabber Mouse, **Super Snooper,** Huck, and **Yogi Bear.**
© HANNA-BARBERA PRODUCTIONS.

shreds the book on child-rearing he had consulted throughout the short. Over the years, things get worse. Donald takes the boys camping in their second outing, *Good Scouts* (1938), and after they laugh at a series of mishaps (Donald trying to chop down a petrified tree and accidentally launching himself into the stratosphere with a bent sapling), he makes a stab at revenge: covering himself with catsup and pretending to be hurt. Quick as lightning, though, the ungrieving boys are on him, proudly displaying their first aid saavy by wrapping him head to toe in bandages. Unable to see, Donald feels something nudge him, and lashes out . . . at a bear. Donald is still primarily an innocent victim in their third short, *Donald's Golf Game* (1938). The boys talk incessantly, but Donald is prepared: He carries clothespins inside his sailor's cap, and clamps their bills shut. Then the lads turn nasty, substituting "goofy clubs" for the real set, thus forcing the increasingly frustrated Donald to play with an umbrella club, a boomerang club, and the like. Then they place a grasshopper inside a hollow ball, causing Donald to chase it and even play a shot underwater (a scene that features exquisite slow-motion animation). The cartoon also highlights a trademark of the trio: one duckling continuing a sentence begun by the other, e.g., "Hello," "Unca," "Donald." After

several more cartoons, Donald really begins to take the offensive against the lads in the likes of *Donald's Snow Fight* (1942) and *Donald's Happy Birthday* (1949)—but, predictably, his efforts backfire. In the first cartoon, he spitefully sleds toward the boys' snowman. They build another, and Donald slides toward it again . . . unaware that they've built this one around a rock. In the second cartoon, the boys— who more and more are subject to fits of affection— have pooled their money to buy Donald a box of his favorite cigars, La Smello Panatellas. Naturally, Donald finds the carton, assumes the boys intended to smoke it themselves, and forces them to do so until they're ill. Only then does he see the birthday note at the bottom of the box. Inarguably their greatest stunt occurred in *Soup's On* (1948). A dispute erupts during a turkey dinner and, while chasing the boys, Donald is knocked out. Outfitting him like an angel, and simulating his remains poking out from a nearby boulder, the boys convince Donald that he's dead. He forgives them, and tells them to enjoy the turkey , . . then attempts to fly. He crashes to earth, the truth dawns, and the chase begins anew. The boys share a bedroom at the house, and on those rare occasions when they sleep, are shown either in separate beds or in one big bed. Today, as the costars of the TV series *DuckTales* (see **Scrooge McDuck**), the

Huey, Dewey, and Louie
set for trick-or-treating.

three nephews are distinguishable at a glance: Huey wears a red cap, Dewey a blue one, and Louie a green one. However, their very high-pitched Donald-type voices have been replaced by less garbled ones (long-time voice man Clarence Nash died in 1985).

Comment. The boys were named after contemporary political figures Huey P. Long of Louisiana and Thomas E. Dewey of New York; Louie came from Louie Schmitt, the friend of a Disney artist. The boys starred in twenty-four theatrical shorts, a TV featurette (*Scrooge McDuck and Money,* 1967), and the theatrical featurette *Mickey's Christmas Carol* (1983). In comic strips, they first appeared in the daily Duck strip on February 23, 1938—one of them did, anyway—crying for a candy cane. Over the years, they were sometimes malicious (mending broken arms using Donald . . . and a sapling for a splint, which springs erect when they're done), sometimes helpful (vainly trying to warn Donald he's rowing toward a waterfall) . . . although in any case, Donald always gets the worst of it. In comic books, the boys have appeared regularly in the Duck's magazine, beginning with a one shot in 1938 (reprinting comic strips); they appeared in various other one shots, and starred in eighty-one issues of their own title, *Huey, Dewey and Louie Junior Woodchucks,* published by Gold Key from 1966 to 1984. The Junior Woodchucks were the comics' important addition to the mythos, and first appeared in *Walt Disney's Comics and Stories* no. 125 in February 1951. The ducklings—who are more industrious than in the cartoons (they even have a paper route!)—joined the Boy Scout-like club and, with its handbook of "inexhaustible" knowledge, can deal with virtually any contingency. As Woodchucks (Duckburg Burrow), they perform simple chores like patroling the Black Forest of Duckburg during droughts to watch out for fires to photographing birds for their clubhouse to tracking lost citizens. On occasion, they're aided by the fleabitten bloodhound General Snozzie, who sports an inflatable "balloon jacket" to investigate treetops, can climb greased poles (why he would want to, with the jacket, is a mystery), and even "wears a special nose filter for deep sea work." The Junior Woodchucks wear coonskin caps with a W on the front, sweatshirts, and red neckerchiefs. They also have a variety of rankings, which range from International Twelve-Star Admiral and Deputy Custodian of the Fountain of Inexhaustible Knowledge to Hawkeyed Ogler of Twigs, Sprigs, Herbs, Oaks, Truffles, Thickets, Eelgrass and Ragweeds to

(take a deep breath) Bellicose Expecter of Limitless Lionization, Esteem, Reverence and Indefatigable, Never-dying Gung-ho, as well as Bedeviller of Unskillful, Lunkheaded Lallygaggers, and Nemesis of Extemporizing Campground Know-no-things. (Check the acronyms of the second and third titles.)

HUMPHREY THE BEAR
Pedigree. Underappreciated Disney bear.
Biography. The large, shambling, naked creature loves fish, is quick to anger, is something of a clod, and speaks by grunting endlessly before finally spitting out a single word. Humphrey first came to the screen in *Rugged Bear* (1953; read the title again if you missed the gag). Not too bright, Humphrey fails to take shelter in a cave before hunting season gets under way. They're all locked and, in desperation, he goes to a hunting lodge owned by **Donald Duck,** and takes the place of a bearskin rug. The rug's open mouth happens to be where Donald cracks nuts and opens bottles; the bear also gets thrown into the washing machine when he gets dirty, and mowed when he emerges with his fur a mess. When hunting season finally ends and the bedraggled Humphrey goes to leave, the original "rug" bounds out and thanks him: It, too, was a bear playing possum. Humphrey's next short, *Grin and Bear It* (1954), set in Brownstone National Park, marked the first of four teamings with prissy Ranger J. Audubon Woodlore. Seems the bears' job at the park is to entertain visitors. Humphrey gets stuck with Donald, who's a bad sport and won't reward the bear with food. The frustrated Humphrey finally pretends he's been run over by Donald, who pays up with food—then sees through the deception and gets into a fight with the bear. Food is strewn all over, which Woodlore makes him clean up. In *Bearly Asleep* (1955), the loudly snoring Humphrey is kicked out of his cave by other bears trying to hibernate, and tries to crash at the pad of Ranger (!) Donald Duck. Needless to say, the two don't get along, although Humphrey manages to get back into the cave by taking a bonnet from Donald's teddy bear and pretending to be a baby. The remaining Humphrey cartoons are *Beezy Bear* (1955; the bear steals honey from Donald's farm), *Hooked Bear* (1956; Humphrey paws for fish, and has a fine moment when he battles a large fish for possession of a smaller one), and *In the Bag* (1956; the ranger forces the bears to clean all the litter in the park).

Comment. Jim Macdonald provided the voice for

the bear. A ferocious bear seen in the **Goofy** cartoon *Hold That Pose* (1950), resembles Humphrey physically, but has a much nastier demeanor. When Disney director Jack Hannah went to work for Walter Lantz, he used Humphrey as the model for Fatso Bear, who had run-ins with Ranger Willoughby in a pair of cartoons in the early 1960s.

THE HUNTER

Pedigree. Detective dog of TV cartoons.

Biography. Also known as the "Booming" Hunter due to his loud voice, the southern-bred, marginally effective bloodhound wears a floppy fedora and trench coat, and is constantly in pursuit of the "wily, witty" Fox, a con artist who comes up with schemes ranging from the simple (robbery) to the more sublime (selling fake autographed baseballs). The Hunter has a nephew, Horrors, who is precocious but a much better detective than his uncle. The Hunter answers to Flim Flanagan, and is fond of exclamations like, "Folderal, son!" His motto is Have Nose Will Hunt.

Comment. The characters first appeared on Leonardo Productions's *King Leonardo and His Short Subjects,* which aired on ABC from 1960 to 1963, then moved to *Underdog,* which was seen on NBC from 1964 to 1966; there were sixty-five cases in all. Kenny Delmar was the voice of the Hunter; Ben Stone was the Fox.

HYACINTH HIPPO

Pedigree. Ballet dancer hippo from the Walt Disney film *Fantasia.*

Biography. Hyacinth and her colleagues dance to the strains of *Dance of the Hours* by Ponchielli. As the curtain rises on a cartoon stage showing a courtyard, the pink-bowed ostrich Mlle. Upanova stretches and wakes nine other sleeping ostriches. Dancing over to a cornucopia, she flings fruit to each of the dancers, saving the grapes for herself—or at least trying to. All the ostriches want them, and the bunch of grapes ends up falling into a pool. They return, held by naked Hyacinth wearing only her ballet slippers. Daintily shaking the water from her feet, she steps from the pool as her hippo attendants arrive bearing her tutu and makeup. She dances now—a pirouette whirling her bulk up to her chin—then reclines on a divan and falls asleep. As she naps, a heard of elephant dancers arrives, use their trunks to draw water from the pool, and begin blowing bubbles; at one point, Hyacinth yawns and gulps down the plentiful bubbles. The elephants blow more bubbles, which float under the divan and carry it, along with the sleeping Hyacinth, into the air. The sofa hovers there until a breeze comes along and lowers it to earth . . . at the same time sweeping the elephants into the sky (!). As Hyacinth's divan settles back to earth, bright eyes appear from the dark atop the surrounding columns: eyes that belong to eleven caped alligators. The animals leap down and surround the still-sleeping hippo. However, before they can do her any harm, their leader Ben Ali Gator leaps down, chases them away, and falls in love with the prima ballerina. Hyacinth wakes and she's afraid, at first, then coy . . . then, in a burst of balletic enthusiasm, runs into the distance and leaps into Gator's arms—flattening him. But he struggles up beneath her, and the two partake in a merry chase, all the other animals joining in. In the end, after catching her and juggling her with his feet, fingers, and tail, Gator places her on the ground and stands triumphantly on top of her as the columns and scenery come falling down.

Comment. The animals' names have been retroactively applied by the studio; the characters are not specifically named in the 1940 film. Hyacinth also made a brief appearance in the 1988 feature film *Who Framed Roger Rabbit?*

INSPECTOR GILL

Pedigree. The most intrepid member of the comic book law enforcement group, the Fish Police.

Biography. A city three miles under the ocean looks like any terrestrial city . . . except that it's inhabited entirely by intelligent fish. Although they swim about, they're dressed in clothing, talk like humans, and even pack heat. Gill is a tough, Serpico-type law officer who is the chief nemesis of the criminal organization S.Q.U.I.D., which is led by Hook . . . a fish that lost its tail, since replaced by a metal hook. Hook, his butler Blophish, and his prawn slaves live in Castle S.Q.U.I.D. Gill is tough, if opinionated (in a restaurant, he complains, "There are *few* things more *disgusting* than watching an octopus eat soup"), and he has a serious weakness for beautiful women. Gill's sustenance consists largely of beer and cheese puffs. Other characters in the strip include Goldie, secretary to the Chief of the Fish Police; her father, the evil scientist Dr. Calamari; and Gill's informant-friend Oscar the Octopus. Lately, Gill's discovered that he has "mystical" powers, although their origin and precise nature are not yet known.

Comment. Steve Moncuse's popular series is colorful, hard edged, and exquisitely drawn. *Fish Police* was first published by Comico in 1985. Warner Books reprinted the first four issues as "The Hairball Saga" in 1987. Apple Comics took over the series with no. 18, and it lasted through no. 26. On a related front, in 1988, Cine Group produced thirteen half-hour-long TV cartoons *Sharky and George,* about a pair of underwater detectives. Unlike *Fish Police,* the syndicated series was aimed at children.

IRWIN THE DISCO DUCK

Pedigree. Record album mascot.

Biography. Nothing is known about the long-haired duck who lives in an otherwise all-human world, save that he hosts the *Dance Party,* rerecordings of hit dance tunes. These are performed by the Wibble Wabble Singers and Orchestra, and are geared toward children.

Comment. The character, created by artist George Peed in 1976, allegedly "wrote" the liner notes for the series of records on which he appeared for Peter Pan Industries. Irwin was also featured in his own poster, and there were plans to star the duck and his girlfriend in comic book adventures, which would have been packaged with his records. Several stories were written—Irwin versus schoolteachers who hate disco, Irwin forming a band of inner city kids—but the project was killed when the disco craze died.

JABBERJAW

Pedigree. Not-so-voracious TV shark.

Biography. The theme song describes Jabberjaw as "the latest, greatest shark you ever saw." That's true, provided you haven't seen any. With a voice like Curly of the Three Stooges—right down to the *nyuk, nyuk, nyuk* and *wooo-wooo-wooo*—Jabberjaw is the drummer (yes, the drummer) of the rock group the Neptunes, which entertains at supper clubs, parks, and the like, and is comprised of human musicians Clamhead, Bubbles, Shelly, and Biff. The humans live in Aquaworld, an undersea settlement in the year A.D. 2021, a world of domed buildings connected by a network of transparent tunnels. Jabberjaw is approximately fifteen feet long, is blue with a white belly, can survive outside the water for an unlimited period, and is able to walk on his tail fin. His escapades with the band involve saving the city more often than giving concerts, battling Dr. Lo, the giant Sourpuss Octopus, the Phantom Kelp, El Eel the Heel, and even a trip into the prehistoric past, where Jabberjaw hypnotizes a tyrannosaurus and brings it to Aquaworld. Jabberjaw enjoys skiing on the enclosed slopes underwater. On such occasions, he dons a beanie, sweater, gloves, and earmuffs.

Comment. The Hanna-Barbera series—inspired by the success of *Jaws*—aired on ABC in 1976. There were sixteen half-hour episodes; Frank Welker provided the shark's voice. Jabberjaw actually made his TV debut on an episode of Bill Cosby's variety show *Cos* in September 1976, a preview of Saturday morning fare. The shark has had cameos in several other cartoon series and also surfaced in small parts in Marvel Comics thirteen-issue run of *Laff-a-lympics* (1978 to 1979). De Patie-Freleng also offered up a *Jaws*-inspired cartoon shark: Misterjaw—Supershark, who appeared in adventures on *The Pink Panther Laff and a Half-Hour* on NBC in 1976. This shark is nearsighted; wears a vest, bow tie, and top hat; has a German accent; and also moves about more on land than in the sea, walking on his fin. He's assisted by the diminutive Catfish the Hunter, who always calls his boss "Chief."

JAKE ANT

Pedigree. Prehistoric ant in the comic strip "B.C."

Biography. Jake Ant lives with his wife, Maude (sometimes called Mildred), their ant kids (only Junior is named, and he's at college) and their full-size chihuahua Poopsie. Mr. and Mrs. Ant are like any middle-class human family, with concerns ranging from keeping Junior from seeing X-rated movies to reflecting on the fact that they're "smaller than practically everything," to musing on the drawbacks of being reincarnated as a dinosaur ("I might step on my kids.") Other ants in the strip are Joyce, Harry, Shirley (who's having an affair with Jake), Hadley, Uriah, the white ant Sidney, Mitch, Willard, Sarah, Claude, the industrious Harvey, Zeke and his heavyset wife, Zelda, Queen Ida—who wears a golden crown and lives in a sand castle—friends Herb and Fred, the megalomaniacal Adolf, the timorous Charlie, Myrtle the "hussy in Hill 75," and the guru Herm. The single best ant strip doesn't identify the two male speakers (the females all have long lashes), but it goes thusly:

> ANT ONE: It's ridiculous the way men discriminate against each other . . . at this rate they will soon destroy themselves, then ants will rule the earth!
> ANT TWO: Red or black?

The ants' second greatest fear is being crushed by falling leaves (prehistoric foliage was heavy!). Their greatest fear is the anteater, who uses his superlong tongue to nab insects with a resounding *Zot!* (he can even snatch them from around corners or behind him, by shooting through his legs). This creature frets about his "ant-breath," and is in love with a lady armadillo, who fails to return his affections. Although not terribly bright, the anteater isn't fooled the one time the ants don tiny anteater costumes. And while the anteater occasionally eats one of the principal players, he or she mysteriously returns in future strips. The anteater's worst experience was on the day that aliens landed on the planet. They turn out to be enormous ants, one of whom looks at him and grins, "Look, Lenny, they got insects." The anteater exercises by doing nose-ups.

Jake and a fatal (but funny!) encounter in "B.C." © PUB-LISHERS NEWSPAPER SYNDICATE.

Comment. Johnny Hart's enduring strip first appeared on February 17, 1958, when the artist was twenty-six years old; it was the success of "Peanuts" (see **Snoopy**) that inspired Hart to create the strip. The characters have been seen in a series of animated TV specials, as well as in computer games.

JANE FELINE

Pedigree. Exercise-hating comic strip cat.

Biography. Although Jane is owned by a (nameless) aerobics teacher who works for the California Aerobics and Tanning Specialists, the cat couldn't be less motivated to work out. She comes to the center and, while her master teaches her classes, Jane suits up, goes to the basement where the other cats are . . . and gossips with the "ladies," ogles the toms pressing weights (cleverly improvised from all kinds of trash), and sharpens her claws. She keeps her weight down by dieting. Jane lives with her master in a townhouse in Tarzana. She's friendly with the fat, matronly cat Victoria who lives next door, is terrified of dogs and spiders, and dislikes most of the men her master dates. Most of all, she hates her master's bossy mother, who's allergic to cats. Jane's passions are TV gossip shows and the tabloid newspapers (she likes to see what the cats of celebrities are wearing).

Comment. The biweekly strip was created by San Francisco artist/writer Nona Bailey, and was syndicated for publication exclusively in health club newsletters from 1982 to 1989.

J. FENIMORE FROG

Pedigree. One of DC Comics's longest-lived funny animals—and a grouch among frogs.

Biography. Dressed in a top hat and often smoking a cigar or cigarette (in a holder), the gruff, conniving Fenimore has many adventures with his trusting, dull-minded, necktie-sporting friend Dunbar Dodo. Fenimore is always trying some new scheme to make money—which invariably backfires, as when he and Dunbar nearly drown while testing a pen that writes underwater. If Dunbar happens on some potentially lucrative business or product (as the time he found a magic wand), Fenimore simply dips into his chest labeled "Disguises for Fooling Dunbar" and tries to relieve him of his delusion.

Comment. These characters first appeared in *Funny Stuff* no. 18 in 1947. The magazine was renamed *Dodo and the Frog* with no. 81 and was discontinued with no. 92 in 1957. The animals also appeared in *Comic Cavalcade* beginning with no. 30 in 1948.

JIMINY CRICKET

Pedigree. Insect star of *Pinocchio* and other Walt Disney cartoons.

Biography. A sharp dresser, even though impoverished when we first meet him, Jiminy wears a blue top hat, yellow ascot, fawn vest, tan knee breeches, a black jacket with tails, brown shoes with tan spats, and he always carries a bumbershoot (which he opens and uses as a parachute, when necessary). A wise little fellow, the inches-tall Jiminy crawls into the shop of woodcarver Geppetto on a cold night, and witnesses the completion of the puppet Pinocchio, whom the kindly Geppetto wishes were a living boy instead of a marionette. That evening, the Blue Fairy comes and animates the wooden figure—with the proviso that he won't become a real boy until he proves himself brave, truthful, and unselfish. The spirit names Jiminy his conscience . . . and, never one to refuse a lovely lady, the cricket accepts. Best able to express himself in song, Jiminy counsels Pinocchio to "Give a Little Whistle" if he's ever faced with a dilemma. But the message is lost on the wide-eyed boy. On day one, when Pinocchio goes off to school, Jiminy is unable to dissuade him from accompanying the conman **J. Worthington Foulfellow.** This sets the puppet off on a series of adventures that culminate on Pleasure Island, where boys are turned into donkeys and sold as laborers. Jiminy is able to spirit Pinocchio away before he's completely transformed, and he and the donkey-eared puppet return home. But Geppetto is long gone, having left (with his goldfish Cleo and cat **Figaro**) to search for the boy. Learning that the woodcarver has been swallowed by Monstro the Whale, Pinocchio and Jiminy jump into the sea and search the ocean floor. (Apparently, Jiminy doesn't need to breathe, and has no trouble speaking underwater.) Finding the huge black whale, the two enter when he opens his mouth. They find Geppetto and, after a happy reunion, make the giant sneeze by lighting a fire inside. The group rides out on a raft, the furious whale in pursuit. Pinocchio is badly hurt in the resultant chase,

and the grieving Geppetto takes the inert puppet home . . . where the Blue Fairy pays another visit. Not only does she reanimate Pinocchio, but she rewards his heroism by turning him into a real boy. As for Jiminy, he gets a badge and ribbon, which declare him an "Official Conscience"—and he sings about the value of hope and dreams in the now-classic "When You Wish Upon a Star." The insect's second screen appearance was in the feature film *Fun and Fancy Free* (1947), in which he hosted the film and bridges the two component featurettes, *Bongo* (about a little circus bear, based on a tale by Sinclair Lewis) and *Mickey and the Beanstalk.* His antics are amusing: He flees from an angry cat after accidentally poking it with his umbrella, and sneaks into a house to listen while Edgar Bergen—with Charlie McCarthy and Mortimer Snerd—tells the Mickey story. However, he is less the slightly stuffy sage of the first film, and more a happy-go-lucky, often self-effacing wit. Following these two features, Jiminy went on to host three different, ten-minute-long series that appeared on *The Mickey Mouse Club* show from 1955 to 1959: *Encyclopedia,* which told viewers about everything from tuna to cork (and featured a theme song that taught us how to spell *encyclopedia*); *Mickey Mouse Book Club,* which unabashedly plugged stories on which forthcoming Disney films were based; and *You,* in which Jiminy lectured on the workings of the human body. Although the Cricket himself was authoritative, the Disney artists always touched the series with humor. For instance, a volume titled *How to Ask Mom for a Quarter* can

J. Fenimore Frog *shows characteristic charity toward Dunbar Dodo.* © DC COMICS.

be found in Jiminy's library, and when the Cricket points out that humans are the only animal that can read, we see a boy enjoying a comic book that he's holding upside down. Jiminy also guest starred on the *Disneyland* show in episodes such as *Donald's Award,* wherein Walt promises **Donald Duck** an award if he can control his temper for one day. To help achieve this, Jiminy serves as the Duck's C Man—Donald's everpresent conscience. Jiminy's most recent appearance was in the 1983 featurette *Mickey's Christmas Carol.*

Comment. *Pinocchio* was based on Carlo Collodi's children's classic, written in 1881 and serialized in the Roman children's magazine *Giornale dei Bambini.* In the original tale, the unnamed talking cricket lives in Geppetto's home. When the insect first tries to warn Pinocchio that his roguish behavior will be his downfall, the puppet crushes the cricket to death. However, the cricket's ghost returns shortly thereafter to serve the same role as Jiminy—Pinocchio's conscience. Also in the original tale, Geppetto was swallowed by a giant dogfish, not a whale. Jiminy's voice was provided by Cliff Edwards, who died in 1971. Jiminy also starred in four issues of Dell's *4-Color* comic book, beginning with no. 701 in 1956 and ending with no. 989 in 1959.

JOHN

Pedigree. Prehistoric turtle in the comic strip "B.C."

Biography. John is "about a hundred" (with a life expectancy of 150), has a long, reptilian tail, and is usually seen in tandem with a Dookey bird (a form of loon), which he transports on his back. (After the two-and-a-half-pound bird makes a particularly hard landing, John says, "I wonder what all the other aircraft carriers are doing?"). If necessary, the bird can fly holding the turtle by its shell (the turtle's eyes light up for night flying). John can leave his shell, which he sometimes does to get away from the loon (who has an annoying habit of doing bird impressions) or just to tapdance on top. John is extremely slow—so much so that snails pass him with ease. As for the talking bird, it has a sideline: Checking on the weather for Peter's Weather Bureau. He also moonlights by carrying love messages from the caveman Thor to his unreceptive lover. Although the bird has a drink now and then, John abstains because he does the driving. Another bird seen in the strip is the fast-running "Apteryx, a wingless bird

with hairy feathers." It eats worms and spends most of the time ruing the fact that it can't fly. Other animals abound, including Madge the worm, her husband Bruce, and their son; a woolly mammoth; a quadrupedal dinosaur that walks around roaring *Gronk!;* the two-legged clams Shirley and her husband, the philandering Harv, who falls in love with everything from a mushroom to a credit card; and Whippo the snake, who lost legs after meeting Adam. Indeed, no one has more hard luck than the snake: When a lightning bolt misses him, he sticks out his tongue at it; another comes, striking and

John and passenger (and wonderful gag!) from Johnny Hart's "B.C." © PUBLISHERS NEWSPAPER SYNDICATE.

forking it. He's constantly getting clubbed by "the fat babe," one of the two "girls" in the strip, who hates snakes, mice, and insects.

Comment. See **Jake Ant** for details of the strip's creation.

JOLLY JUMPER

Pedigree. Valiant steed of the Belgian-created comic book and cartoon cowboy Lucky Luke.

Biography. The white horse is the faithful mount of the unassuming American cowboy . . . and, if the truth be known, is also smarter than his master, not only outguessing criminals but outplaying Luke in chess. Although Jolly Jumper is nonanthropomorphic, he's able to untie knots with his teeth.

Comment. The horse's name derives from his pleasant disposition and graceful leaping ability. The "Lucky Luke" strip was created by Maurice de Bevere (a k a "Morris") in 1946 and, after a one shot tryout, became a regular feature in the weekly *Spirou* magazine. When writer Rene Goscinny (see **Dogmatix**) came aboard, the strip became less comedic as some pretty vile characters traded shots with Luke (e.g., Billy the Kid and Jesse James). Goscinny also introduced Luke's dog Ran-tan-plan, as shivering and inept a canine as ever slunk through a comic

strip. The strip moved to *Pilote* magazine in 1968. There have been two feature-length Lucky Luke cartoons: *Daisy Town* (1971) and *The Ballad of the Daltons* (1978). The horse was also seen on the short-lived Hanna-Barbera TV series, which aired in 1983. Bob Ridgely provided the horse's voice.

JOSÉ CARIOCA

Pedigree. Parrot friend of **Donald Duck**.

Biography. The "Brazilian Jitterbird" with a cigar, undersize Panama hat, bumbershoot (which somehow doubles as a flute!), yellow dinner jacket, and black bow tie, made his debut in the feature-length cartoon *Saludos Amigos* (1943). The Disney artists take a tour of South America, where, in the segment *Aquarela do Brasil (Watercolor of Brazil)*, they tour Rio de Janeiro during carnival time. One of the animators is inspired to draw the natty Brazilian parrot, who comes to life and takes Donald Duck on a tour of the continent. At the end of the trip, José sambas the night away with his duck pal. (An animator's paintbrush fills in the watercolor scenery for the pair as they dance; naturally, self-absorbed Donald walks smack into the bristles and is coated with paint.) José's next screen appearance is in *The Three Caballeros* (1945). Donald gets a book about Brazil for his

Jolly Jumper and his master (although obviously not a chess master) Lucky Luke. *From the feature film* Lucky Luke: Daisy Town. © PRODUCTIONS DARGAUD FILMS.

birthday, and out pops the parrot—only a few inches tall. Splitting into four little Josés, he sings a song about his native land *(Baia)* then clubs Donald with a mallet, shrinking him to José's size so they can enter the book, catch a train, and visit Baia. (Inventively, the train has a square wheel which enables it to hop and "dance" to the beat of the music.) In the city, the birds dance with some locals . . . after which lamps, fountains, and finally the buildings themselves begin to boogie. The book itself begins to bop and slams shut; José squirms out and Donald follows. Plugging his thumb in his mouth, José blows himself up to full size; Donald puffs on his index finger, but only manages to reinflate various portions of his anatomy. José enjoys the spectacle, but finally breaks down and tells Donald he's using the wrong finger. At this point, **Panchito** arrives, and the trio go for a tour of Mexico. José's third film was *Melody Time* (1948), the parrot appearing with Donald in the *Blame It on the Samba* segment. The two birds are bored and blue (not figuratively: They are colored blue!) until **The Aracuan Bird** arrives and livens things up. In the dance that follows, Donald and José are more or less set decoration for the antics of their fellow bird.

Comment. *Carioca* is a word used to describe a native of Rio de Janeiro. The "south of the border" films were made not only to reinforce a "good neighbor policy" in a time of war but also because Disney's normally lucrative European markets had been cut off. South America provided an acceptable substitute. José's voice was provided on film by José Oliveira. Dell published a comic book edition of *The Three Caballeros* (4-Color no. 71), drawn by Walt Kelly of **Pogo** fame. José also has made frequent appearances in comic strips and comic books featuring Donald.

J. RUFUS LION

Pedigree. A henpecked comic book lion.

Biography. The black-maned lion lives in Zooville, (also home to **McSnurtle the Turtle**), in a quaint house surrounded by a chain-link fence. Also living with him are his wife, a bespectacled, bridge-playing chicken, and their nephew, Arsenic, a giraffe. An inventor (his crowning achievement is a "Cigarette Putter Outer") and a "blowhard," Rufus is the Baron Munchausen of Zooville, boasting of distinguished friends the Lions used to have, and great deeds he once performed. Later in the strip, Rufus's life and character change somewhat. Rufus lives alone, wanting only peace and solitude. Unfortunately, the wily Mortimer Mouse is constantly trying to mooch off him, thus preventing the lion from reading the newspaper or his favorite comic book, *Scribbly*. In both versions, Rufus usually dresses in trousers, a T-shirt, and suspenders.

Comment. This strip first appeared in DC Comics's *Funny Stuff* no. 1 in 1944, and later as a back-up feature in *Dodo and the Frog* (see **J. Fenimore Frog**). Mortimer Mouse was the name Walt Disney had originally intended to use for **Mickey Mouse**.

Mortimer Mouse pulls the mane over the eyes of **J. Rufus Lion.** © DC COMICS.

JULIUS THE CAT
Pedigree. Walt Disney's first continuing character.
Biography. Julius is a black cat with a round head, a black, oval nose, small, pointed ears, and a long tail that works like a third arm and has other special properties (see below). He's occasionally drawn with a white belly, walks on two legs or four (usually when he's running), and sometimes smokes a pipe. In 1923, to bolster the fast-fraying finances of his fledgling cartoon studio, Walt Disney began producing silent cartoons featuring Alice, a live girl who interacts with animated animals in a cartoon setting. In the debut adventure, *Alice's Wonderland* (1923), Alice encounters Walt at a drawing board, then enters the cartoon; a cat chased by a dog in the cartoon is the prototype for Julius. Julius himself first appeared in the third Alice short, *Alice's Spooky Adventure* (1924), in which the little girl enters a haunted house and is accosted by a ghost. She plucks away the sheet, and Julius thanks her for saving him from being consigned to "the life of a spook!" Alice accompanies the grateful Julius to a ghostly dance, where he upsets a table on which ghosts are playing mah-jongg. They chase the cat and girl and Julius detaches his tail, swinging it like a club. The two get away, Julius pledges his love for the girl . . . and Alice awakes to find a live-action cat licking her hand. In Julius's next screen appearance *(Alice's Fishy Story*, 1924), he briefly has the screen all to himself as he goes fishing at the North Pole. Using his tail to drill a hole in the ice, then employing it as a fishing rod, he's dumped in the sea by a swordfish and has to be rescued by an Eskimo. Alice arrives, and the two go scavenging through a shipwreck. They find chewing tobacco and, with fish still on his mind, Julius begins dropping it into the sea. The fish take the bait and, removing his tail, Julius bashes them unconscious when they jump up to spit the vile stuff out. Perhaps the most important of the Julius cartoons was his next, *Alice the Peacemaker* (1924), in which the cat battles a mouse for control of an icebox; in appearance and manner, the mouse was virtually a dead-ringer for the early **Mickey Mouse.** The mouse's name was Ike, and Julius was named Mike in this cartoon. Disney was clearly hoping that "Mike and Ike" would catch on and become an ongoing team à la the cat and mouse in **Krazy Kat.**
  Comment. From 1924 to 1927, Julius appeared in from forty-seven to fifty-one shorts in the Alice series. (Not all of the films have survived, and their contents are unknown. It's likely, however, that the four films in question featured the cat in some capacity; in the early Mickey Mouse cartoons that came later, Disney almost always used the same cast of characters.)

JUNIOR
Pedigree. The dog owned by Popeye's "adoptid" child Swee'Pea.
Biography. Nothing is known about this little, yellow "dorg" except that he eats any kind of food—from pickles to popcorn, gumdrops, hamburgers, and, yes, dog food—in any amount.
  Comment. Although Popeye is best known for his appearances in comic strips and cartoons, this character appeared only in the Popeye comic books, and even then, rarely. Far better known was the mythical creature Eugene the Jeep. (The comic strip name was created before the motor vehicle.) A jeep is an animal from a fourth-dimensional world. According to Professor Brainstine, Eugene was created when "a number of jeep life-cells somehow forced through the dimensional barrier into our world [and] combined . . . with free life cells of the African Hooey Hound," whose electrical vibrations were the same as the foreign cell. The jeep has magical powers: If asked a question regarding the past, present, or future he will answer frankly. When he bows, that means yes. If he doesn't bend, the answer is no. The little yellow quadruped with the red bulb of a nose first appeared in Popeye's "Thimble Theatre" comic strip on March 21, 1936, and has also appeared in cartoons. Eugene now lives with 364 other jeeps on Jeep Island in the Eighth Sea. Jeeps live strictly on a diet of orchids. See also the Popeye costar **Bernice, the Whiffle Hen.**

J. WORTHINGTON FOULFELLOW
Pedigree. Wicked fox seen in Disney's *Pinocchio.*
Biography. As the young, animated puppet Pinocchio heads to school, followed by his "conscience" **Jiminy Cricket,** he is greeted by the fox Foulfellow—a k a "Honest John"—and his sidekick Gideon, a doltish, cigar-smoking alleycat, both of whom wear torn top hats, cloaks, and torn, ill-fitting jackets and trousers; they each carry a cane. Foulfellow realizes that a stringless marionette would be worth a fortune to the puppetmaster Stromboli, and singing "Hi-diddle-dee-dee, an actor's life for me," he lures the boy to the puppet show. The ecstatic Stromboli pays the pair and keeps the puppet, locking him in a bird cage when he's not performing. Jiminy Cricket tracks him down and, with the help of the Blue Fairy, Pinocchio is freed. He

promises to be good, and returns home to the woodcarver Geppetto. Meanwhile, the fox and cat are at the Red Lobster Inn, chatting with a coachman who brings boys to Pleasure Island, where they're turned into donkeys and sold. The coachman promises to pay the animals a gold piece for every boy they bring him. The pair encounter Pinocchio once again and, convincing him that he needs a trip to Pleasure Island for his health, they bring him to the coach. Jiminy is able to hop on before it departs, and once again he rescues the puppet.

Comment. See entry on **Jiminy Cricket** for notes about the novel on which the film was based. In the original, Pinocchio skips school to attend a puppet show and is kidnapped by the puppetmaster. But Pinocchio's abductor is persuaded to let him leave, and gives him five gold pieces to boot. The fox and cat meet the boy as he's headed home, and steal the money from him. It is a young boy, and not the fox and cat, who convince Pinocchio to go to Pleasure Island. The fox's voice was provided by Walter Catlett, while the cat's sole sound—a belch—was burped by Mel Blanc.

KABOOBIE

Pedigree. A winged camel of TV cartoons.

Biography. While exploring a cave off the coast of Maine, young twins Nancy and Chuck discover a broken ring with *Shaz* written on one, and *zan* on the other. When they put the halves together, they're whisked to the time of the Arabian Nights, where they meet the sixty-foot-tall genie Shazzan, who gives them the airborne Kaboobie. Alas, the children can't return to the present until they return the ring to its rightful owner. Thus they begin their search through the ancient world, with Shazzan at their service and Kaboobie for transportation. The camel is smart and resourceful. For example, when a curse spirits Nancy away, Kaboobie has the presence of mind to pull a magic rope from a pouch and send it to search for her. Kaboobie's hindlegs pack the kick of a mule, and have gotten the kids out of some tight spots. His vocabulary consists entirely of garbled mutterings.

Comment. Hanna-Barbera's *Shazzan!* aired on CBS from 1967 to 1969. There were thirty-six episodes in all.

KAMIKAZE CAT

Pedigree. Feline comic book sleuth.

Biography. Kamikaze Cat—KC to his friends—is a feline who lives for danger in a *film noir* world of animals. A cigarette-smoking comic book freak, KC wears a trenchcoat and fedora; his girlfriend is a waitress (also a cat) named Boopsie Meow. His perennial foes are the members of WORM: Worldwide Organization of Registered Megalomaniacs. Among their members are the Warbler, a canary; Bearface; Cat-tastrophe, and Woodside Weasel.

Comment. The characters were created by Mark Hamlin and Roger McKenzie, and their short-lived magazine was published by Pied Piper Comics in 1987.

KAT KARSON

Pedigree. Feline cowboy comic book star.

Biography. Astride his white horse Aram, the spunky, black-furred little deputy for hire rides from county to county ("Gunfire Valley shore sounds like a rough town! Let's have a look!"). Finding the sher-

iff, the cat signs onto his team and rids the region of bad guys. The cat's most dangerous foe is Silver Dollar Dan, who's a dead-ringer for the sarsaparilla-drinking kitty.

Comment. Kat appeared in Compix's *Cowboys 'n' Injuns* comic book from no. 2 to no. 8, which was published sporadically during 1946 to 1952. He also appeared in the I. W. Enterprises (publisher Israel Waldman) one-shot reprint *Kat Karson* in 1953. Also appearing in the Compix comic book was Waggin' Weasel (called Wagon Weasel in some issues), a farmer who lives outside of Bloody Gulch and is always looking for the easy way to do things, such as buying a rocket-powered plow that goes berserk. The human characters who had their own strips in the magazine were innocuous figures like the child Jesse Jimmy, who rode the black-spotted white horse Sixty, and the prospector Ol' Smokey, who traveled the north with his sled dogs Clancy, Nancy, Pansy, and Knockwurst.

KATTU

Pedigree. A comic book wolf who rears a human child.

Biography. In the "damp, dark . . . jungle world (of) the dawn lands—a lost valley," a scientific expedition is ambushed by the fierce Balu tribe. During the fight, little Carol London is carried off by an eagle. Meanwhile, the wolf Kattu has gone to the eagle's aerie, where it slays the eagle's mate Ela, "for it was Ela that had killed Kattu's cub." As the wolf finishes off the bird, its mate arrives, carrying Carol. Kattu slays this bird too. While Carol mumbles, "Good doggy! Nice doggy!" the animal is thinking, "Here was a baby come to replace her dead wolf cub." Kattu's tribe adopts Carol, who grows up to be the mighty Cave Girl. When Kattu eventually passes on, Carol becomes the leader of the pack.

Comment. Magazine Enterprises' Cave Girl—beautifully drawn by Bob Powell—was introduced in *Thun'da* no. 2 in 1952, though the saga of Kattu wasn't told until the first of the four issues of Cave Girl's own magazine, published in 1953 to 1954. Among the other animals in the strip are Hortha the boar, Beeta and Lita the monkeys, Lakli and Paath the panthers, and Broog the gorilla.

SNARLING HER HATE, KATTU LEAPED—

GRRRR....

Kattu to the rescue. From the first adventure of Cave Girl.

KERMIT THE FROG

Pedigree. Muppet frog star of television, films, comic strips, and comic books.

Biography. Born in a swamp in Georgia, Kermit—a bipedal frog with a scalloped collar, red mouth, and buttonhole eyes, who can speak both English and Frog—usually sits around singing ballads, accompanying himself on the banjo. Learning of a trade newspaper advertisement for talented frogs, he packs his bags and heads for Hollywood. En route, he meets Fozzie Bear, who's doing terrible stand-up comedy at a local club; the bear revs up his 1951 Studebaker and joins Kermit on his trip west. By accident (*in* an accident, really) they meet the magician the Great Gonzo and his love Camilla the Chicken, who go with them. At a fair, Kermit spots **Miss Piggy**, who falls instantly and madly in love with him, and becomes the next member of the group. Cocktail pianist Rowlf the Dog is the last to throw in with the troupe. The Muppets eventually make it to the West Coast, finagle an audience with movie mogul Lew Lord, and get a motion picture contract. As for that trade advertisement—it was to serve as spokesfrog for the French Fried Frog Legs Fast Food Franchises, something Kermit understandably finds distasteful. (These details were introduced in *The Muppet Movie*). It isn't known how or why, but at some point the group's movie career becomes unrav-

eled. At this time, Kermit moves to Sesame Street where his primary job is as the reporter/host of the "Frog on the Street" segment. Dressed in a trench coat and fedora, holding a microphone, and greeting viewers with his customary, "Hi ho, Kermit *the* Frog, here," he stops "regular folks" and asks them the question of the day. Their inane answers usually frustrate him, revealing Kermit's greatest weakness: his short temper, which results from the frog being something of a stuffed shirt with no sense of humor. (Once, the vampiric Count, who is compelled to count numbers, is running an elevator with Kermit as his passenger. The Count is having such a good time counting off the floors that he neglects to stop at the frog's floor. Kermit immediately throws a tantrum, the likes of which would put even **Donald Duck** to shame.) Kermit is much more at ease when he is alone, singing songs like "It's Not Easy Being Green" ("It's not that easy being green / having to spend each day the color of leaves"). Given his low boiling point, it's surprising to find Kermit showing up next on *The Muppet Show*, in the high-pressure position as master of ceremonies at the Muppet Theater, supervising a vaudeville-style presentation that somehow emerges relatively unscathed from backstage disorder. Kermit has a nephew, Robin, who's in the first grade; the pudgy little fellow was introduced in the Muppets comic strip (see "Comment").

Comment. The Muppets were created by Jim Henson who, as a high-school senior in Maryland, hosted his own local puppet show; in 1955, at the University of Maryland, he and future wife, Jane Nebel, created the show *Sam and Friends,* coining the term "Muppet" for their felt and foam rubber creations, to describe the combination hand puppet and marionettes (rod-articulated from below the stage instead of controlled by strings from above) used in the series. Kermit was created in 1956 and, a year later, was first seen on *The Tonight Show* (with Henson manipulating him and providing the voice) singing *I've Grown Accustomed to Your Face* to a monster, which attempts to devour the frog. The piano-playing dog Rowlf (also Henson's voice) was the first Muppet character to gain regular national exposure, on the variety series *The Jimmy Dean Show,* which aired on ABC from 1964 to 1966. However, the characters and their creator gained their greatest fame with the debut of *Sesame Street,* an educational program for preschoolers that premiered on PBS on November 10, 1969. The show was created by Children's Television Workshop executive director Joan Ganz Cooney, and underwritten by the U.S. Office of Education and various philanthropic foundations. The series is set on a fictional street in New York, in the Bronx, where the humans are all kindly, and they interact freely with Muppets such as **Big Bird** and his best friend, the long-lashed, mastodonlike Aloysuis Snuffleupagus and his sister, Alice, who wears a blue bow in her hair (they're named after their trunks, which are called "snuffles"); Barkley the brown-and-white dog; the inspired opera star Placido Flamingo, whose "singing is for the birds"; and various nonanimal Muppets like Oscar the Grouch, Cookie Monster, Bert and Ernie, and the Dracula-like Count. Kermit's costarring role on *Sesame Street* led to greater fame as the star of *The Muppet Show,* which was filmed in England and shown in syndication. There were 120 episodes produced from 1976 to 1981. In addition to Miss Piggy and the return of the floppy-eared Rowlf, animal characters featured on the show were the gentle and unassuming Fozzie Bear, Sam the Eagle, and Rizzo the Rat (after Ratso Rizzo from the film *Midnight Cowboy*). There were a handful of TV specials, after which the next stop for Kermit and *Muppet Show* colleagues was motion pictures. They starred in a trio of films, which became increasingly more elaborate (read: overproduced) and less successful: *The Muppet Movie* (1979), which traces Kermit's rise from anonymity

to fame; *The Great Muppet Caper* (1981), with the Muppets trying to solve a jewel heist in London; and *The Muppets Take Manhattan* (1984), in which the troupe tries to mount a Broadway play (also the basis for a three-issue Marvel Comics adaptation). When *The Muppet Show* ceased original productions, the reruns continued in syndication, supported by a newspaper comic strip, "Jim Henson's Muppets," by Guy and Brad Gilchrist. The strip moved between typical Muppet egg-on-the-face shtick and out-and-out slapstick (the latter out of character): Miss Piggy receiving flowers in her dressing room, savoring the adoration of the public, then getting an apology from the newspaper for running her obituary; Fozzie Bear and Gonzo having mishaps while hot-air ballooning; Rowlf getting his medical degree to gain respectability, then having to dress up as a clown to work in pediatrics; and Miss Piggy going to a drive-through restaurant and literally driving *through* the place. The notion of the Muppets as infants was introduced in *The Muppets Take Manhattan,* and became an ongoing animated series *The Muppets, Babies & Monsters,* which premiered on CBS in 1985. The Muppets Monsters segment of show was dropped the following year, and the show became *Jim Henson's Muppet Babies.* A Marvel comic book was introduced in 1985. In *The Muppets Take Manhattan,* Miss Piggy states that the characters didn't know each other as children; the series speculates what might have happened if they did. The Muppet Babies live with Nanny and get into adventures both semireal (lost in a museum) and fanciful (climbing a beanstalk). In addition to Kermit in his little sailor's suit and Miss Piggy, there are juvenile versions of Animal, Gonzo, Rowlf, Fozzie Bear, Skeeter, and Scooter. Muppet characters new and old appeared on NBC's *The Jim Henson Hour,* a ratings failure that debuted in 1989. Also that year, the Walt Disney Company bought the Muppets—guaranteeing further exposure and inevitable team-ups. The Muppets are among the few strictly educational cartoon animals—although they aren't the only ones. Prominent in TV is Clifford, a red dog who hosts half-hour animated cartoons that are syndicated and available on videocassette. He teaches through narrative adventures like *Fun with Opposites* and *Fun with Sounds* (he wreaks havoc after getting a job in a movie sound-effects department). Clifford's tales are from Family Home Entertainment. In videocassette only is a more ambitious project known as *The Watchkins Adventure,* a half-hour, million-dollar collection of music videos on educational and "good behavior" themes. These cartoons from UMA Productions feature the likes of Elvis Gorilla, Leon the Frog, and the Ant-rew Sisters.

THE KID'S CAT

Pedigree: Obscure comic strip cat.

Biography. The Cat and his owner, a young boy, live with the boy's parents. The little black cat with the white muzzle and paws is constantly getting into trouble due to its curiosity or short-sightedness. Thinking that a bulge in the sofa cushion is a mouse, the Cat claws at it and gets launched into the air by a spring. Searching everywhere for a mouse, the Cat can't find it—because the mouse is on its back. Following a mouse into a bag of cement, the Cat is trapped there—trapped solid—when it rains. Sometimes, the boy's activities cause the Cat grief, such as rocking a chair on its tail or sitting on it to warm his bottom. The boy is known only as "Baby"; the cat has no name.

   Comment. John Rosol's "The Cat and the Kid" was inadequately circulated by the (Philadelphia) Ledger Syndicate, and lasted only from 1935 to

*The wonderful simplicity of **The Kid's Cat.***

1937. Another short-lived comic strip was "The Radio Catts," which appeared in the middle 1920s and ran on the same page as radio listing. The strip is about young radio fanatic Danny, his older sister, and his parents; the Catts are essentially a human family, dressing and talking like people, and fretting about domestic matters. The strip is notable in that it was written and drawn by Chester Gould, who went on to create "Dick Tracy."

THE KING

Pedigree. Lion inspired by Fonzie of TV's *Happy Days*.

Biography. A 1950s lion with a pompadour-mane, the King travels around in a ramshackle hotrod driven by Skids the alligator (who wears a pail for a helmet), and leads a pack of friends through adventures like *The Riverbed 5000, The First King on Mars,* and *The Carnival Caper.* The gang members include Sheena the lioness (the King's main squeeze), Yuka-Yuka the mole, Big H the hippo, the incredibly dumb Square the gorilla, and the soda shop waitress Zelda the ostrich.

   Comment. Hanna-Barbera's *Heyyy, It's the King* was seen as part of the **C.B. Bears** show; there were thirteen episodes in all. Lennie Weinrib provided the King's voice. Speaking of Fonzie, the original Arthur Fonzarelli came to TV cartoons in 1980 on ABC's *Fonz and the Happy Days Gang,* in which he had a pet dog named—what else?—Mr. Cool.

KING LEONARDO

Pedigree. Saturday morning cartoon potentate.

Biography. Ruler of the African nation of Bongo Congo, Leonardo is a benevolent but stupid lion, his show accurately described in the theme song as, "The kingly cartoon with the kingly buffoon who has his share of woes." Leonardo's reign is constantly threatened by **Biggy Rat** and his flunky, Itchy Brother, who was the king's own brother. Leonardo invariably falls for whatever trick the two villains try to pull. For example, told he has to christen a new rocket ship from the *inside,* the king gladly steps in, the villains lock the door, and Leonardo is launched to Venus. However, his "true blue" regent Odie Colognie, a skunk, always comes to his rescue. The tall, slender monarch stands upright and always wears a robe and crown in matching colors (usually orange or purple). His favorite pastime is watching television. Odie is dressed in just a starched collar and a big *L* medallion, worn like a necklace, which contains the "Royal Odie Decoder" for secret communiqués.

Comment. The characters first appeared on Leonardo Productions's *King Leonardo and His Short Subjects,* which aired on ABC from 1960 to 1963. After that, it became a segment of **Tennessee Tuxedo**'s show. There were 103 episodes in all, several of them two- and four-part stories running fifteen and thirty minutes. Jackson Beck provided the gruff voice of Leonardo, while Allan Swift was the smooth, Ronald Colman-esque Odie. Dell, then Gold Key, published a total of four Leonardo comic books from 1961 to 1963. See **King Leonidas** and **Linus the Lionhearted,** two other lion potentates.

KING LEONIDAS

Pedigree. Lion-potentate in the Walt Disney film *Bedknobs and Broomsticks.*

Biography. In 1940, shortly after the onset of World War II, London children Carrie, Paul, and Charlie are forced to leave the beleaguered city and move to the country. They are given over to Eglantine Price—who happens to be an apprentice witch. Along with Professor Emelius Browne, the four partake in a variety of adventures, which include raising a ghostly army to battle invading Nazis. However, their most wonderful time together involves a trip to the Lost Isle of Naboombu, where they go searching for a magic pendant. Sailing (via bed!) under the sea, they encounter the rather distinguished, cigar-smoking Mr. Codfish, who directs them to Naboombu ("straight up," he says helpfully). En route, the bed is snared by Fisherman Bear of Naboombu, and although it's illegal to catch people, the bear takes the group to see King Leonidas. The king is first introduced by voice only, as the spindly, bespectacled Secretary Bird is blasted from the tent by the lion's roar: The king is displeased because there's no referee for the soccer match he's been looking forward to playing. (And winning. He fancies himself the world's greatest player, and won't hesitate to change the rules in midgame to ensure victory.) When Emilius volunteers to ref, the king doffs his red, ermine-trimmed robe—revealing not just a rather potbellied royal figure, but the pendant worn on a chain around his neck—and proceeds to field his yellow-garbed rhinoceros, wild boar, gorilla, and other rough and tumblers against the timorous likes of the ostrich, kangaroo, and leopard in blue. The blues put up a good fight, but when the ball lands on the rhino's horn, deflates, and goes jetting away,

Leonidas screams for someone to get it: His roar is so loud that it not only blows the leopard's spots from his body, but sweeps all the animals from the field. As the deflated ball drifts down, the king smugly walks to the goal, blows it in, orders Emilius to blow the whistle, and declares the game ended, his team victorious. As Emilius helps the lion on with his robe, he switches the pendant with his referee's whistle, and the humans head back to their bed. Noticing that the "royal star" is gone, the Secretary Bird so informs the king—who not only pounds the bird's head deep into his collar, but shrieks and goes running after the humans. Just as he's about to leap on them, Eglantine manages to conjure up a spell that transforms the lion into a rabbit. His crown falls around his body, and the transformed potentate turns tail and goes hopping away.

Comment. Angela Lansbury starred as Eglantine, and David Tomlinson played Emilius. Lennie Weinrib was the voice of both Leonidas and Secretary Bird, Robert Colt was Mr. Codfish, and Dallas McKennon was Fisherman Bear. A comic book adaptation was published in Gold Key's *Walt Disney Showcase* no. 6. This vastly underrated film with still-magnificent special effects was derived from a pair of novels, *The Magic Bedknob* (1943) and *Bonfires and Broomsticks* (1947) written by Mary Norton. Another lion-king in the Disney film library is Prince John, villain of Disney's next feature film, an all-animal version of *Robin Hood* (1973). Rather more bumbling than Leonidas, John (voiced by Peter Ustinov) is ruling England in the absence of his truly regal brother, Richard. John is a vain, thumb-sucking monarch who is easily manipulated by his regent, the snake Sir Hiss. In that film, Robin is portrayed as a fox, Little John as a bear, and Friar Tuck as a badger.

KISSYFUR

Pedigree. Cuddly little bear of TV cartoons and comic books.

Biography. Circus bears, young Kissyfur and his big, Hoyt Axton–like father Gus slip into a depression when Kissyfur's mother is killed (presumably, during their tightrope act). When the circus train derails during a storm, the two bears steal clothes from a chest to stay warm, and escape down a river. Settling in a swamp, they meet the birds, bunnies, turtles, pigs, racoons, and other animals who are already living there—along with Charles Warthog, who's having trouble dealing with the food shortage as well as the danger represented by Floyd and Jolene, a pair of carnivorous alligators. During a swamp meeting, Gus puts in his two cents about how things can be better run (build a bridge over the river, which will allow them to access new berry supplies *and* avoid the alligators), and is appointed the new leader. (When all else fails, Gus has been known to grab the alligators by the neck, snarl at them, and chase them away.) He also catches the eye of Emmy Lou Bear, who becomes his love interest. Gus and Kissyfur live inside a spacious tree; dressed in a T-shirt, Kissyfur attends school and usually pals around with Toot the beaver. All the animals of the region fear humans, who are usually shown only in shadow; when they are spotted, the village is quickly camouflaged, with shrubs moved into place and roll-down bark dropped in front of the windows.

Comment. The Phil Mendez creation premiered as an NBC cartoon series in 1985; a surprisingly amateurish DC Comic book debuted in 1989. The series was originally going to be called *Bear Roots.*

KITTY
Pedigree. One of the longest-lived comic strip cats.
Biography. Kitty is a light gray alley cat who lives in the household of Paw (Sam'l), Maw, and daughter, Polly Perkins. Extremely fond of birds (he regularly eats the Perkinses' pet canaries), he adores Paw and usually hangs around with him as the elderly man gets into trouble. Now and then, he can be seen standing in the background or at Paw's feet, immitating exactly the way the man stands. Kitty hates it whenever Polly gets it in her mind to enter him in a cat show (she once put a bow on him and he

Kitty with Maw and Paw.

slunk under the sofa to avoid the laughter of the other alley cats), when he has to go to the vet (he files his own claws down to keep from having to go), or when a mouse is able to elude him (once, Paw promised to stock the house with anemic mice to boost Kitty's self-image). The Perkinses briefly owned a police dog named Sherlock.

Comment. Created by the great cartoonist Cliff Sterrett, the cat appeared in "Polly and Her Pals" (originally known as "Positive Polly"), which first appeared in the *New York Journal* on December 4, 1912. The strip lasted forty-six years. From 1926 to 1928, the Sunday entry opened with a one-row comic strip called "Damon and Pythias" (changed, after two months, to the simpler "Dot and Dash"), about the misadventures of a cat and dog.

KITZ 'N' KATZ
Pedigree. A pair of comic book "katz."
Biography. The carefree cats live in the largely rural animal realm of Boomalacka. Although one cat is black, the other white, it is never made clear which is which. The good-natured felines spend their time trying to help those in need (such as stirring up interest in ice cream, to help Kozy, a lovely young cat who runs an ice cream stand), playing music on the banjo, or even (gasp!) visiting the racy Katnip Klub. In their most dramatic tale, a litter drive results in the junk being "fused and ... reborn ... as a giant Robokat!" Fortunately, the entire adventure proves to be a dream. Other characters that appear in the strip are Nootin the Squirrel, who wears a beret shaped like the top of an acorn; the huge cat Bloon; and the cats' lookalikes Fizzy 'n' Fuzzy.

Comment. Bob Laughlin's simply drawn characters first appeared in *Bop* no. 1, from Kitchen Sink Comics (1982). A total of six issues of *Kitz 'n' Katz* have appeared, published by Phantasy, then Eclipse (four issues), and finally by Laughlin himself.

KLONDIKE KAT
Pedigree. TV feline mountie.
Biography. Klondike is a fumbling Northwest Mountie dressed in a bright red uniform and stationed in Fort Frazzle, under the command of Major Minor. Although he has numerous assignments, Klondike's chief responsibility is to try and capture the French mouse Savoir Faire, who steals local stores of food. Despite Klondike's oft-stated vow—"One of these days I'm gonna make mincemeat of

that mouse!"—he never succeeds. The cat's aide is the sled dog Malamutt.

Comment. The Total Television/Leonardo Productions *Klondike Kat* was part of the CBS *Tennessee Tuxedo* show in 1963. It was also aired on the *Go Go Gophers* show on CBS in 1968. There were twenty-six episodes in all.

KOKO THE BEAR
Pedigree. A high-chair decoration that comes to life for comic book adventures.
Biography. Koko begins his existence as a picture on the inside seat back of baby Raymond's high chair. One day, he simply pulls himself off, inviting Kola the panda (who is printed on the back of the chair) to join him. Visiting Raymond in bed, Koko explains, "We can't come down when you are *bad* and don't eat your food." Kola adds, "But when you are *good* and eat all your food and don't get *messy*—then the magic works!" In their first adventure, the masked bandit Muggsy Mouse enters the house and, at gunpoint, orders the trio to open the "cheese safe" (the ice box) and get him cheese. Koko blinds Muggsy by squirting seltzer into his eyes, and Kola clobbers him with a pie (see **Mickey Mouse**, for more on Muggsy). In another adventure, Koko must free Kola when a postage stamp becomes stuck across the back of the chair, trapping him. After each escapade, the animals return to the "magic high chair."

Comment. Koko made his debut in Magazine Enterprises' *Tick Tock Tales* no. 1 in 1945, and stayed with it through no. 34 in 1951. Another character that appeared in that magazine was Goofus the Gopher, who began as a back-up feature in no. 1. Dressed in red trousers, a blue shirt, and a polka dot tie, Goofus is always searching for new ways to make money, be it capturing bandits or working as a valet for a millionaire. Unfortunately, he's too clumsy to pull any of it off: He's unable to turn on a fan without getting caught in the blades. Other bears who surfaced briefly in comic books during the later 1940s and throughout the 1950s were Bozo Bear, who starred in eight issues of Harvey Comics *Nutty Comics* from 1945 to 1947; Kokey Koala, who appeared in his own Toby Press one shot in 1952; Buster Bear, who had ten issues of his own Quality House magazine from 1953 to 1955; and Mighty Bear, a superheroic bear who battled through five issues of his own Star Publishing magazine from 1954 to 1958. (Unrelated to Marvel's Star Comics line.)

KOSMO W. CAT
Pedigree. Detective comic book feline of the future.
Biography. A private eye on a futuristic animal world, Kosmo is assisted by the dog-mechanic Portly, who keeps his spaceship "gassed up an' rarin' to go." The "space-age Ellery Queen" packs a disintegrator gun, wears a jet belt that enables him to fly, can create an energy field to protect himself from harm, drinks milk instead of alcohol, and has an ulcer. Incidentally, the *W* in Kosmo's name stands for Ralph. As he puts it, "My parents learned English from Elmer Fudd cartoons." In his only adventure, he tracks down the thieves who steal a collection of rare *TV Guides*. His only known girlfriend is the shapely Pussy Willow.

Comment. The character appeared just once, in Star*Reach Productions's *Quack* no. 1 in 1976.

KRAZY KAT
Pedigree. One of the great comic strip characters.
Biography. In the beginning of their illustrious career, Krazy Kat and a bulldog pal were seen underfoot in the household of the Dingbat family, pursuing their tit-for-tat business while the Dingbats "carried" the strip. Ignatz Mouse (known, then, as Mr. Mouse) was added after a month, shown heaving a rock at the cat. When the animals got their own space (see "Comment"), the world outside the home grew quickly. Other animals who sauntered in and out of the strip include the gentle Mr. Kroke, a frog; Krazy Katfish, the cat's seagoing "kousin"; Katbird, a winged cousin; the donkey Don Kiyoti; the flippered Mr. Sseell; Joe Stork, who's fond of recounting the time he was delivering the infant Krazy to Mrs. Kat of Katnip Kourt, Kokonino, and had to shoot dice with Santa to see who would go down the chimney first; the nosy duck Mrs. Kwakk Wakk and her chicken friend Mrs. Kakkil; Y. Zowl, the owl M.D.; and major costar, Officer B. Pupp, a canine law officer with a blue police hat and uniform, badge, and nightstick, who is there to throw Ignatz right into jail whenever any bricks are tossed (see below). In addition to keeping an eye out for the mouse, he also employs a special divining rod that only searches out bricks. However, it was the relationship between the blue-black cat with the long, pointy ears and red scarf, and the wiry pink mouse that carried the bulk of the tales—specifically, Ignatz's ongoing efforts to hit the cat with a brick (evolved from the stone): The streaking *zip* followed by a hearty *pow!!* were to become the mouse's trademark. Once, when Krazy was

riding the 20th Century Limited, the mouse had the audacity to stop it just to toss a brick. Another time, to get past the diligent Officer Pupp, he invented both a mechanized brick-tosser and an airborne one. Not that he *always* got his cat. Brick in hand, Ignatz once snuck along a board on which Krazy was sitting; the cat happened to get up and the board, which was balanced like a seesaw on a rock, flung the mouse and brick skyward. Another time, the mouse found a curved object and threw it at Krazy, thus learning about boomerangs; yet another time, Krazy gave Ignatz a brick made of rubber that, when thrown, bounced back and clobbered the mouse. And at a carnival, he was offered a prize if he could hit the cat's head with a ball: Failing time after time, Ignatz finally succeeded when he got himself a brick. It wasn't that the mouse had anything to fear from the cat; he was just an uppity little cuss. Indeed, despite the punishment he took, Krazy genuinely cared for the mouse, and often waxed melodramatic whenever Ignatz was away—"E'en but to gaze at thy picture fairest one, gives big pains to my heart—fain, sweet face, would I kiss thee o'er and o'er." When Ignatz *was* around, Krazy was regularly moved to indulge in poesy, and would sit and tell his pal things such as, "I am the 'jagged rock,' and thou the tender 'violet' 'neath my umbrageous cool . . . I am the 'soaring eagle,' whilst you, ah you a shrinking 'tom tit' be." Ignatz would listen, then hit him with a brick. When he wasn't speaking the King's English, Krazy often lapsed into what appears to be an amalgam of immigrant and regional accents: *Offissa* for "Officer," *heppy* for "happy," *guv* for "give," *pipples* for "people," *hokay* for "okay," *mizzil* for "missile," and so forth. Occasionally, the strip lapsed into pure fantasy, as when Ignatz fancied himself the leader of a band of Robber Rodents, and when prehistoric mice first invented the candle.

Comment. The characters were created by George Herriman. "The Dingbat Family" premiered on June 20, 1910; it became "The Family Upstairs" in August, at which time the animals were separated from the Dingbats, their adventures running in a series of panels along the bottom of the strip. "Krazy Kat and Ignatz" took over the comic's entire space for several weeks in July 1911; they were finally promoted to their own regular series on October 28, 1913; the first Sunday page began on April 23, 1916. The strip was discontinued in 1944 with the death of the artist. Because of the delightful characterizations and Herriman's unmatched wit, the strips are as funny today as they were when they were first published. There were three separate series of silent, Krazy Kat animated cartoons: International Film Service released thirteen in 1916, RC Pictures issued nineteen from 1926 to 1927, and Paramount-Famous Lasky produced forty-one silent short subjects. However, because Herriman's strip art was so animated, the theatrical cartoons were actually superflous!

KRYPTO

Pedigree. Awesome lab-dog from Superman's home world, Krypton.

Biography. Krypto is the pet dog of Superboy. A native of the planet Krypton, the white-furred Krypto has superpowers on earth due to the effect our world's yellow sun has on the dog's body, which was raised under Krypton's red sun. Krypto's abilities are similar to those of his master, although scaled down to a dog: He possesses superstrength, the power to fly, invulnerability, supersenses, and so forth. On Krypton, Krypto belonged to Kal-El (a k a Superboy). When Kal-El's father, scientist Jor-El, became convinced that Krypton was going to explode, he struggled valiantly to build a rocket that would carry his family to safety. To test a prototype, Jor-El sent Krypto into space, intending to recover him; however, a meteor hit the ship and knocked it out of orbit. Despite this setback, Jor-El had no choice but to place Kal-El in another ship and rocket him to earth moments before Krypton exploded. Years after Kal-El landed in Smallville and was adopted by the Kents, Krypto's rocket landed on earth and, thanks to his supernose, he was able to locate his former master. Because people would see Superboy and Krypto performing super deeds together, it was necessary for the dog to adopt his own secret identity when he was with Superboy in his Clark Kent guise. Thus he would apply stain to his back and pose as an earth dog, Skippy; whenever he had a superjob to do, he'd use his heat-vision to erase the mark. When he's on a mission or out with Superboy, Krypto wears a red cape emblazoned with a yellow *S*. If Superboy needs his dog for any reason, he can summon him by whistling on a superultrasonic frequency that only Krypto can hear, or by calling to him with superventriloquism. The dog is a member of the Legion of Super-Pets and, when he needs to be alone, retires to his Doghouse of Solitude, an abode built of meteoroids and located on a small, flat planetoid somewhere in space (a retreat akin to his master's Fortress of Solitude in the Arctic). Although Krypto cannot speak, his thoughts are printed out for readers. In these, Krypto comes across as slightly cocky, such as "Ha, ha! Now *I've* got my own *Doghouse of Solitude!* . . . Pretty slick, ha?") Krypto hails from a line of distinguished Kryptonian dogs: His great grandfather Vypto was unusually intelligent; his grandfather Nypto (who was a light blue, with dark blue spots) was once turned into a giant by an alien; and his father Zypto had wings, the result of a "strange serum" he was given.

Comment. The superdog first appeared in *Adventure Comics* no. 210, published by DC Comics in 1955. He also costarred in *The Adventures of Superboy,* a segment of *The New Adventures of Superman* cartoon show that was produced by Filmation Studios and aired on CBS from 1966 to 1967. Other animal survivors of Krypton include **Beppo the Super-Monkey** and Super-Ape. The latter is sent into space onboard an experimental rocket built by a colleague of Jor-El's, Shir Kan (the name is a tribute to Rudyard Kipling's Shere Khan, a tiger in *The Jungle Book).* The baby ape lands in Africa and is raised by an ape couple. Due to his Kryptonian birth, the ape has superpowers that he uses to protect the denizens of the jungle. Super-Ape appeared in *Action Comics* no. 218 in 1956. Another superdog in the Superboy chronicles was Swifty, who made his debut in *Superboy* no. 105. After abandoning a master who enjoys fox hunting, the dog is found by Superboy. Because Swifty shows remarkable intelligence, Superboy gives him a cape and uses a special serum developed by the Kryptonian scientist Roz-em to give the dog "temporary superpowers." Although Superboy intends for the dog to serve as a playmate for Krypto and to destroy deadly kryptonite (to which Swifty is immune), Krypto is jealous of the dog. Thus Superboy lets Swifty's powers expire . . . although he restores them whenever a second superdog is needed.

KWICKY KOALA
Pedigree. Superfast TV bear.
Biography. The "fastest Australian bear" in the world, Kwicky is a demure, gray koala who wears a red ascot and lives in a small house in the woods. Kwicky's nemesis is Wilford Wolf, a scraggly beast who wants to capture him—not to eat him (not in these days of the puritanical Action for Children's Television!), but to have him as a pet. However, nothing Wilford ever comes up with is fast enough to nab the bear—although he tries everything from a vacuum cleaner to a fast-folding chair. Kwicky's only known relative is his wealthy, late Uncle Jeremiah Koala, for whom Wilford used to work as a butler. Perhaps that explains the wolf's turnabout attitude toward the bear.

Comment. Hanna-Barbera's *The Kwicky Koala Show* joined the CBS Saturday morning lineup in 1981. The characters were created by legendary Warner Brothers director/animator Tex Avery. Although the concepts were vintage Avery, the cartoons lacked the sharp pacing and clean animation of the old classics. Kwicky's voice is provided by Robert Allen Ogle, while the wolf sounds like the late Paul Lynde (John Stephenson). Other segments on the show feature more Avery characters. Joey and George are the Bungle Brothers, one tiny and one gargantuan dog, respectively, who appear in short skits and bungle everything from bouncing on a trampoline to playing the piano to appearing on a game show (Allan Melvin is Joey, Mike Bell is George). Crazy Claws is a lynx who sounds like Groucho Marx and lives on Mt. Kitty in a U.S. national park. In each episode, Crazy must avoid the clutches of a trapper named Rawhide Clyde and his sadistic dog Bristletooth—both of whom, themselves, are trying to stay out of the way of Ranger Rangerford. Not only is Rawhide a clod, and not only will Bristletooth drop whatever he's doing for beef jerky, but Crazy's claws flash at lightning speed, enabling him to do things like whittle a decoy at superspeed. Jim McGeorge was the voice of Crazy, and Peter Cullen was Bristletooth. The fourth character is Dirty Dawg, a hobo dog who talks like Howard Cosell (courtesy of Frank Welker) and lives in a junkyard with his rat aide Ratso (voice by Marshall Efron). Their nemesis is human police officer Bullhorn, who despises the two and is always looking for an excuse to run them in. Dirty is fond of regaling other animals with (presumably fictitious) tales of his glorious past, such as the time he was a professional quarterback.

LADY AND TRAMP

Pedigree. Canine leads in a Walt Disney feature.

Biography. It's Christmas, 1910, in a city reminiscent of Pittsburgh. In a lovely house in the suburbs, a young man gives his wife a cocker spaniel puppy as a gift, the woman declares her to be a "perfectly beautiful little lady." From the start, Lady makes herself an integral part of the couples' lives: Despite repeatedly being placed in her own bed in a separate room of the house, Lady always manages to get out and make her way to the master bedroom. Finally, "Jim Dear" (that's what Lady hears his wife call him) gives in to both "Darling" and Lady and lets the dog sleep in the bed. Six months pass, and Lady is grown. She gets a license and a new collar, and goes out to show these off to her neighbors, the Scottish terrier Jock—who is a kind dog, even though he selfishly hordes bones in his backyard "bank"—and the aged bloodhound Trusty—who used to track criminals with his "grandpappy, Old Reliable" until his nose gave out (although Trusty doesn't acknowledge the fact that his olfactory sense isn't what it used to be). When Jim Dear comes home from work, Lady breaks from her friends and races him home, is rewarded with a biscuit, and cuddles up with the two humans, Darling smiling, "I don't imagine anything could ever take her place in our hearts." Time passes. Cut to the other side of the tracks (literally), where the gray mutt Tramp wakes up in a barrel, drinks from a puddle, and goes off to enjoy the day. He heads to Tony's Restaurant where his friend, the cook Joe, gives him a bone. While he's enjoying it, Tramp sees the dogcatcher. Sneaking over to the truck, he frees his friends Peg and Bull and leads the dogcatcher away before losing him. The chase ends in a fancy neighborhood, which Tramp—in his John Garfield voice—calls the home of "the leash and collar set." Nearby, Lady is in a doghouse (a change, for her), moping to Jock and Trusty about how Jim Dear and Darling have been acting strangely and ignoring her. The dogs listen to the symptoms, and tell Lady that Jim and Darling are going to have a baby. Hearing this, Tramp ambles over and pontificates on the subject of babies as "home wreckers." Jock tells the "mongrel" to leave, and he does—warning Lady (whom he calls "Pigeon") that the worst is yet to come. Months pass, during which Lady is indeed treated as an invisible dog: no walks, no playing ball, nothing. Come April, a baby boy is born, at which point, the pressure off, Jim and Darling are finally more attentive to Lady. But the spaniel's contentment is short-lived. The parents go on a short vacation, and the harsh Aunt Sarah comes to stay . . . along with her troublesome Siamese cats (called Si and Am in trailers for the film). The cats claw curtains, overturn a vase, and try to eat the goldfish— for which Sarah blames Lady. She takes the dog to the pet shop to get a muzzle, and no sooner is it in place than the constricted Lady bursts from the shop and runs off. Her flight carries her to the wrong side of the tracks, where she's cornered by a trio of snarling dogs. Fortunately, Tramp hears the commotion, runs over, and fights the dogs until they retreat. Studying the muzzle, Tramp takes Lady to the zoo. At first, he stops by the alligator pool and asks the toothsome beast to bite it off. He opens his jaws wide, and Tramp pulls Lady away moments before the creature snaps off the muzzle and the spaniel's head. Heading over to a beaver, Tramp can't get him to stop building a dam and chew off the muzzle . . . until he convinces the gnawer that muzzle and leash would make an excellent log-puller. Now the beaver pauses and chews off the restraining strap (and goes flying, hilariously, when the log pulls the muzzle and him down a long hill). Showing off just a bit for his new friend, Tramp takes Lady to his various haunts—explains how, on Mondays, he visits the Shultz family, who feed him and call him Fritzi. On Tuesdays, he's "Mike" at the O'Brien home. But tonight, using his "private entrance" (a filthy alley, in fact), he takes her to the back door of Tony's. Tony and Joe not only set a lovely table and give the couple spaghetti, but they serenade the dogs. Lady and Tramp go to the park, where they spend the night under a beautiful moon. Come morning, Lady wants to go home, and Tramp reluctantly takes her. On the way, however, he sees a chicken coop and persuades her to live a little by chasing chickens just for the fun of it. They do, are nearly shot by the farmer, and flee. As they do, Lady—unbeknownst to Tramp—is nabbed by the dogcatcher. By the time he realizes she's been caught, the truck is gone. At the pound, she's caged with Peg, Bull, Pedro, Toughy, Dachsie, Boris, and the flea-bitten Nutsy—who's taken away and put to sleep in a sobering sequence. Peg sings to try to lift everyone's spirits, but her song only depresses Lady more, for Peg sings about how Tramp "breaks a new heart every day." Sarah bails Lady out and, back at home, the spaniel is chained to her doghouse. Tramp comes to visit. He apologizes for what happened, but she refuses to talk to him; he leaves, dejected. However, before he's gone far, he hears Lady barking. He runs back, and, upset, Lady tells him that a rat has crawled across the yard and into the baby's open window. Using the dog door, Tramp enters the house, runs upstairs, and kills the rodent in a wild fight which ends behind a big chair (a brilliantly animated scene). During the fray the baby's crib is overturned, and Aunt Sarah comes running to see why the boy is crying. Having pulled the chain off the doghouse, Lady, too, runs up. Tramp is sitting there, proud as can be, but instead of getting a reward from Sarah, he's swatted into the closet with a broom; Lady is locked in the cellar, and Sarah calls the pound. Jim Dear and Darling return just as the dogcatcher is hauling Tramp away. They let Lady out, and she leads them upstairs to show them the rat. Sarah realizes she's made a mistake, and Jim and Lady set out by cab to try and find the dogcatcher. So, too, do Jock and Trusty, who've come to see what the hub-bub was about. For once, Trusty's nose works perfectly: He and the terrier find the truck. The dogs bark at the horses, trying to stop them, but only manage to frighten the animals; they rear, and the speeding truck overturns. Tramp is freed, but Trusty is pinned under the wheel, inert, Jock sobbing at his side. Yet, all ends well. Come Christmas, Jock and Trusty—his leg bandaged—visit Lady and her mate, Tramp . . . and their four puppies, three of which look like Lady, and one, Scamp, which resembles Tramp (and acts like him, too, playfully unwinding Jock's new tartan sweater without the terrier realizing it). Although Tramp is wearing a collar and license, something he vowed he'd never do, he's happy with his family. Nor is he the only one who's changed. There's even a Christmas gift from the repentent Aunt Sarah: dog biscuits.

Comment. *Lady and the Tramp,* released in 1955, was based on an original idea by writer Ward Greene. Barbara Luddy was the voice of Lady; Larry Roberts was Tramp; singer Peggy Lee was Peg, Darling, and Si and Am; Lee Millar was Jim Dear; Bill Baucom was Trusty; and Bill Thompson was Jock. In comics, the characters starred in two issues of Dell's *4-Color* comics, and in various one-shots, in-

cluding a fine adaptation of the film. There were several sequences in the comic book that were apparently planned for the film but deleted—for example, an in-character bit in which Tramp sits outside a store at Christmas time, follows a shopper home, waits until he drops a package, returns it to him, then claims a reward. Unlike the genuinely selfless Tramp who attacks the rat, this is the Tramp whose conniving side masquerades as virtue. There's also a scene from the first Christmas when Aunt Sarah sends the couple a portrait of herself, ready for hanging. It would've been a nice way to introduce the self-possessed character in the film. The comic also gave "Darling" a name: Elizabeth. Scamp also had his own eponymous comic book; together, Dell and Gold Key published an amazing forty-five issues (1956–1979) based on the precocious pup.

LINUS THE LIONHEARTED
Pedigree. Cereal mascot promoted to TV cartoon monarch.

Biography. Seated on his throne—a barber's chair—Linus is the king of a tropical island, where the only problems arise from the idiosyncrasies of his crazy subjects, namely Rory Raccoon, the keeper of the corn fields; Billie Bird, a mockingbird who drives everyone crazy; the perpetually miserable bird Sascha Grouse; and the nutty Dinny Kangaroo. The only human visitor to the isle is the mail carrier, Loveable Truly.

Comment. Linus and his subjects first appeared on Post Animal Crackers cereal; the Ed Graham–produced series debuted on CBS in 1964. There were thirty-nine adventures in all. Sheldon Leonard was the voice of Linus, Carl Reiner was Sascha, Dinny, and Rory, and Graham was Billie. Also seen on the show were the adventures of **Sugar Bear.**

LIONHEART
Pedigree. Comic book detective cat.

Biography. Hard-boiled journalist Lionheart, who works for editor Artie of the *Times,* burst on the comic book scene while reporting on the death of film star Dizzy Dog. Dizzy is found pressed flat with fold-marks on a rooftop: "I could remember a time when Dizzy Dog was the *biggest* star in comedy films," Lionheart muses. "Now he was just the widest." After interviewing Dizzy's bitter ex-pal Quacky the Duck (**Daffy Duck**), Hollywood lover Mr. L'Aroma (a parody of Pepe le Pew), and pig costar Porkpie (**Porky Pig**), Lionheart learns that Dizzy was

Lionheart examines the remains of Dizzy Dog. © TOM STAZER.

shot when he tried to stop the pig from torching a gag-prop wearhouse for the insurance. Not only did Porkpie shoot him, he also ran him through a giant typewriter (which is how he got flattened), made a giant "paper airplane" out of him (hence, the folds), and sent him soaring onto the rooftop. In subsequent stories, Lionheart investigates everything from ghosts haunting the small town of Wako to following around movie star Freddie Lucre, a raccoon whom someone is trying to kill. Lionheart is good friends with the local law-rhino, Sergeant Nyarg, and with Mike Barrier, who is literally top dog at Scrutiny Security Service.

Comment. The character was created by Tom Stazer; the first tale bears striking similarities to **Roger Rabbit.** Lionheart's initial adventure appeared in Fantagraphics Books's *Critters* no. 4 in 1986 and was featured irregularly thereafter. *Critters* also featured **Duck "Bill" Platypus, Fission Chicken, Miyamoto Usagi,** and other characters, including Rodney Roadhawg, a pig on the highway; disk jockey and news hound Dirk DuClaw who, while holding an "ancient turquoise dogbiscuit," invokes a Pawnee incantation taught to him by Obi-Wan Coyote and becomes the superhero Blue Beagle (whose foes include the Disney-spoofing Dingy Duck and Rodney Rodent); Quax Bedroom, "the first computer-generated duck"; and Prince Alfon Kashota, a fox, who, with other animals (ducks, horses, raccoons, tigers, and so on) rebel against the evil Tosiu, conquerors of their once-proud country Shartoa, in the *Birthright* series. Fantagraphics Books also published the adventures of **Captain Jack.**

LIPPY THE LION

Pedigree. Homeless lion of TV cartoons.
Biography. Together with his hyena-friend Hardy Har Har, the bipedal Lippy roams the countryside looking for some way—any way—to raise their standard of living. Always the optimist, Lippy never listens to his negative companion, who is forever muttering, "Oh dear, oh my, I just *know* something awful will happen." But Hardy's pessimism usually proves on target: Even when they get themselves arrested in order to eat, they're tossed from prison just before dinner time. Other escapades involve the usual ration of ghosts and monsters, gunfighters, precocious babies, and other animals ranging from mice to sharks.

Comment. Hanna-Barbera's *Lippy the Lion* premiered in syndication in 1962; there were fifty-two episodes. Daws Butler provided Lippy's voice—reminiscent of Joe E. Brown—and Mel Blanc was Hardy. Gold Key published one Lippy comic book in 1963, and the characters were also featured in Gold Key's *Hanna-Barbera Bandwagon* nos. 1 to 3 in 1962 to 1963.

LITTLE BEARS

Pedigree. The first continuing comic strip animals.
Biography. The strip features the very tame adventures of small "California Bears" as they play with human children, attend school, hike, paint, and partake in other pastimes.

Comment. James Guilford Swinnerton (1875 to 1974) is one of the fathers of the newspaper comic strip. At the age of sixteen, he went to work for William Randolph Hearst's *San Francisco Examiner* (Hearst's first newspaper), where he created a cartoon bear cub inspired by the bear on the flag of California. The bear was used to introduce the daily weather report in 1891, and proved so popular that it got its own weekly strip the following year, "Little Bears and Tykes." Shortly after Swinnerton took a job on Hearst's *New York Journal* in 1899, he added tigers to the strip and it became "Little Bears and Tigers." Before long, one tiger took over entirely (see **Mr. Jack**).

LITTLEFOOT

Pedigree. Motion picture dinosaur.
Biography. It's apparently late in the Cretaceous period, and the leaves are dying in an area where Leaf Eaters such as "Long Necks" (apatosaurs, a k a brontosaurs), "Spike Tails" (stegosaurs), "Big Mouths" (duck bills), "Three Horns" (triceratops) and others usually graze. Thus they set out for the west, heading toward the mythical Great Valley where water and foliage are said to be abundant. Apart from starvation, the gravest danger they face along the way are "earth shakes" (earthquakes) and "Sharp Tooths" (tyrannosaurs). Newborn Long Neck Littlefoot goes romping away from his mother and grandparents one day, and meets small Three Horn Cera. Both flee when chased by a hungry Sharp Tooth, and Littlefoot's mother hurries to their defense, batting the powerful carnivore with her tail. Although an earth shake interrupts the proceedings, and Littlefoot's mother is able to nudge the Sharp Tooth from a cliff, she perishes from wounds in-

flicted by the giant's teeth. Before dying, this prehistoric Obi Wan Kenobi tells her son to make his way to the Great Valley, vowing "I'll be with you, even if you can't see me." The earth shake has separated Littlefoot from his grandparents, and Cera from his clan—but the brash Three Horn refuses to travel with the Long Neck as he begins his journey. After meeting an old dinosaur named Rooter, who encourages the grieving Littlefoot to go on, the Long Neck meets, in turn, the goofy little Ducky, a Big Mouth; the hyper pteranodon Petrie, who can't fly; and the big, mute Spike, a Spike Tail. They're also joined by Cera, who had a run in with the still-living Sharp Tooth that fell from the cliff, and—still pretending to be a tough guy—deigns to join them. Along the way, the increasingly confident and plucky Littlefoot sees his mother's image in a leaf and passes a rock formation in her shape, and knows he's going in the right direction. Soon, though, there's dissension in the reptilian ranks. After the group has a narrow escape from Sharp Tooth, Cera wants to take a shortcut through a field of volcanoes, while Littlefoot insists that they continue going the way they're headed . . . the long way. Cera peels off and the others join him, leaving Littlefoot on his own. But not for long. While Cera walks ahead, Petrie falls into a tarpit and the other two dinosaurs are trapped on a rock, surrounded by a sea of lava. Littlefoot hears their cries and comes running. He pushes a boulder across the steaming flow so they can cross to safety, then wades with the others into the tar to pull Petrie free. Meanwhile, a herd of pachycephalosauri corners Cera. As they move in for the kill, and Cera drops his iron man pretense, a strange, tall, black creature appears and scares off the predators: It's Littlefoot, Petrie, Ducky, and Spike, covered with tar and intentionally piled one atop the other. Realizing they can't go on with Sharp Tooth still trailing them, the group decides to do him in. With the rest of the group poised behind a boulder on a cliff overlooking a pond, Ducky goes to the killer and lures him into the water. Although unable to walk in the soft-bottomed pond, Sharp Tooth can still bite; he nearly makes a meal out of Ducky before Petrie—forcing himself to fly—zips down and pecks the monster in the eye. As the little dinosaurs fight with the stubborn boulder, the titan manages to get to the cliff and climbs toward the bold dinosaurs. Finally, with a mighty butt from horned Cera, the boulder crashes down, pinning Sharp Tooth beneath the water. Moments later, the clouds form an image of Littlefoot's

mother and, following it as it drifts through the sky, the dinosaurs reach the Great Valley. There, all are reunited with their families, including Littlefoot with his grandparents.

Comment. The characters appeared in the 1988 Universal film *The Land Before Time,* which featured typically lush animation from the Don Bluth staff—and a typically maudlin and derivative storyline from coproducers George Lucas and Steven Spielberg. Plot elements are not just borrowed from Disney's *Fantasia* and *Bambi;* they resemble a trainwreck between the two, lacking any real heart. Although the dinosaurs talk, effort was put into making them look and act as current paleontological research suggests dinosaurs behaved. Gabriel Damon was the voice of Littlefoot, Judith Barsi was Ducky, Candy Hutson was Cera, Will Ryan was Petrie, Helen Shaver was Littlefoot's mother, and Pat Hingle was both the narrator and Rooter.

LITTLE ROQUEFORT
Pedigree. Mouse of theatrical cartoons and comic books.

Biography. Roquefort is a little, gray mouse, buck-naked, buck-toothed, and bipedal, and Percy is a black cat with a white belly and face. They live together in an unnamed human's house, where Roquefort wants to get into the kitchen and Percy's job is to stop him. However, whether by trapping Percy in the refrigerator, or strapping cakes of soap on his feet and skating by, or creating armor from thumbtacks, Roquefort usually prevails.

Comment. Of all the cat-and-mouse characters, these two were the least exceptional, their actions and situations barely changing from cartoon to cartoon. From 1950 to 1955, Terrytoons produced nineteen cartoons starring the characters; Tom Morrison provided their voices. The cartoons came to television as part of the syndicated *Heckle and Jeckle Show* in 1955. The mouse was a backup feature in various **Mighty Mouse** comic books, and had his own ten-issue run from St. Johns (1952 to 1958).

LOBO
Pedigree. Wolf-companion of Marvel Comics Indian superhero Red Wolf.

Biography. A Cheyenne, Johnny Wakeley stumbles on the tomb of a former superhero known as Red Wolf, a native American who was given superpowers by the wolf spirit Owayodata. The deity appears and grants Johnny the powers of Red Wolf. There, Red Wolf also finds a wounded wolf, whom he nurses back to health. Lobo becomes his faithful but feral companion—a "gift of the wolf spirit." The two become a force for justice in nineteenth-century Montana. Later, in modern times, Cheyenne Will Talltrees becomes the new Red Wolf, raising a wolf cub to be the new Lobo.

Comment. Lobo made his debut (along with Red Wolf) in Marvel Comics's *Marvel Spotlight* no. 1 in 1971, and appeared in all nine issues of Red Wolf's own magazine.

LOOPY DE LOOP
Pedigree. French wolf of motion pictures.
Biography. The juxtaposition of "French" and "wolf" would suggest a womanizer to the extreme. However, Loopy is anything but. Wearing a wool cap and scarf, the bipedal red wolf is actually quite "sharming." He wants only two things in life: to go around doing good deeds and to change people's negative impressions about wolves. As he explains it, "You may look on me and say, 'Yecch! Anothair sneaky, no good scoundrel of a wolf! But zat is not true! Because I am zee good wolf. All heart. Polite to zee fault. Always on zee lookout to do zee good deed." He concludes, "I have zee mission to give zee wolves a good name. Zee wolf can become man's next-to-best friend." Unfortunately, his actions are always misconstrued. Trying to rehabilitate a wolf, he takes a chicken away from it and brings the fowl back to the coop . . . only to be discovered by a dog and beaten to a pulp. Returning a fallen bird to its nest, Loopy is attacked by the mother. Spotting a baby buzzard on the ground, he also returns it to his nest . . . despite the fact that he has to shimmy up a large cactus to get there ("Loopy does not mind zee pain while he's doing zee good deed!"). Loopy is also involved with Sheep Stealers Anonymous and partakes in many adventures that are not part of his crusade, involving crooks, zoos, bears, and other characters. He always carries a Boy Scout knife, and is sometimes accompanied by his half-pint wolf nephew Bon Bon, who dresses the same as Loopy but believes in eating any sheep, chicken, or cow he can lay his claws on. Their most entertaining adventure together involves Loopy's efforts to get rid of a lamb (or a "Baa-baa," as he calls it) that has taken a liking to Loopy—much to the chagrin of the sheepdog that is guarding it.

Comment. Hanna-Barbera produced forty-nine

theatrical Loopy cartoons from 1959 to 1965. Despite some clever scripts and the charming vocal characterization of Daws Butler, the cartoons have the same flat look and limited animation style of the studio's later TV cartoons, such as **Quick Draw McGraw.**

LUCIFER (1)
Pedigree. From *Cinderella,* the nastiest animal in the Disney realm.
Biography. Lucifer is a smug, saw-toothed, overweight, sadistic cat who walks with her nose in the air when she's around Cinderella, and enjoys tormenting the gentle dog Bruno by clawing his face. How did such nice folks end up living with a cat like that? "In a land faraway," a widower remarries so that his young daughter, Cinderella would have a mother. Entering the "stately chateau" with the new Lady Tremaine are her ugly daughters, Anastasia and Drizella, and her kitten, Lucifer. Some ten years pass, during which time Cinderella's father dies and the girl is made the household servant. Cinderella's only friends are her elderly dog Bruno, the horse Major, the nameless songbirds who fly into her room and wake her each morning, and the mice Jaq, Suzy, Blossom, Mert, Bert, Luke, and Perla, who live with other mice in a hole in Cinderella's wall. (The mice are the only ones with whom she can converse.) Each morning, Cinderella must first feed Lucifer his milk, then feed the farm animals. One particular morning, she finds a chubby mouse in the trap, releases him, names him Octavius ("Gus" for short) and introduces him to the other mice. After the mice suffer a close encounter with the smug, overweight, sawtoothed, sadistic cat, word arrives from the palace that the king is holding a ball honoring his son, the Prince. All the "eligible" maidens in the land must attend. While Cinderella rushes to finish her chores, the birds and mice sew her a beautiful gown using remnants of fabric and jewelry pilfered from her stepsisters' rooms. On the night of the ball, the ugly young ladies see how lovely Cinderella looks and realize that if she attends, they'll have zero chance with the Prince. Thus they yank and pull at the dress, reclaiming "their" cloth and trinkets, until it's in tatters. Cinderella runs into the garden, crying, while Lady Tremaine and her daughters set off. Miraculously, Cinderella's fairy godmother arrives and not only creates a new gown but turns a pumpkin into a coach, the mice into horses, Bruno into a footman, and Major into a coachman. She sends the girl

off, with the warning that the "dream" ends at midnight, by which time she must return. The Prince and Cinderella are smitten with each other, and the girl forgets about the time. At the stroke of twelve, she runs away, losing a glass slipper . . . and barely making it into the woods before everything returns to the way it was. Meanwhile, the Prince sends his Grand Duke throughout the kingdom to find the foot that fits the glass slipper. When he arrives at Cinderella's house, Lady Tremaine locks her in her tower room and takes the key. In a daring maneuver, Jaq and Gus sneak into her pocket, get the key, and arduously haul it up the tower . . . only to be met, on top, by grinning Lucifer. The cat traps Gus and the key inside a teacup, and battles off the mice, who gamely attempt to chase him away with forks (he swats them away) and a candle (he blows it out). The birds try bombarding him with dishes, but that too fails. In desperation, Cinderella tells the birds to go to the barn and get Bruno. The aged dog marshals his strength and runs to the rescue, battling Lucifer and forcing the cat from an open window. Lucifer plummets to a well-deserved death, Gus slips the key under the door, and Cinderella gets out just in time to try on the slipper.

Comment. *Cinderella* is a brilliant, unassuming film with a breathless climax that makes many modern movies seem static. The film was released in 1950; June Foray was the voice of the cat, while James Macdonald was Gus, Jaq, and Bruno. Gus's angry mutterings at the mistreatment of Cinderella, and Jaq's charming mispronunciation "Cinderelly" are among the more inspired traits of any Disney cartoon animals. The animals were all added to the original tale by Disney. The story itself goes back at least to the ninth century, when it appeared in the Chinese anthology *Yu Yang Ts Tsu,* which contained stories with a long oral tradition. The tale first appeared in Europe in Basile's *Pentamerone* (1634), in which the heroine Zezolla is nicknamed "The Cat Among the Cinders," i.e., La Gatta Cennerentola . . . whence the name Cinderella. Disney's film was based primarily on the Charles Perrault version of the tale, published in 1697.

LUCIFER (2)
Pedigree. Horse for DC Comics's cult-favorite western hero, El Diablo.

Biography. The "coal-black stallion" of the masked western avenger is unusually intelligent—even by comics horse standards. If its master is hurt or ab-

ducted, Lucifer will stop at nothing to free him. Nor can anyone else ride him. According to the hero, Lucifer "Lets *no* man near him—except *me!*" It would be easier "trying to lasso a *tornado.*"

Comment. The characters first appeared in DC Comics's *All Star Western* no. 2 in 1970. They made their last appearance in no. 19, the magazine having been renamed *Weird Western Tales.*

LUCKY DUCK
Pedigree. The name's a misnomer: Lucky is a comic book disaster area.

Biography. Lucky is a talking green duck who wears a white dickey and black bow tie, smokes using a cigarette holder, and has a spray of red feathers on his head. Billed as "The World's Wackiest Screwball," he's actually a moron, the kind of creature who, when he sees a sign that says "Brake Your Car," gets out a mallet and trashes his automobile. He plays cards with an octopus—and lets the cephalopod hold all the other hands. He's also perpetually broke, always trying new schemes to make a fast buck, and also vindictive. When his friend Rocky Rabbit opens a diner, Lucky is annoyed that he can't have a complimentary meal. Later, puzzled by the fact that not a single customer has stopped by, Rocky ventures outside to find that Lucky has changed the sign out front from, "A Good Place to Dine" to "A Good Place to Die."

Comment. The character appeared in four issues of his own Standard Comics publication, then became a backup feature in comics featuring **Supermouse.**

LUDWIG VON DRAKE
Pedigree. Crackpot uncle of **Donald Duck.**

Biography. The European professor—a grandson of Mother Goose—made his debut on the season opener of *Walt Disney's Wonderful World of Color* on September 24, 1961. The hour-long show (of which Ludwig was only the first half) was *An Adventure in Color: Mathmagic Land,* and Walt Disney himself introduces the duck from Donald's paternal side (the Drakes—"the eggheads of the clan"). Walt reveals that Von Drake is "a brilliant scientist, and world traveler and psychologist," who speaks four languages and holds degrees from Oxford, Cambridge, and Heidelberg. Ludwig arrives, and after exchanging banter with Walt Disney ("You're de fellow who works for my nephew Donald Duck, isn't dat right?"), chatting with a stuffed alligator, and rearranging the furniture (some terrific special effects, here), the balding duck with bushy eyebrows and pince-nez glasses, too long sleeves, too large jacket, too high collar, and pendulous vest, gets into his subject. He returned for a far funnier hour-long show on October 22 called *The Hunting Instinct,* in which he's aided by his assistant Herman, The **Bootle Beetle.** Herman loads the projector and Ludwig shows cartoons (processed in Von Drake Ludwigcolor) about the various aspects of hunting. Between clips, when he isn't playing tic-tac-toe with himself, Von Drake makes observations about the subject at hand . . . and several not at hand. Stating the obvious (his forte), he declares that the moral of one cartoon is, "Keep out of the woods, you nut!" Another time, he all but admits that the emperor is naked, declaring, "Some hunter! I can't find my glasses!" Later, he asks candidly, "Did I confuse you? I don't even know what I said myself!" In other appearances, he is equally candid. For example, referring to his upcoming tome on childrearing, he says that if there's nothing helpful on "the inside, you'll find the outside useful on their little backsides!" As it turns

out, there isn't any subject in which the duck isn't well versed (as he's the first to admit), and over the next five years he appeared in fifteen additional tutorial programs, among them *Kids is Kids, Inside Outer Space, Fly with Von Drake, The Truth about Mother Goose,* and *In Shape with Von Drake.* Most of these consisted of Von Drake providing transitions between classic Disney cartoons.

Comment. The duck appeared in just one theatrical cartoon, the 1962 featurette *A Symposium on Popular Songs,* in which he lectured on the origins of contemporary musical styles. The late Paul Frees provided the character's voice (using an Austrian accent) in most of his appearances. Von Drake began appearing at once in the daily and Sunday Donald Duck comic strips (his September 24 Sunday debut technically preceded his first TV appearance!), often having the spotlight to himself (finding a soda machine out of order, he unpacks his tool kit, repairs it, and gets his drink). Although he starred in just four issues of his own Gold Key comic book (1961 to 1962), he appeared in *Walt Disney's Comics and Stories* from no. 256 to no. 274.

MAC 'N' TOSH

Pedigree. Warner Brothers theatrical cartoon stars.

Biography. The scrupulously polite gophers (Mac: "You've lost five [card games] in a row. Would you like to lose another?" Tosh: "Oh, yes, yes, very much, quite") with high-pitched voices are nonetheless two of the most dangerous animals ever to hit a garden or forest. In their first cartoon, *The Goofy Gophers* (1947), the small, brown, buck-toothed pair continually fend off a dog by using a pumpkin and shovel on its head, fire on the feet, mousetrap to the hand, and so on, in order to have a garden to themselves. (Although they finally succeed in using a rocket to launch the dog into space, they haven't quite won: **Bugs Bunny** arrives to share in the booty.) In *Two Gophers from Texas* (1948), the animals must protect themselves from a dog who comes to the woods and wants to eat them. After various traps fail (including the old radish-attached-to-a-boulder trick), the dog tries to lure them from their hole with music, only to end up imprisoned in the piano with hammers attached to the keys, slugging him as the gophers play. In their last cartoon, *Tease for Two* (1965), they withstand a similar assault from **Daffy Duck,** who's convinced that their hole is a gold mine. His efforts to flood the hole end abruptly when the gophers knot his hose and it explodes, sending the duck past an orbiting Soviet spacecraft. The duo have also matched wits with Charlie the Dog (see **Foghorn Leghorn.**)

Comment. The Warner Brothers characters were parodies of the polite and only slightly less destructive **Chip 'n' Dale** over at Disney. They appeared in nine cartoons.

MAGICA DE SPELL

Pedigree. "The saucy sorceress" seen in **Scrooge McDuck** comic books.

Biography. The witch has long, straight black hair, superlong lashes, a black dress, and black high heels. Her one goal in life is to steal Scrooge's lucky dime, convinced that it will make her "the richest, luckiest duck in the world." Fortunately, Scrooge can always tell when Magica is near, thanks to **Gyro Gearloose,** who built a "special sensor that . . . only responds to Magica's magical vibes." Gyro also came up with one gadget that made life especially tough for the witch: "an anti-magic magnification ray." Calculating the "vertical bombasity and allowing for a severe linear thumptitude," it not only turned the coin into a ten-ton giant dime, but repulsed Magica's witchly shrink beam, bouncing it back and reducing her to the size of a gnat. Magica belongs to Sorcerers Anonymous, and has the power to levitate objects or turn herself into any animal she wishes; many of her potions are mixed using formulae first conceived by the mythological sorceress Circe.

Comment. Magica made her debut in *Uncle Scrooge* no. 36, and later starred in her own one-shot title *(Walt Disney Showcase* no. 30). She is presently a regular on the syndicated TV series, comic book, and magazine *DuckTales*. The witch was created by writer/artist Carl Barks, who felt that he was overusing **The Beagle Boys** as McDuck's nemeses and also felt that a witch would allow him to lampoon "this Superman stuff—the superwitches and the weird things that you find in some of the other comics."

MAGILLA GORILLA

Pedigree. Fun-loving TV cartoon ape.

Biography. No matter how hard he tries, the short, mustachioed Mr. Peebles of Peebles Pet Shop in Los Angeles can't sell or even give away the impish, inadvertently destructive gorilla. Dressed in a bow tie, derby, shoes, and shorts with suspenders, Magilla enjoys roller-skating around the shop (breaking an average of three windows a month) and is fond of speaking in nonsense parables (when asked what one means, he replies, "I don't know, but it's a catchy saying"). If he's having a good time, Magilla has been known to mutter, "This is more fun than a barrel of people." Despite the fact that Peebles professes to loathe the ape, he's heartbroken when Magilla is chosen by the government to be sent by rocket to the moon. (Fortunately, the frightened Magilla is able to abort the mission and return safely to the pet shop.) Magilla's good friend is the little girl Ogee, named for her favorite expression. Among the gorilla's other noteworthy adventures were a stint in the army at Camp Killkare, a run-in with a mad scientist, a visit to the circus, and a trip to the planet Zero.

Comment. The Hanna-Barbera show was first syndicated in 1964; there were thirty-one episodes in all. Allan Melvin was the voice of Magilla, and Howard Morris played Mr. Peebles. Gold Key published ten issues of a Magilla comic book from 1964 to 1968. In Yiddish, "magilla" literally means "big deal" in a sarcastic way; whatever is being referred to usually isn't, really.

MAN-BAT

Pedigree. Mutated comic book villain, foe of Batman.

Biography. Gotham Museum of Natural History scientist Kirk Langstrom is an expert on nocturnal mammals. Hoping to acquire "natural sonar-detection" ability so that he can emulate his hero Batman, Langstrom distills a bat-gland extract that is supposed to do the job. That it does, also giving him superstrength, "animal instincts," and the ability to fly. But it has the unfortunate side-effect of giving him the head of a bat, leathery wings that grow from his arms, clawed hands, and a spotty coat of fur, and causing him to go slowly insane. Although Langstrom helps Batman battle the Blackout Gang, he soon becomes a nemesis of the caped crusader. Langstrom even forces his own fiancée Francine Lee to take the bat-gland plunge, turning her into She-Bat. In time, they have a daughter, Rebecca, who is normal; luckily for her and her parents, Batman comes up with an antidote that purges their system of the bat-extract. Thereafter, by taking a carefully prepared pill, Langstrom briefly becomes a sane, crime-fighting Man-Bat. Francine isn't as fortunate, becoming She-Bat for a brief period after suffering the double-whammy of being attacked by a vampire bat and exposed to the rays of the full moon.

Comment. The DC Comics character first appeared in *Detective Comics* no. 400 in 1970. He was regularly featured in the short-lived *Batman Family* magazine, guest starred in various other titles, and had two issues of his own comic book (1975 to 1976). Other villains who are human-animal hybrids are Armadillo, a scientifically created humanoid armadillo (he first appeared in *Captain America* no. 308, 1985); Batman's foe the Gorilla Boss, born when the brain of an executed thug is transplanted into the body of an ape *(Batman* no. 75, 1953); Spider-Man's nemesis the Lizard, a k a Dr. Curtis Connors, who becomes a lunatic reptile-man after trying to regrow a missing arm by injecting himself with a serum extracted from lizards *(The Amazing Spider-Man* no. 6, 1963); Man-Bull, the swarthy, horned scientifically mutated criminal William Taurens *(Daredevil* no. 78, 1971); Bruto, "the largest gorilla in the world . . . over a ton of pure strength," who is the assistant to the evil Mr. Freek, foe of the scientific superhero Frankenstein *(Frankenstein* no. 2, 1966); Animal-Man's nemesis the Mod Gorilla Boss, a criminal who invents a potion that gives him the body and power of an ape, without sacrificing his human intelligence . . . or sharp haberdashery *(Strange Adventures* no. 201, 1967); Piranha, a genetic mutant and enemy of the seagoing hero Sub-Mariner *(Sub-Mariner* no. 70, 1974); the Shark, a tiger shark who is pushed 1 million years along the "evolutionary spiral" when a nuclear power plant blows up and lands in the sea *(Green Lantern* no. 24, 1963); Super-beaver, humanoid beaver foe of the superhero Power Pie (he appeared just once, in 1966, in the *Power Pie* comic strip, which ran in Stanford University's *The Stanford Chaparral);* and Tse-Tse, a treasure hunter who discovers a long-buried alien device that transforms him into a human fly *(Web Woman* segment of the CBS cartoon series *Tarzan and the Super 7,* 1978). *(Note:* Marvel's Anti-Men, Man-Elephant, Walrus, The Rhino, The Vulture, and Tiger Shark; DC's Turtle Man and the Weasel; and Archie's The Cat Gang, among many others, are all men in costumes.) Finally, among the antiheroes, there's the Tarantula, who gnawed his way through all three issues of Atlas Comics's *Weird Suspense* in 1975. He was actually Count Eugene Lycosa, whose family lives under the curse of a spider cult, a legacy that compels them to turn into green, humanoid, people-eating tarantulas. That's the bad news. The good news is because he has to eat people, Lycosa decides that he might as well become a superhero and eat crooks (giving new meaning to McGruff's "Take a bite out of crime.")

MARMADUKE

Pedigree. Comic strip and TV cartoon dog.

Biography. The Great Dane is as unpredictable as he is unusual. As likely to sublet his sheepskin-lined, air-conditioned dog house (with a TV set and refrigerated water cooler) to a family of skunks as he is to run into a pizza shop and start throwing dough to make his own pie, the big, gangly, brown dog is owned by Phil and Dottie Winslow. Among his other quirks: He's "a peanut butter junkie," convulses with laughter when told to fetch something, steals briefcases from Yuppies, loves human food (punishing him once, Dottie proclaimed, "Eight hamburger patties are missing and you refuse to eat your dinner . . . that's all the evidence I need!"), enjoys pulling children on sleds (he once pulled Phil to work that way as well), and enjoys stopping small cars—with his teeth. Above all, he loves the lady dogs . . . although he's terrible when it comes to keeping his date book straight, and that's gotten him into trouble. Lady Godiva is his girlfriend, although he's rarely faithful to her.

Comment. Brad Anderson's strip debuted in 1954 and continues to this day. Marmaduke was seen in his own cartoon adventures on *Heathcliff and Marmaduke,* which aired on ABC in 1981. The dog was inspired by Bruno, the Great Dane which belonged to Anderson's parents.

MAUD
Pedigree. Early comic strip mule.
Biography. Maud is owned by farmer Si and his wife Mirandy. She was bought by the former for $10. In the first episode, as Si introduces his wife to "Maudie," the mule hauls off and kicks him into the fields. Thereafter, the temperamental mule is constantly being offended by someone for something they say or do. The result: She kicks them into the next week's installment. Occasionally, good comes of this, as when she gets rid of bill collectors or thieves. In one episode, Maud knocks Si's stalled automobile off a train track. Most of the time, though, Si is busy ducking the mule while Mirandy says with resignation, "I'll telephone for the doctor." Si regularly tries to sell the mule, but there are never any takers. Maud's vocabulary consist of *Hee haw,* although she can converse freely with other animals (conversations that the reader is able to understand).

Maud, doing what she does best.

Most of the time, though, it's Maud's hind legs that do the talking.

Comment. Frederick Burr Opper (1857 to 1937) introduced Maud in the "Happy Hooligan" strip on July 24, 1904. She got her own strip, "And Her Name Was Maud," a two-row strip that appeared atop the Sunday "Happy Hooligan" strip, on May 23, 1926. It was discontinued six years later. Another animal that appeared regularly in "Happy Hooligan" was Happy's dog Flip, a white mutt with black spots. Due to their inherently stubborn (and thus unlikable) nature, mules and donkeys have appeared relatively infrequently in comic strips and comic books. The notable exceptions are Benny Burro, who made occasional appearances in Dell's *Our Gang* from no. 3 to no. 59 (1943 to 1949), and the young boy Tito and his Burrito, which ran in many of the books headlined by the Fox and the Crow (see **Fauntleroy Fox**).

MAUS
Pedigree. A gripping comic book retelling of the Holocaust, starring animals.
Biography. Young comic book publisher mouse Artie comes to visit his father, Vladek, in Rego Park, New York. There, during the course of an evening, Artie persuades the elder mouse to tell him about the Holocaust, for a comic book he wants to create. Vladek begins with his youth in Czestochowa, Poland, in the early 1930s, and his courtship and marriage to Anja Zylberberg. Their first son, Richieu, is born in 1937, but the strain of his birth causes Anja to become emotionally disturbed, and she's placed in a sanitarium. Meanwhile, the Nazis have begun violent, anti-Semitic campaigns. In August 1939, Vladek is drafted; when the Nazis invade Poland, he's taken prisoner and put to work in various prison camps. Eventually, bribery from the outside gets Vladek released, and he manages to return to his family. Conditions in Poland worsen, and by 1942 the Jewish mice are moved into cramped apartments in the Stara Sosnowiec quarter. In time, the Nazis begin shipping mice to concentration camps, and Vladek, Anja, and their son flee (wearing pig masks to disguise themselves). Eventually, they're caught and sent to the Auschwitz concentration camp, where the story ends. At present, all that's known of their life after the war is that Art was born in Stockholm in 1948, Anja committed suicide in 1968, and Vladek has remarried fellow Pole, Mala. Artie's wife is named Francoise.

Comment. The Jews are mice, the Nazis are cats,

and other citizens are pigs and dogs. Save for their animal heads, the characters are entirely human, their world is identical to ours, and the story is told literally, without Orwellian metaphors. (Rats, incidentally, are pictured as the scurrying quadrupeds they really are.) The saga was written and drawn by Art Spiegelman. Early, unpolished versions of Spiegelman's tales began appearing in underground comic books, starting with Apex Novelties's *Funny Animals* no. 1 in 1972. One of these was reprinted in Marvel Comics's *Comix Book* no. 2 in 1974. These stories were more graphic and horrifying than the later version. Another difference between these stories and the later version was that the "Art" mouse was called Mickey, and he was a young boy whose father told him the war era stories before he went to bed. The more fully developed work was serialized in Spiegelman's adult comic magazine *Raw* from 1980 to 1985; these stories were collected in book form in 1986 as *Maus: A Survivor's Tale*. A sequel, *Part Two, From Mauschwitz to the Catskills*, covering winter 1944, to the present, is in the works.

MAX

Pedigree. A 2,000-year-old TV mouse.
Biography. The cartoon mouse (who doesn't look his age) was optically combined with live-action footage to teach viewers about great moments in history, ranging from the painting of the Sistine Chapel ceiling to Magellan's circumnavigation of the globe to the journey of Marco Polo.

   Comment. The Steve Krantz series was syndicated in 1969; there were 104, five-minute-long shows in all. A similar historical education theme was used in 1973 in the thirteen-episode Filmation series *Mission: Magic* in which a cartoon version of rock singer Rick Springfield helped school teacher Miss Tickle and her students go on a different historical trek each week. The animals here were Rick's pet owl, Tolamy, and Miss Tickle's cat, Tut Tut.

MAX THE RABBIT

Pedigree. Comic book hare detective.
Biography. Max and his partner Sam, a hound, are the Freelance Police. The only anthropomorphic animals in an otherwise human urban environment, they are "overzealous, brutal, sadistic"; they won't hesitate to shoot—or, in Sam's case, bite—a criminal. When surrounded by bad guys, Sam has also been known to grab little Max by the feet and swing him like a medieval mace ("curiously refreshing" is

how Max describes the experience). Sam is fairly straightlaced and serious, and always wears a suit and fedora; Max is ever ready with a sarcastic quip, and naked. (He vows that they'll be "serving snocones in hell" before he wears clothes.) In their strangest tale, the partners go on vacation and meet a bunch of land buccaneers who travel about on "a Spanish galleon pulled by a legion of rats and the world's largest prairie dog."

   Comment. Creator Steve Purcell served up clever repartee and displayed an off-the-wall sense of humor in these episodic sagas. There were just two issues of *Sam and Max: Freelance Police*, the first published by Fishwrap Productions in 1988, the second from Comico a year later.

MAXWELL

Pedigree. English comic strip cat.
Biography. Maxwell is a sensitive, philosophical cat with a mean streak toward mice and birds. He'll stand in the field and narrate an ode to a robin (then burp feathers) or chase away the mice who've laid siege to his litterbox, then muse philosophically, "Shouldn't it be the *losers* who have to sit in a box full of shit?" The white cat with dark markings on his back and hindquarters belongs to young Norman Nesbitt, a boy who'll do anything for his cat (when Maxwell befriends Peregrine, a panther, Norman nervously allows both cats to share his bed). However, the thrust of the strip is not boy-and-cat *schtick*, but social commentary. For example, Max is chatting with his best friend Delroy, a cat who's escaped from a research center:

   DELROY: They tested all these *cosmetics* . . . on me . . . lilac eye-shadow, beige blusher, magenta lip-gloss.
   MAXWELL: That's *barbaric*—I mean, especially with *your* bone structure.

The "Doonesbury"-style joke makes the point more palatable. A favorite topic is war, personified by Maxwell's battles with Eric and his mice. For example, although the mice have a cruise missile in their hole, after Maxwell eats two of the rodents, they realize the value of a good, preemptive strike. Maxwell's tail is also a character: It is divorced from the snake Lance, with whom it has had children. Other characters that appear in the strip are the Flea (who feels that "drinking blood is *vile* . . . and not only that, but the white corpuscles tend to get stuck in ya teeth!") and George Starkweather the Subversive Mole. The best strip of all: A parody of the *E.T.* ads, in which a small alien is described in successive panels: "He is *adorable* . . . he is *alone* . . . he is *afraid* . . . he is eight million light years from home." Then Maxwell comes along, kills him, and says, "Unfortunately . . . he is also only four centimetres tall."

Comment. The often brilliant strip ran in the *Northants Post* from August of 1979 to October of 1986. It was written and drawn by noted comic book writer Alan Moore, working under the pseudonym Jill de Ray. Another out-of-the-ordinary British cat is Firkin, who turns a keen, voyeuristic eye on human sex in the men's magazine *Fiesta*. The strip began in 1982 and was created by Hunt Emerson.

MAXWELL MOUSE
Pedigree. Comic book mouse.
Biography. A failure in Hollywood of the 1930s (he complains, the "ducks and rabbits get all the good parts"), the five-inch-tall, Gable-like mouse comes to New York to try to find success on the stage. Meeting aspiring mouse actress Monica in an alley, Maxwell opens a nightclub—Chez Maxwell—and Monica goes to work for him as a singer. Thanks to a favorable review by Leticia Titmouse writing in the *New York Daily Mouse,* the club is a hit. Maxwell dresses in a tie, spats, and gloves; Monica wears shoes, gloves, and pearls.

Comment. Maxwell Mouse first appeared in a small, amateur comic book published by creator Joe Sinardi. New Media published an issue of *Maxwell Mouse Follies* in 1981, and Renegade Press offered a brief run in 1986.

McBARKER
Pedigree. TV dog owned by Mr. Magoo.
Biography. The small, white, talking, quadrupedal bulldog is as nearsighted as its master, whom it joins on many adventures. Most of these are caused when the nearsighted Magoo unwittingly ambles into a dangerous situation. Among their escapdes together: *Baby Sitter Magoo, Magoo's Monster Mansion, Mountain Man Magoo, Gold Rush Magoo, Spaceman Magoo,* and *McBarker the Wonder Dog.*

Comment. Although Magoo has a career going back to 1949, his dog was seen only on the De Patie-Freleng series *What's New, Mr. Magoo?* which aired on CBS from 1977 to 1978. There were thirty-two adventures in all; Robert Ogle provided the voice.

McSNURTLE THE TURTLE, THE TERRIFIC WHATZIT
Pedigree. Awe-inspiring comic book superfast superhero, parodying The Flash.
Biography. Merton McSnurtle is the owner of McSnurtle's General Store in Zooville. He's incredibly lazy, but scrupulously honest. Thus the bespectacled turtle is "selected by the gods of another planet to be a force for good on earth . . . as the Terrific Whatzit, the super-super hero of super heroes." McSnurtle is also endowed with an "automatic conscience," a nattily dressed turtle that leaps from his body to prod the slothful animal into action when he's needed. McSnurtle becomes the superhero by slipping out of his shell and into his costume: blue trousers, red boots, a red shirt with a yellow *TW* on the front, and a winged helmet. As the Terrific Whatzit, McSnurtle moves so fast that, under a bar-

Maxwell Mouse: a legend in his own mouse-mind. © 1990 by JOE SINARDI.

rage of gunfire, he can punch each bullet back at the animal that fired it. In one of his most famous tales, he helps the down-and-out boxing kangaroo Kid Botts beat the cheating champion, the gorilla King Klong.

Comment. The turtle is DC Comics's delightful send-up of its own superhero (the turtle's costume is virtually identical to that of the Flash). It first appeared in *Funny Stuff* no. 1 in 1944. The character was created by Martin Nadle, and was a clear inspiration for DC's later Fastback. Nadle also wrote the magazine's occasional text feature, *Ol' Judge Owl*. Another popular DC tortoise was Super-Turtle, which was written and drawn by Henry Boltinoff. These two-thirds–page cartoons appeared in DC's *Superman* and Superman-related comics *(Action, Superboy,* and so on) throughout the late 1950s and early 1960s. These humorous cartoons boasted action themes that ended in a punchline. Super-Turtle was all green, with dark green spots on his shell, and had a red cape with a yellow Superman-like *T* in a shield on the back. Able to fly and endowed with superstrength and supersenses, the turtle helped humans, from police (he once moved a truck involved in an accident from Kosdanskio Street to Elm Street because the officer couldn't spell the former) to working men and women (he saved a lumberjack from under a fallen tree). The one time he needed a rest, he burrowed into the earth, intending to "hibernate for a good long time." He ended up in China, where the locals came crying for his help.

MERLIN, THE MAGIC MOUSE

Pedigree. Latecomer in the Warner Brothers theatrical cartoon lineup.

Biography. Merlin is a magician mouse with a W. C. Fields voice, a magic top hat, and a little mouse assistant named Second Banana. The two tour the country, performing questionable feats of magic that invariably put them in disfavor with someone, and earn them little money. In their debut cartoon *(Merlin the Magic Mouse)* they get in trouble after trying to cut a cat in half with a real saw instead of a fake one. In their follow-up escapade *(Hocus Pocus Pow Wow),* the two are tossed from a train when they haven't got the fare and, in the middle of nowhere, are chased by an Indian who wants Merlin's hat. In subsequent tales, the two have acquired a magic carpet and travel a bit easier. Other cartoons take them smack into a feud between the Hatfields and Mc-Coys; into a boxing match that Second wins thanks

to magic gloves; and to Ireland, where they match wits with a leprechaun.

Comment. There were only five Merlin cartoons. Although there were moments of inspiration (the magic gloves thinking for themselves, for example, to the surprise of Second), the animation and stories were pale compared to the **Bugs Bunny** or Road Runner glory days of Warner Brothers.

MERTON MONK

Pedigree. A comic book monkey who is an inventor/sales-ape.

Biography. A cigar-chomping chimp with unruly hair, Merton is always trying some new, but always legitimate scheme to make money. He sells books (although not many, because he invariably tells prospective buyers the entire plot to assure them they'll enjoy it), invents devices like a rocket camera (it takes a picture of everyone on earth—but the photograph is spoiled when someone moves), and, in his most noteworthy adventure, finds the winged shoes of the Greek god Mercury, which he is utterly unable to control. (When he grabs a bull for ballast, Merton and the animal both fly skyward.) Fortunately, Mercury (a beagle) comes to the chimp's rescue. Merton is never without a sports jacket.

Comment. Throughout the 1950s, Merton appeared as a back-up feature in the comic book starring **Supermouse.** Other comic book chimps have included Jocko and Socko, who starred in the only issue of William H. Wise's *America's Biggest Comics Book* (1944); Itchi the Monk, sidekick of Tom-Tom the Jungle Boy in *Tick Tock Tales* nos. 23 to 34 (1948 to 1951), and then in six issues of their own title; Squeeks, who had five issues of his own comic from Lev Gleason (1953 to 1954); and Zippy the Chimp, who starred in two issues of his own Pines title in 1957.

MERVIN

Pedigree. Comic book mouse; best friend of Spencer Spook.

Biography. Mervin is a kindly, streetwise mouse who lives in a hole in the wall of the first apartment Spencer is assigned to haunt. When the occupant proves utterly unfrightened by Spencer's howls and appearance, the ghost goes to Mervin for help; as it turns out, Dracula's the tenant, and the only thing that scares him is mice. When Mervin walks over, the vampire runs screaming into the night. Spencer's boss thinks the ghost did it, and is so impressed he

The hard-bitten **Mervin** gives his pal Spencer Spook some advice. From 1954. © WALT KELLY ESTATE.

gives Spencer the entire building as his beat. In another adventure, after Spencer's desirable attic apartment is taken over by a bully-ghost named Rocky, Mervin tries to teach Spencer how to box. Spencer proves inept at that, so Mervin shows him how to fire a cannon. When that fails to teach the bully a lesson, Mervin marches into the attic . . . and frightens the ghost away by himself. The mouse speaks (squeaks?) with a Brooklyn accent and is naked, save for his mouse fur. The apartment is located in Middleville.

Comment. The Spencer Spook strip had a healthy run in American Comics's *Giggle Comics* comics from no. 58 (1948) to no. 99 (1955). It became *Spencer Spook* for the next two issues, then expired. Ace Comics brought the characters back for a five-issue run in 1986 to 1987. Unlike the Casper comics, which are for kids only, Spencer had terrific sight gags and some witty dialogue. For much of its original run, the strip boasted expressive, very animated art by Jack Bradbury, who also worked on strips in the 1940s, which included such characters as the portly, domestic, lovable Bagshaw Bear; the brawny,

seagoing "Butch" O'Sparrow; Tuffy the Cat; and Supermouse.

MEWSETTE
Pedigree. Cartoon animal whose voice was provided by Judy Garland.

Biography. Bored with farm life (and with her boyfriend Jaune-Tom), bushy-tailed cat Mewsette and her male friend Robespierre hop on a train bound for Paris; her boyfriend, jilted, good-hearted Jaune-Tom, trails them on foot. In the big city, Mewsette meets the slick, crooked Meowrice, who takes her to Madame Rubens-Chatte's beauty parlor and has her dolled up . . . intending to sell her to an aged bachelor cat in Pittsburgh. Meanwhile, Jaune-Tom finds Robespierre, who's been given the boot, and the two cats search for Mewsette (although just *why* isn't clear, because she's about as endearing as a litterbox). As they search, one of Meowrice's henchcats pushes Robespierre into a sewer; Jaune-Tom saves him, after which they're spotted by Meowrice. Because they don't know who he is, the fiend is able to buy them drinks, get them drunk, and have them placed on a ship bound for Alaska. Back in Paris, Mewsette—still unwittingly being groomed for marriage—moves among the uppermost reaches of society, having a grand old time. Then, like Heathcliff (Bronte's, not Gately's), Jaune-Tom and Robespierre return: They found gold in Alaska and are filthy rich. Resuming their search for Mewsette, they arrive just as the ladycat learns of Meowrice's plans. She runs away, but is caught and placed on a train. Luckily, she's able to leave a message on a wall, which Jaune-Tom and Robespierre find. They chase the train, board it, battle Meowrice, and, rescuing Mewsette, stuff her abductor into the box bound for Pittsburgh.

Comment. The characters appeared in the 1962 feature film *Gay Purr-ee*. In addition to Garland as Mewsette, there were Robert Goulet as Jaune-Tom, Red Buttons as Robespierre, Paul Frees as Meowrice, and Hermione Gingold as Rubens-Chatte. The Warner Brothers film was directed by Abe Levitow (a former animator on **Droopy**, among other classics) with an "executive director" credit for Chuck Jones. Gold Key published a comic book adaptation. Another little-seen, non-Disney feature length film is the episodic *Shinbone Alley* (1970), which is based on Don Marquis's Archy and Mehitabel 1920s newspaper columns about the love of a cockroach, Archy, for a fun-loving cat. (Archy ostensibly wrote the original tales on Marquis's typewriter, at night, in his newspaper office. Everything was in lower case because he couldn't reach the shift key.) The columns were collected as a trio of books that inspired a Joe Darion musical that served as the basis for the film. Carol Channing, Eddie Bracken, and John Carradine provided the voices.

MIAMI MICE

Pedigree. Comic book crime-fighter rodents, caricatures of their human TV counterparts.

Biography. Rocket and Stubo work for Mice Central, a police force in a world consisting of happily coexisting mice and cats. Equally adept with knife or gun, and traveling about in copters shaped like mice, the heroes fight notorious foes such as the Snicaragua Contrats led by Tumeric Squeekle, who collects the ears of defeated mice-cops. Their female associate is the tough Vermousa Ratez.

Comment. Mark Bodé's down-and-dirty characters appear in their own Rip Off Press magazine, which began publication in 1986. The strip's back-up feature stars the perenially hungry Paco,

"Rocket's oversize pet cockroach." Teenage Mutant Ninja Turtles and Cerebus the Aardvark guest starred in no. 4. *Miami Mice* was also an unrelated segment on TV's *Sesame Street*.

MICHIGAN J. FROG

Pedigree. Star of the classic Warner Brothers cartoon short *One Froggy Evening*.

Biography. Although bipedal and a singer, Michigan is otherwise very froglike. As a building from 1892 is being razed, a construction worker finds a box in the cornerstone, and opens it: Out pops a frog, complete with top hat and cane, dancing and singing *Hello! Ma Baby*. The construction worker sees a fortune to be made in the frog. Spending all his money to rent a theater, the man discovers, to his utter horror, that the frog won't sing if anyone else is present: He just lies there and croaks. Broke, the man becomes a bum. When a police officer hears singing in the park, he walks over and asks the man who it is. The man points to the frog; cut to his incarceration in an insane asylum. After several years, the construction worker takes the frog and places him in the cornerstone of a new building which is going up. A century later, ray guns bring this structure down . . . and once again a man sees dollar signs as Michigan emerges, singing and dancing his little frog heart out.

Comment. The frog was nameless in the 1955 cartoon; he was nicknamed later by creator Chuck Jones. Considered by many to be the finest cartoon short ever made—the switches from the realistic frog to the anthropomorphic one are superb, as are the transitions from scene to scene and incredible swings from humor to pathos—*One Froggy Evening* is told without dialogue, except for the frog's songs. While none of Warner Brothers other one-shot characters are quite as extraordinary as Michigan, their numbers are legion. There were cartoons that featured animal parodies of celebrities, such as *The Woods Are Full of Cuckoos* (1937), which starred Eddie Gander, Fred McFurry, Walter Finchell, Bing Crowsby, W. C. Fieldmouse, Lily Swans, and others. Bobo the Elephant starred in *Hobo Bobo* in 1947, the tale of a young pachyderm who sets out from India to join a circus (a mynah bird suggests he paint himself pink if he doesn't want to be stopped, because no one will admit to seeing a pink elephant); Quentin Quail starred in an eponymous cartoon in 1946, vainly trying to get a worm for his baby Toots to eat. One of the most endearing minor characters is Willoughby, a St. Bernard who has to be the dumbest cartoon animal of all time. Joining in on a fox hunt, he finds George the fox, doesn't know he's a fox, and asks for directions. The fox leads the dog straight off a cliff. Although Willoughby realizes that that was the fox and goes to get him, George fools him by wearing a dog costume and sends Willoughby off the cliff once again. And so it goes. Perhaps the most intriguing of the one-shot characters was Rapid Rabbit. Seen in the 1969 short *Rabbit Stew and Rabbits Too*, this was a rabbit version of Warner's successful Road Runner. His nemesis was a fox determined to catch and eat him. Several cartoons featuring the character were planned, but the animation unit was shut down and the series was canceled.

MICKEY MONEY
Pedigree. A cross between the comic books' Richie Rich and Mickey Mouse.
Biography. On Levram, a world of superheroes, earthling Normalman is the only one without superpowers. Leaving, Normalman stumbles on a land of talking animals; in particular, the estate of Mickey Money. The pint-size human has a mouse's snout and ears, and dollar signs instead of pupils: Nothing matters to him except money. He is served by the blue-furred rabbit Rugcleft, who is secretly the ad-

venturer Rags Rabbit (possibly related to **Rags Rabbit**). Other characters that appear in the strip are the dumb Dipstick Duck and the brutish Punky Pig. Eventually, Normalman is rescued from the clutches of the arrogant little rodent by the superhero Captain Everything. When last seen, Mickey and the long-suppressed Rags were engaged in a savage slugfest. Mickey wears a little jacket, blue shorts, a white shirt, and a red bow tie.

Comment. The character appeared in Aardvark-Vanaheim's *Normalman* nos. 4 and 5 in 1984. He was created by Valentino.

MICKEY MOUSE
Pedigree. The one and only.
Biography. Dressed in yellow shoes ("big shoes," Disney once said, "to give him the look of a kid wearing his father's shoes"), white gloves (with four fingers each, making one less finger to animate), velvet shorts (red, when shown in color), with a pair of large pearl buttons on the front, the black-furred, white-faced Mickey made his theatrical debut in *Steamboat Willie* (1928), the first cartoon with a completely synchronized soundtrack. (Earlier cartoons had featured clumsily added music and/or sound effects, to no great commercial or artistic effect). In this historic short subject, Mickey is an ambitious riverboat hand who makes his way to the

Mickey Mouse
in Steamboat Willie.
© THE WALT DISNEY COMPANY.

wheelhouse, from which he's chased by the captain, **Pete.** As the boat pulls from the shore, Mickey spots **Minnie Mouse** and uses a boat hook to grab her (by the panties, no less). When a goat eats Minnie's music and instrument, the two make music using the livestock onboard, rather sadistically performing *Turkey in the Straw* using a cow's udders and teeth, yanking a cat's tail, and banging pots and pans (Mickey uses his tail to bang a basin with a mallet). *Gallopin' Gaucho* (1928) was the next cartoon to be released (although it was made before *Steamboat Willie;* see "Comment"), and had Mickey wooing Minnie in a Mexican setting. *Plane Crazy* (1928) was the second Mickey Mouse cartoon released (although the first to be filmed), and featured Mickey as a rather clumsy flier with Minnie as his panicked passenger. This was a send-up of the public's fascination with aviation in the wake of Charles Lindbergh's historic transatlantic flight. Mickey found his voice in his ninth short, *The Karnival Kid* (1929), in which he operated a hot dog stand and greeted Minnie at one point by "tipping" his ears and the top portion of his head to her. One amusing bit had him chasing a runaway frankfurter and, on catching it, pulling off its skin and spanking it. Scenes like this were indicative of the fact that, like Disney's previous characters **Julius the Cat** and **Oswald, the Lucky Rabbit,** Mickey had a broadly sketched personality. Apart from flashes of irreverence and a desire to have fun, the mouse's only distinguishing trait was a willingness to tackle larger foes—a Chaplinesque toughness born of necessity, not desire. Other than that, the mouse was there simply as a peg on which to hand the gags. But the public loved those gags and, abetted by Disney's affinity for choosing catchy and evocative music (still a novelty in motion pictures), the mouse's popularity grew in cartoons such as *The Barn Dance* (1928), *The Opry House* (1929), *Mickey's Follies* (1929), *The Jazz Fool* (1929), *The Barnyard Concert* (1930), and *Blue Rhythm* (1931). Still, neither Mickey nor Minnie, nor even the overbearing Pete, were strong enough to sustain the cartoons by themselves *ad infinitum.* Even in imaginative fantasies like *Gulliver Mickey* (1934) and *Thru the Mirror* (1936; Mickey experiencing adventures à la Alice in Wonderland), his reactions to the amazing things going on around him are seriously underplayed. The taming of the mouse grew more severe as he became more famous: Any time he did anything even remotely nasty or off-color, parents and censors let the studio know of their displeasure. Disney realized

he'd have a problem if his star became less interesting than whatever was going on around him. The catch-22 was that it was Mickey's Boy Scout nature that made him an ideal licensing property, and the revenue from Mickey Mouse watches, dinner plates, soap, dolls, biscuits, and so on, made Disney disinclined to change him. Thus idiosyncratic but nonnasty characters were developed to support the mouse, such as his dog **Pluto,** the fumbling **Goofy,** and, most important, Mickey's irascible friend **Donald Duck.** [In *The Birthday Party* (1931), Mickey ended up with a water-filled fishbowl over his head . . . and sat there smiling. Can anyone even imagine Donald doing that?] Some characters, like **Clara Cluck,** were introduced, failed to click, and were dropped as future costars. Nephews for the mouse, **Ferdy and Morty,** were tried and also didn't work. But Donald, Mickey, and Goofy interacted perfectly together and were teamed in classics like *Orphan's Benefit* (1934), *The Band Concert* (1935; the first Mickey Mouse film in color), *Mickey's Grand Opera* (1936) (in all, music adding to the appeal), *Alpine Climbers* (1936), *Mickey's Circus* (1936), *Moose Hunters* (1937), and many others. By the 1940s, Donald had become the studio's most popular character, and Mickey was so tame that he was usually seen wearing trousers and a shirt (he'd already begun sporting a straw hat in the early 1930s). But that was no longer a negative: He was now the sane, sensible counterweight to (and often the victim of) the overreactions of Donald and the clumsiness of Goofy. But he also continued to be a solo star, and made one of the greatest shorts of all time: *Thru the Mirror* (1936). In it, Mickey falls asleep while reading Lewis Carroll, and dreams of going through the looking glass. In addition to encountering living furniture and other animate household objects, he does an incredible dance with a deck of cards, which keep shuffling and cutting. Then, after flirting with the queen, Mickey duels the jealous king-card, whose dual torsos both wield swords. Mickey barely escapes back through the mirror before waking. The only mistake Disney made with Mickey was a short-lived attempt in the early 1940s to draw his ears "in perspective," on the sides of his head instead of piled on top of it, regardless of which way he turned. These more natural drawings weren't really Mickey, and they were abandoned. Mickey has remained the conservative "anchor" at the studio, all thirteen pounds and two feet, three inches of him, and costumed Mickeys are the official hosts of the Walt Disney theme parks around the world. The mouse may not be as entertaining as his cartoon comrades, but he *is* an unassuming, good-hearted soul—one of the screen's great Everyman figures.

Comment. After Disney's unscrupulous distributor Charles Mintz gave the cartoonist a take-it-or-leave it deal to remain on the Oswald cartoons, Disney opted to leave. Together with his animator and then-partner Ub Iwerks (see **Flip the Frog**), Disney created Mickey Mouse. At first, Disney had intended to call the new character Mortimer, but his wife, Lillian, convinced him that it was an awful name. [Still, he did get to use the name—several times, in fact. Morty was one of Mickey's nephews; Mortimer was a tall, natty mouse who wooed Minnie in *Mickey's Rival* (1936); and in the Mickey comic strip, Minnie had an Uncle Mortimer.] Late in 1928, Disney and Iwerks made two cartoons, *Plane Crazy* followed by *Gallopin' Gaucho,* but couldn't find a distributor. It occurred to Disney that he might have better luck if he capitalized on a new technology that was proving a hit at the box office: sound. Without knowing quite how they were going to add synchronized sound effects and music, they put a third cartoon, *Steamboat Willie,* into production. The sound problem was solved when Disney joined forces with producer Pat Powers, whose engineers had recently come up with a system known as Powers Cinephone. Even with sound, Walt still couldn't find a distributor. However, he was able to get a two-week booking in New York's Colony theater. That was all he needed. The film was a hit, and it soon went nationwide. The previously produced cartoons were given soundtracks and released (although Mickey didn't have his gloves or shoes in these), and the mouse was on his way to starring in 132 theatrical cartoons, as well as in segments of the feature films *Fantasia* (1940; *The Sorcerer's Apprentice,* as the magician's helper who "borrows" his master's hat, animates a broom to do his chores for him, chops it to pieces when it gets out of hand, then watches helplessly as each piece comes to life), *Fun and Fancy Free* (1940; *Mickey and the Beanstalk,* costarring Donald and Goofy), and the featurette *Mickey's Christmas Carol* (1983), in which he costarred as the long-suffering Bob Cratchit. Over the years, Mickey's voice has been provided by Walt Disney, Jim MacDonald (from 1947), and, most recently, Wayne Allwine. Disney was given his first Oscar in 1932, a special award for the creation of Mickey Mouse; a total of three Mickey shorts have been Oscar nominated. Mickey made his debut in daily comic strips on January 13, 1930, in adventures drawn by Ub Iwerks and Win Smith, and written by Disney. When Smith left, animator Floyd Gottfredson was handed the strip—and, thanks to wonderful dialogue, brisk pacing, and an ongoing storyline involving Mickey and **Pete,** he was able to attain a level of characterization not to be found even in the animated cartoons. A Sunday page began in January 1932, also done by Gottfredson, and familiar cartoon characters such as **Clarabelle Cow** and **Horace Horsecollar** were brought in for support. Gottfredson and his assistant stuck to the formula of having Mickey partake in all kinds of exotic adventures done straight, with foes ranging from the Phantom Blot to Captain Vulture to Eli Squinch, and for two decades the strip had a huge and devoted following. Unfortunately, syndicator King Features ordered the action theme changed in the 1950s to emphasize gag cartoons, a genre that was enjoying a greater popularity; Gottfredson hung on, but the strip was never to return to the approach that made it famous. In comic books, Mickey appeared in five issues of *Mickey Mouse* magazines, which reprinted daily and Sunday strips (1931 to 1934), before moving into his own title consisting of all new stories. Dell published these from 1941 to 1962; Gold Key took over with no. 85, and Gladstone picked up the magazine with no. 219 (1986). Disney itself began a new series in 1990. There have also been numerous one shots published over the years, including Eternity Comics's *The Uncensored Mouse,* two issues of which were published in 1989. These reprint the early comic strips, in which Mickey is often as sadistic as he was in *Steamboat Willie.* He is seen reciting "She loves me, she loves me not" while plucking the feathers from a chicken, and making snide remarks such as this about **Horace Horsecollar:** "Everytime he takes off his hat, the woodpeckers chase him," or this about the talkative **Clarabelle Cow:** "She must have been vaccinated with a phonograph needle!" The meanness aside, the comics are invaluable in that they reprint the first run-in with Pete, his unsavory partner, lawyer Sylvester Shyster, and their efforts to wrest an estate from Minnie. On television, Mickey was the mascot of *The Mickey Mouse Club,* a variety and cartoon children's show hosted by mouse-eared Mouseketeers, which aired on ABC from 1955 to 1959; *The New Mickey Mouse Club,* which featured all new Mouseketeers and was syndicated in 1977; and *The Mickey Mouse Club,* with a third set of dish-eared kids, created for the Disney Channel cable service in 1989. There was also a short-lived syndicated series *The Mouse Factory*

(1972), which featured a celebrity host introducing old Disney cartoons. See also Mickey's pet dog **Pluto the Pup** and his goldfish **Bianca.** While the success of Mickey inspired other cartoon studios and comic book companies to create their own mice, these were far different from Mickey, such as **Herman the Mouse** and **Mighty Mouse.** Among the lesser-known, more Mickey-like rodents that have scurried through brief comic book careers are Bertie Mouse, who appeared in both issues of Marvel's *Komic Kartoons* (1945); the bow-tied Mertie Mouse, costar of Orbit Publishing's *Toy Town Comics,* which lasted seven issues (1945 to 1947); Marty Mouse, who appeared with Nutsy McKrow in seven issues of *Jack in the Box* (1946 to 1947); Merry Mouse, who had a four-issue run of his own title from Avon (1953 to 1954); and Marvin Mouse, who starred in one issue of his own Marvel comic in 1957. The only new wrinkle in the mousecapades was the masked cheese bandit Muggsy Mouse, who appeared in several issues of Magazine Enterprises *Tick Tock Tales* beginning with no. 23, then starred in five issues of his own title (1951 to 1953). See **Koko the Bear** for more on Muggsy.

MIDNITE, THE REBEL SKUNK

Pedigree. Morally upright comic book skunk.
Biography. Humans and talking animals coexist in the seedy world of Midnite. According to the comic, "To the rich, she is a mystery . . . to the poor, she is a Robin Hood, a hero." Little else is known about the cigar-smoking lady skunk who, dressed in a trench coat and magnetic underwear (to attract the guns and knives of would-be killers) prowls the streets of Heluva town, uncovering police scandal, revealing safety violations, and even—something of a change-of-pace for the cigar-chomping lady—transporting Yuppies to another planet. From her hideout in a local dump, she's assisted by the scientist/dog, Lint McFadden. Midnite has been married eleven times.

Comment. The character appeared in two issues of her own Blackthorne comic book (1987).

MIGHTY MANFRED

Pedigree. Dog of TV cartoon do-gooder Tom Terrific.
Biography. Thanks to a tin funnel he wears on his head, young Tom is able to change into anything he wishes. As the theme song puts it, "If you see a plane up high / a diesel engine roaring by / a bumble

*The **Mighty Manfred** gets a lift from Tom Terrific.*

bee / or a tree / 'That's me!' " Tom lives in a treehouse with Mighty Manfred, the Wonder Dog (an intentional misnomer). The two come down to right wrongs, which are perpetrated, more often than not, by the wicked Crabby Appleton. Although the big, sleepy-eyed Manfred has an incredibly sensitive nose, and is called a "relentless pursuer" by Tom, he would rather nap than track.

Comment. Terrytoons's *Tom Terrific* adventures aired on *The Captain Kangaroo Show* from 1957 to 1959. There were twenty-five episodes in all, each consisting of five, five-minute-long cliff-hangers that aired one-a-day and wrapped up at week's end. The series was created by Gene Deitch, who had made his name in TV advertising animation. Several of the stories were written by Jules Feiffer.

MIGHTY MOUSE

Pedigree. The most powerful superanimal that ever lived.
Biography. It may well be the most heart-swelling cry in all of cartoondom: "Here I come to save the day!" When the shout booms from the sky, you know that Mighty Mouse is on the way. Mighty Mouse is actually two completely different characters. In the beginning, he was known as Supermouse (see "Comment"); even then, he had two different origins. In an unspecified human city, the mice are slowly being eradicated by cats. One night, a mouse seeks refuge from an attack by hiding in a supermarket. There, he eats supercelery and supersoup. He cleanses himself with supersoap, then indulges in

*The beauteous **Midnite the Rebel Skunk** makes like Marilyn Monroe, with predictable results.*
© MILTON KNIGHT.

supercheese. As a result, the scrawny mouse suddenly acquires superpowers and a flash costume and becomes Supermouse (in the slightly different origin, he simply gulps down supervitamins). Flying forth, he uses his superstrength to fly the cats to the moon, then returns to protect his fellow mice. When it was decided to change the character from Supermouse to Mighty Mouse, a new origin was devised. On a dark, rainy night, a cloaked stranger leaves a basket on the stoop of a cottage in the woods, just outside of Terrytown (a k a Mouseville). The mouse homeowners emerge and find a baby mouse swaddled inside the basket. They raise it as their own, although they soon discover that this is no ordinary rodent: It has superpowers beyond belief. Over the years, in addition to flight (with his brilliant red contrail—how else could you see the tiny mouse amid the larger cats?), incredible strength (he has moved the earth itself), awesome speed (he's faster than lightning), and imperviousness to bullets and arrows (although an artillery shell and the fiery exhaust of a rocket have been known to send Mighty Mouse somersaulting out of control), the superhero has used X-ray vision, superhypnotic powers (he can turn these on inanimate objects as well, once having forced the raging waters of the Johnstown flood to retreat), and superhearing (while on the planet Pluto, he's heard sounds on earth . . . even through the vacuum of space). He is vulnerable to excessive humidity and certain kinds of poison gas. Mighty Mouse's archenemy is Oil Can Harry, a cat; his girlfriend is Pearl Pureheart—although that hasn't prevented the lusty mouse from kissing many of the lady mice he's rescued over the years. Other foes of the superhero include Catula, Cattenstein (Frankenstein's Cat), Ding

Dong, the Catnip Gang, the Goons from the Moon, the Kilkenny Cats, the Electronic Mouse Trap (a mouse-vacuum the size and shape of a brontosaurus), and the awesome Bat-Cats (bat-winged cats who attack a tribe of mice in the Academy Award–nominated *Gypsy Life*, 1945). Mighty Mouse has also taken time off from mouse-protecting to save the lives of a bunny family attacked by vultures in *Raiding the Raiders* (1945). Many of the mouse's vintage cartoons are done in operatic style, with the hero, villain, and heroine singing while they fight (for instance, Oil Can Harry will sing, "This is the end of Mighty Mouse!" to which the hero sings in reply, "Noooo! This is the end of *yooou!")* The hero's base of operations has varied from cartoon to cartoon: He has had headquarters on the moon, on top of the world's tallest building, on a mountain, and elsewhere. Physically, Supermouse and Mighty Mouse are quite different. Supermouse has pipe-cleaner-thin legs and arms, a kind of goofy head with big ears, and a big, round chest. Mighty Mouse has short, stocky legs, a massive chest, a huge head with intelligent eyes, and thick, powerful arms. Supermouse's costume consists of a blue suit, red trunks, a red cape, red shoes, and white gloves; Mighty Mouse's attire varied in the early cartoons, before he settled on his familiar yellow suit, red trunks, red cape, red shoes, and white gloves.

Comment. The character was created by producer Paul Terry, who took the idea of one of his writers to do a parody of Superman using a fly and turned it around into a serious adventure about a supermouse. The character first appeared as Supermouse in the Terrytoons cartoon *The Mouse of Tomorrow* in 1942. Another five Supermouse cartoons followed, before Mighty Mouse made his de-

Mighty Mouse, the superhero who can do almost everything. Pearl Pureheart looks on as Mighty fesses up. © VIACOM INTERNATIONAL.

but in *The Wreck of the Hesperus* in 1944. Contrary to popular belief, the name change wasn't forced by the publishers of Superman. It came from Terry, who didn't want his cartoons promoting the character **Supermouse**, which ironically, had debuted the same month (Who would pay a hefty licensing fee to do toy and books based on Terry's mouse, when they could get the other one cheap?) When the Terrytoons were sold to television, the words *Mighty Mouse* were dubbed wherever *Supermouse* appeared in the soundtrack of the original five cartoons. As Mighty Mouse, the hero starred in seventy-nine theatrical cartoons through 1967. The earliest of the cartoons came to television in 1955 when CBS began airing *Mighty Mouse Playhouse* (later called *The Mighty Mouse Show*). The series went into syndication in 1967. Tom Morrison provided the voice for the mouse. Filmation produced thirty-one new episodes for *The New Adventures of Mighty Mouse and Heckle and Jeckle*, which aired on CBS in 1979, while Ralph Bakshi was responsible for the lively *Mighty Mouse: The New Adventures*, which came to CBS in 1987. That series came under considerable fire (hysterical and unjustified, for the record) when, in one episode, Mighty Mouse paused to sniff a flower in a way that convinced certain viewers the superhero was snorting cocaine. (One wonders what hallucinogen the critics were on.) The show was canceled. In comics, Mighty Mouse first appeared in *Terry-Toons* [sic] *Comics* no. 38 in 1945, then went on to star in numerous titles, among them *March of Comics* and several incarnations of his own magazine, from Marvel (four issues, 1946 to 1947), St. John Publishing and Pines (seventy-nine issues from 1947 to 1959, including specials such as the world's first 3-D comic, the eye-popping *Three Dimension Comics Starring Paul Terry's Mighty Mouse)*, Gold Key, then Dell (eleven issues from 1964 to 1968), and Spotlight (three issues in 1987). Marvel Comics made Mighty a reporter for WPRL-TV in their new comic book, which began in 1990. They also gave the hero a Ratcave.

MILDEW WOLF
Pedigree. Beleaguered TV predator.
Biography. Mildew is a lanky wolf who is bare chested, wears low-slung overalls, a collar and tie, and a too small brimmed hat. His prey is the small Lambsy, who—unfortunately for Mildew—is under the protection of the big sheepdog Bristle Hound, who dresses in a vest, ascot, and porkpie hat. To his credit, Mildew tries all sorts of schemes to get at the lamb. In addition to the tried-and-untrue ploy of dressing up as Little Bo Peep to spirit Lambsy away from its guardian *(It's the Wolf)*, Mildew has tried to hijack the lamb and get it onto a ship bound for Australia *(When My Sheep Comes In)*, disguised himself as a snowman when the dog and lamb took a vacation at a ski resort *(Winter in Blunder Land)*, erected an amusement park designed to appeal just to the lamb *(Merry-Go-Roundup)*, used high-tech devices to try and spy on the lamb *(Super Scientific Sheep Sitting Service)*, pretended to be a baseball scout interested in having Lambsy play for the Dodgers *(Any Sport in a Storm)*, posed as a TV director to get the lamb to play Red Riding Hood opposite himself as the wolf *(Channel Chasers)*, and constructed a robot wolf in *Smart Dummy*.

Comment. There were twenty-five Mildew Wolf cartoons, which aired on *The Chattanooga Cats (see* entry) on ABC in 1969. This Hanna-Barbera series starred Paul Lynde as the voice of Mildew, Allan Melvin as Bristle, and Daws Butler as Lambsy.

MILDLY MICROWAVED PRE-PUBESCENT KUNG-FU GOPHERS
Pedigree. Mutated comic book animals.
Biography. Snoozing in a hole on the test site of a U.S. government microwave bomb test, four gophers are irradiated when the bomb goes off. Roaming through the desert, they encounter an Eastern mystic, who teaches them how to speak and fight. When their training is complete, they make costumes from his tent, go forth, encounter a writer, and become the stars of their own comic book. In their only altercation with evil, they battled the Devil's Babushkas, a gang of bikers eighty years old and older.

Comment. The characters had no names. They were created by George Macas and appeared in one issue of their own title, published by Just Imagine Graphix in 1986.

MILFORD
Pedigree. Intelligent cartoon pig.
Biography. Maw and Paw and their family live on a farm, and are dumber than just about any humans who ever lived. The only one with any smarts is the big, occasionally bipedal pig Milford. Although Milford can't talk, he can read and is handy with tools, taking care of everything from household chores to reading the mail. He communicates with the others through very clear and concise sign lan-

*Gunshots . . . and a close call for Tintin and **Milou***. © CASTERMAN, PARIS AND TOURNAI.

guage that, more often than not, they can't understand.

Comment. Walter Lantz's *Maw and Paw* series lasted just four cartoons, from 1953 to 1955.

MILOU

Pedigree. Fox terrier owned by the teenage adventurer Tintin.

Biography. Tintin is a reporter, and his investigations carry him not just around the world, but into space. The dog is always at his side and Tintin talks to him—largely as a way to reveal exposition to the reader. Several times in each story, the dog will complain to the reader ("How can a dog get a wink of sleep? Not a minute's peace since he fell for shortwave radio"), and often with good reason: If the small white dog is curled up in a chair, odds are he'll be sat on. If someone doffs their hat, it falls on him. If Tintin packs a trunk, Milou will usually be locked inside. If someone leaves a drugged beverage for Tintin, Milou will get to it first. If Tintin leaves the dog in someone else's care, the person usually turns out to be a nut of some kind. In *The Blue Lotus*, for example, he's in China visiting elderly Wang Chen-yee and leaves Milou with the man's son. When he checks on the dog, Tintin finds him tied to a chair, his muzzle bound shut, the young man about to slice him up with a huge blade. Despite the abuse, Milou sticks by his master, and won't hesitate to attack anyone who tries to hurt him . . . even if the dog is usually knocked out before he can get in his licks. Only the reader can understand Milou when he talks. Everyone else just hears *Wooah!* or a variation thereof.

Comment. When the stories were published in

English, the dog's name was changed to Snowy. *Tintin* was created by Belgian artist Hergé (Georges Remi), and was first published in 1929 in *Le Petit Vingtième,* a weekly comic section of the newspaper *Le Vingtième Siècle.* The first adventure was *Tintin au Pays des Soviets (Tintin in the Land of the Soviets).* The character's popularity inspired the publication of *The Journal Tintin;* dozens of Tintin adventures have been collected in book form. In 1960, Raymond Leblanc, former editor of *The Journal Tintin,* began releasing a series of cartoons, each five minutes long; there are 104 in all. In 1969, he produced a feature-length cartoon, *Tintin et le Temple du Soleil (Tintin and the Temple of the Sun).*

MILTON

Pedigree. Cat nemesis of Disney's **Pluto the Pup.**

Biography. Tan-furred, with a darker head, tail, and paws, the rambunctious Milton made his screen debut in *Puss-Cafe* (1950), entering the yard of **Mickey Mouse** to make meals of the milk, birds, and pondfish therein. Unfortunately for him, diligent **Pluto the Pup** is napping nearby, and—although it isn't easy—the dog finally manages to send the cat packing. Milton not only makes his way back, but in *Cold Turkey* (1951) is actually living in Mickey's home! When the two see a commercial for Lurkey's Turkeys on the television, they get a yen for fowl, and raid the kitchen. As it happens, there's a frozen turkey in the freezer, and the two fight over it. Eventually, their greed results in the turkey being burned to a crisp inside the television (it got there when Milton tried to hide with it), and the frustrated cat and dog ending up beating each other up.

Comment. See also Pluto's cat-nemesis **Figaro.**

MINNIE MOUSE

Pedigree. Inamorata of Mickey Mouse.

Biography. Dressed in a frilly skirt, a hat with a long-stemmed flower tucked in the brim, high heel shoes too wide for her feet, and batting her long lashes, Minnie first meets Mickey in *Steamboat Willie* (1928) when she's a ukelele player and he's a hand on a riverboat. When Minnie misses the boat, Mickey hauls her onboard—where a goat eats her music and instrument. Not one to become dispirited, Minnie turns the goat's tail to grind out music, after which she and Mickey have a cruel jam session using the tails, teeth, and necks of the livestock onboard. In her second screen appearance (*Plane Crazy*, 1928, which was actually made before *Steamboat Willie*; see **Mickey Mouse**), she's a bit warier of the young mouse, watching from the sidelines as Mickey builds an airplane powered by a dachshund and a rubber band—which crashes soon after takeoff. A second plane, made by cannibalizing a car and a peacock, holds more promise. When Minnie offers Mickey a horseshoe for good luck, he invites her for a ride. She accepts; unfortunately, the plane hits a stone while taxiing, Mickey is heaved from the cockpit, and Minnie does little more than scream as the aircraft soars wildly through the skies. Mickey finally manages to get back in and, showing a remarkable lack of tact, tries to steal a kiss from Minnie. She refuses and, out of spite, Mickey puts the plane through maneuvers intended to terrify her into capitulation. Instead, she jumps from the aircraft, her underwear filling with air and floating her gently to the ground. Mickey crashes and, the panties hanging loosely around her legs, Minnie stalks from the wreck. (Mickey hurls her horseshoe away, but it comes back like a boomerang and circles his neck, leaving him literally seeing stars.) Things went somewhat better for the couple in *Gallopin' Gaucho* (1928), as the ostrich-riding Mickey woos singer/dancer Minnie south of the border, and rescues her from the clutches of **Pete**. Over the years, as Mickey gave up his more rambunctious ways, Minnie, too, became much less independent. With exceptions—mostly period pieces like *Brave Little Tailor* (1938), in which Mickey slays a giant to win Princess Minnie— the couple were no longer meeting anew in each cartoon. For example, they were already dating in *The Beach Party* (1931), *The Whoopee Party* (1932), and *Puppy Love* (1933), and in *The Pet Store* (1933) she comes to the shop where Mickey works just to be with him (and ends up being abducted by a gorilla). They were now devoted friends, and have remained such (although kissing was apparently, still, verboten: When Mickey tries to plant one on her in *Mickey's Steam-Roller* [1934], she's deeply offended). Her devotion wavers only in *Mickey's Rival* (1936) when her snappy-dressing former boyfriend Mortimer stops by while she's picnicking with

Minnie Mouse *tickles the ivory. Note Mickey's ears, one of the few times when they were drawn in perspective.*

Mickey. Minnie is smitten by his charm and sense of humor (of which the mortified Mickey is the brunt), and Mickey goes off to brood. However, when a rampaging bull threatens Minnie, Mortimer drives away and it's Mickey who comes to her rescue. All is forgiven, and Mortimer has not returned. Concurrent with her more traditional role—typified by the fact that she's no longer a "disreputable" singer/musician, but a nurse (*First Aiders*, 1944)—Minnie's wardrobe became more feminine. She was almost always seen with a big, fluffy bow on her head, and often wore dresses with a huge bow in the back. By the end of the 1940s, she was always seen in a blouse. Minnie's pet is the goldfish **Figaro**.

Comment. Interestingly, while there's no evidence for this in any of the films, Walt Disney once said about Mickey and Minnie, "In the studio we have decided that they are married, really." He described the Minnie we see on screen as simply "his leading lady." Minnie appeared in sixty-eight cartoons, and was also seen in the 1983 featurette *Mickey's Christmas Carol*. Minnie's voice was provided by Marcellite Garner and, later, by Ruth Clifford. Minnie appeared in theatrical cartoons, and is a regular co-star in the Mickey Mouse comic strip and comic books. (Curiously, unlike **Daisy Duck**, she's never had her own magazine.) Her Uncle Mortimer has also appeared in the comic strip, although never in the movies.

MISS LIL
Pedigree. A Mae West-type comic strip cat.
Biography. Owned by Blanche and Vernon, the chubby Miss Lil is vain (passing a puddle, she describes it as "nature's way of saying, 'Lil, you're gorgeous!' "), self-impressed ("I don't have a superiority complex. I'm just better than everybody else"), amorous ("My whole body is an erogenous zone"), and in love with the cat Nick, who wears an eyepatch and is always fighting ("I like a cat with guts," Lil says, "But did you have to leave them all over the patio?"). Her roommate is Blanche's other cat, the local sex kitten Muffie, who's younger and cuter. Despite her faults, Miss Lil has a sense of humor: Spotting a cat eating candy and dropping the wrappers, she remarks, "Kitty litter." Unlike most cats, Lil's afraid of mice; for all her wit and pith, she insists on calling all birds "chickens."

Comment. Rick Detorie's unpublished comic strips were collected in a paperback from Wallaby Books in 1983.

MISS PIGGY
Pedigree. Muppet star of television, films, comic strips, and a comic book.
Biography. The elegant, pink, blond-haired, long-lashed, seemingly cultured pig (she knows approximately two words of French, "moi" and "vous," but uses them so often you'd think she knows more), is actually an overbearing egomaniac whose love of self is only overshadowed by her love of **Kermit the Frog** (and even *that* is selfishness). Withal, she's so outgoing and hammy it's impossible to dislike her. Besides, Kermit is such an old fogy (old froggy?) it's a pleasure to see him shaken up by the overly and openly demonstrative pig. According to *The Muppet Movie* (1979), the lovers first met at a county fair, where Miss Piggy was being crowned "fairest of the fair." When their eyes locked, that was it. Piggy joined Kermit on his trip to Hollywood, and remained at his side when he went to London to serve as emcee at the Muppet Theater on *The Muppet Show*. She became the star of each show, not only forcing Kermit to mount each weekly presentation, but to make sure his prima donna is never offended. If she is, her fury hath no match. On the show, the pig's greatest achievement has been as the star of the ongoing series *Pigs in Space*, in which she plays a rather promiscuous crewmember onboard the starship *Swinetrek*, in love with Captain Link Heartthrob whose mission is to counter the criminal designs of Dr. Strangepork. While Miss Piggy's thespian abilities are undisciplined, her manner grand, she has no peer when it comes to dominating her "Kermie." Once, when Kermit broached the topic of dating other girls, she seemed unopposed. Kermit sang her praises . . . until, after a moment's silence, she quietly informed him, "I'd break every bone in your body." (She could do it, too, being a master of martial arts.) Not surprisingly, when Rowlf once asked Kermit if he believed in an "all-powerful entity, a guiding force," the frog glanced over at Miss Piggy and muttered, "Yes."

Comment. See Kermit entry for a history of the Muppets. Miss Piggy was also the star of her own prime-time TV special, *The Fantastic Miss Piggy Show,* which aired on ABC in 1982. In it, Piggy demonstrated her own aerobics technique (the "Jelly Roll" consists of raising the chin, straightening the back, raising the roll, and taking a bite), acting as a consumer advocate, and playing a pagan love goddess. Although Miss Piggy was never seen on *Sesame Street* with Kermit, that show *has* used pigs, for example, in the game show parody *Squeal of Fortune.*

MISS PRISSY

Pedigree. Widow chicken of theatrical cartoons.
Biography. Miss Prissy lives on the farm owned by Porky Pig (which is famous for its Hammond Eggs). In her initial outing *(An Egg Scramble)*, it's clear that Miss Prissy has been having difficulty laying eggs. She finally succeeds in producing one, then protectively chases after it when it's sent to market. Eventually, she gets the egg back and hatches a chick-version of herself. In her next two appearances *(Lovelorn Leghorn* and *Of Rice and Hen)*, she courts the very eligible **Foghorn Leghorn**—despite the fact that he belongs to Bachelor's Anonymous. He begins to find her very attractive in her next cartoon *(Little Boy Boo)*, but only because it's winter and she has a very "cozy little roost." Prissy agrees to let him move in, but only if he can be a good father to her son. Unfortunately, the rooster hasn't half the brains of the brilliant little chick (they make paper airplanes, and the boy's shoots Foghorn's down); after blowing himself up with the child's chemistry set, the battered and bandaged Foghorn departs. He moves in with her again later, and although their son is no longer with them, Foghorn has a new adversary (see **Henery Hawk**). Miss Prissy is a slender, bespectacled chicken who is never without her bonnet and big, fluffy bow tie. The name of one of Miss Prissy's few chicken friends is Agnes.

Comment. The Warner Brothers character first appeared in 1950.

MR. AND MRS. RESPECTABLE MOUSE

Pedigree. Costars of the comic strip "The Teenie Weenies."
Biography. The Teenie Weenies are people who are inches tall and live in a Lilliput-like civilization deep in the woods. Mr. and Mrs. Respectable Mouse and their four children are close friends of the village, and Mrs. Mouse frequently joins them around the hearth, at Christmas parties, and the like. (Mr. Mouse is described as "not very sociable," and "too lazy to be useful, for all he does is eat and sleep most of the time.") Although the elder Mouses occasionally wear clothing, talk, and stand on their hind legs, they are otherwise mice in appearance. Because Mrs. Respectable Mouse "is a most ambitious mouse and wants her children to get an education," the little mice go to school with the humans. The mice are "mighty proud of their flowing tails." Mrs. Mouse's cousin, Robow, makes occasional appearances, as do Ginky and Slowsy, who "with a couple of low down mice companions live in the trash heap" and

are "a great annoyance" because they occasionally raid the village for food. At such times, a Teenie Weenie will get on the back of one of the good mice, ride forth, and try to lasso the foul rodent. The comparatively huge Rhyming Rabbit also visits the characters now and then, uttering such verse as, "A rabbit's life is full of strife / His days are short and few, / For dodging shot becomes his lot / From the cradle to the stew."

Comment. William Donahey's strip debuted in the Sunday Chicago *Tribune* in 1914 and lasted until 1969. It consisted of a thick block of text to the left, and a single, very illustrative drawing to the right. *The Teenie Weenies* was inspired by updated Mother Goose strips Donahey had been doing for the Cleveland *Plain Dealer*.

MR. JACK

Pedigree. The first comic strip cat.
Biography. Orange with black stripes, the bipedal, talking tiger has a huge, round head and is the nattiest dresser in the history of cartoon animals. Wearing a variety of impeccable suits and hats, the confident, cigar-puffing womanizer always finds a way to meet women, as when he cuts a dog's leash while its owner is distracted, just so he can catch the animal and return it. ("I could kiss you!" gushes the grateful lady cat. "You may," replies the gallant Mr. Jack). Unfortunately, things rarely work out for the sly cat: In this case, the dog runs away again, the lady chases it and spots a movie star, and Mr. Jack is promptly forgotten.

Mr. Jack prepares to cut loose a lady's dog . . . so that he can return it and win her gratitude.

Comment. See **Little Bears** for details on the strip's creator, James Guilford Swinnerton. Mr. Jack was inspired by the Tammany Tiger, the symbol of the New York Democratic party. Mr. Jack made his debut in 1899, and the strip continued for more than forty years. On Sundays, it usually occupied the top two rows of Swinnerton's "Little Jimmy," a strip about a little boy, which ran from 1905 to 1958. "Little Jimmy" featured its own cast of animals led by the boy's bulldog Beans.

MR. JINKS

Pedigree. Harried TV cat in pursuit of the mice Pixie and Dixie.

Biography. Two small, confident southern mice, Pixie and Dixie relish being the bane of the existence of the cat, Mr. Jinks. As the theme song puts it, "Pixie, Dixie . . . enjoy a spat / with Mr. Jinks the cat." The pair live in a nicely appointed mousehold (a teacup has been turned into a handsome easy chair, a spool into a stool) which is located in the home of an unidentified, well-to-do, elderly "sir" (although the man's butler, to whom Mr. Jinks reports, is named Bagsley). For the mice, getting to the pantry for cheese (their favorite food) or cookies is rarely a problem, because Jinks is one of the most ineffectual mousers ever born. It's not for lack of trying: He just happens to be a clod. Grabbing a handy ewer and announcing, "Here's a vase in the face," he'll throw it, only to have pieces fall away and transform the vase into a boomerang, which comes flying back at him. Designing a new mousetrap, which consists of cheese stuffed with a firecracker, he'll be duped into showing the mice how it works. He's also been known to miss Pixie and Dixie with a shotgun fired at point-blank range. Even when the cat finally wins in one cartoon—stuffing the mice into a box and mailing them to "North Pole, Alaska," (where, he cackles, they'll become "micicles")—Mr. Jinks is forced to trek up there and get them back when Bagsley announces that his services are no longer required. Not that Jinks has a long memory. Reading that a space research center is looking for white mice and chuckling that this is a "once in a nine lifetime opportunity," he ambles over to the gray mice, convinces them that white is the "in" color for mice, helps them paint themselves, then sells them. (Naturally, the space agency ends up putting Jinks in a spaceship instead of the mice). Outside forces such as dogs, bats, and visiting mice also conspire against the cat. In one adventure—

arguably the funniest—Pixie and Dixie's fairy godmother (a mouse in a dress and spectacles) turns them into dogs or crocodiles whenever Mr. Jinks bothers them. (After one such transformation, the disbelieving cat moans, "Somebody musta, ya know, like, turned my record over to the flip side, like.") Indeed, if there's anything that truly distinguishes this cat-and-mouse series from the others, it's the wonderful characterization of Mr. Jinks. Apart from the way he's always wiping egg from his face—self-effacingly, and rarely with an unbridled show of temper—the cat's beatnik language is always amusing. His coinage of the plural "meeces" (as in, "I hate those meeces to pieces") was popular among kids of the late 1950s; his tendency to misspeak is always fun, such as "Abdominal Snowman" and "posolutely." So are his hollow threats, as when he picks up the aforementioned shotgun and calmly states, "You're gonna get air conditioned." For relaxation, Jinks likes to read the newspaper, especially the classifieds. ("Man with frying pan would like to meet lady with cow," he reads. "Object: Hamburgers." Good gag . . . but it was lifted, verbatim, from the **Daffy Duck** cartoon *His Bitter Half*, 1950.) The tawny Mr. Jinks wears only a blue bow tie. Pixie wears a blue bow tie and is the taller of the two mice; Dixie is dressed in a red vest. The cat is most fond of "rich-in-butterfat cream," and has the ability to recover instantly when clobbered.

Comment. Hanna-Barbera's *Pixie and Dixie* aired as part of the syndicated *Huckleberry Hound Show* beginning in 1958; there were fifty-five cartoons featuring the duo. Daws Butler was the voice of Mr. Jinks, and Don Messick was the voice of the meeces. From 1960 to 1963, the characters starred in four issues of Dell's *4-Color* comic, and in one issue of their own *Pixie & Dixie & Mr. Jinks* from Gold Key. A slightly different cat-and-mouse situation can be found in the seven, little-known *Hickory, Dickory, Doc* cartoons produced between 1959 and 1962 by Walter Lantz (**Woody Woodpecker**). Doc is a dapper, cultured cat decked out in a top hat, bow tie, high collar, and cane—although the distinguished look disintegrates whenever he chases the two mice.

MR. MIND

Pedigree. An evil, alien worm and nemesis of the comic book superhero Captain Marvel.

Biography. Mr. Mind is a worm born on a planet of underground-dwelling worms. Possessing a mutant brain far superior to that of any other worm (although his eyesight is awful), Mr. Mind discovers that an alien named Goat-Man has landed on his world. Because he has the ability to briefly transfer his mind into other bodies, and control them, Mr. Mind subjugates the extraterrestrial and uses him to construct eyeglasses and a portable voice amplifier (which he wears around his neck) so he can dominate his own world. He also has the alien build a radio that allows him to listen to broadcasts from earth. Deciding to conquer our world, Mr. Mind flies through space and organizes the Monster Society of Evil, a group consisting of sundry supervillains. Although he is thwarted by the superhero Captain Marvel (see **Hoppy, the Captain Marvel Bunny**) after a battle that lasts two years, Mr. Mind escapes and hides out at a radio station: "and so begins the greatest . . . worm-hunt—in history!" Captain Marvel calls in an exterminator, has every crack in the building sprayed, and eventually, coughing and gagging, the worm slithers out. Captured by the superhero and put on trial, the worm is prosecuted by Marvel himself, accused of "having murdered 186,744 people in cold blood." Mr. Mind's own attorney is so sickened by the worm's atrocities that he mutters, "I hope you get the electric chair"; the jury doesn't even have to leave the courtroom to pronounce a guilty verdict. The tiny villain is summarily strapped into an electric chair and "lamps all over the city grow dim as the switch is closed . . . sending thousands of volts . . . through the evil Mr. Mind's body." The worm is stuffed and placed in a glass case in a museum, Marvel musing, "That's the final and complete end of Mr. Mind! Only a little worm, but he had the whole world worried." However, Marvel is wrong: That's *not* the end of the fiend. As it happens, worms from Mr. Mind's planet can only be stunned by electricity. When he arrived at the taxidermist, the insect took over the man's mind and had him create an artificial worm, while Mr. Mind spun a cocoon and went into hibernation. Awaking after a nap of nearly thirty years, the megalomaniac alien bug resumed his battle with Captain Marvel. Mr. Mind is approximately two inches long and his skin is green, save for a black back and red spots on the side. He has a pair of stubby antennae on his head.

Comment. The nefarious insect first appeared in Fawcett's *Captain Marvel Adventures* in no. 22 (as a voice), and no. 23 (in the flesh). See also Captain Marvel's foe **Mr. Tawky Tawny**, the talking tiger.

MR. PEABODY

Pedigree. Time-traveling dog of TV fame.

Biography. Dressed in a bow tie and glasses, the unflappable, prim Mr. Peabody is a brilliant bipedal beagle scientist, and Sherman is his shrill, nerdy but clever adopted human son. After the dog opens each adventure by declaring, "Hello, out there. Peabody here," he and the boy climb into the Way-Back Machine and visit different historical periods, invariably making certain that events occur as history says they should. (The dog's time-traveling unit is sometimes referred to in print as the WABAC machine, a nonsense acronym parodying early computers such as UNIVAC). Among the diverse historical figures they've visited are Napoleon, the Wright Brothers, Custer, Francis Scott Key, John L. Sullivan, Louis Pasteur, William Tell, James Whistler, Magellan, Jules Verne, Henry VIII, Cleopatra, Beethoven, Sir Isaac Newton, Marconi, Marco Polo, and Lucretia Borgia.

Comment. Jay Ward Productions made ninety-two cartoons for *The Improbable History of Mr. Peabody* segment of *Rocky and His Friends,* which began airing on ABC in 1959; the cartoons were also seen on *The Bullwinkle Show* in 1961. Bill Scott was the voice of Peabody; Walter Tetley, of Sherman. The characters were also seen in stories that ran in comic books featuring **Rocky and Bullwinkle.**

MR. TAWKY TAWNY

Pedigree. A talking tiger befriended by the comic book superhero Captain Marvel.

Biography. When the nontalking Mr. Tawny is a cub in India, his mother is shot by a hunter. Given a home by Thomas Todd, a missionary's son, the tiger is happy—until a man is slain by a tiger and Mr. Tawny is blamed. Fearing for his pet's life, Thomas flees with him into the jungle, where they meet a hermit-scientist who has invented a serum that "will energize his brain and enable him to use his vocal cords for speech." Sure enough, after lapping the serum from a dish, Mr. Tawny looks at his friend and says, "Hello, Tom! Say, it sure is swell to talk like you humans." Finding and killing the tiger that killed the man, Mr. Tawny explains his own innocence to the natives ("See, folks? This paw-print, left by the killer, exactly matches his! That clears me of the crime!") and is exonerated. Soon thereafter, Tom's father is transferred, and the talking tiger goes to live with the hermit . . . who discovers that the serum is causing other changes in Mr. Tawny, enabling him to walk on two legs and turning his paws into hands. In time, Mr. Tawny grows "tired of the jungle" and yearns to see civilization, to experience "clothes and ice cream cones, and movies!" Sneaking onboard a ship (and moaning that the hermit "didn't tell me about sea sickness! *Groan!*"), the tiger comes ashore where he is spotted by Billy Batson, who is secretly the superhero Captain Marvel. Before the tiger has a chance to explain who he is, Marvel socks him unconscious and brings him to the zoo. Ripping apart the bars, Mr. Tawny goes for a stroll. He sits down in a restaurant ("Bring me some meat," he tells the waiter, adding, "Make it raw!"), then goes to a clothing shop and selects a jacket and tie (on his own, because the tailor flees). Upon leaving, he bumps into Captain Marvel again; this time, the tiger gets to explain that all he wants is "to lead a civilized life here among you human beings." With Captain Marvel's help, Mr. Tawny becomes a lecturer on nature and animals at the local natural history museum. In his second appearance, he uses his supersensitive nose to pick up the spoor of a killer after Tom is wrongly accused of murder. In another story, Billy Batson sponsors a contest to find Mr. Tawny a first name; the winning entry is Tawky. The tiger continues to work at the museum, although he also moonlights as a model for the Hubb Clothing Company.

Comment. The chatty cat first appeared in Fawcett's *Captain Marvel Adventures* no. 79 in 1948. In some stories, the character was used as a metaphor for racial prejudice, as when people objected to him moving into their neighborhood. See also Captain Marvel's foe **Mr. Mind.**

MR. WILD WOLF
Pedigree. Nasty TV character who preys on Mapletown.
Biography. Mapletown is an idyllic village ("Each day we laugh and we play," says the theme song) inhabited entirely by anthropomorphic, clothed animals like Bernard Beaver and his daughter Bitsy and son Bucky (the boy has a "strange talent" for being able to predict bad weather), Danny Dog, Bobby Bear, Patty Rabbit, Mayor Lion, Penny Pig, Fanny Fox, Kirby Cat, and the sheriff (a bulldog). The only bummer is that these loving, cheerful animals are regularly troubled by Mapletown's "most wanted criminal," Mr. Wild Wolf. Dressed in a torn, red straw hat and shoes and tattered coat that doubles as a cloak, the raspy-voiced biped has a long, crooked

snout and a tail like a bare twig. Although it isn't known whether or not Mr. Wild Wolf has ever tried to eat any of Mapletown's inhabitants (the show is for *really* young children), he doesn't hesitate to slink from the woods to lie or steal. His ambition is to wreck every building in Mapletown.

Comment. The half-hour episodes of Saban Productions *Mapletown* were first syndicated in 1988. The lush backgrounds and moral-laden stories are undercut by terrible animation (each drawing is photographed on two successive frames of film instead of one, making the characters extremely jerky).

MIYAMOTO USAGI
Pedigree. Sword-swinging bunny bodyguard for hire.
Biography. Usagi lives in a nameless world structured like feudal Japan but inhabited by talking, bipedal pigs, monkeys, cats, bears, and the like. Usagi is originally a devoted retainer to Lord Mifune. When his master is slain by Lord Hikiji in the Battle of Adachigahara Plain, Usagi, now a rabbit ronin (masterless samurai) becomes a nomadic yojimbo (bodyguard). Usually, Usagi is honorable to a fault. Hired to protect the rhino bounty hunter Gennosuke on a dangerous mission, the rabbit has the opportunity to let him die and collect the entire reward. Instead, he fulfills his employment contract—and gets stiffed for the half he was supposed to receive. Some stories are short and humorous, such as Usagi's efforts to get rid of a horse he'd taken from a bandit, not realizing it had been stolen from a town magistrate who is determined to get it back; some are steeped in tragedy, like his struggle with the ninja Shingen, who erroneously blames Usagi for having slaughtered his village. The series also boasts exquisitely sinister characters, such as the giant snake Lord Hebi. The hare dresses in traditional samurai garb and is so fast with a blade that, on one occasion, he slices the points from a pair of spears that have been thrown at him.

Comment. This one's a class act. Stan Sakai's literate, atmospheric creation first appeared in no. 1 of *Albedo,* published by Thoughts and Images in 1985. Usagi moved to Fantagraphics Books's *Critters* with no. 1 in 1986, before getting his own Fantagraphics title, *Usagi Yojimbo,* in 1987.

Miyamoto Usagi *displays his prowess . . . and luck! © Stan Sakai.*

MOBY DICK

Pedigree. TV cartoon whale in continuing adventures, unrelated to Melville.

Biography. When a storm batters their ship *The Sea Explorer,* youngsters Tom and Tubb are saved from sharks by a benevolent white whale. The boys are returned to the magnificent underwater city where they live. Whenever they don their sleek diving suits, venture out, and get into trouble, all they or any nearby sea creature has to do is call "Moby!" and the great, white whale will come. (The boys' pet seal Scooby once croaked out the name when the lads were "swallowed" by a flying saucer disguised as a giant clam, and the whale hurried to save them.) Moby's tail is powerful enough to smash through undersea mountains; if he is stranded on land, the whale has been known to wriggle hundreds of yards to water. The whale is approximately twenty-five feet long. Among the trio's foes have been pirates; the "electrifying Shoctopus"; Aqua-Bats; Moraya

the Eel Queen; Toadus, Ruler of the Dead Ships; the Crab Men; the Shark Men; and the Iguana Men.

Comment. Hanna-Barbera produced eighteen cartoons in all, which aired on the CBS series *Moby Dick and the Mighty Mightor* from 1967 to 1969. Mightor is a prehistoric superhero who works in conjunction with a brave dodo bird named Ork, a winged dinosaur named Tog, and a baby woolly mammoth named Rollo.

MOBY DUCK

Pedigree. Sailor-duck from a Walt Disney TV show and comic books.

Biography. Because **Donald Duck** wears a sailor suit, it was only natural that a real sailor-duck eventually join the duck lineup. Moby has a more rounded bill than Donald, and a more human body; he has thick brown eyebrows, and longish brown hair tumbling down from the sides of his head (none on top, though). Dressed in blue trousers and a black-and-red striped shirt, smoking a corncob pipe and wielding a mean cutlass when necessary, he sails the seas in his small tug, transporting goods, investigating mysteries, singing while he accompanies himself on the accordion, or just fishing and enjoying the sea. Moby has an unparalleled knowledge of the seas, which he shares in his first appearance, as host of *Pacifically Peeking,* an hour-long special that aired on *Walt Disney's Wonderful World of Color* (1967, NBC). Moby has a Long John Silver voice and inflection *(Pacific* becomes "Percific," and his speech is littered with "Aye, mateys!"), but these add to his old salt charm. Moby is scrupulously honest ("I never even robbed an oyster!") and, in the comics, is assisted by his mate Dimwitty, a duck who wears blue coveralls, a navy blue tie, and a green party hat, has half-lidded eyes and a mass of brown hair, and rarely says anything more enlightened than, "Gawrsh," "Duh-h . . ." or "Aye-aye." Also never faraway is Moby's pet porpoise Porpy, who swims alongside their ship.

Comment. The characters were created by animators Ward Kimball, Hamilton Luske, and writer Bill Berg. Paul Frees provided the voice. Moby made his comic book debut in *Donald Duck* no. 112 in 1965, then went on to star in thirty issues of his own title, published by Gold Key from 1967 to 1978.

MORTY THE DOG

Pedigree. Hero of existential comic book.
Biography. A hound, Morty has no idea how he got in jail. Miraculously, though, the prison door is open, and he leaves with his cellmate, a human named Arnie. Morty's goal: To "go out there and kick butt . . . sink our teeth into a leg or two." Burying their jail cell, which is a box in the middle of a plain, they meet various bizarre characters until they find "the end of the rainbow." All they discover there, underground, is their cell . . . although after all the oddballs they met, they're glad to be back.

Comment. There was just one issue of Morty's comic, published by Starhead Comix in 1986. Steve Willis created this unique, little-known character.

MOTLEY THE CAT

Pedigree. Comic strip cat with a mean streak.
Biography. A fluffy white cat, Motley lives in suburbia with Tom and Nancy Kane and their children Sharon and Joey, and is interested in two things: his own well-being, and the discomfort of others. One marvelous strip sums up the latter facet of Motley's personality, as an easy chair reflects on how the cat has "torn the other chairs in this house to shreds." In a fit of blind panic, the seat causes its own springs to pop, and fabric to rip. Motley watches, then walks

A jubilant **Morty the Dog,** who's about to learn that bliss is illusory.
© STARHEAD COMICS AND STEVE WILLIS.

*A typically wonderful (and rambunctious) moment with **Motley the Cat**.*

away contentedly, thinking, "Once you establish a reputation you don't have to work nearly as hard." Motley is strong: He's clawed through the front door when left outside too long, and slashed through the car door en route to the vet. Motley is clever: He pretends to have to go out, makes Tom hold open the door, walks away as Tom screams, "Why did you make me stand here holding this door open?" then settles on a heat vent, thinking, "It's the only way I know of to make the furnace come back on." Motley also loves to capture and eat other animals, especially fish, mice, and birds. Birds, though, regularly give him trouble: Woodpeckers play dentist on his teeth and bluejays dive bomb him and peck his head (then get him with a joybuzzer "to add insult to injury"). One surprisingly strong bird flew off with him and left him stranded atop a statue, and another perched on the top of a tree, bent it down, then released it when Motley climbed up, sending the cat toward a target pinned to a tree. And he once fell for "the old exploding-robin trick," attacking a booby-trapped dummy left by a couple of birds. However, if the cat doesn't feel like moving, the prospect of nabbing an animal won't stir him. Told to chase a mouse

once, he sits still and reflects, "One more mouse this year would put me in a higher tax bracket." Motley also wages war on vacuum cleaners, not only because he hates the noise, but "because we compete for the same food supply." Motley's only known relative is his father, an alley cat who lives on the other side of town and is as violent as any cat ever born.

   Comment. Motley appears in the long-running comic strip "Wright Angles," which was created by Larry Wright in 1980. It's easily the most ingenious of all the contemporary cat strips.

MOTORMOUSE
Pedigree. TV mouse . . . with a twist.
Biography. Motormouse owns and operates the Spin Your Wheels Garage. Autocat is a chunky tan cat who wears a helmet and too tight vest, and likes to race. The cat is constantly egging the mouse on, persuading him to race—and always loses to the rodent. Autocat has a sadistic streak rare even for cartoon cats: Instead of eating him, Autocat yearns to place Motormouse beneath a lift and lower a car onto him. (Would the quivering purists at ACT allow such delicious cruelty today?) The masterpiece of Autocat's arsenal is the huge Mouse Stomper, a

Motormouse *makes a getaway from one of the cockamamy vehicles contrived by Auto Cat.*
© HANNA-BARBERA PRODUCTIONS.

steamroller with feet on it for crushing mice. The cat and mouse both talk and walk upright.

Comment. The characters appeared in thirty-four cartoon adventures, which were seen on Hanna-Barbera's ABC-TV series starring **The Cattanooga Cats.** Reruns were shown on the *Motormouse and Autocat* show, which aired in 1970. Dick Curtis was Motormouse while Marty Ingels provided the voice of Autocat. The animals also appeared in Gold Key's comic *Hanna-Barbera Fun-in* nos. 5, 7, and 9, in 1970 to 1971.

MS. LION
Pedigree. Prissy dog in the Spider-Man comic book.
Biography. Something along the lines of a Lhasa apso, Ms. Lion is the pet dog of May Parker, aunt of Peter Parker, a k a the superhero Spider-Man. The playful pup lives with the elderly woman at Aunt May's Boarding House in Shady Glen, a small town near New York City. She occasionally helps the hero with his cases, as when she found the villainous Kraven the Hunter by following his scent.

Comment. The character first appeared on the 1981 TV series *Spider-Man and His Amazing Friends,* and also costarred in the one-issue Marvel Comics magazine of the same name.

MUMBLY
Pedigree. Sleuthing TV dog.
Biography. Sniggering and muttering like the popular **Muttley** (whom he resembles), the burly Mumbly is a canine version of TV's Columbo, working for Chief Inspector Schnooker, who was clearly inspired

by Kojak. Luck and occasional underhandedness have more to do with his successful crime busting than skill. Among his self-explanatory cases are *Sherlock's Badder Brudder, The Return of Bing Bong,* and *Hyde and Seek.*

Comment. Hanna-Barbera's bland and boring *Mumbly* show debuted on ABC in 1976; there were a total of sixteen episodes. Don Messick was the voice of Mumbly, John Stephenson of Schnooker. When the show was canceled, the character was moved to *Laff-a-lympics* where he became a frankly more interesting bad guy, the head of the Really Rottens.

MUTTLEY
Pedigree. Nasty TV dog, companion to the even nastier human Dick Dastardly.
Biography. In their first cartoon incarnation, the devilish duo enter a variety of races early in this century, driving a souped-up vehicle known as the Mean Machine, and cheating to win. *("Fair?* That's a drag!" Dastardly says at the start of a race.) About the only time Muttley has ever deserted his master is when Dastardly asked him to open the cage of the giant ape King Klong. In their second TV series, the perfidious pair fly their biplane as part of the Vulture Squadron during World War I. Their one and only task: to capture the bold Yankee Doodle Pigeon, a bugle-blowing bird who delivers messages for the Americans. The chunky, yellow mutt doesn't talk: He just snarls and snickers his smug, wheezing laugh. In fantasy segments on the latter series, titled *The Magnificent Muttley,* the dog imagines himself

34

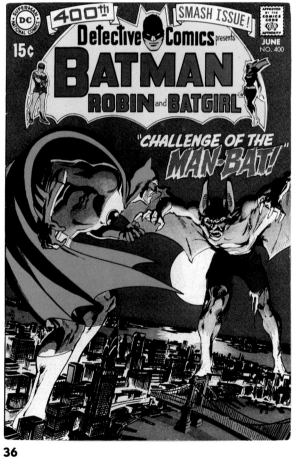

36

34. **KAT KARSON** meets his doppelgänger.
35. **KOKO**, with Koala on the vacuum.
    That's Muggsy Mouse they're chasing.
36. The debut of **MAN-BAT**. © DC Comics.
37. **MAX THE RABBIT** and Sam take pride
    (and delight) in their work. © Steve Purcell.

38

39

40

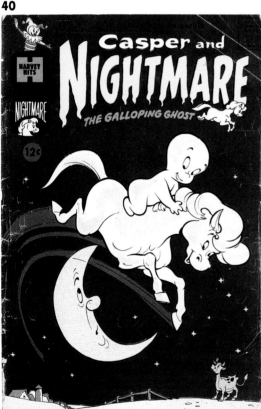

41

42

38. McSNURTLE THE TURTLE, THE TERRIFIC WHATZIT, *"dreams" of wearing his costume, which is identical to that of the 1940s superhero the Flash.* © DC Comics.

39. *From the left:* **MOBY DUCK**, **SCROOGE McDUCK**, *and Dimwitty.* © The Walt Disney Company. *All rights reserved.*

40. NIGHTMARE, *with Caspar the friendly Ghost on its back.* © Harvey Publications.

41. NUGGET, *feeling left out, as usual.* © Big Boy Restaurants.

42. PETER PIG *and Punchy have one of their regular disagreements. Note the hatchet.*

43

46

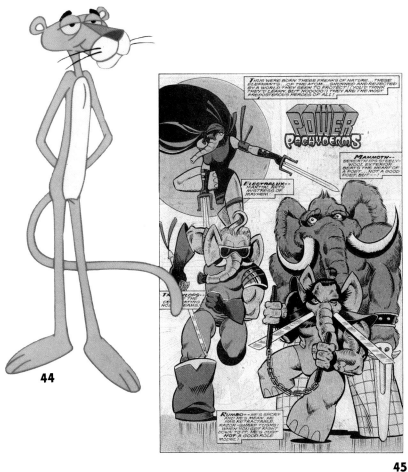

44

45

43. *Lean and sly,* **PETER PORKCHOPS** *is nobody's fool.*

44. *So suave, so cool, so...pink.* **THE PINK PANTHER.**

45. *Even if they weren't superpowered, who'd mess with the*
POWER PACHYDERMS? From their debut issue.

46. *The indomitable* **REX THE WONDER DOG.**

47. **ROON,** *hallucinating that a jackrabbit has become a monster, turns tail and runs. Art by* JACK SPARLING.

47

48

49

51

50

52

48. *The sly, utterly devoted* **RUFFERTO**. © Sergio Aragones.

49. **SAM SIMEON** *on the job.* © DC Comics.

50. *Joe Kubert's superb rendering of* **SGT. GORILLA** *in action.* © DC Comics.

51. *Don't let those cute smiles deceive you:* **SPACE BEAVER** *and Tog know how to use those blasters!* © Darick Robertson.

52. *Walter Lantz's little-known interplanetary hero* **SPACE MOUSE.**
© 1957 by Walter Lantz Productions, Inc.

53

54

55

56

53. *A herd of animal stars that appeared in* **SPIDER-HAM***'s first issue: Hulk Bunny to the right, Captain Americat on the bottom, and Goose Rider on the bottom right.* © 1991 MARVEL ENTERTAINMENT GROUP. *All rights reserved.*

54. **SUN**, **THE 4-D MONKEY** *surrounded by Karate Pig and Ninja Flounder.* © LEUNG'S PUBLICATIONS.

55. **SUPER CHICKEN** *playing free and easy with Fred's life.* © WARD PRODUCTIONS. *Courtesy Jay Ward.*

56. *The gallant, poetic* **SUPERMOUSE** *and Mabel.*

57

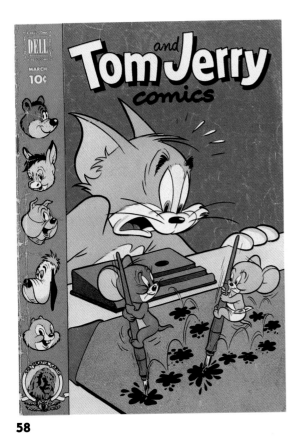

59

58

57. **THE THREE MOUSEKETEERS**, *old style...and new.* © DC Comics.
58. **TOM AND JERRY**: **JERRY** *(left) and Tuffy up to no good. On the left-hand side of the page (from the top) are* **BARNEY BEAR**, *Benny Burro, Spike,* **DROOPY**, *and Wuff the Prairie Dog.* © Turner Home Entertainment.
59. *Timorous* **TOMMY TURTLE**, *whose shell always looks as if it's about to slide off.*
60. **TOP CAT** *and his brood (clockwise from his right): Choo Choo, Fancy-Fancy, Benny the Ball, Spook, and Brain.* © Hanna-Barbera Productions.

60

61

62

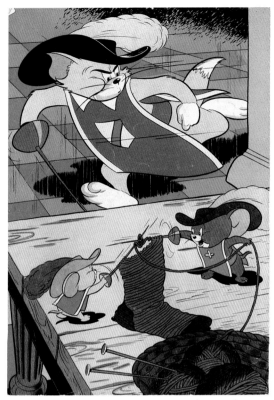

61. What constitutes a crisis for **TOP DOG**? Being struck speechless. © 1991 MARVEL ENTERTAINMENT GROUP. All rights reserved.
62. The practical **TWO MOUSEKETEERS** and their nemesis. © TURNER HOME ENTERTAINMENT.
63. **UNDERDOG**, with Sweet Polly Purebred. © LEONARDO-T.T.V.
64. **WACKY DUCK**, brashly making his own rules. Note the squared-off bill to make him different from earlier screen and comic book ducks. © 1991 MARVEL ENTERTAINMENT GROUP. All rights reserved.
65. **WEAKHEART (2)**. The "whine line" says it all. © WESTERN PUBLISHING CO.

64

65

66. *A brilliant little portrait of* **WONDER WART-HOG**.
© 1971, 1988 *by* GILBERT SHELTON. *Used by permission. Reprinted from*
Underground Comics no. 5 published by Rip Off Press, Inc.

67. *A rare comic book panel showing* **WOODY WOODPECKER** *(right) with*
(from the right) Knothead, Splinter, and Winnie. © UNIVERSAL PICTURES.

68. **YOGI BEAR** *(right) and* **BOO BOO BEAR** *pictured on the first issue of their*
Marvel Comics magazine © HANNA-BARBERA PRODUCTIONS.

69. **THE ZOO CREW** *on the cover of their first issue (from the left): Rubberduck,*
Fastback, Alley-Kat-Abra, Captain Carrot, Yankee Poodle, and Pig-Iron. That's
Superman, bound in chains of kryptonite. © DC COMICS.

to be dog versions of great figures of fact and fiction, e.g., The Masked Muttley (a Lone Ranger parody), Mutt-Dini, Leonardo De Muttley, Wild Mutt Muttley, Astromutt, and others.

Comment. The Hanna-Barbera villains were seen on the series *The Wacky Races*, thirty-four episodes of which ran on CBS from 1968 to 1970; and on *Dastardly and Muttley in Their Flying Machines*, thirty-four cartoons airing on CBS from 1969 to 1971; there were sixteen cartoons in *The Magnificent Muttley* series. Don Messick provided Mutley's voice. Gold Key published seven issues of *The Wacky Races* comic book (1969 to 1972); the flying-machine incarnation appeared in *Hanna-Barbera Fun-in* nos. 1, 5, 7, 9, and 10. In 1976, an almost identical dog surfaced on ABC in Hanna-Barbera's *Mumbly (see* entry).

MUTTSY
Pedigree. The army dog of the *Sad Sack* comic book.

Biography. The military dog wasn't consistently the same kind of mutt, or even the same color—but he was always wearing the same blanket with his name on the side, along with K-9 dog tags. Initially, Muttsy was mostly window dressing, looking on as the soldiers interacted. Later, to give him more of a

role in the strip (especially when he got his own comic book), Muttsy acquired the ability to talk. Like most army dogs (see **Otto**), Muttsy's primary concerns are eating (hot dogs are a favorite), sleeping, chasing cats, and fighting with other dogs (he was zero help while serving as a sled dog, because he spent all his time nipping at the rougher, bigger huskies).

Comments. "Sad Sack" made its debut in 1942, in the army's *Yank* magazine. It was created by George Baker, a former Disney animator. Muttsy wasn't added to the lineup until Harvey Comics began a successful line of Sad Sack comic books in 1949—including *Sad Sack's Muttsy, The Talking Dog,* which was featured in nineteen issues of the *Harvey Hits* title from 1963 to 1967. *Harvey Hits* also published five issues titled *Little Sad Sack* (which ran from 1963 to 1964; *Little Sad Sack* then started its own nineteen-issue run from 1964 to 1967). Featured was the small dog Pupsy, who also wore an embroidered blanket.

MYRON MOOSE
Pedigree. Underground comic book moose.

Biography. Myron is a moose with a "sinus condition," which causes his nose to run incessantly. Many of the one-to-four page gags describe the un-

*The apologetic **Myron Moose.** © BOB FOSTER.*

assuming moose's efforts to control the drip . . . and the inevitable failure of these remedies, such as corks and knots popping, buckets overflowing, and so on. (Only once was the problem beneficial: when he couldn't get his **Mickey Mouse** watch to work, and the "drip" did the trick.) Other pages are devoted to Myron in parodies of popular books, films, and comic books, such as Bat Moose (Batman), Plastic Moose (Plastic Man), Little Orphan Moose (Little Orphan Annie), Fritz the Moose (**Fritz the Cat**), Citizen Moose *(Citizen Kane)*, Steamboat Moose (Mickey Mouse's *Steamboat Willie)*, *The Shneen in the Latrine (The Cat in the Hat* spoof), and the send-up of a classic EC Comics cover from *Weird Science-Fantasy* as *Weird Moose-Fantasy*, featuring the moose as a barbarian.

Comment. Myron Moose Comic Book Works published two issues of *Myron Moose Funnies* (1971 and 1973); Fantagraphics Books published two issues in 1987. The character was "created, written, and drawn by that darn Renaissance man" Bob Foster. A different Myron, a quadruped, was seen in Vince Davis's *Travels with Myron*, which appeared in Marvel's *Comix Book* no. 1 in 1974. In it, an idealistic youth mounts the moose and rides off in search of the real America. Unfortunately, not long after he sets out, Myron is repossessed because of late payments. This moose doesn't speak.

NAIVE INTER-DIMENSIONAL COMMANDO KOALAS

Pedigree: Comic book koala bear musicians.

Biography. Rock musicians in Australia of another world, the koalas are all named Bruce. In the midst of playing "the *loudest* song they have written to date," they're suddenly transported to our earth. Pelted with fruit by angry New Yorkers (who think the koalas are from Philly), the animals eventually fall into the hands of the military and become secret operatives.

Comment. The characters had a short run in their own Independent Comics Group magazine, published in 1986; **The Adolescent Radioactive Black Belt Hamsters** guest starred in the first. The "joke" of calling all the animals Bruce was derived from a Monty Python TV skit in which all the soldiers in an Australian unit were named Bruce.

NAPOLEON

Pedigree. Early dog comic strip.

Biography. Napoleon is a skinny, awkward black-and-white mutt who is taken in by the portly Uncle Elby. At first, the duo became involved with the likes of the sailor Singapore Sam and partook in his fanciful adventures. Later, the characters became stay-at-homers whose escapades were geared to gags or slapstick.

Comment. Clifford McBride's cartoon dog is based on a big St. Bernard which was owned by MacBride's uncle, Elby Eastman (the prototype for Uncle Elby). Napoleon and Elby first appeared on May 5, 1929 in a nameless McBride strip; they were brought back a number of times, and proved so popular that they were given their own strip, "Napoleon and Uncle Elby," on June 6, 1932. The strip had a remarkable run of twenty-eight years.

NATO, THE SAMURAI SQUIRREL

Pedigree. A sword-swinging squirrel in a barbaric comic book world.

Biography. Nothing is known about this character's origins, or about his world. Nato and his brother Malik are bold warriors in a primitive world dominated by the evil of Emperor Mordak, a rat, whose brutish soldiers they're only too happy to slay. ("My best guards tricked by a *squirrel!*" Mordak roars at one point.) Nato has an extremely well-developed sense of smell.

Comment. The character appeared in two issues of *Samurai Squirrel*. He was created by Kelley Jarvis and published by Spotlight Comics in 1986. That same issue featured the one adventure of the Nuclear Spawned Martial Arts Frogs, in which an atomic reactor leaks radiation into a pond, causing tadpoles to evolve into highly intelligent frogs. Finding a book on martial arts, they teach themselves the skills and decide, "Since it was *man* who made us, so it will be *man* we defend." The frogs were part of the post–**Teenage Mutant Ninja Turtles** radiation boom, as was yet another samurai animals series: the saga of Zatoichi Walrus, who is entirely human, save for his walrus head. He's also blind. His adventures in the contemporary world of humans was chronicled in two issues of Solson Publications unimaginative *Bushido Blade of Zatoichi Walrus* (1987). More interesting than the steady "Zato" is one of his nemeses, the lisping assassin-duck Panju, who truly loves his work.

Nato, the Samurai Squirrel. © KELLEY JARVIS.

NAZRAT

Pedigree. Comic book rat and insurrectionist.

Biography. The claustrophobic rat and his sidekick Kipper, a humanoid dog, live in the medievallike Great Empire of England in the times of King Hank IV. Possessing a lean, human body with a rat's head and tail, Nazrat is "an excitable sort [who] always thinks with his spleen, never with his noggin." Enemies of the monarch, the snide Nazrat and jolly Kipper spend much of their time on the lam, relying on Kipper's nose to tell them who smells "right" and can be trusted. Nazrat is friends with several revolutionary humans.

Comment. Eternity Comics published five issues of Jerry Frazee's gritty *Nazrat* in 1986 to 1987.

Nazrat: Not your typical Mickey Mouse–style rodent! © JERRY FRAZEE.

NEIL THE HORSE

Pedigree. A simple-minded, talking comic book horse.

Biography. Neil is a black horse with big, black eyes and pipe cleaner–thin legs; his inseparable companion is gruff Soapy the cat. According to the strip, Neil's "good qualities include: stupidity, gluttony, gullibility, naivete, strong legs, a big smile." As for the cigar-smoking Soapy, his "good points are: greed, cynicism, base cunning, sarcasm, alcoholism, violence, dishonesty, and a soft heart." The two first meet when Neil is out looking for food, and Soapy agrees to show him to an unlocked barn. Shortly thereafter, Neil is abducted by carnival owner Adam Footstool, fitted with false fangs, and put on display

Neil the Horse and Soapy. Note similarity of the artistic style with the early *Oswald, the Lucky Rabbit*. © 1990 BY ARN SABA.

in a sideshow as a saber tooth tiger (!). Soapy rescues him, although the cat negotiates a fee for Neil to inhale helium and pose as an elephant. Unfortunately, he floats away, with Soapy on his back, and they have a run-in with the insane dog-barnstormer Gaston Piston. Surviving that, they have other adventures among the walking, talking animals and few humans of their world (Hell's Ducks and Canine the Barbarian). They are joined, later in the series, by the sweet marionette Mam'selle Poupée. Among the threesome's most harrowing exploits is a space flight to the Soft Universe, where they're arrested by plush toys "for failing to meet common standards of softness [as] dictated by the Ministry of Corrective Reupholstery." They escape with the help of a soldier-doll who falls in love with Mam'selle.

Comment. Neil was created by Arn Saba and first appeared in Canadian newspapers in 1975. The artwork is, at times, reminiscent of the best of Winsor McCay and Will Eisner; perspective and animation are superb. Neil's first comic book publication was in *Charlton Bullseye* no. 2 in 1981; he got his own comic book in 1983, published by Aardvark-Vanaheim (to no. 10; by Renegade Press thereafter). There were paper dolls in no. 13. Along with **Cerebus the Aardvark** and a handful of other characters, Neil helped to establish the viability of comic books published by companies other than the giants Marvel and DC.

NELLIE
Pedigree. Temperamental comic strip horse.
Biography. Texas Slim and Dirty Dalton work for modernday rancher Mr. Akers in Texas. Nellie is Slim's brown, fleet, brave, but easily angered horse. After the strip's hiatus (see "Comment"), the horse returned looking more realistic and having much less personality. Texas's love interest is Jessie Akers; another animal seen in the strip was "Miss Jessie's" tenacious little brown dog, Valentino, who was sent to her by her uncle in Boston.

Comment. Ferd Johnson's "Texas Slim" debuted in the Chicago *Tribune* on August 30, 1925 and ran until 1928; it was revived as "Texas Slim and Dirty Dalton" and ran from 1940 to 1958.

NEWTON, THE RABBIT WONDER
Pedigree. Extradimensional, very human comic book hare.
Biography. When earth's pollution threatens to seep into a dimension of anthropomorphic animals, the monkey Fenton goes through the dimensional "hole-

gap" to examine the problem. When he fails to return, Newton, the Rabbit Wonder is sent to find him. Learning that Fenton was mistaken for a lab animal and sent into space, the jackrabbit goes to the research center and, posing as an earth rabbit, is launched into space with human passengers. Resetting the course to Antares, Fenton's destination, Newton uses his martial arts skills to overcome the captain (who is already rather nonplussed, having just exclaimed, "Holy shit! A talking rabbit!"). Befriending the other crewmember, Monica, Newton locates the world on which Fenton landed. It happens to be a planet populated entirely by female monkeys . . . and Newton generously allows Fenton to stay behind. In his next "dimensional jump" adventure, he finds himself on a primitive world where he battles the Barbarian Bunny; the adventure of the cowbunny Range Rabbit followed.

Comment. The character first appeared in Star*Reach Productions's *Quack* no. 2 in 1977. Other characters that appeared in *Quack* during its five-issue run included the comic book aficionados, the Beavers; Kerwin Keystone, "half aardvark, half platypus," a castaway on the Planet of the Ducks; and E. Z. Wolf, part of an ensemble of hillbilly characters including Sis Fox, insane artist Vincent Van Hogh ("I'm using my own feces as a base for th' pigments," the pig says, explaining that he can paint all he wants, as long as he eats), the pig Sheriff Alabama, Brer Bill Goat and his dog Huncher, and Denver Goose, a singer ("So I went to the desert / to go swimming / there I saw sweet Jesus / and he jus' splashed that water"). (The Ted Richards character actually had its start in the underground press several years earlier.)

NIGHTMARE
Pedigree. Ghost-horse featured in Casper comic books.
Biography. Nicknamed "the galloping ghost," the all white Nightmare is that wonderful rarity: a dead cartoon animal. Nightmare lives on our world, can speak to other ghosts, has the power to become invisible, fly, pass through solid objects, talk to clouds, and even catch bullets in its teeth. One of Nightmare's closest animal friends is Harry the (dead) Horsefly. Whenever people are around, Nightmare becomes invisible so as not to scare them. The horse is especially fond of apples.

Comment. The spectral steed first appeared in Harvey Comics's *Casper the Friendly Ghost* no. 19 in 1954. *Nightmare and Casper* began publication in 1963 and lasted forty-six issues (Casper got top billing starting with no. 6). Another animal who pops up in the Casper strip is the young Bertie Bear. Now and then, Harvey Comics also features the horse Danny Dobbin, who is white with black spots and a black mane. Danny, who can speak, appears in the Stumbo the Giant strip.

NIGHTWIND

Pedigree. Mount for long-running western hero, the Rawhide Kid.

Biography. Perceived as an outlaw, Rawhide is actually a force for justice in the old west. Like most comic book cowboys, he talks a great deal to his valiant white horse for the sake of exposition. ("Nightwind! Looks like we're just in time! Those rannies just robbed the *bank!*")

Comment. Nightwind arrived early in the 151-run of Marvel Comics popular western hero, which lasted from 1957 to 1979. Prior to Nightwind, the Kid rode the horse Apache. See other Marvel cowboy horses **Banshee, Cyclone,** and **Steel.** See also **Sandy** (2) for two different horses named Nightwind.

NOOZLES

Pedigree. TV koalas, one of whom is magic.

Biography. Blinky and Pinky are a brother and sister pair of koalas who leave Koalawalaland and move in with a young girl named Sandy Brown. The two-foot tall, rational male Blinky is an ordinary koala; the one-foot-tall, extremely temperamental female Pinky has a small shoulderbag in which she keeps magic artifacts. These include a wandlike lipstick that allows her to create a portal to Koalawalaland, and a magic compact that she can use to look at objects anywhere in the world. Pinky can also fly and starts to sneeze whenever people are talking about her. Blinky is the more responsible of the two bears, always encouraging the reluctant Pinky to do everyday things without the use of magic; being lazy, Pinky argues and resists. The only time they band together is when there's danger, as when Sandy's archaeologist father is lost in Egypt. When anyone else is around, Blinky pretends to be a doll, and Pinky vanishes. As for Koalawalaland, humans are not allowed to visit there (the one time Sandy goes, she has to dress as a koala). *Why* anyone would want to go there is a mystery. One of several worlds (Kangarooland is another) hanging in a perpetually blue sky, it's a Brave New World where Koalas are all raised in incubators, don't have real mothers, and live in communal stone houses. The population is kept in line by the Eucalyptus Patrol, which flies through the skies in small "pods" and looks like the Gestapo. A platypus is in charge of the immigration office.

Comment. The half-hour *Noozles* episodes from Saban Productions began airing in syndication in 1988. Like the company's *Mapletown* (See **Mr. Wild Wolf**), the animation is subpar, although the backgrounds are exquisite and the stories are relatively sophisticated.

NUGGET

Pedigree. Dog companion to Big Boy hamburger mascot.

Biography. The dog—apparently a terrier of some kind—is the companion of Big Boy, mascot of the restaurant chain of the same name. Nugget talks directly to the reader, often fretting over his master's nutty undertakings or complaining about being left behind on an adventure. The white dog has black ears and a black spot on its back.

Comment. The dog appeared regularly in *The Adventures of Big Boy,* a giveaway comic book that made its debut in 1956 and remains in publication.

NUTSY SQUIRREL

Pedigree. A fun-loving, not-very-bright comic book squirrel.

Biography. Sometimes an inventor of useless objects (like the Galunk, a funnel that rolls a bowling ball with a loud *ga-LUNK,* hence the name), sometimes an imp (he once hitched himself to Santa's sleigh, just to romp alongside the reindeer), the good-natured Nutsy is most often found hitting up humans and animals alike for food. So doing, he becomes caught up in whatever adventure they're involved in. The blue-furred Nutsy wears orange trunks and a long red-and-white tie. Other animals in Nutsy's world include Hector the Collector, a pig, and Grover the Grocer, a dog. A human, the Professor, is also a regular (in one story, Nutsy unwittingly cooked and ate a dinosaur egg that was "800 zillion years old" and had to find a replacement).

Comment. Created by Rube Grossman, Nutsy made his debut in DC Comics's *Funny Folks* no. 1 in 1946. The magazine was renamed *Nutsy Squirrel* with no. 61 in 1954; the last issue was no. 72, in 1957. The character also appeared in *Comic Cavalcade* beginning with no. 30 in 1948.

THE ODDBALL COUPLE

Pedigree. TV cartoon, all-animal spoof of *The Odd Couple.*

Biography. Fleabag and Spiffy are reporters, but that's about all they have in common. Spiffy is a neat, thin, prissy cat; Fleabag is a pot-bellied, hopelessly messy dog. When they aren't nagging one another in domestic adventures such as *Spiffy's Nephew, A Day at the Beach,* and *Fleabag's Mother,* they manage to work on stories such as *Klondike Oil Kaper, Who's Afraid of Virginia Werewolf?, A Royal Mixup, Hotel Boo-More,* and *Jungle Bungle.* Their secretary, Goldie, is usually caught in the middle of their arguments.

   Comment. The De Patie-Freleng series aired on ABC from 1975 to 1977; there were thirty-two episodes in all. Paul Winchell was the voice of Fleabag (no one does a "slob" voice better than Winchell), and Frank Nelson was Spiffy.

OLD RED

Pedigree. Pet in the comic strip "Gasoline Alley."

Biography. The big, gangly bloodhound belongs to Walt Wallet and family, a typical middle-class group whose domestic escapades have delighted readers for decades. Other dogs in the strip are Sieg and Kleine, a Great Dane and Doberman pinscher, owned by Slim and Clovia Skinner. Also seen now and then is the baby donkey Torchy, who rides around in a cart with junkmen Joel and Rufus.

   Comment. The strip was created by Frank King and first appeared on November 24, 1918; the Skinner dogs and Torchy didn't arrive until the late 1960s, when Dick Moores took over the strip.

OLD WHIFF

Pedigree. One-of-a-kind cartoon dog.

Biography. Old Whiff is a bloodhound who loses his sense of smell and finds it again with the help of the human Inspector Dribble.

   Comment. Made in 1959, *The Tale of Old Whiff* not only has the distinction of being the first animated short subject filmed in 70 mm but the only one ever shot in Mike Todd, Jr.'s Smell-O-Vision process. It played in a handful of theaters equipped to show the Todd feature *Scent of Mystery.* Among the odors that accompanied the fifteen-minute subject were sausage, chocolate candy, a field of flowers, a horse (!), mustard, soap, and soup.

OLIVER THE CAT

Pedigree. Star of the Disney feature *Oliver & Company.*

Biography. When a group of kittens is set outside a market for passers-by to take, all but little Oliver are claimed. It begins to rain and, cold and hungry, the sad cat decides to leave the box. Soon, he meets the Dodger, "New York's coolest canine," a dog wearing a neckerchief and sunglasses. The streetwise mutt and Oliver plot to raid a hot dog cart at the corner: While the cat distracts the vendor by running up his apron, Dodger steals some food and runs off . . . without Oliver. Dodger heads to the barge owned by the human Fagin, for whom he robs wallets, food, and other items with the rest of the dogs—a gang consisting of Tito the Chihuahua, Francis the bulldog, the dumb Great Dane, Einstein, and the Afghan, Rita. However, Oliver has followed him and accidentally crashes through the weather-beaten roof. The dogs are impressed by the plucky cat, as is Fagin, who arrives shortly after. But the goodwill is short lived, as evil Sykes and his fierce Dobermans Roscoe and DeSoto show up. Fagin owes Sykes money, and while he begs for more time to pay, DeSoto goes to bite Oliver. Much to the dog's surprise, the kitten fights back, scratching his nose. A chase follows, and the cat is cornered by the Dobermans. Dodger leaps between them, but the dogs are undeterred: They say they'll have Dodger for the main course and the cat for dessert. But Sykes is finished with his business and, as he isn't one to be kept waiting, the dogs depart—promising to get the dog and cat "next time." The dogs go out early the next day, determined to get Fagin the money he needs. Spotting a limousine, Einstein and Francis occupy the chauffeur while Tito and Oliver slip inside the car to get the radio. But Oliver trips an alarm and becomes tangled in the wires; unable to escape with the dogs, he watches as a partition slides open and a little girl looks out from the back seat. The girl, Jenny, takes to the kitten at once. She brings him home, gives him cream and a collar with a name tag . . . and makes her family's spoiled pet poodle, Georgette, extremely jealous. While the poodle is busy admiring herself in the mirror, Fagin's dogs creep up beside her. When her screams subside, they explain that they want the cat back, and Georgette is only too happy to help. The poodle leads them to Jenny's room, where the cat is curled at the sleeping girl's side; the dogs shove him in a pillowcase and carry him back to the barge. Oliver is less than thrilled, and the angry Dodger tells him to go back to Fifth Avenue, if he wants. Hearing "Fifth Avenue," Fagin sees the prospect of reward money. He gets the address from Oliver's tag, and sends word to Jenny. She comes at once; seeing the affection between the girl and the cat, Fagin can't take money from her. Sykes, however, is not so munificent. He comes calling for his money, spots Jenny, and abducts her, convinced that someone will pay a handsome ransom. Fagin, the dogs, and Oliver pile into a sputtering motorbike and follow the kidnapper to his warehouse. They improvise a catapult to hurl Oliver inside, and the kitten opens the door to let in the rest of the dogs. They find Jenny tied to a chair—and, unfortunately, Sykes and the Dobermans find them. But before the villains can attack, Fagin charges in with his scooter, and the animals and Jenny climb aboard. They zoom off, Sykes and his dogs pursuing in their car. The vehicles end up racing along on train tracks, where the villain manages to catch up, grab Jenny, and pull her to the car; Oliver bites his hand and he releases the girl, but the cat ends up in the backseat of the car with the Dobermans. Dodger jumps in through the sun roof to save him—moments before a train comes barreling down the tracks. Fagin is able to avoid it, but Sykes does not. Dodger steps from the wreckage, the limp form of Oliver in his mouth. Jenny rushes over and strokes the cat—who revives, meowing weakly. The following day there's a party at Jenny's home, where the dogs celebrate their victory, and Oliver celebrates his new home.

Comment. The 1988 film was loosely but imaginatively based on Charles Dickens's *Oliver Twist* (originally serialized from 1837 to 1839). Voices (and songs) for the feature were provided by pop stars Bette Midler, Billy Joel, Cheech Marin, and others.

OMAHA THE CAT DANCER

Pedigree. Adult comics cat.
Biography. Omaha is an entirely human female (and voluptuously so), save for her cat head and long tail.

A dancer/stripper, she lives with a tabbylike cat-man named Chuck and toils at the Kitty Korner Klub in Mipple City, Minnesota. When strict new laws force the club to shut down, Omaha's dancer-friend Shelley gets her a gig: Restaurateur Charles Tabey is opening an expensive cafe and she's asked to dance there. On opening night, Charles's rival Andre DeRoc drugs the liquor, causing the guests to become violent. They chase the dancers, and in the ensuing confusion a killer hired to shoot Tabey plugs Shelley instead. After a series of close calls with the assassin, Chuck and Omaha head for San Francisco. Their car breaks down en route, and they're given a lift by the crooked poodle Sasha, and her equally sleazy bulldog pal Al. This sets them off on adventures that include Omaha's friendship with Senator Bonner, who is assassinated—a killing that puts the cat on the run, alone, leading her to a new low that includes (as of this writing) dancing at a bar in Wisconsin.

Comment. Created by Reed Waller, Omaha made her debut in the final issue (no. 9) of Kitchen Sink Comix comic book *Bizarre Sex* in 1980. She went on to star in her own title, which Steeldragon Press inaugurated in 1984; Kitchen Sink is now once again her publisher, and the strip is being written and drawn by Waller and Kate Worley. Coincidentally, an erotic dancer was also featured in the comic strip "Hepcats," which was created by Martin Wagner and ran in the University of Texas /Austin paper *Daily Texan* from 1987 to 1989, and got their own Double Diamond Press comic book in 1989. The stars of that strip are Joey and Gunther, a cat and rhino who are college roommates. The genus of the dancer, Erica, is indecipherable.

OPUS THE PENGUIN

Pedigree. Penguin-star of the comic strip "Bloom County."
Biography. Opus weighs thirty-six pounds, stands two feet, eleven inches, wears a red bow tie, plays the tuba, and was born on King George Island in Antarctica. Put up for adoption, he was raised in the Falkland Islands. He entered the comic strip (with a smaller, more pointed bill than he had later) as the pet of schoolboy Binkley. Initially, Opus is an inquisitive sort, but also wary of whatever he's told. At an antinuclear rally, a cockroach sidles over to him and touts its ability to survive a nuclear war, bragging that it's "indestructible." Opus listens, then squooshes the cockroach. (Eduardo and Ahmed the

cockroaches subsequently appear in the strip, trying to infest suburbia with cockroach-kind.) When, on a park bench, an old-timer complains about hating left-wingers, Opus looks at his left wing and remarks, defensively, "Well maybe they don't care for you either." The truth is, Opus is a great listener, even if his philosophy tends to be rather obvious and simplistic. When lovesick Steve Dallas asks rhetorically, "What could be worse than being dumped by a dame?" Opus replies, "Being eaten by a walrus." His immaturity surfaces in other ways as well: He hangs out with crippled Vietnam vet Cutter John so they can play *Star Trek* on his sleek wheelchair (Opus in the Mr. Spock role). Later, however, Opus becomes a miserably unhappy sort, not just pessimistic about the future of the world, but distressed by everything from the sorry state of his complexion to the absence in his life of females (a k a "snugglebunnies"). He resents being "a damp and dumpy water fowl," and although he hates how his breath smells, he just can't resist herring— particularly Del Monte Herring Chunks. [Opus also has been known to drink Herring Wallbangers at bars, has ordered herring Whoppers at Burger King ("hold the head"), and eats anchovy and herring sandwiches at the local diner. However, he shuns Kentucky Fried Chicken, because "some of my best friends are chickens."] Through the years, and in his increasingly rare moments of stability, Opus has exhibited a talent for writing. He writes poetry ("A leaf . . . so bright, so precious . . . / bird poop . . . so nice, so—"), and has held several positions with *The Bloom Beacon*, from film critic to personal column editor, and has gathered gossip for *The Ear*. He's also dabbled in politics, running for vice president on the National Radical Meadow party ticket headed by **Bill the Cat**. In the closing days of the comic strip (see "Comment"), Opus is knocked unconscious and lies near death after being hit by "an errant piece of space litter." He returns to the land of the living, only to face the ultimate disappointment: the publication of his autobiography *Naked Came I*. Not only have extensive revisions been made in the manuscript, but it becomes a TV movie with Gary Coleman playing the penguin. Throughout the run of the strip, Opus's good friends are the rather goofy groundhog Portnoy and the rabbit Hodge-Podge. The ineffective aerobics instructor "Big Pig Peaches" also appears from time to time. In November of 1986, the question was raised whether Opus is a penguin or if he is, in fact, a puffin, which he more closely resembles. The matter was never successfully resolved.

Comment. "Bloom County" was launched in December 1980; writer/artist Berke Breathed was awarded a Pulitzer Prize for the strip in 1987. The strip ended on August 6, 1989. Breathed explained: "The ugly truth is that in most cases, comics age even less gracefully than their creators. 'Bloom County' is retiring before the stretch marks show." After literally walking into the sunset, Opus made a subsequent appearance in the "Ziggy" strip (see **Fuzz**) on August 14, applying for work, and can now be seen in "Outland."

ORSON THE PIGLET

Pedigree. Pig star of the "U.S. Acres" comic strip.

Biography. When Orson is born, he's the runt of the litter. His larger brothers enjoy playing "runtball" with him (a volleyball variant using Orson as the ball), as well as squash (they jump on Orson and flatten him). However, there are advantages to being small: When the pig steals their corn, he can "fit under fences" and make a getaway. Early in his life, Orson's nameless master (pictured only by his feet) can't keep him, and the pig ends up on a farm, the special pet of a little girl. There, he meets a curious bunch of animals. There's Roy the Rooster, a fowl with back-up systems: If his cry doesn't wake people, he uses a bugle; if that doesn't work, he stomps on them. There's Booker the baby chick, who thinks Orson is his mother because the pig hatched his egg after mama chicken walked off the job. There's Sheldon, Booker's brother, who walks around with just his feet sticking from his eggshell ("I read the newspapers," he says, and refuses to come out); Sheldon eats by shoving food up his leghole, and flies using a balloon or parachute. There's Wade the Duck, a "panophobe" (he's afraid of everything); he won't blink because he's afraid of the dark, he hates his garden, convinced that a "plant's out to get me," and he walks around wearing an inner tube, because he fears water more than anything. There are Lanolin, a ewe with a violent temper (she enjoys ripping the bills off Roy and Wade), and her timid mate Bo. There are Orville, Sylvia, Woodrow, and Fred, worms Booker is constantly trying to catch. And there are Cody the Dog, who describes himself as "an egg sucking meat eater," and Blue the Cat, both of whom enjoy terrorizing the animals. Orson loves two things most of all: wallowing in mud (he eventually persuades Wade to come on in) and fantasizing that he gobbles down "power corn" and becomes the costumed superhero Power Pig, "keeping the world safe for pigs everywhere."

Comment. Jim Davis created "U.S. Acres," which debuted in March 1986. It was inspired by his own youth on a farm in Indiana. Despite being launched in an incredible 505 newspapers, the strip never achieved the success of Davis's **Garfield.** The characters were featured on the 1988 CBS Saturday morning series *Garfield and Friends.*

OSWALD, THE LUCKY RABBIT

Pedigree. Pre-Mickey Mouse Walt Disney cartooncharacter.

Biography. Except for his fluffy tail and long rabbit ears (which, along with the top of his scalp, he can detach in a tip-of-the-hat gesture) Oswald *is* the early Mickey in appearance—an all black body, white face, and short pants. In his screen debut, *Trolley Troubles* (1927), Oswald is a trolley driver who must deal with shoddy tracks, a stubborn cow, a formidable hill, and other obstacles on his route. Along the way, Oswald manages to lose most of his animal riders, including an adoring lady-rabbit; by the time the trolley rockets from the last of several tunnels (which, inexplicably, ends in the face of a cliff!), he's the only one left onboard. The trolley plunges into the sea, and Oswald is last seen rowing away. (Fanciful as all this is, it's no match for the sequence in *Bright Lights* [1928] in which Oswald falls and breaks into nearly a dozen pieces—each of which becomes a mini-Oswald! That cartoon also has Oswald entering a theater without paying by hiding under a patron's shadow.) Oswald goes to school in his second cartoon, *Oh, Teacher* (1927), and in *The Mechanical Cow* (1927), not only does he try to milk a cow to feed Mrs. Hippo's hungry baby (contorting the poor cow's udders), but he rescues his girlfriend from a monster. (In early cartoons such as *Sky Scrappers* [1928] and the ice-skating delight *Sleigh Bells* [1928], Oswald almost always consorts with lady cats rather than with rabbits. Pressure from the very conservative censors is rumored to have been responsible: Because "jackrabbits" are synonymous with prolific sexual activity, it may have been too suggestive for them to share the screen.) As much as Oswald isn't tied to reality, neither is he bound to one locale or era. He ventures into the jungle in *Africa Before Dark* (1928), heads west in *Sagebrush Sadie* (1928), goes to the northwest in *Ozzie of the Mounted* (1928), and in *Oh,*

Oswald, the Lucky Rabbit, *as originally drawn by Disney animators . . .*

. . . and as portrayed twenty years later in comic books.

What a Knight (1928), the plucky rabbit is a medieval minstrel who rescues a lovely lady cat from the prison tower of the villainous **Pete.** But whatever the era, the series retains its wonderful surrealism: Oswald unreels more and more of the lass's arm from her blouse so he can keep on kissing it and, in the climactic swordfight, lets his shadow continue the duel while he resuscitates himself by kissing the fetching prisoner. Oswald returned to this era, defeating the evil Black Knight and marrying a queen in *Kings Up* (1934), an operatic cartoon done entirely in song. One of the more innovative cartoons, *The Puppet Show* (1936) starred Oswald as a puppeteer controlling the strings of live-action marionettes. Unfortunately, in all of the Oswald shorts—especially through the early 1930s—the rabbit is basically a cipher, a pawn to trigger the nonstop gags which are the cartoon's *raison d'etre.*

Comment. Former Warner Brothers secretary Margaret Winkler had been the distributor of Disney's early Alice short subjects (see **Julius the Cat**). When she married Charles Mintz, her husband took over running the company and convinced Disney to come up with an all-animated series. Together with animator Ub Iwerks, Disney invented Oswald. In the first Oswald cartoon Disney produced, *Poor Papa,* Oswald is a grouchy old rabbit; Mintz hated the unpleasant character and sent Walt back to the drawing board (literally) with instructions to create a more appealing character. *Poor*

Papa was given a bum's rush of a release almost a year later. After nearly a year and twenty-six successful productions, the New York–based Mintz not only refused to give Disney more money to make the cartoons, but hired away much of his staff and continued to produce the series himself. Disney and Iwerks created Mickey Mouse and went their own way. In 1929, the distributor (and legal owner) of the character, Universal Pictures, pulled the rug out from under Mintz by turning production of the cartoons over to Hollywood-based Walter Lantz. Lantz continued the cartoons, modifying Oswald's appearance and personality over the years (he became cuter and cuddlier, his adventures far less frenetic), producing a whopping 158 of them from 1929 to 1938. In comics, Oswald starred in the very first DC publication, *New Fun Comics* no. 1 (1935), and between 1943 and 1961 appeared in twenty issues of Dell's *4-Color* comic (in which his girlfriends, at long last, were always rabbits). In his run in *New Funnies* from no. 65 to no. 78 (1942 to 1943), he was obviously married, because he had precocious sons named Floyd and Lloyd. Bunnies who had a less hare-raising career in comic books include Johnny Rabbit, who romped through all four issues of Victory Publishing's *Jingle Pals* (1946), and Kid Carrots, who starred in one eponymous issue from St. Johns (1953).

OTTO

Pedigree. Cheeky dog in the comic strip "Beetle Bailey."

Biography. Otto is the puglike pet of Sergeant Orville Snorkel of Camp Swampy. He has one lower fang that juts prominently over his upper lip, dresses in the same military threads as his owner (right down to the spotted boxer shorts—although there's a small hole in these and in the pants for his stubby tail), and considers himself very much a human: He walks upright, occasionally suffers from insomnia, and enjoys lounging on Snorkel's cot when the sergeant's away . . . watching television, drinking soda, and eating dog biscuits and popcorn (when Snorkel's

around, Otto has his own bed-box, pillow, and blanket). Otto requires a good ten hours of sleep at night, and gets ready with the men each morning. At muster, he stands beside the sergeant; if he hears, "Men, today we are going on a twenty-five mile hike," he returns to bed and says, "Thank God I'm not a man." Otto is a finicky eater and goes grocery shopping with Snorkel. However, his culinary tastes notwithstanding, he'll go down the aisle and "always take the one with the foxy babe on the box." He usually dines with the men in the mess hall, and grades the food with one to four *woofs*. Also on the base is Sergeant Louise Lugg, who's in love with the Snorkel (who loves only food and Otto). Unfortunately for Otto, when his master goes out with Louise, it ends up being a double date with the dog taking Louise's spoiled white cat Bella. (When no one but the cat is looking, Otto has been known to stick out his tongue at her, stick out his derriere, and even lift up a leg in her direction.)

Comment. "Beetle Bailey" was created by Mort Walker and debuted on September 3, 1950. Otto was also seen in the shortlived series of Beetle Bailey cartoons released theatrically under the *Comic King* banner in 1962; others were produced the following year and aired on the syndicated *King Features Trilogy* show. There were fifty cartoons in all. Dell, Gold Key, Charlton, and Whitman have all shared the publishing of the 132 *Beetle Bailey* comic books which lasted from 1953 to 1980. Otto was a regular in many of these. In a 1954 comic strip, Walker introduced Beetle's sister, Lois, when the soldier was home on leave. She and her husband Hi Flagston were given their own strip, "Hi and Lois," in October of that year; it was drawn by Dik Browne. As a typical suburban family, it was only natural that they have a dog: The honor fell to the big white sheepdog, Dawg. "When I was little," the animal reflected on one occasion, "I wanted to be loyal and obedient like Lassie . . . strong and courageous like Rin Tin Tin . . . cute and cuddly like Benji. Now," he continues, "I'm content to be what I am . . . fat and lazy."

PADDLEFOOT
Pedigree. Dog who finds adventure with TV's Clutch Cargo.

Biography. Paddlefoot is a bold little dog who joins his master, Spinner, and blond adventurer Clutch on adventures around the world.

Comment. The characters were created by cartoonist Clark Haas; the Cambira Studios series was syndicated in 1959, each daily episode running five minutes, the serialized adventure wrapping up at week's end. There was very little animation, but one notable, if freakish-looking, gimmick: Syncro-Vox, in which human mouths are superimposed over the cartoon characters. Paddlefoot didn't have a dog mouth superimposed, however. Margaret Kerry provided the voice.

PANCHITO
Pedigree. Mexican rooster and friend of **Donald Duck**.

Biography. The tall, slender rooster in an ivory sombrero and a red waistcoat is about as unstoppable a figure as any in animated film history. In *The Three Caballeros* (1945), Donald and José Carioca open one of the duck's birthday presents, a box from Mexico, and out pops—more accurately, explodes—Panchito. Six guns blazing, color exploding everywhere, he flips the weapons skyward, his holsters stretching sideways to catch them when they fall. Then he launches into the wonderful *Three Caballe-ros* song, which salutes the kinship between the three birds. He holds the last note so long his companions get sick of it and try in vain to shut him up: They pour a bucket of water down his throat, surround him with fast-growing hedges and set them ablaze, and even cut a hole in the floor to drop him through (his small circle remains standing, while the rest of the floor collapses). Finally ending the song, Panchito produces a *piñata* for the duck to swat. (Naturally, Panchito ropes the paper jar with his lariat and hoists it here and there, confusing and frustrating the blindfolded duck). Afterward, he summons a magic serape and takes Donald and José on a tour of Mexico—at one point, handing the duck a telescope that he produces with a wave of his hand. After returning to Donald's home, the energetic rooster plays bullfighter to Donald's bull, piercing the duck's costume and ending the cartoon in a rain of confetti and color.

Comment. This was the memorable character's only screen appearance. Panchito's voice was the work of Joaquin Garay.

PANDA KHAN
Pedigree. Genetically engineered comic book panda.

Biography. In the future, Asia has dominated the world and spread its influence into space. Hundreds of years after earth has colonized the planet Da Tu, the "small, lush planet" becomes one of the fore-

Panda Khan *brings his martial arts training to bear.* © DAVE GARCIA AND MONICA SHARP.

most outposts for "bio-design": the genetic alteration of animals to replenish earth's flora and fauna, and also to survive on other worlds. The pandas like Po Ye are the most intellectually advanced such creatures, the creation of the brilliant scientist P'an Ku. When the biodesign facility is invaded by Tong raiders, the pandas are evacuated. At the foot of Wu-Kung Shan, the Caterpillar Mountains, they build a fortress and become fierce warriors. The various animal races battle each other until the pandas rule the world. Generations pass, and many Panda Khans lead the tribe . . . although all are subservient to their god, P'an Ku. The present Panda Khan is Li Yang. His bitter foes are the bears known as the Ursii, and the human Shibo, a former associate of P'an Ku's, who is aided by monster bats.

Comment. One of the most sprawling and intricate fantasies of any kind to appear in comics, the stories are steeped in Asian lore and tradition. The use of pandas gives the otherwise realistic tales a beauty and pathos they wouldn't have with human characters. The pandas first appeared in the fan magazines *FANtasy,* in 1983, and then in *Interfan Showcase.* "Panda Khan" was a back-up feature in WaRP Graphics's *A Distant Soil* nos. 6 to 9, then graduated to its own title via Abacus Press. It is published, on average, once a year. The character was created by Dave Garcia and Monica Sharp.

PAT TH' CAT
Pedigree. Underground comics cat.
Biography. Pat is a black cat who walks upright, talks, and is more resourceful than his nerdy human roommate Nard. Most of their adventures involve economic or ecological concerns, for instance, buying "food producin' insects" as a hedge against starvation in the coming depression. Nard affectionately calls his pet "Kitty-Kat," and lets him share his bed. One of Pat's good friends is the sleazy rodent Ratso who, in one escapade, helped Pat earn money by pimping for him.

Comment. The characters were created by noted underground comics cartoonist Jay Lynch, who says they were modeled after a couple of friends, "A religious nut and what Agnew would call a radical liberal." They first appeared in the mid-1960s in the underground newspaper *Chicago Seed,* although they took on more balanced, middle-class personalities when they appeared in the first issue of Krupp Comics Works's *Bijou Funnies,* which started its eight-issue run in 1968. One issue of the characters'

own magazine appeared in 1974, and another in 1981.

PECKERS, THE
Pedigree. Comic book rock musician chickens.
Biography. The Peckers consist of crabby lead guitarist Crank, skinny keyboardist Rik, hefty drummer and boss Harry, lead singer Bunni, and tiny, timid bass guitarist Orvil. In their first adventure, the band is stranded in Transylvania while on a concert tour of Eastern Europe. They seek shelter in the castle of the lunatic frog-man Dr. Anton S. Wartbelly—who just happens to be trying to create the perfect robot rock star, so he can make a fortune. Aided by his snake aide Feedback and his duck androids, the Quackbots, he attempts to transfer the brains of the Peckers into the bodies of his Quackbots. Unfortunately for him, he tries to kiss the captive Bunni, which turns her into the mighty Sensuous She-Chick. Crank finds weapons in the castle, and war erupts; the quintet manage to fight their way out and escape. But—surprise! Their next tour is also cursed, as they face the wicked Catnip and his League of Ninja Assassins in Japan.

Comment. The characters appeared in just two issues of *Those Crazy Peckers* from Solson / U.S. Comics in 1987. They were created by James Hallett and Kent Bivens.

PENGUIN AND PENCILGUIN
Pedigree. Comic book penguins.
Biography. The penguins are brothers who work for their father, Dadguin, proprietor of an ice cream shop that offers such treats as sea urchin splits, cod liver oil sherbet, and squid syrup. Whether through daydreams or storytelling, the penguins transport themselves and the penguins around them into fanciful settings. The most imaginative of these takes place "One thousand years ago, in Ancient Japan [when] the mighty shoguins controlled great armies." One such leader, the penguin father of Penguin and Pencilguin, develops a revolutionary new weapon of war: the ice cream cone. Says the shoguin: "You take careful aim [and] fling the scoop with total concentration and discipline." Because Shoguin owns the only ice cream factory in Ancient Japan, he controls all the weapons of war. And when he sees how messy his warriors become during battle, he also toys with the idea of opening a dry-cleaning business. Alas, too many penguins end up eating the weapons, so the shoguin goes into a new business:

producing VCR's with the clan of Sonyguin, and "motor powered vehicles" with Nissanguin, Toyotaguin, ad nauseam. Another fun tale involved Aladguin and 1,001 flavors. Other penguins of the stories include Dadguin's sister Auntie Arktic, the twinguins Glenguin and Gwenguin, and comedian Punguin who "studied under Henny Younguin."

Comment. The characters first appeared in 1987 in Fragments West's clever, light-hearted, but naggingly infrequent *Penguin and Pencilguin* comic book.

PEPE LE PEW
Pedigree. Warner Brothers's romantic skunk.
Biography. Pepe is the **Wile E. Coyote** of love: a predator who simply doesn't grasp his limitations. The French lover is as smooth as his own coat of black-and-white fur, so sure-footed (and sure-handed) with the ladies of any species that it's clearly *their* problem when they don't respond to his charms. Never once does it occur to him that it might have something to do with his incredible stench. The skunk arrived on scene in *Odor-able Kitty* (1945), although he's different from the later stinker: The French accent is affected, and his name is Henry, not Pepe. Still, his amorous personality is the same. Hoping to get some food by scaring away competition, a cat disguises himself as a skunk. "Henry" mistakes him for a female and chases him all over—until the real skunk's wife and children show up and drag him home. The skunk is family-free in his second cartoon, *Scenti-mental Over You* (1947), in which he leaves his treehouse in New York to court a lady Mexican hairless who just got a skunk-fur coat. There's no romance in *Odor of the Day* (1948), in which Pepe and a dog battle for possession of a warm bed during winter, but it's back to mush for the skunk in the Oscar-winning *For Scent-imental Reasons* (1949), with Pepe romancing the cat who's been given the task of tossing him from a perfume shop ("I am zee locksmith of love," the smarmy skunk declares at one point to his "leetle luff bundle"). A few of the more interesting Pepe cartoons are *Little Beau Pepe* (1952), which places him in the Foreign Legion, where he's not only left to defend the fort alone (his odor chases everyone else away), but he once again falls for a cat who resembles a skunk (due to a brush with a newly painted ladder); *Wild Over You* (1953), where he pursues an escaped wildcat around the Paris Exposition of 1900; and *Louvre Come Back to Me* (1962), in which a newly

painted flagpole "transforms" a cat into a skunk and attracts Pepe's attention. The best scene: the subjects of masterpieces turning, complaining, or simply falling to paint chips as the potent skunk passes.

Comment. Pepe starred in seventeen cartoons. Pepe's name was inspired by Charles Boyer's character from *Algiers* (1938), Pepe Le Moko. Mel Blanc provided the skunk's voice.

PETE
Pedigree. The oldest Disney character still appearing in the cartoons and comic books.
Biography. Even the Disney people aren't sure whether Pete is a cat, a dog, or even a big, hefty rat (most likely a cat). They're not even consistent regarding his name. He was Peg Leg Pedro in *The Cactus Kid* (1930), was Pierre the Trapper in two separate **Mickey Mouse** cartoons, *The Klondike Kid* (1932) and *Timber* (1941), was impressario Sylvester Macaroni in *Symphony Hour* (1942), fought **Goofy** as Pistol Pete in *Two-Gun Goofy* (1952), battled **Donald Duck** as boxer Peewee Pete in *Canvas Back Duck* (1953; his last short to date), to name just a few of his alter-egos. Regardless, the black-furred, pot-bellied, pointy-eared, gravel-voiced, sometimes peg-leg nemesis of Mickey and his friends is one of the most intimidating cartoon characters of all-time. The "Pittsboig"-born Pete was introduced in *Alice Solves the Puzzle* (1925), the fifteenth adventure in Walt Disney's "Alice" series (see **Julius the Cat**). Known as Bootleg Pete, he's a crossword puzzle collector who tries to steal a puzzle from young Alice. Julius comes to the girl's rescue and Pete chases them to the top of a lighthouse, where the cat defeats the bully. But you can't keep a good antagonist down, and the snarling scoundrel returned in several other Alice shorts, usually menacing Alice and falling before the heroic efforts of Julius. Pete went on to star as a foe of Disney's **Oswald the Lucky Rabbit**. However, Pete's place in history was assured not by these cartoons, but by his costarring role in the first Mickey Mouse cartoon, *Steamboat Willie* (1928). As the captain of the riverboat on which Mickey is an undisciplined hand, Pete is actually well within his rights to chase him from the wheelhouse. (And it's hardly an insult when Pete glares at the spindly mouse and calls him a "little rat!" although Mickey does take offense at that.) Pete's got less noble intentions in their next team-up, the second Mickey cartoon, *Gallopin' Gaucho*, in which he tries to make off with entertainer Minnie

Mouse. Among Pete's other appearances, the most memorable are as the surly victim of *dis*service in *Mickey's Service Station* (1935; Pete had a slight German accent this one time only); as an unsympathetic sheriff who evicts Mickey in *Moving Day* (1936); as a heartless dogcatcher in *The Worm Turns* (1937); as a sadistic construction company foreman and Donald's boss in *The Riveter* (1940); as an abusive train conductor who not only tries to keep **Pluto** from boarding with Mickey in *Mr. Mouse Takes a Trip* (1940), but punches tickets with his teeth; and as a frustrated sponsor who, in *Symphony Hour* (1942), becomes so disgusted with the live radio performance of Mickey's orchestra that he literally eats the arm of the easy chair in the listening booth. One of Pete's best roles was in *The New Neighbor* (1953), as a Ralph Cramden sort whose tit-for-tat battle with neighbor Donald Duck escalates until both move from their homes.

Comment. Pete appeared in forty-one cartoon shorts, as well as in the 1983 featurette *Mickey's Christmas Carol*—playing the Ghost of Christmas Yet-to-Come (smoking a cigar, Pete's frequent prop). His voice was provided by Billy Bletcher in the shorts, and Will Ryan in the featurette.

PETER PANDA
Pedigree. Comic book bear from the 1950s.
Biography. The sensible little black-and-white bear was a precursor to **The Care Bears:** Interacting with human children, he invariably finds one with a problem, like the boy whose sailboat has sunk to the bottom of the sea, or the Crooked Man from the Mother Goose rhyme who left Crooked Town and is lost. Then he gets involved in often magical adventures as he tries set the situation right. When not helping people, Peter likes to relax by fishing.

Comment. Peter troubleshot his way through thirty-one issues of his own DC Comics magazine from 1953 to 1958.

PETER PIG
Pedigree. An industrious, but klutzy, comic book pig.
Biography. Clever Peter and his rough-and-tumble pig pal Punchy live in Pigville and are always looking for ways to earn money, such as painting Bozo Bear's house with disastrous results, or competing against champion Backstroke McBull, a bulldog, for the prize money in a swimming meet. Unfortunately, the two swine invariably wing it and make a mess of

things. Peter always wears glasses, a black vest, and a cap; Punchy's clothing consists of a worker's cap and sweatshirt.

Comment. Throughout the 1950s, Peter appeared as a backup feature in the comic book starring **Supermouse.** He starred in two issues of his own Standard Comics title in 1953.

PETER PORKCHOPS
Pedigree. Like the wisest of the three little pigs, this comic book swine is hot as a drop of bacon grease.
Biography. The clever, ambitious Peter is the owner of Peter Porkchops Clothing Shoppe. The pig's nemesis is Archimedes the Wolf, a k a Wolfie, who is always trying to cheat Peter out of clothing or attempting to "mess up" whatever project the pig has undertaken. In one of their most famous escapades, Wolfie tampers with the chemicals Peter is using to manufacture spot remover, causing an explosion that blasts them back to ancient Rome (no. 15). Peter is usually dressed in orange overalls with a blue T-shirt underneath. His preferred newspaper is *The Forest News,* and he enjoys fishing and photography. The baker Mr. Floogle, a dog, has a shop down the street from Peter.

Comment. Created by Otto Feur, the character was introduced in DC Comics's *Leading Comics* no. 24 in 1946. He appeared in most of the remaining issues until the title was discontinued with no. 41, then starred in sixty-two issues of his own magazine from 1949 to 1960. Peter underwent a dramatic change in 1982. While working at a steel mill in Piggsburgh, he was hit on the head by a meteorite, which fell, with Peter, into a vat. The interaction of the space rock and "the goopy stuff" in the tub turned Peter into a superpowerful, hulking brute encased in a metal skin. Renaming himself Pig-Iron (a k a the Swine of Steel), he became a crime-fighting partner of Captain Carrot. Other animals which appeared in *Leading Comics* included Nero Fox, the "jive-jumping emperor of ancient Rome," and the medieval lion-potentate King Oscar.

PETER POTAMUS
Pedigree. TV's famous hippo adventurer.
Biography. Decked out in a white safari jacket and yellow pith helmet and piloting the Magic Flying Balloon, the big, grinning, purple Peter travels around the world and through time with his monkey companion So So, in search of exotic adventure.

Among the foes they've faced are Clankenstein, the Kookie Spook, and the Eager Ogre. Peter once posed as Big Red Riding Hood to save Little Red Riding Hood from the wolf, and although you won't find it in any history books, he also helped Columbus find the New World. Whenever the hefty hippo gets in a jam, he employs a secret weapon: his Hippo Hurricane Holler, which blasts away any and all enemies.

Comment. Hanna-Barbera syndicated twenty-seven episodes of *The Peter Potamus Show* in 1964. Daws Butler provided Peter's voice, and Don Messick was So So. Gold Key published one issue of a Peter comic book in 1965.

PETER PUPP
Pedigree. Innocent comic book dog thrown into dangerous adventures.
Biography. Peter and his small, thumbsucking pal Tinymite are Bedlington terriers who talk and wear human clothing. In their first adventure, the pups are sharing a bed at home when they're knocked out by a rat and taken to the castle of "the mad scientist," Watt A. Dogg. The reason? Watt has "always wondered . . . whether the moon is made of cream [sic] cheese," and needs someone to go and find out. The dogs' adventures in space (beginning with a stopover on a "planet colony" where an old man offers them soup) are more surreal than anything ever faced by Flash Gordon! Back on earth, Tinymite wants only to grow up to be a firefighter.

Comment. Peter Pupp first appeared in Fiction House's *Jumbo Comics* no. 1 in 1938. The character was created by Bob Kane, whose more famous brainchild, Batman, followed by a year.

PETUNIA PIG
Pedigree. Pig inamorata of **Porky Pig**.
Biography. In her screen debut *(Porky's Romance)*, Petunia is a shrewish swine who cares more about candy than about poor, lovesick Porky. That grating characterization was quickly abandoned, and by her second appearance *(The Case of the Stuttering Pig)* she's more likable—although less independent, as the duo face a timid lawyer who becomes a monster when he drinks a potion. By the next cartoon *(Porky's Double Trouble)*, Petunia is chasing Porky (quite an about-face, considering that these shorts were all released the same year!) They were very much in love in the handful of appearances that followed, usually making goo-goo eyes or singing to one another to the exclusion of all else. Petunia's

physical appearance quickly evolved from a chunky, bald pig with ruddy cheeks and big lashes, to a slightly more petite pig who looks a lot like Porky, save for the lashes, the black hair with bowed pigtails worn on the side of her head, and the dresses.

Comment. Warner Brothers's lady pig was introduced in 1937. She costarred in only a half dozen cartoons over the next two years, more or less being ignored once **Daffy Duck** became Porky's semiregular costar and foil.

THE PIGGLYS
Pedigree. Contemporary comic strip family of pigs.
Biography. The Pigglys consist of Papa and Mama Piggly, and their sons Petey and Pudgy, and daughter Pinky. Each strip has the family involved in an activity that poses an arithmetic problem which the young reader must solve, for example: "Papa Piggly has had 180 at bats this season. He has 45 hits. What is Papa's batting average?" or "Papa Piggly has spent 15 dollars this week on ice cream. If each ice cream costs $1.25, how many days have [the three children] had ice cream?" Little is known about the Pigglys' personal lives, save that they own a boat named Pigasus, that Papa Piggly "has terrible aim," that they enjoy watching mud-wrestling contests (Bash-Boom Bull and Slam-Bang Boar are favorites), that they've been to the moon to visit their cousin Lunar Larry, and that the kids enjoy going to Arnie's Arcade to play videogames. On August 6, 1989, they rented a room in their home to the newly unemployed **Opus the Penguin** ("Papa Piggly says he can have a room here for 56 dollars a week. How much would it cost the visitor per day?").

Comment. The Pigglys are a one-panel segment of Bob Weber, Jr.'s *Comics for Kids* Sunday page. Sharing the page with them is Slylock Fox, a sleuth dressed in a suit, cloak, and deerstalker hat, who solves crimes with his assistant Max Mouse. In his one-panel adventures, Slylock listens to clues about a crime, then reaches a decision (as does the reader) regarding who's responsible. Other animals who have appeared in Slylock's strip include regulars Chief Mutt, the wicked Shady Shrew, Granny Squirrel, Mandy Mink, Kenny Kangaroo, Buster Beaver, Steven Stork, Wanda Weasel, Sir Hound and Lady Hound, and the mad (human) scientist Dr. Weirdly. The American-made strip was originally introduced overseas, syndicated to thirty newspapers and magazines in 1986. It was finally distributed in the United States in 1987.

PIGGY

Pedigree. Early cartoon character from Warner Brothers.

Biography. Piggy is a short, cheerful swine who engages in a series of mostly musical adventures. In his first cartoon *(You Don't Know What You're Doin'),* Piggy and his girlfriend Fluffy go to a vaudeville theater, where Piggy razzes a performer and gets into trouble. In his second cartoon *(Hittin' the Trail to Hallelujah Land),* he's captain of a riverboat, which is the scene for a performance by a black band. Getting carried away by the music and falling overboard, Piggy wrestles with a crocodile, skeletons rise from a graveyard, and a snarling baddie puts in an appearance.

   Comment. Both cartoons were released in 1931. Piggy was superseded by Warner's next cartoon swine, **Porky Pig.**

THE PINK PANTHER

Pedigree. Feline star of cartoons and comic books.

Biography. The tall, lanky feline with half-lidded eyes and Groucho Marx eyebrows first slunk his way through the opening credits of the 1964 feature film *The Pink Panther.* The "real" Pink Panther was a diamond sought by the cat burglar the Phantom (David Niven) who, himself, was being pursued by the dim-witted Inspector Clouseau (Peter Sellers). When critics remarked about the excellence of the credits featuring a cartoon panther and Clouseau (and a sly Henry Mancini score), United Artists asked animators DePatie-Freleng to spin off a theatrical cartoon. They did, and *The Pink Phink* (1964), in which he torments the Clouseau-like Inspector, won an Oscar. The ensuing series features sight gags in which the Panther either nags the Inspector (not necessarily on the job but also in his leisure moments), or is faced with a problem that he attempts to solve, resulting in a series of slapstick catastrophes. The Panther almost always triumphs, even if it means wrecking a house to get rid of a fly. The cartoons unspool to the tune of the Mancini music. Among his many adventures are *Super Pink* (1966), with the Panther attempting to emulate his favorite superhero; *Pink-A-Rella* (1969), in which he played fairy godfather to Cinderella; *Pink Plasma* (1975), where the Panther is haunted by ghosts; *Pink at First Sight* (TV), in which he works as a singing and dancing Valentine's Day messenger; as well as *Pinkfinger* (1965), *Pink Panzer* (1965; a title that *had* to come before the plot), *Super Pink* (1966), *Pinknic* (1967),

Pinkadilly Circus (1968), *The Pink Quarterback* (1968), *Prehistoric Pink* (1968), *G.I. Pink* (1968), *Pink Pest Control* (1969), *Fly in the Pink* (1971), *Trail of the Lonesome Pink* (1974), *Sherlock Pink* (1976), and *Rocky Pink* (1976). Even the Inspector could guess the subjects of these from their titles.

   Comment. The character was featured in a series of black-out-type gags in the opening credits of seven of the eight "Pink Panther" comedies (he did not appear in *A Shot in the Dark*), the later ones created by animator Richard Williams (best of them all: Williams's *The Pink Panther Strikes Again,* 1976, in which the feline mugs his way through the opening titles imitating movie legends such as Buster Keaton, Bela Lugosi, George Raft, Gene Kelly, and the shark from *Jaws*). DePatie-Freleng Enterprises produced ninety-five separate cartoon shorts in all; Freleng had been a Warner Brothers animator who had worked on many of the classic cartoons starring **Bugs Bunny,** among others. The theatrical cartoons have been shown on television, along with the occasional new cartoons, on *The Pink Panther Show* (NBC, 1969), *The New Pink Panther Show* (NBC, 1971), *The Pink Panther Laff and a Half-Hour* (NBC, 1976), *Think Pink Panther!* (NBC, 1978), *The All-New Pink Panther Show* (ABC, 1978), and *Pink Panther and Sons* (NBC, 1983). The latter show introduced Pinky and the toddler Panky, curious little panthers who are constantly getting into trouble. Their friends are the Rainbow Panthers: Chatta, Anney O'Gizmo, Rocko, Murfel, and Punkin. Each is a different color. They occasionally run afoul of Finko the Fang and the Howl's Angels, a bunch of delinquent lions. Billy Bowles was the voice of Pinky, B. J. Ward was Panky and Punkin, Jeannie Elias was Anney, Shane McCabe was Murfel, and Frank Welker was Finko. Dad also starred in several prime-time specials, among them *Pink Panther's Christmas* (1978) and *Pink Panther in Olym-Pinks* (1980). Gold Key (later, Whitman) published eighty-seven issues of the *Pink Panther* comic book, along with sundry one shots, from 1971 to 1984. The Panther was able to speak in the comic books, and was a fairly middle-class sort who held a job as a teller at a bank and regularly jogged in the park. Tangentially, in 1972, DePatie-Freleng tried to recapture past glory by producing a series of theatrical cartoons titled *The Blue Racer,* featuring a blue snake whose attempts to capture a Japanese beetle consistently end in failure. There were fifteen adventures produced until the series petered out in 1974.

PLUTO THE PUP

Pedigree. Pet dog of **Mickey Mouse.**

Biography. Pluto is a tan bloodhound with black ears and a red collar. In his first cartoon, *The Picnic* (1930), Pluto was named Rover and he belonged to **Minnie Mouse.** (Some Disney scholars consider *The Chain Gang,* released earlier that year, to be Pluto's debut. Not so. For one thing, there are *two* "Plutos" in the film. For another, while they look like Mickey's future pet, they're doggedly chasing escaped prisoner Mickey—hardly in character for the benign Pluto. While it's possible that one of them was subsequently befriended and tamed by Mickey, that's stretching things a bit for the sake of including the cartoon in Pluto's repertoire.) During the picnic, Pluto chases rabbits and generally makes it impossible for Mickey to woo Minnie. Between this cartoon and the next, the dog went to live with Mickey (although he would visit Minnie many times on his own; see below) and got a new name. (Always one for alliteration, Disney considered Pal the Pup and Pluto the Pup before deciding on the latter.) Mickey and Pluto first teamed as dog and master in *The Moose Hunt* (1931), which was also the first of the many cartoons in which they "enjoyed" the great outdoors together, others being *Fishin' Around* (1931), *The Duck Hunt* (1932), *On Ice* (1935), *Beach Party* (1931)—in one scene Mickey uses Pluto to inflate an inner tube by pumping his tail—*Alpine Climbers* (1936), *The Pointer* (1939)—the two go hunting, only to end up being stalked, themselves, by a bear—*Canine Caddy* (1941), and others. Then there were the "domestic" comedies, in which the home and its environs were the setting, shorts that included *Mickey Cuts Up* (1931)—in which Pluto becomes attached to a lawnmower and chases a cat, mowing not just the lawn but also a tree and, finally, the cat—*Mickey's Garden* (1935), and *Mickey's Surprise Party* (1939). But there were also many enjoyable cartoons in which Pluto was either the star or the focus of attention. Usually, these have him at odds with another animal (assuming one doesn't count Mickey, **Donald Duck,** and pals as "animals"), as in *Mickey's Orphans* (1931; Pluto must cope with some unwanted, very frisky baby cats), *Mickey and the Seal* (1948), *Bone Bandit* (1948, Pluto versus a gopher), *Pluto's Fledgling* (1948, Pluto helps a baby bird named Orville [Wright?] learn to fly), *Pluto and the Gopher* (1950; a rematch), and *Cold Storage* (1951; Pluto battles Fred Stork, who's overturned Pluto's doghouse to use as a bed). The funniest of these was *Pluto at the Zoo* (1942), in which the dog's efforts to steal a huge bone from a lion's cage lead him to run-ins with a kangaroo, a gorilla, and alligators, not to mention the lion itself. Ironically, Pluto never does get the bone: In the end, he must use it to prop open the lion's jaws so he isn't chewed up. The most touching of the Pluto/animal shorts is the Oscar-winning *Lend a Paw* (1941), a color remake of the black-and-white cartoon *Mickey's Pal Pluto* (1933). *Lend a Paw* proves that Pluto isn't just a dumb dog who instinctively chases animals and also happens to be a klutz: He's a dog with real heart. Pulling a sack from the river, Pluto is grossed-out to discover that there's a kitten inside. Pluto tries to shoo the foul little creature, but it follows him home, where Mickey treats it like royalty. Jealous, Pluto is tortured by his conscience (pictured as small, bipedal angel and devil Plutos) who urge him to be charitable and assertive, respectively; he bows to the wishes of the devil, tries to get the kitten in trouble, and is thrown outside, in the dead of winter, when Mickey finds out what's up. Playing with a ball, the cat follows it outside and tumbles down a well; this time, the angel Pluto prevails, and the dog once again rescues the kitten, earning not just the thanks and love of his master, but a kiss from the cat. Among the other animals with which Pluto has interacted over the years have been **Butch, Figaro,** and **Milton.** Then there are the two loves of Pluto's life: Fifi and Dinah. The former is a little brown dog with a tan breast, large black tail, and black ears, who costarred in three cartoons. In *Puppy Love* (1933), her relationship with Pluto is brief but torrid, the highlight of which occurs when Pluto replaces a gift he had for Fifi with candy Mickey was going to give to **Minnie Mouse.** Naturally, Minnie is slightly peeved when she gets a bone. In *Pluto's Quin-Puplets* (1937), the two dogs are married and have five offspring (Pluto's dog house reads, "Mr. and Mrs. Pluto and family"). Spotting a butcher trailing sausage links as he walks whistling past the yard, Fifi goes "shopping," leaving dad-of-the-year loser Pluto at home with the puppies. Following an inchworm, the pups get into the cellar and pry a hose from a compressed air tank; suffice to say by the time Fifi returns home, Pluto has gotten drunk and the pups are covered with paint. At the fadeout, Fifi is snarling and angry in the doghouse, while Pluto and his progeny are curled up inside a nearby barrel. Not only does Fifi reveal an unforgiving streak but there's a look that goes with it: Not only does she put on a batlike sneer but her ears cock up, like big, bushy satanic brows. *Society Dog Show* (1939) skips back in time (it has to; the dogs obviously have no future!) recalling a time when Fifi and Pluto were both entered in a dog show; Pluto's passion for the lass turns the show into a comic disaster until a fire breaks out, and the cartoon turns serious. Pluto rescues Fifi, winning her heart. Fifi made cameo appearances in two more cartoons, but otherwise the spotlight was turned on Dinah. In *The Sleepwalker* (1942), Pluto provides food and shelter to the brown dachshund and her pups; three years later, he rescues her from the dog pound and helps her get back to her puppies in *Canine Casanova*. *In Dutch* (1946) has the pair living together, puppy-free in Holland (or maybe they're just on vacation) when they spot a hole in a dike. While Dinah plugs it, Pluto runs to the village to get help. But no one will come, and, desperate, Pluto becomes a thief to get the villagers to chase him. He leads them to the dike, the hole is repaired, and the dogs are hailed for their courage. Pluto and Dinah are simply courting in *Pluto's Heart Throb* (1950), with Butch also vying for her attention. Finally, in *Wonder Dog* (1950), Pluto tries to become as acrobatic as Dinah's hero Prince, the Wonder Dog, hoping she'll fall for him. He fails . . . until Butch chases him. While making his escape, Pluto performs a series of miraculous athletic feats, which Dinah happens to notice. Impressed, she gives herself to Pluto heart and soul. As for family members, it's not known by whom Pluto was the father of *Pluto, Junior* (1942), although clearly it wasn't Dinah, whose first appearance Pluto, Jr. predates by several months. Junior—a deadringer for his dad—lives in a small doghouse beside his father's. Unable to sleep, he tangles with a ball and a balloon (disturbing his father), then gets himself hauled skyward by a bird and dropped onto a clothesline, from which he has to be rescued by Pluto. This was the small dog's only appearance; however, it's not surprising to find that in his very next cartoon, *The Army Mascot* (1942), Pluto joined the army. It had to be more peaceful there. [He also served in *Private Pluto* (1943), where he crossed paws with **Chip 'n' Dale**.] Similar to *Pluto, Junior* is *Pluto's Kid Brother* (1945), in which this second small lookalike gets into even more trouble than Pluto's son, stealing hot dogs and fighting with a cat and also with Butch.

Comment. Pluto has been featured in 102 theatrical cartoons, had his own Sunday comic strip late in the 1930s, and is a regular in the Mickey Mouse comic strip. Pluto has also had a healthy comic book career, not only costarring with Mickey, but headlining ten issues of Dell's *4-Color* from 1952 to 1962.

POGO POSSUM

Pedigree. Star of comic books, comic strips, television, and a motion picture.

Biography. Originally, Pogo was just a minor character in the lineup of critters in the Okefenokee Swamp (on the Florida-Georgia border), one of the many timorous foils for the aggressive **Albert the Alligator**. He didn't even look much like the round-headed, bulb nosed Pogo of later days; rather, he was a ratty, skinny fellow with a long, pointed snout, a

From the left: Chug Chug Curtis, **Pogo Possum, Albert the Alligator,** *Porky Pine, Boll Weevil, Howland Owl, Churchy La Femme, and Beauregard Bugleboy. From a 1949 strip.* © WALT KELLY ESTATE.

head of matted hair, and a gnarled tail. However, he broke from the pack and began to change, physically, when he became friendly with the carnivore. The thoughtful, gentle Pogo was a perfect foil for the overbearing crocodilian (they've been described as everything from Mutt and Jeff to Ego and Id); in short order, Pogo became the reader's proxy in the swamp, the more-or-less sane eye of the storm. These mad goings-on ranged from lopsided sports events (149–0 is not an uncommon baseball score) to finding ways to avoid work to elections (crooked although they may be: When one of Albert's cigar ashes burns all but one of the ballots—a vote for Pogo—rival Howland Owl intentionally misreads it). Because unorthodoxy is the rule rather than the exception, it's not surprising that Pogo is anything but "a regulation 'possum," as he puts it. He dresses in a vertically striped shirt and doesn't even hang by his tail: The one time he tried, he slipped and fell. ("I is more the human bean type," he insists. "This is a job for a monkey.") Pogo is surrounded by other humans (with human failings) in animal form. Over the years, the other major and minor players in the strip (along with some of their self-assessments) have included the duck Chug Chug Curtis, "the mail man" (not the brightest bird in the world, Chug Chug once fell in the water, found a fish in his mailbag, and angrily tossed it back for lack of postage); Porky Pine, who "don't like anybody or anything"; Howland Owl, who can't even spell but imagines himself "a natural born scientist what knows practical [sic] everything" and is usually seen wearing a wizard's cap; the Rackety Coon family; the scheming P. T. Bridgeport, the bear; Beauregard Buglebov, the bloodhound who is "A-lert . . . A-ware and A number one in perspicacity," yet doesn't understand why he can't budge until Pogo points out that he's standing on his own floppy ear; the turtle Churchy La Femme, who wears a pirate hat and has a piratical way of maneuvering himself into other animals' business; the conbugs Boll Weevil and Deacon Mantis McNulty (they sell tickets to the Atomic Bowl game, then try to convince the dumb animals that they can't see it because atoms are playing in it); the even shadier Deacon Muskrat, whose hypocrisy is underscored by the Gothic lettering of his word balloons, reminiscent of religious texts; the desirable French polecat Mam'selle Hepzibah; Seminole Sam, the deceitful fox; the "piggy-hog" Solid MacHogany; the cute little Bun Rab; and the corncob-pipe smoking Miz Beaver, among others.

Comment. Created by former Disney artist Walt Kelly, the characters first appeared in Dell's *Animal Comics* no. 1 in 1941. Originally, the black boy Bumbazine was the costar with Albert, a youth who lived in the swamp and had discovered how to speak with the animals. However, Kelly dropped him because "being human, he was not as believable as the animals." In addition to starring in various one shots—such as the *Our Gang* appearance—Albert and the other animals were featured in Pogo's own title, *Pogo Possum,* of which there were sixteen issues from 1946 to 1954. There were also two issues of *Albert the Alligator and Pogo Possum* (1946 and 1947). The "Pogo" comic strip debuted on October 4, 1948 in the New York *Star;* the paper folded in January of 1949 and, beginning in May, Pogo went into national syndication. It became famous for its sharp political satire in 1952, when it introduced the rifle-toting Simple J. Malarkey, "a good wing shot" and an on-target parody of Senator McCarthy. During the presidential election years of 1964 and 1968, Kelly went so far as to offer newspapers two strips for the same day—one with political content, the other focusing on less controversial topics (such as an Easter Bunny convention). When the cartoonist died in October 1973, the art and writing were taken over by Kelly's wife, Selby (Sundays), and by son, Stephen, and assistant Don Morgan (dailies); both were canceled on July 20, 1975, then revived by the team of Doyle and Sternecky on January 8, 1989. The new incarnation has a strong political thrust, but only occasional flashes of the sharp Kelly wit. In other media, an animated TV special aired in 1969; better known is the 1980 film *I Go Pogo,* starring clay puppets brought to life with stop-motion animation. Skip Hinnant was the voice of Pogo about that time, every four years, when "every fool and his frog wants Pogo Possum to run for president." Although Pogo insists he won't run ("I don't even like to walk that much!"), he does indeed mount a campaign. The notion of Pogo running for president began with the 1952 American election, when grassroots support originated on college campuses. The slogan I Go Pogo was coined for the 1956 campaign.

POKEY
Pedigree. Clay TV horse.
Biography. Pokey is an orange horse with a black mane and tail and bug eyes. He's the long-suffering companion to the green clay boy Gumby of Storybook Land (a k a Toyland), a place where adventures

happen simply by walking into books (*The Small Planets, Neat Stuff, The Kingdom of Roo,* and so on). In all of the duo's adventures, the talking Pokey is the conservative voice of reason, although he seldom dissuades the impulsive Gumby from a reckless course of action. The duo live with Gumby's parents: His father is Gumbo, who works at a fire station, and his mother is Gumba. Other animals who pal around with the two are Trixie the triceratops and Prickle, the fire-breathing dragon. Pokey is the drummer in Gumby's rock band. The one place Pokey hates uncategorically, and refuses to visit, is the city, with its "traffic jams, noise, expensive parking, mugging, and the concrete jungle." Pokey stands half as tall as his green pal.

Comment. Surreal, and with characters unlike any that had been created for television, Gumby and company were the brainchildren of Art Clokey. They made their debut on *The Howdy Doody Show* on NBC in 1956; their own series, *The Gumby Show,* ran from March to November of 1957, hosted first by Bobby Nicholson (who played the clown Clarabell on *The Howdy Doody Show),* and then by comic Pinky Lee. Gumby has had an impact far beyond its brief run due to endless reruns and the recent syndication of new episodes. The characters also hosted *The Puppetoon Movie* (1987). The Gumby characters were made of clay and shot a frame of film at a time, with incremental movements made by hand between frames; this, years before the arrival of Claymation and the California Raisins. In addition to countless Gumby and Pokey products, a must-have 3-D Gumby comic book began publication in 1986 from Blackthorne.

PONGO AND PERDITA

Pedigree. Dog stars of the novel and Walt Disney film *One Hundred and One Dalmations.*

Biography. Roger Radcliff is an aspiring songwriter based in London, and the human "pet" of the male dalmation Pongo. Spotting a lady dalmation (Perdita) and her "pet" (Anita), Pongo grabs his leash and hounds Roger to take him for a walk in Regents Park. The beleaguered Roger agrees, and Pongo manages to wrap his leash around the couple to bring them together. Although they topple into a pond, love blossoms between the human couple . . . and also between the dogs. (The dogs pledge their troth outside the church where their human companions are wed.) Soon, fifteen puppies are born to the dogs. However, all is not well: Anita's former classmate, rich, rotten Cruella De Vil arrives and offers to buy the puppies, from which she intends to make a coat. Her request is refused, but Cruella is undeterred: The dogs and the Radcliffs go for a walk; Cruella sends thugs Jasper and Horace Badun to steal them. When Pongo and Perdita learn of the theft, they send word of the crime throughout the countryside using the Twilight Bark, a relay system in which one dog howls to a neighboring dog, and so on, until the news has gone far and wide. Eventually, word reaches distant Suffolk. In a barn, English sheepdog the Colonel, the cat Tibs, and the horse the Captain listen intently. The hard-of-hearing Colonel is confused: He doesn't understand who would want to kidnap "fifteen spotted puddles." The cat corrects him, then adds that he heard barking over at Hell Hall, De Vil's old, abandoned mansion. The animals investigate the place and find the puppies . . . along with eighty-four others. They use the bark to send word to London, and Pongo and Perdita set out. Forging through the snow, given shelter by dogs along the way, the anxious parents make the trip in two days. They arrive at Hell Hall none too soon: Jasper and Horace have been told to kill the puppies that night. With the help of the three barnyard animals, they liberate *all* the youngsters—well-placed kicks from the Captain taking care of the two baddies. However, Cruella is on her way up to collect her pelts. She encounters her flunkies, who managed to pull themselves together and get into their van; Cruella is furious, and the two vehicles set off in pursuit of the animals. Not far away, a dog has learned that a truck is headed for London, and tells Pongo and Perdita there's room enough for all the dogs. As they wait in a blacksmith's shop, they see Cruella's car, the evil woman's eyes searching all about. Covering themselves with soot, the dogs all pretend to be Labradors, and climb onto the truck. However, drops of melting snow hit the back of the last of the puppies as its being pulled onboard; Cruella sees the soot wash away, and gives chase. In her frantic pursuit, Cruella drives like a madwoman and, after several close calls, she's finally undone when her thugs' van crashes into her car and both vehicles end up in a ditch. The Radcliffs are thrilled with their expanded family, and Roger sits down and writes a song about their "Dalmation plantation." Other dogs seen in the film are two involved in the Twilight Bark: Danny, the Hampstead Great Dane, and Towser the bloodhound and his pal Lucy Goose. Also in the film is Thunderbolt, a heroic collie, whose exploits on television fascinate the puppies. On the road home, the cows Queenie, Princess, and Duchess offer milk to the exhausted puppies.

Comment. The film was released in 1961, and was the first feature that employed animator Ub Iwerks's invention Xerography. This photocopying process accomplished two things: It enabled Disney to transfer animators' pencil-on-paper sketches directly onto the clear cels (which are then colored and filmed), thus eliminating the costly and time-consuming process of hand-tracing the pencil drawings onto cels using ink; and it also allowed one, single drawing to be replicated to create many, many puppies in the crowd scenes. It is this process that gives the animation its "scratchy" pencil line, instead of the cleaner, bolder ink line of earlier films. Actor Rod Taylor was the voice of Pongo, and Cate Bauer was Perdita. Lisa Davis and Ben Wright were Anita and Roger. Dell published a comic book adaptation of the film. Dodie Smith's novel was serialized in *Woman's Day* Magazine in 1956 as *The Great Dog Robbery.* Disney's scenario hews closely to the original. The author wrote another dog tale, *The Starlight Barking,* in 1967.

POOCH (1)
Pedigree. Soldier dog who fought in World War II, comic book style.

Biography. Pooch is a white German shepherd and "the best sniffer" in the K-9 Corps during World War II. He's so well rounded that during one battle, he's able to sniff his way through a mine field . . . then drag a wounded soldier to safety. Serving with marines Gunner and Sarge, Pooch completes "that unique trio the enemy hates to kill." Pooch is the litter mate of **Rex, the Wonder Dog.**

Comment. The dog appeared regularly in DC Comics's *Our Fighting Forces.* Gunner and Sarge began their run in no. 45 (1958) and ended with no. 94.

POOCH (2)
Pedigree. The beloved "doggie *and* . . . lover" of the underground comic character Ingrid the Bitch.

Biography. When the older-than-her-years youngster Ingrid runs away from home, she meets Pooch in the street. It's "love at first sight"; anyone who tries to tell them that their love "is sinful, immoral, illegal, and disgusting," is rewarded with a bite from the dog. Initially, the two spend a lot of time getting thrown out of bars, where the dog tries to order

The expressive **Pooch (2)** *with Ingrid.* © DENIS KITCHEN.

Pabst. They are separated, briefly, when Ingrid is kidnapped by the Masked Molester. Pooch scours the city in search of her—although he's briefly distracted by the luscious Cindy Sue, who takes the "well-hung" dog back to her apartment and seduces him. (Pooch introduces himself as "R. Pooch," although that's the only time the initial is ever used.) When Pooch leaves, he stumbles on the Molester's lair by accident and rescues Ingrid. Among his other talents, the dog plays the banjo.

Comment. The "Origin Story" of Ingrid and Pooch was told in *Mom's Homemade Comics* no. 3, published by Kitchen Sink Enterprises in 1971. It was the magazine's final issue. The character was created and drawn by underground comics legend Denis Kitchen.

POOSY GATO
Pedigree. Cat from the comic strip *Gordo.*

Biography. Gordo is a Mexican farmer turned tour bus driver whose frisky white Poosy Gato stars in many of the adventures. Above all, the cat loves to sleep, although playing is a close second. Unfortunately, Poosy doesn't always pay attention to what he's doing. He's the kind of cat who'll grab a piece of fabric being dragged along the ground, not realizing it's a kite tail until he's sailing through the air. Balls of yarn and cords hanging from window shades have

Poosy Gato *and her long-suffering master.* © UNITED FEATURE SYNDICATE.

also been known to leave him completely tangled. Poosy's favorite resting place is the summit of a telephone pole; topping his hate list is rain. Thought balloons allow readers to know what Poosy is thinking. Other animals in the strip are the black kitten Bete Noire, the big black cat P.M. (as in post meridiem?), Popo the Rooster, Senor Dog, and Senor Pig.

Comment. Gus Arriola's strip made its debut in 1941, was put on the back burner during the war, and returned in 1946.

PORKY PIG

Pedigree. The one and only stuttering pig; a pink, curly tailed porcine legend.

Biography. Barely recognizable as the contemporary Porky, the pig made his screen debut in the 1935 cartoon *I Haven't Got a Hat*. In that modest, black-and-white cartoon, he was truly fat: Built roughly as round as a basketball, with a slightly smaller pig head, Porky had two chunky legs ending in bright hooves, and wore a sweatshirt. There's no story, really, just a schoolhouse musicale in which Porky is called forward to recite, from memory, *The Midnight Ride of Paul Revere*. He quickly becomes flustered and abruptly switches to *The Charge of the Light Brigade*; that's his entire role! Other charac-

ters introduced in the cartoon (all of them given more screen time, and most of them not heard from again) were Miss Cud, the cow teacher; a tough, troublemaking cat named **Beans** (Porky and Beans were conceived as a team, and made several cartoons together); the intellectual musician Oliver Owl; Tommy Turtle; Miss Kitty, a demure little cat; and the puppies **Ham** and **Ex.** Porky was brought back the following year in *Gold Diggers of '49*, although it was Beans who was really the star. In it, a gold rush in 1849 leads to theft of a precious package belonging to Porky, who promises to give Beans his daughter if he can get it back. Beans sets out by car (remember the year?), and manages to recover the parcel: The hungry pig's lunch! So much for Porky being named Father of the Year. However, the humor and pathos of the stuttering Porky made him endearing, and after another teaming with Beans he was given his own cartoon: *The Blow Out,* in 1936. In it, Porky wants to buy an ice cream soda, but doesn't have the money. Hoping to earn change by returning objects that people have dropped, he returns a clock to a man . . . not realizing that the clock is a bomb, and the man is a lunatic trying to blow up the city. The dogged Porky keeps returning the explosives until the madman is destroyed; the pig gets a reward, and stuffs himself silly with sodas. (Porky's insatiable appetite does, however, get him into trouble on one occasion. While out fishing in *Fish Tales* [1936] he spots a donut and sinks his teeth into it, only to find himself drawn to the bottom of the ocean. Turns out the donut was bait set by a fish, and when Porky is in the hungry fish's fins, he's stripped and shoved into an oven. Porky barely escapes with his life, but does he swear off donuts? Not Porky. Upon surfacing, he swears off fishing. In fact, in *Pigs Is Pigs* [1937], Porky's infatuation with food is so great that it causes him to dream he's in the clutches of a machine, the sole purpose of which is to shove as much food as possible into the pig. In the end, Porky is released . . . but can't resist a piece of chicken. He eats it and explodes, which causes him to wake up.) Porky's love, **Petunia**, was introduced in *Porky's Romance* (1937), and his cute but violent baby nephew Pinkie made his debut in *Porky's Naughty Nephew* (1938). Cousins Peter, Percy, and Portus, and Porky's late uncle Solomon Swine, were seen briefly in *The Case of the Stuttering Pig* in 1937. However, one of the most significant events in Porky's early life (indeed, in the history of Warner Brothers itself) was the day of *Porky's Duck Hunt* (1937), when the pig and his dog encounter **Daffy Duck.** The truly looney Daffy proved more popular than other characters that had appeared in try-out cartoons with Porky, namely Dopey the Ape and Lulu the Ostrich (who star with Miss Cud in *Porky's Moving Day* (1936); diminutive **Gabby Goose;** or the loud **Gabby Goat.** Porky's physical appearance changed over the years, but it wasn't until the late 1940s that he became the Porky we know and love today. (According to cocreator, animator Bob Clampett, "We thought Porky would be cuter and more loveable if we slimmed him down a bit.") Personality-wise he also continued to evolve, although he was fairly well established by the end of the 1930s. No longer primarily a glutton, he became easygoing, shifting between a square and a milquetoast; a slow-on-the-uptake kind of pig who can be pushed around quite a bit before he gets his dander up. Even when the world is falling apart around him, he rarely explodes like some of his cartoon peers. Although Porky's adventures span the centuries, his life in the modern day has regularly been set on a chicken farm (see **Miss Prissy**) or in the woods, where he hunts Daffy. Among the splendid cartoons in which the pig has appeared over the years are *The Lone Stranger and Porky* (1939), in which he rides alongside the great western hero; *Kristopher Kolumbus Jr.* (1939), as the intrepid sailor; *Porky's Last Stand* (1940), with the pig and Daffy as short-order cooks; *Porky's Preview* (1941), in which he runs a theater (a skunk tries to get in but can't, because he only has one scent); *My Favorite Duck* (1942), the best of the Porky versus Daffy cartoons, as Porky tries to camp out and Daffy torments him, the pig being hamstrung by the fact that there's a $5,000 fine against hurting a duck (when duck season finally opens, Daffy's saved by a break in the film); *Porky Pig's Feat* (1943), in which pig and duck share a hotel room and try to get out without paying; the marvelous *Baby Bottleneck* (1946), starring Porky and Daffy as the pair hired to help the exhausted stork get through the postwar baby boom (after various foul-ups, the two end up getting shipped to Africa, where they are placed with Mrs. Gorilla); *One Meat Brawl* (1947), with Porky hunting wily Grover Groundhog; *The Wearing of the Grin* (1951), a tale of Porky's run-in with leprechauns in Ireland; the classic *Duck Dodgers in the 24½th Century* (1953), an outer-space classic in which Porky and Daffy fly to Planet X (see **Daffy Duck** for more). That one was Porky's last costarring appearance in any cartoon. Fond of dogs,

Porky rarely has the same one from cartoon to cartoon. Among them has been Rover, Flat Foot Flookey, Mandrake, Black Fury, and Charlie (see **Foghorn Leghorn**). These are more or less "lifelike" dogs who can do nothing but bark, unless they're talking to other dogs. Clothes-wise, Porky usually wears a little jacket and bow tie. Even in period pieces, although he usually has on a vest or jacket of that era, he rarely wear pants. (If he were *too* human, he'd be like the fully clothed **Mickey Mouse** of the 1940s: too real to be appealing.) When pictured with humans, Porky stands approximately three feet tall. Perhaps Porky's most unusual attribute is his valentine-shaped heart; in times of stress, it can be seen beating in his chest.

Comment. Warner Brothers produced 157 "Looney Tunes" cartoons starring Porky; the pig made cameo appearances in five other short subjects, and in one film (see **Roger Rabbit**). Mel Blanc provided what is inarguably one of the most famous voices in motion picture history, although it was quickened a bit, electronically, for the screen. (Joe Dougherty did the voice in the first few cartoons. However, he was a real stutterer and couldn't plan Porky's stutters for humor's sake, the way Blanc could). One of the clever character traits with which Blanc endowed the pig was to have Porky discard a word whenever he got stuck on it. As Blanc puts it, "I'd say things like, 'Say, have you got a nick-, eh ni-nick-, eh-ni-nick, eh-ni—spare five cents?' " (The one obvious exception to this rule: The immortal tagline to the series, "Eh-th-, eh-th-, eh-th-, eh-that's all, folks!" The name "Porky" was the nickname of childhood friend of animator-director Friz Freleng. (Freleng latter became head of the studio that created **The Pink Panther**). Porky has been a valuable licensing property since his inception and has also appeared in a number of comic books. The most significant of these was *Porky Pig*, Dell (later, Gold Key) published a total of 109 issues (1942 to 1984); and Dell's *Looney Tunes and Merrie Melodies Comics*, which lasted 246 issues (1941 to 1962). The comics introduced another of Porky's nephews, Cicero, who dresses like his uncle and is much less obnoxious than Pinkie.

POSSIBLE POSSUM
Pedigree. Easygoing TV hillbilly.
Biography. Possible Possum regularly faces adventure that has a way of finding out-of-the-way Happy

Hollow swamp. Along with his buddies Macon Mouse, Billy Bear, and Owlawishus Owl, the drawling, laid-back Possible has to deal with the likes of the Popcorn Poachers, pirate treasure, the Red Swamp Fox, and a case of "rootin' tootin' pumpkin lootin'." When the problem is solved, he sits down with his guitar, which he dearly loves to strum.

Comment. Terrytoons produced thirty-seven tales of the Possum, which aired on the syndicated *Astronut Show* (about a loony visitor from space) in 1965. Also seen on the show were the adventures of the dog secret agent James Hound, who battled the likes of Dr. Ha Ha, Baron Von Go-Go, and Mr. Winlucky (seventeen episodes); and Sad Cat, a rather ratty feline who lives in the woods with pals Letimore, Fenimore, Impressario, and Gadmouse, and has adventures that involve fishing, mountaineering, racing, and so on (thirteen episodes).

POUND PUPPIES

Pedigree. Toys turned TV and motion picture stars.
Biography. Approximately ten centuries ago, a young boy named Arthur and his dog Digalot were playing fetch when their stick hit the evil knight McNasty. There was a chase through the woods, which ended when a circa fifteen-foot-tall sheepdog named Big Paw frightened the knight off—but not before he witnessed Arthur pull a sword from a stone, thus becoming the future King of England . . . and Digalot pull the Bone of Scone from a neighboring stone and acquire Puppy Power for himself and all his descendants. This power enables their dogtalk to be understood by humans (Digalot rather arrogantly tells the amazed Arthur, "I could *always* talk. *Now* you can understand me!"). The bone is presently in a museum near the pound where the dog's line now resides (although the kindly young owners allow them to come and go at will). The dogs operate Pound Puppy Mission Control, whose job it is to save stray dogs. The canines get to the outside world via a tunnel, pulling the fur over the eyes of their human guardian Holly. The Pound Puppie's number includes Cooler, Nosemarie, and their newborns; the tall-tale teller Whopper; Reflex who, because of having undergone training by scientists, starts shouting "I love you" and kissing everyone in sight when he hears a bell; Bright Eyes; Howler, who has quite a bark; Florence; Colette; and, among other dogs, the cats Hairball and Charlemange [sic]. If the dogs aren't rescuing ownerless and/or lost dogs and dealing with the evil dogcatcher Dabney and the

nasty young Katrina and Brattina Stoneheart and their feline Cat Gut, they're fighting the modern-day Marvin McNasty, who wants to steal the Bone of Scone in order to control all of dogdom and thus conquer the world. One noteworthy supporting player is the fairy dogmother Zazu, who makes timely appearances. An annoyingly derivative aspect of the show that deserves mention is the Grapevine Howl, with which the dogs communicate throughout the city. This was clearly inspired by the Twilight Bark (see **Pongo and Perdita**)—right down to being used, at one point, to help determine the location of some kidnapped dogs.

Comment. The Tonka toys were first introduced in 1985, at the same time as Hanna-Barbera's Saturday morning ABC-TV series. Dan Gilvezan was the voice of Cooler, Ruth Buzzi was Nosemarie, Bobby Morse was Howler, B.J. Ward was Whopper, and Frank Welker was Cat Gut. The toys were designed to serve as dog versions of the popular Cabbage Patch Kids: Not only did they have that same pinched-fabric face, but they came with Puppy Care Sheets and certification papers. There was also a feature-length Pound Puppies film *Pound Puppies and the Legend of Big Paw* (1988), which recounted the saga of Digalot. Mattel had tried a similar toy/movie synergy with their *Poochies* line the year before. The "caring" dogs (à la **Care Bears**) flopped in toy stores and as a syndicated hour-long special, in which advice columnist Poochie and aide Hermes receive a letter from an archaeologist's son who is lost in Egypt.

POWER PACHYDERMS

Pedigree. Marvel Comics's animal parody of their own popular superheroes the mutant X-Men.
Biography. As luck would have it, a circus train passes through an atomic test site just as the bomb goes off. The radiation causes four elephants to give birth to four mutated elephants; because they can talk and walk upright, and have human arms, the elephants are sent to live with human families. But the elephants are more than simply half-human. They also have amazing powers. The sole female member, Electralux, is the "martial arts mistress of mayhem"; Trunklops can fire "devastating nose-beams" (only the ruby-quartz plug stuck in his snoot keeps him from leaking destructive rays); Rumbo has "retractable razor-sharp tusks"; and Mammoth, a towering brute has the power to turn "to solid steel." Rumbo and Electralux meet by chance and, rounding up the

others, decide to fight evil. They establish their headquarters in a Chinese junk anchored in New York harbor, a vessel with six lower levels containing everything from sleeping quarters to a torpedo room to workout and recreation areas. Their chief foe is the evil Clarinetto, head of the Brotherhood of Evil Musicians (a spoof of Magneto and the Brotherhood of Evil Mutants).

Comment. The *Power Pachyderms* comic book first appeared in 1989. Originally, the team was going to be called Adult Thermonuclear Samurai Elephants, playing on the success of **Teenage Mutant Ninja Turtles.** However, obviously wanting to be perceived as an industry leader and not a follower, Marvel changed the derivative name. The characters were created by Marvel editor in chief Tom DeFalco and artist Adam Blaustein.

PRECIOUS PUP
Pedigree. Seemingly gentle TV dog.
Biography. Wealthy Granny Sweet loves her little Precious, although the dog is anything but tame and demure. Whenever she's not looking, he attacks everyone in sight, from burglars to other dogs to birdwatchers to would-be kidnappers, then snickers about it while Granny pets him. Precious is a very scruffy brown mutt with a mass of red hair on his head.

Comment. The Hanna-Barbera characters appeared in their own segment of *The Atom Ant Show,* which debuted on NBC in 1965; there were twenty-six cartoons in all. Don Messick was the voice of Precious Pup, and Janet Waldo was Granny.

PRE-TEEN DIRTY-GENE KUNG-FU KANGAROOS
Pedigree. Mutated comic book school kids.
Biography. At an unspecified time in the future, while touring the Presto Bio-Genetic Labs in Emeryville, California, five Australian exchange students are caught in an explosion that causes them to interact with organic computer chips known as "bio-chips." Although the accident gives the teenagers "fantastic powers," it also, unfortunately, turns them into kangaroos. Contacting Rootin Slagg, a teacher and former soldier, the kids ask him to be their mentor, and become superpowered crime fighters. The five Kangaroos are Meep, the leader, who wields a deadly boomerang; Kayo, who is not only a computer whiz but has a tail that "packs the wallop of a ten ton truck at 85 miles an hour"; Matsu Mike, a martial-arts master specializing in Toe Fu; the big,

powerful Mr. K.; and Snurfette, who is described as "a real glamour puss" and has a pouch stocked with all kinds of tools and weapons, from land mines to a Vegamatic. Their first foe is the megalomaniacal Nez Pierce, Bossrat of Federated Conglomerat, and leader of the monster mooses, the Mooseketeers.

Comment. In addition to their own short-lived Blackthorne comic book, which was published in 1986, the characters were seen in the magazine *Laffin' Gas,* which also featured **Adolescent Radioactive Black Belt Hamsters.** Other characters that appeared in *Laffin' Gas* were the Colossal Nuclear Bambino Samurai Snails (Wilbur, Darryl, Koichi, and Eddie), masked, giant, talking, "warrior born gastropod mollusks" created when a young man tries to kill snails "with some glowing liquid I found in the garage"; Adolescent Maniacal Samurai Hares (named after famous animal animators Jones, Freleng, Clampett, and Avery), who take up swords to kill the Guerrilla Gophers who have been growing carrots laced with cyanide; Geriatric Glowing Gas-Pumping Geckos; and Radioactive Wrestling Rodents (Mr. TV, Bulk Bolshevik, and The Kung Fu Kid—respectively, a lab rat raised on television action shows, a squirrel fed steroids, and a chipmunk raised in a Tibetan Monastery). Marvel Comics checked in with *Brute Force* in 1990, a team featuring the superintelligent, power-suit-wearing, bioengineered lion Lionheart, eagle Soar, dolphin Surfstreak, bear Wreckless, and kangaroo Hip Hop. The comic ran for four issues. Other publishers offered up mutants of staggering variety, from the Puerile Phosphorescent Pugilistic Prairie Dogs *(Boris the Bear)* to the Infant Alien Karate Sloths *(MythAdventures)* to the truly over-the-edge Gesticulating Non-Breathing Hyperactive Over-Developed Old-Aged Pensioner Zitzoid Gecko Something Or Other *(Cyborg Gerbils).* All were inspired by the success of **Teenage Mutant Ninja Turtles.** The Kangaroos were created by Lee Marrs.

PRINCE
Pedigree. Dog owned by the comic strip kid Tiny Tim.
Biography. Tiny Tim is a young boy who can shrink with the help of an enchanted amulet. In both sizes, he has many adventures alone (such as the case of the mysterious veiled lady), but when he comes home he likes playing with the dog. Prince is loving, but he has pride. When Tim shrinks and stages a neighborhood circus, he presents the trained dog . . .

then takes credit for the tricks. Hearing this, Prince picks the boy up and drops him in his water dish. Prince is white with a dark spot on his back.

Comment. Stanley Link's "Tiny Tim" ran from 1932 to 1958. The strip was inspired by the fantasies of Link's own son; it was discontinued when Link died.

PROFESSOR OWL

Pedigree. TV owl seen in two Walk Disney short subjects.

Biography. An absent-minded, wheezy, chatterbox of a teacher dressed in a blue vest, jacket, and trousers, with a starched collar and huge spectacles, the blue-feathered Professor Owl lectures his class (and theatergoers) about music in the films *Adventures in Music: Melody* (1953), and in the informative and innovative *Toot, Whistle, Plunk, and Boom* (1953). In the first film, Owl tells his students—among them vivacious Suzy Sparrow, dunce Bertie Birdbrain, the triplets the Canary Sisters, and the bookish Penelope Pinfeather—about music in the world around us, both natural and human-made. He himself can play the piano and fly with one wing while pointing with the other. This carton was the first of Disney's very few shorts filmed in 3-D. The second cartoon—an Oscar winner—presents the history of music in a series of entertaining vignettes. The title represents the four basic sounds known to prehistoric music makers, and Owl relates how a quartet of cave dwellers evolved into a modern symphonic orchestra. Both cartoons, especially the latter, were drawn in a very sparse, occasionally abstract style that, far from appearing rushed or catchpenny, brought a spontaneous new look to the screen. As narrator, Professor Owl was heard more than he was seen in both films.

Comment. Another Disney owl was Archimedes, pet of the magician Merlin in the 1963 feature *The Sword in the Stone* (based on the three-part section of that name from T. H. White's 1938 masterpiece *The Once and Future King*). Where Merlin is flighty, the bird has both feet on the ground; it is he who remembers where things are and which incantations do what. See also **Bambi** for Disney's Friend Owl, and **Tod and Copper** for Big Mama. Except for **Doctor Whoot** and the detective Whoo-Doodit, an infrequent supporting character in Premium Group's *Frisky Fables* which was published from 1945 to 1949, owls have been in the background in comic strips and movies. The principal reason is that it's difficult to break the stereotype of the "wise owl,"

which doesn't give artists and writers much leeway. Mules suffer a similar disadvantage (see **Maud**).

PUP STAR

Pedigree. Space dog of TV cartoons.

Biography. Pup Star is the dog belonging to the Space Kidettes (Scooter, Snoopy, Jenny, and Countdown), little kids who fly through space in a convertible ship, and have a clubhouse that resembles a discarded Gemini capsule. Their ongoing nemesis is the rotten Captain Skyhook. Pup Star is a resourceful animal who is often called on to save the Kidettes, such as when he blew up an inflatable Space Spook and used it to scare Skyhook. Pup Star is usually dragged behind the spaceship, attached to a leash. The tiny dog is white with a black spot on its back, and has black ears. It's naked, save for a space helmet.

Comment. The dog appeared on Hanna-Barbera's *Space Kidettes,* twenty episodes of which aired on NBC in 1966. Don Messick provided Pup Star's bark.

PUSSYFOOT

Pedigree. Cat star of several Warner Brothers theatrical short subjects.

Biography. The tiny gray kitten with big eyes is the foil of the bellicose brown bulldog Marc Antony. In their first cartoon, *Feed the Kitty* (1952), Pussyfoot is so innocent and unafraid, not only doesn't Marc chase it, he actually takes it home with him. However, fearing that his owner Blanche Morton wouldn't let him have the cat, he's forced to conceal it in a number of clever (?) ways, for example, pretending it's a toy or powder puff. But Pussyfoot goes off on his own and falls into a batch of cookie mix; unaware that the cat has climbed out, Marc presumes his little friend has been baked. Depressed beyond words when he's handed a cookie that happens to be shaped like Pussyfoot, he's overjoyed when the real cat appears . . . even though Blanche finds out about it. Happily, she lets the kitten stay. In *Kiss Me Cat* (1953), the house is plagued by mice and the mistress announces that Pussyfoot must catch them or be replaced. Desperately, Marc tries to tutor the cat—and, failing that, tries to fool Blanche (at one point, he petrifies the mouse using a jack-in-the-box, and places the stunned rodent in Pussyfoot's mouth to show the woman). However, things backfire when the mouse abducts the kitten and demands cheese as a ransom (Marc capitulates). It finally takes Pussyfoot's face seen through a magnifying glass to scare the mouse family into leaving. The two friends are faced with the wicked **Claude Cat** in their next cartoon, *Feline Frame-Up* (1954). Claude has moved in and tries to take advantage of Pussyfoot at every turn. The cartoon is actually a battle of wits between Marc and Claude, as one looks to get rid of the other. Their last appearance was in *Cat Feud* (1959). It's as if the two hadn't met before. Marc is a sentry at a construction site who finds the homeless Pussyfoot

and gives him a sausage to eat. A Claude-like cat spots the food, covets it, and spends the rest of the cartoon battling Marc to get to it. Meanwhile, Marc must also watch out for Pussyfoot, who goes for a stroll high atop the building.

Comment. The "big brother" theme in the Pussyfoot cartoons proved far less popular than the adversarial relationships seen in other Warner Brothers series starring the likes of **Tweety Bird** or **Wile E. Coyote.** Mel Blanc provided the animal voices.

QUICK DRAW MCGRAW

Pedigree. Horse hero of cartoons and comics.

Biography. According to the theme song, Quick Draw is "the high-falootin'est, fast a-shootin'est, cowboy you ever saw." Brave, gallant, but stupid, Quick Draw is a horse law officer in New Mexico. (Although the narrator declares that it's "the old west," the hero occasionally drives a jeep. In one episode, *Big City Kabong,* he steps off a train into a modern metropolis. Must there be logic in a series about a crime-fighting horse?) Originally a scout— Quick Draw blazed the trail for the first railroad— the hero later became sheriff. Before deciding to write his memoirs—hanging up his six-shooters and other weapons, such as the minicannon he's been known to wear under his hat—Quick Draw fought such foes as Big Chief Little Runt, the diminutive Sundown Sam, the pirate Walker de Plank, the con man Slippery Earl Slick, the Bow-Wow Bandit, and most notably his criminal twin, Horse Face Harry. He helped friends in need such as wild west show operator Mild Bill. When it's necessary to operate undercover, the hero assumes a variety of disguises. Most often, he'll pose as a guitar-strumming minstrel in order to spy on his prey . . . then dons the black cape, the broad-brimmed hat, and (sometimes) the mask of the superhero El Kabong, so-named because he clubs his foes with the guitar. (Kabong—a spoof of the then-popular Walt Disney TV show *Zorro*—also "Robs from the rich and borrows from the middle class.") Quick Draw has been known to pose as the black-masked hero the Masked Avenger, as a baby, and as Bumbershoot Bam, a distinguished gentleman who carries an umbrella with which he clobbers his foes. At the local saloon, Quick Draw's favorite beverage is parsnip juice. With a white or light blue coat (it varies), and a black mane and tail, Quick Draw wears a red hat and blue neckerchief. He's an expert with a lariat, a brilliant trickrider, and does superb bird calls. Among his weaknesses are his habit of murdering the English language (such as "recognicize"), his inability to swim, the fact that his gun frequently gets stuck in his holster (when it doesn't, he's just as likely to twirl it and fire, without realizing it's pointing at his head), and his stubborn reluctance to listen to his loyal, more intelligent, pint-size burro aide Baba Looey (whom he calls "Baba boy"). Quick Draw will follow his own faulty plans to their usually disastrous conclusion, at which point Baba usually steps in and wins the day. Baba wears a yellow sombrero and neckerchief, and speaks with a Mexican accent (he calls his boss "Queeks-Draw"). Both animals walk upright on their hind legs. Quick Draw's pet phrase is the admonition to Baba, "I'll do the thin'in' [*thinking*] around here, and dooooon't you forget it!" They're sometimes assisted by the bloodhound Snuffles, a k a "the biscuit-hungry hound." The dog always gets his prey . . . but only after wasting time eating a biscuit and writhing in ecstasy. Quick Draw's girlfriend is the amorous filly Sagebrush Sal, to whose advances (in true western-hero fashion!) the stallion is ambivalent.

Comment. The character's syndicated, half-hour show was produced by Hanna-Barbera and debuted in 1959 (also seen on the show were cartoons featuring Snooper and Blabber, and **Augie Doggie**). Daws Butler provided the voices for both characters. There were forty-five episodes in all. Created by Mike Maltese, Quick Draw was very loosely based on Red Skelton's goofy character Sheriff Deadeye. Baba Looey was named after Desi Arnaz's theme song, "Baba Loo." Quick Draw had his own comic book from 1959 to 1972: Dell published twelve issues, followed by three from Gold Key and eight from Charlton.

R

RACCOON KIDS

Pedigree. Good-natured comic book raccoon brothers who live in an idyllic forest.

Biography. Rudy and his brother Rollo live with their Uncle Percy in a house at the edge of the woods. The lads aren't malicious, but trouble has a way of finding them: Once, when lost in the forest and hungry, they went to steal duck eggs from a nest, only to find out that they were crocodile eggs . . . with a mad parent determined to protect them. Another time, the mischievous woodchuck Muggsy volunteered the Kids to ride a bull in a rodeo. Rollo wears a red shirt and black trousers; Rudy wears red trousers and a blue shirt.

Comment. Created by Otto Feur, the characters first appeared in DC Comics's *Animal Antics* no. 1 in 1946. It became *Raccoon Kids* with no. 52 in 1954, and ceased publication with no. 64, three years later.

RAGS RABBIT

Pedigree. Fun-loving, benevolent comic book bunny.

Biography. With his pint-size brothers Jesty and Pesty, Rags will do anything to have a good time, from going to the circus (where he gets on the bad side of a watchdog) to sledding (and discovering a kingdom of snowmen living underground). He's also

*The usually even-tempered **Rags Rabbit** loses it after getting crowned by a snowball.*

a monumental liar. Out for a walk, once, he finds a bearskin, brings it home, and brags to his siblings about how he slew the animal. (When the small bunnies sneak inside the skin and animate it, Rags runs for his life!) The brown-furred (later, blue-furred!) Rags wears either a black derby or a red baseball cap and a red sweatshirt, occasionally adorned with a bow tie. The smaller rabbits wear sweatshirts with their initials.

Comment. The hare first appeared in Harvey Comics's *Nutty Comics* no. 5 in 1947. Over the years, he appeared in other Harvey titles including *Junior Funnies* and *Harvey Wiseguys*. *Harvey Hits* no. 2 was all Rags.

RALPH, THE RIGHTEOUS, RADICAL, RASSLIN' RHINO

Pedigree. Comic book rhinoceros described thusly: "He's rough! He's tough! He's horny!"

Biography. Managed by the crow Dik-Dik, Ralph is a has-been wrestler who's planning a comeback. He spends half his time musing about the past and thinking of ways to promote himself (he breaks into a TV studio, and lifts the anchor desk during a newscast), and half the time finally meeting and beating Hoagy the Hunk Hammar. ("I be bad!" he salutes himself after finally butting his adversary from the ring.) Ralph has a hulking, humanoid body with a rhino's head; he dresses in a green, skintight uniform when he fights, and in street clothes the rest of the time. Most of the characters in the strip are human.

Comment. The characters appeared just once, in Blackthorne's *Mad Dog* comic-book (1986). Other features in the magazine were a *Top Gun* spoof *Top Lop*, the story of rabbit test pilots; and Electrik Eel, the tale of a humanoid eel-assassin (a send-up of Marvel Comics's popular Elektra character).

RAPID RABBIT

Pedigree. One-shot star of a Warner Brothers theatrical cartoon.

Biography. In *Rabbit Stew and Rabbits Too* (1969), Quick Brown Fox is in the mood to eat rabbit. He consults a cookbook, realizes that first he has to *catch* a rabbit, then sets out to do so—using everything from a cannon to a mallet, among other devices, all of which backfire on the hapless fox. The hare in question—Rapid Rabbit—says nothing as he blazes through the forest, but simply honks a horn as he passes—à la the *Beep, beep* of the Road Runner (see **Wile E. Coyote**).

Comment. This was the only cartoon in what was intended to be a new series.

RAT FINK

Pedigree. Ugly rat of T-shirt fame.

Biography. Practically nothing is known about this character, save that he likes to hotrod and has driven everything from gas-fueled motorcycles to bikes driven by toxic waste.

Comment. The big-mouthed rat with bulging, blood-shot eyes was created in 1962 by Ed "Big Daddy" Roth. Though the term "rat fink" had been around for years, no one had ever *drawn* such a thing. Roth did so, but for a peculiar reason: He spent a great deal of time creating T-shirt designs, and was so overwhelmed with work that he decided to create one so ugly people wouldn't want it. Rat Fink was the result. But instead of decreasing, the demand for Roth's shirts grew. Rat Fink was licensed widely throughout the decade. However, it wasn't until 1990 that he finally got a comic book, appearing with an equally grotesque set of supporting characters in *Rat Fink Comix,* from World of Fandom.

RENEGADE RABBIT

Pedigree. Comic book hare freedom fighter.

Biography. The rabbit colony is located on a parallel earth in the near future, a world ruled for eighty-four years by the oppressive Borg regime. Tired of living in a virtual ghetto, Winston Longears III, a rabbit colony representative to the governing general assembly, decides to mount a rebellion. Donning a dashing blue outfit and calling himself Renegade Rabbit, he rallies a few brave rabbits (and one bear) around him, intent on overthrowing their humanlike oppressors. The hare's chief weapon is a rocket-sled from which he drops giant carrots.

Comment. The character starred in the short-lived (seven issues) Printed Matter Comics's *Renegade Rabbit* in 1986 to 1987. Craig Miller's story and art were excellent, as was the back-up feature in no. 1: Darebunny, a smart parody of Marvel Comics's superhero Daredevil. In it, a rabbit comic book fan becomes a crime fighter. Although Daredevil is blind, Darebunny isn't: Unfortunately, in imitating his hero, the rabbit made the costume without eyeslots, and stumbles around attacking the wrong people and running into poles.

THE RESCUE RANGERS

Pedigree. Sidekicks of Disney's **Chip 'n' Dale.**

Biography. Headquartered in the upper reaches of a huge, hollow tree, the Rescue Rangers are a secret team that tackles local and international crimes and mysteries. In addition to the chipmunks, the group consists of three other members. Monterey Jack is a giant, muscular mouse from Australia who wears flier's goggles, a sweatshirt, and finds his adventures with the Rangers "more fun than riding a kangaroo bareback." His one weakness is cheese. When he smells is, his moustache stiffens, he goes into a semihypnotic state, and he must search out the "chu-eez-uh" at all costs. Gadget is another mouse, a lady with light brown hair and a blue jumpsuit. The brightest member of the team, she can tinker together any tool that might be needed at any time. Chip and Dale both vie for her affections, although she doesn't care about anything except for justice and gadget making. The final member is Zipper the fly. He's blue, wears a red sweatshirt, and has huge, yellow eyes. Zipper flies at incredible speeds, and communicates with the others through buzzes and sign language. His most moving case was when he became emotionally involved with the queen bee whose swarm was enslaved by an exterminator who wanted to be a rock and roll singer and needed the bees to steal instruments. Although Monterey counseled Zipper on how to win a woman's heart, the interspecies romance was not meant to be. The Rangers travel about in their Ranger Plane, a gondola attached to a hot dog–shaped balloon with flapping wings. Chief among the foes they've faced are Fat Cat, a czar of crime who is based in a casino at a cat food plant and is served by an army of bugs, rats, reptiles, and other cats.

Comment. *Chip 'n' Dale's Rescue Rangers* began airing on cable television's the Disney Channel in March of 1989. The half-hour adventures continue to air.

REX, THE WONDER DOG

Pedigree. Comic book dog of exceptional intelligence and physical prowess.

Biography. Born in 1941, the white German shepherd is tutored in the K-9 Army Dog Training Corps, serving with valor in both World War II and Korea. Because his master is missing and presumed dead, Rex is sent to live with Phillip Dennis and family in the United States. When Dennis is accused of murder, Rex turns his talents to finding the real killer and intimidating him into confessing. Linking up with Phillip's kid brother, Denny, Rex travels the world with him, a hound of fortune, taking adventure where he finds it (even on the moon, in one story) as "the four-footed champion of justice." Occasionally, Rex is loaned out to those who need a dog of his intelligence, agility, and talent for detecting "the scent of evil." In one story, Rex partakes in "a police mission on the west coast," while in another he becomes "Rex—Airline Detective" when thugs hijack the commercial plane on which he's a passenger. (The dog has a seat in the passenger compartment; when it becomes apparent the plane's in trouble, Rex does handstands to distract his fellow flyers.) Thought balloons reveal what Rex is thinking. To wit: While attending the circus, he sees the tightrope walker lose her balance and thinks, "Got to grab that pole and save her from falling!" Another time, watching a pair of armed thugs, he reasons, "If I push those men . . . they may shoot me . . . and then I won't be of any help to the good humans out there!" He also stars in motion pictures, such as *Four-Footed Defenders of the West* with Jim Pardee and his horse Tex. While appearing at a local circus benefit, he meets **Bobo the Detective Chimp**, his biggest fan. When the receipts of the show are stolen, Rex and Bobo track the criminal's scent to a boat, and end up in Bimini. They follow the felons to a swamp, where Rex is wounded by a crocodile. Bobo brings him water . . . and suddenly, Rex is healed. Bobo also drinks and, when they capture the crook and return to civilization, a vet discovers that the animals have somehow acquired the health of eighteen month olds! They'd discovered the Fountain of Youth, and Rex begins a new career: joining Danny in the astronaut corps. In time, Lieutenant Colonel Daniel Dennis and Rex take part in a lunar landing. Rex's brother is **Pooch (1)**.

Comment. DC Comics's *The Adventures of Rex, the Wonder Dog* lasted forty-six issues, from 1952 to 1959. The comic book was played straight and, nutty as it could be, it had dash. The credibility-straining moon landing was in *DC Comics Presents* no. 35. Another, although much less successful comics-only dog hero was Duke, who starred in just one issue of Gold Key's *Duke of the K-9 Patrol* in 1963.

RICOCHET RABBIT

Pedigree. Superspeed TV hero of the old west.
Biography. Aided by his slowpoke deputy Droopalong Coyote, the high-velocity sheriff takes off after bad guys with a *ping-ping-ping* and a cry of,

"Ricochet, and away!" In addition to his great speed, the rabbit is armed with an astonishing array of bullets. These don't kill his foes, but do just about everything else: They open up to hit them with hammers, lasso them, or knock them off their feet with water. Among the ne'er-do-wells who have felt his wrath are Annie Hoaxley, Itchy-Finger Gunslinger, and El Loco, Loco, Loco, Loco Diablo. Ricochet wears a vest with a sheriff's star, and a flat-topped hat. His long ears are usually seen flying behind him.

Comment. The adventures of Hanna-Barbera's hare aired on *The Magilla Gorilla Show,* which was syndicated in 1964. There were twenty-three cartoons in all. Don Messick was the voice of Ricochet, while Mel Blanc was his sidekick (a send-up of the Chester character from *Gunsmoke).* The character was to some degree inspired by the success of the studio's **Touché Turtle.**

ROCKET RACCOON
Pedigree. Space-faring comic book hero.
Biography. At sometime in the future, Halfworld is established as "an institutional world" for insane humans. Psychiatrists there are given robots to do all the labor, and animals to amuse the inmates. Eventually, the doctors leave. When radiation from a nova socks the planet, it changes the robots' programming. No longer willing to serve illogical humans, they genetically alter the animals to become intelligent keepers of the Loonies. Eventually, Rocket Raccoon becomes the world's chief law officer. Dressed in a green leotard, the pipe-smoking Rocket is assisted by Llyla the otter, his lover; Pyko the superintelligent tortoise; Blackjack O'Hare, a rabbit who was the former leader of the Black Bunny Assassins; and Wal Rus the walrus, who has prosthetic tusks ranging from Tool Tusks (wrenches and more) to Martial Molars (which fire disintegration beams) to his "sharpshooting" Terror Tusks. The group travels through space onboard their spaceship, the *Rack 'n Ruin,* covering shorter distances using their Rocket Skates. In Rocket's first (and, to date, only) adventure, he becomes embroiled in a trade war between the toymakers Judson Jakes (a mole) and Lord Dyvyne (a snake).

Comment. The character appeared in Marvel Comics's *Rocket Raccoon* comic book, which lasted four issues in 1985, and, prior to that, in *The Incredible Hulk* no. 271. Rocket was created by Bill Mantlo and Keith Giffen.

ROCKY AND BULLWINKLE

Pedigree. TV and comic book stars in a class all their own.

Biography. The wily, small, buck-toothed, gray Rocket J. Squirrel—a k a Rocky the Flying Squirrel—wears a blue, World War I pilot's cap and goggles atop his head, and is partnered with big, dumb Bullwinkle J. Moose. They hail from Frostbite Falls, located in Koochiching County, Minnesota, and live in a small cabin on the edge of a cliff that overlooks the town proper. (Gossipy Chauncy and Edgar are the only other townspeople to appear regularly.) Rocky is a graduate of the Cedar Yorpantz Flying School, while Bullwinkle's alma mater is Wossamatta U. Adventurers, the pair are always crossing paths with humans, from the dizzy Captain Peter "Wrongway" Peachfuzz to the evil Boris Badenov and Natasha Fatale (a Garbo lookalike), spies-for-hire from the Eastern European nation of Pottsylvania. These two baddies answer to the neo-Nazi Fearless Leader who, in turn, works for the dwarfish Mr. Big, based in the Krumlin. Among the

duo's greatest adventures are *Jet Formula* (their first saga, a quest for the rare mooseberry bush that is used in the manufacture of votane, ran a whopping forty segments long; see "Comment"), *Upsidaisium*, *Metal Munching Mice*, *Buried Treasure*, and *The Last Angry Moose*. Bullwinkle is the proud owner of the famous Kirwood Derby, a magic bowler that never seems to work right (instead of pulling a rabbit from it, he pulls a lion). The hat was originally created by moon creatures, members of the same race that bred the square-headed lunarians Gidney and Cloyd, with whom Rocky and Bullwinkle have had numerous adventures.

Comment. Jay Ward's characters were created for a cartoon series that was to be called *Frostbite Falls Follies*. However, Ward (who had been a producer of **Crusader Rabbit**) was unable to find a sponsor for the show. The moose and squirrel sat on a shelf for a few years, after which Ward and his partner Bill Scott, with the Bob Hope/Bing Crosby "Road" pictures in mind, revamped the premise to get the characters out of Minnesota and into adventures in

Rocky and Bullwinkle.

exotic locales worldwide. Rocky was named after the fast-punching Rocky Graziano, while Bullwinkle came from Berkeley used-car salesperson Clarence Bulwinkle [sic]—whose name amused Ward. Note that both characters have the same middle initial, J.—their producer's first name. Gidney and Cloyd were based on Ward and Scott themselves, and named for the first names the two "would least like to have," according to Scott: Floyd and Sidney. The *Rocky and Bullwinkle* cartoon aired on the series *Rocky and His Friends*, which premiered on ABC as a fringe prime-time series (5:30 to 6:00) in November 1959 (cartoons featuring **Mr. Peabody** were also seen on the program). Each cartoon was part of a serial and ended with a cliff-hanger; five to forty segments comprised an entire story and there were twenty-eight different sagas in all, with a total of 325 episodes between them. Through September of 1961, the network shifted the series to various time periods. With the old cartoons and a handful of new ones, *The Bullwinkle Show* premiered in prime time on NBC in September of 1961, went over to ABC in 1964, and remained on the network (albeit, as a morning show) until 1973. The cartoons are presently in syndication. The characters returned, briefly, to the NBC lineup on *Bullwinkle,* which premiered in 1981. Bullwinkle was also seen in his Mr. Know-It-All persona, answering questions and solving problems on *The Hoppity Hooper Show* (see **Hoppity Hooper**), dealing with such topics as How to Tame Lions, How to Open a Jar of Pickles, How to Escape from Devil's Island, How to Disarm a Live TNT Bomb, How to Avoid Tipping the Waiter, and How to Make the Neighbors Quiet. These segments also featured Rocky, and were reruns of the earlier shows. In all the cartoons, the voice for Rocky was provided by June Foray, with Bill Scott doing the honors for Bullwinkle. Ms. Forway was also Natasha, and the late Paul Frees was inimitable as Boris. The compelling narration was provided by actor William Conrad. As a tribute to how important the voices were to the success of the cartoons, Rocky and Bullwinkle have had a relatively undistinguished comic book career. They starred in six issues of Dell's *4-Color* (1960 to 1962), five issues of *Rocky and His Fiendish Friends* from Gold Key (1962 to 1963), in nine issues of Marvel's *Bullwinkle and Rocky* (1987 to 1989), and in various one shots such as Blackthorne Publishing's *3-D Bullwinkle and Rocky.* During the mid-1960s, the characters were featured in cartoon and comic book–style print

advertisements for General Mills' Cheerios cereal ("Cheerios 'n' milk give us people muscle-makin' protein . . . and lots of go . . . go . . . *go!*" Bullwinkle enthuses as he parachutes from a plane in one ad. Getting tangled in an old woman's laundryline, he notes, "But they should watch where they're going!").

ROGER RABBIT
Pedigree. Rabbit hero of a novel turned film star in the 1988 movie *Who Framed Roger Rabbit?*
Biography. In the 1940s, 'toons—animated cartoon characters—work at various Hollywood studios, then return at night to their homes in Toontown. Dressed in red coveralls and bright, polka-dotted bow tie, Roger Rabbit, along with Baby Herman, are 'toons acting in the short cartoon *Somethin's Cookin',* in which the stuttering, accident-prone rabbit is sitting for the precocious toddler. When Roger botches a take (he's hit on the head and sees birds instead of stars), the crew breaks. Roger is on edge because he believes that his voluptuous 'toon wife Jessica is cheating on him. Enter detective Eddie Valiant, who's been hired by Maroon Cartoon head R. K. Maroon to find out if it's true. (Eddie has his problems about working with 'toons: His brother, Teddy, was killed by one several years before.) He finds Jessica romancing Marvin the gag king, a human who sells props to cartoon makers—and, shortly thereafter, Marvin is killed when a safe falls on his head . . . a 'toon-style murder if ever there was one, and the same way that Eddie's brother died. All clues point to Roger, and the local prosecutor, Judge Doom, wants the hare. But Eddie doesn't believe that Roger is guilty, and hides him—even when Doom's weasel goons Smartguy, Psycho, Stupid, and company come calling. Undaunted by their sniffing around, Eddie continues his investigation, which takes him to Toontown. There, he learns that Jessica had met Marvin in order to take his will for safekeeping: His will stipulates that, upon his death, Toontown will be bequeathed to the inhabitants . . . something that *someone* doesn't want to happen. Turns out that "someone" is Judge Doom. He reveals himself to be a 'toon, and not just any 'toon but the dirty rat who killed Eddie's brother. Doom killed the gag king when Marvin wouldn't sell out to him: The fiend intends to use a 'toon-destroying mixture known as "dip" to level Toontown and build freeways in its place, so he can rake in money on gas stations, motels, and restaurants. Jessica and

Roger Rabbit *in a typical fix from the 1989 short subject* Tummy Trouble.

Roger are captured and bound in front of the dip-spraying dipmobile, which is set loose toward Toontown. As death and destruction nears, Eddie and Doom battle, the sleuth triumphing when he unleashes dip on the megalomaniac. Roger is cleared, and he, Jessica, and all of Toontown rejoice. Throughout most of the film, Roger is a skittish figure—understandable, given the pressure he's under as a murder suspect, and the torture he endures believing that his wife, whom he adores, is unfaithful. Otherwise, the white-furred star is a born ham and comedian. He can't resist performing if there's a crowd, can survive all kinds of abuse (plates and hammers crashing over the head), and can't pass up a joke even if time is short. (Handcuffed to Eddie, he waits until the detective starts hacking away at the shackles before simply slipping his hand out. When Eddie asks why he didn't do that before, Roger replies that he had to wait until "it was funny.") In fact, Roger's closest call occurs because of his compulsion to yuk it up: At one point, Doom comes searching at the bar where Roger's hiding, and keeps tapping out notes from that 1914 chestnut "Shave and a Haircut" (a k a "Rum Diddle-de-um Bum," named for the opening bars)—knowing that a card like Roger can't resist jumping in with the cli-

mactic "Bum bum!" Sure enough, after fighting to curb his impulses, Roger vaults from hiding, proudly sings the last two notes, and is nabbed. (He's saved from dip only because Eddie is able to slip him a drink, knowing that booze causes the Rabbit to fly around like a skyrocket.) Roger and Baby Herman return in a short subject *Tummy Trouble* (1989), in which Roger once again baby-sits for Herman. The three year old swallows a rattle, and the frantic rabbit rushes him to the hospital, where things go awry for Roger. A follow-up, *Roller Coaster Rabbit,* was released in 1990. A new feature film, a prequel entitled *Who Discovered Roger Rabbit?*, is in production for a Christmas 1993 release. It tells hows Roger and Jessica met.

Comment. Roger was created by author Gary Wolf, and first appeared in the novel *Who Censored Roger Rabbit?* in 1981. The setup in the novel is fundamentally the same, only there are two villains in the piece. One is Roger himself, who's actually responsible for the murder of unscrupulous cartoon syndicate head Rocco DeGreasy. The other is an evil genie whom Roger unwittingly releases from a lantern. The djinn shoots Roger dead well into the novel; in a final showdown, Valiant coaxes a confession from the genie while holding him over salt water—his one weakness. With the document in hand, the detective drops the genie into the liquid. The Roger in the novel is "close to six feet, but only if you counted his eighteen-inch ears." Like all 'toons, he speaks using word balloons. (In 1991, author Wolf wrote a sequel, *Who P-P-Plugged Roger Rabbit,* revealing how Roger lost the part of Rhett Butler to Clark Gable.) The film version was directed by Robert Zemeckis, with Roger's voice provided by Charles Fleischer. Marvel Comics published a comic book adaptation, and Disney began its own Roger comic book in 1990. A follow-up Marvel comic book adaptation included *Tummy Trouble* and a new story, *The Resurrection of Doom,* in which Maroon Cartoons turns to inexpensive animation techniques, which leaves Roger, Jessica, and other quality Toons unemployable. While animation and live action have been combined for decades (see **Julius the Cat**), the Roger Rabbit story has a direct predecessor in the 1940, black-and-white **Porky Pig** cartoon *You Ought to Be in Pictures.* When the animators break for lunch, **Daffy Duck** persuades Porky to leave cartoons and go into live-action features. Porky visits producer Leon Schlesinger, quits, hops in his (cartoon) car, and heads to the feature soundstages. Chased by a guard, the pig disrupts a huge musical number, gets caught in a western-set stampede, and finally, contritely, returns to the animation stand. A related theme can be found in Eclipse Comics's *Crossfire* no. 8 (1985), in which cartoon animals escape from a character's subconscious and invade our world; and in DC's superhero comic book *Blue Devil* no. 27 (1986), in which the animated character Godfrey Goose comes from Cartoon Land on the silver screen and begins turning everyone he meets into cartoon animals.

ROOBEAR
Pedigree. TV Koala in an anthropomorphic world.
Biography. Roobear is the son of Mr. and Mrs. (Koala) Bear, and the brother of little Laura Bear. Like the other animals in their world—including Floppy Rabbit, Nick Penguin, and various dogs, cats, and birds—the Bears live in a quaint thatched house in the middle of the woods. Their adventures are not especially dramatic, ranging from the search for an extinct Moa bird to getting Mr. Bear on a diet (he just loves those eucalyptus cakes) to playing soccer and skateboarding. Kiwi Bird is a permanent house guest of the Bears's; the family's favorite beverage is tomato juice.

Comment. *The Adventures of the Little Koala* was produced by Tohokushinsha (Japan) and Cinar Films; the half-hour adventures went into syndication in 1987. Steven Bednarski was the voice of Roobear. It's never explained why every other animal in the series has a "normal" name, except for Roobear. (Didn't his folks think Roobear Bear might be a trifle redundant?)

ROON
Pedigree. Pet jackal of comic book native Naza.
Biography. Naza and his small Stone Age tribe are nomads in search of a home; Roon is his faithful jackal. In addition to fighting skills, Roon sniffs vegetation they encounter. If it's okay to eat, the brown jackal wags its tail. Whenever the tribe is in unknown territory, Naza looks to him: If Roon's fur bristles, there is danger ahead. Roon was named after the sound he makes when howling; his nickname is Warm Eyes.

Comment. Roon appeared in most of the stories published during the nine-issue run of Dell's *Naza, Stone Age Warrior* from 1963 to 1966.

ROSCOE THE DAWG, ACE DETECTIVE
Pedigree. Comic book canine.
Biography. Roscoe is a cigarette-smoking, gun-toting, low-keyed dog-detective living in a human world. His cases tend to be relatively mundane (such as the theft of a valuable stamp), but the mysteries and characterizations are memorable.

Comment. Renegade Press published three issues of *Roscoe!* in 1987. The character was created by Martin Trengrove, whose art has a lot of the hyperactive flavor of the early *Mad* magazine stories by Harvey Kurtzman.

RUDE DOG
Pedigree. Saturday morning cartoon TV dog.
Biography. Rude Dog is a fox terrier who has a black right eye, a red left one, a green studded collar, and red spots on his side. Like a canine Riff in *West Side Story,* he's the uncontested leader of the Dweebs—seven dogs of varying degrees of ineptitude. The British dog Winston is always painfully proper and also painfully dumb ("Keep your eyes peeled," Rude Dog advises the Dweebs at one point, Winston replying, "Couldn't we try something less disgusting, sir?"); Reginald is a snide Jack Nicholson type; Tweek is a clumsy Chihuahua; Barney is a dull-witted bull terrier with a country-

western manner; Caboose is a nervous bloodhound with a Southern drawl; and Satch is a very naive Great Dane. The one "Dweebette," a pug named Kibble, is both bright and very attached to Rude Dog. Also in the cast is the very nasty blue cat Seymour, who enjoys terrorizing the dogs, and the evil dogcatcher Herman and his mumbling dog Rot. A street-smart wiseacre, Rude Dog endures the Dweebs because they let him run the show—and although he gets angry with them now and then (like when they go out to get a pet goldfish, and come back with a cow), the Dweebs are so good-natured that Rude Dog invariably mutters, "How can I stay mad at these little guys?" The dogs live in the city, in an abandoned auto shop that has been converted into a fifties-style "pad." Rude Dog has a nice room upstairs, while the other dogs crash below. They get about in a flashy red Cadillac, which only Rude Dog is allowed to drive. In his leisure time, Rude Dog enjoys watching sports on television.

Comment. The Sun Sportswear mascot—and update of the old **Top Cat** theme—came to CBS via Marvel Productions in September 1989. Each segment of *Rude Dog and the Dweebs* was fifteen minutes long. This was the first cartoon series since **Count Duckula** that both adults and children could enjoy; the highly stylized designs were also noteworthy. Rob Paulsen was the voice of Rude Dog, Ellen Gerstell was Kibble, Frank Welker was Caboose, Rot, and Seymour, Peter Cullen did an exceptional job as Herman and Winston, Dave Coulier was Barney, Jim Cummings was Satch, Mendi Segal was Reggie, and the characters' creator Hank Saroyan was Tweek.

RUFF
Pedigree. Pet dog of the comic strip "Dennis the Menace."
Biography. Ruff is a big, white dog who is, according to his owner Dennis Mitchell, "part Great Dame,

Dennis the Menace and **Ruff.** © HALL SYNDICATE.

"SURE IS FUNNY THAT WE'D *BOTH* GET HUNGRY FOR PEANUT BUTTER SAMWICHES AT THE SAME TIME!"

part Irish Set-up, an' . . . he's got a lotta puddle in him, too." He's also terrified of cats. Ruff shares Dennis's love for peanut butter, and the two regularly go to the malt shop together ("Chocolate soda and a pan of water, please"). Dennis has Ruff trained to lick houseguests until they hand over a nickel; whenever Dennis is forced to sit in the corner for punishment, Ruff curls up beside him. Ruff never speaks or thinks . . . although once in a rare while, when he's confused, a "?" will appear over his head. The Mitchells also have goldfish named Charley and Thelma, and a canary named Caruso.

Comment. Hank Ketchum's one-panel strip (multipanels on Sunday) debuted on March 12, 1951, inspired by the antics of his own four-year-old son. Dennis and Ruff have also appeared in a number of *Dennis the Menace* comic books, most notably from Standard and Fawcett (a run of seventy-five issues from 1955 to 1969), and from Marvel Comics (thirteen issues from 1981 to 1982).

RUFF AND REDDY

Pedigree. TV's second cartoon animals.

Biography. The theme song admits, "They sometimes have their little spats / even fight like dogs and cats," but the tall, drawling bulldog Reddy and his diminutive, bow-tied companion cat Ruff always pull together when there's danger. Riding about on their small scooter (Ruff perches on the handlebars), the two have battled everything from the robot inhabitants of the planet Muni-Mula (spell it backwards) to the menace of the Chickasaurus. Reddy has a white coat with a shock of red hair; Ruff is brown with a blue bow tie, and often talks in rhymes (e.g., "In a blue suit to boot!").

Comment. Hanna-Barbera's *The Ruff and Reddy Show* was the second show to feature cartoons with continuing characters produced expressly for television (**Crusader Rabbit** was the first). The animation in the six-minute cartoon was limited—there were a whopping 90 percent fewer drawings than in a comparable theatrical cartoon—but the characterizations were good. The newly formed Hanna-Barbera (this was their first TV series) produced 138 cartoons in all, most of the cartoons were chapters in larger adventures. *The Ruff and Reddy Show* ran on NBC from 1957 to 1964; Don Messick and Daws Butler were the voices of Ruff and Reddy, respectively. Del, then Gold Key, published twelve Ruff and Reddy comic books between 1958 and 1962.

RUFFERTO

Pedigree. A "spotted dog" that looks more like a jackal, Rufferto is the comic book companion of Groo the Wanderer.

Biography. Groo is a barbarian famed for his strong arm and sheer idiocy. Rufferto is equally as brave and just as dumb. Residing in the realm of King Kassabist, they wander about in search of work and sustenance. Rufferto cannot speak, but thought balloons reveal whatever he's thinking to readers. In his most notable adventure (no. 45), Rufferto is left alone while Groo goes to work. Captured while trying to rescue a pack of dogs from dog traders, Rufferto is sold to pirates. He manages to leap overboard, avoids a monstrously huge shark, is captured by an eagle and carried toward is aerie, bites the bird and is dropped into the jungle, lands on a sacrificial altar, runs, is caught by a maiden who throws him to her pet dragon, manages to avoid its snapping jaws, and makes it back to Groo's side . . . where he falls asleep, only to have Groo remark, "You have it so easy while I do all the daring work, you lazy dog!"

Comment. The droll Groo was created by *Mad* magazine artist Sergio Aragones. He first appeared in *Destroyer Duck* no. 1 in 1982, before getting his own magazine—first from Pacific Comics in 1982, then from Marvel in 1985. Rufferto didn't join the barbarian until the Marvel days.

RUFUS, THE RED-BLOODED AMERICAN REPTILE

Pedigree. Beleaguered underground comics character.

Biography. Roaming the nation and observing, Rufus—apparently an alligator—finds pigs in power everywhere he turns, and *Oink* the solution to every problem. (Serious problems in need of candy-coating are solved with a musical *Oinque.*) The most pointed strip regarding the state of law enforcement found Rufus hauled into court for littering, not because he dropped a banana peel on the highway, but because it "was from an out of state banana."

Comment. Typical of late 1960s, early 1970s pessimism, Bill Crawford's creation appeared in the only issue of the Print Mint's *High-Flyin' Funnies Comix and Stories* (1970).

RUSTY

Pedigree. Sidekick to TV's bizarre Turbo-Teen.

Biography. When Brett Mathews loses control of his car, he crashes into a government lab where a "molecular transfer ray" is being tested. He and his sports car are blasted; as a result, any time he becomes hot, Brett is automatically transformed into the auto. Conversely, when the car cools, it turns back into Brett. The teen tools around Hillmont with his sheepdog Rusty and friend Alex, wooing the ladies, racing, fighting criminals like the Dragon, and trying to avoid the mysterious Dark Rider, who wants "to prove that Brett Mathews is his car," and learn the secret of his transforming ability. Rusty usually does little more than use his sniffing ability like a bloodhound. However, Rusty does have one desperate adventure—indeed, it's a new high in horror for pet animals—when the Dark Rider kidnaps a scientist and steals a potion that turns animals into their prehistoric ancestors. He turns Rusty and two other dogs into large-fanged, slavering beasts, and sends them forth to kidnap Brett. Brett turns into the car in his kitchen and gets away; when his mother comes downstairs (she doesn't know about his powers) she looks at the carnage and wonders why her son can never clean up after himself. Eventually, the pack of prehistoric dogs attacks the high school during a football game, and Turbo-Teen nabs them after a wild chase around the field. Rusty gets away and the teen chases him into a hotel, through a banquet hall and up the stairs, before Alex is finally able to administer the antidote. Rusty returns to being his old self, just sitting in the backseat with his tongue hanging out.

Comment. Ruby-Spears's *Turbo-Teen* joined ABC's Saturday morning lineup for a brief run in 1984. Another dog who got into dangerous adventures with its master was Bib of *Here Comes the Grump* (NBC, 1969). When the sour Grump places the Curse of Gloom on a fairyland, teenager Terry Dexter and Bib are magically whisked to the enchanted kingdom. Fighting various foes, they help Princess Dawn search for the Cave of the Whispering Orchids, hiding place of the Crystal Key which can free them.

S

SALEM

Pedigree. The cat owned by Sabrina the witch, of Archie comics fame.

Biography. The tabby cat is the pet of Sabrina, the good witch of Riverdale. Although the two don't communicate, balloons reveal the cat's thoughts to the reader. Like its master, Salem has the ability to perform tricks of white (good) magic.

Comment. The cat appeared regularly in the *Sabrina* comic book from 1971 to 1983; Sabrina herself debuted in *Archie's Madhouse* no. 21 in 1962. Another animal in the series is the white, flying Cloud Stallion, which belongs to head witch Della. Salem and Sabrina have been seen on many cartoon shows, beginning with *The Archie Comedy Hour with Sabrina* (CBS, 1969), and including her own series *Sabrina, The Teenage Witch* (CBS, 1971) and *Superwitch* (NBC, 1977). Her adventures are presently in syndication on *The Archies*. Salem co-starred with **Super Duck** in *Laugh* no. 24 in 1990.

SALOMEY

Pedigree. Pig pet of the comic strip's Li'l Abner.

Biography. Li'l Abner is a six-foot, three-inch, nineteen-year-old, happy-go-lucky hillbilly denizen of Dogpatch, U.S.A. With the possible exception of his girlfriend (later, wife) Daisy Mae Scragg and their two children (Honest Abe and Tiny), no living creature matters as much to Abner as the Hammus Alabamus, Salomey. When Abner isn't around, the pig usually hangs out with his father, Pappy Yokum. Her most dangerous adventure occurred in 1969, when "King of Pork" J. Roaringham Fatback decided to make pork and beans our national dish (displacing pizza) . . . and no pig tastes better than a Hammus Alabamus. Daisy Mae warned Salomey, "Don't grunt to *no* strange hawgs, don't take *no* garbage fum no strange swine." However, Fatback used plastic surgery (including a snout job) to transform the wild boar Porknoy the Complainer into a gentleman, who successfully wooed the lady. Luckily, as Salomey tells Porknoy (she can only talk to other pigs), "No one can cook me once they look into my big brown eyes." While Fatback looks for a chef immune to Salomey's charms, Abner's mother Mammy Yokum arrives and persuades Fatback that a "hoomin bean" will taste better than a Hammus Alabamus. Devoted to the art of cooking, Fatback jumped into the beanpot himself. Other animals in the strip—less lovable by far—are the turnip ter-

Salem, and her witch-master Sabrina.
© ARCHIE PUBLICATIONS. *Courtesy* MICHAEL SILBERKLEIT.

Salomey gets a lecture from Daisy Mae, girlfriend of the pig's owner, Li'l Abner. © UNITED FEATURE SYNDICATE.

DELL
12c
12-740-602
FEBRUARY
Sinbad Jr
SINBAD JR. AND SALTY DISCOVER THE MAD SCIENTIST AND HIS INFERNAL MACHINE!
STOP! YOU'LL DESTROY THE WORLD!
LOOK OUT, SINBAD! HE SEES US!
© 1965, AMERICAN INTERNATIONAL PICTURES

mites, who regularly descend on Dogpatch and destroy the town's sole crop.

Comment. Al Capp's "Li'l Abner" debuted on August 20, 1934. The characters were also featured in five theatrical cartoons released in 1944 to 1945. Other pigs that have appeared in comic books and cartoons are Ziggy Pig, who starred in various Marvel Comics titles throughout the 1940s (usually paired with Silly Seal); Puffy Pig, another Marvel swine who drifted in and out of various comic books; Pudgy Pig, who appeared in two issues of his own Charlton Comics magazine in 1958; and Squeely, who was a military commander in charge of those irrepressible recruits Laverne and Shirley in the 1982 ABC cartoon series *Laverne and Shirley with the Fonz,* which took the *Private Benjamin*-ish twist of having the young women in the army. Ron Palillo provided the voice for the officer pig.

SALTY

Pedigree. A macho parrot of comics and television, sidekick to Sinbad, Jr.

Biography. Salty is a green, talking parrot who is the mate onboard the sailboat *Seafarer*—the only other passenger being Sinbad, Jr., a young man who gains superpowers by activating a magic belt. Although Salty tends to be a little sloppy about his work, he is an accomplished scuba diver, and "when it comes to dropping anchor, I'm the best around!"

Comment. Salty appeared in the cartoon series *The Adventures of Sinbad, Jr.,* a k a *Sinbad Jr., the Sailor.* Mel Blanc provided the voice. The half-hour Hanna-Barbera Production was aired via syndication in 1966, and there were eighty cartoons in all. Dell published three issues of a *Sinbad, Jr.* comic book; Salty was featured in all of them. Another comic book parrot was Cracky, who starred in *Wacky Adventures of Cracky* in *Gold Key Spotlight* no. 5 (1977) and also appeared in house ads promoting Gold Key comic books.

SAM SHEEPDOG

Pedigree. Star of several Warner Brothers theatrical shorts.

Biography. The title is irresistible: *Don't Give Up the Sheep.* Something had to be made using it; fortunately, in 1953, director-animator Chuck Jones came up with a winner, a series of blackout gags in which Ralph Wolf—a deadringer for **Wile E. Coyote**—preys on a flock guarded by Sam Sheepdog. What's particularly inspired about the cartoons, however, is that before and after hours, and sometimes during breaks, the two foes chat amiably; the adversarial relationship is strictly professional. In the first cartoon, Ralph waits until Sam arrives for work in the morning, replacing Fred. The wolf pushes the clock ahead so it says noon, and Sam leaves to have lunch. Ralph tries to make off with a lamb, but Sam isn't as dumb as he looks (and he does look dumb, with eyes perpetually covered by bangs and an otherwise vacant expression). He trails the wolf and smashes him. Next, Ralph tries to get the dog to take a nap—and gets pummeled. Approaches by tunnel and vine work no better, nor does swimming underwater: Sam casually pokes a stick of TNT down Ralph's snorkel! Their second cartoon together, *Sheep Ahoy* (1954) opens with Sam pushing a boulder onto Ralph, and goes downhill (for the wolf) from there. This cartoon concludes not just with Fred arriving for the nightshift, but the wolf George showing up as well. The two dutifully take their positions, Fred bashing George just as Sam was beating Ralph.

Comment. There were seven Sam cartoons in all.

SAM SIMEON

Pedigree. Simian sleuth, and costar of his own DC comic book.

Biography. The truth is, this comic book was a lot like the late ABC TV series *Moonlighting.* It starred a clever blond and a hulking, muscular male, who headed up their own detective agency, O'Day and Simeon. Only in this case, the male doesn't just act like an ape . . . he *is* one. Most of the time, Sam is a cartoonist, equally adept drawing with his hands or feet. However, when friend Angel O'Day needs his help, he drops his pen and joins her on a case. Angel is fluent in ape, which is the only language Sam talks. (It does bear some semblance to English, though. For example, "Gushabuh! Yukkubinkle!" is "Got you buddy! You could've been killed!") The gorilla possesses an "awful temper," a supersensitive nose (he can follow the trail of a candybar–eating criminal), and awesome strength. He bathes only once a month, and it's remarkable that criminals don't smell *him* coming, too! The ape can usually be found munching on a banana, even while swinging from ledge to ledge to beat city traffic. Sam dresses in a suit, shirt, tiny fedora, and loud ties when he's on assignment. Although he isn't immune to women's charms, he is ever the professional. Glancing at a pinup poster, he muses, "I've never seen such beautiful color reproduction."

Salty stating the obvious. Then again, Sinbad Jr. isn't the brightest tar on the seven seas.

Comment. The ape's name is a play on William Randolph Hearst's California estate. The characters first appeared in *Showcase* no. 77, 1968, then went on to star in six issues of their own title, *Angel and the Ape* (1968 to 1969). They returned in a four-issue mini-series in 1991.

SAMURAI PENGUIN
Pedigree. Somber, comic book defender of penguins in the South Pole.
Biography. Serving Yoshi, "Lord and Master of the Antarctic Penguins," the bold young Samurai Penguin protects his clan from predators, such as sharks and skuas. Meanwhile, Artimus Walrus moans that the warrior is "messing up the entire food chain." His seal aides Stan and Ollie don't understand why that makes Artimus so angry, and he explains, "If the penguin colony is allowed to grow then they will eventually dry up the other available food supply." The struggles between the hero and villain comprise the bulk of the action.

Comment. The short-lived (eight issues) *Samurai Penguin* was the creation of Dan Vado and Mark Buck, and was first published by Slave Labor Graphics in 1986. Buck's angular artwork and continuity is exceptional, and Vado's characterizations are well thought out. The publication deserved far greater success.

SANDY (1)
Pedigree. Pet dog of the comic strip immortal Little Orphan Annie.
Biography. When the sour-tempered Mrs. Warbucks goes to the orphanage and brings home eleven-year-old Annie—just to prove to her "society pals what a hot charity worker" she is—the girl's only friends are the Warbuckses' Peke-type dog One Lung, and Mrs. Warbucks's husband, the benevolent Oliver "Daddy" Warbucks. Mrs. Warbucks quickly comes to detest the precocious girl, and takes her back to the home; but "Daddy" loves her and gets her back, and this time she comes with her "orphan" dog Sandy. Not long thereafter, Sandy bites the evil Count de Tour, who was secretly out to destroy the Warbuckses' fortune. Outraged, the very proper Mrs. Warbucks orders two of the servants to put Sandy in a bag and shoot him. Only the timely arrival of Daddy Warbucks prevents Sandy's demise. However, Annie is so upset that she, Sandy, and her doll Emily Marie run away. The trio are caught in a blinding snowstorm, which gives Sandy one of his

finest moments: They spot a stack of straw, in which cows have burrowed a dry niche. Sandy chases them away, and silently stands guard while Annie sleeps and the cows glower. Meanwhile, the frantic Daddy drives around, looking for Annie, and finds her. Not long thereafter, Mrs. Warbucks is gone. In time, Daddy Warbucks is transformed from a bored millionaire arms manufacturer to a globe-hopping adventurer, and the stories center around the efforts of Annie and Sandy to find him, or he them. Sandy is tan with a white muzzle, a black left ear, and a black spot on his back. His vocabulary consists of three different barks: One *Arf* means he agrees with Annie, two means there's danger, and *Gr-r-r* means he's angry. If anyone tries to hurt Annie, nothing will stop the dog from biting or treeing them.

Comment. For four years, Harold Gray had been an assistant to cartoonist Sidney Smith (on *The Gumps*) when he submitted his own cartoon strip to Captain Joseph Medill Patterson, cofounder of the *New York News*. Patterson had Gray change the hero of the strip to a heroine, and *Little Orphan Annie* debuted on August 5, 1924. Gray died in 1968,

*An early, slender **Sandy (1)** with Little Orphan Annie.*
© CHICAGO TRIBUNE/NEW YORK NEWS SYNDICATE.

and the strip has continued—as a failed attempt to make Annie more contemporary, as reprints, and, now, as a return to its roots written and drawn by Leonard Starr. Perhaps the most noteworthy event in Sandy's life occurred in 1933. When the dog vanished, the publisher of the *New York News* received the following telegram: PLEASE DO ALL YOU CAN TO HELP ANNIE FIND SANDY STOP WE ARE ALL INTERESTED (signed) HENRY FORD. Annie and Sandy have been featured in numerous comic books from 1926 to 1948, many of them being reprints of the comic strips.

SANDY (2)
Pedigree. Realistically portrayed comic book mount.
Biography. Judge Mark Colt is the law in Fort Smith, Arkansas in the 1870s—both behind the bench and behind a gun. The sandy-colored Sandy is always ready to help him.
Comment. There were four issues of Gold Key's *Judge Colt* from 1969 to 1970. Sandy appeared in them all. Other obscure comic book characters with even more obscure mounts were the Sundance Kid's Buckshot (*The Sundance Kid*, three issues in 1971 from Skywalk Comics); Arizona Ames and Thunder, who appeared in *Crack Western* in the early 1950s (Ames's sidekick Spurs could be found astride Calico); Whip Wilson and Bullet, who had their own three-issue run in 1950; the Whip, a masked hero who rode Diablo in the pages of *Flash Comics* beginning with no. 1 in 1940; the Wyoming Kid and Racer, who first appeared in *Western Comics* no. 1 in 1948, and Nighthawk and his horse **Nightwind,** who arrived in no. 5; the Apache Kid and *his* stallion Nightwind (both unrelated to the Rawhide Kid's **Nightwind**), who starred in nineteen issues of their own magazine from 1950 to 1956; Kamesa, the "war pony of the Commanche Kid," who costarred in the only issue of Atlas Comics's *Western Action* (1975); the Western Kid and Whirlwind, from *The Western Kid* (1954 to 1957); Gunhawk and his horse Blaze who galloped through *Wild Western* beginning with no. 15 (1949); the Outlaw Kid and Thunder, stars of nineteen issues of *The Outlaw Kid* (1954 to 1957); Bill Elliot and his steed Stormy, who started a short ride through the west in *4-Color* no. 278 in 1950; Durango Kid and Raider, who thundered through the cowboy's own title from 1949 to 1955; White Rider and the not-really-super Super-Horse, who debuted in *Blue Bolt* no. 1 in 1940, and

finally had six issues of their own from 1950 to 1951; the Indian Straight Arrow's horse Fury, who first appeared in *A-1 Comics* in 1954; Monte Hale and Pardner, who went from the movies to a *Monte Hale Western* comic book which lasted fifty-nine issues (1948 to 1956); and the Ringo Kid, who saddled up Arab in twenty-one issues of his own magazine from 1954 to 1957. See **Black Fury,** for a listing of horses who had their own comic books.

SCAREBEAR
Pedigree. Occasional TV companion to Yogi Bear.
Biography. When Yogi joins the outer space racing circuit, his long-time sidekick Boo-Boo is replaced by Scarebear. The short engineer bear has shaggy fur, a pear-shaped body, and is as hyperactive as they come. Somehow, he and Yogi always make it through such matches as *The Saturn 500, The Neptune 9000, The Spartikan Spectacular, The Race through the Planet of the Monster, The Mizar Marathon,* and others. After abandoning the competitive life, the duo spend time solving intergalactic crimes involving the likes of the Purloined Princess, the Vampire of Space, the Clone Ranger, and Tacky Cat. The bear is naked, save for a small, futuristic vest with flared shoulders.
Comment. The Hanna-Barbera character was seen on *Yogi's Space Race,* which began on NBC in September of 1978; he and his cartoon-mates got their own show, *The Galaxy Goof-Ups,* in November of that year. There were thirteen different segments produced for each show. Joe Besser (one of the latter-day Three Stooges) provided the voice in both versions. **Huckleberry Hound** and the inept law officer Quackup, a dizzy duck with a propeller beanie, are also seen in the series.

SCOOBY-DOO
Pedigree. Popular dog of TV cartoons and comic books.
Biography. The theme song poses the question, "Scooby scooby doo, lookin' for you; scooby dooby doo, where are you?" The answer: hiding or running. A big, brown Great Dane with black spots on its back and a long tongue always hanging from the side of his mouth, Scooby is a coward. Thus it isn't clear why Scooby hangs out with four teenage amateur detectives. Handsome leader Fred, brainy Velma, gangly and long-haired Shaggy, and pretty but unlucky Daphne travel around in their mod Mystery Machine, a van, becoming caught up in ee-

rie mysteries such as *Strange Encounters of a Scooby Kind, The Scary Sky Skeleton, The Night Ghouls of Wonderworld, The Neon Phantom of the Roller Disco, The Sorcerer's a Menace, The Hairy Scare of the Devil Bear, The Demon of the Dugout,* and *Twenty Thousand Screams Under the Sea.* Not the stuff for which Scooby's frail nerves were made! Scooby's fumbling, lookalike, bumpkin cousin Scooby-Dum arrived on *The Scooby-Doo/Dynomutt Hour;* the timid Scooby-Doo was joined by his shorter, but much bolder nephew in a later series, *Scooby and Scrappy-Doo.*

Comment. Scooby's first series, *Scooby-Doo, Where Are You?* debuted on CBS in 1969 and was a huge hit. The Hanna-Barbera show remained with the network until 1976, and moved briefly to ABC in 1978. There were forty-one episodes in all. Subsequent series were *The New Scooby-Doo Comedy Movies* (twenty-four episodes, CBS, 1972 to 1974); *The Scooby-Doo/Dynomutt Hour* (twenty-four episodes, ABC, 1976; see **Dynomutt**); *The Scooby-Doo/Dynomutt Show* (the previous show with a new name, ABC, 1976 to 1977); *Scooby's All Star Laff-A-Lympics* (ABC, 1977 to 1978; see below for episode information); *Scooby's All Stars* (ABC, 1978 to 1979); *Scooby and Scrappy-Doo* (ABC, 1979 to 1980); *Scooby's Laff-A-Lympics* (ABC, 1980); *The Richie Rich/Scooby and Scrappy-Doo Show* (ABC, 1980 to 1982); *Scooby-Doo Classics* (ABC, 1981 to 1982); *Scooby, Scrappy, and Yabba Doo* (ABC, 1982 to 1983); *Scooby and Scrappy-Doo* (ABC, 1983 to 1984); *The New Scooby-Doo Mysteries* (ABC, 1984 to 1985); and *The 13 Ghosts of Scooby-Doo* (ABC, 1985 to 1986). Don Messick was the voice of Scooby in all, Lennie Weinrib was Scrappy-Doo, and Daws Butler was Scooby-Dum. The biggest of the shows in terms of the cast of characters was *Scooby's All Star Laff-A-Lympics,* which was created to cash in on the publicity generated by the 1976 Olympics. There were sixteen half-hour adventures (eight more for *Scooby's All Stars* the following year), in which the characters went around the world competing in such events as airboat racing (Florida) and rickshaw-pulling (Hong Kong) for the Laff-A-Lympics Gold Medallion. There were three teams in the competition, each made up of characters from other Hanna-Barbera series: the Scooby-Doobies—consisting of Scooby, Shaggy, Scooby-Dum, the Blue Falcon and Dynomutt, Tinker and Speed Buggy, **Hong Kong Phooey,** Babu (a

genie), and Captain Caveman (see **Cave Bird**)—the Yogi Yahooeys—composed of **Yogi Bear, Boo Boo Bear, Cindy Bear, Super Snooper, Huckleberry Hound, Grape Ape, Quick Draw McGraw** (no Baba Looey), **Wally Gator, Mr. Jinks** (with Pixie and Dixie), **Augie Doggie** (and Doggie Daddy), **Yakky Doodle** (sans Chopper and Fibber Fox), and **Hokey Wolf** (without Ding-a-ling)—and (boo-hiss) the Really Rottens—made up of **Mumbly** (who used to be a good guy!) and the Dread Baron; the magician Great Fondoo and Magic Rabbit; backwoods Daisy Mayhem and her huge companion Sooey Pig (who wears a patch over one eye); the Creeply Family (monsters); Orful Octopus; and the gun-toting Dalton Brothers. Announcing the games were **Snagglepuss** and Mildew Wolf. Presently in syndication is the animated series *A Pup Named Scooby-Doo,* which chronicles the adventures of the dog, Shaggy, and the other kids and their Scooby-Doo Detective Agency. In comics, Gold Key published thirty issues of *Scooby Doo . . . Where Are You?* (retitled *Scooby Doo Mystery Comics* with no. 17; name not hyphenated) from 1970 to 1975; Charlton published eleven issues of plain, old *Scooby Doo* from 1975 to 1976, and Marvel offered nine issues of *Scooby-Doo* from 1977 to 1979. Marvel also published thirteen issues of *Laff-A-Lympics* (1978 to 1979), in which **Jabberjaw** occasionally appeared as a judge.

SCROOGE MCDUCK

Pedigree. Miserly uncle of **Donald Duck.**

Biography. Scrooge lives in a mansion in Duckburg (see Donald's entry), adjoining a massive vault known as the Money Bin: In it are three cubic acres of money, over 6 septillion dollars . . . virtually every cent the tightwaddler has ever made. (The inside walls of the bin are marked like a swimming pool, showing the depths of the money.) McDuck's greatest pleasure in life is to enter the bin and literally swim in his money—which is why, he says, he likes "to keep my assets liquid." He recognizes each piece of money he owns: Shown a randomly selected fistful of bills, he squawked, "Yes! I made these dollars ten years ago, when I owned Duckburg's only door-to-door butcher company." Usually dressed in a silk top hat (there's money tucked underneath it), a red broadcloth coat (purchased in Scotland in 1902), spectacles, and spats, and occasionally a walking stick, the duck belongs to the Clan McDuck of Scotland. Little is known of his ancestors, although Ad-

Scooby-Doo and Shaggy. Scooby is now the cartoon animal with the longest running show still on the air (in one incarnation or another). © HANNA-BARBERA PRODUCTIONS.

miral Sir Drake McDuck was a bold seaman of the mid-eighteenth century. As for Scrooge himself, he first struck it rich in the golden hills of the Klondike in 1899, partnered with the burly Sourdough Sam, a human-dog hybrid. (Decades later, Scrooge found an IOU from Sam for one dollar, and flew back to the icy wastes to collect it.) McDuck increased his wealth by opening banks, mom-and-pop grocery stores, hardware stores, hot dog stands, cold dog stands, a Christmas tree stand (he charges Donald for the family tree), a gumball factory, and other canny enterprises—such as a pottery stand situated on a dangerous curve (business is "A bang-up success"). His portfolio also contains oil wells in Australia, pearl beds in Japan, and he's also rumored to be involved in the feather business in downtown Duckburg. He has a "Tycoon Diploma," and one unbreakable rule: Unless a doctor is in attendance, no one is permitted to mention income tax in his presence. For all his wealth, Scrooge's most precious possession is his "lucky dime," the first ten cents he ever made, which he keeps in a glass case. Among his other holdings are the world's largest emerald, which he "bought from the emperor Hung Tu Soon," as well as the McDuck Building in downtown Duckburg. Although Scrooge loves sitting at home and counting his money or taking baths in it, he'll embark on wild adventures if there's money in it (such as diving for sunken gold, braving rugged mountains for legendary treasures, looking into lost mines, and so on). To this end, he even owns an "automatic digitator," a computer that keeps him abreast of "the location of everything of value in the world." However, vacations per se tend to be a drag for the duck: Once, on a beach, the dunes reminded him of his money, and he had to have it shipped to him, pronto, so he could "wallow in my mounds." In the matter of marriage, Scrooge was pursued by Minny Pearl, a Southern belle of a duck whom he spurned. Indeed, McDuck has this to say when **Daisy Duck** asks why he hasn't considered marriage: "I have. I consider it a nuisance." Daisy goes on to say that a bachelor has no one to tell his troubles to, to which Scrooge replies, "Why should a bachelor *have* any troubles?"

Comment. Uncle Scrooge first appeared in *4-Color* no. 178 in 1947. Carl Barks created him because Donald was going to camp in the mountains: "Somebody had to own this cabin he was going to," says Barks, "so I invented Uncle Scrooge as the owner." At first, Scrooge was an unlikeable misan-

thrope; he evolved quickly, however, into a cheerful penny-pincher whose philosophy was simply stated: "People that spend money . . . don't know how to enjoy it." There have been 236 issues of his own magazine, published by Dell (to no. 39), Gold Key (to no. 209), and Gladstone thereafter; there have been various one-shot comic books as well. Scrooge has been a regular in the Donald Duck comic strip since 1960. (In his first appearance, we learn how near he is: He carries his own bag at the airport, walks rather than take a cab, and gives **Huey, Dewey, and Louie** a dime for Christmas.) Prior to his TV series *DuckTales* (see below), Scrooge made only two animated appearances: in the 1967 TV cartoon *Scrooge McDuck and Money*, and as the star of the 1983 featurette *Mickey's Christmas Carol*. Bill Thompson and Alan Young provided the Scottish voice in these, respectively. Beginning in 1988, Scrooge was seen in both the syndicated TV series and Gladstone comic book *DuckTales*, and in a quarterly text-and-comics magazine *DuckTales*. On the TV series, assisted by his comrades (see below), Scrooge battles such foes as the evil Captain Bounty of the Bermuda Triangle, a rampaging robot who seizes control of the Money Bin, the leprechaun Far Darrig (whose treasure Scrooge tries to obtain), Dr. Nogood and his organization FOWL (Foreign Organization for World Larceny), a lemming that steals the locket containing the combination to Scrooge's new safe, and, while searching for a valuable old crown once owned by Genghis Khan, Scrooge and company have a run-in with an abominable snowwoman. He also battles two recurring enemies: the thieving **Beagle Boys** and **Magica de Spell**. (The most inventive of the Beagle Boys episodes had Scrooge suffering from a nightmare in which he must serve the Boys as the Cinderella-type domestic Scroogerello.) About the only kind of foe Scrooge doesn't face are solicitors; no doubt they're intimidated by the sign beneath the loudspeaker at his front gate, which reads, "Salesmen and fundraisers will be ridiculed." Also seen on the show are **Gyro Gearloose; Huey, Dewey, and Louie;** Scrooge's butler, the stuffy but devoted dog Duckworth; kindly, white-haired, heavyset housekeeper Mrs. Beakley; her niece, the little duck Webbigail (a k a Webby); the portly duck Doofus, who wears thick eyeglasses, a coonskin cap, and is a member of the Junior Woodchucks (see **Huey, Dewey, and Louie);** the prehistoric Bubba Duck and his pet triceratops Tootsie; and the strutting, virile-voiced Launchpad

McQuack. Launchpad is the real "find" of the show: a tall, strapping, red-haired pilot-duck who runs Launchpad Limited from an airfield on the outskirts of Duckburg. He dresses like a 1930s aviator, with a cap, goggles, scarf, jacket, breeches, and boots (shaped just like his webbed feet), and while he isn't the brightest duck in the world, he can pilot most kinds of aircraft—even though he has trouble keeping them aloft. (He and Scrooge recently celebrated their 100th crash together.) Launchpad is also in charge of steering Scrooge's yacht, SS *Glitter O' Gold,* and any other vehicle the tycoon may need. For instance, when extraterrestrials steal the Money Bin to melt down the precious metals therein, he's able to scare up *and* fly a rocketship. On the two-hour special *Super DuckTales* (shown on NBC's *Magical World of Disney* in April 1989), Scrooge's new accountant Fenton was introduced, a young duck who lives with his TV-addicted mother in a trailer park and lisps like **Daffy Duck.** Although a whiz with numbers, Fenton is dumber than any other member of the group (he once made a phone call with Scrooge's lucky dime). Fenton was also, briefly, Gizmo Duck (see **Gyro Gearloose** for more).

SCRUBBY BEAR
Pedigree. TV hygiene spokesbear.
Biography. The brown bear has a tiny red heart on the left side of its chest, and has only one goal in life: To get kids to wash their hands. As the song puts it, "Wash your hands / Wash your hands / There's more dirt than you might think / Put them in the bathtub / Wash them in the sink."

   Comment. The character began appearing in public service spots in 1988, sponsored by the U.S. Department of Health and Human Services.

SEABERT
Pedigree. TV cartoon seal.
Biography. Seabert works with the human boy Tommy and girl Aura to "protect endangered animals." Based in Greenland, the three travel the world protecting whales, elephants, alligators, seals, leopards, and other hunted breeds. Although he can't talk, Seabert can make a trilling sound; although he can't walk, he can flipper along at top speeds (even on land), sliding into villains or dropping on them from above. He's also just; however, in one episode, he positioned himself in front of a hunter to prevent angry animals from tearing him to pieces. Despite the serious theme of the cartoons, the filmmakers manage to inject questionable humor: While preventing a hunter from setting a trap, he causes the trap to spring and hurl both of them into the air; while reacting with shock to a film showing the abuse of animals, Seabert paws at the film, becomes tangled in it, and is flung across the room by the spinning reels. The activist is blue, approximately two feet long, and incredibly intelligent.

   Comment. The thirteen cartoons were produced in 1985 by Sepp-Inter and BZZ films. The character was created by Marc Tortarollo. For all their good intentions, the filmmakers are undermined by bad scripts and even worse animation.

SEADOG
Pedigree. Advertising mascot for Cap'n Crunch cereal.
Biography. Seadog is the dog first mate of the SS *Guppy,* the ship commanded by the intrepid Cap'n Crunch. Other crewmates include the children Brunnhilde, Alfie, Dave, and Carlyle. In addition to traveling the world, the group tries to keep their precious cereal cargo out of the clutches of the pirate LaFoote. Another animal occasionally featured in the commercials was Smedley the elephant, who later became the mascot for a short-lived peanut butter-flavored version of the cereal.

   Comment. The characters were introduced in 1963 in the advertising and on packaging for the Quaker Oaks Company cereal. They're still used for both. Jay Ward Productions (**Rocky and Bullwinkle**) handled the animation.

SEBASTIAN (1)
Pedigree. TV and comic book cat.
Biography. Sebastian is the pet of the teenage Josie and, later, the mascot for her all-girl rock group the Pussycats. For the most part, the cat merely tags along on the girls' adventures around the world and in space.

   Comment. The Archie comics character appeared in the *Josie* comic book, which began publication in 1963 and was discontinued in 1982 after 106 issues; it also appeared on Hanna-Barbera's *Josie and the Pussycats,* which aired on CBS from 1970 to 1972, and on *Josie and the Pussycats in Outer Space,* which ran on CBS from 1972 to 1974. Don Messick purred the voice in both series; there were sixteen cartoons produced for each. An animal seen on the second series is Bleep, a ducklike creature whose quack is an offensive weapon.

SEBASTIAN (2)
Pedigree. Animated cartoon crab.
Biography. The red crustacean, who speaks with a Jamaican lilt and sings reggae, is the guardian and friend of Ariel, a headstrong mermaid and the daughter of Triton, the king of the sea. Falling in love with a surface-dwelling young man, Ariel makes a deal with the sea-witch Ursula: She trades her lovely voice for legs. On land, Sebastian continues to look after her, eventually helping her to get her voice back, win her heart's desire, and destroy Ursula. Helping Sebastian are his fish friend, Flounder, and the perpetually befuddled seagull, Scuttle.
Comment. Sebastian first appeared in the magnificent 1989 Walt Disney Pictures cartoon *The Little Mermaid,* and though the character wasn't in Hans Christian Andersen's original tale, he *should* have been! The voice of the scene-stealing crab was provided by Samuel E. Wright, a magnificent singer who was inexplicably and wrongly denied the opportunity to sing the Oscar-nominated "Kiss the Girl" and "Under the Sea" from the film at the Academy Awards ceremony!

SECRET SQUIRREL
Pedigree. TV secret agent with buck teeth.
Biography. Dressed in a trenchcoat, his hat pulled low, the not-very-imposing Agent 000 fights a variety of criminals and enemy operatives. Aided by his driver Morocco Mole (a Peter Lorre soundalike), the squirrel races forth to the cry of "Heroes to the rescue!" then suffers countless setbacks—especially when the gadgets hidden in his coat misfire. However, he always ends up triumphing against such foes as Yellow Pinky, the Masked Granny, Robin Hood and His Merry Mugs, and Captain Kidd.
Comment. Hanna-Barbera's *The Secret Squirrel Show* premiered on NBC in 1965 (after his introduction with **Atom Ant** in a prime-time special, *The World of Secret Squirrel Show*); there were twenty-six episodes. These were later syndicated as part of *The Banana Splits and Friends.* Mel Blanc provided the squirrel's voice, and Paul Frees was Morocco. Also seen in his own adventures on the show was one of the least physically appealing cartoon animals in memory: Squiddly Diddly, a squid who entertains crowds at the Bubbleland aquarium. Squiddly's driving ambition is to become a celebrity, although along the way he encounters everything from ghosts to a robot squid to an upstaging seal. Gold Key published one *Secret Squirrel* comic book (1966), which also boasted a Squiddly story.

SGT. GORILLA
Pedigree. DC Comics soldier: "The only non-com who ever escaped from a zoo to join the marines."
Biography. Charlie the ape and his trainer, Sgt. Pinky Donovan, a former marine, travel through the South Pacific entertaining troops during World War II. The gorilla wears fatigues and a helmet, and carries a rifle and bayonet. Since Pinky plays a Japanese soldier in the act, Charlie learns how to fight him off using weapons and martial arts. When Pinky is called back to active service, Charlie stows away on the ship. The marines are chopped up when they storm a beach and Pinky is pinned down, so Charlie races to his rescue. But Charlie doesn't stop there. Scooping up a machine gun, he storms the Japanese nest and cleans it out. Later, he climbs a tree and shakes out the enemy snipers. Finally, he scales a sheer cliff, pulling the marines behind him like "a hair escalator." Reaching Japanese artillery at the edge of the cliff, the ape uproots and tosses it into the sea—then raises the American flag, Iwo Jima style. After musing, "How in blue blazes do you pin a medal on a gorilla?" the C.O. promotes the ape to sergeant.
Comment. The heroic ape appeared just once, in *Star Spangled War Stories* no. 126, 1966. Screwy as the story is, artist Joe Kubert—who drew the Green Berets newspaper comic strip, as well as the Tarzan comic book—was the only artist who could have made it all *look* plausible.

SHAMUS
Pedigree. Dog assistant to the TV gumshoe Q. T. Hush.
Biography. Q. T. has a most remarkable ability: He can work as a human private eye, or as a separate shadow known as Quincy. His aide Shamus, a private nose, accompanies him in both guises. Among their foes have been kidnappers Yo Yo and Ping Pong, the art crook One Ton, gangster Al Cologne, Dr. Tickle and Mr. Snide, and nuclear materials thief Professor Zappo.
Comment. Filmation produced the adventures of *Q. T. Hush,* which went into syndication in 1960. There were ten adventures consisting of ten chapters, each three and a half minutes long. Another Filmation pooch sidekick was Trouble, the aide to the black superheroes Super Stretch and Micro Woman, who appeared in their own segment of *Tarzan and the Super 7* (CBS, 1977). (Speaking of Tarzan, for his three different Filmation series, the hero's movie companion, the chimp Cheetah, was replaced by the spider monkey Nkima.)

SHARPIE

Pedigree. Advertising mascot for Gillette.

Biography. Squawking the praises of Gillette's Blue Blades, Sharpie appeared in TV commercials that appeared almost exclusively on sporting events. The exuberant parrot, who never talked, was originally animated over live-action footage of sporting events. Later, he usually suited up and partook in animated sports, although occasionally he conducted the product's "Look Sharp" music.

Comment. The parrot was created by the Maxen Agency and first appeared in 1952. He last appeared in 1960. Another popular advertising bird (species unknown) of the 1950s was Wally, who drank champagne and smoked cigarettes with a holder in Western Airlines commercials (his name was derived from the phrase, "Western Airlines Loves You").

SHERLOCK MONK

Pedigree. A hapless monkey-sleuth of comic book "fame."

Biography. Sad, but true: Although it's the chimp Sherlock who smokes the pipe and wears the deerstalker cap (a shock of red hair curls dramatically from beneath the brim in front), it's his aide Chuck the Duck who's the brains of the outfit. How dumb *is* Sherlock? Show him a full-length mirror, and he'll deduce that someone else is standing there; if he drops his pipe while in hot pursuit of a criminal, he'll go back and get it. He has no better luck with the English language, as when he undertakes a stake-out by assuring a new client, "We'll be quiet like a moose." (Actually, that's about how quiet they are. They hide in a closet to watch a thief; when the crook pours plaster under the door, the duo is forced to pound on the walls for help.) Still, the simian is gallant: He once stooped and retrieved jewels dropped by a crook and gave them back . . . to the thief. Arguably, his greatest achievement was apprehending the Bantam of the Opera, a fowl who was robbing theatergoers. Sherlock's motto is, "Big or small, we solve them all!"

Comment. Sherlock first appeared in Fawcett's *Funny Animals* no. 1 in 1942. For other animals that appeared in the magazine, see **Hoppy, the Captain Marvel Bunny** entry.

SHOE

Pedigree. Comic strip duck.

Biography. Shoe—a k a P. Martin Shoemaker—is a cigar-smoking, blue-feathered editor of the *Treetops Tattler Tribune*, which is based in a treetop and dis-tributed among the local fowl. His chief political reporter and close friend is Perfesser Cosmo Fishhawk. The two have known each other for more than a decade, and while they're devoted to their work, Shoe laments to his friend, "Maybe you haven't noticed, but all the big dough goes to dogs and cats in this business." Muffy Hollandaise is another reporter, somewhat naive, who often needs help from the other birds. (When she can't get continuing character Senator Battson D. Belfry on the phone, Shoe calls and says, "This is the Wild Weasel Massage Parlor . . . we found his socks." The senator gets right on the line.) Shoe is a gruff, cynical editor who vascillates between sensationalism (a falling air-conditioner is headlined as "Death from the Skies!") and flashes of legitimacy (he decries one of Cosmo's stories about a giant mutant radish). The overweight Cosmo is the more likable character, a bird who also vascillates—between wanting to work and goofing off. He makes insincere efforts to exercise, goes fishing with friend Irving—the local junk dealer—and is an avid Chicago Cubs fan who frequently skips work to go to games. He also has the messiest desk on earth. When his computer goes down from an "information overload," it means the towering stacks of paper have fallen over and crushed it. On the plus side, Cosmo paints and is working on a novel . . . although whether he'll ever finish a canvas or a chapter is questionable. Other characters include Cosmo's young, bespectacled nephew Skyler and the boy's would-be girlfriend, cheerleader Mary Beth Malarkey, both seventh graders at Treetops High School; Roz, waitress and owner of the divey Roz's Restaurant; accountant Abacus; the cockeyed skywriting pilot Loon, who's also a photographer and delivery bird for the newspaper; and the hostile dogs who regularly grab their rifles and go duck hunting. The birds in the strip all wear human clothing.

Comment. Three-time Pulitzer Prize–winner Jeff MacNelly created the strip "Shoe" in 1977.

SIDNEY SPIDER

Pedigree. Would-be conquerer of Tatter Town.

Biography. When her insufferably mean doll Muffet runs away, little Debbie follows it, accompanied by her (living) stuffed animals, the blue Dog and the derby-wearing teddy bear Harvey. They track the doll to Tatter Town, a place where all the world's forgotten objects come to rest, from broken toys to bent instruments to wrecked appliances. Meanwhile, Muffet stumbles on Sidney, a big, red-nosed, green-eyed, top hat–wearing, cigar-smoking spider who's being razzed by Tatter Towners for trying to make off with a doll. Muffet shrieks at the villagers and chases them away, then introduces herself to the impressed Sidney as Muffet the Merciless. Explaining that he's been trying to take over Tatter Town for a long time, he invites her to join his crusade. She agrees, and he leads her to his headquarters in the Deadster Zone, where "unsavory characters" such as war toys and television sets abide. Muffet quickly takes over the Zone, Sidney becoming her second-in-command (which means he has little to do other than play with a yo-yo and try on her regal robes and crown, which he covets). Sidney's former aide, the Fly, becomes her eyes in Tatter Town. Spying on the village, the Fly sees Debbie organizing the downcast toys to celebrate Christmas. Muffet is livid: She *hates* Christmas, a time when dolls are hugged, squeezed, and twisted. She decides to attack at once. Disguising herself as Santa, she forces Sidney to wear a reindeer costume and pull her sleigh through the skies, her army of planes and flying ammo behind her; the Fly is barely helping Sidney stay aloft. As Muffet nears Tatter Town, the real Santa arrives on his sleigh; the hate-filled doll turns to attack him and confuses her soldiers, who crash one into the next and explode. Santa thanks her for the thoughtful firework display, and leaves. More furious than ever, she urges Sidney and the Fly onward. But Debbie puts on Bing Crosby singing "White Christmas" and, reduced to tears, the arachnid and insect are unable to continue. They stop in midair, flinging the doll downward, into prison.

Comment. The characters were seen in the syndicated half-hour special *Christmas Comes to Tatter Town* in 1988. This original, wonderfully animated, uninhibited cartoon was produced by Ralph Bakshi (see **Fritz the Cat**). Another spider was Jake, who wore a porkpie hat and starred in one-page gags in Archie Comics's *Tales Calculated to Drive You Bats*, eight issues of which were published from 1961 to 1966.

SIDNEY THE ELEPHANT

Pedigree. Depressed theatrical and TV pachyderm.
Biography. Sidney is a big, clumsy, forty-two-year-old orphan elephant who sucks his trunk instead of a thumb, and doesn't have brain one. Living in the jungles of Africa, the two-ton animal complains, at first, that the jungle is too noisy for him. When all the animals are carted off by hunters, he complains that it's too quiet (*Sick, Sick Sidney,* 1958). In his

second cartoon—*Sidney's Family Tree,* 1958 (an Oscar nominee)—the pachyderm gets himself adopted by a pair of monkeys. In later cartoons, he acquires permanent friends named Stanley the Lion and Cleo the Giraffe, who do their best to cheer up the unhappy elephant . . . and keep the oaf from razing the jungle.

Comment. This Terrytoons character, created by Gene Deitch, appeared in nineteen cartoons produced between 1958 and 1963. They were released theatrically, and also aired on *The Hector Heathcote Show* on NBC in 1963. The character is also known as Silly Sidney. Sidney costarred in Dell, then Gold Key's *New Terrytoons* comic book, fifty-four issues of which were published from 1960 to 1979.

THE SKATEBIRDS

Pedigree. Costumed actors portraying birds on television.
Biography. These roller-skating or skateboarding birds starred in live-action vignettes and introduced cartoons, one of which featured animals (see **Woofer and Whimper**). The Skatebirds are Scooter the Penguin, who wears aviator goggles and a scarf; Satchel the Pelican, who's dressed like a postal carrier; and Knock Knock the Woodpecker, who's dressed only in a vest and shoes. Their nemesis is the skating Scat Cat; they're occasionally rescued by the dopey dog Chester. In between the skating action, the birds pause to deliver sung messages about everything from education to honesty to pollution.

Comment. Hanna-Barbera's *The Skatebirds* had a short run on CBS in 1977. The voice for Scooter was Don Messick (Joe Giamalva wore the costume), Satchel was Bob Holt (Ken Means in the suit) and Knock Knock was Lenny Weinrib (Bruce Hoy inside).

SMILIN' ED SMILEY

Pedigree. Rodent star of adult comic books.
Biography. A young bipedal rat who dresses in a sweatshirt, jeans, and sneakers, and speaks with a Brooklyn accent, Ed gets into adventures around town, often with his good friend Delbert, a cat. Short-tempered, he's only at ease when he's with his friends at Chuck's Place, a bar, or is watching a bad horror movie. In fact, Ed's wildest adventure has him falling in with talent agent Argyle, a dog, who gets him into a horror movie, starring as the costumed monster Edzilla. Tragically, Ed can't get the costume off, and, being the excitable rodent that he is, he panics and rampages through the studio

*The perennially disgruntled **Smilin' Ed Smiley.***
© FANTACO.

dressed as the monster. It takes Delbert and a movie memorabilia collector, the Count of Crud, a fox, to rescue him. (A mouse technician, Ray Merrymausen, is a tip of the hat to special effects genius Ray Harryhausen.) In other tales, he has worked as a "D.J. for a Day," and has also been a contestant on the game show *Hollywood Squirrels,* where he got involved in a torrid, highly publicized romance with costar Brazilia, a Charo-like squirrel.

Comment. FantaCo Enterprises *Smilin' Ed* comic book was first published in 1980, and lasted four issues. It was created by Tom Skulan and Raoul Vezina.

SMOKEY THE BEAR
Pedigree. Mascot of the U.S. Forest Service.
Biography. Beginning in 1944, the bear with the kindly face, overalls, and ranger hat with his name on the front appeared in posters, carrying a shovel and warning about the danger of forest fires. With the advent of television, he moved into animated commercials, produced with the help of the Advertising Council. His deep voice and slogan, "Only *you* can prevent forest fires," have become part of the nation's social conscience. He was copyrighted in 1952 and his likeness licensed to manufacturers, the profits used to further the cause of fire prevention.

Comment. The bear made his first comic book appearance in the *Forest Fire* one-shot, published by Commercial Comics in 1949. He went on to star in nine issues of Dell's *4-Color* comic book, published from 1955 to 1961. The "real" Smokey seen for

years in Washington D.C.'s National Zoo was a seriously burned cub discovered in the Lincoln National Forest (New Mexico) in 1950. He died in 1976. The C.B. radio term "Smokey" for state trooper derives from the similarity of their hats. Other public service cartoon characters include Woodsy Owl, a Robin Hood–hatted mascot for the U.S. Forest Service in their ongoing "Give a hoot. Don't pollute" campaign (and starred in ten Gold Key comic books from 1973 to 1976); Conservation Charlie, a red bird who wears a ranger hat and overalls and asks us to "Keep America's Songbirds Singing: Feed the Birds"; and McGruff, the piano-playing dog who urges people to "Take a Bite Out of Crime" for the U.S. Department of Justice. Since 1988, in animated TV commercials and through cartoon brochures, the trenchcoat-wearing hound has worked especially hard to convince kids not to use drugs.

SNAGGLEPUSS
Pedigree. Melodramatic TV lion.
Biography. Snagglepuss is a lion with a voice like Bert Lahr (the Cowardly Lion from *The Wizard of Oz)* and an uncontrollable need to ham it up whenever he's in the spotlight, or to find an excuse to *get* into the spotlight. For example, when reading about Robin Hood, he decides to become a real-life Robin Hood "to help the poor woodland creatures from the hunter's gun [so] the cheery chipmunk can once again chip amongst us, unafraid." (This development shouldn't have come as a surprise: In an earlier cartoon, he revealed that he's been taking that ever-popular correspondence course, "How to Be a Musketeer.") Although he regularly has run-ins with hunters, gangsters, and even abandoned babies, Snagglepuss never loses his poise, even if his life is in jeopardy. However, the lion's poetic soul doesn't prevent him from murdering the language ("Let's considerate this thing") not to mention classic dialogue, such as "All the world's a stage, with matinees on Wednesdays and Saturdays," and "What light through yonder window breaks? Who threw that stone?" Only rarely does he question what he's saying, as when he utters with a flourish, "I'll see what the mailman bringeth," then quickly adds, "or it is brungeth?" Most characters are known for one catchphrase, but it's fitting that the theatrical Snagglepuss has two. His well-known declaration of surprise is "Heavens to Murgatroyd," although he's also been known to shout a "Heavens to Nimrod" and similar "Heavens to . . ." exclamations. But his better-known line is uttered whenever he beats a

quick retreat. Snagglepuss shouts (as when he fails to collect a reward) "Exit—empty pocketed—stage right!" or (when he's wearing a Santa Claus disguise to elude a hunter), "Exit—beard, jelly belly, and all—stage left!" Snagglepuss lives in a cave on Cave Street in an unspecified suburban locale. All that's known about his past is that he was raised somewhere along the Susquehanna River, a region hardly famous for its lions. The slim, orange-furred feline stands upright, is approximately six feet tall, and wears cuffs, a collar, and a string tie.

Comment. Hanna-Barbera's Snagglepuss aired as a segment of *Yogi Bear,* and first went into syndication in 1958; there were thirty-two episodes in all. Daws Butler provided the character's voice. Murgatroyd is also the name of the invisible horse ridden by the Galloping Ghost in his Hanna-Barbera series (see **Buford**).

SNERT

Pedigree. Comic strip dog of Hagar the Horrible.
Biography. Here's a typical exchange between the brawny but hot air–filled Hagar and his self-possessed retriever:

> HAGAR: Look at how Snert watches me! He can't take his eyes off me. He *lives* to please his master. *That's* love in its purest form.
> SNERT: *(thinking)* I'm wasting my time . . . he hasn't got any food for me.

The dog is also terrible when it comes to fetching, although there's a method to his intransigence: As he sits there, lady dogs invariably come trotting over with whatever Hagar has tossed. Snert is white with a brown spot on his back, a brown beard, brown ears, and a brown tail. Like his master, the dog wears a horned Viking helmet. Another important animal in the strip is Kvack, the duck that belongs to Hagar's wife, Helga. Hagar would like nothing better than to see the bird "on a platter surrounded by potatoes and sprigs of parsley," and no wonder. Not only does he have to walk her (on a leash), but he can't even enjoy an egg without her glowering and "laying a guilt trip" on him. When Helga's not around, Hagar enjoys tormenting the duck by filling her water dish with wild rice and l'orange sauce. Kvack, too, wears a horned helmet. She has three ducklings and doesn't like to get her feet wet.

Comment. "Hagar the Horrible" was created in 1973 by cartoonist Dik Browne (after whom Hagar himself is modeled). On Browne's death in 1989, son Christopher took over.

SNIFFLES

Pedigree. A cute, little mouse with a "code in da nose," which causes it to run.
Biography. One of a pack of perenially runny-nosed mice, Sniffles gets into a variety of adventures both related and unrelated to his proboscis. In his first cartoon *(Naughty but Nice),* he goes to a pharmacy in search of a cold remedy and drinks one saturated with alcohol. Quickly becoming drunk, he strikes up a friendship with an electric shaver (which also gets a cold and drunk!). When a cat stumbles on the mouse, Sniffles is saved by the brave razor. In his

Dik Browne's Hagar the Horrible and **Snert.**
© KING FEATURES SYNDICATE.

most fanciful and delightful adventure *(Sniffles and the Bookworm,* 1939), the mouse comes to the rescue of the timorous, bespectacled Bookworm who is being chased by the Frankenstein Monster (our hero sends the monster flying off the shelf). Sniffles has a round head, big ears, huge eyes, tiny cheeks, a button nose, and a short tail. He usually wears a hat.

Comment. This rather ordinary Warner Brothers character appeared in twelve cartoons from 1939 to 1946. Bernice Hanson provided the voice. Sniffles was the first character supervised by the studio's soon-to-be-legendary director Chuck Jones.

SNOOPY

Pedigree. Comic strip dog owned by the youngster Charlie Brown.

Biography. The pride and joy of the Daisy Hill Puppy Farm, Snoopy, a white beagle with black ears, is owned by young Charlie Brown—although he once briefly belonged to a young girl named Lila (as friend Linus Van Pelt remarks, "You got a used dog, Charlie Brown!"). Snoopy actually has a contract with Charlie Brown, forbidding the boy from getting rid of him. Not that the boy doesn't have just cause: Snoopy is so self-absorbed, he can't even remember his owner's name. He refers to him, simply, as "the roundheaded kid." The following conversations are typical of Snoopy's limited world view (Snoopy thinking, because he can only speak one word, his expression of exasperation, *Augh!!,* or converse with other animals):

> CHARLIE BROWN: The world is getting worse all the time! Murder, robberies, automobile accidents, blackmail, all sorts of terrible things.
> SNOOPY: Don't forget about kicking dogs.

And:

> CHARLIE BROWN: We not only like each other, but we respect each other.
> SNOOPY: Don't forget the supper dish.

In general, Snoopy's philosophy can be summed up thus: "I wonder why some of us were born dogs while others were born people. Why should I have been the lucky one?" Snoopy's canine-centered view of things derives not just from the fact that he's a dog, but because he fancies himself an elite, suave, and heroic Renaissance individual. In his fantasies (which often take hold of him for days), he dons the appropriate costumes and/or mien and imagines himself a World War I ace riding his Sopwith Camel, fighting "brave duels" with the Red Baron (shout-

ing, "Curse you, Red Baron!" when he crash-lands in his supper dish), and recounting his exploits at the aerodrome officer's club; Joe Cool, a campus hotshot, who gives the ladies the eye from behind his shades; a spinoff persona, Joe Gloat, who doesn't have to go to school and snickers at kids who do; the Easter Beagle, dispensing eggs in a flashier fashion than the Easter Bunny (for example, mounting a unicycle and crashing from inside a giant egg); a "world famous surgeon"; a vulture, glowering down at the world from atop his doghouse; an attorney; a beagle scout who leads Woodstock and his other bird friends on unparalleled nature hikes; artistic director of the Pawpet Theater, which has presented everything from *War and Peace* to *Ben-Hur* (when his posters announce a "cast of thousands," that's just what patrons get: A puppet named Joe Thousands); and, of course, a brilliant author of both nonfiction *(A History of the World)* and maudlin, overwritten fiction *(A Sad Story, Small Women, The Broken Heart,* and so on). When he's just being himself, Snoopy enjoys dancing (feet pat-a-pattering, arms splayed, a big smile beneath what Lucy Van Pelt calls his "banana nose"), skateboarding (as hip Joe Skateboard), golfing, surfing, playing tennis (he has a terrible temper), ice-skating, throwing a football, and playing shortstop on Charlie Brown's baseball team. He jogs, although he hates it (when he yells at his feet to get going, they answer with a small *hee hee hee hee* and don't budge), and he also has an odd recreation: Whirling his ears and taking off from his Ace Helicopter Pad, flying around with Woodstock as a passenger—although the bird is wise enough to pack a parachute. His musical instrument is the trombone (he likes the *um PAW PAW),* and he considers it a sign of "real maturity" that he doesn't feel compelled to bite cats or chase rabbits. A finicky eater, he likes bread best "when they cut the crusts off," and finds it "impossible to eat dog food when your stomach is all set for Shrimp Louie." However, he also enjoys a good pizza, loves root beer, and likes cooking marshmallows (he uses a metal rake in the name of efficiency and gluttony). The worst prospect, for him, is the thought of becoming a vegetarian. Regardless of the meal, Snoopy gets very pushy when his supper is late (he'll punt his dish into the kitchen, walk around with the bowl in his mouth or on his head, and so on). Snoopy's base of operations is his doghouse, which also doubles as his Sopwith Camel and is equipped with great works of art (including a Van Gogh and a Wyeth, or so he says), and a pool table. There's nothing the dog likes better than lying on top of the house, sleeping . . . although he *does* allow himself to be "the hill" in the winter, letting Woodstock and his bird friends ski down his head while he lies there. Snoopy's only nemesis is the "Stupid Cat" who lives next door, and is never seen—except for the aftermath of its rending claws, the cat slashing away with all four sets, leaving various shapes cut in Snoopy's doghouse: a Christmas tree on December 25, a candle-bedecked cake on his birthday, and the numerals of the new year on December 31. As for responsibilities, the dog has just one. On Halloween, when the Great Pumpkin rises from the pumpkin patch to bring toys to children, Snoopy must get on a hobby horse and "be kind of a Paul Revere . . . and ride through the countryside spreading the news." Snoopy has several known relatives. His grandmother was fond of proverbs. His father is retired and living in Florida and has a big, white moustache. Snoopy credits this wise beagle for his own civilized nature: "In the evening . . . dad never chased rabbits. He'd invite them over to play cards." Of his eight litter-mates, the only ones named are his brothers Spike, Marbles, and Olaf, and his sister Belle. Belle ran off with a "worthless hound" and lives in Kansas City with her very tall teenage son. Marbles has a mottled back, and "was always the smart one in our family." Spike, who is older and thinner, lives in Needles, inside a cactus, and sells real estate in the desert. He's just a little crazy from the isolation: He plays baseball by himself (the scoreboard reads "Me" and "Nobody Else") and he argues with the calls made by his umpire, the cactus. Spike wears a fedora and has a thin, drooping moustache. As for the portly Olaf, Snoopy hasn't seen him in years. The two big loves of Snoopy's life have been Fifi, a dog from deep in his past; and a nameless dog whom he was about to marry. However, Spike—his best man—ran off with the bride, who, in turn, abandoned him for a coyote. Snoopy has forgiven his brother; in fact, after downing a few diet doughnuts, the dog had virtually forgotten the incident. His closest friend, outside of Charlie Brown, is Woodstock. Presumably, Snoopy is more friendly and charitable toward the bird because Woodstock looks up to him (the bird is his caddy, holds an umbrella when it rains, and so on).

Comment. Snoopy was inspired by the black-and-white dog Spike, which creator Charles Schulz was given at the age of thirteen. However, Schulz says, "Snoopy is not a real dog. He is an image of what people would like a dog to be." Snoopy's arrival on the comic pages didn't come easily. After be-

ing rejected by syndicate after syndicate, the strip finally appeared on October 2, 1950—although the United Feature Syndicate *did* change the title from "Li'l Folks" to "Peanuts." There have been more than thirty TV specials featuring Snoopy and company (most of them a half hour) beginning with *A Charlie Brown Christmas,* which first aired on CBS on December 9, 1965, and including the Emmy Award–winning *A Charlie Brown Thanksgiving* (1973). Other notable entries in the series have included the classic *It's the Great Pumpkin, Charlie Brown* (1966), *He's Your Dog, Charlie Brown* (1968), *It's the Easter Beagle, Charlie Brown* (1974), *Be My Valentine, Charlie Brown* (1975), *It's Arbor Day, Charlie Brown* (1976), and the hour-long *Happy Anniversary, Charlie Brown* (1976) and *Happy Birthday, Charlie Brown* (1979). There's also been a series of feature-length animated cartoons, beginning with *A Boy Named Charlie Brown* (1969). The second of these, *Snoopy Come Home* (1972), was devoted primarily to the runaway pooch and his repeated, frustrating encounters with "No Dogs Allowed" signs. Animator Bill Melendez has provided the voice of Snoopy throughout; Jason Serinus provided the whistling for Woodstock. A short-lived cartoon series, *Charlie Brown and Snoopy,* premiered on CBS in 1985. "Snoopy vs. the Red Baron," by Dick Holler and Phil Gernhard, was a hit song in 1966 and *Snoopy* was the name of the lunar module on the Apollo 10 moon mission in 1969. *Snoopy* magazine, consisting of comic strips, puzzles, and activities for children, has been published since 1987.

SONNY

Pedigree. Advertising mascot for Cocoa Puffs cereal.

Biography. A cuckoo bird, the big-beaked Sonny (who has a fondness for loud sweaters) is sedate and in control—until he sees anyone eating Cocoa Puffs cereal. Then he goes positively loony, bouncing around and shouting over and over, "I'm Cuckoo for Cocoa Puffs!"

Comment. The General Mills character was hatched in the early 1960s by the same creative team responsible for the **Trix Rabbit.** It remains an important part of the cereal's advertising. Originally, a bearded bird, Gramps, intentionally triggered Sonny's reaction by showing him the cereal. However, this was deemed sadistic and he was dropped in favor of live-action children.

SPACE BEAVER

Pedigree. Comic book science fiction hero.
Biography. "Beave" and his turtle sidekick Tog are intergalactic law officers who, armed only with pistols, tackle the might of the drug czar Lord Pork, a pig. (Pork's second-in-command is the Commander Foxx, leader of the Foxguards.) The hero's love interest is Jackie, a rabbit whom he met a year before when she was waitressing at Max's bar, Beave's favorite hangout. Also seen in the strip is Joshua Rat, a drug-hating rodent who helps lead Beave on an invasion of Pork's command ship; and Euripides, the beaver's mentor—a koala bear.

   Comment. Ten-Buck Comics published just one issue (1986) featuring the Darick Robertson creation.

SPACE MOUSE

Pedigree. Space age comic book mouse.
Biography. A native of the planet Rodentia, Space Mouse is a soldier in the service of the king of Camembert Castle. Most of the time, this means flying through space onboard his saucerlike ship the *Lunar Schooner* (which gets 6,000 miles to the gallon) and watching out for cat invaders from the planet Felinia. However, when summoned over his "electra-belt viewer," Space Mouse is also ready to serve the king's sometimes quirky desires, such as the time the potentate had "a sudden hunger for Plutonian pickles" and Space Mouse went to fetch them. But watching the cats is his primary job, and it can be dangerous: The felines have been known to litter space with giant magnetic mousetraps. Once snared, the trap and the ship with its mouse occupant are hauled to Felinia's capital city of Catolina for trial. If found guilty—which the mice always are—they're sent to the world Nothing, "a planet with no food, no water, no rocks, no trees, no people, no nothing . . . just a round ball." Among the clever ways Space Mouse has attacked the cats has been to send dogs from the Dog Star after them; blast the cats' space ships with catnip balls; and use a "zorch torch" to fry their whiskers. Space Mouse dresses in a purple spacesuit with a tight-fitting cowl, which doesn't cover his ears or face; he never wears a helmet. When he's not fighting cats, there's nothing Space Mouse likes more than to play his trumpet or go "cruising through the wide open . . . outer spaces . . . with the top down" on his ship. Another prominent citizen of Rodentia is Dr. Rodent Rocket, a space scientist; another nearby world is Planet Sludge, "the muddiest

planet in the universe," and home to a population of pigs.

   Comment. Space Mouse was created by Walter Lantz and appeared in two issues of Dell's *4-Color* comics in 1960 and 1962 before moving on to five issues of its own Gold Key title (1962 to 1963). He appeared in just one animated cartoon, *Space Mouse*, in 1959. The character is unrelated to a previous Space Mouse, which had appeared in five issues of his own Avon title (1953 to 1954) along with three issues of *Funny Tunes* and two issues of *Space Comics*, costarring with Super Pup and Merry Mouse. While on the subject of space animals, Power Comics published one issue of *Space Kat-Ets* in 1953, a 3-D comic book about a trio of cats (one big and smart, another small and cute, the third medium-size and goofy) who travel through the stars in a tiny spaceship.

SPARK PLUG

Pedigree. Comic strip horse.
Biography. The knock-kneed race horse is owned by well-to-do Barney Google, sports fan extraordinaire. Over the years, Barney manages to win a little on Spark Plug (like when he gives the horse a "goat gland," then holds tin cans in front of him), although more often than not he loses. The jockey is a black man, a crossword puzzle buff named Sunshine who's devoted to the nag. Once, when Sunshine fell ill, Barney was forced to bring the horse to his upper-floor apartment to lift the jockey's spirits. For a while, Spark Plug's stallmate was an ostrich named Rudy, which Barney also trained for the track; an-

Spark Plug visiting its master at the hospital . . . the hard way. © KING FEATURES SYNDICATE.

other of Barney's horses is Pony Boy. In 1934, while fleeing the authorities, Barney hid in the Kentucky hills where he met Snuffy Smith (see **Bullet**).

Comment. Spark Plug appeared in Billy De Beck's "Take Barney Google, for Instance," which premiered in the Chicago *Herald-Examiner* June 17, 1919. (The title was later shortened to "Barney Google.") Spark Plug arrived in 1922; the Sunday pages were often titled "Barney Google and Spark Plug."

SPEEDY GONZALES

Pedigree. Warner Brothers's fleet Mexican mouse.
Biography. Although Speedy was thin, unkempt, and lacked his trademark sombrero in his screen debut, *Cat-Tails for Two* (1953), he was not without his tornado-quick takeoff (his business card describes him as the "fastest mouse in all Mexico"). He hardly needed the speed, however, as Benny and George, two very "smelly" cats, board a ship in search of Mexican food and try to eat him. After the two nearly self-destruct on several occasions (Benny mistakes gas for water, drops anvils on George's head, and so on), the two try to use a pipe and lighted dynamite to blow Speedy from his mousehole—not knowing that the mouse has turned the pipe to where they're standing. End of cats. After a two-year vacation, Speedy returns—with his golden sombrero, red neckerchief, and white outfit—to battle the long-suffering **Sylvester the Cat** in the Oscar-winning *Speedy Gonzales*. Sylvester is a guard at a cheese factory in Mexico, where his record of kills is impressive. Enter Speedy who, something like **Mighty Mouse**, comes whenever his countrymice need him. He not only gets past all the traps Sylvester sets, but at one point runs into the cat's mouth and out his tail. In the end, the frustrated Sylvester blows up the factory—only to be bested yet again when the cheese rains down on the mice. Another classic from the character's early days is the Oscar-nominated *Tabasco Road* (1957), in which Speedy must help his drunk pals Pablo and Fernando avoid the claws of a cat. During the early 1960s, Speedy spent much of his time battling Sylvester, in cartoons like *West of the Pesos* (1960), where Speedy saves lab mice being guarded by Sylvester; the Oscar-nominated *The Pied Piper of Guadalupe* (1961), with Sylvester reading about the Pied Piper and using music to trap mice, whom Speedy must rescue; the wonderful *Mexican Boarders* (1962), costarring Speedy's cousin Slowpoke Rodriquez,

whom Speedy repeatedly saves from Sylvester; *Chili Weather* (1963), wherein Sylvester is the watch-cat at the Guadalajara food processing plant which Speedy and his friends invade; *A Message to Gracias* (1964), in which the mouse is summoned by skyrocket (which advises him to come "queeck") and is charged with hand-delivering a message from El Supremo, ruler of the Mexican mice, to his general, Gracias (when Speedy completes the treacherous journey, he learns it's just a birthday poem. He then frees Sylvester, who was tied to a tree, and lets him chase the general and El Supremo); and *Nuts and Volts* (1964), a saga of Sylvester's consistently backfiring attempts to use robotics and electronics to catch the mouse. Not surprisingly, Sylvester become tired chasing Speedy and passed the baton to **Daffy Duck** in *It's Nice to Have a Mouse around the House* (1965). In that cartoon, Sylvester's owner Granny frets that the cat is overexerting himself, and phones Daffy's Jet Age Pest Control to deal with Speedy. He fails, and the two meet again when stranded on a desert isle in *Moby Duck* (1965). In *Assault and Peppered* (1965), Daffy is the sadistic owner of El Rancho Rio Daffy who tries to chase the mice from his property, only to be taught a lesson by Speedy. Their third team-up of that year, *Well Worn Daffy,* has Daffy as the selfish owner of a desert oasis. By the end of the cartoon, it's Speedy and his two mice friends who have the water and the duck who's dying of thirst. Typically, the bouts with Daffy end with a turnabout of this sort, as in *Snow Excuse* (1966), when what begins with Speedy asking Daffy for a fireplace log in the dead of winter ends with Speedy having all the wood, Daffy's cabin wrecked, and the duck having to disguise himself as a mouse to come to Speedy's to get warm. Roads burn up whenever Speedy really pours on the gas (along with whatever was in his way, i.e., Sylvester), and he's much more of a showoff than that other famous Warner Brothers speedster, the Road Runner (see **Wile E. Coyote**). But his flamboyance is part of his charm and, under any conditions, it's tough to muster much sympathy for Sylvester and Daffy. Speedy's trademarks are exuberant cries of, "Andale!" "Ariba!" and "Yeee-*haaah!*", shouted various times in numerous combinations.

Comment. Speedy starred in forty-seven cartoons, and costarred on the 1981 NBC cartoon series *The Daffy/Speedy Show.* Mel Blanc provided his voice. He is the only one of Warner Brothers's male cartoon animals who wore clothing.

SPIDER-HAM

Pedigree. Marvel comic book parody of Spider-Man.

Biography. Spider-Ham is a bipedal, talking pig who fights crime on a world of animals. He can climb walls and spin webs, which he uses for swinging from building to building and for snaring villains. He also possesses "spider sense," which alerts him when danger is near. Spider-Ham is actually teen-aged Peter Porker, who lives with his aunt May Porker and works as a photographer for J. Jonah Jackal, publisher of the *Daily Beagle*. His girlfriend is Mary Jane Waterbuffalo, although he also has a soft spot for Jackal's secretary Batty Brant. When he goes into action, Spider-Ham wears a red-and-blue costume covered with a black-web motif. Other heroes in Spider-Ham's world are Captain Amerikat (Captain America), Hulk Bunny (The Hulk), Goose Rider (Ghost Rider), Deerdevil the Cloven-Hooved Mammal without Fear (Daredevil the Man without Fear), Croctor Strange (Doctor Strange), the Fantastic Fur (Fantastic Four), X-Bugs (X-Men), Iron Mouse (Iron Man), Silver Squirrel (Silver Surfer), the Asinine Torch (the Human Torch), Sub-Marsupial (Sub-Mariner), and Nick Furry, Agent of S.H.E.E.P. (Nick Fury, Agent of S.H.I.E.L.D.). Villains battled by the hero include heavy metal rocker Ozzy Ostrich, the vampire duck Quakula, Dr. Chickenstein, the Moooomy, and the towering monster Hog-zilla.

Comment. The character made its debut in the first issue of *Marvel Tails Starring Peter Porker the Spectacular Spider-Ham* in 1983. "Marvel Tails Starring" was later dropped. Peter Porker was also a pig character in *Funny Funnies* (1943), which lasted one issue from Nedor Publishing. Harry Hare, Tubby Bear, Ozzie Ostrich, Lester Lion, and Granpa Scotty (a dog) were the costars of that comic book.

SPIKE

Pedigree. Claymation rabbit in a Michael Jackson film.

Biography. Singer Michael Jackson finds himself at the MJJ movie studios when fans and photographers descend on him ("Would you autograph my tummy?" shouts one adoring kid). Ducking into a wardrobe room, Jackson dons a rabbit head and biker clothes and is transmogrified into Spike, who walks upright, dances like Jackson, wears yellow pants and a leather jacket, has Jackson's hair . . . but has a rabbit head with buck teeth and blue fur. Leaving the wardrobe room, Spike grabs a bicycle, which turns into a motorcycle, and he roars away. The adoring masses follow him into the nighttime street. Transforming himself into Sylvester Stallone (and the bike into a jackhammer), Spike pretends to work on the street and the gang shoots past him. Becoming Spike again, he leads another pack onto the river, where his motorcycle turns into a jet-ski and he becomes Pee-wee Herman to throw them off the trail. Finally, the jet-ski becomes a rocket-backpack, and Spike goes soaring through the clouds. When he lands, the rockets become the motorcycle and he tools from the city into the desert. There, Jackson doffs the rabbit head and clothing—which come to life. The two do a dance until a police officer comes by. Spike vanishes and Jackson gets a ticket for boogying in a no-dancing zone. Jackson is unable to convince the officer that he was dancing with someone else. When the officer leaves, a nearby mountain transforms into Spike's head, and the rabbit winks at Jackson, who smiles.

Comment. The character was seen in a ten-minute segment of Michael Jackson's 1988 film *Moonwalker*, which was a string of music videos linked by concert footage. The song accompanying the adventure is "Speed Demon," from Jackson's *Bad* album. The segment was directed by Jerry Kramer; Spike was animated by Will Vinton Productions using the Claymation process. *Moonwalker* was intended as a theatrical release, but went right to video in the United States.

SPIRIT

Pedigree. Steed of the toy-turned-multimedia heroine She-Ra.

Biography. The world of Etheria lies in a dimension other than our own. There, based in the Crystal Castle, Princess Adora defends her world against the evil forces of Catra. She does this by holding aloft an enchanted sword, uttering the incantation, "For the honor of Grayskull," and becoming the warrior She-Ra. When she points the sword at her horse —who is white, with an orange mane and tail—it grows blue wings, is covered with armor, and gets a new name: Swift Wind.

Comment. Other animals who cavort with She-Ra are Arrow, the flying horse owned by the archer Bow, Catra's horse Storm, and the giant swan Enchanta. On the parallel world of Eternia, Adora's brother, Prince Adam, performs a similar ritual and becomes the brawny He-Man. When he levels his blade at his cat Cringer, the cowering, green, tiger-size feline is transformed into the powerful, rip-snorting Battle Cat, complete with saddle and armor. Their foes are the wicked Skeletor and his minions. These characters came into existence as part of the Mattel toy lineup Masters of the Universe, introduced in 1982. Filmation's popular syndicated series, *Masters of the Universe,* debuted the following year, and spawned the 1985 animated film *Secret of the Sword* that introduced She-Ra and her horse. A syndicated cartoon series, *She-Ra,* was introduced that same year. Mattel introduced other animals in the lineup—the Meteorbs, a group of "comet creatures" who had egg-shaped bodies and animal heads and limbs. These were Ty-Grrr, Astro Lion, Comet Cat, Tuskor, Crocobite, Rhinorb, Orbear, and Gore-illa. They failed to make it into the TV series. Hoping to duplicate Mattel's success, Hollywood's Lorimar-Telepictures created the *SilverHawks* TV series in 1987 and licensed the characters as toys. These characters were a group of humans and one animal who underwent the "superandroid" process and became the cyborg SilverHawks. The one animal was the soaring bird Tally-Hawk. The heroes had a feisty nemesis in the vile Mon-Star, but the toys and show were duds. Meanwhile, trying to duplicate the success of *She-Ra* on television, CBS introduced the Saturday morning series *Wildfire* in 1986. The magic horse was the star here, helping a young princess battle a witch who's trying to take away her throne. Who says innovation is dead? John Vernon was the horse's voice. Mercifully, some action toys/dolls never made it past the toy stage, e.g., Remco's Mikola with his Mighty Stallion (1983), their Conan with his War Stallion (1984), and Hasbro's Ninja Warriors, Enemies of Evil series, featuring Oji San and his horse Windspirit (1987).

SPOOKY

Pedigree. Cat from the classic "Smokey Stover" comic strip.

Biography. Spooky is a scrawny black cat with a red bandage tied to the tip of its tail. The strip reveals many sides to the character. He's a resourceful cat: Locked outside, he wails until neighbors throw enough junk at him so he can climb to an open window. He's an impish cat: Tossed from the house, he carries a no-parking sign over to where his master's car is parked, and a passing officer gives it a ticket. He's a wily cat: Chasing a mouse and accidentally smashing a milk bottle on the porch, Spooky re-

places it with a bowling pin. He's an unlucky cat: Sent to the store to buy a soup bone, he sees a sign which says "free bone," goes in, and gets tossed out (an open door was blocking the rest of the sign, which offered free trombone lessons). But most of all, he's a cat who gets his comeuppance. Told to stay inside, he blithely leaps from an open window . . . and lands inside a sack hanging from the laundry line, where he's trapped. Called for a bath, he runs away . . . and gets splashed by a department of sanitation truck. Cockily approaching a rooster, he doesn't realize that it's Battling Buford, and gets his brains knocked out. Running single-mindedly after a meat truck, he falls in a manhole. Walking past a bucket, he hears a mouse inside and leaps after it, only to get drenched; a ventriloquist walks by, laughing (this gag was later recycled in *U.S. Acres,* see **Orson the Piglet**). The cat's rival is a tabby who is constantly trying to steal fish from him, and vice versa; Spooky's master is Fenwick, a lazy boob.

Comment. Bill Holman's "Smokey Stover" debuted in March of 1935; Spooky had his own one- or two-row strip, which ran at the end of the Sunday comic strip. Concurrently, the cat was usually seen hanging around Smokey Stover's firehouse. The separate Spooky strip ended in 1945, and the cat was featured in both "Smokey Stover" and in the one-panel daily adventures "Nuts and Jolts," which continued into the 1950s; usually, the cat was simply an observer to some outrageous bit of business (like a mugger forcing a penniless victim to borrow money to give him), and—although he couldn't speak in the other strips—made asides like, "Watch out!" and "Hot number!" Holman's sense of humor was often cruel, usually off the wall, and never dull. Possibly the best strip of all: The painter who accidentally drops a bucket of paint on the cat. Climbing down, the man looks at the white cat and says with apparent remorse, "Gee—that's a shame—I'll have to do something about that." Last panel: Spooky unhappily walking off with a "Wet Paint" sign hanging from his tail.

SPOT

Pedigree. TV frog.

Biography. This one is for supertrivia buffs and completists: Spot was the pet frog of Jerry Lewis's sister Geraldine on his short-lived TV cartoon series.

Comment. There were seventeen episodes of Filmation's *Will the Real Jerry Lewis Please Stand Up?* They aired on ABC in 1970.

SPOTTY

Pedigree. The dog owned by comic book legend Archie Andrews.

Biography. The mutt lives in Riverdale with its master. While Spotty just hangs around most of the time, he won't hesitate to leap to Archie's defense—as when the boy was baby-sitting for a cat that had inherited millions of dollars, and an angry heir tried to kill it. Spotty is also devoted to other dogs. Falling for a poodle, he risks his own freedom to rescue her when the purebread is captured by dognappers. Spotty is light brown with big black spots; he hates being dressed up in any kind of doggie clothes, and does a crummy job fetching newspapers intact.

Comment. The character was introduced in *Little Archie,* which began publication in 1956.

SQUEAK THE MOUSE

Pedigree. Tough-to-kill comic book mouse.

Biography. Squeak is a small, brown, bipedal mouse who wears white gloves and white shoes. In his very first adventure, he's caught by a nameless black cat, who, after a frantic chase, catches the mouse, rips off his head, dashes it against a brick wall, and eats the body. That night, at a party, the mouse returns inexplicably as a zombie and begins killing cats in horrible ways: Shoving a spear up through the bed, burning one with scalding water in the shower, using a chain saw to bisect a couple in a torrid embrace, electrocuting another loving pair, and so on. The cat finally finds the mouse, sets him ablaze, and runs home. There, the zombified cats come after him, along with the horribly burned dead mouse. Catching him inside a blender, the cat turns it on and pours the liquid zombie mouse down the drain. But that's not the end. The mouse returns during an orgy and starts cutting the ladies up. Frantic, the cat turns on the gas and runs from the house, which explodes. Picking himself up and dusting himself off, he spots another mouse, gives chase . . . and the saga begins anew.

Comment. The character was created by Massimo Mattioli, and his adventures were first published in 1982. A book collection came to the United States in 1985—although there was a brief delay in distribution through Catalan Communications because the U.S. government charged the publication with being obscene. A trial justifiably cleared the publication.

STEEL

Pedigree. Horse belonging to Marvel Comics's western hero, Kid Colt.

Biography. The gunmetal gray steed is ridden by Kid Colt, Outlaw—who isn't really. He's just misunderstood, and actually fights for the law. Naturally, exposition is delivered through the Kid's conversations with Steel. ("Whoa, Steel! A deputy's got the drop on us!")

Comment. Steel was with the Kid from no. 1 of his 229-issue run. The publication lasted from 1948 to 1979. See other Marvel Comics cowboy horses **Banshee, Cyclone,** and **Nightwind.**

STEVEN WOLF

Pedigree. Underground comics wolf, a k a "Stoned Wolf."

Biography. Because he keeps having the same horrible dream—that he is given a good neighbor award—Wolf fears that the "civilized middle class lifestyle [is] making me lose my natural savagery." He decides to pay a visit to his father in a nursing home (where the elder Wolf flips a nurse the bird when she tries to take away his copy of *Little Pigs in Leather).* Upon arriving, the young wolf tosses an anvil at the frail old wolf, who falls down the stairs. Satisfied that he can still be a feral predator, Steven leaves. Going to sleep that night, he has the same dream as before—only this time, he beats the fur off everyone on the dais. Alas, Steven is awakened by his father: The battered old wolf has attached a rope to his legs, lashed him to a TV set—and throws the latter from a second-floor window. It drags Steven behind, and as the wizened wolf leaves, he says to his mangled son, "You fool around with your mother, it's incest . . . you fool around with your father—it's curtains!"

Comment. This marvelous character appeared in Last Gasp Eco-Funnies's *No Ducks* no. 2 in 1979. Also appearing in the magazines two-issue run were Star Rats and their adventure on Dante's, the Sin Planet; Chasney Zweibach, the aggressive dog detective of "Have Nose Will Sniff" ("Miranda decision? *Fuck* the Miranda decision! Kick the little pus head's *face* in!"); and Bill the Bunny and Barny Blowfly and the menace of the Mad Bats, who are trying to turn every animal into a bat.

STORM

Pedigree. A TV cartoon seahorse.

Biography. Storm is the approximately ten-foot-long seahorse ridden by the seagoing superhero

Aquaman. The animal has no special power, other than the ability to swim quickly underwater. Aquaman's sidekick, Aqualad, rides the seapony Imp; he also has a pet walrus named Tusky.

Comment. The animals appeared on Filmation's *The Superman/Aquaman Hour of Adventure,* which aired on CBS in 1967. None of these animals appeared in the *Aquaman* comic book. Another undersea creature was Splasher, the pet dolphin of Marine Boy on the Japanese series of that name, which was syndicated in 1966. Obviously, Splasher was one of the few dolphins to escape the Japanese fishing nets. A dolphin was also one of the cast members of *Sealab 2020,* a Hanna-Barbera cartoon that ran for thirteen episodes and aired on NBC in 1972. The dolphin, Tuffy, is owned by young Gail, a youngster who lives in the undersea settlement of the future.

STREAKY THE SUPER-CAT
Pedigree. Mutated earth cat, pet of the comic book superhero Supergirl.
Biography. When the superhero Supergirl tries to find a cure to the lethal radiation of the extraterrestrial rock kryptonite, she inadvertently creates X-kryptonite, and throws the isotope into the woods. Shortly thereafter, in her secret identity as Linda Lee Danvers, she finds an orange cat with a white lightning bolt on either side of its body. The cat is cornered in an alley, being attacked by "a vicious dog," and she rescues it. Streaky trails her home, and she adopts the animal. That night, the cat goes sniffing around the woods, finds the small ball of X-kryptonite, and is "struck by the full force of X-kryptonite's delayed full-effects." Suddenly, the cat can fly. Bumping into a Superman doll left outside by a child, Streaky acquires a cape. Possessing superstrength, the cat immediately flies over to the Creamy Dairy Company and spills a truckload of milk into the street "for starving cats." Then he chases away a dog and saves chicks from an eagle. Streaky's other powers include the ability to let loose "a super-loud meow . . . magnified 50 times louder than usual," although all of his powers last only for a few hours after exposure to X-kryptonite. Streaky enjoys playing with huge spools of telephone cable instead of balls of yarn, and has his own "playroom" in Supergirl's Fortress of Solitude, which is located in an "Arabian desert." The room is stocked with giant rubber balls. Supergirl loves the cat, but regards him as "a little dickens [who] should learn to use your super-powers to do useful things." Despite her assessment, Streaky does partake in many ad-

ventures with Supergirl and with the Legion of Super-Pets, an organization that also consists of **Beppo the Super-Monkey, Comet the Super-Horse,** and **Krypto.** Readers always know what Streaky's thinking thanks to thought balloons. In Streaky's most unusual adventure, the cat briefly acquires the ability to speak when the fifth-dimensional imp Mr. Mxyzptlk subjects the city of Metropolis to a "zoophonic force." In another bizarre escapade, the cat steals Krypto's bone and the dog gives chase so rapidly that the two break the time barrier. In the thirtieth century, Streaky's descendant Whizzy has telepathy.

Comment. Streaky first appeared in DC Comics's *Action Comics* no. 261 in 1960.

STRIPE
Pedigree. Pet dog in the comic strip "Tiger."
Biography. Stripe is a brown dog with black spots. Fond of running and dragging young Tiger behind him whenever he goes for a walk, and frequently getting loose because of this, Stripe loves begging for scraps from the dinner table, enjoys sleeping on Tiger's bed (even though he has one of his own), and hates being alone. The cast of characters includes Tiger's young brother Punkinhead and his pal Hugo.

Comment. The long-running strip debuted in May of 1965, written and drawn by Bud Blake.

SUGAR BEAR.
Pedigree. Mascot for Post Sugar Crisp cereal.
Biography. With his Bing Crosby voice and casual manner, one would think that Sugar Bear is a push-

The cool, unflappable **Sugar Bear.** Sugar Bear is a trademark of GENERAL FOODS CORPORATION.

Suicide Squirrel *lectures Humbug, the ant . . . who is concerned with matters other than personal integrity.* © R. L. CRABB.

over. Wrong! Whenever a person or animal tries to steal his favorite cereal, Sugar Crisp, he pops a handful and is endowed with a "vitamin-packed punch," which enables him to deck all comers, be they wolves, bees, or other thieves. The brownfurred Sugar Bear wears only a T-shirt, which often rides up over his pale bear belly. When he's not chowing down, the bear sings, "Can't Get Enough of that Sugar Crisp."

Comment. Introduced in 1964, the bear was featured on both the packaging and in print and animated TV advertisements for the cereal. He was put into hibernation in 1984, then returned in 1987 for a successful and ongoing campaign. The bear has also been associated with Sugar Crisp spin-off cereals, such as Super Sugar Crisp and Super Golden Crisp. The character was also seen as the star of his own cartoon series, which aired on **Linus the Lionhearted** (see entry). On the show, the temperate bear went around singing songs and interacting with other woodland animals. Sterling Holloway provided his voice.

SUICIDE SQUIRREL
Pedigree. A depressed, moribund comic book animal.
Biography. Chronically drunk, the squirrel feels as though he's "jus' one amongsht many of th' disenfranchtized of thish whird . . . I don' half no va . . . vadil . . . valibity ash an *imdivibajul!*" His drink-

ing partner is sometimes Junior Jackalope (see "Comment"), and sometimes Humbug, a very wise ant. In his most socially relevant escapade, Suicide is recruited by activist Carl the Mole for Anti-Social Anarchist Animals Anonymous. (The mole says dirt tainted his childhood. "We *lived* in it . . . *ate* in it . . . *slept* in it! Is it any wonder why my self-esteem is so low?"). But Suicide is too besotted to help the mole in his crusade to create "true equality" by making every animal miserable. He leaves the clubhouse to continue drinking. The squirrel is dressed in a hillbilly hat.

Comment. Suicide Squirrel is a supporting character in R. L. Crabb's wonderful *Tales of the Jackalope* comic, which Blackthorne began publishing sporadically in 1986. A Jackalope is a fanciful creature that's half rabbit, half antelope.

SUN, THE 4-D MONKEY
Pedigree. Hero of comic books published in Hong Kong.
Biography. In the year 2988, Dr. Wise uses a "Memory Retracking Machine" to successfully duplicate the ancient Monkey King of China (see "Comment"), whom he dubs Sun, the 4-D Monkey. Using a computer, he also tinkers genetically with a pig and fish, creating Boaro, the Karate Pig, and Fishy, the Ninja Flounder. Trained by the martial arts master Robot Commander, Sun and Fishy are endowed with additional powers: Sun can fly, surround him-

self with a "protective bubble," and turn strands of his fur into whatever he wills simply by blowing on them (he can even create duplicates of himself); Fishy can transform himself from humanoid back to fish. Unknown to the trio, Dr. Wise sets up an elaborate scheme in which he poses as a deadly alien from space based in a fortress in South America. He sends the heroes to defeat the menace and, when they're victorious, he deems them ready to become superheroes, responsible for "defending the earth and protecting the peaceful people who live on other planets in the universe." After preventing a war between the planets Pluto and Mars, the heroes battle the marauding robots of the evil Dr. Ambit.

Comment. Produced by Leung's Publications in 1988, the comic book is available in English. Monkeys have a long history in both the lore and cartoons of Asia and the Orient, dating back to the Hindu legends of Hanuman (circa 200 B.C.), the monkey general who serves Sugriva, King of the Monkeys, and is made an aide to the demigod Rama. His most famous adventure is the rescue of Rama's wife, Sita, from the evil Ravana. In China, a related character, the Monkey King (the same who's the "father" of Sun), is featured in a popular series of animated cartoons that are based on stories hundreds of years old. Another comic book featuring a mighty simian, *Trickster King Monkey* (published in 1988), is based on the sixteenth-century Chinese folktale "Hsi Yu Ki." The comic is about a monkey who erupts from inside a stone, spends centuries traveling the world—arming himself with knowledge and weapons—and finally does battle with Yama, King of Death. The same tale served as a springboard for the feature-length Japanese cartoon *Saiyu-ki* in 1960, released in the United States ten years later as *Alakazam the Great*. After being born from the boulder, the monkey (call Goku in the Japanese version, not Alakazam) becomes king of the monkeys, but is sentenced by Buddha to spend 500 years in the wilderness for the crime of practicing magic. Goku is freed by a priest and fights a vile sorcerer, heroism that earns him the forgiveness of Buddha.

SUPER CHICKEN
Pedigree. Bumbling superhero pullet of TV cartoon legend.
Biography. According to the cartoon's theme song, "When you find yourself in danger / when you're threatened by a stranger / when it looks like you will take a lickin' / there is someone waiting / who will hurry up and rescue you / just call for Super

Chicken." The fact is, however, you'd be wiser to call for **Courageous Cat.** A graduate of Harvard, millionaire Henry Cabot Henhouse III monitors crime from his penthouse apartment in Pittsburgh. Whenever something's amiss, he has his lion aide Fred prepare supersauce (in liquid or paste form) and becomes the well-meaning, but incredibly stupid, hero. (The sauce apparently does little for the bird, except to give him a small measure of superstrength and make him impervious to harm.) Costumed in a purple cape and boots, with a black mask and musketeer hat, the mighty fowl wields a rapier, flies about in his egg-shaped Supercoop, and has been known to wear a rocket under his cape. He also has a bolt-throwing lightning rod, which he rarely uses. Although Super Chicken is always confronted by intellectually superior foes such as the Noodle, the Zipper, Dr. Gizmo, Rhode Island's Apian Way (one of the Ways of Providence), and Briggs Bad Wolf, the hero always manages to triumph . . . by accident rather than design. Fred accompanies his boss on each mission, and always goes along with Super Chicken's schemes, no matter how little faith he has in them (like dressing as Red Riding Hood to fool Briggs into thinking he's a desirable young woman). As Super Chicken often admonishes his leery companion, "You knew the job was dangerous when you took it!" When he takes to the skies in the Supercoop, Super Chicken always clucks out a charge. Henry's only known hobby is writing plays in his spare time.

Comment. Super Chicken's adventures, characters, and dialogue are among the wittiest ever devised for TV cartoons. The hero was created by the Jay Ward Studios, and appeared in his own cartoon on the ABC-TV series *George of the Jungle*. There were sixteen cartoons in all; the show aired on Saturday mornings from 1967 to 1968. Bill Scott was the voice of the chicken, and Paul Frees provided the voice for Fred. The characters also appeared in the two issues of Gold Key's *George of the Jungle* comic book (1968 to 1969).

SUPER DUCK
Pedigree. Costumed comic book superhero turned misanthrope.
Biography. By gulping down vitamins, an ordinary duck becomes superpowered—but not for long. After just a few issues, the duck stops becoming a superhero and opens a market, though he's still called Super Duck. (Dr. Brayne, a psychiatrist-dog, rationalizes keeping the name: "You let people bully

and take advantage of you! So, you must *fight!!!* Remember—you are *Super Duck!*") Unfortunately, Super Duck's assertiveness manifests itself as the quickest and hottest temper possessed by any animal on earth. When the doctor presents his bill, Super Duck socks him. When the bird tries earning a living as an inventor, his bread-buttering toaster doesn't work so he takes an ax to it. When he goes bowling and doesn't like his score, he hacks down the scoreboard. Super Duck's constant companion in Fauntleroy, a decent young duck whose relationship with "Supe" is never explained. Super Duck's long-suffering girlfriend is the blond duck Uwanna; she has a sweet nephew named Kant, who usually breaks in on them at the wrong time. The favorite food of the ill-tempered bird is blackberry pie; appropriately enough, the stinker's license number is PU2. Super Duck usually wears red shorts with suspenders, a felt hat that's much too small, a black shirt, and spats. In his brief superhero days, the duck wore a red cape and shirt, blue trousers, and a yellow band across his chest with a black *SD* in the middle. Unlike most cartoon ducks, who have pear-shaped bodies, Super Duck is lean and long-legged. Animals, not humans, are all that live in the duck's world. Super Duck returned in 1990, appearing in *Laugh* no. 24. This time out, he was actually the *son* of Super Duck: Clifton Webfoot, a timid teacher at the Little Reed Schoolhouse. When pollution turns an ordinary duck into the evil RoboDuck, Clifton is persuaded by the other animals of Riverdale Marsh to munch down his late father's "quackers," which endow him with superpowers. This Super Duck wears a yellow costume with a blue *SD* on the chest, blue boots and gloves, and a red cape. Costarring in the story was the magical cat **Salem.** His girlfriend is sculptress Delta Duck, his close friend is Crazylegs the frog, and his mentor is the wise Owlbert Einstein. Other characters in the strip include the Houseless Mouse and Merle and Merly Squirrel.

Comment. Super Duck first appeared in Archie Comics's *Jolly Jingles* no. 10 in 1943, and remained super powered through no. 15. When the comic book was discontinued the following year, *Super Duck Comics, The Cockeyed Wonder* began and lasted for ninety-four issues, until 1960. It also spawned three issues of *Fauntleroy Comics,* published from 1950 to 1952. No reason has ever been given for the abrupt change from a comical superhero strip, though weak sales were the probable cause. Making the character more like the irascible **Donald Duck** obviously worked! The best of the stories were written and drawn by Al Fagaly. *Jolly Jingles* no. 10 also featured the debut of a character named Woody the Woodpecker, who was different from the earlier **Woody Woodpecker.** Other characters that appeared in the *Super Duck* comic books were Fauntleroy's best friend Ham Burger, a very goofy dog who occasionally starred in short strips of his own; and Cubby the Bear, a city dweller who gets into various adventures with his nephew Junior and tries to woo the lovely bear Petunia.

SUPER GOOF

Pedigree. Superheroic secret identity of **Goofy.**
Biography. When Goofy isn't getting into trouble on his own or with his friends **Donald Duck** and **Mickey Mouse,** he's busy righting wrongs in his own singularly inept fashion. Based in Duckburg (see Donald's entry), Goof gobbles down peanuts known as Super Goobers—which he grows in his backyard peanut patch—and thus becomes superpowered . . . although he only gets a few minutes of might from each peanut. His array of powers is truly amazing . . . although his ability to wake people with supershaking is of questionable worth. He has telescopic vision and microvision, X-ray vision and spotlight vision, and can pick up TV signals with his eyes; he can fly through air and space, hovering or moving at superspeeds; he has superhearing (he can eavesdrop on a chat in England), a supernose (he can track "helicopter exhaust lingerin' in thuh air"), supersuction (which he creates by rotating his hands), invulnerability, and superstrength (he can lift a car with his hands, or an elephant with his teeth). Needing a great deal of sleep, Goof won't hesitate to pop a few Super Goobers to induce supersleep; unfortunately, these also cause him to become a supersnorer, and he wreaks widespread destruction. Indeed, Goof is a bit of a clod even when he's awake: He has to beware when he dances that he doesn't cause earthquakelike tremors. Super Goof works closely with Duckburg's Police Chief O'Hara, a dog, and wears red longjohns with a white *SG* on the front, a blue cape, and a blue stovepipe hat. These appear magically when he pops his Goobers . . . although he never does so in public, and has been known to slip into a handy trashcan when no other place of concealment was available. The longjohns inspired his stirring slogan, "Crooks beware . . . I'll chase yuh in muh underwear!" Goof's girlfriend is **Clarabelle Cow;** Mickey Mouse is a neighbor. His foes include **The Beagle Boys;** the hu-

man Super Jokester, who distracts people with gags while his thugs take their wallets; the human Dr. Stigma, the "super-thief" who made off with the Leaning Tower of Pizza [sic] (the newspaper headline announced, "All Tours Cancelled!"); and the costumed supervillain the Red Arrow, who hypnotizes people (even Super Goof) into heading whichever way the arrow on his chest is pointing. Super Goof is descended from the medieval superhero Mighty Knight who, dressed in armor, orange tights, and a blue cape, flies through the air on his yellow-colored horse Hayburner. He is assisted by his squire, **Gus Goose.** Mighty's chief asset is his "push button sword," which can be transformed into a variety of weapons, most notably a can opener to open armor.

Comment. The character first appeared in the second issue of the comic book *The Phantom Blot,* published by Gold Key in 1964 (the Phantom was a shrouded crook who regularly teamed with **The Beagle Boys**). Super Goof went from there to his own title, of which there were seventy-four issues published by Gold Key from 1965 to 1982. The character never appeared in any animated cartoons. Mighty Knight adventures appear in many issues.

SUPERKATT
Pedigree. Looniest of all the comic book cat superheroes.
Biography. Superkatt is the pet of the baby, Junior. Possessing no superpowers, just uncanny good luck, the black feline is the self-appointed guardian of the dog Humphrey the Hound and other helpless animals. Whenever there's danger (and whenever Junior's black nanny, Petunia, turns her back), Superkatt grabs Junior's bonnet, bow tie, and diaper, shouts, "Make way for the cat what is super!" and launches himself into the fray. If foes run, it's because there's a truck roaring down at them from behind Superkatt (he doesn't know this, of course), or a skunk has wandered into the room.

Comment. The cat first appeared in American Comics's *Giggle Comics* no. 9 in 1944 and was created by Fleischer animator Dan Gordon, who signed his work "Dang." The magazine was taken over by Spencer Spook in 1955. Another supercat is Super Pamby, a blue-costumed, red-caped black cat who starred in his own comic book in Spain in the early 1960s.

SUPERMOUSE
Pedigree. The first superpowered animal hero.
Biography. As an ordinary mouse, our hero lives in a small suburban house with his bride Mabel, a downhome type mouse whom he wed after a long romance with his redheaded girlfriend mouse Annabel. (Mabel is a connoisseur of museums and classical music, in particular the swine violinist Pigetti; Annabel is a wild lass who preferred the rodeo.) In his nonsuper state, Supermouse gets around onboard a little blue airplane named the *Supercheese Special.* Supermouse doesn't seem to hold a job of any kind, and never removes his costume. When the unassuming little mouse takes a bite of the supercheese that's tucked in his back pocket, he's granted amazing powers: flight, invulnerability, X-ray vision, superstrength, superventriloquism, superhearing, and the ability to survive without breathing. (Even a sniff of the cheese is enough to rouse him from unconsciousness.) His "worst enemy" is the evil cat Terrible Tom, though the foul Spud McWolf of the Bar Fly Ranch has also been known to give him trouble. In their most challenging confrontation, Tom used a "reducing potion" to shrink the nonsuper Supermouse and place him in a bottle. Shattering the prison by singing a high note, Supermouse calls a bug army to help him bring Tom to justice, then returns to normal size. The most dangerous weapon in Tom's arsenal is his Terrorplane, which, in one adventure, he uses to cause more than a week of rain and flooding. Perhaps the most bizarre foe the mouse ever faced was the surreal Esuomrepus: his own distorted reflection, which crawls from a funhouse mirror and is as powerful as he is. (He defeats him rather ingeniously by eating Supercheese, reasoning that "things work in reverse here! That cheese made you *weak* instead of strong.") Supermouse's costume consists of red tights and a red cape, a blue shirt and shoes, and white gloves. Originally, the emblem on his chest was a wedge of cheese with a ? in the ceneter; this was replaced with a yellow S. The hero is nicknamed the Mouse of Stainless Steel, although his friends call him nothing more imposing than "Soupie." The local foodstore—the Super (Mouse) Market—is named after him.

Comment. Supermouse flew into the pages of history in Standard Publishing's *Coo Coo Comics* no. 1 in 1942. He was given his own magazine in 1948, and it survived an impressive ten years. The best of the stories featured superb, very lively art by Milton Stein. A few of the lesser-known animals that appeared in *Coo Coo Comics* were Harold the Hound, who doggedly guarded the chickens of Farmer Bear against onslaughts by Shifty Fox; Sparks, the chimp firefighter; Windy Willy (a k a Wacky Willy), an affluent pelican; Fin 'n' Butch, a pair of tough fish who delight in tormenting the overbearing Pool Shark; Al Gator, an alligator sailor; the Bold Knight, an armored dog who rides the steed Sliver and serves a lion-king in medieval times; Ham Swift, a scientist-pig; the Buttinsky, a billy goat who's always minding other animals' business; Lil' [*sic*] Herkimer, a hapless bear; Colonel Punchy Penguin, a "really wacky" bird who wears a Confederate cap, speaks with a southern accent, and has various adventures in the North Pole with his friend Petey Polar Bear (who wears a white bow tie); the kilt-wearing Scottish dog Duncan and his pipesmoking cat friend Douglas, and their money-making schemes in a city of anthropomorphic animals; Tuffy the Cat (a **Sylvester the Cat** lookalike), who is always trying to get around the guard-dog Herman to eat a (nameless) caged canary; Silly the dog, a mongrel; and the one-of-a-kind Dodger, "Da Squoil from Brooklyn," who sits on a jaloppa tree overlooking Ebbets Field and gets into adventures with his favorite baseball team, the Brooklyn Dodgers (e.g., preventing the team owner from cutting down his tree to make baseball bats). Some of the animals who had their own strips in *Supermouse, the Big Cheese* include **Buster Bunny**; **Merton Monk**; **Tommy Turtle**; Roscoe Mouse, a playful rodent; the adventuresome young trio of Randy Raccoon, Jim Squirrel, and Billy Beaver; golf fanatic Goofy Gander; and the well-to-do Cuffy Cat, who's always being bothered by his thimble-witted friend Pesky Pooch.

SUPER SNOOPER

Pedigree. Cat TV detective.

Biography. Dressed in matching white trenchcoats, the detective cat Super Snooper (in a deerstalker cap) and his assistant Blabber Mouse (in a fedora) tackle big-city crime as well as the occasional ghost or monster. Both animals walk upright; Blabber is roughly half the size of Snooper, though thanks to his constant palaver he's never overshadowed by his taciturn partner. Among the more important cases of the Super Snooper Detective Agency are *Puss and Booty, Big Diaper Caper, Disappearing Inc.* (a wonderfully inspired title, a play on Murder, Inc.), *Case of the Purloined Parrot, Person to Prison,* and *Desperate Diamond Dimwits.* The duo is aided by their secretary, Hazel.

   Comment. The Hanna-Barbera characters appeared in separate segments of the syndicated show *Quick Draw McGraw,* beginning in 1959; there

were forty-five cartoons in all. Daws Butler provided the voices for both characters.

SUPERSWINE

Pedigree. Pig hero of comic books.

Biography. Falling-down drunk one night in Dream City—home of anthropomorphic animals—a good-for-nothing, chain-smoking pig curls up on the front stoop of the bar. When a bandit tries to rob the place, he trips over the prone pig, and the swine is declared a hero. Because of the media attention and reward (free pizza and beer), the pig decides to make superheroing his life. He sews himself a blue bodysuit with a red cape, red gloves, and a black mask, and becomes Superswine. Unfortunately, he's basically lazy and tries to bum cash, food, and drink from people by virtue of who he is ("Hey, buddy! Hows'bout contributin' to yer friendly neighborhood sooper hero?"). After a while, the act wears thin and he becomes little more than a costumed bum. The only thing that gets his goat is being mistaken for the genuine superhero, Powerpig.

   Comment. Created by Gary Fields, the character costarred in the only issue of *Kaptain Keen and Kompany,* published by Canada's Vortex Comics in 1986, and starred in Fantagraphics Books's *Christmas with Superswine* in 1988. In that magazine, the pig and his friend Drab, an ant, rescue Santa, who's been abducted by a hippo known as the Green Mist. The strip is well drawn, but offensive: In this era of enlightenment about the dangers of tobacco and alcohol, it's perplexing why anyone would want to look for humor in a drunk chain-smoker.

SUPERTED

Pedigree. Teddy bear star of comics and television.

Biography. On the teddy bear assembly line, workers find "something wrong" with one bear, and toss him into a stockroom. He's found there by an explorer from the planet Spot: Spotty (a k a Spottyman), who has a yellow body and hot dog–shaped head, is covered with green spots, and sports an orange Mohawk. The extraterrestrial sprinkles the bear with "cosmic dust," which brings him to life, then carries him to a cloud. There, seeing the potential for good in the bear, Mother Nature gives him a potion: "By whispering a magic word that only he knows," the teddy bear obtains superpowers, including flight, superstrength, invulnerability, and the ability to survive (and talk!) in outer space. With Spotty, SuperTed establishes a space station "deep in outer space" and, flying about using a space scooter,

SuperTed and Spottyman. Note the space station in the background. © PETALCRAFT DEMONSTRATIONS LTD. AND S4C.

a rocket ship, or stripped down to yellow rocket boots, SuperTed travels the universe, fighting evildoers. When he goes into action, SuperTed dresses in a red bodysuit and cape, his yellow boots, and a white and yellow "flame" symbol on his chest. He wears these under a fake bearskin, it being easier to change out of the skin than into the costume. In his leisure moments, SuperTed enjoys eating the spotted pan

cakes fixed by Spotty, or playing with the puppy Miff.

Comment. The character was created by Mike Young and was first seen in ten-minute-long cartoons produced by Siriol Animation in Cardiff, Wales, in 1979. He later debuted as a comic strip in England's *Pippin* magazine, and he's also been featured in a number of children's books, among them

SuperTed and the Green Planet, SuperTed Meets Zappy and Zoppy, and *SuperTed and Nuts in Space.* In the United States, SuperTed's adventures are available only on videocassette and in children's books. (Peripherally, the character Superteddy, a toy bear with a cape, was introduced in the comic strip "For Better or Worse" in August 1989. It belongs to young Elizabeth, who's fond of shouting, "Hi-yaah Superteddy!!" and throwing the inert bear at people, as if it were a crusading crime buster.) Other characters from the United Kingdom which have enjoyed some success in the United States include **Count Duckula** and **Danger Mouse.** In recent years, one of the United Kingdom's foremost breeding grounds for cartoon animals has been the weekly IPC comic magazines *Whoopee* and *Wow!*—which have introduced characters such as Hairy Henry, pet dog of the young terror Sweeny Toddler; Kid Kong, the friendly ape; Ossie the Ostrich, who constantly tries to remain one step ahead of the zookeeper; TV star Ronald Rodent; and one-shot strips that have included minor classics like *The Ducks of Hazard.* See also **Captain Teddy.**

SYLVESTER THE CAT
Pedigree. Warner Brothers cartoon star.
Biography. The lisping, bird-craving black-furred white-bellied cat began his screen career in *Life with Feathers* (1945), walking along trash cans in an alley, a tray (actually an overturned lid) in his hand, as though the cans were a buffet. The short marks a delightful twist on the soon-to-be-familiar theme of Sylvester chasing **Tweety Bird** or mice: A henpecked parakeet tries to commit suicide by getting into Sylvester's mouth, but the cat will have none of it, fearing that the bird may be poisoned. The cat suffers various painful indignities as the bird tries to pry open his maw. He also utters his soon-to-be characteristic "Sufferin' succotash" in the cartoon. Order is restored to the cat-eat-bird universe in the next cartoon, *Peck Up Your Troubles* (1945) as the feline preys on a woodpecker (Sylvester's stilts get pecked, as does the branch on which the cat climbs). After several other failed assaults, Sylvester is blown up by the dynamite he'd intended to use on the woodpecker. *Kitty Kornered* (1946) offers Sylvester one of his few victories, as he and four other cats are pitted against Porky, who's trying to get them out of his home. The cat (here called Thomas, not Sylvester!) meets his gravest threat yet in his fourth film, *Tweetie Pie* (1947), in which the placid but sadistic

canary **Tweety** [*sic*] **Bird** is taken in from the cold by the cat's owner, and kitty spends the rest of the cartoon trying to get to its cage and eat it (Tweety saws down the furniture Thomas stacks up, unplugs the electric fan he's using as a propeller, and so on). Sylvester and Tweety slugged it out in a total of forty-four adventures, including *Home Tweet Home* (1950), set in a park where Tweety is trying to bathe in the birdbath while Sylvester stalks him; *All Abir-r-rd* (1950) in which they fight on a train headed to Gower Gulch; *Canary Row* (1950) which not only has a brilliant title but a great concept: Tweety is in a hotel that bans cats and dogs, but not birds, and Sylvester's trying to sneak in; *Tweety's S.O.S.* (1951), the saga of a battle on a cruise ship; *Bird in a Guilty Cage* (1952), in which a department store after hours is the battleground; *Sandy Claws* (1955), a tale of conflict on the beach; and *A Pizza Tweety Pie* (1958), set in Venice, with the Italian-accented cat making repeated efforts to cross the canal and get to Tweety. Granny, Sylvester's and/or Tweety's elderly owner (it varies), is occasionally seen in the cartoons—often warning the cat at the outset that nothing better happen to the bird while she's away, then swatting Sylvester with a broom when something *does* happen. When he isn't fighting with Tweety, Sylvester had his hands full with another menace: **Hippety Hopper,** a baby kangaroo, which, in many of their dozen cartoons, Sylvester repeatedly mistakes for a giant mouse . . . always to his detriment. In several of the Hippety cartoons, beginning with *Pop 'Em Pop* (1950), Sylvester was joined by his son, Sylvester Junior. The purpose of the boy (who looks like a miniature version of dad) is to coax him into battle when any sane cat would have given up ("You want to destroy a child's faith in his father?" the tad asks). Sylvester's other foes have included Wellington Bulldog (*Doggone Cats,* 1948); a nameless mouse plaguing Sylvester's temporary owner Boris Borscht of Slobovia in *Mouse Mazurka* (1949); Mike the bulldog, a friend who's shamed by a mouse into fighting the cat in *Stooge for a Mouse* (1950); Timmy Mouse, who plays *Little Red Rodent Hood* (1952) to Sylvester's wicked "wolf"; Spike the bulldog in *Tree for Two* (1952), a marvelous cartoon in which Spike is goaded by the adoring little dog Chester into attacking Sylvester—yet every time he tries, he ends up tangling with an escaped panther instead; **Speedy Gonzales** in the Oscar-winning *Speedy Gonzales* (1955); and Sam the Cat, a neighbor, who competes with Sylvester to try and eat

Tweety in *Trick or Treat* (1959). Sylvester isn't as excitable as Warner's other perennial loser, **Daffy Duck,** nor is he as quietly determined as the much-battered **Wile E. Coyote.** He's simply a cat who does what he must do, bearing up like a good and usually even-tempered soldier.

Comment. Sylvester starred in 104 cartoons. Animator Friz Freleng says that the cat was designed "subtly like a clown [with] a big red nose and a very low crotch . . . to look like he was wearing baggy pants." Mel Blanc provided the cat's voice. See **Tweety Bird,** for a rundown on Sylvester in the comic books.

TADPOLE

Pedigree. Teddy bear companion to TV's Spunky.

Biography. Spunky, as his name implies, is a go-get'em kid whose comrade-in-arms is the talking, marginally intelligent Teddy bear Tadpole, who's the only animal in the adventures. Spunky enjoys solving mysteries, and their investigations not only carry them around the world, from the Casbah to the North Pole, but into outer space as well. Tadpole wears no clothing and has a voice that drips from his mouth like running molasses.

Comment. The Beverly Film Corporation Production was syndicated in 1960. There were fifteen adventures, each of which consisted of ten episodes lasting three and a half minutes each, all but the last ending in a cliff-hanger. Don Messick and Ed Janis provided Tadpole's voice.

TASMANIAN DEVIL

Pedigree. "A vicious, ravenous brute with powerful jaws like a steel trap," a worthy opponent to **Bugs Bunny.**

Biography. When the Devil chases animals past Bugs Bunny's hole, the rabbit looks up the creature in an encyclopedia. He needn't have bothered: The Devil drops in to eat the rabbit, thus providing Bugs with one of the only foils worthy of his mettle. Although the rabbit tries to bury the Devil ("What for you bury me in the cold, cold ground?" the carnivore demands after whirling his way out), and fails to send him floating away with a mixture of bicarbonate and bubble gum disguised as a chicken, nothing works until Bugs summons a female Tasmanian Devil, who whisks the male Devil away. (All of this takes place in *Devil May Hare.)* In their second meeting *(Bedevilled Rabbit),* Bugs stows away in a box of carrots and is dropped off in Tasmania. When they meet, Bugs pretends to be a monkey, which the Devil claims not to enjoy eating—although the creature realizes, "You got little powder puff tail like rabbit." When Bugs dresses as a woman, Mrs. Devil comes to his rescue, clubbing her husband with a rolling pin. In the Devil's third appearance, **Daffy Duck** goes hunting for him to claim a reward. The creature is mostly head and torso, with a massive jaw, tiny legs, gangly arms, and a short tail. His one

vulnerability (except for an onslaught from Mrs. Devil) is sung music, which tends to soothe him.

Comment. The Warner Brothers character was seen in six cartoons from 1954 to 1979.

TAWN

Pedigree. The pachyderm pal of the comic book hero Wambi, the Jungle Boy.

Biography. Wambi is a young native who, with "his favorite friend" Tawn, keeps an eye on the corrupt doings of "white campers" who come to the jungle, and also uses Tawn to break up fights between animals. Tawn is loyal to his young master, charging through huts, trees, or armed men when he hears Wambi whistle.

Comment. Wambi and Tawn appeared frequently in Fiction House's *Jungle Comics,* beginning with no. 1 in 1940. The first issue also featured a surprisingly moving story about Simba the lion, and his decline as the King of the Lions.

TEENAGE MUTANT NINJA TURTLES

Pedigree. Comic book heroes who became multimedia superstars.

Biography. Twenty years ago, in Japan, Hamato Yoshi is "the greatest shadow warrior" in a ninja clan known as the Foot. His closest "friend" is a pet rat, Splinter, whom he keeps in a cage nearby when he works out . . . unaware that the rat is mimicking his movements. Yoshi and warrior Oroku Nagi compete "fiercely . . . for the love of a young woman, Tang Shen." But the woman loves Yoshi and, in a jealous rage, Nagi tries to kill her. Yoshi comes to her rescue and murders his fellow clansman; dishonored, he takes Shen and his rat and moves to New York, where he founds a martial arts school. Meanwhile, Nagi's brother Oroku Saki vows vengeance. Coincidentally, Saki is sent to New York to found an American limb of the Foot. There, as the Shredder, he moves the league into "drug smuggling, arms running . . . and their specialty, assassination." Surprising Yoshi in his apartment, Saki slays him and Shen. During the altercation, the rat cage is smashed and Splinter flees. One day, while rummaging through trash cans, the rat witnesses a young man leap in front of a truck to save a blind man; as the truck brakes, a canister of radioactive muck bounces out, strikes a jar of baby turtles being carried by a young boy (straight from Shelly's Pet City), and falls, with the turtles, into an open manhole. Inside the storm drain, the "glowing ooze" covers the turtles bodies. The rat runs over, scoops them into a coffee can, and cares for them ... watching as they grow and mutate. After a year, the foursome have become fully humanoid turtles averaging five feet tall and 150 pounds, with three-fingered hands, two-toed feet, powerful chests, and the ability to speak. Splinter, too, has become more intelligent, although only slightly humanlike (apparently, he was already too mature for the mutagen to fully affect him). Seeking revenge against the Shredder, Splinter begins to teach the upright turtles all that he'd learned watching his master back in Japan. He also chooses names for the turtles: Leonardo, "the super cool, sword wielding leader"; Raphael, "the jokester, hurling manholes and one-liners in rapid succession," who also carries daggerlike sai; Donatello, "the brain behind the brawn" who wields a "simple wooden staff [which] can disarm any adversary"; and Michael-angelo, "the ice cream, pizza gobbling party animal" who does battle with nunchakus (two pieces of wood connected by a length of chain). Dressed in silk ribbon masks with matching bands around their arms, wrists, and knees, belts with golden initials on the front, able to speak, and fond of pizza and cola, the Turtles become crime fighters, with the Foot and the fiendish Shredder as their first adversaries. They issue a challenge to the villain and his flunkies, and in a brutal showdown on a rooftop, the Turtles vanquish the Foot and slay the Shredder. Based in apartments located in the sewers, the Turtles and their master continue to battle crime. (In a subsequent retelling of the tale, the story is slightly different. Yoshi is a teacher, and, when a student, Oroku Saki, frames him for the attempted murder of the clan's master, the teacher is banished. He flees to the United States where he is "forced to live in the sewers." One day, a boy trips and drops a jar containing four turtles. The animals fall through a sewer grate, land on Yoshi, and, along with sewer rats, become his companions—although not for long. In Japan, Saki has transformed the Foot into a criminal league. Obtaining a "powerful mutagen," he endeavors to destroy Yoshi by having the "strange glowing liquid" poured through a drain near his home in the sewer. The poison coats the animals and transforms the turtles into the "animal they had most recently been in contact with"—a human. But the ooze also touches Yoshi, who had most recently been with

sewer rats. Thus Yoshi becomes a man-size, upright rodent, while the turtles become our heroes. Realizing that the turtles will "be outcasts," Yoshi trains them to be ninja warriors. They name him Splinter, and he, in turn, names them "after my favorite Renaissance painters.")

Comment. The characters were created by Kevin Eastman and Peter Laird, and were first seen in their eponymous Mirage Studios magazine in 1984. The young men first came up with the idea in 1983, while watching television. Eastman (who was working as a cook), inspired by a recent DC comic book *Ronin,* sketched a picture of a wrinkled, masked, bipedal turtle carrying nunchackus and dubbed it a ninja turtle. Laird, a free-lance artist, threw in the "teenage mutant" aspect, which parodied the origins of the Marvel superhero Daredevil. He also took over the art chores, and the single turtle became four. Of their naming, Laird says that despite the Turtles' "Japanese fighting methods ... we didn't want to make up Japanese names, because we thought they'd seem too strange or silly to American readers." Instead, they went with names of great European artists. Using their meager savings and borrowed money, they printed a semiprofessional comic book that might have gone relatively unnoticed had a UPI reporter not received a press release from the creators, interviewed them, and written up a story. The 3,000-copy first printing sold out, and subsequent issues had increasingly larger press runs (up to 135,000 by no. 8, in which **Cerebus the Aardvark** guest stars). The parodic tone of the first issue was largely discarded by the second, the Turtles becoming bona fide heroes. Each of the characters had one-shot titles in 1986, and a companion comic book, *Tales of the Teenage Mutant Ninja Turtles,* was introduced in 1987. Archie Comics has published their own licensed versions of the characters in a three-issue miniseries in 1988, and a regular bimonthly title in 1989. The Archie titles are the only Turtles comic books in color. A successful syndicated, animated TV series first appeared in 1988, produced by Murakamie Wolf Swenson Inc. Several episodes were edited together to form the feature-length *The Epic Begins* for videocassette. A daily newspaper strip was inaugurated in 1991. In addition to licensing—which includes everything from top-selling Nintendo videogames to a popular line of action figures from Playmates (see below)—the characters were featured in the live-action Golden Harvest motion picture directed by Steve Barron and released in 1990, and a sequel released the following year. Several new characters were introduced to the mythos (and the toyline) in 1989: Ace Duck, a duck-headed, web-footed human who was pilot Ace Conrad before being struck by an energy beam with which Shredder was trying to send a terrestrial duck to Dimension X; Rocksteady, a rhino-man mutant born in the La Brea Tar Pits, and now Shredder's number one thug; Bebop, a boar-man; Leatherhead, an alligator who was transformed into a humanoid reptile by an orange mutagen in a Florida swamp; the tyrannical Genghis Frog; and Baxter Stockman, who has the mind of a man and the body of a fly, created when a disintegrator beam malfunctioned. **Miyamoto Usagi** and **Panda Khan** were also added to the toy line. For the curious, take a look at the 1989 "graphic novel" featuring **The Adolescent Radioactive Black Belt Hamsters,** for a Turtles parody featuring Van Gogh, Picasso, Pollock, and Warhol. In May 1991 the same creative team introduced *The Mighty Mutanimals* comic book, featuring Leatherhead, along with other humanoid, talking animals: Jagwar, the skateboard-riding Mondo Gecko, the seagoing Man Ray, the wolf Dreadmon, the bat Wingnut, and the mosquito Screwloose, a k a Little 'Skeeter.

TENNESSEE TUXEDO

Pedigree. Antarctic penguin of TV fame.
Biography. Exhibits at the Megopolis Zoo, the sarcastic Tennessee and his dull, clumsy friend Chumley the Walrus get into many adventures while trying to improve the lot of animals at the zoo. It's mostly standard cartoon dramatics: Trouble with a rocket, circus, toothache, dinosaur, crime, and one novelty, the zoolympics. Unique about the show was its intentional educational value. Before undertaking any project, the two animals would go and visit their human friend, scholar Phineas J. Whoopee, who would review the engineering, scientific, and/or mathematic principles involved. Naturally, Chumley (with an assist from zookeeper Stanley Livingston and his klutzy assistant Flunky) usually manages to mess things up. Skinny Tennessee wears a collar, bow tie, and hat; Chumley is dressed in a hat and necktie.
  Comment. Leonardo Productions *Tennessee Tuxedo and His Tales* aired on CBS from 1963 to 1966; there were sixty-nine episodes. Don Adams—later of *Get Smart* fame—provided Tennessee's voice. Bradley Bolke was Chumley. Late in the show's run, the segment *Yak and Baldy* was introduced, featuring a steer and an eagle.

TERRY BEARS

Pedigree. One papa bear and two boys in a theatrical cartoon series.
Biography. The titles of the Terry Bears cartoons are misleading: *Papa's Little Helpers, Papa's Day of Rest, Plumber's Helpers,* and so on are anything but. Living in a cottage in the woods, the twin bears cause their father no end of trouble; never intentionally, but that doesn't matter. Their short-fused dad rarely takes kindly to abuse. If the father's repairing the roof, chances are good a barrel of nails will fall into the lawnmower the kids are using and fly back like machine gun fire. If dad agrees to help the cubs make a championship-caliber bow, odds are he's going to launch himself into the woods, like an arrow. If the kids toss a boomerang, the only way it's coming back is in dad's hand—to whack them with, after it's hit him in the head. When papa bear tries to relax, he enjoys reading the newspaper and playing the violin (badly). The bears walk upright, talk, and wear clothes, and have a hen house, which apparently provides them with a living. There's no clue about what happened to mama bear, but given the precocious kids and volatile father, it wouldn't be surprising to learn she packed her bags and left.
Comments. Terrytoons produced seventeen cartoons starring the Bears from 1951 to 1955. The voices were provided by Roy Halee, Doug Moye, and Phillip A. Scheib. The characters also appeared in various **Mighty Mouse** comic books as one- or two-page back-up features.

THE THREE BEARS

Pedigree. Warner Brothers theatrical stars inspired by the classic fairy tale.
Biography. A trio in which the young, dumb, diapered, Junior Bear is twice the size of short, fat Papa Bear, with Mama Bear in between. Having nothing else to do in *Bugs Bunny and the Three Bears* (1944), Papa, Mama, and Junior decide to use food to sucker Goldilocks to their house, then eat her. However, the carrot soup Mama makes brings only **Bugs Bunny,** but the canny rabbit is not about to become anyone's dinner. Pitching woo to Mama Bear, he turns her into his staunch defender, and leaves in one piece . . . and well fed (although he's a little alarmed to find Mama in his rabbit hole when he gets there). In *What's Bruin' Bruin* (1948), the bears hibernate—except for Papa (he now has a name: Henry), who is bugged by everything from a leaking roof to Mama's snoring. By the time he falls asleep, spring has arrived . . . but Papa's angry scream sends it away, and winter

returns. Henry and Junior have trouble with bees when they try to replenish their honey supply in *The Bee-Deviled Bruin* (1948), while in *Bear Feat* (1949) they painfully brush up old circus acts in response to an ad for trick bears—only to notice, in the end, that the ad is twenty years old. The bears' last screen performance was in *A Bear for Punishment* (1951), in which the best intentions of Mama and Junior go awry, and Papa has a Father's Day he'll never forget.

Comment. The bears' voices were provided by Mel Blanc and Billy Bletcher (Papa), Bea Benaderet (Mama), and Stan Freberg (Junior). Warner Brothers also produced *Goldilocks and the Jivin' Bears* in 1944, in which King-Size Bear, Middle-Size Bear, and Wee Little Bear are jazz musicians who, on returning home from a gig, find Goldilocks being chased by a wolf. Thinking the two are jitterbugs, they break out their instruments and jam. Goldilocks boogies with the wolf as an unwilling partner, whipping him every which way and making him rue the day he became a predator. The story of the Three Bears was first published in 1837, in Robert Southey's *The Doctor,* in which the title character tells the tale of the Little, Small, Wee Bear, the Middle-sized Bear, and the Great, Huge Bear, and the old Woman who comes to their home. The story was repeated orally prior to Southey, although it's provenance is unknown. Goldilocks (originally known as Silver Hair) was not introduced until Joseph Cundall's *Treasury of Pleasure Books for Young Children* in 1850. The traditional version has been filmed numerous times, most impressively with animated puppets in the 1954 Czech short *Goldilocks.* A different set of Three Bears were featured in EC's *Tiny Tots Comics,* which ran for ten issues from 1946 to 1947. The magazine, in fact, had a three fixation, not only featuring the adventures of the bears, but also the Three Blind Mice, the Three Little Kittens, the Three Little Pigs (not Disney's) and the Three Billy Goats. The magazine boasted fine art by Walt Kelly, who went on to create **Pogo Possum.**

THE THREE MOUSEKETEERS

Pedigree. Comic book mice who are more like the Three Stooges than like Porthos, Athos, and Aramis.

Biography. The bold trio consists of "strange mice [who] can read and write," a talent they acquired by attending a school they discovered while out searching for food. The Mouseketeers are the tiny, adventurous Minus, who wears a baseball cap and T-shirt;

the dumb, tall, lanky, and naked Patsy; and their leader, the portly "captain" Fatsy, a bright but volatile mouse who wears a sailor's suit and cap. Our heroes live in the Secret Club House, a U-shaped underground tunnel that is accessed by a tin tomato can lying at the foot of the Old Elm Tree in the middle of a meadow. When they aren't dodging human intruders (a k a "Big Feets"), the mice are busy partaking in adventures that range from sailing the seas (aboard a ship stolen from a bottle) to flying around on their rubber band–propelled Mousekeplane to taking a flight onboard the rocketship of Professor Niddleswitch of Luke University. The Mouseketeers keep their tools and weapons beneath a mushroom, which is marked "Secret Hiding Place for Rescue Equipment." Cowardice and stupidity among the mice are penalized with "demerits," which are tabulated on a chart pinned outside the clubhouse. If a mouse receives the ultimate demerit, a Black Ball, he's kicked out of the group until he performs a brave deed. Other denizens of the meadow include Mrs. Ladybug, the sarcastic Herman Hop-Toad, the Ed Norton-ish Sherm the Worm, Buzz-Buzz the Bee, and the mouse-eating Hamilton Hawk.

Comment. Created by Sheldon Mayer, the characters first appeared in DC Comics's *Funny Stuff* no. 1 in 1944. Early in their run, the mice actually were Musketeers, complete with plumed hats, swords, spurs, and moustaches. Living in France of King Looey XIV (a dog), and aided by the clever D'Artagmouse, the "stout Mouseketeers" fought various cat-foes of the king—when they weren't busy winking at the pretty lady-mice or engaging in snappy repartee ("Slug him with all your might," says one. "You use your *might*," says another, "I'll use my *fists!*"). It isn't known why the characters were changed, although it may have been a combination of sluggish sales and possible litigation from Walt Disney (see below). The Mouseketeers' own magazine ran for twenty-six issues from 1956 to 1960, then again for seven issues in 1970 to 1971. *Note:* Pearl S. Buck was on the publisher's advisory board. See also the similar **The Two Mouseketeers.** All three dress in red musketeer uniforms with blue hats and white plumes, carry words . . . and wear sunglasses. Physically, one is tall and lean, the other chunky, the other tiny and rascally. Their foe is Captain Katt (a k a **Pete**), a feline who wears an eyepatch and tries repeatedly to nab the mice, only to be thwarted by their blind dumb luck (e.g., they blithely and unwittingly cross a floor blanketed with mousetraps, and accidentally pop the cork from champagne bottles, fortuitously smiting the cat). In the end, the cat flees from the mice.

THUNDERBUNNY

Pedigree. Comic book rabbit superhero.

Biography. Bobby Caswell is a teenage comic book fan who dreams of being a superhero. While vacationing in Rutland, Vermont, in 1980, he sees a fireball strike Bald Mountain. Bicycling over to investigate, he finds a spaceship with a holographic-style message from Doctor Bar-ko—a humanoid dog, and Director of the Energy Institute on his home world, a planet of anthropomorphic animals. Bar-ko explains that his world is "growing cold. Even the superhero of our world cannot prevent this." However, Bar-ko adds that "we are not a selfish race." Thus he's brought the superhero's "energy force" to earth within a "power box," so that someone on our world can become Thunderbunny—a being with a human body and a rabbit's head. All Bobby needs to do to effect the transformation is to clap his hands and picture Thunderbunny in his mind. However, Bar-ko warns him, "the *longer* you keep the *form* . . . the *harder* it will be to change back," which requires clapping his hands and picturing his human form. In his superheroic state, Bobby can fly, possesses superstrength (he can lift a bus with ease), and is impervious to bullets. He stands approximately six feet tall. In his first adventure, the heroic hare wears a light blue cape and tights, white gloves and boots, white trunks, and a navy blue shirt with a white lightning bolt down the center. The shirt and tights are red in his second appearance.

Comment. Created by Martin Greim, the character first appeared in Charlton Comics *Charlton Bullseye* no. 6 in 1982. The character moved over to Red Circle (Archie) Comics (1984), and is presently being published by Apple Comics.

THE TIJUANA TOADS

Pedigree. Hillbilly frogs of theatrical cartoons.

Biography. Poncho is a chunky, basically lazy Mexican frog, and Toro is his slim, inexperienced friend. The two live on a pond where the seasoned Poncho instructs his companion on everything from how not to become a meal for the big, dumb crane that's always after them, to the best ways of catching flies. Naturally, things always go wrong in this relationship, which owes a great deal to Laurel and Hardy.

Comment. The De Patie-Freleng characters were known as the Tijuana Toads when their seventeen adventures were shown theatrically between 1969 and 1972. When the cartoons were shown on *The Pink Panther Laff and a Half-Hour* (NBC, 1976), they were renamed the Texas Toads, and their new names, Fatso and Banjo, were dubbed in. The voices were provided by Don Diamond and Tom Holland. Although the cartoons were not very imaginative, the titles were usually great: *A Dopey Hacienda* (say it fast), *Snake in the Gracias,* and *Never on Thirsty.*

TIGE

Pedigree. Dog owned by the comic strip kid Buster Brown.

Biography. Dressed like Little Lord Fauntleroy, the ten-year-old Buster Brown is no angel: He's constantly playing tricks on family members and servants in his well-to-do home, and on police officers, kids, and others in the neighborhood. His constant companion is his talking brown bulldog Tige, who usually doesn't partake in the pranks but serves as a Greek chorus, chatting with us ("I'm no mind reader but I'll bet he has an idea now") and then reacting to whatever Buster's done, grinning at us, holding his belly with laughter, doing paw-stands (and even tail stands, balancing on the tip of his tail), etc.

Comment. Tige—in likeness, if not in name—first appeared in artist Richard Outcault's strip "The Yellow Kid" in 1897, staring at a group of kids who'd fallen into a snow drift. Outcault's wildly popular "Buster Brown" strip debuted on May 4, 1902 and lasted until 1920; the artist made a fortune from licensing the characters, especially for the Buster Brown line of shoes ("I'm Buster Brown. I live in a shoe. This is my dog Tige. He lives there too!"). The characters also appeared in a successful comic book, thirty-nine issues of which the Brown Shoe Company published from 1945 to 1959. There was also one issue of *My Dog Tige,* published in 1957.

TIME BEAVERS

Pedigree. Comic book beaver soldiers.

Biography. Captain Slapper is the leader of Busy Company, a military unit consisting of Doc, Shiner, and Mac. They belong to a race of anthropomorphic beavers who have "mastered the sciences." Their enemies are the Radere Sappers, rodents who "developed along a more *arcane* course—worshippers of chaos." Busy Company, a k a the Timeguard, is responsible for protecting the Great Dam of Time, the function of which is to regulate "dimensional time streams and keep the universal crosscurrents in check." Of course, the rats want to destroy the dam so their "prionic magics can feed and flourish in the planes beyond this place." Learning that the rats have gone to different periods in the history of the planet Earth, Busy Company boards a Time Scout, a vehicle capable of making "timejumps" in order to stop them, lest they "change earth's history." The beavers go first to the era of Cardinal Richelieu and prevent the death of a young soldier named D'Artagnan—thus inspiring the tale of the Three Musketeers. Heading to 1863, they prevent the rats from killing Abraham Lincoln at Gettysburg. Jumping to 1945, they prevent the rats from delivering an atomic bomb to Hitler. However, there, the rats abduct Shiner and make off with him. Hypnotizing the beaver, the rats use him to lead their ships "through the outer defense system which encircles the accursed time dam." Approaching the dam, they draw a bead with their all-powerful Great Gun. But the self-sacrificing beaver lights a red flare at the heart of the gun's power source, and the beaver defenses blast it, destroying the enemy and Shiner, but saving the dam. He is replaced in Busy Company by Fifi, daughter of the beaver ruler, the Great Walter XIII.

Comment. The characters have appeared just once, in the *Time Beavers* graphic novel published in 1985 by First Comics. They were created by writer/artist Timothy Truman and cowriter Mark Acres. Apart from the clever use of the beaver-dam theme, there's nothing terribly original here, although the art is quite good.

TIPPIE
Pedigree. Pet dog owned by young Cap Stubbs.
Biography. Tippie is hybrid, a little sheepdog with a terrier's head. The fun-loving, affectionate dog is never entirely at rest (even when it's sitting, an ear is usually cocked), and forms part of an endearing triangle with the Tom Sawyerish Cap and his stern but loving Gran'ma Bailey. The amusing slice-of-life stories are usually built around a domestic theme—for example, Tippie insisting on kissing or jumping on Gran'ma while she's trying to rest. The dog is portrayed realistically, with no anthropomorphic traits.

Comment. "Cap Stubbs and Tippie" was created by Edwina Dumm in 1921. One of her early works (1917) was a strip titled "The Meanderings of Minnie" for the *Columbus Daily Monitor,* which chronicled the adventures of a young girl and her dog (years before the coming of *Little Orphan Annie* [see **Sandy**]). The strip was noticed by a syndicate executive, who liked the dog and the art but no Minnie; Edwina left Ohio for New York to come up with something new. The result was the Tippie strip.

Edwina did a weekly, Tippie-esque strip for *Life* magazine about the dog Sinbad, and also created the newspaper feature "Alec the Great," which consisted of a dog drawing with a short poem. In 1967, at the age of seventy-four, Edwina retired from comic strips to paint . . . dogs. The canine also starred in two issues of his own comic books, *Tippie and Cap Stubs,* published by Dell in 1949.

TIPPY-TOES
Pedigree. Horse of TV cartoon star Lariat Sam.
Biography. Fond of reading poetry, the horse and his cowboy master partake in adventures on and off the plains (such as at the circus, in Toyland, and so on).

Comment. There was little violence in these stories aimed at very young children. *The Adventures of Lariat Sam* was a five-minute-long cartoon segment of *The Captain Kangaroo Show* (CBS); Terrytoons produced thirteen episodes, which aired in 1961 to 1962. Dayton Allen provided the voice for both characters.

TITANO THE SUPER-APE
Pedigree. Towering gorilla foe of Superman.
Biography. When he was three years old, Titano was Toto, a performing monkey. As a publicity stunt, his manager arranged with the U.S. government to have Toto fly into space on a week-long mission. Once he was aloft, uranium and kryptonite collided near his capsule: The resultant rays bathed Toto. Reporter Lois Lane is onhand when Toto's round capsule parachutes safely back to earth. Upon emerging, Toto begins to grow and, nearly fifty feet tall, he scoops the journalist in his hand. "I . . . I'll re-name him *Titano!*" she utters, as though there were no more pressing concern on earth, adding, "These may be the last words I ever speak . . . *gulp* . . . unless Superman comes to save me." Sure enough, Superman arrives—but Titano blasts him with green rays from his eyes: "Kryptonite vision," which debilitates the Man of Steel. But canny Lois gets the ape to mimic her: She puts on glasses, and Titano dons glasses lined with lead. Thus protected, Superman grabs the giant and flings him back through the time barrier, into prehistoric times, commenting, "Titano is now among giant creatures his own size." However, the ape doesn't stay put. Inadvertently returned to Metropolis by an alien time machine, he is far more feral than before. "Mightier than a thousand gorillas," he doesn't just grab Lois but also destroys buildings and cars. This time, two prehistoric coco

nuts obtained by Superman prove the monkey's undoing. While Titano drinks them, Superman knocks him out and returns him to the past. After additional battles with Superman, Titano is transported to a world of giants in the Ashtar system; there, he's eventually found by the evil Atomic Skull, who subjugates Titano by implanting a mind-controlling device in his brain. Sent to destroy Superman, Titano is left docile when the Man of Steel renders the Atomic Skull unconscious. The ape is returned to his new world. In one of the most offbeat Titano stories, **Krypto** becomes furious when, on a rampage, Titano destroys one of his bones; flying into the past, the superdog plays various tricks on the hirsute horror, ultimately deeming Titano to be "stupid—but lovable!".

Comment. Created by editor Mort Weisinger and writer Otto Binder, Titano first appeared in DC Comics's *Superman* no. 127 in 1959. In a revisionist story published in *Superman Annual* no. 1 in 1987, the ape becomes a giant due to "super-science" energy experiments. Before Superman can capture the beast, the scientists shoot and kill him with a fission ray gun. Another giant ape from the Superman chronicles is King Krypton. A scientist on Superman's native world, he becomes an ape when his "evolution accelerator" accidentally shifts into a deceleration mode. The researcher has an assistant send him into space, hoping that cosmic rays will return him to normal. Instead, he ends up on earth where he terrorizes Africa and battles Superman until exposed to the rays of kryptonite, which return him to human form . . . and kill him. King Krypton appeared in *Action Comics* no. 238. Equally dangerous was Superboy's foe Chandu the giant gorilla, who was captured in Africa and brought to Smallville, USA in *Adventure Comics* no. 219. Because he drank from a kryptonite-poisoned lake in Africa, the gorilla has X-ray and heat-ray vision, which are triggered by lightning. Breaking from his cage, Chandu goes on a rampage; because of the ambient kryptonite in his rays, Superboy can't get near him. The superhero's finally able to stop him by building a giant battery to sap the clouds of lightning, then using jiu-jitsu to pin and cage the ape. Away from the lake, the ape's supervision fades.

TOAD
Pedigree. Underground comic strip frog.
Biography. Human except for his toad's head, Toad (a k a the Toad and Mr. Toad) is "quick to anger,"

"beyond obnoxious," and unable to make friends—not exactly mutually exclusive problems. (After a young man has lectured him about hostility, Toad remarks, "Pal, I hope you like *Spam,* 'cause I'm pressing a slice into your right shoulder.") A former law officer, Toad has since tried his hand at a number of ventures, few of them legitimate. ("I've already taken out *ads* for that phony *tour package.* We aim it at gullible types, then we leave 'em high 'n dry in Cleveland.") Toad's one friend is the clownlike simpleton, Zippy the Pinhead. Whenever he's had his fill of society, Toad visits the sequestered Toadette Pond, where he chats with his all-frog "support system," Todd, Tad, Ted, Nanette, Nonette, and Nurnette. Toad tends to be a natty dresser, as befits his egomania.

Comment. There were three issues of *Tales of Toad* (1970 to 1973). Bill Griffith's Toad, Zippy, and company are best known for their long-running King Features cartoon strip. They have also appeared in various underground comics, including *Arcade* (1975), *Yow* (1978), *Zippy* (1980), and others. In 1988, Zippy was briefly transformed into a parakeet nicknamed Puffy.

TOBY THE BADGER
Pedigree. Star of the British comic strip "The Hayseeds."
Biography. Toby and his talking, mostly bipedal, naked friends live in a rural area and get into a variety of situations involving social mores—in other words, behaving more like people than like animals. Among the other characters are Lizzy Lizard, Ern the Owl, Homer the Snail, and Braithwaite the Bird.

Comment. Inspired by **Pogo Possum,** although much less political, the strip was created by Harry Hargreaves, and began appearing in *The Evening News* on July 1, 1968. Hargreaves created a number of successful animal strips, including *Comet,* which features the dog Scamp (1958); *Harold Hare* (1950); *Ollie the Merry Mouser,* a cat who enjoys catching mice (1951); and *Sammy Squirrel* (1968).

TOD AND COPPER
Pedigree. The titular stars of a novel and of Disney's film *The Fox and the Hound.*
Biography. When a vixen is shot by a hunter, Big Mama—an owl—goes over and has a look at something the fox hastily left in the tall grasses. It's a cub, and, aided by the sparrow Dinky and the woodpecker Boomer, she brings the cub to the home of the

gentle Widow Tweed. The woman adopts the "tod-dler" and names him Tod. In a nearby house, the nasty hunter Amos Slade lives with his equally crabby dog Chief and a new puppy, Copper. One day, Copper heads into the woods and meets Tod. The two play, and vow to "be friends, forever." Alas, Slade isn't happy that his dog went off, and lashes him to a barrel. When Tod comes to see why his friend didn't show up, he wakes Chief, who gives chase. Tod bounds into the chicken coop, which causes a ruckus and brings Slade running, shotgun in hand; luckily, Widow Tweed is passing by, and Tod is able to leap into her truck. Slade threatens to blast the fox if he ever sees him again, and unhappily, Widow Tweed is forced to keep Tod inside. Come winter, Slade and his dogs set out on a season-long hunting trip, and Tod is allowed to roam once more. When Slade returns, the grownup Tod and Copper meet once again. Copper says they can't be friends any longer, because he's "a huntin' dog," but lets

Tod go this once, and leads the nearby Chief and Slade in another direction. However, Chief picks up Tod's trail and tracks him to a railroad trestle. A train comes roaring at them, and although the fox is able to duck beneath it, Chief is struck and knocked from the bridge. Racing to his wounded friend, Copper vows to pay Tod back for what he's done. When a furious Slade comes to see Widow Tweed, she refuses to let him in . . . but also realizes that it's no longer safe for Tod to live with her. Tearfully, she brings the fox to a game preserve. Big Mama literally takes him under her wing, and the dejected Tod's spirits perk when he meets the girl-fox Vixey. However, Slade knows where Tod is, and, undeterred by the No Hunting signs, enters the preserve with Copper. He sets out traps for the fox, and starts a fire outside Tod's and Vixey's den. However, instead of smoking out the animals, he attracts a towering and meanspirited grizzly bear. The monster swats away Slade's gun, and when Copper tries to protect his

Tod and Copper *in their innocent youth.* © 1981

master, he, too, is brushed away. The wounded Copper howls, and Tod hears his cries. Hurrying over, he lures the bear away, onto a tree growing over a deep valley. The weight of the bear dislodges the tree, dropping him and Tod into the raging river below. Tod manages to crawl ashore . . . only to find Slade standing there with his shotgun, still bent on slaying the fox. However, Copper stumbles between the two and refuses to move; the selflessness of both the fox and the hound causes Slade to realize that he's been a bloodythirsty fool, and he lowers his gun. Not only do Copper and Tod become friends again (along with the mending Chief), but the "born again" Slade and Widow Tweed form a lasting friendship.

Comment. Mickey Rooney was the voice of Tod (Keith Mitchell spoke for him as a child), Kurt Russell was Copper (Corey Feldman was little Copper), Pearl Bailey played Big Mama, Sandy Duncan was Vixey, Pat Buttram played Chief, Dick Bakalyan was Dinky, and the ever-splendid Paul Winchell was Boomer. Jeanette Nolan was Widow Tweed, and Jack Albertson was perfect as Slade. The well-plotted if visually unarresting film (save for the vivid bear-fight) was based on the 1967 novel of the same name by Daniel P. Mannix. One of the funniest characters in the film is the unheralded Squeeks, a caterpillar, whom the inept Dinky and Boomer are constantly trying to eat. The insect is finally able to escape them for good by becoming a butterfly. As for the bested birds, they throw up their wings and head south. The characters starred in a Whitman comic book adaptation of the film, and in a lengthy version which appeared in the Sunday comic strip "Walt Disney's Treasury of Classic Tales."

TOM AND JERRY

Pedigree. Cat and mouse adversaries of theatrical and TV cartoons and comic books.

Biography. In early cartoons, Tom is quite sinister looking: Light gray with a round face, he's bearded, has tiny, pointed ears and four sharp fangs; his tail operates as a tentacle, able to hold his prey or probe mouseholes. Jerry is little and brown, looking much like he does today. In their first adventure, the 1940 charmer *Puss Gets the Boot* Tom (here called Jasper) has obviously been tormenting the mouse (who has no name in the cartoon). When Jasper's owner Mammy (a k a Mammy Two Shoes) goes out, the cat is warned not to break anything in the house or he'll get the boot. The mouse sees this as a chance to make the cat suffer and runs amok, threatening to break

things unless Jasper stays out of his fur. Jasper gets in his licks, but it's the mouse who finally gets the last laugh: Cornered, he writes out a will and leaves the cat his sole worldly possession, a custard pie. As soon as Tom finishes reading the document (aloud, in an Arnold Stang-type voice) he gets it . . . right in the kisser. The cartoon was intended to be a one shot, but when it proved an audience pleaser and earned an Oscar nomination, a series was born, and the characters' names were changed to Tom and Jerry. The theme was the same from cartoon to cartoon: Tom chasing Jerry, Jerry defending himself (closing Tom's tail in a waffle-iron, for example), with a constant seesawing of who has the upperhand. One of their landmark appearances is the 1947 Oscar winner *The Cat Concerto,* in which a tuxedoed pianist Tom (now the leaner, bat-eared, more contemporary cat) gives a recital of Liszt's *Hungarian Rhapsody* while Jerry romps across and under the keyboard. The highlight: Tom's slow burn culminates in him grabbing the mouse and shoving him inside the bench, which Jerry cranks up, forcing Tom to contort himself in order to reach the keys. Other classics include *Flirty Birdy* (1945), in which Tom matches wits with a hawk who wants to make a meal of Jerry; *Mouse Cleaning* (1948), a misnomer, as Jerry tries to mess up the newly cleaned house so Tom will get in trouble with Mammy; *Heavenly Puss* (1949), wherein Tom dreams he's died and gone to heaven, only to be told that he's going to hell (where a bulldog Satan awaits) unless he can get Jerry to sign a Certificate of Forgiveness for all the suffering Tom caused (the cartoon ends with Tom waking and kissing a befuddled Jerry); *Nit Witty Kitty* (1951), in which Tom suffers amnesia and thinks he's a mouse; and *Little Runaway* (1952), in which a baby seal makes life difficult for them both. Other characters who made regular appearances in the series were the little mouse Nibbles, the big bulldog Spike (who first appeared in the fifth cartoon, *Dog Trouble,* in 1942), and his son, the little bulldog Tyke. In addition to their cartoons, Jerry made cinema history by performing a wonderful dance with Gene Kelly in the feature film *Anchors Away* (1945), while, together, Tom and Jerry swam with Esther Williams in *Dangerous When Wet* (1953).

Comment. MGM's Tom and Jerry cartoons first brought together the team of producers Joe Hanna and William Barbera, who remained theatrical producers until 1957, when they went into television with **Ruff and Reddy.** The team made 113 theatrical

Tom and Jerry cartoons from 1940 to 1958, which won an unprecedented seven Oscars. There were 47 additional theatrical cartoons created by other producers from 1960 to 1967, but these are, in a word, uninspired. The characters' old cartoons were aired on TV's *The Tom and Jerry Show,* which was syndicated in 1965; 48 new and abyssmal cartoons were seen on *The New Tom and Jerry/Grape Ape Show,* which aired on ABC in 1975. The show metamorphosed to *The Tom and Jerry/Grape Ape/Mumbly Show* in 1976, *The Tom and Jerry/Mumbly Show* later that year, and became *The Tom and Jerry Comedy Show* when it moved to CBS in 1980. Because of the popularity of kid versions of popular characters such as the Muppets/Muppet Babies, the fall of 1990 saw the advent of *The Tom and Jerry Kids* on TV. (What were they before? Grown-ups?) In addition to Tom, Jerry, Spike, and Tyke, the show introduced the cat Kyle to bedevil them. In comic books, the duo made their debut in Dell's *Our Gang Comics* no. 1 in 1942; the subtitle *With Tom and Jerry* was added with no. 39, and the magazine became *Tom and Jerry Comics* with no. 60 in 1949. Gold Key took over publication with no. 213, and the comic lasted until 1982 and no. 344. Tuffy Mouse costarred in many of the duo's stories (see **The Two Mousketeers**). **Barney Bear** and **Droopy** were featured in the comic, along with other costars: Wuff the Prairie Dog, who got into desert adventures with his pals prairie dog Sammy, Archie Armadillo, and their carnivorous foe Charlie Coyote; Flip 'n' Dip, a pair of young monkeys who live on a houseboat with Ma and Pa Simian and become embroiled in playful adventures with other animals in the African jungle; Benny Burro, who lives with Barney Bear in his comic stories, in which they're usually trying to keep the conniving Mooseface from stealing their food; and the cute, blue Bertie Bird, who hunted for worms or helped birds in need in text and cartoon stories. "Big" Spike and "Little" Tyke appeared in stories as well, and went on to star in twenty-five issues of their own *MGM's Spike and Tyke* comic book, which lasted from 1953 to 1962. They live in a doghouse (the outside reads "Pop 'n' Pup") and their stories either starred animals only (Tyke lost in the woods, a criminal bulldog who looks like Spike), or adventures with their unnamed "Mistress" and her baby boy, tales of the "I'm-going-shopping-and-I-want-you-two-to-watch-the-house" or "Careful-because-baby's-in-the-bath" variety. Also seen in the bulldog strip were the bloodhound Schnoz who

lived next door ("the best private nose in the business") and the little white kitty Snowball. Tangentially, Hanna-Barbera also animated the animals in the Sinbad segment of the 1957 film *Invitation to the Dance,* in which Gene Kelly performed a surreal dance with a huge serpent. An historical note: In 1981, plans to star Tom and Jerry in a feature-length documentary about MGM special-effects films were mercifully canned. The scenario called for the two to chase each other through famous special effects sequences: in chariots for *Ben-Hur,* in spaceships for *2001: A Space Odyssey,* and so on.

TOMMY TURTLE

Pedigree. Comic book terrapin.

Biography. Tommy is a tiny, bespectacled turtle who enjoys sitting at his suburban home, doing domestic chores or reading. However, he invariably gets pulled into local adventures, either treasure hunting or looking into reports of ghosts. When he does, his inherent wariness serves him in good stead: As he himself has said, "I'd like to find that treasure . . . but I'd also like to live to enjoy it!" Tommy has a large shell, flared at the top, and wears a red vest beneath it as well as a small, red cap.

Comment. The character appeared irregularly as a back-up feature in **Supermouse**.

TONY THE TIGER

Pedigree. Advertising mascot for Frosted Flakes cereal.

Biography. Originally, the orange, black-striped, blue-nosed Tony would step off a cereal box and, standing just six or seven inches tall, would make his pitch. As the years passed, Tony grew to his current height of six and one half feet. He is famous for his shouted assessment of the merits of Frosted Flakes: "They're grrreat!" The only clothing Tony wears is a red neckerchief with his name on the bottom. A young tiger character, known only as "boy" and then as "son," was also introduced in the early commercials. He was later referred to as Tony, Jr., and became the mascot of Frosted Rice cereal. During the 1960s, Tony was involved in wild, slapstick commercials in which he'd fall into a Marineland tank and get tossed around by a dolphin, or go skydiving and bounce off the tops of the parachutes of fellow jumpers. In the 1970s, he became more sedate and conservative, a husband and father to both Tony, Jr., and an infant daughter.

Comment. The Kellogg's tiger made his debut in

1955. He was designed by children's book illustrator Martin Provensen, and remains the cereal's symbol to this day. The tiger's distinctive voice was provided by Thurel Ravenscroft.

TOOTER TURTLE

Pedigree. Physically and intellectually slow TV turtle.

Biography. Dressed in a straw hat, collar, and necktie, Tooter is a naive, bipedal turtle who is full of "what ifs": What if he went to work in a certain occupation, what if he lived in a different era, and so forth. To satisfy his curiosity, he goes to visit Mr. Wizard, who lives in a box at the base of a tree in the woods. The lizard always gives a few words of advice (when Tooter wants to try his hand at duck hunting, the wizard says, "The first thing a duck hunter needs . . . is his head examined"), then uses magic to let Tooter experience firsthand the era or occupation of his choice. Over time, Tooter has been a gunfighter, highway patrol officer, knight, quarterback, skydiver, reporter, foreign legionnaire, sailor, and others. Invariably, Tooter learns that he's better off just being an unassuming turtle. The lizard is a diminutive fellow who speaks with a German accent and is decked out in a sorcerer's hat and robes. In order for Tooter to have an audience with him, the wizard shrinks the turtle to his own size. (How the turtle got to be the size of a human being in the first place is never explained. His name is also a mystery, because he doesn't toot.)

Comment. The characters first appeared on Leonardo Productions's *King Leonardo and His Short Subjects,* which aired on ABC from 1960 to 1963. After that, they became part of **Tennessee Tuxedo**'s show. There were thirty-nine episodes in all. Allan Swift was the voice of Tooter; Frank Milano was the Wizard.

TOP CAT

Pedigree. Popular TV cat.

Biography. Top Cat is a good-natured con artist, the kind of cat who attaches a thread to a coin before tipping someone, so he can yank the money back. The feline and his gang live off Mad Avenue in the 13th Precinct, making their homes in trash cans in one of the 500 alleys in New York. There—using a police call box to make their calls—they constantly plot to improve their standard of living through various scams (impersonating a visiting maharajah, gambling, and so forth) or legitimate fund-raisers

(holding a circus in their alley . . . although Top Cat neglects to tell his helpers they'll be flying high above the air on a trapeze, with no net). Top Cat regularly delegates authority, although when his fellow cats fail him, he will mutter something like, "What am I doing sending children out to do a man's job?" and go forth to blow things himself. Invariably, the cats always end up back in their alley, no better or worse for their efforts. The unflappable Top Cat is prone to verbal overkill, to wit: "Go like the wind boy, go, go, go, Mercury—fly, fly!" The group's activities are closely monitored by the beleaguered Officer Dibble. The first five members of Top Cat's gang were Choo Choo, Spook, the Brain, Fancy Fancy, and Top Cat's chief aide, the rolly polly Benny the Ball. Later additions were Goldie and Pierre. Called "T.C." by his friends, Top Cat wears a vest and a flat-topped hat with holes in the brim for his ears, and often carries a cane. The tan cat walks on his hind legs, stands approximately three feet tall, can't swim, and sleeps with a mask on his eyes. Underhanded as he is, it's impossible to dislike the guy.

Comment. Inspired by Phil Silvers and his Sergeant Bilko characterization (with a dash of *West Side Story),* Top Cat was produced by Hanna-Barbera and aired on ABC from 1961 to 1962. There were twenty-eight half-hour episodes in all. Arnold Stang provided the voice for T.C. A *Top Cat* comic book lasted thirty-one issues from Dell (through no. 3) and Gold Key (1962 to 1970), then twenty issues from Charlton Comics (1970 to 1973).

TOP DOG

Pedigree. Marvel Comics dog star.

Biography. The little brown dog (apparently a cocker spaniel) is owned by young Joey Jordan, the only one who knows that the dog can speak. His sister is constantly trying to catch them conversing . . . but the dog is always able to cover (when she hears him finish a sentence with ". . . at you" and accuses him of talking, he simply pretends to have been sneezing). Likewise, nasty Mervin Megabucks is also keen to prove that the dog talks, and regularly spies on Joey (on one occasion, Top Dog is able to turn "take a bow" into "a bow! Bow wow!"). In addition to facing such foes as Mervin, teaming with the superhero Spider-Man (no. 10), battling the mad scientists Frank 'n' Stein, and fighting his own evil twin, Dirty Dog, Top Dog has dealt with mundane problems such as helping Joey impress a girl by in troducing her to a rock star and trying to keep his doghouse clean. In addition to his sharp mind (and sharp tongue), Top Dog can impersonate voices, play the guitar, and walk bipedally (although he does so only when no one else is around).

Comment. *Top Dog* starred in fourteen issues of his own magazine (under the Star imprint) from 1985 to 1987, after which he became a back-up feature in Marvel's *Heathcliff* comic book, beginning with no. 23 (see **Heathcliff**).

TORNADO

Pedigree. Comic strip dog owned by Brenda Starr.
Biography. Brenda Starr is a gutsy, globe-trotting reporter who works for the newspaper *The Flash*. Often her brave little dog accompanies her—his thoughts revealed to the reader. For relaxation, Tornado loves making a mess of clothing ("I wasn't named Tornado for nothing!") and, as the animal itself admits, there's "nothing I like better than opening packages." The dog was most active in *The Mystery of the Black Orchid* (1945), helping to find the missing Brenda . . . and earning the admiration of the Afghan, Gharboo. Tornado is white with black on the tip of its ears and tail.

Comment. Dalia "Dale" Messick's *Brenda Starr Reporter* made its debut on June 30, 1940.

TOUCAN SAM

Pedigree. Advertising mascot for Froot Loops cereal.
Biography. With a voice like Ronald Colman, the big-beaked bird extolled the delights of the cereal in TV ads, referring to the brand, in pig latin, as "Ootfray Oops-lay."
Comment. The bird first appeared in the early 1960s, created for Kellogg's by the Leo Burnett agency. Other cereal characters the Burnett team came up with for Kellogg's were Sugar Pops Pete, a gun-toting prairie dog who promoted Sugar Corn Pops in the late 1950s; Coco the monkey, who wore a panama hat and said of Cocoa Krispies (in the middle 1950s), "It tastes like a chocolate milkshake, only crunchy"; Dig 'Em the frog, who hopped around the breakfast table on behalf of Honey Smacks; Smaxie the seal, decked out in a sailor suit for Sugar Smacks; and Cornelius the rooster, crowing the praises of Corn Flakes. Another advertising bird is the yellow-feathered Early Bird, which is featured in TV ads (an actor in a costume) for McDon

ald's, and in the giveaway activity magazine *McDonaldland Fun Times*.

TOUCHÉ TURTLE

Pedigree. Swashbuckling TV tortoise.
Biography. Naked, save for his (bent) rapier and white Musketeer hat with a big red feather, Touché and his big, similarly attired, sheepdog assistant Dum Dum lend their heroic "skills" to those in need. With a cry of "Touché and away!", the turtle charges or swings on a rope or vine, followed by the blindly loyal dog—who, blind in other ways as well, invariably runs into a tree or other obstacle. The daring duo tend to pop up in any era that suits the writers. Thus their stories have revolved around the likes of Napoleon, Custer, Robin Hoodlum, Billy the Cad, Aladdin, ghosts, and a superfast hare titled Rapid Rabbit (quite similar to the studio's later **Ricochet Rabbit**). Touché's slogan is, "Hero work done cheap, all credit cards accepted."

Comment. Hanna-Barbera made fifty-two cartoons, which began airing in syndication in 1962. Bill Thompson provided the voice for Touché, which was inspired by the timid character Wallace Wimple on the radio series *Fibber McGee and Molly*. Alan Reed was Dum Dum. The turtle appeared in Gold Key's *Hanna-Barbera Bandwagon* nos. 1 to 3 in 1962 and 1963.

TRIX RABBIT

Pedigree. Advertising mascot for Trix cereal.
Biography. In his first commercial, the rabbit explained, "I'm a rabbit, and rabbits are supposed to like carrots. But I hate carrots. I like Trix!" From that point forward, he tried every trick and disguise imaginable to try and obtain a bowl of cereal. He always came close: Whether disguised as a magician, a cowboy, or a coal miner, he always got his hands on a bowlful, and was able to savor the nearness of the "raspberry red, lemon yellow, and orange orange." Unfortunately, kids in the cartoon would always discover that he was a rabbit (his ears would usually fall out of whatever hat he was wearing), and they'd take back the bowl with the admonition, "Silly rabbit! Trix are for kids." In 1976, to coincide with the presidential election, a boxtop ballot election was held to decide whether or not the rabbit would finally get to eat the cereal. More than 99 percent of the votes were pro-rabbit, and he got to dig in. Then, holding out his empty bowl, he was told to wait until

*The **Trix Rabbit** in a typical print advertisement from 1964. TM and © GENERAL MILLS.*

the next election. Since then, the rabbit has been back to his losing ways. The floppy-eared, four-foot-tall white Trixophile is also pictured on the cereal box.

Comment. The rabbit debuted in 1961, and remains the cereal mascot to this day. He is also seen (wearing a scarf and earmuffs) on a line of Trix ice pops. The character and ads were cocreated by General Mills and by the Dancer, Fitzgerald & Sample advertising agency. Another well-known advertising rabbit is the Quik Bunny. The pink-furred mascot of Nestlé's Strawberry Quik powdered milk mix was introduced in the mid-1960s. He later shifted, in a brown-furred version, to Chocolate Quik (the Strawberry rabbit was given a strawberry to wear on his head, presumably as an aid to the color blind). Predictably, the rabbit goes into fits of ecstasy when drinking flavored milk in TV ads ("You can't drink it slow—'cause it's Quik!"). However, the rabbit played a more interesting role as a comic book hero, starring in the one-shot comic book *Superman Meets the Quik Bunny,* which was published by DC in 1987. In it, the rabbit (chocolate version) raids the Quik Qlubhouse Qitchen for Quik, and gets caught up in a battle between Superman and the evil Weather Wizard.

TRYPTO THE ACID DOG
Pedigree. Vengeful comic book superpup.
Biography. Dr. Benjamin Martin and his wife, Alison, are environmentalists who, after gathering in

formation against the Toxicem corporation of rural Kirby, Indiana, are murdered one night by Gino Catelli, a hitman. Then, as the family dog Trypto watches, horrified, their young son, Dewey, comes downstairs to investigate and is also shot dead. Enraged, the little bull terrier leaps from hiding, attacks the man, and is also shot. Stumbling from the house before Gino blows it up, the dog falls into the polluted Kentston river . . . just as Toxicem makes "another illegal nocturnal emission." As the dog sinks in the poison, a bolt of lightning happens to strike the waters; the combination transforms Trypto into a superdog, "fueled with a hunger for revenge" and adorned with a cape (actually, a Toxicem bag that had been floating in the water). Picking up the killer's scent, he follows it to Toxicem where he finds Gino with the company's boss, Sherman Bursky ("First a kid, then a dog," the murderer complains. "I was waitin' for Mother Theresa to show up!"). Trypto crashes through a window, and Gino's bullets bounce from his body. The dog kills the murderer, then turns on Bursky . . . suddenly transforming himself into a giant dog. As the canine glowers at the fiend, other Toxicem victims rise from the water (a police officer among them), and toss him into a vat of his own poison. Trypto shrinks to normal size and returns to the burned-out shell of his home, where he's found by Dewey's friend Robbie, and given a new home.

Comment. There was just one issue of this extremely well written Renegade Press comic book

(1988). The character was created by writers Bill Mumy (former star of the *Lost in Space* TV series) and Miguel Ferrer, and drawn by Steve Leialoha.

TWEETY BIRD

Pedigree. Warner Brothers's star canary.

Biography. When we first meet the docile bird in *A Tale of Two Kitties* (1942), he is pinkish rather than yellow, has no name (though he was dubbed "Orson" by the production staff), and is jowly rather than simply pudgy-cheeked like the later canary. Otherwise, he's the same little bird as the present-day Tweety, with three hairs on his head, oversize feet, huge and innocent eyes topped by long lashes, and a little baby voice. Living in a nest atop a tree beside a barn, he's awakened when the cats **Babbit and Catstello** try to get him. Uttering his immortal, "I tawt I taw a putty tat," he's not only unflappable as the cats try every way they can think of to get at him, he demonstrates quite a cruel streak—for example, as Catstello hangs from a clothesline by his toes, the bird plays "This Little Piggy" (technically, "Dis Widdy Piddy") and lets him fall, then generously throws him a rope—with anvil attached. Another time, when Catstello ascends on a pair of springs, Tweety hits him with a handy club on his first bounce, bashes him with other objects on subsequent bounces, and finally gives him a lighted stick of dynamite to take down with him. In his second cartoon, *Birdy and the Beast* (1944), Tweety is in a new nest and being stalked by a cat. However, he's lost none of his flair for causing suffering: At one point, he enters the cat's mouth, strikes a match, and sets it aflame. The thoughtful bird runs and gets a hose . . . and pumps gasoline into the animal's fiery maw. The cat blows up—then blows up again when he reaches into Tweety's nest for the bird and finds himself holding a hand grenade. As the cartoon fades out, Tweety remarks, "I lose more putty tats dat way." After matching wits with a pair of cats in the 1945 cartoon *A Gruesome Twosome* (it's no contest, really), Tweety was first teamed with his perennial foe **Sylvester the Cat** in the 1947 short *Tweetie Pie* [sic], which won an Oscar. It's winter, and the homeless bird is attacked by the cat—whose master comes to investigate, finds Tweety, and takes him in. Sylvester tries various means to reach the birdcage, but Tweety (with a seemingly bottomless bag of tricks) uses everything from a pin to a shovel to a blowtorch to keep him at bay. When Tweety tweets and the master comes to

investigate, the cat gets thrown out; he reenters via the fireplace, in which (surprise!) Tweety has lit a blaze. The two meet again in *I Taw a Putty Tat* (1948), the weapons being a hammer, dynamite, and a "putty dog," which Tweety hits with a hammer (making it look like Sylvester did it) then locks in the birdcage with the cat. By their next row, in *Bad Ol' Putty Tat* (1949), the bird is living in a birdhouse surrounded by barbed wire. Sylvester uses a girdle to bounce up, Tweety attacking him each time (repeating the Catstello gags verbatim), after which there's an innovative double cross: Tweety leaves his house by scooting down a clothesline, which happens to be fastened to a tooth in Sylvester's gaping mouth. But the cat doesn't get to eat the bird: Tweety's fastened the other end of the line to a rocket, which takes off . . . with Sylvester's teeth in tow. Several additional encounters end with Tweety riding Sylvester like a train and driving him into a brick wall. Although his arsenal (which is always pulled from "thin air" off-screen) has a lot to do with his survival, and Tweety often has a dog nearby to protect him (or an entire dog pound's worth in *Dog Pounded*, 1954), the bird is the definition of cool under pressure—even more so than his wily Warner's mate **Bugs Bunny**.

Comment. There have been forty-seven Tweety cartoons in all. Mel Blanc provided the bird's voice. The name Tweety was inspired by the birds Twick 'n' Tweet, once drawn by animator Bob Clampett. The look of the bird was inspired by a nude baby picture of Clampett. Interestingly, the first Sylvester/Tweety film had been designed to star the cat and a woodpecker from the 1945 cartoon *Peck Up Your Troubles,* but the substitution was made because Tweety was a better known and more interesting character. In 1986, *The Bugs Bunny and Tweety Show* debuted on ABC and proved to be a surprise powerhouse. It has remained on the top of the Saturday morning ratings. Dell published 37 issues of a *Tweety and Sylvester* comic book from 1952 to 1962, while Gold Key/Whitman published 119 issues from 1963 to 1984. By the way, the spelling *Tweetie* is correctly applied to the genus of the bird, while *Tweety* is the character's name.

THE TWO MOUSEKETEERS (A K A THE MOUSE MOUSEKETEERS)

Pedigree. Swashbuckling alteregos of Jerry (from Tom and Jerry) and his young friend Tuffy.

Biography. Sporting Musketeer garb—Tuffy talking with a French accent—the mice live in seventeeth-century France, in the "little kingdom" of Charmant, whose oppressed peoples they try to liberate (they help humans, not mice). Without fail, they are confronted by the king's guard, Poosycat (Tom), who's dressed in a red tunic and black hat (based on the dress of Cardinal Richelieu's elite guards). Although Poosycat is constantly threatened with a trip to the guillotine for failing to capture the mice, he's never beheaded. By the end of their careers, the mice and cat degenerated into typical Tom and Jerry antics, with the trio working as servants for the king, the mice trying to avoid hard labor or attempting to steal cheese from the larder. When the mice were fighting injustice, their slogan was "I'm for you and you're for me."

Comment. The characters first appeared in MGM's 1952 cartoon *The Two Mouseketeers*. They went on to star in twelve issues of Dell's *4-Color* comic from 1953 to 1962. The last nine issues were titled *The Mouse Mouseketeers,* reportedly under pressure from the copyright holders of **The Three Mouseketeers**. Costarring in their comic book were the Three Little Kittens, the further adventures of the Mother Goose cats, and Nibbles the Mouse, a tough little country mouse who doesn't get along with the other farm animals.

TYG

Pedigree. Leader of a group of heroic little TV animals.

Biography. "Who do you call when you're caught in a jam?" asks the theme song. The answer is these six little animals. Rick the raccoon, Pammy the panda, Tyg the tiger, Digger the mole, Kip the kangaroo (who has the ability to balance on the tip of her tail), and Bogey the orangutan (who talks like Humphrey Bogart) stand approximately two feet tall, wear skimpy T-shirts, and live with Mr. Dinkle, a guide at the Oak Tree Park in the center of a city. When Tyg raises his hand and declares, "It's Shirt Tale Time!", the group is bathed in light, their wits and strength increase and their magical shirts become larger and acquire the (dubious) ability to reveal exactly what's on the animals' minds, e.g., flashing "Yum, Yum!" when they eat something delicious or, "Let's Split!" when danger threatens. After surviving a particularly tough adventure, the animals line up and each one's shirt flashes one word: "That," "Was," "A," "Close," "One." More useful are their wrist communicators, which are miniature TV sets, and their jet car. Hidden in the base of a statue in the park, the car can be transformed from a land vehicle to a jet to a rocket, and has such useful gadgets as a laser lasso and extendable arms. The animals get into adventures all around the world, from rescuing Dinkle when he's trapped inside a runaway rocket, to fighting the evil Fire God while searching for treasure on the Island of Mora Mora.

Comment. The Hanna-Barbera production was inspired by characters from Hallmark Cards. It premiered on NBC on Saturday mornings in 1982. Steven Schatzberg was the voice of Tyg, Nancy Cartwright was Kip, Pat Parris was Pammy, Bob Ogle was Digger, and Fred Travalena was Bogey. Galoob produced an unsuccessful line of toys in 1983.

UNDERCOVER ELEPHANT

Pedigree. Pachyderm spy of TV cartoons.

Biography. An international secret agent who reports to the Chief, Undercover Elephant gets his orders from tape recorders that promptly explode (à la TV's *Mission: Impossible*). Ordinarily dressed in a fedora and ill-fitting trench coat, the big, ungainly elephant adopts various (amateurish) disguises . . . although, miraculously, his enemies are even dumber than he is and usually fail to recognize the elephant until his partner Loud Mouse inadvertently gives him away. His missions have inclined *The Moanin' Lisa, Dr. Doom's Gloom,* and *Perilous Pigskin.*

Comment. There were thirteen cases in all, and they aired on *C.B. Bears* (see **C.B. Bears**) in 1977. Daws Butler was the voice of Undercover Elephant, Bob Hastings was Loud Mouse, and Mike Bell played the Chief.

UNDERDOG

Pedigree. Heroic canine of TV and comics.

Biography. Whenever timid, eager-to-please Shoeshine Boy learns of a crime, he slips into a phone booth, dons a red suit and blue cape, gulps down energy pills stored in a ring, and emerges as the powerful Underdog, hound-hero of Washington, D.C. Speaking in rhyme, the amazing pooch has the ability to fly and possesses superstrength, X-ray vision, and superhearing. His oft-uttered phrase is, "Never fear! Underdog is here!" Underdog must frequently rescue his girlfriend, Sweet Polly Purebred, a (dog) reporter, who, when in danger, always chants, "Oh where, oh where, has my Underdog gone?" His chief nemesis is the bald human scientist Simon Bar Sinister, although the pirate Riff Raff, the giant ape Fearo, the vampire Batty Man, and the evil Captain Marblehead have also been pains in his tail. When Underdog needs to get away from it all, or conduct secret research, he heads to his Shack of Solitude (a parody of Superman's Fortress of Solitude). Also spoofing Superman is the show's opening, in which onlookers utter, "Look in the sky! There's a plane! It's a bird! It's a frog . . . a frog?" Swooping along, Underdog corrects them by saying (in couplet form, of course), "Not plane, not bird, or even frog . . . it's just li'l ole me, Underdog!"

Comment. The character's show was produced by Total Television Productions and Leonardo Productions, and premiered on NBC in 1964. It moved to CBS in 1966, then back to NBC in 1968, where it remained for five years. There were thirty-two adventures in all, most of them four-parters. Reruns of the series are presently in syndication. Wally Cox provided the voice for Underdog, while Norma MacMillan was Polly. In the comics, Underdog was featured in his own title for twenty-three issues, from Charlton (1970 to 1972) and then Gold Key (1975 to 1979). Spotlight Comics published three issues in 1987. The well-known Underdog balloon made its first appearance in the annual Macy's Thanksgiving Day Parade in 1965.

URBAN GORILLA

Pedigree. The comic book "primate protector of animal inhabitants of . . . Socal City."

Biography. Socal City is the home of the world's greatest zoo. There, "easy-going" Griswold Gorilla resides with "the libidinous Gorgonzelda and her son Skippy." But whenever he's needed outside the zoo, "the avenging anthropoid" dons a "wrinkleproof" business suit and fedora, leaves a dummy likeness of himself in his grotto, sneaks through a "secret exit," and either helps animals in distress (dogs locked in a hot car, ducks trying to cross a busy street, and so forth) or takes in an old Tarzan movie. Other talking animals in the strip are Tattler, the "paranoid stool-pigeon pigeon," Bruno the police dog, and Naif the Waif, a cat version of Oliver Twist.

Comment. The only appearance of Scott Shaw's go-get-'em character was in the one issue *Amusing Stories,* published by Renegade Press in 1986. A companion strip, "Moby Drip," was announced but never appeared.

Following page: *The resourceful **Urban Gorilla**.* © SCOTT SHAW.

VIDEO VICTOR

Pedigree. Comic strip superhero bee.

Biography. Victor Bumble is a bee who, as fate would have it, is allergic to pollen. Although he possesses an IQ of 200, he says he'd "rather be a *busy* bee than a *spelling* bee." Unfortunately, only the clean, sterile air of shopping malls gives him relief. Visiting a Noah's Arcade in a nearby shopping center, he notices a loose wire in a *Strong Samuel* videogame a kid named Goodrich is playing. Victor uses his stinger to complete the circuit so the kid won't lose his score. Result: He's zapped by electricity and becomes a living "bee-cell battery." Superpowered to the max, he can fly at incredible speeds, has awesome strength, and is no longer allergic to pollen. Flying from the arcade, Victor vows to go out and thrash the bees who'd laughed at him for being so frail. Flying to the hive, he beats up bugs ("That's the first time I've ever *seen* bee-flat," comments one insect after a bee is trounced), and is about to trash more when, back at the arcade, Goodrich stops playing . . . and Victor reverts to his wimpy, old self. The bee realizes he's only superpowered as long as Goodrich is playing, and is unceremoniously thrown from the hive. Disconsolate, he goes searching for the vidkid. Aided by the mystic insect Bussam

("Ever since I was zapped by a radio while listening to Jack Armstung, All-American Bee, I've been battling the adversaries of technology"), Victor rescues Goodrich from antitechnology pickets at the arcade, and goes home with him. When "Goody's" mother berates him for "wasting money your poor father won at the track," the youth grabs a portable videogame (which also gives Victor superpowers) and leaves the house for good with Victor at his side. Among the foes they face are "the evil and malignant Yabba of the Dabba Wasps" and an army of flower children who hate technology. Victor's favorite expression is "Buzzooka!"

Comment. The character was created by artist Nona Bailey, and first appeared in Ion International's *Videogaming Illustrated* Magazine no. 4 in 1983. The full-page strip changed creative hands regularly, beginning with the second installment, as noted comic strip artist Gill Fox took over; famed science fiction writer Ron Goulart wrote the third adventure; artist John Costanza began drawing the strip with the fourth installment, and writer Bob Sodaro came aboard with the fifth episode. Pretty amazing for a strip that ran just nine issues (vanishing with the demise of the magazine).

THE WABBITS

Pedigree. Board game and comic book rabbits.

Biography. The Wabbits live in tunnels under a farmer's carrot field, and consist of Dirty, siblings Casey and Racey, Snowshoe, and their families. When the carrots are harvested prematurely, the Wabbits and their ally Barley Rat must make their way into the farm and steal enough to live, all the while surviving attacks from a bulldog, the farmer's hand, and the farmer himself, who's armed with a shotgun and a powerful tractor. Using everything at their disposal—a pitchfork, a scarecrow's belt transformed into a slingshot, a chainsaw—the Wabbits are able to achieve their goal, although Racey dies saving another Wabbit from the tractor. The Wabbits can walk upright and talk among themselves, although humans can't understand what they're saying.

Comment. These hard-edged characters were created by Steve Sullivan for Pacesetter Ltd.'s 1985 board game *Wabbit Wampage* and its sequel, *Wabbit's Wevenge.* They appeared in one issue of Amazing Comics's *Wabbit Wampage* in 1987.

The Wabbits make weady to ambush a foe. © STEPHEN SULLIVAN.

WACKY DUCK

Pedigree. A quick-tempered comic book duck.

Biography. With his oversize sweatshirt and hat with its upturned brim, the rough-edged Wacky could well pass for a duck version of one of the Bowery Boys. Although he's always ready to fight anyone who looks at him askance, Wacky does have one soft spot: He's infatuated with the delightful duck Florence. Only three things prevent him from winning her hand: his rival, the cultured, portly duck Reginald; Florence's kid brother, who's constantly bugging them in order to force Wacky to bribe him to stay away; and his own proclivity to fly into rages, as when a waiter has the audacity to suggest that the couple order food instead of just sitting in a restaurant, talking.

Comment. This Marvel Comics character was introduced in 1945. Known as Dopey Duck in the first two issues of his magazine (in which guise he wore either a propeller-beanie or porkpie hat), he became Wacky Duck for the next four issues, and remained Wacky Duck in three other brief incarnations of his magazine. See also **Wonder Duck**, which basically recycles the character. Other comic book ducks from this period, cut from the same cloth, were **Lucky Duck**; the big-eyed Dickie Duck, who wears a Little Lord Fauntleroy outfit and got into mischief in the occasional issue of *Funny Pages* (a Comics Magazine Company publication which ran from 1936 to 1940); Buck Duck, a cowboy duck who doesn't behave as though he's living in a modern, urban world, and appeared in eleven issues of Marvel's *It's a Duck's Life* (1950 to 1952) and his own four-issue title in 1953; Dizzy Duck, who wore a Jughead Jones-type cap (and had a Jughead Jones appetite), star of Nedor's *Barnyard Comics,* which began in 1944 and became *Dizzy Duck* with no. 32 (and died seven issues later); and one modern-day counterpart, the star of *Crazy Duck,* which was published by Canada's Lave Press in 1982, and lasted only one issue.

WACKY SQUIRREL

Pedigree. Minor comic book star.

Biography. The buck-toothed rodent resides in a dimension filled with anthropomorphic animals, and

Wacky Squirrel *uses his ever-present mallet to silence Keyhole, a UFO expert.* © DARK HORSE COMICS.

lives to find "some *dope* out there . . . that I can have some fun with." In Wacky's debut tale, Harold (a rabbit) spots the squirrel and pulls a series of pranks on himself (pushing a pie in his own face, setting his own foot on fire, and so on) thereby spoiling Wacky's fun. Frustrated, the squirrel enters a dimensional rift in a park and comes to the world of **Boris the Bear,** who's "always good for a laugh." Not this time. Boris is busy killing rival comic book characters and mounting their heads on a wall. Finding a plaque reserved for his own head, Wacky realizes he'd better take the offensive. He creates a costume based on the hero of the *Black Cross* comic book and ventures forth, mallet in hand, a bomb strapped to his hip, as the avenging *Black Wack.* After Wacky locates the bear, the two slug it out, the squirrel gets hold of his foe's submachine gun, and Boris is blown away. The mallet becomes a fixture of Wacky's, serving him especially well in issue no. 3, when he goes south to Antarctica to battle the martians that are stealing earth's ozone. Wacky's only known relative is his nephew, Sonny Squirrel.

Comment. The character was created by writer Mike Richardson and artist Jim Bradrick. He appeared in four issues of his own Dark Horse comic book (1987 to 1988), as well as in a pair of one shots, *Wacky Squirrel Summer Fun Special* and *Wacky Squirrel Halloween Adventure Special,* both 1987.

WAGS
Pedigree. Early comic book dog.
Biography. Wags is owned by the good-hearted boy Pee Wee, who lives in small, rustic Boonville where, on his go-cart (the Jet Purpeld Express), he and his dog get into various innocent adventures, from delivering paint to a local theater and getting locked in a ventriloquist's trunk (Pee Wee becomes a hit on Broadway as a dummy!) to trying to keep the boy's cousin Philip from constantly losing balloons. Wags, a wire fox terrier, tags along and *arf-arfs* whenever he's lost or if there's something that Pee Wee has overlooked.

Comment. The Pee Wee strip was created by artist Samuel Maxwell "Jerry" Iger for the first issue of *Famous Funnies* (1935), one of the first comic books ever published.

WALDO KITTY
Pedigree. Cat version of James Thurber's *The Secret Lives of Walter Mitty.*
Biography. Waldo and his girlfriend Felicia have a problem: They're constantly being pushed around by the bulldog Tyrone and the members of his pack. To deal with the humiliation, Waldo regularly slips into fantasies and imagines himself in combat against desperate villains, either as the superhero Catman; the jungle hero Catzan of the Apes; the western hero the Lone Kitty; the legendary archer

Robin Cat; or the brash Captain Herc, commander of the starship *Secondprize* in one episode, *Cat Trek*.

Comment. Filmation produced thirteen adventures of *The Secret Lives of Waldo Kitty*, which aired on NBC in 1975. Howard Morris provided the voice for Waldo, Jane Webb for Felicia, and Allan Melvin for Tyrone.

WALLY GATOR

Pedigree. TV cartoon alligator.

Biography. The theme song declares, "Wally Gator is the swinging alligator in the swamp. / He's the greatest percolator when he really starts to romp. / There has never been a greater operator in the swamp!" However, truth is, Wally is good-natured, eager to please, and nonviolent (when rival alligator Beau wants to duel to the death, Wally suggests "Mudpies at 20 paces!" Beau responds, "That's dirty fighting!" and Wally helpfully says they should try "nasty looks" instead). With a singsong voice like Ed Wynn and a perpetually sunny disposition, all Wally wants is to get out of the zoo, where he does odd jobs like bathing the elephants, and is checked, with regularity, by the short, mustachioed zookeeper Twiddles. Only when he's been very good is Wally allowed to have a weekend pass (the origin of the prison furlough system?), although he has managed to get out through other means, such as launching himself from a cannon, dressing as a woman and walking out at closing time, and pretending to be ill and getting taken out by ambulance (after which the problem becomes how to escape from the hospital). And he *always* finds a way out in the spring, which, says Twiddles, is when Wally "gets Everglades fever" and has to return to the swamp for a visit. Among his adventures are a run-in

with the big, burly aforementioned Beau when both woo the same lovely lizard lass; a battle with a witch; trouble with a powerful ape; a stint as a sheriff; a brush with Gosh Zilla; and a battle with his own conscience, personified by little angel and devil alligators. The green Wally wears a pink hat, white collar, and French cuffs, is approximately six feet long, and walks upright. He's fond of saying, "fiddle-dee-doo," as in "Fiddle-dee-doo, it's always the same kind of dull day. Nothing exciting ever happens in a city zoo!" He occasionally smokes a cigar.

Comment. Hanna-Barbera produced fifty-two cartoons for syndication in 1962. Daws Butler was the voice of Wally, and Don Messick was Twiddles. Butler accurately described the voice as "sloppy, like eating a sandwich through a picket fence." Wally appeared in the first three issues of Gold Key's *Hanna-Barbera Band Wagon* (1962 to 1963), and did guest shots in other Hanna-Barbera titles over the years.

WALLY WALRUS

Pedigree. Cartoon nemesis of **Woody Woodpecker** and **Andy Panda**.

Biography. Wally isn't a malicious character: It's fate that puts him at odds with other characters. He's usually seen as Woody's long-suffering landlord and/or neighbor, to wit: In *Ski for Two* (1944) he happens to run the lodge where the pesky bird is vacationing; in *Bathing Buddies* (1946), Woody drops a dime down the bathtub drain and wrecks Wally's building trying to get it; and in *Sleep Happy* (1951), the walrus tries to get some rest despite living next to the noisy bird (see **Woody Woodpecker** for details). In addition to other costarring roles, Wally starred in a cartoon of his own: *Overture to William Tell* (1947), part of the Musical Miniature series, in which there's no real story, just gags set to pieces of classical music. Always wearing clothes of some sort, the bipedal Wally has webbed feet, a Swedish accent, and a big, droopy moustache. In comic books, Wally was also there to serve as a brunt for Woody's activities.

Comment. Reminiscent of movie second-bananas like Alan Hale and Andy Devine, the hulking Wally is as close as cartoon stars come to being character actors. Somewhat more sinister than Wally is Woody's big, powerful foe Buzz Buzzard, who plays a bandit in the western cartoon *Stage Hoax* (1952), a sailor who hates the scrappy bird in *Alley to Bali* (1954), and so on, and is only slightly less contemptuous in the Woody Woodpecker comic books, where he's been everything from a rival student at

Wags, snacking at the local soda shop.

the Footindoor School of Salesmanship to a scrap iron dealer who not only won't buy Woody's antique cannon ball, but decides to use it against the bird. Buzz usually wears a red-and-black sweatshirt and black trousers.

WEAKHEART (1)
Pedigree. The dog belonging to early animated cartoon character Dinky Doodle.

Biography. The black, floppy-eared dog is the companion of a young boy, who gets into adventures with their creator, Walter Lantz (the animation was combined with live action). The trio meet many fairy tale characters (Little Red Riding Hood, the Pied Piper, Cinderella, and Robinson Crusoe), and also partake in more mundane adventures in the circus, out west, in the army, and so forth.

Comment. The dog was inspired by the popular and heroic silent film dog Strong Heart. The Bray Company characters appeared in twenty-three cartoons from 1924 to 1926. Lantz went on to create Woody Woodpecker.

WEAKHEART (2)
Pedigree. Comic book dog who is an adventurer-cum-lover.

Biography. Pauline Peril, reporter for the *Daily Noose,* travels around the world covering oddball stories. She is frequently accompanied by her "old, shaggy, whining, and faithful" mutt, who frequently saves her life. His one weakness is stylish bitches; he fell particularly hard for Pasha Poodle in one escapade.

Comment. The purple (!) pooch appeared in all four issues of Gold Key's *The Close Shaves of Pauline Peril,* from 1970 to 1971.

WILE E. COYOTE
Pedigree. Perennial loser in the battle of wits with the Road Runner.

Biography. The lean (make that skinny) and scraggly Carniverus Vulgaris—a k a Famishius Famishius, Hardheadipus Delirius, Evereadii Eatibus, Appetitis Giganticus, Hungrii Flea Bagius, Overconfidentii Vulgaris, among other appellations—has made a career (albeit, an unwelcome one) out of trying in vain to snare the Acceleratii Incredibilus, a k a Burnius Roadibus, Disapperialis Quickius, Burn-em Upus Asphaltus, Digoutis Hot-Rodis, Super Sonicus, Fastius Tasty-us, Velocitus Incalculus, Speedipus Rex—or, simply, the Road Runner. The cartoons consist of a series of blackout gags, each of which ends with Wile E. Coyote not only caught in whatever trap he's laid for the bird, but being battered by some additional element he hasn't considered (if he's poised on the edge of a cliff and tries to fire himself from a cannon to overtake the bird, not only will the weapon shift and fire him straight down, it will fall and land on top of him). The pair made their debut in the 1949 short *Fast and Furry-ous,* in which eleven different schemes backfire on the Coyote, among them a boomerang that returns (sans the bird); the ever-present tunnel-painted-in-the-side-of-a-cliff (the bird passes through it, the Coyote does not); a masterful invention consisting of the Coyote on skis and a freezer/sprinkler contraption strapped to his back, spreading snow ahead of him (alas, he shoots past the Road Runner and goes off a cliff, the snowmaker stalls, the ice bridge it was making ends, and down he goes—the snowmaker coming to life again and sprinkling flakes on his head, which is all that's jutting from the ground); rocket shoes that are so fast he constantly overshoots the bird; and the final indignity, the hungry beast successfully using a shortcut to pass the bird, raising his hatchet when he hears the Road Runner's characteristic *Beep Beep,* and getting flattened by a truck. The Coyote obviously needed some time off after the battering he took, and didn't return until 1952, at which point his prey wasn't the Road Runner but **Bugs Bunny.** In *Operation: Rabbit,* the Coyote (named Wile E. for the first time) goes over to the hare and, in a very civilized voice, announces that he's a "genius . . . more muscular, more cunning, faster, and larger than you are," and that the rabbit would be wise to save them both a lot of trouble and simply surrender. Bugs declines, of course, and Wile takes a licking: He fires a cannon into Bugs' hole, but the rabbit redirects the cannonball at him; he fills carrots with nitroglycerine, but before he's finished Bugs has moved the Coyote's workshop into the path of a train and Wile E. is blasted; and so on. His confidence still unshaken (Wile E. actually carries silverware for the anticipated feast), the Coyote tries and fails to nab the Road Runner in their second cartoon together, *Beep, Beep* (1953), in which he suffers indignities such as riding a fireworks rocket into the stratosphere, getting run over by a train (at a fake railroad crossing he'd set up, no less!), and lighting a match in a cache of explosives. Things get even worse in their next outing, *Zipping Along* (1953), in which the Coyote tries to snare the bird using a slew of mousetraps (the Road Runner's rapid passage simultaneously triggers them and sends them flying in the air, landing on the Coyote), chopping down a telephone pole (it falls all right, pulling another right on top of Wile E.), cutting the ropes holding up a rope bridge (the mountain collapses!), and so on. Their last clash to date has been *Soup or Sonic* (1980), in which everything from flypaper to exploding tennis balls fail to stop the bird. However, in the end, the Coyote does finally catch him. The only problem: Wile E. has been shrunk to inches in height by a very constrictive pipe through which he's passed. As he hangs on to the bird, the Coyote holds up a sign that reads, "You always wanted me to catch him. Now what do I do?"

Comment. Originally, the carnivore was to be known as Don Coyote. Animator Chuck Jones's idea to create a coyote cartoon star was inspired by Mark Twain's *Roughing It* (1872), which featured a chapter on coyotes. He originally considered having the coyote chase a jackrabbit (also written up by Twain), but Warner Brothers already had Bugs Bunny. Thus he settled on road runners, which are "all over Southern California." The Coyote and the Road Runner made forty-two cartoons together, the best of which were seen in the 1962 featurette *The Adventures of the Road Runner* and the 1979 compilation film *The Bugs Bunny/Road Runner Movie* (which consists of the best moments only from sixteen different cartoons). On television, *The Road Runner Show* aired on CBS on Saturday mornings from 1966 to 1972, showing reruns of the theatrical cartoons. *The Bugs Bunny/Road Runner Show* was seen on CBS in prime time in 1976, then shifted to Saturday mornings the following year, where it remained until 1981. In comic books, Dell and then Gold Key published 105 issues of *Beep Beep, the Road Runner* between 1958 and 1983. A Warner Brothers character virtually identical to the Coyote, Ralph Wolf, tangled with **Sam Sheepdog**. Incidentally, in real life, roadrunners are not only fleet (they can sustain fifteen miles an hour over considerable differences—just three miles an hour less than human sprinters), but they are among the canniest birds extant. *Natural History* magazine praises them for their "sophisticated survival tactics" (for example, surrounding a sleeping snake with thornbushes and letting it impale itself upon awaking)—something fans of the cartoons have observed for years!

WILLIE THE WHALE
Pedigree. Costar of Walt Disney's feature *Make Mine Music*.
Biography. When a "ghostly opera-singing" voice is heard at sea, experts blame it on a "trick of the radio air waves." However, opera maven Professor Tetti Tatti is convinced that an opera star has been swallowed by a whale, and sets out to find the singer. Meanwhile, the seagull Whitey notices a newspaper that quotes the professor, and brings it to the real singer: Willie, a black whale with a light brown belly (and a shape less like a whale than like a loaf of bread). Assuming that the professor wants to find him to put him in an opera, Willie seeks out Tetti Tatti's ship. He sings for him, and the professor is horrified: He orders his crew to slay the leviathan and rescue the singer. But the sailors are enjoying the concert—especially when Willie *concurrently* sings tenor, baritone, and bass parts from *The Marriage of Figaro*—and refuse to harm him. As Willie sings, the audience sees his fantasies: performing a succession of classic parts at the Met. Alas, Tetti Tatti mans the harpoon himself and slays Willie—who, literally, finishes his concert in Heaven (behind an SRO sign on the Pearly Gates).

Comment. Willie appeared in the segment *The Whale Who Wanted to Sing at the Met* in the 1946 film. Nelson Eddy provided the whale's voice.

WILLIE THE WORM
Pedigree. A cute comic book wriggler.
Biography. Dressed in a black bow tie with green dots, white gloves, and a stovepipe hat, the playful, pink Willie (who has arms, but no legs) lives in a cozy house built inside a tree trunk, and gets into harmless adventures with his friends Sammy Skunk and the bear Reddy Dough. During World War II, Willie joined the army and became Private Willie, partaking in solo adventures with Captain Bull (who is, of course, a bull). Willie's girlfriend in these later adventures is Winnie Worm, an adoring little insect who wears a bonnet and white gloves.

Comment. Willie first appeared in Fawcett's *Funny Animals* no. 1 in 1942; many of his adventures were reprinted in the **Atomic Mouse** comic book in the 1950s. The early Willie strips boasted one character that, while not an animal, deserves mention as one of the oddest figures in comics: Mr. Bottle, an empty bottle with arms and legs, a yellow vest, an Eton collar, and a detachable head. As odd as Willie was, slightly odder yet was Wiggles the

Wonderworm, who first appeared in Orbit Publications's *Taffy Comics* no. 1 in 1945, and appeared on and off in the magazine's twelve issues. Wiggles became a costumed superhero and battled villainous bugs whenever he said the magic word "Omygosh!" He had little legs and arms and stood upright, boasted small antennae and a humanlike face, and dressed in a blue cape and tights, a yellow T-shirt with a red W on the front, and white gloves. Wrapping up the insect kingdom, we can't ignore Freddy Firefly, a bug version of the superhero Human Torch. Freddy appeared in E.C. Publications's *Animal Fables* 1 to 7 from 1946 to 1947.

WILLOUGHBY WREN

Pedigree. Superheroic bird of theatrical cartoons.
Biography. Shaped rather like a hot dog with a pair of tail feathers, a sickle-shaped comb, thick arms, and skinny legs, Willoughby is a timid, unassuming bird who becomes superpowerful whenever he dons a hat that contains hair cut from the head of Samson.

Comment. Columbia Pictures made only four of the well-animated, sadly underrated Willoughby cartoons: *Willoughby's Magic Hat* (1943), *Magic Strength* (1944), *Carnival Courage* (1945; a bout with the circus strongman Klondike Pete), and *Cockatoos for Two* (1947).

WINNIE THE POOH

Pedigree. Bear of literature, adapted to the screen by Walt Disney.
Biography. To date, there have been five featurettes, each approximately a half hour long, recounting the adventures of "the bear of no brain at all" and his equally hapless animal companions who live in the Hundred Acre Wood. In *Winnie the Pooh and the Honey Tree* (1966), we find Winnie—who also goes by the name of Mr. Sanders—warming himself by the fire outside his house in a tree trunk. Going inside for honey, he finds there's only a little left. Just then, a bee buzzes by Pooh's ear and, realizing that where there are bees there's honey, he follows the insect back to a tree. It enters a hole on top, and Pooh begins to climb. But he can't make it to the top, and goes to ask his friend Christopher Robin for advice. Pooh returns to the tree with a balloon in hand and, rolling in mud, floats to the hole: as he rises, he mutters, so the bees will hear, "I'm only a little black rain cloud. Pay no attention to little me." Despite the fact that Christopher has an umbrella and is walking around muttering. "Tut-tut, it looks like rain," the bees aren't fooled. As the bear reaches for honey, they attack him and the balloon deflates, dropping the bear to earth. He says philosophically, "You never can tell with bees," and gives up the idea of having honey. Instead, he goes to the home of his friend Rabbit and mooches lunch. Alas, when the bear tries to leave, he becomes stuck in the hole; although the lanky rabbit, Christopher Robin, and Pooh's sorry-looking donkey friend Eeyore yank hard, they're unable to get him out. The solution: leave him there until he gets thin enough to exit. This they do (Rabbit having a heck of a time trying, meanwhile, to decorate the derriere in his living room), and when they're finally able to pull Pooh out, he rockets right to the honey tree, where his head gets stuck in the bee hole. His sudden arrival causes the alarmed bees to skeedaddle, and this time Pooh is only too happy to remain wedged where he is. In Pooh's next outing, *Winnie the Pooh and the Blustery Day* (1968), "windsday" in the Hundred Acre Wood proves to be just that, as Pooh and his tiny friend Piglet (who's wrapped tightly in a red shirt with black stripes, and has the biggest ears this side of **Dumbo**) are blown into the skies and scuttled on Owl's home. No sooner do they get inside than the winds whip the house and send it crashing to earth. Eeyore offers to go and find Owl another home, and sets out. That night, while the howling winds batter Pooh's home and he cowers within, the rambunctious Tigger comes bouncing in, knocking Pooh over (he does this with most everyone he meets, then stands on their chest to talk to them). After tasting some of Pooh's honey (and not liking it very much), he warns the bear to be on the look out for the honey-thieving Heffalumps and Woozles. Pooh suspects that he really means elephants and weasles but, in any case, he takes his popgun, sits guard that night, falls asleep . . . and has a nightmare about creatures as bizarre as the names Tigger concocted. When he wakes up, he's in far worse straits as floodwaters wash him and his precious honey pot away. Meeting Piglet in the roiling waters, he saves the diminutive animal's life by poking him inside the honeypot. When the storm ends, Christopher arranges a party to celebrate Pooh's heroism. Just then, Eeyore reports that he's found that ideal new home for Owl . . . not knowing that the place is Piglet's home. The self-sacrificing pig says nothing, and the party becomes a "two-hero" celebration. The next film, *Winnie the Pooh and Tigger Too* (1974) is about the problems everyone in the woods has with

Tigger incessantly bowling everyone over. Rabbit, Pooh, and Piglet agree to lead Tigger into the woods and lose him; they reason that when he returns, he'll be so happy to see everyone he'll stop thumping them to the ground. Naturally, after they get rid of Tigger, the trio gets lost. They try to get home by following Pooh's stomach, which he reasons will lead them to his honey pot. This flops, and they're more than happy when Tigger bounces Rabbit down, announcing that he can get them home because "Tiggers do not get lost." When they return, Tigger and the baby kangaroo Roo bounce to the top of a tree, where the feline suffers from vertigo; turning to the narrator, Tigger promises never to bounce anyone again if he'll get him out of the tree. The narrator obliges by tipping the picture so Tigger can slide down. Unable to bounce for joy, Tigger becomes miserable. Because they hate to see their friend in this state, the other animals self-sacrificingly agree to let him bounce. Finally, it's Eeyore's birthday in *Winnie the Pooh and a Day for Eeyore* (1983), which begins with Pooh, Rabbit, and Piglet playing Pooh-sticks (toss a stick off one end of the bridge, and the player whose stick emerges from the upstream side first wins). When Eeyore floats by, the trio learns that he was bounced there by Tigger. When he emerges on the shore, he explains that it was only insult added to injury: The day was already ruined because no one remembered that it was his birthday. Pooh and Piglet feel for their friend, and try to set things right. Pooh goes and gets him honey in a honey pot, and although he eats the contents on the way home, he figures the donkey will enjoy the pot. Piglet brings him a balloon, which he manages to puncture along the way. However, Eeyore is content: He now has a nice pot *and* a memento to put inside. Tigger, Rabbit, and Christopher arrive for a party, which climaxes with Pooh-sticks, at which Eeyore is repeatedly victorious.

Comment. Sterling Holloway is the voice of Pooh, Paul Winchell is Tigger, Ralph Wright is Eeyore, Clint Howard and Dori Whitaker are Roo, Barbara Luddy is his mother Kanga, John Fiedler is Piglet, Hal Smith is Owl, Junius Matthews is Rabbit, and Howard Morris is Gopher, a minor character invented for the cartoon series. A succession of people have provided the voice for Christopher Robin, while narration was provided by the late Sebastian Cabot. Author A(lan) A(lexander) Milne (1882–1956) wrote two books about the characters, *Winnie the Pooh* (1926) and *The House at Pooh Corner*

(1928). The second book introduced Tigger, who starred in three of the ten stories. Several of the characters were based on toys owned by Milne's son Christopher: The boy got Pooh when he was one, although the name was adapted from a swan they had met during a vacation. Winnie was also a borrowed name, taken from an American black bear cub that came to the London Zoo in 1914. Toys Piglet and Eeyore were also toys of Christopher's; his parents gave him Tigger, Kanga, and Roo, the real-life Christopher recalls, "not just for the delight that they might give to their new owner, but also for their literary possibilities." As much as young Christopher based his play adventures on his father's stories, the elder Milne also watched his son's play for potential stories. The author's wife, Daphne, contributed many ideas. In 1982, Benjamin Hoff published *The Tao of Pooh,* his thesis being that Pooh's attitudes and principles are similar to those "envisaged long ago by the Chinese founders of Taoism." The Disney animators closely followed the designs of original Pooh artist E. H. Shepard. The initial three Pooh featurettes were edited together to form the 1977 feature-length film *The Many Adventures of Winnie the Pooh.* Regular TV shows featuring the bear are *Welcome to Pooh Corner,* half-hour adventures that feature actors in costumes and air on the cable service The Disney Channel, and *The Gummi Bears and Winnie the Pooh Hour,* which features new cartoon shorts and debuted on NBC in 1989. In comics, Gold Key, then Whitman, published thirty-three issues of a Winnie comic book from 1977 to 1984.

WINSTON
Pedigree. Pet of theatrical and TV cartoon hero Hector Heathcote.
Biography. Thanks to a time machine, lanky Hector and his dog are able to travel back to the Revolutionary War era and other crucial eras in American history and make sure events turn out the way they're supposed to (e.g., Paul Revere's ride, the Boston Tea Party, the forging of the Liberty Bell). Looking very much like Winston Churchill, Winston helps his master whenever possible.

Comment. The characters were created by writer Eli Bauer. Terrytoons produced thirty-five cartoons in all. The first, *The Minute and a Half Man,* was released to theaters in 1959. *The Hector Heathcote Show* premiered on NBC in 1963. Gold Key published one comic book in 1964. Also seen on the show were **Hashimoto** and **Sidney the Elephant.**

WONDER DOG

Pedigree. Member of TV's Superfriends.

Biography. The Superfriends are a team of super-heroes—Superman, Batman, Robin, Wonder Woman, and Aquaman—who are assisted by nonpowerful teens Marvin White and Wendy Harris and their pet Wonder Dog. Despite the fact that he wears a green cape, the blue Wonder Dog has no powers . . . although he's brave, an expert at running for help, and very good at getting underfoot to trip up bad guys.

Comment. The Hanna-Barbera creation was seen on *Superfriends* on ABC, from 1973 to 1975 (although the series itself ran through 1980). There were sixteen separate adventures in all; Frank Welker was the dog's voice. Wonder Dog was also seen in DC Comics's *The Super Friends,* which was published from 1976 to 1981. He appeared in no. 1, and in scattered issues through no. 47. The teens and dog were replaced on *The All-New Superfriends Hour* (1977) and in the comic book by teens Zan and Jayna, the shape-changing Wonder Twins from the planet Exor. With their Exorian, purple-caped, orange-costumed, blue-skinned pet monkey Gleek (named after the only word in its vocabulary) they remained with the Superfriends for the duration of the show's run. Mike Bell provided the monkey's sounds.

Wonder Dog *with Marvin and Wendy. It's a toss-up as to whether Marvin or the canine is runner-up in the brains deparment.* © HANNA-BARBERA PRODUCTIONS.

Wonder Duck, *about to become an ex-cartoon animal.*
© 1991 MARVEL ENTERTAINMENT GROUP. *All rights reserved.*

WONDER DUCK

Pedigree. An inept, timid comic book duck.

Biography. Wonder—that's really his name—lives in a spacious house with his nephew Dizzy; Wonder's girlfriend is Wilma, whom he affectionately calls "Dream Duck." Wonder's stories involve either domestic problems (how not to fix a squeaky door, how to deal with a vacuum cleaner salesdog, and other situations that suburban ducks face each day) or problems at the office. Wonder works in the Tam Building, employed by a hard-hearted pig investment broker named Giltly; he's also pushed around by his coworkers, Horrible Harry the office boy (bear, actually), and the big dogs who work on either side of him. (Tellingly, all the women who work in the office are human women. Either the comic book was telling us that all men are animals, or that women were lower than dogs, a duck, and pigs.)

Comment. Wonder Duck first appeared in Marvel Comics's two-issue run of Film Funnies in 1949. Those were also three issues of Marvel Comics's *Wonder Duck*, which lasted from 1949 to 1950. The strip was written by Stan Lee, who went on to cocreate the bulk of the classic Marvel superheroes.

Lee also wrote the back-up strip, *The Rabbit and the Fox* (it appeared in both comic books), about a clever hare who's always trying to cheat a stupid fox (such as by selling him oyster rights on a public beach). The one time the Rabbit genuinely tries to reform—upon the advice of his goat-psychiatrist—and offers to take the Fox to the movies *(Film Funnies* no. 2), the Fox is so suspicious that by the time they get there, he clubs the hare.

WONDER WART-HOG

Pedigree. Classic underground comic strip super-hero.

Biography. Philbert Desenex (also written Desanex) is a "timid, mild-mannered reporter" for the *Muthalode Morning Mishap.* Although Philbert runs at the "mere mention" of danger, his terror isn't genuine: He's running so he can gulp down a power-capsule, pull off his clothes and humanlike mask, and fight crime as Wonder Wart-Hog. The wart-hog battles evil with his powers of flight and super-strength *not* to see justice done, but because it makes him "sorta famous, and if you're famous, you get lotsa dates." Moreover, Philbert can use the reward money. (If there isn't any, he keeps whatever the crooks have robbed and lets them go.) If Wonder Wart-Hog encounters wood, steel, Portland cement, or strawberry rhubarb pie, his strength is sapped and he's left as "worthless as teats on a boar hog." When the superswine is needed by the police, they crank up the Hogsignal, which sends out a rattling loud *Soooooooeeeeeepigpigpig!* If the hero himself is ever in trouble, he gives the same cry and pigs from around the city ("The Bacon Brigade") come galloping to his aide. Wonder Wart-Hog also gets about on his Hog cycle. When he needs to reflect or relax, he heads to his secret Wonder Cave hideout. The superhero is garbed in a blue costume with brown trunks, brown boots, a brown cape, and a black domino mask (these colors have varied over the years). A large *WW* graces his massive chest. As Philbert, he's in love with fellow human reporters Melody Lane and Lois Lamebrain. (Watching Lois pass one day, Philbert longingly reflects, "What if I ripped off my *Philbert Desanex* disguise and said, 'I'm *Wonder Wart-hog!* Let's *fuck?*' ") The fact is, the Wart-hog is impotent, and makes love with his formidable snout.

    Comment. Gilbert Shelton's creation first appeared in the University of Texas, Austin, student magazine *Bacchanal* in 1962. It was also published in *The Texas Ranger,* followed by newsstand exposure in *Drag Cartoons* and two issues of *Wonder Wart-Hog, the Hog of Steel* (1967), among other underground comics.

WOODY WOODPECKER

Pedigree. One of the great cartoon birds of theatrical shorts and comics.

Biography. Over the years, Woody Woodpecker has evolved from being a complete lunatic to being a pest to being a beleaguered middle-class bird. In his first cartoon, *Knock Knock,* he pokes through the roof of **Andy Panda** and his father, with his signature, "Guess who? Ha-ha-ha-*ha*-ha!" After escaping the pandas' best efforts to capture him, the bird surfaces in his own starring vehicle, *Cracked Nut* (a k a simply *Woody Woodpecker).* This little masterpiece has Woody as a certifiable lunatic, from the moment he bounds out singing, "Everybody thinks I'm crazy / yesiree, that's me, that's me! / That's what I'm cracked up to be / I chop a hole in every tree!" After annoying other woodland animals (he tells a bird to "go lay an egg," and it does . . . right on his head), then rapidly turning a tree into a totem pole, Woody tries to repeat that feat with a marble statue. The failed effort rattles his brains, and he decides that maybe he is crazy and should see a psychiatrist. As it happens, the analyst, a fox named Dr. Horace N. Buggy, is nuttier than Woody, and the two end up heckling each other until Woody finally falls off the screen into the audience. The wonderful lunacy of the two characters must be seen to be appreciated. In this and other early cartoons, Woody looks only marginally like the bird we've come to know, with his elongated face and body, blue feathers, and red belly. And he *looks* crazy, with his eyes crossing constantly and his tongue hanging from the side of his beak. In his fourth cartoon, *Pantry Panic* (1941), the bird is so hungry that when he spots a wolf, he decides to eat him (there's a twist!), sadistically slamming his head in a waffle iron at one point. In the sort-of sequel, *Fair Weather Friends* (1946), he manages to lure the wolf into a meat grinder! In *The Screwball* (1943), he's tooling along and is stopped by a police officer. Telling the officer, "Hold that pose," the insane bird whips out a camera. To no one's surprise (except the officer) the lens pops open, a huge boxing glove flies out and decks him, and Woody drives away laughing. By Woody's eleventh cartoon, *The Barber of Seville* (1944), he has evolved, physically, into the more modern Woody, with a shorter body, smaller head, and white belly—although he's only slightly less crazed. Finding Tony Seville's barbershop deserted, Woody decides to take care of the customers himself. After an Indian chef is driven mad, a construction worker shambles in. While Woody sings "Largo al factotum" from Rossini's *The Barber of Seville* (the barber Figaro's famous, appropriately self-aggrandizing aria), he wields a razor the size of a meat cleaver, lathering and shaving everything from the customer's head to his shoes. Woody was tamed considerably when he acquired a semiregular victim, **Wally Walrus**: It was more by accident than by design that the woodpecker bugged him. For example, in *Smoked Hams* (1947), Wally sleeps during the day. Waking up one morning, Woody decides it's a perfect day to mow the lawn, thus making it impossible for Wally to sleep. When the incensed walrus corners Woody and facetiously demands, "Could you possibly make any *more* noise?", the bird is only to happy to oblige: He breaks out a one-man band and begins playing. Things escalate, Wally flinging a hand grenade at Woody, who tosses it back (Woody has the good sense to keep a slingshot in his hip pocket for just such an emergency). The walrus finally waits until Woody goes to bed, then straps him in a "Tit-for-Tat Machine," which subjects the helpless Woody to every noise he himself had created that day. In *Sleep Happy* (1951), Woody is even less malevolent than before, as his innocent snoring keeps roommate Wally awake. The woodpecker literally sleeps through the entire cartoon—even when Wally hurls him through the night like a javelin, Woody landing beak-first in a telephone pole. (Yes . . . the snores come back to the house over the phone line.) Most of the Woody/Wally cartoons are superb entertainment, although Woody simply isn't as wonderfully uninhibited and unique as before. One of the few classic Woody cartoons from the waning years of the series is *Three Little Woodpeckers* (1965), in which a big, bad wolf tries to get at Woody. Over the years, Woody's cartoons also featured him in wildly diverse times and locales, from outer space to the wild west to the piratic high seas. The taming of Woody was even more complete in his comics, where his nephew and niece Knothead and Splinter had their own strip and became the antagonists, constantly getting into trouble while Woody's trying to relax (chasing a rabbit through the yard while Woody is in the hammock, for instance). The two are miniature versions of Woody, except for the fact that his niece has her head feathers in a pony tail and wears a skirt (an odd conceit, seeing as how it covers nothing, nor is there anything to cover!). Woody's girlfriend, in the comics, was Winnie. She wears a dress *and* blouse!

Comment. Walter Lantz has long maintained that he was inspired to create Woody when a woodpecker was hammering incessantly on the roof of his honeymoon cottage. Whatever producer Lantz's contribution may have been, writer/director Ben Hardaway had a lot to do with the genesis of the character. Woody appeared in 193 theatrical short subjects between 1940 and 1972. These came to television in 1957 when *The Woody Woodpecker Show* premiered on ABC. At first, Mel Blanc was the voice of the woodpecker; when he agreed to work only for Warner Brothers (**Bugs Bunny**, et al.), various artists were brought in. Lantz's wife, Grace Stafford, finally got the job; reportedly, her husband selected the speeded-up voice, not knowing it belonged to Grace. Woody appeared in 201 issues of his own comic book, which was published, in succession, by Dell and Gold Key from 1947 to 1984; he also starred in Dell's *New Funnies*, beginning with no. 87 and lasting through no. 288 (1944 to 1962). Knothead and Splinter first appeared in no. 182.

WOOFER

Pedigree. Canine sidekick to the outré Winky Dink.
Biography. Woofer is just an ordinary dog, but Winky Dink is a real oddity: Dressed in a harlequin's suit, he has a head twice the size of his body, each eye is as large as his torso, and his hair is cut in the shape of a flat, five-pointed star. That aside, the duo got into all manner of cliff-hangers (raging river in front of them, no way out of a burning building, no exit from a cave, and so on) from which viewers provided the only escape. Using transparent screens placed over the TV picture tube (millions were sold at 50 cents), kids had to draw whatever was needed to save the pair (if you were a cynic and didn't do the drawing, Winky Dink and Woofer escaped just the same).

Comment. *Winky Dink and You* was an Ariel Production, which was seen on CBS from 1953 to 1957; there were fifty-two black-and-white episodes in all. New, color cartoons were syndicated in 1969, but failed because of widespread concern about being so close to the television. Dayton Allan was the voice of Woofer; Mae Questel was Winky Dink. Jack Barry cocreated and hosted the show.

WOOFER AND WHIMPER

Pedigree. TV bloodhounds.

Biography. "Just give the old pro a whiff of a clue, and the nose goes," boasts the long, gangly Woofer, the more aggressive of the two Southern dogs who solve crimes alongside the all-human kids of the Clue Club (Larry, D.D., Pepper, and Dotty). The dumpy Whimper prefers sleeping to searching for clues. Dressed in a deerstalker cap and walking on all fours, Woofer is white with a black spot on his back. Whimper is tan with a brown spot on his back. The two dogs can talk, but only to one another. Woofer frequently mutters threats under his breath when a person is obviously lying.

Comment. The characters appeared on Hanna-Barbera's *Clue Club* adventures, which aired on CBS in 1976; there were sixteen half-hour episodes in all. The following year, the characters resurfaced on *The Skatebirds* in a regular segment titled *Woofer and Whimper, Dog Detectives,* before returning as *Clue Club* the following year. Paul Winchell provided the voice for Woofer, Jim McGeorge for Whimper. These cartoons were played relatively straight, with the dogs used as occasional comic relief. Woofer and Whimper appeared in no. 2 of Marvel Comics's *TV Stars* (1978).

WUZZLES

Pedigree. Hybrid animals of a Walt Disney TV cartoon.

Biography. The Land of Wuz is a place that looks a lot like Disneyland: clean streets, brightly colored trains, and homes made of pastel-colored wood and stone, with vibrant flowers everywhere. (Even the furnishings look as though they were carved from rainbows, like the colorful Steinwuz piano.) This is also a place where, according to the song, "Every single thing is really two-in-one." Among the animals (all of whom have small, colorful, flylike wings), Butterbear is a bear with antennae, Bumblelion is a lion with bee-parts (who roars with a hum!), Eleroo is an elephant with kangaroo limbs, Rhinokey is a rhinoceros and monkey (and a crackpot inventor, who comes up with gadgets like an exploding doorbell), Hoppopotamus is a hippopotamus with rabbit ears, Moosel is a moose with a seal's lower-quarters, Woolrus is a lamb and a walrus, Pandeaver is a panda and a beaver, Tycoon is a raccoon and tiger, Piggypine is a porcupine and a pig, Koalakeet is a koala and parakeet, and Skowl is a skunk and an owl. The vegetation here also consists of hybrids: Appleberries are the animals' favorite food. (Naturally, when a Wuzzle is accidentally coated with preserves, he moans, "This is another fine appleberry jam!") The only dark clouds on the environment are the nasty Croc, a nonhybrid crocodile who wears a sailor's cap, his aide Brat, a **Tasmanian Devil**-like frog and dragon combo with horns and a spiked tail, and the frog-lizard mixture Flizard. Even these blighters aren't so bad, though: The worst they do is change dustjackets on library books to confuse patrons, steal fruit from Butterbear's appleberry garden, or stand outside the grocery store with a "free sampling" sign, then taste food from the shopping bag of anyone dumb enough to stop by.

Comment. The series debuted in the ABC Saturday morning lineup in 1985; there were thirteen episodes in all. It was one of two cartoon shows created expressly for network television by the Walt Disney studios (the other being *Gummi Bears),* and the animation is high-quality, fluid, and strong on characterization. Stan Freberg provided the narration for these half-hour adventures, reminding kids what they may have forgotten during the commercials. Henry Gibson provided the voice of Eleroo, Joanne Worley was Hoppopotamus, Bill Scott was Moosel, and Brian Cummings was Bumblelion. The characters were featured in the comic book *Walt Disney's Comics and Stories* beginning with no. 511. Another set of fanciful animals was seen on ABC in 1983: the Monchhichis, based on a less-than-popular line of dolls from Mattel. Like the Wuzzles, these creatures are fanciful—although not identifiable as any known species. Vaguely monkeylike, they have names like Moncho, Kyla, Tootoo, Patchitt, and Thumkii; they talk, live in cloud-piercing trees, get about by gliding on wooden wings, and fight the evil Grumplins—who have scuzzy sounding names like Gonker, Shreeker, and Scumgor.

YAKKY DOODLE

Pedigree. TV cartoon duck.

Biography. The smallest cartoon duck of all, Yakky has a big round head, yellow feathers with a blue back, wings, and tail feathers, and a high, **Donald Duck**-type voice. The duckling roams about with his big pal Chopper—a gruff, bipedal bulldog who wears a red necktie and calls Yakky "little feller." Chopper, whose only fear is ghosts, constantly protects the innocent Yakky from harm, most notably from the fox Fibber, who's constantly trying to eat the duck. As Yakky's name implies, the "little feller" never shuts up, which can be annoying to foes and viewers alike.

  Comment. Hanna-Barbera produced thirty-two Yakky cartoons, which aired as part of the syndicated *Yogi Bear Show* in 1958. The voice belonged to ventriloquist Jimmy Weldon, who simply adapted a voice he'd used for the duck puppet Webster Webfoot on his NBC series *Funny Boners* four years earlier. Gold Key published one *Yakky Doodle and Chopper* comic book in 1962.

YELLOW BEAK

Pedigree. Walt Disney comic book parrot.

Biography. In his debut story, Yellow Beak is a pegleg parrot with a flowing black cloak, pirate's hat, and red vest and bandana. One night, he shows up at the Bucket o' Blood Sea Food Grotto, owned by **Donald Duck** and his nephews **Huey, Dewey, and Louie**. Yellow Beak explains that he saved a sailor's life in Singapore and the grateful sailor told the parrot that the ghost of Morgan the Pirate had informed him of a treasure map hidden in the Bucket o' Blood. The parrot finds it and, with the four ducks, makes plans to hire a boat and sail to the treasure island. Unknown to them, the evil Black Pete (a k a **Pete**) is eavesdropping, and makes sure to have a ship available for them at a bargain price. En route, the Pete and his two rat thugs get ahold of the map and force Yellow Beak and Donald to walk the plank. Fortunately, the duck's nephews had the foresight to build a raft and float under to catch them. Also fortunately: Before they left port, Yellow Beak took the precaution to cut the exact location of the treasure from the map and had it tatooed on his chest. Thus they are the first ones to reach Skeleton Tree and find the crossed bones that mark the spot. They uncover the treasure—unaware that Pete and his tugs have also arrived and are watching to let the birds do the "woik." Once again, though, Donald's nephews are one step ahead of the group: They've climbed a tree, and when Pete steps out to claim the treasure, the little ducks drop a coconut on his head. The three crooks go back home in chains, and the birds return wealthy. For Yellow Beak's second appearance, the story was largely recycled as, one rainy evening, the bird stumbles into the cottage of Snow White's Seven Dwarfs. Now two-legged and lacking his cloak, he's dressed in a red-and-white striped shirt, pirate's hat, blue trousers and gloves, and an earring. Curiously, his beak is orange. He introduces himself as the skipper of the boat *Crimson Crate*, and explains that he was out looking for a crew when he was caught in the storm. He offers the Dwarfs a chance to join him on a treasure hunt, and they accept (says Doc: "I would like to buy Snow White something *really fine* for her *birthday*"). Meanwhile, the Old Witch learns of the treasure from her Magic Mirror, and transforms herself into a mouse so she can get onboard. During the voyage, the only trouble Yellow Beak encounters is with Sleepy, since the skipper has an iron-clad rule: "If you *snooze* on the job . . . it means the *brig!*" Eventually, they're shipwrecked on Nothing Atoll, where they find both the treasure and a prospector who's there with his cat, Abercrombie. When Yellow Beak and two of the Dwarfs are turned into food by the witch, Dopey swaps the prospector the treasure for his cat, then lets Abercrombie eat the witch. His friends are restored, and they leave the island on the back of a whale. The story was reused yet again when the Darling family of *Peter Pan* fame rent a home at the seashore . . . a home that comes complete with a caged parrot. The parrot does nothing but sleep until the fairy Tinker Bell arrives and sprinkles him with pixie dust. She reports that the mean Captain Hook overheard her master, Peter Pan, talking about a treasure; donning his pirate hat and red cape, Yellow Beak explains that years before, he and Pan saved an old sailor in a shipwreck (deja vu!). The man was so grateful he told them where they could find a treasure map. "That's why I dropped anchor in this house," says the parrot. "I've been waitin' for Pan to give the order to start the search." Retrieving the map from the fireplace, he's unaware that Hook is watching. The next day, when Yellow Beak and the Darling boys Michael and John set out to rent a boat, they inadvertently hire Hook's hurriedly disguised vessel. They set out, and events proceed exactly as before (right down to Michael and John catching Yellow Beak on a raft when he walks the plank, and the center of the map being tatooed on the bird's chest). On the island they're met by Pan, make their way to Skeleton Tree and the crossed bones that mark the spot, and unearth the treasure chest. Hook follows them, young Michael climbs a tree and bops him and his mate Smee with coconuts, and the boys and parrot return home, rich. The lads use their money to buy the seaside house their father had rented.

Comment. Yellow Beak was created for a feature-length animated cartoon *Morgan's Ghost,* which was to have gone into production in 1942. Called *Pieces of Eight, or The Three Buccaneers* when it was first conceived in 1939, the story had **Mickey Mouse,** Donald, **Goofy,** and **Pluto** heading off on the adventure against Pete; Yellow Beak was simply Pete's pet in this version. The title was changed and the story was altered and sketched out in story-boards (drawings that show the entire action of the film, comic book style). In this version, Yellow Beak assumed the role he would have in the comic book. However, Disney chose to devote studio resources to creating films for the war effort, so the film was shelved. However, the story was recycled by Carl Barks as a comic book (Dell's *4-Color* no. 9: *Donald Duck Finds Pirate Gold,* August, 1942), which featured basically the same story except that it involved Donald and his nephews **Huey, Dewey and Louie** instead of Donald, Mickey, and Goofy. The lesser-known adventure with the dwarfs was published in *4-Color* no. 227, *The Seven Dwarfs,* in 1949, while the Captain Hook tale appeared in *Walt Disney's Peter Pan Treasure Chest* in 1952. The parrot also appeared, unauthorized, his name and appearance unchanged, in *Woody Woodpecker* no. 76 in 1963, in a shortened version of the tale.

YELLOW DOG
Pedigree. Mascot for the long-lived underground tabloid/comic book *Yellow Dog.*
Biography. There is no personal history to the long-eared, ever-smiling dog: It simply appears on the

front of almost every issue, urinating on one thing or another. At first, it was seen wetting the wooden leg of Captain Ahab (who was shouting, "Have you seen the Yellow Dog?"). Later, the yellow animal could be found relieving itself on fire hydrants, the title, and anything else that was handy. On rare occasions, the dog would appear in a brief strip, as when it discovers god by looking into a mirror (dog reversed) . . . and proceeds to urinate on him.

Comment. The dog was originally going to be called Puck, but Hearst had had a comic strip character by that name. According to the dog's cocreator, Don Schenker, the dog is intended "to show contempt for symbolism. Instead of 'What fools these mortals be,' he's saying, 'Piss on them.' " First published by the Print Mint in 1968, *Yellow Dog* lasted until 1973, a record run (twenty-five issues) for an underground comic book.

YIPPIE
Pedigree. Early animated cartoon dog; one of the first female cartoon animals.
Biography. The white dog with a black spot on its back and an oversize terrier head (it's slightly larger than the rest of her body!) is the beloved pet of the young button-eyed boy Scrappy. In their very first escapade, Scrappy becomes frantic when he thinks Yippie is dying. After searching desperately for Dr. Woof's Dog Tonic, the boy is relieved to find that Yippie isn't dying but is about to give birth. In most of the other adventures, Yippie more or less just tags along with her master.

Comment. The first of Columbia's Scrappy cartoons was *Yelp Wanted,* released in 1931. There were 112 cartoons released before the series ended in 1940. The character was cocreated by animator Dick Huemer, who was just coming off the cancellation of his eleven-cartoon series about Toby the Pup, a frankly unlikable little dog.

YIPPIE, YAPPIE, AND YAHOOEY
Pedigree. A trio of ineffective TV guard-dogs.
Biography. Dressed like Musketeers, the sword-swinging Yippie, Yappie, and Yahooey are assigned to protect a (nameless) king from his enemies, though the king more often laments, "I need guards to protect me from my guards." Among the foes and difficulties they somehow overcome are dragons, enchantments, and the like. The characters were informally—although not inappropriately—known as the Goofy Guards. Yippie is tall and purple,

Yappie is fat, big, and white, and Yahooey is small and brown.

Comment. Hanna-Barbera syndicated twenty-seven episodes of *The Peter Potamus Show* in 1964. Daws Butler did the voices for Yappie and Yahooey, with Hal Smith playing Yippie.

YOGI BEAR
Pedigree. Classic cartoon bear of TV, movies, and comic books.

Biography. Yogi wears a small green or blue porkpie hat, a matching tie, and a white collar. He walks upright, speaks, and lives in Jellystone Park, which overlaps the states of Montana and Wyoming. He has a large, private cave, and always finds it difficult to wake up after a "long winter hibernation." Once he does, however, Yogi is single-minded in his quest for food. (He can even eat underwater, if he has to.) Although it's forbidden for picnickers or campers to feed the bears, Yogi does everything in his power to steal food: He poses as a food inspector and checks baskets at the gate ("Too many calories," he says, taking a pizza from one camper), he has trained ants that march up baskets and steal food, he uses a bow and arrow to spear meals, swings on a vine to make passes over picnic tables, sneaks into trailer refrigerators, robs car trunks, and even snatches fish when pictures of a prize catch are being snapped. When all else fails, he begs . . . piteously. Confronting campers, once, he moaned, "Help! I'm starving! I haven't eaten for weeks! A bowl of broth! A pizza pie! A roast chicken! I just gotta get some food in my shrunken stomach!" (Listening to all of this, his good friend and constant companion **Boo Boo** turns to the camera and says, "This is embarrassing.") Meanwhile, Chief Ranger John Smith and his assistant Ranger Anderson do everything in their power to keep Yogi from the campers—although the bear usually finds a way to outsmart Smith, even if it means locking him in the closet of the ranger station. Yogi prides himself on being "smarter than the average bear," and while he *is* resourceful when it comes to thievery and panhandling, he has a tendency to murder the language (like his namesake, baseball great Yogi Berra). To wit: "pick-a-nick baskets," outsmarting the rangers using "psick-ol-cology," commenting—after falling on his head—"I never get hurt when I land on my numbskull," observing that he sees things simply and, ergo, is "simple-minded," and remarking to the lovestricken **Cindy Bear**, "What's on your mind . . . as if it isn't oblivious?"

Above all, Yogi is good-natured and unflappable—certainly more endearing than the average bear.

Comment. Yogi made his debut as one of the component episodes of *The Huckleberry Hound Show* (see **Huckleberry Hound**) in 1959. There were forty-eight episodes in all. He proved so popular that *The Yogi Bear Show* was introduced in 1961 (nineteen new episodes, plus reruns). It was changed to *Yogi and His Friends* in 1967, after which Yogi made the switch from syndication to network. *Yogi's Gang* premiered on ABC in 1973 (sixteen episodes) and got Yogi (along with Huckleberry Hound, **Peter Potamus, Wally Gator,** and most of the major figures in the Hanna-Barbera menagerie) out of Jellystone Park and into a dirigiblelike Ark Lark. Traveling the nation, they fought apathy about ecology and social concerns, battling the likes of Mr. Bigot, Lotta Litter, Mr. Smog, The Sheik of Selfishness, and the Envy Brothers. It was relevant, but it wasn't Yogi. *Yogi's Space Race* aired on NBC in 1978 (thirteen episodes) and went in a different direction entirely: In the wake of *Star Wars* mania, Yogi was teamed with **Scarebear** and partook in interplanetary races onboard the Supercharged Galactic Leader, competing against teams of Hanna-Barbera characters such as Huckleberry Hound and the duck Quackup, Captain Good and Clean Cat, **Jabberjaw** and **Buford,** and the evil Phantom Phink and his dog Sludge. *The Yogi Bear Show* is presently in syndication. A feature-length film, *Hey There, It's Yogi Bear,* was released in 1964. Written by William Hanna, Joe Barbera, and Warren Foster, and directed by Hanna-Barbera, it's actually a two-part tale. In the first half, Yogi wakes from hibernation and tries every way he can think of to get food. Fed up, Ranger Smith orders him shipped to the San Diego Zoo . . . although Yogi gets out of it by convincing dull-witted Cornpone Bear to take his place. Yogi then goes into hiding deep in the forest, stealing food as the Brown Phantom. Meanwhile, Cindy tosses a pizza pie in Ranger Smith's face, hoping she'll be sent to San Diego to be with Yogi. Instead, she's crated and sent to St. Louis. En route, she's abducted by the Chizzling Brothers Circus, whose compact, vicious dog Mugger forces her to perform as the High Wire Bear by chasing her up the pole. (Mugger's other pastime is chewing on the arm of Snively Chizzling.) Learning of Cindy's fate, Yogi and Boo Boo race to her rescue—escaping Jellystone via an inflatable raft, which Yogi keeps stashed in a tree for emergencies. Yogi fills it with helium so they can fly out fast, leading to some wonderful aerial sequences, including one in which Yogi clings to the outside of the cockpit of a commercial airliner. ("I would like to report a bear on the windshield," the pilot deadpans in this very funny sequence.) Eventually, the Chizzlings capture the inept Yogi and lock him in a cage with Cindy, guarded by Mugger. Thus it's up to Boo Boo to outwit the dog and help his friends escape. This they do in a clown car, which leads—through a Rube Goldberg-style series of events—to the trio being trapped by the police atop a skyscraper. Only the timely arrival of Ranger Smith saves them. There have been other, less entertaining Yogi features. *Yogi's Great Escape* was released in 1986. With the parks scheduled to close, the bears are all due to be sent to a zoo. Thus it's up to Yogi, Boo Boo, and the cubs Bopper, Yapper, and Bitsy, to find a way to keep it open. Even less impressive were *Yogi and the Magical Flight of the Spruce Goose* (1987) and *Yogi and the Invasion of the Space Bears* (1988), although the latter, at least, had some fun with the change-of-pace science fiction theme. On television, specials have included *Yogi's Ark Lark* (1 and 2, in 1972 and 1973), the two-hour *Yogi's First Christmas* (1980), and *Yogi Bear's All-Star Comedy Caper* in 1982. In the original shows and in most of the films, Daws Butler was the voice of Yogi, Don Messick was Boo Boo, and Julie Bennett was Cindy. In recent cartoons, which have been shown in syndication, Greg Burson has replaced the late Mr. Butler. Burson is good, but the animation has deteriorated along with the plots: Yogi joining a Top Gun training program, for example, depends not on timeless gags and Yogi's quest for food, but on familiarity with the film *Top Gun*. Yogi has had a healthy life in comic books, starring in forty-two issues of *Yogi Bear* from 1959 to 1970 (from Dell through No. 9, Gold Key thereafter), thirty-five issues from 1970 to 1976 (Charlton), nine issues from Marvel (1977 to 1979), and various one-shots.

YOU-ALL GIBBON
Pedigree. A comic book monkey who loathes healthful foods.
Biography. Known as "the junk-food monkey," and "the master of malnutrition," the white-haired You-All is a chimp who smokes a pipe, wears a plaid vest, and enjoys nothing more than "a bombasto-burger with all th' trimmings." You-All was raised in a zoo in the south, where he ate nothing but junk food until he was twelve. As a result, he "turned allergic to real food," and became an expert and proselytizer for synthetic sustenance. His adventures involve him with either the purveyors, opponents, or victims of junk food. Other animals that appeared in the strip during its run were the horse Graham Crackers, TV's Gallopin' Gourmet; the pig Mack Grabgrease, the fast-food king; Pig Boy, another fast-food entrepreneur; revolutionary Ratty Hearst; the giant monster Dogzilla; game show host Monty Halibut; the prehistoric boar Pig-Foot; and You-All's pure-food advocate nephew, singer Buffalo Chimps (to whom You-All is—you got it!—a monkey's uncle).

Comment. The character first appeared in Star*Reach Productions's *Quack* no. 1 in 1976, and starred in the next two issues as well. He also appeared in the only issue of *Wild Animals* (see **Ducky Duckbill**).

YUKK
Pedigree. Dog sidekick of TV's Mighty Man.
Biography. "The ugliest dog in the world," Yukk is a modern-day Medusa, the real power behind the team. Mighty Man is actually wealthy playboy Brandon Brucester, who uses a laser beam to shrink himself to the inch-high superhero Mighty Man. When the two go out to fight crime, Yukk wears a small doghouse on his head. Encountering criminals, the dog removes the doghouse and causes their prey to collapse in horror. Buildings, too, have a way of collapsing; this is one ugly mug! Among the duo's foes are Magnet Man, Goldteeth, Babyman, Glueman, Beach Bum, Catman, Kragg the Conquerer, Krime Clown, Evila, and the Malevolent Marble Man.

Comment. Ruby-Spears produced thirty-two episodes of *Mighty Man and Yukk*, which aired on *The Plastic Man Comedy Adventure Show* on ABC in 1979.

Z

ZERO

Pedigree. Pet dog of comic strip character Little Annie Rooney.

Biography. Annie is a twelve-year-old orphan who is adopted by the Robins family; Zero accompanies her on her many adventures around the world ("anyplace where there ain't hungry tigers that eat girls"). Originally, Zero was a big, long-muzzled dog. After two years, he was given the "cute" treatment, his size diminished and his muzzle shrunken.

Comment. An attempt to imitate the success of *Little Orphan Annie* (see **Sandy**), *Little Annie Rooney* was created by Brandon Walsh and debuted on January 10, 1929. It was discontinued in 1966. Although the theme was derivative, the exceptional, very cinematic artwork was always worth a look.

THE ZOO CREW

Pedigree. Comic book superheroes.

Biography. The Zoo Crew is a team of superheroic animals who reside on the world Earth-C in a parallel dimension—a world identical to our own, save that it's inhabited by anthropomorphic animals. (The C simply indicates that the animals' home isn't the only world like ours in another dimension.) The six animals become superheroes through a curious chain of events. While battling the starfishlike villain Starro the Conqueror, the superhero Superman rushes to intercept a deadly ray beamed at the C dimension. He grabs a meteor to use as a weapon, but the interaction of the beam and Superman's own alien energies metamorphose the space rock into something else. Chunks fall to the planet. One piece lands near cartoonist Roger Rodney Rabbit (not *that* Roger Rabbit), and it gives him the ability to "Bunny Hop" great heights, superstrength, the power to cause destructive shockwaves by stamping his feet, and supersenses. He dons a yellow bodysuit, red cape, cowl, and boots, and green trunks, and becomes Captain Carrot. Another piece comes down where metaphysics student Felina Furr is meditating. It turns a nearby chalkboard pointer into a wand from which, simply by willing it, she can gain the powers to peek into the near future, communicate telepathically, create small amounts of matter, levitate, teleport herself and others (even in the vacuum of space), and paralyze objects. She dons a red bodysuit and mask and assumes the superheroic identity Alley-Kat-Abra. Slowpoke turtle Timmy Joe Terrapin of Kornsas is the beneficiary of a third chunk of meteor. After quitting his job as a firefighter, he's racing to catch a bus when the rock arrives: In an explosion of speed, he passes the bus and finds that he can run nearly 1,500 miles an hour, create tornados and waterspouts by running in a circle, and even speed across water. He dons a blue bodysuit, cowl, gloves, and boots, and becomes the heroic Fastback. Rubberduck is born when a rock lands near actor Byrd Rentals while he's hot-tubbing at his Bel-Airedale mansion, giving an interview to gossip columnist Rova Barkitt. Byrd gains the ability to stretch to any length and shape, and dons a green bodysuit in honor of his new identity. The rock also transforms Rova into the superhero Yankee Poodle, who can repel objects with stars fired from her right paw, and attract them with stripes radiated from her left. The white-furred poodle with a red bodyshirt and blue trunks can also form a roadway through the skies with the stripes and propel herself along it using the stars. The last piece lands near **Peter Porkchops**, transforming him into Pig-Iron. The six heroes learn about each other from appearances on the TV news and, banding together as the Zoo Crew, they fight crime from their Z-shaped Z-Building in Gnu York. Captain Carrot is the leader of the Crew. He stands two feet, six inches and weighs forty-seven pounds. Among their many foes have been the huge and brawny Shaggy Dog, the wizard Feline Faust, the towering armadillo Armordillo, the malevolent mole Digger O'Doom, the evil owl Dr. Hoot, the giant monster Frogzilla, the extraterrestrial Bunny from Beyond, and the chimeric Amazoo, who is part elephant, gorilla, alligator, lion, and more. The heroes also teamed, once, with superanimals from Earth-C (who have recognizable human counterparts in our own world): Super Squirrel, Batmouse, Wonder Wabbit, Aquaduck, The Crash (i.e., the Flash), and Green Lambkin (Green Lantern).

Comment. Writers Roy Thomas and Gerry Conway and artist Scott Shaw created these characters, which debuted in a special insert in DC Comics's *New Teen Titans* no. 16 (1982). Their own title, *Captain Carrot and His Amazing Zoo Crew,* lasted twenty issues (1982 to 1983).

APPENDIX

Below is a list of all the animals in this book, grouped according to species. Major subspecies such as Super Cats and Vampire Ducks have been given their own headings.

Animals written in boldface letters have their own entries. All others can be found by consulting the entry following their name.

Aardvarks
Aarnie (Boner's Ark)
The Aardvark
Cedric (Bert Raccoon)
Cerebus the Aardvark
Cyril Sneer (Bert Raccoon)
Kerwin Keystone (also half platypus)
    (Newton: The Rabbit Wonder)

Alligators and Crocodiles
Albert the Alligator
Al Gator (Supermouse)
Beau (Wally Gator)
Ben Ali Gator (Hyacinth Hippo)
Big Tooth (Hong Kong Phooey)
Brer 'Gator (Brer Rabbit)
Crocobite (Spirit)
Croctor Strange (Spider-Ham)
Gate Gator (Atomic Mouse)
Gummy
Leatherhead (Teenage Mutant Ninja Turtles)
Mr. Knox (Bert Raccoon)
Rufus, The Red-Blooded American Reptile
Skids (The King)
Stan Croc (Fritz the Cat)
Wally Gator

Ants
Action Ant
Addam Antt (Hamster Vice)
Adolf (Jake Ant)
Anastasia Antnik (Atom Ant)
Ant (The Aardvark)
Ant-rew Sisters (Kermit the Frog)
Atom Ant
Charlie (Jake Ant)
Claude (Jake Ant)
Drab (Superswine)
Fred (Jake Ant)
Hadley (Jake Ant)
Harry (Jake Ant)
Harvey (Jake Ant)
Herm (Jake Ant)
Humbug (Suicide Squirrel)
Jake Ant
Joyce (Jake Ant)
Junior (Jake Ant)
Karate Ant (Atom Ant)

Larva 69 (Fritz the Cat)
Lyle (Garfield)
Maude (Jake Ant)
Mitch (Jake Ant)
Myrtle (Jake Ant)
Queen Beatrice (Action Ant)
Queen Ida (Jake Ant)
Shirley (Jake Ant)
Sidney (Jake Ant)
Uriah (Jake Ant)
Willard (Jake Ant)
Zeke (Jake Ant)
Zelda (Jake Ant)

Armadillos
Archie Armadillo (Tom and Jerry)
Armadillo (Man-Bat)
Armeil O'Dill (Bucky O'Hare)
Armordillo (Zoo Crew)
Colt: The Armadillo That Won the West

Badgers
Friar Tuck (King Leonidas)
Toby the Badger

Bats
Aqua-Bats (Moby Dick)
Bat Bat (Cutey Bunny)
Batfink
Belfry
Belfry Q. Bat (Crusader Rabbit)
Dingbats (Captain Jack)
Fidget (Basil of Baker Street)
Mad Bats, The (Steven Wolf)
Man-Bat
She-Bat (Man-Bat)

Bears (see also Koalas, Pandas, and Polar Bears)
Abner and Bridget Bear (Buttons Bear)
Bagshaw Bear (Mervin)
Baloo
Barney Bear (1)
Barney Bear (2)
Bearface (Kamikaze Cat)
Bearzanboltz (Duckula)
Benjamin Bear
Benny Bear (Chauncey Chirp)
Berenstain Bears (Care Bears)
Biggety Bear (Goofy Goose)
Billy Bear (Possible Possum)
Blackie Bear
Bobby Bear (Mr. Wild Wolf)
Bongo
Boo Boo Bear
Boris the Bear

Bozo Bear (Koko the Bear)
Bozo Bear (Peter Pig)
Brer Bear (Brer Rabbit)
Bruno Bear (Atomic Mouse)
Buddy Bears (Captain Teddy)
Buster Bear (Koko the Bear)
Buttons Bear
Calvin and The Colonel
Captain Teddy
Care Bears
C.B. Bears
Cindy Bear
Corban the Barbearian (Boris the Bear)
Crow of the Bear Clan
Cubby the Bear (Hot Dog)
Cubby the Bear (Super Duck)
Doc (Benjamin Bear)
Emmy Lou Bear (Kissyfur)
Farmer Bear (Supermouse)
Filmore Bear (Hoppity Hooper)
Fisherman Bear (King Leonidas)
Flabby (Gabby)
Fozzie Bear (Kermit the Frog)
Fuzzy Bear (Billy the Kid)
Gummi Bears
Gus (Kissyfur)
Hair Bear Bunch, The
Hamm's Bear, The
Harvey (Sidney Spider)
Hillbilly Bears
Horrible Harry (Wonder Duck)
Humphrey the Bear
Junior (Super Duck)
Kissyfur
Kit Cloudkicker (Baloo)
Koko the Bear
Lil' Herkimer (Supermouse)
Little Bears
Little Flying Bears (Care Bears)
Lulubelle (Bongo)
Lumpjaw (Bongo)
Maggie Bell (Calvin and the Colonel)
Mighty Bear (Koko the Bear)
Molly (Baloo)
Oliver Bear (Benjamin Bear)
Orbear (Spirit)
Petunia (Super Duck)
P.T. Bridgeport (Pogo Possum)
Rebecca Cunningham (Baloo)
Reddy Dough (Willie the Worm)
Roscoe Bear (Cosmo Cat)
Samson Bear (Big Bird)
Scarebear
Scrubby Bear
Smokey the Bear
Sue (Calvin and the Colonel)

Sugar Bear
SuperTed
Superteddy (**SuperTed**)
Tadpole
Terry Bears
Three Bears, The
Tubby Bear (**Spider-Ham**)
Wally (**Benjamin Bear**)
Winnie the Pooh
Wreckless (**Pre-Teen Dirty-Gene Kung-Fu Kangaroos**)
Yogi Bear

Beavers
Arthur the Beaver (**Bucky O'Hare**)
Beau Beaver (**Big Bird**)
Beaverlee (**Felix the Pig**)
Beavers, The (**Newton, the Rabbit Wonder**)
Benny Beaver (**Billy the Kid**)
Bernard, Bitsy, and Bucky Beaver (**Mr. Wild Wolf**)
Bill Beaver (**Billy the Kid** and **Hoppy, the Captain Marvel Bunny**)
Billy Beaver (**Supermouse**)
Bingo (**Care Bears**)
Buster Beaver (**Pigglys**)
Dicky Beaver (**Garfield**)
Miz Beaver (**Pogo Possum**)
Space Beaver
Time Beavers
Superbeaver (**Man-Bat**)
Toot (**Kissyfur**)

Bees
Billy and Bonnie Bee (**Chilly Willy**)
Bumble, the Bee-tective (**Hot Dog**)
Buzz-Buzz (**Three Mousketeers**)
Buzz-Buzz Bee
Honey (**Hoppity**)
Honey Nut Cheerios Bee (**Buzz-Buzz Bee**)
Mr. Bumble (**Hoppity**)
Video Victor

Beetles
Bootle Beetle
C. Bagley Beetle (**Hoppity**)

Birds
Birds (see also Buzzards, Canaries, Chickens, Condors, Crows, Dodos, Ducks, Eagles, Falcons, Geese, Hawks, Magpies, Myna Birds, Parakeets, Parrots, Pelicans, Pigeons, Ravens, Seagulls, Sparrows, Storks, Swans, Toucans, Turkeys, and Wrens)
Abacus (**Shoe**)
Apteryx (**John**)
Aracuan Bird
Bertie Bird (**Tom and Jerry**)
Bertie Birdbrain (**Professor Owl**)
Billie Bird (**Linus the Lionhearted**)
Braithwaite the Bird (**Toby the Badger**)

Cave Bird
Chauncey Chirp
Conservation Charlie (**Smokey the Bear**)
Dookey Bird (**John**)
Henri (**Feivel Mousekowitz**)
Humboldt Hummingbird (**Augie Doggie**)
Irving (**Shoe**)
Johnny Jay (**Chauncey Chirp**)
Katbird (**Krazy Kat**)
Kiwi Bird (**Roobear**)
Little Beeper (**Hamton**)
Mary Beth Malarkey (**Shoe**)
Miss Finch (**Big Bird**)
Muffy Hollandaise (**Shoe**)
Penelope Pinfeather (**Professor Owl**)
Pino (**Big Bird**)
Road Runner (**Wile E. Coyote**)
Robin (**Gnatrat**)
Roz (**Shoe**)
Sascha Grouse (**Linus the Lionhearted**)
Secretary Bird (**King Leonidas**)
Skyler (**Shoe**)
Sonny
Talon (**Bucky O'Hare**)
Tuki-Tuki Bird (**Ape**)
Wally (**Sharpie**)
Wernher von Bluebird (**Cap'n Catnip**)
Woodstock (**Snoopy**)

Bugs
Bugs (see also Bees, Beetles, Butterflies, Cockroaches, Crickets, Fleas, Flies, Grasshoppers, Ladybugs and Worms)
Andy (**Goofy Goose**)
Barny Blowfly (**Steven Wolf**)
Boll Weevil (**Pogo Possum**)
Bucky Bug (**Big Bad Wolf**)
Bugaloos (**Cattanooga Cats**)
Deacon Mantis McNulty (**Pogo Possum**)
Julius (**Goofy Goose**)
Mighty Mantis (**Action Ant**)
Mr. Bug (**Boner's Ark**)
Mr. Creeper (**Hoppity**)
Mr. Stinkbug (**Hoppity**)
X-Bugs (**Spider-Ham**)

Bulls
Bash-Boom Bull (**Pigglys**)
Elmer the Bull (**Elsie the Cow**)
Ferdinand the Bull
Man-Bull (**Man-Bat**)

Butterflies
McQueen Butterfly (**Duck "Bill" Platypus**)

Buzzards and Vultures
Beaky Buzzard
Beaumont (**Epic**)
Ben Buzzard (**Beaky Buzzard**)
Blast Off Buzzard (**The C.B. Bears**)
Brer Turkey Buzzard (**Brer Rabbit**)
Buzz Buzzard (**Wally Walrus**)
Gaylord

Igor (**Count Duckula**)
Montrose (**Gaylord**)
Pappy and Elvis (**Beaky Buzzard**)
Vultor (**American Rabbit**)

Camels
Kaboobie

Canaries
Big Bird
Canary Sisters (**Professor Owl**)
Coronary Canary (**Bullet Crow**)
Dagmar
Flippity (**Flop**)
Harry the Canary (**Ducky Duckbill**)
Nanny (**Count Duckula**)
Sweetie (**Hamton**)
Tweety Bird
Warbler, The (**Kamikaze Cat**)

Cats
Cats (see also Super Cats)
Alley-Kat-Abra (**Zoo Crew**)
Ambrose, the Robber Kitten (**Big Bad W**
Aristocats
Attila (**Grimm**)
Aunt Evelyn (**Garfield**)
Aunt Reba (**Garfield**)
Autocat (**Motormouse**)
Azrael
Babbit and Catstello
Bad Cat (**Augie Doggie**)
Baggypants
Bat-Cats (**Mighty Mouse**)
Beans
Bella (**Otto**)
Benny the Ball (**Top Cat**)
Bete Noire (**Poosy Gato**)
Beverly (**Fumbles**)
Big Bertha (**Fritz the Cat**)
Bill the Cat
Black Cat (**Courageous Cat**)
Blue the Cat (**Orson the Piglet**)
Boo
Boom Boom Pussini (**Heathcliff**)
Boopsie Meow (**Kamikaze Cat**)
Brain, The (**Top Cat**)
Captain Amerikat (**Spider-Ham**)
Captain Jack
Casual T. Cat
Catfather, The (**Heathcliff**)
Cat Gut (**Pound Puppies**)
Cattanooga Cats
Cattenstein (**Mighty Mouse**)
Catula (**Count Duckula**)
Catula (**Mighty Mouse**)
Charlemange (**Pound Puppies**)
Choo Choo (**Top Cat**)
Chops the Cat (**Augie Doggie**)
Chuck (**Omaha the Cat Dancer**)
Cinderkitty (**Count Duckula**)
Claude Cat
Comet Cat (**Spirit**)

Corporal Bruiser (**Heathcliff**)
Count Gatto (**Atomic Mouse**)
Creepy Cat
Cuffy Cat (**Supermouse**)
Delbert (**Smilin' Ed Smiley**)
Della Pussywillow (**Fritz the Cat**)
Delroy (**Maxwell**)
Desdemona
Doc (**Mr. Jinks**)
Douglas (**Supermouse**)
Drak Batfang (**Hot Dog**)
Erma Felna
Fancy Fancy (**Top Cat**)
Fat Cat (**Rescue Rangers**)
Fat Freddy's Cat
Fatkat
Feline Faust (**Zoo Crew**)
Felis (**Defiants**)
Felix the Cat
Fencer (**Foofur**)
Figaro
Firkin (**Maxwell**)
Flop
Fluffy (**Garfield**)
Fraidy Cat
Frankenstein's Cat (**Mighty Mouse**)
Fritz the Cat
Furrball (**Hamton**)
Gabrielle (**Fritz the Cat**)
Garfield
Gertie (**Atomic Mouse**)
Gideon (**J. Worthington Foulfellow**)
Goldie (**Top Cat**)
Guido (**Garfield**)
Hairball (**Pound Puppies**)
Heathcliff
Henry (**Heathcliff**)
Henry's Cat
Horse (**Dog [2]**)
Inky and Dinky (**Felix the Cat**)
Jane Feline
Jaune-Tom (**Mewsette**)
Jenny (**Bucky O'Hare**)
Joey (**Omaha the Cat Dancer**)
Julius the Cat
Kamikaze Cat
Kat Karson
Katnip (**Herman the Mouse**)
Kid's Cat, The
Kilkenny Cats (**Mighty Mouse**)
Kirby Cat (**Mr. Wild Wolf**)
Kitty
Kitty (**Dagmar**)
Kitty (**Doctor Whoot**)
Kittycat (**Barfy**)
Kitty Cuddles (**Buzzy the Crow**)
Kitz 'n' Katz
Klondike Kat
Korky the Cat (**Homeless Hector**)
Kosmo W. Cat
Kozy (**Kitz 'n' Katz**)
Krazy Kat

Kyle (**Tom and Jerry**)
Lionheart
Lola (**Bucky O'Hare**)
Lucifer
Madame Rubens-Chatte (**Mewsette**)
Manx (**Fred**)
Maxwell
Mehitabel (**Mewsette**)
Meowrice (**Mewsette**)
Mewsette
Milton
Miss Kitty (**Porky Pig**)
Miss Lil
Mr. Jack
Mr. Jinks
Mrs. Kat (**Krazy Kat**)
Mostly (**Bitsy**)
Motley the Cat
Ms. Arda Chevious (**Bucky O'Hare**)
Muffie (**Miss Lil**)
Naif the Waif (**Urban Gorilla**)
Nermal (**Garfield**)
Oil Can Harry (**Mighty Mouse**)
Oliver the Cat
Oliver Wendell McDuffy (**Bulldog Drumhead**)
Ollie the Merry Mouser (**Toby the Badger**)
Omaha the Cat Dancer
O'Malley the Alley Cat (**Aristocats**)
Pat Th' Cat
Percy (**Little Roquefort**)
Pete
Pierre (**Top Cat**)
P.M. (**Poosy Gato**)
Poosy Gato
Punkin Puss (**Hillbilly Bears**)
Pussy (**Hubie and Bertie**)
Pussyfoot
Pussy Willow (**Kosmo W. Cat**)
Puttypuss (**Houndcats**)
Radio Catts (**Kid's Cat**)
Reddy (**Ruff and Reddy**)
Sad Cat (**Possible Possum**)
Salem
Scat Cat (**Aristocats**)
Scat Cat (**Skatebirds**)
Scratch (**Biskitts**)
Sebastian (1)
Seymour (**Rude Dog**)
Shadow (**Atomic Mouse**)
Shelley (**Omaha the Cat Dancer**)
Siamese Twins, The (**Heathcliff**)
Si and Am (**Lady and Tramp**)
Silver Dollar Dan (**Kat Karson**)
Snowball (**Tom and Jerry**)
Soapy (**Neil the Horse**)
Sonja (**Heathcliff**)
Sourpuss (**Gandy Goose**)
Spook (**Top Cat**)
Spooky
Spot (**Hong Kong Phooey**)

Streaky the Super-Cat
"Stupid Cat" (**Snoopy**)
Stutz (**Houndcats**)
Super Snooper
Sylvester the Cat
Terrible Tom (**Supermouse**)
Three Little Kittens (**Three Bears**)
Tibs (**Pongo and Perdita**)
Tiger (**Feivel Mousekowitz**)
Tom (**Tom and Jerry**)
Top Cat
Tuffy the Cat (**Mervin**)
Tuffy the Cat (**Supermouse**)
Uncle Barney, a k a Aunt Bernice (**Garfield**)
Victoria (**Jane Feline**)
Vocal (**Cyborg Gerbils**)
Waldo Kitty
Waldo the Cat (**Fritz the Cat**)
Whizzy (**Streaky the Super-Cat**)
Winston (**Fritz the Cat**)
Wizard of Paws (**Count Duckula**)
Zipper (**Care Bears**)

Chameleons
Cold Blooded Chameleon Commandos

Cheetahs
Chester Cheetah

Chickens, Hens, and Roosters
Bantam of the Opera (**Sherlock Monk**)
Barbequed (**G.I. Jackrabbits**)
Battling Bantam (**Billy the Kid**)
Bernice, the Whiffle Hen
Booker (**Orson the Piglet**)
Camilla the Chicken (**Kermit the Frog**)
Charlie Chicken (**Andy Panda and Homer Pigeon**)
Clara Cluck
Cleo Elizabeth (**Augie Doggie**)
Dr. Chickenstein (**Spider-Ham**)
Egbert
Fission Chicken
Foghorn Leghorn
Gyro Gearloose
Lady Baden-Baden (**Bert Raccoon**)
Miss Prissy
Mrs. Kakkil (**Krazy Kat**)
Nadine (**Garfield**)
Nuke Chicken (**Fission Chicken**)
Panchito
Peckers, The
Popo the Rooster (**Poosy Gato**)
Rooster Squad (**Hamster Vice**)
Roy the Rooster (**Orson the Piglet**)
Rudy Rooster (**Dinky Duck**)
Rupert the Chick (**Homeless Hector**)
Sheldon (**Orson the Piglet**)
Super Chicken

Chipmunks
Chip Chipmunk (**Dizzy Dog**)
Chipettes, the (**Chipmunks**)
Chipmunks, The
Chip 'n' Dale
Clarice (**Chip 'n' Dale**)
Kung Fu Kid (**Pre-Teen Dirty-Gene
    Kung-Fu Kangaroos**)

Clams
Harv (**John**)
Shirley (**John**)

Cockroaches
Ahmed (**Opus the Penguin**)
Archy (**Mewsette**)
Arnie (**Domino Chance**)
Digit (**Feivel Mousekowitz**)
Domino Chance
Eduardo (**Opus the Penguin**)
Paco (**Miami Mice**)
"Troubles" Galore (**Domino Chance**)

Condors
Cal Condom (**Duck "Bill" Platypus**)

Cows
Calvin Cow (**Goofy Goose**)
Captain Bull (**Willie the Worm**)
Clarabelle Cow
Duchess (**Pongo and Perdita**)
Elsie the Cow
Esmeralda (**Homer Pigeon**)
Miss Cud (**Porky Pig**)
Moooomy, The (**Spider-Ham**)
Princess (**Pongo and Perdita**)
Queenie (**Pongo and Perdita**)
Yak (**Tennessee Tuxedo**)

Coyotes
Calamity Coyote (**Hamton**)
Charlie Coyote (**Tom and Jerry**)
Colonel Kit Coyote (**Go Go Gophers**)
Droopalong Coyote (**Ricochet Rabbit**)
Wile E. Coyote

Crabs
Crab Men (**Moby Dick**)
Crusty (**Henry Limpet**)
Sebastian

Crickets
Jiminy Cricket

Crows
Blackie Crow (**Atomic Mouse**)
Brer Crow (**Brer Rabbit**)
Bullet Crow
Buzzy the Crow
Crawford Crow (**Ducky Duckbill**)
Crawford C. Crow (**Fauntleroy Fox**)

Dik-Dik (**Ralph, the Righteous, Radical,
    Rasslin' Rhino**)
Flip the Bird
Ho-Ho (**Boner's Ark**)
Nutsy McKrow (**Mickey Mouse**)
Punchy (**Atomic Mouse**)
Skywalker (**G.I. Jackrabbits**)

Deer
Bambi
Deerdevil the Cloven-Hooved Mammal
    Without Fear (**Spider-Ham**)
Faline (**Bambi**)
Great Prince (**Bambi**)
Ronno (**Bambi**)

Dinosaurs
Alice Saurus (**Ducky Duckbill**)
Amber (**Dink**)
Bronto
Bronty the Brontosaurus (**Ducky Duckbill**)
Cera (**Littlefoot**)
Denver, the Last Dinosaur (**Dink**)
Dink
Dinny the Dinosaur
Dino the Dinosaur
Ducky (**Littlefoot**)
Ducky Duckbill
Flapper (**Dink**)
Gertie the Dinosaur
Glomb (**Bronto**)
Hoppy the Hopperoo (**Dino the Dinosaur**)
Littlefoot
Petrie (**Littlefoot**)
Rex (**Boner's Ark**)
Rooter (**Littlefoot**)
Scat (**Dink**)
Shyler (**Dink**)
Snoots (**Dino the Dinosaur**)
Spike (**Littlefoot**)
Tog (**Moby Dick**)
Tootsie (**Scrooge McDuck**)
Trixie (**Pokey**)

Dodos
Bobo (**Duck "Bill" Platypus**)
Dodo Family (**Big Bird**)
Dunbar Dodo (**J. Fenimore Frog**)
Ork (**Moby Dick**)

Dogs
Ace, the Bat-Hound
Adam Fink (**Captain Jack**)
Alpo (**Gnatrat**)
Amos Goofy (**Goofy**)
Annabel
Argyle (**Smilin' Ed Smiley**)
Ashley (**Farley**)
Astro
Augie Doggie
Augie the Dog (**Atomic Mouse**)
Aunt Matilda (**Goofy**)

Backstroke McBull (**Peter Pig**)
Bandit
Barfy
Barkley (**Big Bird**)
Barkleys, The
Bar-ko (**Thunderbunny**)
Barky (**Bucky O'Hare**)
Beagle Boys, The
Beagles, The (**Banana Splits, The**)
Beans (**Mr. Jack**)
Beauregard Bugleboy (**Pogo Possum**)
Beegle Beagle (**Grape Ape**)
Beezlebub (**Captain Jack**)
Belle (**Snoopy**)
Belvedere
Bib (**Rusty**)
Big Paw (**Pound Puppies**)
Bimbo
Biskitts
Bitsy
Black Fury (**Porky Pig**)
Black Terrier (**Hot Dog**)
Blue Beagle (**Lionheart**)
Bold Knight (**Supermouse**)
Boris (**Lady and Tramp**)
Bow Wow Bandit (**Quick Draw McGraw**)
Bowzer
Boy
Bozo
Brain
Brandon (**Dozer**)
Braveheart
Bristle Hound (**Mildew Wolf**)
Bristletooth (**Kwicky Koala**)
Broo (**Bert Raccoon**)
Bruno (**Lucifer**)
Bruno (**Urban Gorilla**)
Bubbles
Buffalo Bill Goofy (**Goofy**)
Buford
Bull (**Lady and Tramp**)
Bulldog Drumhead
Bullet
Bullseye and Tricky John
Bumper (**Bitsy**)
Bungle Brothers, The (**Kwicky Koala**)
Buster (**Bowzer**)
Butch
Butch the Pup (**Hot Dog**)
Canine the Barbarian (**Neil the Horse**)
Canis (**Defiants**)
Captain Bark Rogers (**Hot Dog**)
Captain Cleo (**Hero**)
Captain Ebeneezer Goofy (**Goofy**)
Carl (**Grimm**)
Caveman Goofy, aka Neanderthal Goofy
    (**Goofy**)
Charlie Dog (**Foghorn Leghorn**)
Chasney Zweibach (**Steven Wolf**)
Chester (**Skatebirds**)
Chester (**Sylvester the Cat**)
Chief (**Tod and Copper**)

Mop Top (Dozer)
Morty the Dog
Ms. Lion
Mumbly
Musselmutt (Houndcats)
Muttley
Muttsy
Nancy (Kat Karson)
Napoleon
Napoleon (Aristocats)
Nugget
Nutsy (Lady and Tramp)
Nypto (Krypto)
Oddball Couple, The
Odie (Garfield)
Officer B. Pupp (Krazy Kat)
Olaf (Snoopy)
Old Black Goofy (Goofy)
Old Red
Old Reliable (Lady and Tramp)
Old Whiff
Orbit (Dozer)
Otto
Paddlefoot
Pajamas (Epic)
Pansy (Kat Karson)
Pasha Poodle (Weakheart [2])
Paw Paws (Biskitts)
Pedro (Lady and Tramp)
Peg (Lady and Tramp)
Pepe (Foofur)
Percival Goofy (Goofy)
Pesky Pooch (Supermouse)
Pete the Pup (Fido [1])
Peter Pupp
Pilgrim Goofy (Goofy)
Pip (Homeless Hector)
Pluto the Pup
Pluto, Jr. (Pluto the Pup)
Police Chief O'Hara (Super Goof)
Police Dog (Fido [1])
Pongo and Perdita
Pooch (1)
Pooch (2)
Poochie (Dagmar)
Poochies (Pound Puppies)
Poopsie (Jake Ant)
Popski (Homeless Hector)
Pound Puppies
Precious Pup
Prince
Prince, the Wonder Dog (Pluto the Pup)
Prince Charles (Dog [2])
Professor Invento (Atomic Mouse)
Professor Shaggy Dog (Courageous Cat)
Pup Star
Pupsy (Muttsy)
Rex, the Wonder Dog
Rhubarb (Houndcats)
Ribbons (Bitsy)
Rita (Oliver the Cat)
Rivets (Bitsy)

Rocki (Foofur)
Rodney (Fatkat)
Roscoe (Oliver the Cat)
Roscoe the Dawg, Ace Detective
Rot (Rude Dog)
Rover (Bugs Bunny and Porky Pig)
Rover (Fifi)
Rowlf the Dog (Kermit the Frog)
Rude Dog
Ruff
Ruff (Ruff and Reddy)
Rufferto
Rusty
Sam (Barfy)
Sam (Flop)
Sam (Maxwell)
Sam Sheepdog
Sandy (1)
Scamp (Lady and Tramp)
Scamp (Toby the Badger)
Schaeffer (Bert Raccoon)
Schnoz (Tom and Jerry)
Scooby-Doo
Scooby-Dum (Scooby-Doo)
Scrappy-Doo (Scooby-Doo)
Seadog
Senor Dog (Poosy Gatto)
Shaggy Dog (Zoo Crew)
Shamus
Sherlock (Kitty)
Sieg (Old Red)
Silly the Dog (Supermouse)
Sir Cedric Goofy (Goofy)
Sir Cumference (Goofy)
Sir Hound and Lady Hound (Pigglys)
Sir Loinsteak (Goofy)
Smidgen (Bugs Bunny)
Smilie (Bitsy)
Snapper (Buzzy the Crow)
Snert
Snoopy
Snuffles (Quick Draw McGraw)
Sonar (Bullseye and Tricky John)
Sophia (Bert Raccoon)
Sourdough Sam (Scrooge McDuck)
Spike (Droopy)
Spike (Heathcliff)
Spike (Snoopy)
Spike (Sylvester the Cat)
Spike (Tom and Jerry)
Spot (Boner's Ark)
Spotty
Spotty the Pup (Hot Dog)
Stripe
Super Goof
Sweet Polly Purebred (Underdog)
Swifty (Krypto)
Thunderbolt (Pongo and Perdita)
Thunderclap (Hero)
Tige
Tinymite (Peter Pupp)
Tippie

Tito (Oliver the Cat)
Toby (Basil of Baker Street)
Toby the Pup (Yippie)
Top Dog
Tornado
Toughy (Lady and Tramp)
Towser (Pongo and Perdita)
Tramp (Lady and Tramp)
Trouble (Shamus)
Trusty (Lady and Tramp)
Trypto the Acid Dog
Tyke (Tom and Jerry)
Uncle Fernando (Foofur)
Uncle Joe Goofy (Goofy)
Underdog
Valentino (Nellie)
Virgil (Bitsy)
Vypto (Krypto)
Wagger (Homeless Hector)
Wags
Watt A. Dogg (Peter Pupp)
Weakheart (1)
Weakheart (2)
Wellington Bulldog (Sylvester the Cat)
Whimper (Woofer and Whimper)
Wilbur Goofy (Goofy)
Winston
Winter (G.E.R.M.IN Shepherd)
Wonder Dog
Woofer
Woofer and Whimper
Wyatt Goofy (Goofy)
Yankee Poodle (Zoo Crew)
Yellow Dog
Yippie
Yippie, Yappie, and Yahooey
Yukk
Zero
Zypto (Krypto)

Dolphins
Surfstreak (Pre-Teen Dirty-Gene Kung-Fu
    Kangaroos)

Donkeys, Jackasses, and Mules
Aunt Sukey (Bullet)
Baba Looey (Quick Draw McGraw)
Benny Burro (Maud)
Benny Burro (Tom and Jerry)
Burrito (Maud)
Don Kiyoti (Krazy Kat)
Doubtful Donkey (Boris the Bear)
Eeyore (Winnie the Pooh)
Flying Donkeybird (Donald Duck)
Maud
Torchy (Old Red)

Ducks (see also Vampire Ducks)
Ace Duck (Teenage Mutant Ninja Turtles)
Alien Ducklings
Aquaduck (Zoo Crew)
Baby Huey

Bleep (Sebastian)
Bubba Duck (Scrooge McDuck)
Buck Duck (Wacky Duck)
Captain Huey (Cutey Bunny)
Chuck the Duck (Sherlock Monk)
Chug Chug Curtis (Pogo Possum)
Colonel Jones (Erma Felna)
Crazy Duck (Wacky Duck)
"Crowbar" McQuack (Baby Huey)
Daffy Duck
Daisy Duck
Daphne/Fanny (Gus Goose)
Daphne Duck (Daffy Duck)
Darkwing Duck
Dead-Eye Duck (Bucky O'Hare)
Delta Duck (Super Duck)
Dick Duck
Dickie Duck (Wacky Duck)
Dicky Duck (Homeless Hector)
Dildo Duck (Fritz the Cat)
Dimwitty (Moby Duck)
Dingy Duck (Lionheart)
Dinky Duck
Dipstick Duck (Mickey Money)
Dirty Duck
Dizzy Duck (Wacky Duck)
Donald Duck
Doodles Duck
Doofus (Scrooge McDuck)
Dorie Duck (Atomic Mouse)
Drakestar (Bucky O'Hare)
Duckaneer
Duckbots
Ducks of Hazard, The (SuperTed)
Duke "Destroyer" Duck
Dumbella (Huey, Dewey, and Louie)
Dumphy Duck, the No-Luck Duck (Ducky Duckbill)
Edwina Duck (Buttons Bear)
Fauntleroy (Super Duck)
Fenton/Gismo Duck (Gyro Gearloose and Scrooge McDuck)
Gertrude (Dozer)
Grandma Duck
Howard the Duck
Hell's Ducks (Neil the Horse)
Huey, Dewey, and Louie
Irwin the Disco Duck
Kant (Super Duck)
Kvack (Snert)
Launchpad McQuack (Darkwing Duck)
Lucky Duck
Ludwig Von Drake
Magica de Spell
Man-Drake the Musician (Duke "Destoyer" Duck)
Midnite Mallard (Duke "Destroyer" Duck)
Millard Mallard (Duke "Destroyer" Duck)
Moby Duck
Mrs. Beakley (Scrooge McDuck)
Mrs. Kwakk Wakk (Krazy Kat)
Muddlefoots (Darkwing Duck)

Platterpuss (Felix the Pig)
Plucky Duck (Hamton)
Quackmore (Donald Duck)
Quackup (Scarebear)
Quacky the Duck (Lionheart)
Quax Bedroom (Lionheart)
Rubberduck (Zoo Crew)
Scrooge McDuck
Shoe, a k a P. Martin Shoemaker
Sir Drake McDuck (Scrooge McDuck)
Super Duck
Uwanna (Super Duck)
Wade the Duck (Orson the Piglet)
Wacky Duck
Webigail, a k a Webby (Scrooge McDuck)
Webster Webfoot (Yakky Doodle)
Wonder Duck
Yakky Doodle

Eagles
Avenger
Baldy (Tennessee Tuxedo)
Edmond Eagle (Bullet Crow)
Emil Eagle (Gyro Gearloose)
Ethel and Egbert Eagle (Grover Groundhog)
Legal Eagle (Avenger)
Sam the Eagle (Kermit the Frog)
Soar (Pre-Teen Dirty-Gene Kung-Fu Kangaroos)

Eels
Electrik Eel (Ralph, the Righteous, Radical, Rasslin' Rhino)
El Eel the Heel (Jabberjaw)

Elephants and Mastodons
Alice and Aloysuis Snuffleupagus (Kermit the Frog)
Babar the Elephant
Baby Snoots
Catty (Dumbo)
Celeste (Babar the Elephant)
Dolores
Dumbo
Eleroo (also part Kangaroo) (Wuzzles)
Elfalump
Elmer Elephant (Big Bad Wolf)
Ghoonga (Daro)
Giggles (Dumbo)
Jum the Elephant (Homeless Hector)
Jumbo the Elephant (Homeless Hector)
Matriarch (Dumbo)
Mrs. Jumbo (Dumbo)
Ollie Elephant (Flip the Bird)
Packy (Fraidy Cat)
Power Pachyderms
Prissy (Dumbo)
Rollo (Moby Dick)
Shep (Ape)
Sidney the Elephant
Snorky (Banana Splits)

Tawn
Undercover Elephant

Falcons
Redwing (Hero)

Ferrets
Ferrence the Fencing Ferret (Dizzy Dog)

Fireflies
Freddy Firefly (Willie the Worm)

Fish (see also Eels, Goldfish, Octopi, Sharks, Squids, and Tunas)
Blophish (Inspector Gill)
Brer Fish (Brer Rabbit)
Catfish the Hunter (Jabberjaw)
Fin 'n' Butch (Supermouse)
Fishy, the Ninja Flounder (Sun, the 4-D Monkey)
Flounder (Sebastian [2])
George (Inspector Gill)
Henry Limpet
Hook (Inspector Gill)
Inspector Gill
Katfish (Krazy Kat)
Ladyfish (Henry Limpet)
Mr. Codfish (King Leonidas)
Monty Halibut (You-All Gibbon)
Piranha (Man-Bat)
Splash (G.I. Jackrabbits)

Fleas
Ferocious Flea (Atom Ant)

Flies
Baxter Stockman (Teenage Mutant Ninja Turtles)
Fearless Fly
Ferocious Fly (Fearless Fly)
Florrie (Fearless Fly)
Fly, The (Sidney Spider)
Harry the Horsefly (Nightmare)
Horsie the Horsefly (Fearless Fly)
Lady Deflylah (Fearless Fly)
Napoleon Bonefly (Fearless Fly)
Swat the Fly (Hoppity)
Tse-Tse (Man-Bat)
Zipper (Rescue Rangers)

Foxes
Brer Fox (Brer Rabbit)
Captain Stone (Doctor Whoot)
Colonel, The (Calvin and The Colonel)
Colonel Hitzok (Erma Felna)
Commander Foxx (Space Beaver)
Count, The (Egbert)
Count of Crud (Smilin' Ed Smiley)
Ding-a-Ling (Hokey Wolf)
Don Karnage (Baloo)
Fanny Fox (Mr. Wild Wolf)
Fauntleroy Fox

Fibber (**Yakky Doodle**)
Fox (**Hunter**)
Fox (**Wonder Duck**)
Foxy
Foxy Fagan (**Fauntleroy Fox**)
Horace N. Buggy (**Woody Woodpecker**)
Jennifer Dawn Logan (**Bucky O'Hare**)
J. Worthington Foulfellow
Kes Jurorko (**Bucky O'Hare**)
Krystal Kringle
Lamont Red (**Crow of the Bear Clan**)
Nero Fox (**Peter Porkchops**)
Prince Alfon Kashota (**Lionheart**)
Quick Brown Fox (**Rapid Rabbit**)
Red Swamp Fox (**Possible Possum**)
Rusty Fox (**Buttons Bear**)
Seminole Sam (**Pogo Possum**)
Sharpy Fox (**Fauntleroy Fox**)
Shifty Fox (**Supermouse**)
Sis Fox (**Newton, the Rabbit Wonder**)
Slylock Fox (**Pigglys**)
Tod (**Tod and Copper**)
Varcel (**Bucky O'Hare**)
Vicky
Waldo the Fox (**Hoppity Hooper**)
Whitey (**Crow of the Bear Clan**)

Frogs
Baron Silas Greenback (**Danger Mouse**)
Brer Frog (**Brer Rabbit**)
Brother Froghorn (**Duck "Bill" Platypus**)
Burger Kingpin (**Gnatrat**)
Conrad
Crazylegs (**Super Duck**)
Flip the Frog
Freddie
Freddie the Frog (**Cattanooga Cats**)
Fremont Frog (**Ducky Duckbill**)
Frog (**Courageous Cat**)
Genghis Frog (**Teenage Mutant Ninja Turtles**)
Herbie (**Garfield**)
Herman Hop-Toad (**Three Mouseketeers**)
Hoppity Hooper
J. Fenimore Frog
Kermit the Frog
Leon the Frog (**Kermit the Frog**)
Lucifer (**Bullet**)
Michigan J. Frog
Mr. Frog (**Bunson Bunny**)
Mr. Kroke (**Krazy Kat**)
Nanette (**Toad**)
Nonette (**Toad**)
Nuclear Spawned Martial Arts Frogs (**Nato, the Samurai Squirrel**)
Nurnette (**Toad**)
Robin (**Kermit the Frog**)
Robin Hood (**King Leonidas**)
Spot
Tad (**Toad**)
Tadpole (**Gnatrat**)
Ted (**Toad**)

Tijuana Toads
Toad
Toadus (**Moby Dick**)
Todd (**Toad**)

Geese
Agnes (**Gandy Goose**)
Charolette (**Bucky O'Hare**)
Denver Goose (**Newton, the Rabbit Wonder**)
Dr. Von Goosewing (**Count Duckula**)
Gabby Goose
Ganda (**Bucky O'Hare**)
Gandy Goose
Gladstone Gander
Godfrey Goose (**Roger Rabbit**)
Goofy Gander (**Supermouse**)
Goofy Goose
Goose Rider (**Spider-Ham**)
Gus Goose
Lucy Goose (**Pongo and Perdita**)
Luke the Goose (**Gus Goose**)
Mom (**Boner's Ark**)
Mrs. Gobblechin (**Donald Duck**)
Sis Goose (**Brer Rabbit**)
Vanna Von Goosewing (**Count Duckula**)

Gerbils
Cyborg Gerbils
Geriatric Gangrene Jujitsu Gerbils
Womble, the Wonder Gerbil (**Cap'n Catnip**)

Giraffes
Arsenic (**J. Rufus Lion**)
Cleo the Giraffe (**Sidney the Elephant**)
Georgie Giraffe (**Homeless Hector**)
Lookout (**Boner's Ark**)

Goats
Billy the Kid
Brer Bill Goat (**Newton, the Rabbit Wonder**)
Buttinsky (**Supermouse**)
Gabby Goat
Kid Gloves (**Billy the Kid**)
Three Billy Goats (**Three Bears**)

Goldfish
Alvin (**Dagmar**)
Bianca
Cleo (**Figaro**)
Finny the Goldfish (**Buzzy the Crow and Herman the Mouse**)
Goldie (**Inspector Gill**)
Lassie (**Grimm**)

Gophers
Goofus the Gopher (**Koko the Bear**)
Gopher (**Howard the Duck**)
Gopher (**Winnie the Pooh**)
Gopher Gus (**Duke "Destroyer" Duck**)
Go Go Gophers
Guerrilla Gophers (**Pre-Teen Dirty-Gene Kung-Fu Kangaroos**)

Mac 'n' Tosh
Mildly Microwaved Pre-Pubescent Kung-Fu Gophers
Space Gophers (**Cutey Bunny**)
Vincent Van Gopher (**Deputy Dawg**)

Gorillas
Ape
Bing Bong (**Mumbly**)
Bingo (**Banana Splits, The**)
Bruto (**Man-Bat**)
Chandu (**Titano, the Super-Ape**)
Congorilla
Djuba the Red Gorilla
Dopey the Ape (**Porky Pig**)
Dum-Dum (**Boner's Ark**)
Elvis Gorilla (**Kermit the Frog**)
Fearo (**Underdog**)
Gore-illa (**Spirit**)
Gorgonzelda (**Urban Gorilla**)
Gorilla Boss (**Man-Bat**)
Gorilla Grodd
Grape Ape
Kid Kong (**SuperTed**)
Killer Diller Gorilla (**Atom Ant**)
King Klong (**McSnurtle the Turtle, the Terrific Whatzit**)
King Klong (**Muttley**)
King Krypton (**Titano, the Super-Ape**)
Kios (**Gorilla Grodd**)
Konko (**Duck "Bill" Platypus**)
Magilla Gorilla
Mod Gorilla Boss (**Man-Bat**)
Mrs. Gorilla (**Porky Pig**)
Nazi Gorilla (**Dirty Duck**)
Ping Pong (**American Rabbit**)
Sam Simeon
Sgt. Gorilla
Skippy (**Urban Gorilla**)
Solovar (**Gorilla Grodd**)
Square (**The King**)
Super-Ape (**Krypto**)
Titano, The Super-Ape
Tracy (**Belfry**)
Urban Gorilla

Grasshoppers
Hoppity
Wilbur (**Goofy**)

Groundhogs
Grover Groundhog
Grover Groundhog (**Porky Pig**)
Guerrilla Groundhog

Hamsters
Adolescent Radioactive Black Belt Hamsters
Alien Hamsterlings (**Alien Ducklings**)
Amster the Hamster (**Dizzy Dog**)
Hamster Vice
Penfold (**Danger Mouse**)

Hawks
Cosmo Fishhawk (**Shoe**)
Hamilton Hawk (**Three Mouseketeers**)
Henery Hawk
Humphrey "Blowhard" Bohawk (**Chauncey Chirp**)
Tally-Hawk (**Spirit**)

Hippopotamuses
Big H (**The King**)
Green Mist, The (**Superswine**)
Henrietta the Hippo (**Cattanooga Cats**)
Hippo (**Boner's Ark**)
Hoppopotamus (also part Rabbit) (**Wuzzles**)
Hyacinth Hippo
Lasagna Loves (**Gnatrat**)
Mrs. Hippo (**Oswald, the Lucky Rabbit**)
Peter Potamus
Tub (**Duck "Bill" Platypus**)
Tubby Hippo (**Atomic Mouse**)

Horses
Arab (**Sandy [2]**)
Aragorn (**Hero**)
Aram (**Kat Karson**)
Arrow (**Spirit**)
Banshee
Bertram
Betsy (**Fifi**)
Black Fury
Blaze (**Sandy [2]**)
Buckshot (**Sandy [2]**)
Bullet (**Sandy [2]**)
Calico (**Sandy [2]**)
Captain (**Horace Horsecollar**)
Captain, The (**Pongo and Perdita**)
Captain Itzak Arrat (**Erma Felna**)
Comet, the Super-Horse
Cyclone
Cyril Proudbottom (**Horace Horsecollar**)
Danny Dobbin (**Nightmare**)
Diablo (**Hero**)
Dobbin (**Grandma Duck**)
Epic
Francis the Famous Talking Mule (**Black Fury**)
Frou-Frou (**Aristocats**)
Fury (TV horse) (**Black Fury**)
Fury (**Sandy [2]**)
Graham Crackers (**You-All Gibbon**)
Gunpowder (**Horace Horsecollar**)
Harry Horse (**Flip the Bird**)
Hayburner (**Super Goof**)
Hero
Horace Horsecollar
Horse Face Harry (**Quick Draw McGraw**)
Hurricane (**Hero**)
Jolly Jumper
Kamesa (**Sandy [2]**)
L'Ming (**Bucky O'Hare**)
Lucifer (**2**)
Major (**Horace Horsecollar**)

Mighty Stallion (**Spirit**)
Mister Ed (**Black Fury**)
Murgatroyd (**Snagglepuss**)
Neil the Horse
Nellie
Nightmare
Nightwind
Nightwind (**Sandy [2]**)
Old Moe (**Horace Horsecollar**)
Pardner (**Sandy [2]**)
Percy (**Horace Horsecollar**)
Pokey
Pony Boy (**Spark Plug**)
Pronto (**Fearless Fly**)
Quick Draw McGraw
Racer (**Sandy [2]**)
Raider (**Sandy [2]**)
Rover Boy no. 6 (**Horace Horsecollar**)
Sagebrush Sal (**Quick Draw McGraw**)
Samson (**Horace Horsecollar**)
Sandy (2)
Silver (**Black Fury**)
Sixty (**Kat Karson**)
Sliver (**Supermouse**)
Snapshot III (**Horace Horsecollar**)
Spark Plug
Spirit
Starlite (**Care Bears**)
Steel
Storm (**Spirit**)
Stormy (**Sandy [2]**)
Super Horse (**Sandy [2]**)
Thunder (**Hero**)
Thunder (**Sandy [2]**)
Thunderbolt (**Horace Horsecollar**)
Tippie-Toes
Trigger (**Black Fury**)
Valinor (**Hero**)
War Stallion (**Spirit**)
Whirlwind (**Sandy [2]**)
White Wind (**Hero**)
Widowmaker (**Horace Horsecollar**)
Wildfire (**Spirit**)
Windspirit (**Spirit**)
Winged Victory (**Hero**)

Hyenas
Hardy Har Har (**Lippy the Lion**)
Hyena (**Boner's Ark**)

Jackals
Jackals, The (**American Rabbit**)
J. Jonah Jackal (**Spider-Ham**)
Roon

Jaguars
Jagwar (**Teenage Mutant Ninja Turtles**)

Kangaroos
Battling Barney (**Beans**)
Bingo (**Hero**)
Boomer Blue (**Erma Felna**)

Dinny Kangaroo (**Linus the Lionhearted**)
Eleroo (also part Elephant) (**Wuzzles**)
Gracie (**Hippety Hopper**)
Hippety Hopper
Hip Hop (**Pre-teen Dirty-Gene Kung-Fu Kangaroos**)
Kanga (**Winnie the Pooh**)
Kenny Kangaroo (**Pigglys**)
Kid Botts (**McSnurtle the Turtle, the Terrific Whatzit**)
Kip (**Tyg**)
Peach Pluckin' Kangaroo (**Deputy Dawg**)
Pre-Teen Dirty-Gene Kung-Fu Kangaroos
Roo (**Winnie the Pooh**)
Sub-Marsupial (**Spider-Ham**)
Susie Spring and Junior (**Chauncey Chirp**)

Koalas
Cubcake (**Boner's Ark**)
Euripides (**Space Beaver**)
Jeremiah Koala (**Kwicky Koala**)
Koalakeet (also part Parakeet) (**Wuzzles**)
Kokey Koala (**Koko the Bear**)
Kuddly Koala (**Duck "Bill" Platypus**)
Kwicky Koala
Laura Bear (**Roobear**)
Mr. and Mrs. Koala Bear (**Roobear**)
Naive Inter-Dimensional Commando Koalas
Noozles
Roobear

Komodo Dragons
Komodo (**Defiants**)

Ladybugs
Mrs. Ladybug (**Hoppity**)
Mrs. Ladybug (**Three Mouseketeers**)

Lions (see also Lynxes, Panthers and Tigers)
Astro-Lion (**Spirit**)
Brutus
Bumblion (also part Bee) (**Wuzzles**)
Drooper (**Banana Splits, The**)
Finko the Fang and the Howl's Angels (**Pink Panther**)
Fred (**Super Chicken**)
Itchy Brother (**Biggy Rat**)
J. Rufus Lion
King, The
King Leonardo
King Leonidas
King Oscar (**Peter Porkchops**)
Leo the Lion (**Beaky Buzzard**)
Leo the Lion (**Homeless Hector**)
Leon the Lyin' Lion (**Atomic Mouse**)
Lester Lion (**Spider-Ham**)
Linus the Lionhearted
Lionheart (**Pre-Teen Dirty-Gene Kung-Fu Kangaroos**)
Lippy the Lion
Louie the Lion (**Buzzy the Crow**)
Lyle (**Boner's Ark**)

Pigeon Pete (Grover Groundhog)
Tattler (Urban Gorilla)
Yankee Doodle Pigeon (Muttley)

Pigs, Boars, and Warthogs
Bacon Brigade (Wonder Wart-Hog)
Bebop (Teenage Mutant Ninja Turtles)
Boaro, the Karate Pig (Sun, the 4-D Monkey)
Captain Link Heartthrob (Miss Piggy)
Cicero (Porky Pig)
Crackle the Pig (Homeless Hector)
Dr. Strangepork (Miss Piggy)
Felix the Pig
Fluffy (Piggy)
Giltly (Wonder Duck)
Ham Swift (Supermouse)
Hamton
Hector the Collector (Nutsy Squirrel)
Hog-zilla (Spider-Ham)
Lord Pork (Space Beaver)
Mack Grabgrease (You-All Gibbon)
Milford
May Porker (Spider-Ham)
Miss Piggy
Ol' Snort (Bullet)
Orson the Piglet
Penny Pig (Mr. Wild Wolf)
Percy (Porky Pig)
Peter (Porky Pig)
Peter Pig
Peter Porkchops
Peter Porker (Spider-Ham; not the same as
    Spider-Ham's secret identity)
Petunia Pig
Pigetti (Supermouse)
Pig-Foot (You-All Gibbon)
Pigglys, The
Piggy
Piggypine (also part Porcupine) (Wuzzles)
Piglet (Winnie the Pooh)
Pig Newton (Deputy Dawg)
Pinkie (Porky Pig)
P. J. McBrine (Donald Duck)
Plastic Spam (Cutey Bunny)
Porkpie (Lionheart)
Porky Pig
Portus (Porky Pig)
Priscilla (Boner's Ark)
Pudgy Pig (Salomey)
Puffy Pig (Salomey)
Punchy (Peter Pig)
Punky Pig (Mickey Money)
Salomey
Senor Pig (Poosy Gato)
Sheriff Alabama (Newton, the Rabbit
    Wonder)
Slam Bang Boar (Pigglys)
Sooey Pig (Scooby-Doo)
Solid MacHogany (Pogo Possum)
Solomon Swine (Porky Pig)
Spider-Ham
Squeely (Salomey)

Superswine
Three Little Pigs (Big Bad Wolf)
Three Little Pigs (Three Bears)
Tusk (Crow of the Bear Clan)
Vincent Van Hogh (Newton, the Rabbit
    Wonder)
Wonder Wart-Hog
Ziggy Pig (Salomey)

Platypuses
Duck "Bill" Platypus
Kerwin Keystone (also half aardvark)
    (Newton, the Rabbit Wonder)
Ovide (Duck "Bill" Platypus)
Prudence Platypus (Atomic Mouse)

Polar Bears
Breezly (Breezly and Sneezly)
Petey Polar Bear (Supermouse)

Porcupines
Piggypine (also part Pig) (Wuzzles)
Porky Pine (Pogo Possum)
Portia (Care Bears)

Porpoises and Dolphins
Porpy (Moby Duck)
Tuffy (Storm)

Prairie Dogs
Puerile Phosphorescent Pugilistic Prairie
    Dogs (Pre-Teen Dirty-Gene Kung-Fu
    Kangaroos)
Wuff the Prairie Dog (Tom and Jerry)

Rabbits (see also Super Rabbits)
Babs Bunny (Hamton)
Bill Bunny (Steven Wolf)
Billy Rabbit (Garfield)
Blackjack O'Hare (Rocket Raccoon)
Bluebelle Rabbit (Buttons Bear)
Bo Bunny (Dizzy Dog)
Bonnie Bunny (Bullet Crow)
Brer Rabbit
Bucky O'Hare
Bugs Bunny
Bungalow Bill Bunny (Ducky Duckbill)
Bunny and Claude
Bunny From Beyond (Zoo Crew)
Bunny O'Hare (American Rabbit)
Bun Rab (Pogo Possum)
Bunson Bunny
Buster Bunny
Buster Bunny (Hamton)
Chris Rabbit (Henry's Cat)
Clyde (Bugs Bunny)
Crusader Rabbit
Daisy Lou (Bugs Bunny)
Fenton (Newton, the Rabbit Wonder)
Floppy Rabbit (Roobear)
Floyd and Lloyd (Oswald, the Lucky Rabbit)
G.I. Jackrabbits

Goofy Rabbit (Atomic Mouse)
Harold (Wacky Squirrel)
Harold Hare (Toby the Badger)
Harry Hare (Spider-Ham)
Herman (Bugs Bunny)
Honey Bunny (Bugs Bunny)
Hoppopotamus (also part Hippopotamus)
    (Wuzzles)
Hulk Bunny (Spider-Ham)
Jack Bunny (Cap'n Catnip)
Jackie (Space Beaver)
Jake (Bitsy)
Jesty and Pesty (Rags Rabbit)
Johnny Rabbit (Oswald, the Lucky Rabbit)
Joyous Jackrabbit (Fission Chicken)
Kid Carrots (Oswald, the Lucky Rabbit)
Lepus (Defiants)
Mammy Rabbit (Brer Rabbit)
Max Hare (Big Bad Wolf)
Max the Rabbit
Millie (Hoppy, the Captain Marvel Bunny)
Miyamoto Usagi
Moe Hare (Buzzy the Crow)
Newton, the Rabbit Wonder
Oswald, the Lucky Rabbit
Patty Rabbit (Mr. Wild Wolf)
Quik Rabbit (Trix Rabbit)
Rabbit (Winnie the Pooh)
Rabbit (Wonder Duck)
Rags Rabbit
Rags Rabbit (Mickey Money)
Range Rabbit (Newton, the Rabbit Wonder)
Rapid Rabbit
Rhyming Rabbit (Mr. and Mrs. Respectable
    Mouse)
Renegade Rabbit
Ricochet Rabbit
Robert Rabbit (Homeless Hector)
Roger Rabbit
Skipper Rabbit (Buttons Bear)
Slippers (Garfield)
Snowball (Barfy)
Spike (Spider-Ham)
Thumper (Bambi)
Trix Rabbit
Wabbits
Wilfred (Homeless Hector)

Raccoons
Bert Raccoon
Fred and Janet (Captain Jack)
Freddie Lucre (Lionheart)
Melissa (Bert Raccoon)
Ralph (Bert Raccoon)
Raccoon Kids
Rackety Coon (Pogo Possum)
Randy Raccoon (Supermouse)
Rick (Tyg)
Rocket Raccoon
Rory Raccoon (Linus the Lionhearted)
Shep (Crow of the Bear Clan)

Ty Coon (**Deputy Dawg**)
Tycoon (also part Tiger) (**Wuzzles**)

Ravens
Eb'nn the Raven

Reindeer
Rudolph the Red-Nosed Reindeer (**Grover Groundhog**)
Stubby (**Grover Groundhog**)

Rhinoceroses
Gunther (**Omaha the Cat Dancer**)
Mr. Mammoth (**Bert Raccoon**)
Ralph, the Righteous, Radical, Rasslin' Rhino
Rataxes (**Babar the Elephant**)
Rhinokey (also part Monkey) (**Wuzzles**)
Rhinorb (**Spirit**)
Rhinos, The (**Crow of the Bear Clan**)
Rocksteady (**Teenage Mutant Ninja Turtles**)
Sgt. Nyarg (**Lionheart**)

Seagulls
Scuttle (**Sebastian** [2])
Whitey (**Willie the Whale**)

Seahorses
Storm

Seals
Mr. Sseell (**Krazy Kat**)
Moosel (also part Moose) (**Wuzzles**)
Seabert
Sneezly (**Breezly and Sneezly**)
Stan and Ollie (**Samurai Penguin**)

Sharks
Jabberjaw
Mister Jaw (**Jabberjaw**)
Pool Shark (**Supermouse**)
Shark, The (**Man-Bat**)
Shark Men (**Moby Dick**)
Sharky (**Inspector Gill**)
Sub-Moron (**Cutey Bunny**)

Sheep and Rams
Admiral Kilda (**Bucky O'Hare**)
Blackie the Lamb (**Buzzy the Crow**)
Bo (**Orson the Piglet**)
Green Lambkin (**Zoo Crew**)
Lambsy (**Mildew Wolf**)
Lanolin (**Orson the Piglet**)
Nick Furry, Agent of S.H.E.E.P. (**Spider-Ham**)
Rambaba (**Henry's Cat**)
Retro Ram (**Bucky O'Hare**)
Woolma (**Care Bears**)
Woolrus (also part Walrus) (**Wuzzles**)

Shrews
Shady Shrew (**Pigglys**)

Skunks
Cinder (**Crow of the Bear Clan**)
Fifi (**Hamton**)
Flower (**Bambi**)
Keystone (**Bucky O'Hare**)
Mam'selle Hepzibah (**Pogo Possum**)
Midnite, the Rebel Skunk
Mr. L'Aroma (**Lionheart**)
Odie Colognie (**King Leonardo**)
Pepe le Pew
Sammy Skunk (**Willie the Worm**)
Simon Skunk (**Atomic Mouse**)
Skowl (also part Owl) (**Wuzzles**)
Infant Alien Karate Sloths (**Pre-Teen Dirty-Gene Kung-Fu Kangaroos**)

Snails
Colossal Nuclear Bambino Samurai Snails (**Pre-Teen Dirty-Gene Kung-Fu Kangaroos**)
Homer the Snail (**Toby the Badger**)

Snakes
Crazy Legs (**The C.B. Bears**)
Cy the Snake (**Duck "Bill" Platypus**)
Lord DyVyne (**Rocket Raccoon**)
Merv (**Bogey**)
Sir Hiss (**King Leonidas**)
Snooky (**Boner's Ark**)
Whippo (**John**)

Sparrows
"Butch" O'Sparrow (**Mervin**)
Dinky (**Tod and Copper**)
Suzy Sparrow (**Professor Owl**)

Spiders
Jake (**Sidney the Spider**)
Mandok Spydor (**Hamster Vice**)
Sidney Spider
Spike the Spider (**Beans**)
Tarantula (**Man-Bat**)

Squids
Cal Calamari (**Guerrilla Groundhog**)
Dr. Calamari (**Inspector Gill**)
Squiddly Diddly (**Secret Squirrel**)

Squirrels
Brazilia (**Smilin' Ed Smiley**)
Bulk Bolshevik (**Pre-Teen Dirty-Gene Kung-Fu Kangaroos**)
Clarence the Squirrel (**Bucky O'Hare**)
Dodger (**Supermouse**)
Granny Squirrel (**Pigglys**)
Jim Squirrel (**Supermouse**)
Merle and Meryl Squirrel (**Super Duck**)
Nato, the Samurai Squirrel
Nutsy Squirrel

Rocky (**Rocky and Bullwinkle**)
Sammy Squirrel (**Toby the Badger**)
Secret Squirrel
Shorty Squirrel (**Atomic Mouse**)
Silver Squirrel (**Spider-Ham**)
Skippy Squirrelheart (**Fission Chicken**)
Suicide Squirrel
Super Squirrel (**Zoo Crew**)
Wacky Squirrel
Zeke Squirrel

Storks
Joe Stork (**Krazy Kat**)
Mr. Miggle (**Albert the Alligator**)
Sandy (**Boner's Ark**)
Steven Stork (**Pigglys**)

Super Cats
Cap'n Catnip
Cosmo Cat
Courageous Cat
Ms. Kitty (**Cap'n Catnip**)
Super Cat (**Cosmo Cat**)
Superkatt
Super Pamby (**Superkatt**)
Tiger (**Cap'n Catnip**)
Watchcats (**Captain Jack**)
Wonder Cat (**Garfield**)

Super Mice
Atomic Mouse
Danger Mouse
Mighty Mouse
Supermouse

Super Rabbits
Adolescent Maniacal Samurai Hares (**Pre-Teen Dirty-Gene Kung-Fu Kangaroos**)
American Rabbit
Atomic Bunny a k a Atomic Rabbit
Barbarian Bunny (**Newton, the Rabbit Wonder**)
Captain Carrot (**Zoo Crew**)
Cutey Bunny
Darebunny (**Renegade Rabbit**)
Ether Bunny (**Fission Chicken**)
Flash Rabbit (**Cosmo Cat**)
Hoppy, the Captain Marvel Bunny
Renegade Rabbit
Thunderbunny
Wonder Wabbit (**Zoo Crew**)
Wunner Bunny (**Cutey Bunny**)

Swans
Enchanta (**Spirit**)

Tasmanian Devils
Dizzy Devil (**Hamton**)
Mrs. Devil (**Tasmanian Devil**)
Tasmanian Devil

Termites
Godzilla Termite (**Atom Ant**)

Tigers
Baby Puss (**Dino the Dinosaur**)
Cool Cat
Cringer (**Spirit**)
Hobbes
Mr. Tawky Tawny
Rags (**Crusader Rabbit**)
Tammany Tiger (**Mr. Jack**)
Tiger Tim (**Homeless Hector**)
Tigger (**Winnie the Pooh**)
Tony the Tiger
Tony, Jr. (**Tony the Tiger**)
Tycoon (also part Raccoon) (**Wuzzles**)
Tyg
Ty-Grrr (**Spirit**)

Toucans
Toucan Sam

Tunas
Charlie the Tuna

Turkeys
Terrible Turk Brothers (**Billy the Kid**)

Turtles
Barney the Invisible Turtle
Bert the Turtle
Cecil Turtle
Chester (**Cecil Turtle**)
Churchy La Femme (**Pogo Possum**)
Crusty (**Dink**)
Fastback (**Zoo Crew**)
Gertrude Turtle (**Buttons Bear**)
John
McSnurtle the Turtle, the Terrific Whatzit
Middle-Age Generic Mutant Tortoises
    (**Fission Chicken**)
Otto (**Dagmar**)
Pyko (**Rocket Raccoon**)
Slinx (**Doctor Whoot**)
Super-Turtle (**McSnurtle the Turtle, the
    Terrific Whatzit**)
Teenage Mutant Ninja Turtles
Toby Tortoise (**Big Bad Wolf**)

Tog (**Space Beaver**)
Tommy Tortoise (**Buzzy the Crow**)
Tommy Turtle (**Porky Pig**)
Tommy Turtle
Tooter Turtle
Touché Turtle

Vampire Ducks
Count Duckula
Count Quakula (**Count Duckula**)
Duckula
Quacula (**Count Duckula**)

Walruses
Artimus Walrus (**Samurai Penguin**)
Chumley the Walrus (**Tennessee Tuxedo**)
Sgt. Tusk (**G.I. Jackrabbits**)
Tuskor (**Spirit**)
Tusky (**Storm**)
Wally Walrus
Wal Rus (**Rocket Raccoon**)
Woolrus (also part Sheep) (**Wuzzles**)
Zatoichi Walrus (**Nato, the Samurai
    Squirrel**)

Waterbuffalos
Mary Jane Waterbuffalo (**Spider-Ham**)

Weasels
Brooklyn (**Doctor Whoot**)
Psycho (**Roger Rabbit**)
Smartguy (**Roger Rabbit**)
Stupid (**Roger Rabbit**)
Waggin' Weasel (**Kat Karson**)
Wanda Weasel (**Pigglys**)
Woodside Weasel (**Kamikaze Cat**)

Weevils
Mr. Weevil (**Bunson Bunny**)
Weevil (**Dirty Duck**)

Whales
Moby Dick
Willie the Whale

Wolves
Archimedes the Wolf (**Peter Porkchops**)
Big Bad Wolf, The
Bon Bon (**Loopy de Loop**)

Devil (**Hero**)
Dreadmon (**Teenage Mutant Ninja Turtles**)
E. Z. Wolf (**Newton, the Rabbit Wonder**)
Hokey Wolf
Kattu
Li'l Bad Wolf (**Big Bad Wolf**)
Lobo
Loopy de Loop
Mildew Wolf
Mr. Wild Wolf
Ralph Wolf (**Sam Sheepdog**)
Spud McWolf (**Supermouse**)
Steven Wolf
Wilford Wolf (**Kwicky Koala**)

Woodchucks
Muggsy (**Raccoon Kids**)

Woodpeckers
Boomer (**Tod and Copper**)
Knock Knock (**Skatebirds**)
Knothead and Splinter (**Woody Woodpecker**)
Willie the Woodpecker (**Chauncey Chirp**)
Winnie Woodpecker (**Buttons Bear**)
Woody Woodpecker
Woody the Woodpecker (**Super Duck**)

Worms
Bookworm (**Sniffles**)
Fred (**Orson the Piglet**)
Inchy Inchworm (**Buzzy the Crow**)
Madge and Bruce (**John**)
Mr. Mind
Orville (**Orson the Piglet**)
Sherm the Worm (**Three Mousketeers**)
Squoimy the Woim (**Hot Dog**)
Sylvia (**Orson the Piglet**)
Wiggles the Wonderworm (**Willie the Worm**)
Wiggy Worm (**Boris the Bear**)
Willie the Worm
Winnie Worm (**Willie the Worm**)
Woodrow (**Orson the Piglet**)

Wrens
Willoughby Wren

Zebras
Fruit Stripe Zebras

INDEX

Note: Names of cartoon characters, including human characters, are not inverted in the index. For example, Bruce Wayne (Batman's alter ego) and Betty Cooper (of the Archie comics) both appear under the *B*s. This method, while unorthodox in Bruce Wayne's case, makes the most sense generally. Consider Betty Cooper, whose last name is likely to be known only by trivia buffs. Indeed, most characters that have last names are known best by their first name or by their name as a whole, and to invert a name such as "Ham Gravy" is to miss the point. Rather than arbitrarily inverting some names and not others, the more straightforward method was chosen: that of not inverting any cartoon names. This policy extends to titles as well, so that Madame Bonfamille (of *The Aristocats*) appears under the *M*s. Names of actual human beings, such as the creators and voices of the characters, are inverted as usual. Characters with identical names are generally not distinguished, and only characters receiving a substantive discussion are listed in the index. For a comprehensive listing of characters by animal type, see the Appendix.